INTERNATIONAL TRADE THEORY
IN A DEVELOPING WORLD

*Other symposia published for the
International Economic Association*

*

THE BUSINESS CYCLE IN THE POST-WAR WORLD
Edited by Erik Lundberg

CLASSICS IN THE THEORY OF PUBLIC FINANCE
Edited by R. A. Musgrave and A. T. Peacock

THE ECONOMIC CONSEQUENCES OF THE SIZE OF NATIONS
Edited by E. A. G. Robinson

ECONOMIC DEVELOPMENT FOR AFRICA SOUTH OF THE SAHARA
Edited by E. A. G. Robinson

ECONOMIC DEVELOPMENT FOR LATIN AMERICA
Edited by Howard S. Ellis assisted by Henry C. Wallich

ECONOMIC DEVELOPMENT WITH SPECIAL REFERENCE TO EAST ASIA
Edited by Kenneth Berrill

THE ECONOMICS OF INTERNATIONAL MIGRATION
Edited by Brinley Thomas

THE ECONOMICS OF TAKE-OFF INTO SUSTAINED GROWTH
Edited by W. W. Rostow

INFLATION
Edited by D. C. Hague

INTERNATIONAL TRADE THEORY IN A DEVELOPING WORLD
Edited by Sir Roy Harrod and D. C. Hague

STABILITY AND PROGRESS IN THE WORLD ECONOMY
Edited by D. C. Hague

THE THEORY OF CAPITAL
Edited by F. A. Lutz and D. C. Hague

THE THEORY OF INTEREST RATES
Edited by F. H. Hahn and F. P. R. Brechling

THE THEORY OF WAGE DETERMINATION
Edited by J. T. Dunlop

INTERNATIONAL TRADE THEORY IN A DEVELOPING WORLD

Proceedings of a Conference
held by the International Economic Association

EDITED BY
ROY HARROD

ASSISTED BY
DOUGLAS HAGUE

MACMILLAN
London · Melbourne · Toronto

ST MARTIN'S PRESS
New York
1965

First Edition 1963
Reprinted 1964, 1965

MACMILLAN AND COMPANY LIMITED
Little Essex Street London WC 2
also Bombay Calcutta Madras Melbourne

THE MACMILLAN COMPANY OF CANADA LIMITED
70 Bond Street Toronto 2

ST MARTIN'S PRESS INC
175 Fifth Avenue New York 10010 NY

PRINTED IN GREAT BRITAIN

CONTENTS

Contents

vi

LIST OF PARTICIPANTS

Professor O. D' Alauro, Facoltà di Economia e Commercio, Università degli Studi, Genoa, Italy

Professor A. Bechin, Institute of World Economics, Moscow, U.S.S.R.

Dr. James Washington Bell, American Economic Association, Evanston, Ill.

Mr. J. N. Bhagwati, Nuffield College, Oxford, U.K.

Professor I. Bowen, University of Western Australia, Nedlands, Western Australia

Professor M. Byé, Institut de Science Économique Appliquée, Paris

Professor D. J. Delivanis, University of Thessaloniki, Athens, Greece

Professor L. Fauvel, Faculté de Droit, University of Paris, France

Dr. Romulo Ferrero, Lima, Peru

* Mr. K. Forcart, Social Sciences Division, UNESCO, Paris, France

Professor H. Giersch, University of Saarbrücken, Germany

Professor E. Gudin, Rio de Janeiro, Brazil

Professor G. Haberler, Harvard University, Cambridge, Mass., U.S.A.

Professor D. Hague, Duke University, Durham, N. Carolina, U.S.A.

Sir Roy Harrod, Christ Church, Oxford, U.K.

* Mr. R. Hellberg, United Nations, Geneva, Switzerland

Professor E. James, University of Paris, France

Professor H. G. Johnson, Dept. of Economics, University of Chicago, U.S.A.

Professor W. A. Johr, St. Gallen, Switzerland

Professor V. Kaigl, Institute of Economics, Academy of Sciences, Prague, Czechoslovakia

Professor C. P. Kindleberger, Massachusetts Institute of Technology, Cambridge, Mass., U.S.A.

Professor H. Kitamura, Economic Commission for Asia and the Far East, Bangkok, Thailand

Mr. A. Lamfalussy, Banque de Bruxelles, Brussels, Belgium

Mr. H. H. Liesner, Emmanuel College, Cambridge, U.K.

Professor E. Lipinski, Warsaw, Poland

Professor E. Lundberg, Stockholm, Sweden

Sir Donald MacDougall, Nuffield College, Oxford, U.K.

Professor A. Mahr, University of Vienna, Austria

* Observers

vii

List of Participants

Mr. A. Maizels, National Institute for Economic and Social Research, London, U.K.

Dr. V. A. Marsan, Istituto per la Riconstruzione Industriale, Rome, Italy

Professor R. F. Mikesell, University of Oregon, U.S.A.

Professor T. Morgan, University of Wisconsin, U.S.A.

Dr. H. Myint, Rangoon University, Burma

Professor Ichiro Nakayama, Tokyo, Japan

Professor F. Neumark, Frankfurt-am-Main, Germany

Professor B. Ohlin, Stockholm School of Economics, Stockholm, Sweden

* Dr. García Olano, Buenos Aires, Argentine

Dr. I. G. Patel, International Monetary Fund, Washington 25, U.S.A.

Mr. Léo Rip, Belgrade, Yugoslavia

Professor E. A. G. Robinson, Cambridge University, U.K.

Dr. K. M. Savosnick, Manchester University, U.K.

Dr. V. P. Sergeyev, Moscow, U.S.S.R.

* Dr. G. Skorov, Chief, Division for International Development of Social Sciences, UNESCO, Paris, France

Professor E. Sohmen, Frankfurt, Germany

* Dr. K. Szczerba-Likiernik, International Social Science Council, Paris

Professor Shigato Tsuru, University of Rochester, N.Y., U.S.A.

Professor J. Weiller, University of Paris, France

* Observers

PROGRAMME COMMITTEE

Austin Robinson (President I.E.A.)
Roy Harrod (Chairman)
Fritz Neumark (Treasurer I.E.A.)
Maurice Byé   Sune Carlson
Charles Kindleberger   K. N. Raj

ACKNOWLEDGEMENTS

THE International Economic Association wishes to thank all those who did much to ensure the success of the Conference recorded in this volume. Special gratitude is due to the management and staff of the Grand Hotel, Brissago, Switzerland, where the Conference was held in conditions admirably conducive to good-humoured but vigorous discussion.

The Conference received financial support from UNESCO and welcome assistance from officers of that organization. It was supported also by funds available from the general grant to the Association made by the Ford Foundation. Without the support of these two bodies it could not have been held.

It need scarcely be added that the success of a Conference rests primarily on the quality of the papers and the discussion contributed by its participants. To all those who contributed in that way both to the Conference itself and to this volume the International Economic Association expresses its sincere gratitude.

INTRODUCTION

By R. F. HARROD

No excuse is needed for the choice of international trade and investment as the subject for discussion at the Conference organized by the International Economic Association, which met at Brissago, Switzerland, on September 1-9, 1961. Forty-seven persons were present, drawn from twenty-two countries.

Problems connected with international trade and investment are coming into the forefront of consideration in relation to economic policy making. Correct solutions could guide statesmen in their decisions, not only about policies specifically concerned with external relations, but also about matters seemingly related to the internal conditions of each country only. It is becoming ever more apparent how much may be gained if nations come together and see the pattern of world development as a whole. Only in the light of this will it be possible to see in correct perspective what ought to be done by each nation separately. And this is not only looking at the matter from the point of view of pure altruism ; the self-interest of each country also requires that its policy should be appropriate in relation to the wider setting. Gone is the time when it could be considered sufficient for national economic policy makers to regard their duties on the external side as bounded by the precept that they must keep their balances of payment in good order. Import policy, for instance, should be assessed, not only by what a given country needs for its own purposes, but in relation to balanced growth in the world as a whole.

Even more important than the relevance of a given topic to pressing practical problems is its relation to the progress of economic science. For, if such progress is achieved, that can help the solution of problems over an indefinite future. The Programme Committee felt that the relation of dynamic theory to international trade theory might be a key question. Such modest progress as dynamic theory has so far made has been in the main confined to the analysis of closed economies. Apart from a small number of brilliant journal articles, the task of extending dynamic concepts into the field of international trade theory has hardly been started. There are virgin lands to be explored.

It was naturally not expected that, however much trouble authors took in preparing their papers, firm foundations for a theoretical structure could be provided at an international conference. Rather it was hoped that an interchange of views among distinguished economists of various age groups might stimulate those present to further work upon the subject. Moreover it could also help in guiding its direction. For, although the prolonged discussions did not lead to the emergence of agreed conclusions of a specific character on any topic, there did gradually emerge some common views about what types of problem were important and what modes of approach likely to be more useful than others.

It is also hoped that, through the presentation of this volume, the interchange of ideas at Brissago may be helpful to a much wider range of research workers. The reader should not expect to find ready-made conclusions in the papers submitted, nor any summings up of the weight of the various arguments presented around the table. Although the proceedings were lengthy, there was not enough time even to make a beginning of sorting out and correlating the many ideas that were presented at the meeting. But I believe that the careful student of this volume will find, not only many original ideas, but also many striking convergences of thought among the economists, even when they were approaching problems from entirely different angles from one another, and even indeed when they were not formally concerned with the same problems. The inconclusiveness of many of the debates should itself be a challenge to researchers for their future work.

It was felt that there should be one initial paper on the most recent findings within the static theory of international trade. Professor Paul Samuelson consented to do such a paper, but his participation in the Conference was unhappily prevented by serious illness in his family. Accordingly Mr. J. Bhagwati was asked, at very short notice, to contribute such a paper. Readers will find that his summary of recent developments is executed with fine proficiency, a very remarkable achievement in a short space of time.

This paper was much appreciated by the Conference. Readers will, however, find that it was subjected to a barrage of criticism. This phenomenon recurs in the case of many of the papers. The members were naturally anxious to get down to their business with despatch, and expressions of appreciation, even if recorded, appear somewhat perfunctory in cold print. It must not be supposed that the general attitude to the various papers was as unsympathetic as the record may sometimes make it seem.

A striking feature of Mr. Bhagwati's paper was that, while the analysis was firm and sharply defined, its conclusions in relation to public policy were somewhat agnostic. This result, which may be taken fairly to represent the present stage of static theory, is in striking contrast with the traditional outlook. Foreign trade is a sphere in which, from Adam Smith to Marshall and Taussig, and indeed subsequently, economics has been rather strongly affirmative in its practical recommendations. The prevailing agnosticism is no doubt due to a more searching examination of presuppositions. In opening the discussion on this paper, I appealed to Professor Haberler, foremost exponent of traditional theory, to try to help the meeting back, after Mr. Bhagwati's chilling agnosticism, to a more positive attitude about these matters. Professor Haberler's response is on the record. Under the fierce limelight of so many fine theoretical minds, we all of us tended to be a little cautious on purely theoretical matters.

It does appear that, in the present phase of static theory, its exponents can no longer derive from it confident recommendations for helping humanity. The first fresh flush of zeal has departed.

It was thought expedient to preface the systematic exploration of dynamic theory by the cold douche of a statistical examination of certain past trends. In this historico-statistical field, agnosticism seemed also to be the order of the day. Such seemed to be the combined effect of the two intensely interesting papers by Mr. Maizels and Professor Morgan. Generalizations, such as the trend to a worsening in the terms of trade for primary producers, were not substantiated. These two papers certainly provide a challenge to further work in the light of comments upon them.

The central paper on dynamic theory was presented by Professor H. Johnson, a contributor already of important advances in this field. It may not be inappropriate in this introduction to refer to a specific feature of it, since this is so very central to much of the work that is being done at present in foreign trade theory. It is a natural starting-point for an analysis to take the case of two commodities and two factors of production. While this appears to be simple and natural, and one is inclined at first to suppose that the addition of more factors and commodities will not normally substantially alter the basic relations revealed by the simpler model, I believe this not to be so. The two-commodity, two-factor, approach has been yielding paradoxical conclusions, and Professor Johnson's paper contains one, viz., the proposition that an innovation as regards the production of a certain commodity, which economizes in the use of the factor that is intensive in the production of that commodity, will raise the price of that factor in the economy as a whole. I believe that such paradoxes spring essentially from the use of the two-factor, two-commodity, model and that it is absolutely essential, as a matter of principle, in order to reach correct conclusions, to take as the simplest case a three-factor, two-commodity, model (or $n+1$ factors and n commodities). A controversy arose on this topic, which is in part recorded.

Professor Ohlin, from whose original work so many recent developments in the theory of foreign trade stem, was present at the conference and made a number of important contributions. With a scientific detachment, which all admired, he deprecated an excessive focusing of attention on the theory with which his name is regularly associated, and pleaded that the central theory of foreign trade should be approached from a number of different points of view, bringing other factors into the reckoning.

The other papers ranged over various central topics pertaining to international economics in the context of a theory of growth. It should be recorded that there was a recurrent note coming from some of the participants that one or other of the problems at issue could be quite adequately solved by methods of comparative statics. In some cases this view struck me as unacceptable ; thus one aspect of the Conference was a confrontation of minds, as regards the problem of how radical a change in concepts is required by the essential nature of growth theory, as contrasted with statics or comparative statics.

The papers and discussions were not only devoted to many theoretical questions, but also touched on immediate practical problems. The special problems of the developing countries came into the discussions more prominently than is shown by the titles of the papers.

Around the table was a whole spectrum of opinion, ranging from those who favoured total planning to those who were inclined to favour the nearest approximation possible in modern conditions to non-interference. Even in the nine days of the Conference it seemed that both sides were coming to understand the opposite point of view better. On the one hand the stark problems of the developing countries were put forward in a vivid way. Those inclined to favour non-interference were insensibly drawn into addressing their minds to the problem — what shall we *do* about them ? Were their balance of payments problems, for instance, so readily to be solved by the application of orthodox medicines ? On the other side, those inclined to over-facile remedies by control must have been impressed by the weight of the various arguments continuously pressed against specious solutions. While most members recognized the need for a rather far-reaching use of planning in one form or another,

Introduction

I judge that the balance of opinion did not favour protection as a prime instrument for stimulating growth.

We had the benefit of the presence of participants from Communist countries, including three Russians, one Czech and one Pole. Relations between all members of the Conference were of the friendliest. Much mutual knowledge was gained. Some who represented a 'bourgeois' ideology were eager to extract information about how certain very real problems are solved within the framework of the socialist state, and sometimes felt that the explanations of the socialists were rather too *general* for their satisfaction. As a bourgeois myself, I could not help suspecting that the socialist members may have sometimes felt that we were making very heavy weather about certain problems that they would solve quite easily by a stroke of the pen. I have no doubt that mutual interest was aroused by what was said on both sides, and that further interchanges of views in the objective and scientific atmosphere of the International Economic Association would lead to a deepening of mutual understanding.

I believe that this report should provoke further research, both in theoretical and applied economics. Lifelong economists brought into the arena the thoughts that, after very extended reflection, they felt to be most important in relation to each matter discussed; younger economists struck new notes. There was no attempt, and could not have been, to gather these various thoughts into a Procrustean bed of specific findings. The student will not regret this, for it leaves it to him to gather together, to synthesize, to develop, and to subject to statistical and empirical tests, the various opinions of the distinguished economists, young as well as old, who were present.

Chapter 1

SOME RECENT TRENDS IN THE PURE THEORY OF INTERNATIONAL TRADE

BY

J. BHAGWATI

University of Oxford

I. INTRODUCTION

THE main purpose of this paper is to isolate certain quite recent trends in the development of that part of the theory of international trade which is generally described as 'pure', in the sense that it has arisen out of the application of the neo-Walrasian analysis of value and welfare to the classic questions of trade theory.[1]

The pure theory of trade has traditionally been concerned with questions belonging to two different spheres. On the one hand, there are conundrums that fall into the field of 'positive economics' : these are concerned with the explanation and prediction of events. Why does a country trade the way it does ? What effect will a shift in demand have on the terms at which the country trades ? Is growth likely to increase or diminish the volume of trade ? On the other hand, one finds questions concerning trade and welfare ranging back to the time of Adam Smith and Ricardo, when, in the aftermath of the mercantilist debate on the advantages of trade, the study of international trade seriously began.

In positive analysis, the recent trend towards empirical verification, and, in welfare theory, the insistence that economic analysis should be a guide to practical policy, have come to discipline a small, but growing, segment of the recent growth of knowledge. This is in striking contrast to the theory of the 'traditional' persuasion, which is concerned with the investigation of the equilibrium properties of well-defined economic systems.[2] The bulk of this paper, Sections II

---

[1] When I say 'recent', I mean the last three decades. Practically all the important developments since Marshall are centred in that period.

[2] 'Traditional' theory is concerned totally with 'logically true' propositions which, taken thus, cannot be empirically refuted. Such a proposition, for instance, is Samuelson's well-known theorem, that factor prices are equalized under trade if certain conditions are satisfied ; P. A. Samuelson, 'International Trade and the Equalisation of Factor Prices', *Economic Journal*, Vol. 58 (June 1948), pp. 164-84.

(on positive analysis) and IV (on welfare propositions), is addressed to a critical analysis of much of the literature in this important new mould. Section III, however, surveys a single aspect of tariff theory, typical of the 'traditional' contributions; this section is designed partly as a recognition of the indisputable fact that the bulk of the recent developments *are* still 'traditional', but also as a contrast to the new tendencies.

II. POSITIVE ANALYSIS

The theory of comparative advantage, construed as a doctrine explaining the *pattern of trade*, offers an excellent illustration of the tendency towards formulation of economic theory so as to permit empirical verification; and, indeed, of the reverse process, of formulation of theories to 'explain' observed patterns in economic phenomena.

The traditional general equilibrium approach to the explanation of the pattern of trade (and, quite generally, the entire configuration of equilibrium prices and quantities) begins with the innocuous proposition that trade, and the pattern of trade, depend on pre-trade differences in (relative) prices. Pre-trade prices, however, reflect the interaction of supply and demand within each country. Supply reflects the domestic availability of (i) resources ('factor endowment') and (ii) techniques ('production functions').[1] Demand reflects (iii) 'individual tastes' and (iv) the 'distribution of ownership of resources' (which determines the distribution of earned income and hence the weighting of individual tastes). The pattern of trade is thus determined by these four parameters, within each nation in the international economy, working in the context of (v) the 'given institutional framework': for instance, perfect competition, utility maximization, profit maximization, governmental policies of intervention, the pursuit of a successful policy of full employment of resources. This constitutes the essence of the neo-classical theory of comparative costs, designed as an explanation of the pattern of trade. The early work of Leontief, Lerner and Haberler is based implicitly on perfect competition, full employment and the maximization of profits and utility;[2] the work of the later modern theorists

---

[1] It is debatable whether items like 'weather' should be classified as a factor of production or accounted for by altering the shape of the production function. I find myself in agreement with the view that it should be the latter, in so far as the calculus of imputation is not applicable to it as to factors of production. However, logically, either procedure is adequate.

[2] W. Leontief, 'The Use of Indifference Curves in the Analysis of Foreign Trade', *Quarterly Journal of Economics*, Vol. 47 (May 1933), pp. 493-503; A. P. Lerner, 'The Diagrammatical Representation of Cost Conditions in International Trade', *Economica*, Vol. 34 (August 1932), pp. 346-56, and 'The Symmetry

2

admits, among other things, state-imposed 'distortions' and transfers of income.[1] The central objection to this type of formulation, however, is that it does no more than offer a categorization of the factors that affect pre-trade prices. We are offered no proposition that can be refuted by reference to the world. It is difficult not to feel that, for all practical purposes, one has not gone appreciably beyond arguing that the pattern of trade depends on pre-trade differences in prices.[2]

An alternative approach to the problem would be to advance, quite explicitly, meaningful theorems, in Samuelson's sense, theorems which *can* be empirically refuted. This would imply, in this context, pegging a proposition concerning the trade pattern on a few 'key' parameters abstracted from the exhaustive catalogue of 'supply' and 'demand'. Such propositions *have* recently been offered and, what is more important, tests have been attempted with reference to trade patterns actually obtaining in the world.[3]

One such theorem springs directly out of the *Ricardian* analysis of comparative advantage. Ricardo's theory can be construed as either a highly simplified construction designed to establish the welfare case for free trade [4] or an attempt at the explanation of the pattern of trade. If the latter interpretation is chosen, and if the celebrated Portugal-England example is used as a guide, the Ricardian hypothesis can be construed as the following, rather 'strong' proposition : the pattern of trade is determined by the differences in the relative labour productivities in different activities. Looked upon as a 'logically true' proposition, the restrictive assumptions of two commodities, single input (labour) and constant returns to scale (within each activity) represent sufficient conditions for the theorem to be true ; [5] and, indeed, these are the assumptions of Ricardo's example. In a slightly 'weaker' form, that the comparative labour

between Import and Export Taxes', *ibid.* Vol. III (N.S., August 1936), pp. 306-313 ; G. Haberler, *The Theory of International Trade*, London, 1936.

[1] J. E. Meade, *Trade and Welfare (The Theory of International Economic Policy*, Vol. II), Oxford, 1955 ; and *Mathematical Supplement (Trade and Welfare)*, Oxford, 1955.

[2] Cf. Mill's pertinent remark (*Principles of Political Economy*, ed. W. J. Ashley, 1917) : 'But there are many things which, though they could be produced at home without difficulty, and in any quantity, are yet imported from a distance. The explanation which would be popularly given of this would be, that it is cheaper to import than to produce them : and this is the true reason. *But this reason itself requires that a reason be given for it*' (p. 574). (Italics are mine.)

[3] Obviously, the tests refer to trade patterns for particular regions, and specific periods. A hypothesis which is refuted for certain data may none the less be 'verified' by others. This is no argument, however, against the methodological demand for testable theories.

[4] A detailed argument in support of this thesis has been given elsewhere by me ; see 'The Theory of International Trade', *Indian Economic Journal*, Vol. 8 (July 1960), pp. 1-17.

[5] The last two assumptions collapse into one if it is argued that the former implies the latter.

3

productivity of a country's exports exceeds that of her importables, the Ricardian hypothesis follows logically without having to make the two-commodity assumption. However, it is much more fruitful to look upon such hypotheses as empirically refutable propositions, based on the 'hunch' that labour productivities dominate prices and hence the pattern of trade. In fact, it has been so done by some recent writers.[1]

The (weaker) Ricardian hypothesis can be presented neatly in a general form. If $X_1 \ldots X_n$ are the commodities exported from country II, and $M_1 \ldots M_m$ are I's imports from II, then we should find that

$$
(1) \qquad \frac{\dfrac{{}^{0}X_i}{\text{I.}}}{\dfrac{{}^{L}X_i}{\text{I.}}} \Bigg/ \frac{\dfrac{{}^{0}}{\text{II.}}}{\dfrac{{}^{L}X_i}{\text{II.}}} > \frac{\dfrac{{}^{0}M}{\text{I.}}}{\dfrac{{}^{L}M_j}{\text{I.}}} \Bigg/ \frac{\dfrac{{}^{0}M_j}{\text{II.}}}{\dfrac{{}^{L}M_j}{\text{II.}}} \qquad \begin{aligned} i &= 1, \ldots n, \\ j &= 1, \ldots m \end{aligned}
$$

where $\dfrac{{}^{0}X_i}{{}^{L}X_i}$ is the labour productivity (total output divided by man-hours employed) in X_i, $\dfrac{{}^{0}M_j}{{}^{L}M_j}$ in M_j, and the superscripts refer to the country.[2]

However, it is possible to construe the Ricardian theory as based on a labour theory of value in the sense that prices after all reflect essentially labour costs ; and that trade, therefore, would be determined by labour costs. Hence follows the testable hypothesis : '. . . each country will export those goods for which the ratio of its output per worker to that of the other exceeds the ratio of its money wage rate to that of the other'.[3] The hypothesis then is modified to read : [4]

$$
(2) \qquad \frac{\dfrac{{}^{0}X_i}{\text{I.}}}{\dfrac{{}^{L}X_i}{\text{I.}}} \Bigg/ \frac{\dfrac{{}^{0}X_i}{\text{II.}}}{\dfrac{{}^{L}X_i}{\text{II.}}} \cdot \frac{\dfrac{W_i}{\text{II.}}}{W_i\,\text{I.}} > 1 \quad \text{and} \quad \frac{\dfrac{{}^{0}M_j}{\text{I.}}}{\dfrac{{}^{L}M_j}{\text{I.}}} \Bigg/ \frac{\dfrac{{}^{0}M_j}{\text{II.}}}{\dfrac{{}^{L}M_j}{\text{II.}}} \cdot \frac{\dfrac{W_i}{\text{II.}}}{W_j\,\text{I.}} < 1
$$

where W_i is the average wage rate in industry i.

[1] J. Bhagwati, 'The Theory of International Trade', *Indian Economic Journal*, Vol. 8 (July 1960), pp. 1-17 ; R. E. Caves, *Trade and Economic Structure*, Cambridge, Mass., 1960 ; I. B. Kravis, ' "Availability" and other Influences on the Commodity Composition of Trade', *Journal of Political Economy*, Vol. 64 (April 1956), pp. 143-55.

[2] The test would naturally have to employ the labour productivities *after* trade, the only observable statistics.

[3] G. D. A. MacDougall, 'British and American Exports : a Study suggested by the Theory of Comparative Costs', Part I, *Economic Journal*, Vol. 61 (Dec. 1951), pp. 697-724, at p. 697.

[4] The hypothesis, as set out notationally, allows for the wage rate to be that in the particular industry. If it is sought to take the average wage rate for the economy as a whole, the W's can be so defined. MacDougall tests hypotheses under both assumptions ; *loc. cit.* and *idem*, Part II, *Economic Journal*, Vol. 62 (Sept. 1952), pp. 487-521.

Both these Ricardian hypotheses *can* be empirically verified. Two divergent approaches to such testing are available in the literature. One approach has been to start with the identity that the unit cost of production (i.e. unit price) is equivalent to the product of the average wage rate, the ratio of total cost to the wage bill, and the reciprocal of labour productivity. The Ricardian hypothesis (1) has then been thought to be tested by investigating the international 'similarities' in the inter-industrial structure of the average wage rate and of the ratio of total cost to wages.[1] However, the procedure is unsatisfactory. Caves[2] draws upon Kravis' results[3] — that the comparison of the Japanese and United States data shows that the ranking of industries by hourly earnings of workers is almost identical — to deduce that these results 'sustain the classical hypothesis that relative labour productivities are very important factors determining comparative advantage'. However, this already implies that the inter-industrial structure of the ratio of wages to total costs is also 'similar' between Japan and the United States — a proposition which requires empirical support. Moreover, there can exist a correlation between comparative labour productivity and the trade pattern, as stated by hypothesis (1), even if there were international differences in the inter-industrial structures of wage rates and of the ratio of wages to total costs : for these differences could be offsetting. Hence it is impossible, even in principle, to refute the Ricardian hypothesis (1) merely by observing whether these structures are 'similar' between countries.

The only valid procedure is to subject the proposition to a direct test. MacDougall's careful study adopts this procedure.[4] However, the hypothesis tested, with some success, while it can be described as Ricardian 'in principle', is not identical with the ones described so far. Analysing the relative shares, in third markets, of American and British exports of 'identical' commodities, MacDougall finds statistical support for the hypothesis that :

$$(3a) \quad \text{if } \frac{{}^{o}Y_i}{{}^{L}Y_i} \bigg/ \frac{{}^{II.}{}^{o}Y_i}{{}^{II.}{}^{L}Y_i} \cdot \frac{W_i}{{}^{II.}{}_{I.}W_i} > 1, \text{ then } \frac{{}^{E}Y_i}{{}^{II.}{}^{E}Y_i} > 1 \text{ and } i = (1, \ldots q).$$

---

[1] For an unsatisfactory attempt, see K. Forchheimer, 'The Role of Relative Wage Differences in International Trade', *Quarterly Journal of Economics*, Vol. 62 (Nov. 1947), pp. 1-30.

[2] *Op. cit.* p. 272.

[3] I. B. Kravis, ' "Availability" and other Influences on the Commodity Composition of Trade', *Journal of Political Economy*, Vol. 64 (April 1956), at pp. 145-6.

[4] British and American Exports : a Study suggested by the Theory of Comparative Costs', Part I, *Economic Journal*, Vol. 61 (Dec. 1951), pp. 697-724 ; Part II, *ibid.* Vol. 62 (Sept. 1952), pp. 487-521.

$$\left. \frac{{}^{0}Y_i^{\text{I.}}}{{}^{L}Y_i^{\text{I.}}} \middle/ \frac{{}^{0}Y_i^{\text{II.}}}{{}^{L}Y_i^{\text{II.}}} \cdot \frac{W_i^{\text{II.}}}{W_i^{\text{I.}}} \right. \text{ is positively correlated with } \frac{{}^{E}Y_i^{\text{I.}}}{{}^{E}Y_i^{\text{II.}}}$$

where Y_i is the commodity exported, to third markets, by I and II and E is the quantity of exports.[1]

This hypothesis is clearly based on the Ricardian hypothesis (2). But it is possible to formulate, and test successfully, with the data furnished by MacDougall,[2] a hypothesis allied to (1) and relating to labour productivity alone :

$$(3b) \qquad \left. \frac{{}^{0}Y_i^{\text{I.}}}{{}^{L}Y_i^{\text{I.}}} \middle/ \frac{{}^{0}Y_i^{\text{II.}}}{{}^{L}Y_i^{\text{II.}}} \right. \text{ is positively correlated with } \frac{{}^{E}Y_i^{\text{I}}}{{}^{E}Y_i^{\text{II.}}}.$$

It is possible, however, to move entirely away from the Ricardian theories and formulate alternative approaches to the problem. A well-known proposition, attributed to Heckscher and Ohlin, is that *a country's exports use intensively the country's abundant factor.* Once again we can either look upon this as a purely deductive proposition and devise the conditions under which it will be logically true, or alternatively construe it as a deliberate abstraction, focusing on one key factor, differences in relative factor endowments, to explain the pattern of trade. It is known that, provided one defines factor abundance in terms of prices,[3] international identity of production functions and non-reversibility of factor-intensities (in the framework of Samuelson's model [4]) ensure the logical truth of this theorem. Curiously enough, looked upon as logically true propositions, the Ricardian (1) and Heckscher-Ohlin theorems rest upon totally diverging premises : (i) whereas the former assumes one factor and thus renders the factor supply irrelevant in explaining the pattern of trade, the latter assumes two factors and makes differences in factor supplies the dominant explanatory factor in predicting the pattern of trade ; and (ii) whereas the former explicitly makes international differences in production functions (the invariant labour productivities in each activity) the dominant factor deter-

---

[1] He finds support for this hypothesis also when he takes the average wage rate for the economy instead of wage rates in each individual industry.

[2] 'British and American Exports', Part I, p. 703.

[3] This is what the Swedish authors appear to have assumed ; W. Stolper and P. A. Samuelson, 'Protection and Real Wages', *Review of Economic Studies*, Vol. 9 (Nov. 1941), pp. 58-73. Cf. also J. Bhagwati, 'Protection, Real Wages and Real Incomes', *Economic Journal*, Vol. 69 (Dec. 1959), pp. 733-48 ; and H. G. Johnson, *International Trade and Economic Growth*, London, 1958, Chapter I.

[4] P. A. Samuelson, 'International Trade and the Equalisation of Factor Prices', *Economic Journal*, Vol. 58 (June 1948), pp. 163-84.

mining comparative advantage, the latter invokes identity of production functions between nations.

However, viewed as an empirically refutable proposition, the Heckscher-Ohlin (hereafter referred to as H-O) theorem invites direct testing. And this is exactly what Leontief [1] has done for the United States and Tatemoto and Ichimura [2] for Japan. Both studies take 'capital' and 'labour' as the factors in terms of which 'abundance' and 'factor-intensity' are defined. They both turn up what appear to be startling results : the U.S.A. emerges as importing capital-intensive commodities and exporting labour-intensive ones, and Japan has labour-intensive imports and capital-intensive exports. Neither study actually compares the factor endowments of the trading partners and, to that extent, neither provides a *completed* test of the H-O theorem. However, the general consensus that the United States has the highest amount of capital per head may be accepted ; in which case, the H-O theorem has indeed been refuted for the United States — unless objections can be made against Leontief's statistical material and techniques. Objections do, in fact, exist. To take but one telling example, aggregation on the scale involved in Leontief's input-output exercise could have vitiated his estimates of relative factor-intensities. Balogh has argued that the labour-intensity of the export industries could be spurious and attributable to aggregation with labour - intensive, non - export activities ; [3] how far this produces a crippling bias, if any, cannot be determined, however, until at least a sample of export activities in Leontief's exercise has been examined for this purpose.

But if the refutation is accepted one has the option of modifying the *form* of the hypothesis or of redefining the concepts which enter the hypothesis while retaining its form. The latter is a valid scientific procedure, for the hypothesis, with the concepts redefined, can be subjected again to empirical verification. As it turns out, there are at least three ways in which, while preserving the form of the H-O hypothesis, the definitions of 'capital', 'labour' and 'factor endowment' in the Leontief exercise can be altered so as to offer some possibility of verifying the H-O hypothesis.

H-O Adaptation (1). One may argue, for instance, that the average labour efficiency varies between countries and hence 'labour' should be defined in terms of 'standard', as distinct from natural,

[1] 'Domestic Production and Foreign Trade : the American Capital Position re-examined', *Economia Internazionale*, Vol. 7 (1954), pp. 9-45.
[2] 'Factor Proportions and Foreign Trade : the Case of Japan', *Review of Economics and Statistics*, Vol. 41 (1959), pp. 442-6.
[3] 'Factor Intensities of American Foreign Trade and Technical Progress', *Review of Economics and Statistics*, Vol. 37 (Nov. 1955), pp. 425-7.

units. Leontief himself used this argument to contend that the American labourer, on the average, is three times as efficient as an average labourer elsewhere (presumably her trading partners) and that 'spread thrice as thinly as the unadjusted figures suggest the American capital supply per "equivalent worker" turns out to be comparatively smaller, rather than larger, than that of many other countries'.[1]

Leontief merely asserts this, however, without elaborating (i) how the figure of threefold efficiency was arrived at; and (ii) in regard to which of her trading partners the U.S.A. would, by this adjustment, become labour-abundant. Both these questions require extensive statistical analysis which Leontief has not supplied. Leontief's argument in support of his assertion concerning the efficiency of American labour is merely that, in its absence, it would not be possible 'to explain the comparative surplus of labour which our figures unmistakably reveal' (p. 28). But this argument must be rejected because (i) it already assumes that the H-O theorem provides a valid explanation of the American pattern of trade when, in fact, the question being asked is precisely whether it does; and (ii) it also assumes that only the hypothesis about threefold efficiency of American labour can reconcile the results with an H-O type hypothesis when, in fact, there *are* other ways in which such reconciliation could be attempted.

There is no substitute for an actual empirical testing of the hypothesis that American labour is more efficient than foreign labour. From ordinary observation, the traditional method of empirical investigation, it would appear that except (i) in jobs where sheer physical brute force has a direct impact on productivity (as, for instance, in mining) and (ii) in countries where levels of consumption are so low as to affect productivity per man-hour in a variety of occupations (as, for instance, may be the case in certain sectors of Asian and Latin-American economies), one would expect differences in efficiency to be attributable to differences in entrepreneurial, management and organizational ability which affect the efficiency of *both* capital *and* labour probably equally. But, since he seeks to establish that America has more labour *relative* to capital than her trading partners, Leontief needs threefold efficiency of American labour *after* making allowance for any increased efficiency of both capital and labour due to better organization and management. Casual empiricism, therefore, tends to run counter to Leontief's assertion.

[1] 'Domestic Production and Foreign Trade: the American Capital Position re-examined', *Economia Internazionale*, Vol. 7 (1954), at p. 26.

TABLE I
COMPARATIVE CAPITAL-INTENSITY FOR SELECTED COUNTRIES

Countries	Home production in billions of I.U.	Working population in millions	Capital stock per head of working population in I.U.*	Capital stock domestically engaged in billions of I.U.	The previous variables P, L and C expressed in our units			Productivity coefficients (x)	Working population on U.S. labour equivalent basis	Comparative capital intensity	Productivity coefficients (y)	Capital on U.S. equivalent basis	Comparative capital intensity
					P	L	C	α=0·75	1	c/1	'Standard' Capital		
								'Standard' Labour	(10= 7÷9)	(11= 8÷10)			
(1)	(2)	(3)	(4)	(5)	(6)	(7)	(8)	(9)	(10)	(11)	(12)	(13)	(14)
United States (1939)	96·5	46·1	5626	259·36	1·000	1·000	1·000	1·000	1·000	1·000	1·000	1·000	1·000
Canada (1939)	7·04	3·76	5500	20·68	0·073	0·0816	0·0797	1·15	0·0710	1·1225	1·525	0·0523	0·6409
Great Britain (1939)	29·15	20·4	5478	111·75	0·3021	0·4425	0·3784	1·58	0·2081	1·3509	3·935	0·0962	0·2174
Netherlands (1938)	3·18	3·04	4920	14·96	0·0330	0·0659	0·0577	2·40	0·0275	2·0982	13·925	0·00415	0·0629
France (1938)	12·38	17·3	4055	70·15	0·1283	0·3753	0·2705	3·75	0·1001	2·7023	52·67	0·0051	0·0136
Norway (1939)	1·018	1·13	2737	3·09	0·0105	0·0245	0·0119	2·43	0·0101	1·1782	14·395	0·0008	0·0325
Italy (1938)	6·89	15·6	890	13·88	0·0714	0·3384	0·0535	4·30	0·0787	0·6798	79·77	0·00067	0·0019

* Excluding foreign investments.

Note : x=Non-standard labour   y=Non-standard capital

$$\frac{\text{Standard labour}}{\text{Standard capital}}$$

Source : Diab, *The United States Capital Position and the Structure of its Foreign Trade* (1956), for cols. 1–11.

9

Can statistical testing be employed to provide support for Leontief's hypothesis? Diab claims to have done precisely this.[1] He believes that he has demonstrated (subject only to two limitations : (*a*) the authenticity of Colin Clark's figures that he uses ; and (*b*) the correctness of the assumption that the Cobb-Douglas production function obtains in the countries studied) that the U.S.A. possesses, in terms of 'standard' labour, a lower stock of capital relative to labour than Canada, Great Britain, Netherlands, France and Norway (column 11 in Table I). His procedure is to assume that (i) labour must be reduced to 'standard' units in each country ; and (ii) the exact Cobb-Douglas production function, identical for all countries studied, is known for *standard* labour and capital. Given, therefore, this production function and the values of national output and capital, there is one equation to determine one unknown, standard labour.[2] Diab's procedure, however, is arbitrary and must be summarily dismissed. It amounts to positing a hypothetical production function (involving standard labour), deducing the quantity of standard labour by feeding known values of capital and output into it, and attributing the discrepancy between known labour (in natural units) and the deduced (standard) labour to 'efficiency'! But one could equally well use this procedure to deduce the 'efficiency' of management, of capital, indeed of anything at all! And yet striking answers! Thus, if we assume standard units for capital, rather than labour, the equation used by Diab will yield the quantity of standard capital in each country and the capital-labour endowment can be calculated afresh.[3] The results of this exercise have been presented in columns 12-14 of Table I, using Diab's figures. The United States turns out to be overwhelmingly capital-abundant after all![4]

[1] M. A. Diab, *The United States Capital Position and the Structure of its Foreign Trade*, Amsterdam, 1956.

[2] With the quantity of non-standard labour known for each country, the 'conversion factor' can be determined quite easily as the ratio of standard to non-standard labour. Diab, however, *first* determines this conversion factor, *then* uses it, with the known quantity of non-standard labour, to derive the quantity of *standard labour* (for each country) when, in fact, the equation would give the quantity of standard labour *directly*. The equation is of the following form : $P=(L)^{\alpha}(C)^{1-\alpha}$, where P is output, L is standard labour and C is capital. With α assumed to be known, L can be estimated for any country provided C and P are known. Cf. Diab, *op. cit.* pp. 42-5.

[3] The equation now reads : $P=(L)^{\alpha}(C)^{1-\alpha}$, where P is output, L is labour and C is *standard capital*. Now, we determine standard C with the equation. Actually, the assumption of differing efficiencies of C may not be so far-fetched, especially as technological progress varies so much between countries, and it is quite possible that America, which has had high rates of innovation since the war, may have more efficient capital and that this efficiency has not been allowed for in measuring capital. It is well known how deflation procedures used by statisticians do not make adequate allowance for improved quality.

[4] Since the assumption of differing factor-intensity is made in the H-O analysis, Diab should, in any case, as Terence Gorman has pointed out to me, have used

H-O Adaptation (2): It could also be argued that skilled labour embodies capital investment ; that, therefore, the amount of capital engaged in an activity is not fully reflected by the traditional concept and measure employed by Leontief. Measuring capital so as to allow for this kind of capital may help to reverse the present refutation of the H-O hypothesis. As yet, no statistical exercise estimating (i) the capital costs of skilled labour of different types and (ii) the precise adjustments to be made to Leontief's figures has been attempted. The former computation, which must be the foundation of the latter, would involve an estimate of the full cost of providing the education facilities (minus an allowance for such value of education as is regarded, admittedly in European tradition, as consumption) over the period of education, plus the loss of income to the economy in view of the opportunity lost of employing the students in gainful employment over this period (allowance again being made for the 'self-financing', through part-time employment, of education). That such an exercise may be rewarding, from the viewpoint of rehabilitating the H-O hypothesis, is indicated by Diab, who observes that American export industries employ relatively more non-agricultural labour ; [1] and that agricultural labour may be safely assumed to embody less educational and training capital than non-agricultural labour.

H-O Adaptation (3): Another possibility of restating the H-O theorem is suggested by reflecting on its logical derivation. As a logically true proposition, the H-O theorem is developed in the context of economies without any non-traded goods sector. Hence, from the viewpoint of predicting the trade pattern, one takes the *over-all* factor endowment in each economy. However, when a non-traded goods sector is admitted into the formal model, the H-O theorem is logically true, under the usual assumptions, only if the

two different Cobb-Douglas production functions, one for import-substitutes and the other for exportables. With two equations, he could then have determined the 'conversion' ratios (from standard to non-standard units) of *both* capital and labour. Some check on the results so secured could then be obtained by deriving such ratios from similar exercises with different pairs of activities and seeing whether these ratios show any degree of constancy.

[1] Leontief gives the following distribution of labour per million dollars between agricultural and non-agricultural labour :

	Exports	Import Replacements
Agricultural labour (man years)	22·436	40·934
Non-agricultural labour (man years)	159·872	129·069
Total labour	182·308	170·003
Capital ($, 1947 prices)	2,279,500	2,599,831

('Domestic Production and Foreign Trade', *Economia Internazionale*, Vol. 7, 1954, pp. 9-45). Cf. Diab, *The United States Capital Position and the Structure of its Foreign Trade*, pp. 52-3.

factor abundance is defined with reference to the factors employed (in equilibrium) in the traded goods sector alone. This latter might be named the 'residual' endowment since it is obtained by deducting, from the over-all endowment, the factors engaged (in equilibrium) in the non-traded goods sector.[1]

In an economy where trade covers a relatively small range of the activities embraced by domestic production, as no doubt the American economy may be assumed to be, such an interpretation of the H-O theorem is clearly called for. It would be interesting to investigate whether, in residual terms, the U.S.A. is in fact labour-abundant. This test would be fairly straightforward if the traded goods sector was clearly distinguishable from the non-traded goods sector. Complications, however, arise from (i) the existence of indirect requirements (so that even 'domestic' industries such as electricity and railways must be regarded as partly engaged in the traded sector in so far as they provide inputs to the traded sector); and (ii) the very high degree of aggregation of industries in input-output tables which leads to the depiction of practically every 'industry' as having either exports or imports (and usually both!) and hence to the grotesque minimization (if not elimination) of the non-traded goods sector (so that some disaggregation to sort out the non-traded goods from the traded ones would be necessary).[2] In view of these complications, it would be sensible to disaggregate initially in order to demarcate the traded goods sector, and then to revert to an aggregated input-output table to estimate the capital and labour engaged, directly and indirectly, in supporting its given levels of output. It is to be hoped that either Leontief or Tatemoto and Ichimura can be persuaded to undertake this exercise.[3]

[1] In fact, this is an instance of how logical theorizing may suggest testable hypotheses. The two-good, three-factor case, which results from the introduction of the non-traded goods sector, can be analysed rigorously to support the arguments in the text.

[2] For instance, if boilers and tractors happen to be put together under the heading 'machinery', one would want to break this down into (1) boilers : traded ; and (2) tractors : non-traded. Only a detailed analysis, with (no doubt) some arbitrariness inherent in the concept of a commodity, can help here. The value of the traded sector output thus discovered by disaggregation (in this case, the value of the boiler output), the total direct and indirect requirements of capital and labour for producing that output may be estimated by applying Leontief's procedure and using an aggregated input-output table.

[3] It should be emphasized that, in any case, what is relevant is the quantity of factors *engaged* in production in the trading countries and *not* their ownership. Thus, although the U.S. may be capital-abundant in terms of the ownership of capital, if there is a substantial migration of her capital to her trading partners, her trading partners could quite conceivably emerge as capital-abundant for the purposes of the H-O theorem. This would be particularly so if the capital that was so transferred went primarily into the *traded* goods sector. This, indeed, may be the case with the U.S. ; as Kravis has shown, a significant portion of American direct investment abroad, which altogether totals nearly $12 billion, has gone into

Kravis has recently suggested an approach that departs from the Ricardian and H-O types that we have examined.[1] In his view, the commodity composition of world trade is determined largely by 'availability'. Tariff policies and cartelization *tend* to rule out commodities that are available at home even though at 'slightly'higher cost.[2] Hence trade tends to be confined to commodities which are 'not available at home' — in the sense that *either* these items are 'unavailable in the absolute sense (for example, diamonds)' *or* 'an increase in output can be achieved only at much higher costs (that is, the domestic supply is inelastic)'.[3] Unavailability, in turn, can be traced to 'lack of natural resources (relative to demand)' or to technological change (and product differentiation) that confers temporary monopoly of production to the innovating country (until the foreigner learns to imitate efficiently).

While Kravis does not state any testable hypotheses himself, several do, in fact, follow from his suggestive ideas.[4] Provided 'inelasticity' of supply is explicitly defined, one testable hypothesis would be that a country's imports are characterized by inelasticity of domestic supply. One of Kravis' remarks, '. . . it is the elasticity of supply abroad and its inelasticity at home that gives rise to [the American pattern of imports]',[5] suggests a related hypothesis that a country's imports will be characterized by the excess of foreign over domestic elasticity of supply. These hypotheses, while testable in principle, would be immensely difficult to test in practice ; for they would demand statistical effort, at computation of elasticities, of considerable magnitude. It would be easier to formulate hypotheses which directly involve the 'scarcity' of natural resources and technical progress. To take the latter, one hypothesis, based on Kravis' own remarks, would be that a country's export industries show rates of technical progress higher than the national average. It would seem to me to be probably more useful to formulate a hypothesis involving *comparative* rates of technical progress, in Ricardian fashion ; for, after all, that is what would determine very largely the relative competitiveness of the same activities in two economies in so far as

---

development of natural resources which have become scarce in the U.S. and which she now imports (I. B. Kravis, ' "Availability" and other Influences on the Commodity Composition of Trade', *Journal of Political Economy*, Vol. 64 (April 1956), at p. 149).

[1] ' "Availability" and other Influences on the Commodity Composition of Trade', *Journal of Political Economy*, Vol. 64 (April 1956), pp. 143-55.

[2] *Ibid.* p. 155.   [3] *Ibid.* p. 143.

[4] This is an example of how hypotheses can be suggested by induction — Kravis' examination of the 1947 United States pattern of trade and 'casual empiricism' about tariffs and cartelization.

[5] ' "Availability" and other Influences on the Commodity Composition of Trade', *Journal of Political Economy*, Vol. 64 (April 1956), p. 150.

the elements associated with product differentiation are concerned. One such hypothesis would be that a country's export industries show higher rates of technical progress than the same industries in the trading partners.

An immensely rich field is thus opening up in the theory of comparative advantage with the trend towards empirical verification. We are, indeed, a long way from the sterile, 'logical' statement of the doctrine of comparative advantage. This shift in approach is to be found reflected also in the study of other problems in trade theory. Thus, for instance, Steuer has recently found that cross-section variations in the ratio of imports to national income (M/Y), comparing countries, can largely be accounted for by the population (P) and geographical area (A) of the countries. He derives an expression of the form : $M/Y = \dfrac{a}{b\sqrt{AP}}$ where a and b are parameters. One could 'explain' the correlation, with plausibility, by adducing arguments such as that the bigger the area, 'the greater the transport costs on average to randomly selected points within the area on goods moved from outside the area'.[1]

As with the study of other economic theory, however, this stress on empirical verification and on the formulation of theory so as to be testable is relatively new in trade theory. A substantial volume of the recent literature still concerns the derivation of logically true propositions in the context of well-defined models ; to this we must now turn.

III. NON-DISCRIMINATORY TARIFF CHANGES

In the traditionalist contributions to the pure theory of trade, two types of propositions can be found : (*a*) the 'static' propositions that describe the properties of equilibrium in a defined situation ; and (*b*) propositions in 'comparative statics' which concern the difference in the equilibrium configuration between two situations.[2] The classic, and almost solitary, instance of the former is Samuelson's theorem which states the sufficient conditions for the international equality of factor prices under free trade.[3] An equally renowned

---

[1] M. D. Steuer, 'Imports as a Function of Population and Area' (unpublished, Lent 1961), at p. 1.

[2] 'Dynamic' propositions, in *any* acceptable sense of the term, are still unknown in the pure theory of trade. For an exception, by way of an aside, see Mundell, 'The Pure Theory of International Trade', *American Economic Review*, Vol. 50 (March 1960), pp. 67-110 ; at pp. 72-3, n. 5.

[3] P. A. Samuelson, 'International Trade and the Equalisation of Factor Prices', *Economic Journal*, Vol. 58 (June 1948), pp. 163-84.

example of the latter is the theorem which defines the conditions under which protection will raise the real wage of the scarce factor. Among the latter, again, two types of propositions can be distinguished : (*b* (i)) those that concern the effect, on equilibrium prices and quantities, under a *pre-defined* trade situation, of an autonomous change in one of the following parameters : production functions, factor endowments, tastes and distribution of factor ownership (e.g. shift in tastes ; growth of capital ; technological change) ; and (*b* (ii)) those that concern the effects, while ruling out any *autonomous* shifts in these parameters, of a change in the trade situation (e.g. introduction of free trade ; increase of a tariff ; discriminatory reduction of a tariff).

This section centres exclusively on an analysis of a typical (*b* (ii))-type problem in comparative statics : the effect of non-discriminatory tariff changes. This decision is prompted partly by the fact that satisfactory and recent surveys of the other major questions have already appeared, while the literature on this problem has not been put together in quite the way that one should like ; [1] but partly also because it is sufficient, from the viewpoint of contrast with the new trends, to analyse the range of traditionalist conclusions on a single and, indeed, much-discussed question.

The most influential analysis of the effect of non-discriminatory tariff changes has been attempted in the context of the familiar two-good, two-factor, 'well-behaved' technology (i.e. linear and homogeneous production functions with diminishing returns along

---

[1] For useful surveys, the reader may refer to Lipsey for the theory of discriminatory tariff changes ('The Theory of Customs Unions : a General Survey', *Economic Journal*, Vol. 70 (Sept. 1960), pp. 496-513) ; myself and Johnson for the effects of autonomous shifts in demand and factor supplies ('Notes on some Controversies in the Theory of International Trade', *Economic Journal*, Vol. 70 (March 1960), pp. 74-93) ; and Caves for a lucid account of the factor price equalization theorem (*Trade and Economic Structure*, Harvard Univ. Press, 1960). (Professor Johnson has also commented on the effects of shifting technology in his paper to the Conference.) With reference to Caves (*op. cit.*), however, two points must be made. (i) There is nothing in the traditional literature on what happens to the *rate of interest* under trade ; we are merely assured that the rentals on factors are equalized by trade under specified conditions. As I have argued elsewhere, giving priority to a stimulating unpublished paper by Ramaswami, there is no equation in the model to answer this question ('The Theory of International Trade', *Indian Economic Journal*, Vol. 8 (July 1960), pp. 1-17) ; so that when Harrod, arguing within the traditional framework, puts the interest rate in his diagram instead of the factor price-ratio, he is stepping outside the limits of his model ('Factor-Price Relations under Free Trade', *Economic Journal*, Vol. 68 (June 1958), pp. 245-55). Samuelson, in a still unpublished paper ('Equalisation by Trade of the Interest Rate along with the Real Wage', 1960), has *subsequently* shown how the model can be extended to show the equalization of interest rates also, provided certain inequalities which arise with zero gross capital formation are ruled out. (ii) Whereas the traditional literature establishes the 'sufficient' conditions for factor price equalization, Reiter claims to have investigated the necessary conditions for this result as well ('Efficient International Trade and Equalization of Prices', *International Economic Review*, Vol. 2 (Jan. 1961), pp. 29-64).

isoquants) in each good, full employment, profit maximization and perfect competition model. This model, while implicit in Leontief [1] and Lerner,[2] was first employed formally, to the best of my knowledge, by Stolper and Samuelson,[3] then extensively used by Samuelson,[4]) and has now come to be the framework of most modern trade theorists.[5]

The 'comparative statics' propositions that can be uncovered with its aid may be classified as follows : (1) free trade *vs.* no trade (comparisons) ; (2) restricted trade *vs.* free trade ; (3) restricted trade *vs.* no trade ; and (4) restricted trade *vs.* less restricted trade. Within each category, it will be useful to distinguish further propositions according as they relate to (i) *internal* commodity price-ratio, (ii) *external* commodity price-ratio, (iii) factor price-ratio, (iv) absolute real incomes of factors, (v) relative shares of factors in total real income, and (vi) quantity of production of either commodity.[6]

A. *Free Trade* vs. *No Trade*

(i) *Commodity price-ratio.* If the price-ratio is defined as the price of unit importables divided by the price of unit exportables (as it will be throughout this section), it will be lower under free trade than under no trade.[7]

(ii) *Factor price-ratio.* With the assumed technology, Samuelson has established the nature of the relationship between factor and commodity price-ratios.[8] Short of inequalities arising with complete specialization in production, the (relative) price of the factor

[1] 'The Use of Indifference Curves in the Analysis of Foreign Trade', *Quarterly Journal of Economics*, Vol. 47 (May 1933), pp. 493-503.

[2] 'The Diagrammatical Representation of Cost conditions in International Trade', *Economica*, Vol. 34 (August 1932), pp. 346-56 ; and 'The Symmetry between Import and Export Taxes', *Economica*, n.s., Vol. III (August 1936), pp. 306-13.

[3] 'Protection and Real Wages', *Review of Economic Studies*, Vol. 9 (Nov. 1941), pp. 58-73.

[4] 'International Trade and the Equalisation of Factor Prices', *Economic Journal*, Vol. 58 (June 1948), pp. 163-84 ; and 'International 'Factor Price Equalisation once again', *Economic Journal*, Vol. 59 (June 1949), pp. 181-97.

[5] For a lucid survey of some of the logically true propositions in the pure theory of trade, using this model, see Mundell, 'The Pure Theory of International Trade', *American Economic Review*, Vol. 50 (March 1960), pp. 67-110.

[6] Moreover, the analysis could be extended to other questions such as, for instance, the effect on factor proportions in each activity (which depends on the shift in the factor price-ratio) and on the volume of trade (where a distinction must be drawn between the volume of exports and of imports). It should be noted also that the phrase 'restricted trade', in this section, refers to trade restricted by a non-prohibitive tariff (or export tax ; A. P. Lerner, 'The Symmetry between Import and Export Taxes', *Economica*, n.s., Vol. III (August 1936), pp. 306-13).

[7] This statement rules out the possibility of multiple equilibria in consumption at the same price-ratio. In the 'large' country case, the change in the price-ratio may be negligible.

[8] 'International Trade and the Equalisation of Factor Prices', *Economic Journal*, Vol. 58 (June 1948), pp. 163-84.

used intensively in the production of a commodity rises with an increase in the price of that commodity.[1] Hence free trade will increase the price of the factor used intensively in the production of the exportable good when incomplete specialization is not eliminated ; but the factor price-ratio may be unchanged when inequalities occur with complete specialization.

(iii) *Absolute real income of factor.* Again a distinction must be drawn between situations where trade does not eliminate incomplete specialization and the rest. (*a*) Where the former obtains, the Stolper-Samuelson argument shows that, by raising (lowering) the marginal product of the factor in terms of each good, an increase (decrease) in the price of a factor unambiguously raises (lowers) the real income of that factor.[2] Hence free trade will raise the real income of the factor used intensively in the exportable good and lower that of the other. (*b*) Where inequalities occur with complete specialization, half of this neat conclusion breaks down. Since any lowering of the commodity price-ratio beyond the level at which complete specialization in the production of exportables occurs will benefit *both* factors, it is no longer logically true to argue that free trade will lower the real income of the factor used intensively in the importable good.

(iv) *Relative share of factors in total real income.* Since the supply of factors is fixed, the change in the share of each factor in total income can be deduced from the conclusion about absolute incomes and the proposition that free trade is superior to no trade. The share of the factor used intensively in the exportable good will rise with free trade, and that of the other factor fall, when trade does not eliminate incomplete specialization. But nothing can be said in general about the case where inequalities occur.

(v) *Production.* In view of the (not necessarily strict) convexity of the production possibility curve, obtaining under the assumptions of the model, the production of the importable (exportable) good will not increase (diminish) with the transition to free trade.

B. Restricted Trade vs. Free Trade

(i) *Internal commodity price-ratio.* A tariff, imposed on a free trade situation, can raise, lower or leave unchanged the internal commodity price-ratio. The 'paradoxical' possibility that a tariff

---

[1] The careful reader will notice that I have assumed *neither* differing factor-intensity for the two goods *nor* the non-reversibility of factor-intensity. Neither of these assumptions is necessary for the argument of the text. Cf. [5], [16], [17, Chapter I].

[2] 'Protection and Real Wages', *Review of Economic Studies*, Vol. 9 (Nov. 1941), pp. 58-73.

may lower the internal price of the imported good is attributed to Metzler,[1] but was analysed earlier by Lerner.[2] The conditions under which any of the results will occur can be rigorously established, involving the marginal propensity to spend, from tariff proceeds, on exportables, and the elasticity of foreign demand for exports.[3]

(ii) *External commodity price-ratio.* This again can register any behaviour. A rise, however, would be 'paradoxical' and Lerner must be assigned priority for an analysis of this possibility.[4] The rigorous formula governing the direction of the change in the external price-ratio can be established, involving the marginal propensity to spend on imports from the tariff proceeds and the home country's elasticity of demand for imports.[5]

(iii) *Factor price-ratio.* The Samuelson relationship between commodity and factor price-ratio holds.[6] Hence restricted trade can increase, decrease or fail to affect the price of either factor (depending directly on how internal commodity prices are affected).

(iv) *Absolute real income of factors.* With restricted trade, the real *income* of factors depends not merely on the real *wage* in employment, which we have discussed hitherto, but also on transfer incomes from redistributed tariff proceeds (or alternatively the public consumption provided by the state). Thus the problem is more complicated than under the free trade *vs.* no trade comparison. However, it is not as difficult as it looks. It is still possible to say that the movement in the real income will be in the same direction as the change in the real wage, *provided* the country as a whole has not benefited from the imposition of the tariff; for then, the factor whose real wage has fallen cannot be over-compensated by a transfer of the tariff revenues. Hence two cases can be distinguished. (*a*) Where the external price-ratio does not fall with the restriction of trade, the country cannot benefit from the restriction; hence the conclusions from the real wage are valid for changes in the real income as well. (*b*) Where the external terms of trade improve, the

[1] Tariffs, the Terms of Trade, and the Distribution of National Income', *Journal of Political Economy*, Vol. 57 (Feb. 1949), pp. 1-29.

[2] 'The Symmetry between Import and Export Taxes', *Economica*, n.s., Vol. III (August 1936), pp. 306-13.

[3] J. E. Meade, *A Geometry of International Trade*, London, 1952; L. Metzler, 'Tariffs, the Terms of Trade, and the Distribution of National Income', *Journal of Political Economy*, Vol. 57 (Feb. 1949), pp. 1-29; R. A. Mundell, 'The Pure Theory of International Trade', *American Economic Review*, Vol. 50 (March 1960), pp. 67-110.

[4] 'The Symmetry between Import and Export Taxes', *Economica*, n.s., Vol. III (August 1936), pp. 306-13.

[5] The exact formulae for the effect on the external commodity price-ratio can be deduced from those given below, p. 15, n. 1, by making the tariff rate $t=0$.

[6] P. A. Samuelson, 'International Trade and the Equalisation of Factor Prices', *Economic Journal*, Vol. 58 (June 1948), pp. 163-84.

country *may* benefit from trade and it *may* be possible to over-compensate, with tariff revenue, the factor whose real wage happens to have fallen.[1]

(v) *Relative share of factors in total real income.* The conclusion concerning shares is also correspondingly complex. Since restricted trade may be superior or inferior to free trade, two cases may be distinguished. (*a*) Where the external price-ratio does not fall with the imposition of the tariff, the tariff must bring a loss to the country and hence the shares of factors must rise or fall in the same direction as their real wage and income. (*b*) Where the external terms of trade improve, nothing definite can be said.[2]

(vi) *Production.* The change in production will be related, as before, to the change in the internal commodity price-ratio. The production of importables will not decrease or increase according as the internal commodity price-ratio rises or falls with the restriction of trade.

C. Restricted Trade vs. No Trade

(i) *Commodity price-ratio.* The (internal) commodity price-ratio must be lower under restricted trade than under no trade.

(ii) *Factor price-ratio.* The price of the factor used intensively in the exportable good must be correspondingly lower, and of the other factor higher, under restricted trade, except that there may be no change if inequalities occur with specialization.

(iii) *Absolute real income of factors.* The distinction between real wage and real income is relevant here. (*a*) The real wage of the factor used intensively in exportables will rise ; and hence also its real income. (*b*) However, the real wage of the other factor will fall when restricted trade does not eliminate incomplete specialization and may actually rise when inequalities occur with specialization. Where its real wage falls, redistribution of tariff proceeds may over-compensate the loss.

(iv) *Relative share of factors in total real income.* Restricted trade is superior to no trade. Hence the share of the factor used intensively in the exportable good must rise and that of the other

---

[1] J. Bhagwati, 'Protection, Real Wages and Real Incomes', *Economic Journal*, Vol. 69 (Dec. 1959), pp. 733-48.

[2] Metzler, in his well-known analysis (*op. cit.*), is in error on this conclusion. Like Stolper and Samuelson ('Protection and Real Wages', *Review of Economic Studies*, Vol. 9, pp. 58-73), he proceeds to deduce the effect on relative shares from the effect on real wage in employment. Whereas this procedure is valid, as it turns out, for the former authors who argue in terms of (1) free trade *vs.* no trade and (2) restricted trade *vs.* free trade *under the assumption that the country cannot affect her external terms of trade*, it is not so — as argued in the text — when no restriction is imposed on the direction of the change in the country's external terms of trade.

factor fall when the latter factor has suffered a loss of real income. From the immediately preceding analysis, however, it is clear that possibilities exist, from the presence of inequalities and of tariff revenue, of the latter factor actually gaining in real income with the introduction of restricted trade.

(v) *Production.* The production of importables (exportables) will not increase (decrease) with the introduction of restricted trade.

D. Restricted Trade vs. Less Restricted Trade

(i) *Internal commodity price-ratio.* This ratio can register any behaviour when the tariff is increased. The conditions which determine the direction of the change have been established by Metzler [1] and, with different assumptions, by myself and Johnson,[2] the free trade *vs.* no trade formulae appearing as special cases.[3]

(ii) *External commodity price-ratio.* This ratio also can move in all possible directions. The formulae defining the conditions for a move in any given direction can be established.[4]

(iii) *Factor price-ratio.* The Samuelson relationship between factor and commodity price-ratios holds.

(iv) *Absolute real income of factors.* The distinction between real wage and real income applies. But even the small degree of correlation established between the movements in real wage and real income of the factor whose real wage increases with the change now disappears. The reason is that tariff revenues now exist in both the initial and the post-change situations ; hence the distinction between wage and income obtains in both situations. A beneficial movement in the real wage may be more than offset by an adverse movement in the share in tariff proceeds. No universally valid conclusion can be reached, therefore, concerning the effect on absolute

---

[1] 'Tariffs, International Demand, and Domestic Prices', *Journal of Political Economy*, Vol. 57 (August 1949), pp. 345-51.

[2] 'A Generalized Theory of the Effects of Tariffs on the Terms of Trade', *Oxford Economic Papers*, Vol. 13 (Oct. 1961), pp. 1-29.

[3] Traditionally, the formulae have been derived under two alternative assumptions : either the government spends the tariff proceeds or the private sector does. In the former case, the external price-ratio will fall or rise according as

$$[g-(1+gt)\frac{c}{\pi}-\xi' \cdot \frac{1+gt]}{\pi} \gtrless 0$$

and in the latter case, as

$$\frac{\xi'}{1+(1-c)t} \gtrless 0,$$

where c is the private sector's marginal propensity to spend on importables at the domestic price of importables (π), g the government's marginal propensity to spend tariff revenue on imports at the international price of imports and ξ' the compensated elasticity of private demand for imports. The derivation of these and similar formulae for the effects on the internal price-ratio can be found by the interested reader in the paper by myself and Johnson, 'A Generalized Theory of the Effects of Tariffs on the Terms of Trade', *loc. cit.*   [4] *Ibid.*

real incomes of factors, without putting arbitrary restrictions on the way in which tariff revenues are shared between factors.

(v) *Relative share of factors in total real income.* Since no generally valid conclusion can be reached concerning absolute incomes, it follows that nothing can be stated concerning changes in relative shares as well.

(vi) *Production.* The change in production will be related to the movement in the internal commodity price-ratio. Hence the production of importables will not diminish or increase according as the internal commodity price-ratio rises or falls with the increase in tariff.

This is the range of conclusions that can be squeezed out of the specified model. The model itself *can* be changed and the analysis re-worked when one of the assumptions made in the model is 'relaxed'. Thus, for instance, recent contributions by Kemp and Jones, and by myself and Johnson, analyse the effects of letting factor supplies vary with their prices in the context of a model otherwise identical with that employed here.[1] Quite inevitably some of the results have to be altered ; the formulae for changes in the price-ratios get revised,[2] and so do the propositions concerning changes in production.[3] Some results, however, *do* survive ; for instance, the relationship between commodity and factor price-ratios remains intact because it depends purely on technology.[4]

These exercises are certainly challenging and hence interesting. They are also useful in so far as they often dispel naïve beliefs held by sophisticated people — for instance, Metzler's classic analysis demonstrated that a tariff *could* lower the domestic price of the imported good ; [5] the Stolper-Samuelson result showed that, contrary to the consensus of opinion, one *can* predict, given certain assumptions, the effect of free trade on the real wage of factors *without* having to bother about consumption patterns ; [6] and Samuelson

[1] M. C. Kemp and R. Jones, 'Variable Labour Supply and the Theory of International Trade', 1960, unpublished ; J. Bhagwati and H. G. Johnson, 'A Generalized Theory of the Effects of Tariffs on the Terms of Trade', *Oxford Economic Papers*, Vol. 13 (Oct. 1961), pp. 1-29.

[2] J. Bhagwati and H. G. Johnson, 'A Generalized Theory of the Effects of Tariffs on the Terms of Trade', *loc. cit.*

[3] M. C. Kemp, 'The Gain from International Trade', 1960, unpublished.

[4] One other contribution of interest should be mentioned : Kemp's analysis of the effect on income distribution in the context of Keynesian under-employment, in his article, 'Tariffs, Income and Distribution', *Quarterly Journal of Economics*, Vol. 70 (Feb. 1956), pp. 139-55.

[5] 'Tariffs, the Terms of Trade, and the Distribution of National Income', *Journal of Political Economy*, Vol. 57 (Feb. 1949), pp. 1-29.

[6] 'Protection and Real Wages', *Review of Economic Studies*, Vol. 9 (Nov. 1941), pp. 58-73.

managed to show, to the astonishment of many of his contemporaries, that trade *could* equalize factor prices between countries.[1] But do they have any further scientific value? A critique comes readily to mind, in view of the analysis of Section II: the propositions deduced are all logically true and cannot be empirically refuted *if treated as such*. That they are so treated is beyond doubt. However, this need not be so. Is there anything to prevent one from taking Metzler's formula, for the direction of the change in the domestic terms of trade with a change in the tariff, and treating *that* as an empirically refutable hypothesis? Indeed, a veritable flood of fairly *sophisticated* hypotheses, testable in principle, would emerge from the propositions deduced from well-defined models.[2] Moreover, by forging new concepts in dealing with new problems, as for instance in extending the propositions of trade theory to the case of variable factor supplies,[3] the theorist provides useful ways of organizing thought on complex questions and, provided these concepts have operational significance, can prepare the way for fresh, empirically testable propositions.

IV. WELFARE PROPOSITIONS

In welfare theory, as in positive analysis, one can discern a new trend, though it should be emphasized that this trend is quite recent and represents departure from a tradition that begins, for all practical purposes, with Samuelson's classic paper of 1939.[4] Prior to Samuelson's work, there *is* much discussion, no doubt, of the gains from trade and their division between countries, in the classical literature,[5] and also in the work of the neo-classicals, Marshall and Edgeworth.[6] But none of it acquires any rigour or much clarity until the beginning of the 'new welfare economics'.

[1] 'International Trade and the Equalisation of Factor Prices', *Economic Journal*, Vol. 58 (June 1948), pp. 163-84.

[2] This already presumes, of course, that one can quantify concepts like the 'elasticity of demand for imports', with all their attendant assumptions. There *is* one point of view, not wholly without persuasive arguments, which challenges the possibility of quantifying such equilibrium concepts at all in the world as we know it.

[3] J. Bhagwati and H. G. Johnson, 'A Generalized Theory of the Effects of Tariffs on the Terms of Trade', *Oxford Economic Papers*, Vol. 13 (Oct. 1961), pp. 1-29; M. C. Kemp and R. Jones, 'Variable Labour, Supply and the Theory of International Trade', 1960, unpublished.

[4] 'The Gains from International Trade', *Canadian Journal of Economics and Political Science*, Vol. 5 (May 1939), pp. 195-205.

[5] J. Bhagwati, 'The Theory of International Trade', *Indian Economic Journal*, Vol. 8 (July 1960), pp. 1-17; J. S. Mill, *Principles of Political Economy*.

[6] Surveyed in J. Bhagwati and H. G. Johnson, 'Notes on some Controversies in the Theory of International Trade', *Economic Journal*, Vol. 70 (March 1960), pp. 74-93, at section III.

Let me say right away that the new trend I am referring to is the *measurement* of welfare changes. It originates with the work of Meade [1] and has since gained converts.[2] Since it involves a compromise with the problem of income distribution, it is in contrast to the 'superior-for-all-income-distributions' approach to welfare associated with the name of Samuelson, in terms of which the few early welfare propositions in trade theory are certainly cast.

I think one can distinguish between two reasons for this growing shift in approach to welfare propositions : both of them related to the need to formulate economic theory as a guide to policy. The simplest reason, of course, is that policy-makers, it so happens, are interested in asking questions that *do* demand quantification of changes in welfare. The 'economic cost' of adopting a particular trade policy is frequently the sort of figure one wants to know in order to assess whether the other benefits claimed for the policy are worth the loss of welfare entailed.[3] However, there is a reason, more subtle, but no less significant, which makes the new trend inevitable even if one were, in principle, content to ask questions about the *direction* of the change in welfare : questions of the form, 'Is a specified change in trade policy desirable from the viewpoint of economic welfare ?' can be answered, without contradiction, for *all* possible distributions, in the full Samuelson sense, only for a very restricted range of changes. Unless, therefore, one is willing to throw up one's hands in the face of policy-makers' questions concerning choices that lie outside the select group that satisfies the Samuelson criterion, one *must* adopt criteria, less demanding than Samuelson's, which take income-distribution directly into their fold. Once this is done, it is easy to show that, for determining the direction of the change in welfare in any of these choices, the need to measure economic relationships arises ; and once this compromise is made, the calculus of measurement of welfare changes becomes available as well.

[1] J. E. Meade, *Trade and Welfare* (*The Theory of International Economic Policy*, Vol. II), Oxford Univ. Press, 1955 ; *Mathematical Supplement* (*Trade and Welfare*), O.U.P., 1955 ; *The Theory of Customs Unions*, Amsterdam, 1955.

[2] W. M. Corden, 'The Calculation of the Cost of Protection', *Economic Record*, Vol. 33 (April 1957), pp. 29-51 ; H. G. Johnson, 'Discriminatory Tariff Reduction : a Marshallian Analysis', *Indian Journal of Economics*, Vol. 38 (1957), pp. 39-47 ; *idem*, 'Marshallian Analysis of Discriminatory Tariff Reduction : an Extension', *Indian Journal of Economics*, Vol. 39 (Oct. 1958), pp. 177-81 ; *idem*, 'The Cost of Protection and the Scientific Tariff', *Journal of Political Economy*, Vol. 68 (August 1960), pp. 327-45 ; J. Wemelsfelder, 'The Short-term Effect of the Lowering of Import Duties in Germany', *Economic Journal*, Vol. 70 (March 1960), pp. 94-104.

[3] Thus, for instance, one wants to know how much a given tariff costs, so that one can make up one's mind whether it is worth worrying about the pressure groups that manage to have it adopted.

More must be said concerning this issue. Propositions concerning comparisons of trade policies *defined unambiguously in terms of degrees of restriction* (no restriction, total prohibition, 5 per cent tariff, 10 per cent tariff etc.), which satisfy the Samuelson criterion, can be classified under two headings, national welfare and world welfare. With reference to *national welfare*, there are two such propositions, *provided convexity of the production possibility curve and the satisfaction of the standard 'first-best' conditions are assumed*: (1) free trade (no restriction) is superior to no trade (total prohibition) ; [1] and (2) restricted trade is superior to no trade.[2] It should be noted that it *cannot* be shown that the actual *bundle* of goods consumed under free trade, for instance, is superior to the actual bundle of goods under no trade for all hypothetical distributions. What *can* be shown is merely that the utility-possibility curve corresponding to the free trade *situation* is uniformly outside (though it may touch) the utility-possibility curve corresponding to the no trade *situation*.[3] We thus have a unique ranking of these trade policies, *regardless* of the income-distribution we may choose. The policy-maker, provided he accepts the Samuelson criterion, can be confidently told to adopt free trade in preference to no trade as long as convexity and the standard 'first-best' conditions are verified to hold for the economy. As for *world welfare*, three propositions appear to hold : (1) free trade is superior to no trade ; (2) restricted trade is superior to no trade ; and (3) free trade is superior to restricted trade.[4]

---

[1] P. A. Samuelson, 'The Gains from International Trade', *Canadian Journal of Economics and Political Science*, Vol. 5 (May 1939), pp. 195-205 ; M. C. Kemp, 'The Gain from International Trade', 1960, unpublished.

[2] See Kemp, *ibid.* Samuelson's well-known proof of the former proposition is for a country with given external terms of trade. However, as Kemp ('The Gain from International Trade') has shown, no such limitation is necessary. Further, it should be noted that the proposition that free trade is superior to no trade is nothing but the welfare side of the theory of comparative advantage. It is *not* to be confused with the problem concerning the explanation of the pattern of trade as it obtains in the real world. For instance, the H-O theorem is meant to predict the pattern of trade ; and is not a theorem with welfare implications. Chenery has recently fallen victim to a muddle in this respect : 'The Heckscher-Ohlin version of the comparative cost doctrine . . . states that a country will *benefit* from trade by producing commodities that use more of its relatively abundant factors of production'. (My italics.) See his article, 'Comparative Advantage and Development Policy', *American Economic Review*, Vol. 51 (March 1961), pp. 19-20.

[3] R. E. Baldwin, 'A Comparison of Welfare Criteria', *Review of Economic Studies*, Vol. 21 (1953–54), pp. 154-61 ; I. M. D. Little, *A Critique of Welfare Economics*, Oxford Univ. Press, 1957 (2nd ed.).

[4] The first proposition has been established, for instance, by S. Reiter, 'Efficient International Trade and Equalization of Prices', *International Economic Review*, Vol. 2 (Jan. 1961), pp. 29-64. Whereas, to the best of my knowledge, no proofs, of the latter two propositions have yet been advanced, I think they are valid. It should be noted further that none of these propositions require the assumption of a fixed supply of resources, as demonstrated by Samuelson, 'The Gains from International Trade', *Canadian Journal of Economics and Political Science*, Vol. 5 (May

Once, however, we get away from this select group of trade policies, which can be ranked independently of distributional considerations in the Samuelson sense, the situation becomes quite fluid. It turns out that the *ranking of trade policies is affected by the income-distribution chosen.* Take, for instance, national welfare again. Let us say that we wish to rank two non-discriminatory tariffs, one at 5 and the other at 10 per cent. Their mutual ranking could be reversed for two alternative distributions. One just cannot go along to the policy-maker and tell him, without getting into distributional questions, that a 5 per cent tariff is better than one twice that size — unless, of course, one imposes sufficient restrictions on the system to eliminate the problem of contradiction (as can be done, in this instance, by making the 'small' country assumption). It is only when the income-distribution is given that one can proceed to rank all tariffs ; as is done, for instance, in the typical geometrical rendering of commercial policy.[1] Of course, one can argue that, for a *variable tariff rate,* the utility-possibility curve for an optimum tariff situation will lie outside that for the free trade situation. This proposition is valid and does satisfy the Samuelson criterion. However, it is irrelevant from the viewpoint of economic policy which asks questions concerning changes in trade policy and hence aims at ranking, among other things, different tariff rates.

The problem is confounded when the standard 'first-best' conditions do not obtain (as they certainly appear not to in the real world) — when the desirability of a change in trade policy must be decided in the face of unalterable 'distortions' such as a tax on a commodity, monopoly pricing of a factor or (if one is thinking of world welfare) a tariff elsewhere. Once these 'distortions' are admitted, even the few propositions which manage to rank certain trade policies by the formidable Samuelson criterion cease to be valid in general.[2]

Faced with these difficulties, we should prefer to meet the problem of distribution head on, instead of giving up discussing the welfare implications of changes in trade policy which constitute potential policy decisions. This is precisely what has happened.

1939), pp. 195-205 ; and recently reiterated by J. Vanek ('An Afterthought on the "Real Cost : Opportunity Cost" Dispute', *Review of Economic Studies,* Vol. 26 (June 1959), pp. 198-208) and by V. C. Walsh ('Leisure and International Trade', *Economica,* n.s., Vol. 23 (August 1956), pp. 253-60).

[1] H. G. Johnson, *International Trade and Economic Growth,* London, 1958, chapter II.

[2] Similar chaos is caused by the loss of convexity : R. C. O. Matthews, 'Reciprocal Demand and Increasing Returns', *Review of Economic Studies,* Vol. 17 (1949-50), pp. 149-58 ; J. E. Meade, *A Geometry of International Trade,* London, 1952. I should affirm again that I am not denying that sufficient restrictions (reducing generality) can be imposed so as to rescue some propositions that pass the Samuelson test.

The standard theoretical procedure has been to set up a community welfare function which already assumes that the State adopts a policy of lump-sum income transfers to fix the income-distribution at some 'desired' level, and then to evaluate the change in welfare in terms of that function (and hence *that particular* income-distribution).[1] Alternatively, one can adopt Meade's procedure of explicitly combining equity and efficiency in a single welfare function by assuming cardinality and the possibility of inter-personal comparisons of welfare;[2] this enables us to judge the change in welfare between two situations for the actual market income-distributions achieved and, indeed, without having to conjure up a state of lump-sum transfers.

In either case, the way opens up for an evaluation of welfare changes that depends on specific income-distributions, which the State deems desirable and maintains or which are explicitly assigned 'distributional weights' in the Meade fashion. And the evaluation extends not merely to the direction of the change but also to the magnitude. That the former, ordinalist approach yields actual measurement of changes in welfare can be demonstrated,[3] and its systematic application to the measurement of the cost of protection (purely at a theoretical level) has recently been provided by Johnson.[4] Meade, on the other hand, has applied his cardinalist method to the analysis of numerous second-best variety of problems, inclusive of the theory of customs unions.[5]

[1] This is the only sensible way in which one can justify the standard practice of trade theorists, and particularly the practitioners of geometry. For an explicit statement of this assumption, see H. G. Johnson, 'The Cost of Protection and the Scientific Tariff', *Journal of Political Economy*, Vol. 68 (August 1960). Sometimes, however, a community welfare function, defined purely in terms of the quantities of goods available, is maximized as though the community were identical with an individual (see R. G. Lipsey and K. Lancaster, 'The General Theory of the Second Best', *Review of Economic Studies*, Vol. 24, 1956–57, pp. 11-32), a procedure that is certainly unwarranted except in a Crusoe economy or under the assumption of a redistribution policy by the government which fixes the distribution of income at some desired level.

[2] J. E. Meade, *Trade and Welfare (The Theory of International Economic Policy*, Vol. II); and *Mathematical Supplement (Trade and Welfare)*.

[3] J. Bhagwati and H. G. Johnson, 'Notes on some Controversies in the Theory of International Trade', *Economic Journal*, Vol. 70 (March 1960), pp. 74-93, at Section III.

[4] 'The Cost of Protection and the Scientific Tariff', *Journal of Political Economy*, Vol. 68 (August 1960), pp. 327-45.

[5] *Trade and Welfare (The Theory of International Economic Policy*, Vol. II); and *Mathematical Supplement (Trade and Welfare)*. Meade's method of measuring welfare changes is developed in the context of, though not limited to, world welfare. The method amounts basically to estimating gains (losses) as the increase (decrease) in the volume of transactions in each commodity multiplied by the excess of utility derived by the buyer over the utility of that commodity to the seller, a divergence that is measured, for instance in the case of a tax, by the rate of the tax on the assumption that the price paid equals the marginal utility derived by the buyer and the price received the utility to the seller. Johnson's alternative

As for the empirical applications of these theoretical developments on the front of welfare measurement, these are still quite rare. On the question of the *direction* of change in welfare when the trade policy is changed, there is the classic, though totally unsatisfactory, attempt of Marris to recommend protection to British agriculture on the ground that the marginal rate of transformation of British exports into imports is less than the domestic rate of transformation in production.[1] Such a comparison implies not merely the acceptance of the 'first-best' and convexity assumptions, but also a willingness to assume either that the State pursues an income-distribution policy or that the market income-distribution that accompanies the change is acceptable in terms of a calculus like Meade's. In the matter of estimates of *magnitudes* of welfare change, there are attempts by Verdoorn, Scitovsky and Johnson at estimating the gains from European integration, which use in substance Meade's method.[2] There is one striking recent example, a study by Wemelsfelder,[3] of the short-term effect of the lowering of import-duties in Germany, which also uses a method identical with Meade's except that it is cast in a different mould and adapted for large changes while Meade's method is developed for marginal changes.

The trend towards measurement is thus quite noticeable in the recent work, both theoretical and applied, on changes in welfare consequent on the adoption of specific trade policies. Having isolated it and analysed the reasons why it must be judged both necessary and desirable, I wish now to close with a brief analysis of a question which I believe to be of some importance in a 'developing world' and which is thus an appropriate note on which to end this survey.

Economists associated with planning for growth in the developing countries often question the validity of the welfare propositions of trade theory in the context of economic expansion. This is a

method of measurement, based on the ordinal approach, yields a measure that is identical except for differences which are attributable to the fact that Johnson, unlike Meade, is not confining himself to marginal changes. See 'The Cost of Protection and the Scientific Tariff', *loc. cit.* A partial equilibrium, surplus approach has also been used sometimes, as a method of measurement, by Corden ('The Calculation of the Cost of Protection', *Economic Record*, Vol. 33 (April 1957), pp. 29-51), and by Johnson ('Discriminatory Tariff Reduction', *Indian Journal of Economics*, Vol. 38, pp. 39-47; 'Marshallian Analysis of Discriminatory Tariff Reduction', *ibid.*, Vol. 39, pp. 177-81); but it is subject to well-known drawbacks which need not be repeated : see I. M. D. Little, *A Critique of Welfare Economics*, and E. J. Mishan, 'A Survey of Welfare Economics', *Economic Journal*, Vol. 70 (June 1960), pp. 197-265.

[1] R. L. Marris, 'The Purchasing Power of British Exports', *Economica*, n.s., Vol. 22 (Feb. 1955), pp. 13-28.

[2] R. G. Lipsey, 'The Theory of Customs Unions : a General Survey', *Economic Journal*, Vol. 70 (Sept. 1960), pp. 509-11.

[3] 'The Short-term Effect of the Lowering of Import Duties in Germany', *Economic Journal*, Vol. 70 (March 1960), pp. 94-104.

pertinent question which demands careful examination. It can be fruitfully examined by analysing the status of the proposition, concerning national welfare, that free trade is better than no trade.

Fatal objections can certainly be raised against this proposition, which rest on external economies (inclusive of 'infant industry'), divergences arising out of surplus labour at positive wage, urban-rural wage differentials,[1] and such like features of some under-developed economies.[2] However, these factors have to do with underdevelopment; they are irrelevant from the viewpoint of our problem which deals with growth *per se*.

At first sight, it appears that the mere fact of economic expansion, whatever be its cause, should raise no problems. In principle, why can we not apply the proposition that free trade is superior to no trade both before and after the change? And this, indeed, is a tenable view. It underlies the recent treatment of growth by trade theorists,[3] although they cast their argument in terms of the net effect on real income of an *autonomous* change such as an increment in a homogeneous capital stock.[4]

Within this framework, the proposition that free trade is superior to no trade certainly remains unimpeached. It must be admitted, however, that these models, in discussing capital accumulation, abstract from those very difficulties that arise with the phenomenon of time and multi-period optimality. (i) Since the increment in capital stock is autonomous, the question of the optimality of the *saving decisions* that generated the total savings and investment is evaded. (ii) Since capital is further assumed to be homogeneous, one also eliminates the problem of inter-temporal optimality that arises with the fact that the current period's *composition of the capital*

---

[1] G. Haberler,' Some Problems in the Pure Theory of International Trade', *Economic Journal*, Vol. 60 (June 1950), pp. 223-40 ; J. E. Meade, *Trade and Welfare* (*The Theory of International Economic Policy*, Vol. II).

[2] A divergence between private and social marginal rates of transformation which may arise in a typical under-developed country with insufficient channels of communication has not yet been emphasized in the literature on trade theory. Take, for instance, the case of an economy which imports machines. It may have cheap iron ore deposits which would make the production of machines domestically quite economic. However, no machines are produced at home because there is no production of steel at home ; and no steel is produced because no machines are being produced. Lack of co-ordination leads to a divergence between private and social rates of transformation between other things, on one hand, and steel plus machines on the other.

[3] J. Bhagwati, 'Immiserizing Growth: a Geometrical Note', *Review of Economic Studies*, Vol. 25 (June 1958), pp. 201-5 ; H. G. Johnson, *International Trade and Economic Growth*, London, 1958.

[4] Ingenious papers by Ramaswami ('The Effects of Accumulation on the Terms of Trade', *Economic Journal*, Vol. 70 (Sept. 1960), pp. 514-18) and by Samuelson ('Equalisation by Trade of the Interest Rate along with the Real Wage', 1960, unpublished) extend the argument to models which treat capital as a *produced* factor.

stock, which becomes the following period's factor endowment, will limit the range of outputs that are feasible in the latter period and thus affect, in this fashion, the entire time-profiles of output that are open to the economy in the future.

Do these difficulties affect the proposition that free trade is superior to no trade ? I am afraid they do — in the same way as the introduction of any second-best variety of restraints. If perfect foresight does not obtain, no optimality can be read into individual decisions. The marginal utility of current saving, when spent later, is a function of how much others have saved, the pattern of current investment and such-like factors which the individual has no means of guessing correctly. The Fisherian calculus of two-period equation of marginal utilities thus amounts merely to an unverified description of how individuals save. Similarly, the pattern of investment currently chosen, while optimal in the current period, may be inappropriate for the kinds of demands generated later — unless, of course, perfect foresight rules again. But perfect foresight is only a theoretical dodge ; in the strict sense in which it is defined, it is unlikely ever to grace the real world with its presence. With the restraint of imperfect foresight, we are then back to the unfortunate conclusion that the proposition that free trade is superior to no trade is no longer valid.

However, it would be a *non-sequitur* to conclude from this that efficiency in trade, when *planning* for capital accumulation, is not a meaningful or helpful concept. Planners often do *not* worry about the optimality of the savings decision, treating it as a 'political' matter. And they also plan in terms of a definite time-horizon and assumed knowledge of the future which comes to much the same thing as assuming perfect foresight. If so, the proposition that free trade is superior to no trade certainly retains its validity ; and so does the proposition that restricted trade is superior to no trade. Thus, for instance, a recent model of efficient capital accumulation [1] demonstrates, for a closed economy, how an optimal time-path of outputs can be formally defined, which *maximizes the quantity of terminal capital stocks*, given (1) the initial conditions, (2) the time-horizon to which the plan extends, (3) the time-profile of consumption in each period, (4) technology over the planning period and (5) the structural composition of the terminal capital stocks (e.g., the ratio in which they are to be held). This model evades the problem of optimality in savings and also, in effect, assumes perfect foresight. It is not surprising, therefore, that this model can be used to

---

[1] Dorfman, Samuelson and Solow, *Linear Programming and Economic Analysis*, New York, 1958.

demonstrate the superiority of free trade (and restricted trade) over no trade in the sense that free trade (or restricted trade) will lead to a *greater* quantity of terminal capital stocks being left over from the former policy, *while satisfying the same time-profile of consumption.*[1] The welfare propositions of trade theory thus do retain their validity in the framework within which plans for capital accumulation are usually cast.

[1] It also follows that the *efficient* pattern of trade (and domestic production) for any one period cannot be determined except as part of the determination of the efficient time-path over the *entire* length of the planning period. Chenery ('Comparative Advantage and Development Policy', *American Economic Review*, Vol. 51, pp. 18-51) offers an able and lucid explanation of the techniques of programming for development which explicitly adopt the planning approach underlying the theoretical model discussed in the text. The caveat may be entered, however, that I have not discussed here the limitations to which any planning approach, based on the assumption of perfect foresight, will be subject. Finally, mention may be made of a recent unsatisfactory attempt by Raj and Sen to set up an analysis of the problem of trade and domestic production policy in the context of a country with limited export earnings ; the analysis seems to me to obscure the crucial and elementary question of efficiency in trade ; Raj and Sen, 'Alternative Patterns of Growth under Conditions of Stagnant Export Earnings', *Oxford Economic Papers*, n.s., Vol. 13 (Feb. 1961), pp. 43-52 ; cf. Bhagwati, 'The Theory of International Trade', *Indian Economic Journal*, Vol. 8 (July 1960), pp. 1-17.

Chapter 2

RECENT TRENDS IN WORLD TRADE

BY

A. MAIZELS

National Institute of Economic and Social Research, London

I. INTRODUCTION

THE principal aim of this paper is to highlight some of the major trends in the pattern of world trade over the past decade, with special regard to the trading relationships between the industrial countries and the primary-producing areas. The latter group should, more strictly, be called the 'primary-exporting' countries, since it includes countries — like Australia and New Zealand — whose economies are now largely industrialized, as well as mainly agricultural economies, like the poorer, under-developed countries. Industrial countries, in this context, include Japan with a relatively low national income per head.

This distinction between the two groups of trading countries is not, of course, the same as that between trade in industrial goods and primary products. The industrial countries are also major exporters of primary products, and compete directly in this field with many primary-producing countries. The primary-producing countries also export a certain amount of manufactures, though relatively few do so as yet. The varying fortunes of the two groups of countries have nevertheless depended very largely in the past on trends in the world market for manufactures and for primary products, respectively. It is not too much to say that the post-war financial difficulties of the primary-producing countries — and particularly those embarked on industrialization programmes — stem very largely from the failure of their exports to keep pace, either with world trade in total, or with economic activity in the industrial countries, which are the main consuming areas for primary products.

The slower rate of growth in the volume of world trade in primary products than in manufactures has, in fact, been a notable feature of world trade since the mid-1930s (see Table I). However, the movement in the immediate pre-war years was essentially a cyclical recovery from a sharp depression which hit the volume of

31

trade in manufactures more than that in primary products. The movement since 1948–50, however, reflects a decade of rapid expansion during which there have been three periods of recession in the United States, and one recession (1952–53) in Western Europe.

A further important difference between post-war and previous periods is that before the war a relative movement in the volume of trade in primary products and manufactures was almost invariably accompanied by a reverse movement in their relative prices. This resulted in an extraordinary stability in the relative value of trade in the two groups of commodities. In the post-war period, however, the proportion represented by manufactures in total world trade has steadily risen, from 44 per cent in 1948 to 54 per cent in 1959.[1]

An analysis of the causes of this 'perverse' association of relative volume and price over the past decade is of considerable importance for any assessment of probable future trends in the exports of the primary-producing countries. Part of the answer appears to be that supply difficulties during the war and the immediate post-war period helped to push up prices of many primary products to levels at which production of substitutes (either natural or synthetic) became profitable in the main consuming areas (particularly in the United States). But perhaps the more important reason has been that the pattern of demand (and of output) in the industrial countries has changed in such a way as to result in a smaller growth in demand for primary products than for manufactured goods. These points are discussed further in later sections.

The retarded rate of growth in trade in the post-war period was even greater for the countries dependent mainly on primary commodity exports than is suggested by the global comparisons made above. For both primary products and manufactures, exports from the primary-producing countries have risen substantially less than exports of similar commodities from the industrial countries since the early 1950s (see Table II). Indeed, the major flow of exports from the primary-producing countries — namely, their exports of primary produce to industrial countries — rose from 1953 to 1958 at only half the rate of exports of primary produce from the industrial countries. By contrast, the intra-trade among the primary-producing countries rose at a rate not far short of that of the industrial countries.

This slow growth in exports of primary produce to the industrial countries was concentrated in food and industrial materials. In food, the percentage rise over the period was only one-third of that in exports from the industrial countries, while in materials, the value of exports from the primary-producing to the industrial countries

[1] U.N. *Statistical Yearbook, 1960*, New York, 1961.

showed an absolute, as well as a relative, decline (see Table III). Only in fuels did the reverse relationship hold ; here, the percentage increase in exports from primary-producing to industrial countries was considerably greater than that in exports from the industrial countries.

The poor export performance of the primary-producing areas has been one of the major trends in the development of world trade over the past decade. Another has been an unusually rapid expansion in trade among the industrial countries ; unfortunately, this trend is partly obscured in the GATT series on which Table II is based, since 1958 was not a year of good trade, the intra-trade of industrial countries rising relatively sharply in 1959, as it had done also in the years 1950–53. Some of the main influences tending to retard the growth of exports from the primary-producing areas are discussed in the next section. Then, in section III, the trends in exports in the reverse direction (from industrial to primary-producing areas), are discussed, followed by a brief consideration of trade between the Soviet bloc and the primary-producing countries (section IV). Finally, section V deals with the growth in the intra-trade of the industrial countries.

II. CONSUMPTION AND NET IMPORTS OF THE INDUSTRIAL COUNTRIES

Some light can be thrown on the poor post-war export performance of the primary-producing areas by relating their exports to demand in the main industrial countries. A convenient way to do this is to take apparent consumption (i.e. production plus net imports) in the industrial countries as representing demand and net imports as representing exports from primary producers. This has been done for two recent periods,[1] for the main foods, industrial materials and fuels, and the results are given in Tables IV-VI. In each case, the quantities have been valued at world prices, or national wholesale prices, as appropriate.[2]

(a) Food, Beverages and Tobacco

A selection of eight groups of items was taken, covering about 70 per cent of total exports of food, beverages and tobacco from the primary-producing to the industrial countries. The main traded items are tropical beverages and sugar, whereas (by value) the main

---

[1] Unfortunately, the periods are not identical for the three groups of commodities. [2] Thus, net imports are valued at rather more than c.i.f. value.

items of consumption are meat and cereals. From 1948–52 to 1957–1959, the volume of net imports of the sample commodities rose proportionately rather less than consumption (one-fifth as against one-quarter), while, owing to a sharper fall in import unit values, the rise in the value of net food imports was only marginal (see Table IV).

The fall in the import-content of consumption was due in part to a shift in the pattern of demand, and in part to substitution of home output for imports. The main features of the demand shift have been the relatively small increases in consumption of tropical beverages and vegetable oils, each of which has a high import-content, and the relatively large increase in meat consumption, with a low import-content. The small increase in tropical beverages is mainly due to the static level of *per caput* consumption of coffee in the United States ; while that for vegetable oils was due partly to a shift in consumer demand from soap to synthetic detergents, particularly in the United States and Britain, and partly to the substitution of animal fats (tallow) for vegetable oils in soap-making.

Apart from tallow, the great expansion in United States soya bean output, as a result of price support schemes, has been a major factor reducing the demand for oilseeds from the primary-producing countries. The United States is now a major net exporter of oilseeds, whereas pre-war that country was a net importer.

The rise in consumption of cereals has been mainly in animal feed, resulting from the increase in demand for meat. The industrial areas are essentially self-sufficient in grain feed, but Western Europe is a net importer of bread grain from the primary-producing areas. The expansion in wheat production in the EEC countries (30 per cent in the period covered) resulted in a sharp drop in their import requirements.

Another important substitution has been beet for cane sugar. Production of beet sugar in the EEC countries increased by 80 per cent over the period, and net imports of cane sugar were considerably reduced. The degree of protection of beet-sugar output in the industrial countries has increased substantially since 1950, with the fall in the price of sugar.

With the general rise in real income per head since the early 1950s, demand in the industrial countries has also shifted into more expensive qualities and varieties of the different foods. This shift is not expressed in the tonnage figures, on which Table IV is based, but it is an additional reason for the fall in the import-content of consumption, since the better qualities are in some cases produced within the industrial countries themselves (e.g. cheese and butter).

These comparisons show clearly the importance for the export prospects of the primary-producing countries of government policies in the industrial countries. The more important of these policies — apart from the import tariff — are quantitative restrictions on the import of cereals, dairy produce and other foodstuffs, and the support by subsidy or minimum price regulations of home production of beet sugar and oils and oilseeds. Fiscal taxes (e.g. on coffee and tea) are also of importance in reducing the demand for imports from the primary-producing areas. Failing changes in these policies, the prospects for a substantial increase in earnings of the primary-producing countries from exports of foods and beverages are not good.

(b) Industrial Materials [1]

For industrial materials, the pattern of change as it affects the primary-producing countries has been similar to that for foods. But the reasons lie less in protection and fiscal policies than in the changing structure of industry and in technical development — the latter being only a minor factor for foodstuffs.

Between 1950–52 and 1955–57, imports of the main industrial materials into the industrial countries rose only fractionally in value. This was, however, a period of falling prices, particularly for the agricultural materials like rubber, wool and jute, and there was an increase in volume of about one-fifth (see Table V). This very modest rise occurred during a period of rapid economic expansion in the industrial countries.

There appear to have been two major reasons for the poor showing of this sector of trade. First, the changing pattern of demand in the industrial countries has led to big changes in their pattern of manufacturing output. The most important changes have been sharp increases in production in the engineering and chemicals industries, and small increases in the textile industry. From 1950–1952 to 1955–57, the period covered by Table V, engineering and chemicals production in the industrial countries each rose by about 40 per cent, textiles by only 10 per cent. These divergent movements are, of course, a continuation of a long-term trend. In the OEEC countries, for example, the rise from 1900 to 1929 in engineering and chemicals production was some 230 per cent, compared with about 35 per cent in textiles ; and, again, from 1937 to 1950 the percentage increases were 90 and 30 per cent, respectively. Similar divergences in rates of growth are evident in the United States and Japan also. The main factors at work have been an increase in the

---

[1] This subsection draws heavily on an article, 'The Demand for Industrial Materials, 1950–57', *National Institute Economic Review*, No. 5, Sept. 1959.

proportion of final expenditure devoted to investment (and armaments) and to durable consumer goods, including cars ; and the switch in the pattern of import demand by the primary-producing countries towards engineering products. This last trend results both from an increasing emphasis on economic development in these countries, and from the progress of industrialization, which tends to be concentrated in textiles and other lightly processed manufactures in its earlier phases of development.

This shift in output pattern in the industrial countries has had a substantially adverse effect on the exports of the primary-producing countries, because the import-content of engineering and chemicals production is very small, while that of textiles is relatively large. Moreover, the greater part (about two-thirds) of the net imports of industrial materials from the primary-producers consists of agricultural materials (cotton, wool, jute and natural rubber), the consumption of which in the industrial countries rose only fractionally. The traditional non-ferrous metals are next in importance in the exports of primary-producers, and their consumption rose by less than the average. The increase of nearly one-third in steel consumption required only minor imports of iron ore, while that in aluminium required an even smaller increase in bauxite imports. The rise in imports of forest products should be discounted in the present context, since the supplying countries (Scandinavia) are more properly regarded as industrial than as primary producers.

The magnitude of the effect of the shift in industrial structure can be judged by calculating what net imports in the later period would have been, had consumption of each of these materials risen in the same proportion as the total (i.e. by 27 per cent). In this case, net imports by the industrial countries would have been higher than they actually were in 1955–57 by $1·1 billion (one-sixth).[1]

The second operative factor has been the substitution of materials processed mainly in the industrial countries themselves for imported 'raw' or 'natural' materials. The main substitutions have been aluminium for copper and — to a lesser extent — for steel and other materials ; man-made fibres for cotton and wool ; synthetic for natural rubber ; and plastic materials for a wide range of traditional uses of textiles, paper, wood and metals. This process of substitution has gone much further in the United States than in the other industrial countries. In the United States, the consumption of 'processed' materials rose three times as fast as the total consumption of industrial materials between 1950–52 and 1955–57, while in other

[1] This calculation implies no change over the period from 1950–52 in the import-content of consumption of each group of materials.

industrial countries it rose twice as fast. United States' consumption of 'natural' materials, other than wood-pulp, did not increase at all over this period, in spite of a 20 per cent growth in manufacturing production.

There was, however, one major trend in the development of the industrial countries in the 1950s which was distinctly favourable to the primary-producing areas. This was the more rapid economic growth of the EEC countries and Japan (where the import-content of consumption of materials is relatively high), compared with the United States (where the import-content is relatively low and has been falling). The EEC countries and Japan together were responsible for the whole of the increase in consumption of agricultural materials during the period and for most of the increase in consumption of the older non-ferrous metals. In Britain, too, though the rate of growth was slower, there was a significant increase in consumption of some agricultural materials (wool and jute, but not cotton) and non-ferrous metals. Had each of the industrial countries grown at the same rate as the average (which was heavily influenced by the relatively slow growth in North America), their net imports of industrial materials would have fallen in volume over the period, instead of rising by one-fifth.

It seems likely that this disparity in rates of growth, which was due in part to the economic reconstruction and recovery in West Germany and Japan, will be reduced in the coming decade. To this extent, the marginal propensity of the industrial countries taken as a whole to import industrial materials will be reduced. Moreover, the trend to substitute 'processed' for 'natural' materials, so marked in the United States, is almost certain to spread increasingly to Western Europe and Japan. Finally, the pattern of manufacturing production is likely to continue to change in favour of engineering and chemical output. Taken together, these tendencies would indicate that the primary-producing countries would be unwise to expect a faster increase in demand for industrial materials in the 1960s than occurred in the 1950s. They also indicate that the 'perverse' relationship between volume and price is likely to continue. However, one possible way in which the primary-producing countries might increase their export income in this field is to export materials in more processed forms, e.g. aluminium instead of bauxite, though the possibilities of doing so on a substantial scale are limited.

(c) Fuels

In terms of coal-equivalent, apparent consumption of energy rose by 15 per cent between 1951–52 and 1957–58 in the industrial countries. The rise was rather larger, 18 per cent, in terms of values at constant prices (see Table VI). Within the total, some drastic changes in pattern have taken place. Consumption of solid fuel fell by over 30 million metric tons (3 per cent) between the two periods, whereas petroleum consumption and hydro-electricity production rose by one-third and natural gas output by nearly one-half. This switch in pattern was of great benefit to the non-industrial petroleum-producing countries, since the import-content of petroleum consumption is relatively high (about one-quarter in 1957–58), and that of solid fuel is negligible. The development of natural gas and hydro-electricity (both of which have a negligible import-content) was relatively small in relation to that in petroleum consumption, and so had little effect on net import demand. Of even greater importance, however, than the change in consumption pattern has been the growing dependence of the industrial areas on imports for their petroleum supplies. This has happened in spite of the great expansion in their refinery output (particularly in EEC countries and the United States), since production of crude petroleum in the industrial areas supplied only 35-40 per cent of the increase in requirements in this period.

The trend towards oil and away from coal is likely to continue. A recent authoritative review of the probable future trend in energy demand and supplies in the OEEC area [1] estimates the potential indigenous coal supplies in the area in 1975 at 430-495 million tons, compared with 477 million tons in 1955 — an increase, at best, of only 4 per cent. Potential imported supplies of oil, however, are estimated to rise from 146 million tons, coal-equivalent, in 1955 to between 380 and 500 million tons in 1975 — an increase of 160-240 per cent. The 'newer' forms of energy — natural gas, hydro-power and nuclear energy — are all expected to show substantial increases; in 1955, they contributed some 8 per cent to total energy consumption in the OEEC area, but by 1975 the proportion is expected to rise to almost 20 per cent. Even so, and allowing for the inevitable margin of error, it seems clear that a substantial part of Western Europe's expansion in energy requirements over this period will have to be met by imports of oil.

For the United States, too, the prospects are for an upward trend in oil imports, notwithstanding the likely expansion in natural gas and hydro-electric power. A major reason for this is the much lower production cost of imported, than of home-produced, oil. The further growth in oil imports into the industrial areas will, however,

---

[1] *Towards a New Energy Pattern in Europe* (Report of the Energy Advisory Commission), OEEC, Paris, 1960.

benefit only a few of the primary-producing countries, and some of these have very limited possibilities for putting the extra income to a useful purpose.

(d) Manufactures

The usual classification used for 'manufactures' (the United Nations' *Standard International Trade Classification*, Sections 5-8), includes non-ferrous metals which have already been discussed along with other industrial materials. Of the other manufactures exported from primary-producing countries, textiles are easily the most important, India (cotton and jute goods) and Hong Kong (cotton goods) being the largest exporters, their combined exports amounting to about $1 billion a year. Other exports of manufactures (under $\frac{1}{2}$ billion a year in total) are divided among a number of countries, only Australia, Pakistan, South Africa, Israel and U.A.R. (Egypt) being of any great importance.

The relatively small increase in this flow of trade between 1953 and 1958 (30 per cent in value), compared with total world trade in manufactures (up by 50 per cent), is due to two distinct tendencies at work. First, textiles are faced with a much lower income-elasticity of demand than are manufactures as a whole, and this alone would largely explain the slower rate of growth in manufactures exports (other than metals) from the primary-producing countries so far in the post-war period. However, as these countries develop industrially, a wider range of manufactures should become available for export, such as lightly processed metal goods, including some electrical appliances and specific types of mechanical equipment, which have much better long-term prospects than textiles.

The second factor has been that, in the majority of industrial countries, domestic industries have been protected by tariffs from competition by 'cheap' imports. The import of Indian and Hong Kong cotton textiles into Britain is one of the few cases where primary-producing countries have been able to find a mass market for their manufactured goods in the industrial countries. But though limits to this trade (negotiated between the industries concerned) have been applied, the import of large quantities of textiles at low prices has resulted in a considerable contraction of the British cotton industry. Under a government scheme, the amount of plant in the industry has been reduced, and the remaining plant is now running much more nearly at full capacity.

Any substantial increase in imports of lightly processed manufactures from the primary-producing areas may well require compensating adjustments in the pattern of output in the industrial countries. Such adjustments would not only allow for a higher rate of growth in the exporting country but for a more economic allocation of resources in the industrial areas. Adjustments such as these are politically difficult to make because of temporary unemployment that may be caused, but such temporary difficulties are minimized if the adjustments are made in a period of economic expansion such as the industrial areas have enjoyed since the early 1950s.

III. EXPORTS FROM INDUSTRIAL TO PRIMARY-PRODUCING COUNTRIES

Though this flow of trade consists largely of manufactured goods, exports of *primary produce* are also substantial. In 1958 exports of primary produce from industrial to non-industrial countries amounted to $4·9 billion (against $18·9 billion in the reverse direction), the greater part of the flow from the industrial countries consisting of foodstuffs (see Tables II and III). The considerable increase since 1950 has been reflected in the main shipments of surplus commodities from the United States under Public Law 480 and other aid programmes. In 1957, the United States accounted for one-half the exports of primary produce from the industrial to the primary-producing countries, as against only one-quarter before the war.

This expansion of United States exports has been of short-term benefit to a number of industrializing countries, such as India, which have an increasing need for food or which suffer periodically from bad harvests. In the short-term, such commodity aid has the effect of supporting the currency reserves of the beneficiary country, so allowing it to proceed with its development plans, largely unhampered by a sudden shift in import needs from capital goods to food. However, there are also a number of disadvantages to this arrangement. First, as regards the beneficiary country, the availability of large-scale commodity aid may induce a complacency about urgently required changes in the technology and social structure of the agricultural sector, and possibly about the need to curb the rate of growth in population. Secondly, such aid necessarily has an adverse effect on the export of similar commodities by other primary-producing countries. Finally, it tends to create a vested interest in high farm output in the United States, and in the price support policies of the United States Government.[1]

---

[1] In a recent review of the implications of U.S. commodity aid exports, Mr. B. C. Swerling, of Stanford University, suggests that greater exports of farm machinery, equipment and fertilizers might be more effective aid to under-developed countries than the surplus farm output which such equipment helps to produce in the United

Exports of *manufactures* from the industrial to the primary-producing countries are almost as large in value as the intra-trade of the industrial countries. In analysing the trends in this stream of trade, it is important to distinguish exports to the industrializing primary-producing countries from exports to the rest. Before the war, exports to the main industrializing countries represented about half the total exports of manufactures to primary-producing countries, but the industrializing group accounted for less than one-third of the increase over the twenty years up to 1957 (see Table VII).

There have been two main influences at work here. First, there has been a substantial substitution of local manufacturing output for imports in the industrializing countries. Had the import-proportion of supplies remained unchanged between 1937 and 1957, imports of manufactures into this group in the latter year would have been $4·8 billion (at 1955 prices), or 65 per cent higher than they actually were. In 1913, these countries were largely dependent on imports for their supplies of manufactured goods, but the shortages and transport difficulties experienced during the First World War caused a number of them to turn to local manufacturing. The process was greatly stimulated by the economic crisis of the 1930s, which resulted in a sharp adverse movement of the terms of trade (see Table I), and a drastic curtailment of the inflow of foreign capital. By the outbreak of the Second World War, the dependence of this group of countries on imports for their supplies of manufactures was under 30 per cent as against about 60 per cent in 1913. Since 1950, their import proportion has been reduced further.

One important feature of the development in the industrializing group of primary-producing countries has been that the increase in their demand for manufactures has generally more than offset the adverse effects of import-substitution on their trade. This has been true both of the period since 1950, and of a comparison of 1959 with any pre-war period. The major interruption of the process came in the 1930s, when imports of manufactures were reduced, but this appears to have been due to the pressure of abnormal events in that period.

In the non-industrializing primary-producing countries (Table VII), total demand for manufactures has risen by much the same proportion since 1937 as in the industrializing group, but the proportion imported remained at 55-60 per cent — the same as in the industrializing countries in 1913. However, a major influence at

States (B. C. Swerling, 'Some Inter-relationships between Agricultural Trade and Economic Development', a paper prepared for Conference on Relations between Agriculture and Economic Growth at Stanford University, Nov. 1960).

work has been the development of the oil industry in the non-industrial primary-producing areas. This development, though confined to a few countries, has necessitated large shipments of equipment of various kinds from the industrial countries. It is not possible to give accurate figures of this trade, but it no doubt accounts for an appreciable proportion of the increase in imports into this group since 1937, as shown in Table VII.

Taking both groups of primary-producing countries together, the past decade has seen a substantial increase in their imports of manufactured goods. According to GATT estimates,[1] imports of manufactures into the primary-producing countries from North America and Western Europe rose by $5·6 billion between 1953 and 1958. Their total exports in the reverse direction rose by only $2·7 billion, while their payments for freight and interest on foreign investments rose by $1·5 billion, so that the increase in their net current earnings over the period was only $1·2 billion. However, their net borrowings from the industrial countries (including the international agencies) rose by $4·3 billion (to $6·1 billion in 1958), and it was this rise which mainly financed the expansion in their imports of manufactured goods.

The economic growth of the primary-producing areas over the past decade has thus been dependent to an important extent on increased borrowing rather than on increased exports. If exports fail to expand appreciably in the coming decade — and the previous discussion gives some ground for doubt for primary commodities other than fuel — there is a very serious danger that the growing burden of interest and debt-repayment will severely restrict the further expansion of imports for developing purposes.

IV. TRADE BETWEEN SOVIET COUNTRIES AND THE PRIMARY-PRODUCING AREAS

Trade between the Soviet countries and the primary-producing areas is still relatively small, but it has been increasing at a faster rate in recent years than the trade of the primary-producing countries with North America, Western Europe and Japan. This trade is directed essentially towards the less-developed primary-producing countries, and the trade turnover (imports plus exports) between these and the Soviet countries nearly trebled in value between 1953 and 1959 (Table VIII).

Imports into the Soviet Union and Eastern Europe consist mainly

[1] *International Trade*, 1959 (Table 10), GATT Geneva, 1960.

of raw materials and fuels ; finished manufactures represent only a very small fraction of the total. Exports to the less-developed areas consist mainly of manufactures (two-thirds of the total in 1958). The prospects for further growth in import demand by the Soviet countries depend in part on the rate of development of natural and synthetic substitutes for imported primary commodities. The recent trends here have in many ways been similar to those in western industrial countries, particularly in expanded output of synthetic materials and plastics. Plans for the period up to 1965 indicate substantial further increases in production of tea, rice, oils and oil-seeds and sugar.[1] A further problem, paralleling that of the western industrial countries, is the extent to which the Soviet countries can absorb increasing quantities of the simpler types of manufactured goods from the less-developed areas. To the extent that the rate of economic growth is higher than in the western industrial countries, it should be less difficult for the Soviet countries to effect such a change in import pattern. On the side of exports to the less-developed areas, a further important factor will be the extent to which the Soviet countries are willing to increase the present level of long-term credits.[2]

V. INTRA-TRADE OF THE INDUSTRIAL COUNTRIES

The other major trend in world trade in the post-war period has been the rapid expansion in the trade between industrial countries, particularly trade in manufactured goods. From 1950 to 1959 the total volume of intra-trade among the industrial countries rose by about 90 per cent, compared with a rise of about 50 per cent in volume in all other sectors of world trade (other than exports from the Soviet countries). Within the total intra-trade, the increase for manufactures (120 per cent) was more than twice as great, proportionately, as that for primary products (see Table IX). By contrast, of the exports of the industrial countries to the rest of the world, the increase was the same (about 45 per cent) in this period, for both manufactures and primary products.

It is of some importance to consider whether this high rate of growth in the intra-trade in manufactures contains a large 'once-for-all' element, or whether we can expect it to continue to grow in future much faster than world trade or economic activity as a whole. It is evident from the historical experience summarized in Table IX

[1] *Economic Survey of Europe in 1960*, United Nations, Geneva, 1961.
[2] The total amount of credits accorded by the Soviet Union in the period 1956–59 was 5·8 billion roubles (G. Skorov, 'L'Aide économique et technique de l'U.R.R.S. aux pays sous-développés, *Tiers Monde*, Paris, 1960).

that the post-war rate of growth in the intra-trade in manufactures was exceptionally great. It also appears that this was the sector of trade which was hardest hit, in volume, by the economic depression of the early 1930s and its aftermath of trade- and currency-restrictions. By 1937, the intra-trade in manufactures was still some 30 per cent below the 1929 peak, compared with a short fall of only some 5 per cent in the volume of exports of manufactures from the industrial countries to the rest of the world. An additional factor depressing the intra-trade in manufactures in the late 1930s was the autarkic policy of Germany, reflecting the movement of that country towards a war economy.

Trade in the early post-war years was also beset with quantitative and currency restrictions and the year 1950 — so often taken as a post-war 'base' year — is hardly representative of years of 'normal' trade, such as 1929 or 1959 when restrictions on international trade were relatively minor. Between 1950 and 1955, many of these restrictions were dismantled, and there was further liberalization of trade — including dollar liberalization — in the late 1950s. Moreover, the economic recovery of West Germany since 1950 was closely associated with a rapid expansion of her trade with other industrial countries in continental Western Europe. For both these reasons trading conditions in the late 1950s were quite dissimilar from those twenty years earlier, while part of the expansion in the intra-trade from 1950 to 1959 appears to be due to trade liberalization, which can be regarded as a 'once-for-all' gain.

Had there been no liberalization in this period, trade in manufactures among the industrial countries would have expanded in any event because of the economic growth that took place. It is not possible to say with any precision how much of the growth in intra-trade was due to one factor or the other. But an approximate answer can be had by relating the imports of manufactures of the main industrial countries to their total supplies of manufactures available for domestic use or for export. It is convenient here to separate the 'large' industrial countries from the 'small' ones, since the former depend only marginally on imports for their total supplies, whereas the smaller industrial countries are heavily dependent on manufactured imports. Table X sets out the trends in imports and supplies for each of these groups, for selected years since 1913. For the large industrial countries, 1950 appears to have been even more abnormal than 1937, and the rise of the import-proportion from 2·8 per cent in 1950 to 4·4 per cent in 1959 appears to reflect essentially a return to a more 'normal' relationship between production and trade. At the same time, it seems that there is a long-term downward trend in the import-proportion in the large industrial countries. Unfortunately, the data are too scanty to make an estimate of what the 'trend' position would be for 1959, but it seems probable that the actual proportion in that year was not much, if anything, below it.

For the small industrial countries, there was also some recovery in the import-proportion after 1950, though the recovery was relatively much smaller than for the large countries. Moreover, the rate of growth in total supplies was also less than in the large countries, reflecting the latter's sharper rate of economic expansion.

Of the total increase of some $12½ billion, c.i.f., in the imports of manufactures into the industrial countries, both large and small, between 1950 and 1959, about one-half was due to the expansion in demand (as measured by total supplies available), the other half resulting from the rise in the import-proportion to more 'normal' levels. If this general argument is right, then we should expect the intra-trade in manufactures to grow in the coming decade at only about half the rate of the past decade, in relation to the rate of growth in supplies (or in real income) in the industrial countries. A new factor which might, however, result in a rather faster rate of growth in the intra-trade than would be expected on the basis of past trends alone is the establishment of freer trading groups (EEC and EFTA) within Western Europe.

VI. CONCLUSION

Recent trends in the volume and commodity pattern of world trade seem to point to an increasing insulation of the industrial, from the primary-producing, countries. This has been due, in the main, to changes in the pattern of demand in the industrial countries; to technological developments, particularly the use of synthetic for natural materials in industry; and to fiscal and protectionist policies in the field of foodstuffs, beverages and manufactures which limit the expansion of exports of these goods from the primary-producing countries.

Over the past decade, the retarded rate of growth in export earnings of the primary-producing countries would have resulted in a severe limitation in their rate of economic growth had there not been a marked increase in the flow of loans and aid from the developed countries (including the international financial agencies). However, the flow of financial assistance has hardly grown fast enough to offset indefinitely the results of the slow growth in exports. The future development of the primary-producing areas requires a much more rapid growth in their exports than they appear likely to achieve, if the recent trends in their trading relationships with the industrial countries continue in the future.

To the extent that their difficulties arise from changes in demand patterns and from technological development, the recent trends cannot be expected to reverse themselves. But to the extent that they arise from government protectionist and fiscal policies in the industrial countries, changes in such policies may well be of greater importance for the economic progress of the primary-producing areas than any other single measure.

Meanwhile, the reduction of trade barriers between the industrial countries will increase their intra-trade, though this is not likely to rise as fast — in relation to economic activity — as in the 1950s. But, for world economic development in the broad sense, the reduction of trade barriers among the industrial countries seems a less important objective than the breaking down of trade barriers between the industrial countries and the primary-producing countries.

TABLE I

TRENDS IN WORLD PRODUCTION AND EXPORTS, 1913–59 *
(1913 = 100)

Period	Production		Export volume		Export unit values †		Export values †	
	PP	*M*	*PP*	*M*	*PP*	*M*	*PP*	*M*
1926–30	123	141	123	113	128	145	157	164
1931–33	120	110	116	81	68	100	79	81
1934–35	125	133	114	84	85	117	97	98
1936–38	135	158	125	100	93	120	116	120
1948–50	156	238	116	132	259	223	300	294
1951–53	176	297	133	178	289	248	385	442
1954–56	191	341	156	216	271	244	423	526
1957–59	201	381 ‡	181	251	254	261	460	655

* Excluding Soviet Union throughout, and excluding other Soviet countries from 1948.
† In terms of U.S. dollars. ‡ 1957–58.

Note : *PP*=primary products ; *M*=manufactures.

Sources : *Industrialization and Foreign Trade*, League of Nations, Geneva, 1945 ; W. A. Lewis, 'World Production, Prices and Trade, 1870–1960', *Manchester School*, Vol. XX, No. 2, May 1952 ; E. Lerdau, 'Stabilization and the Terms of Trade', *Kyklos*, Vol. XII, 1959, Fasc. 3 ; U.N. *Statistical Yearbook*, 1959, New York, 1960.

TABLE II

EXPORTS OF PRIMARY PRODUCE AND MANUFACTURES FROM PRIMARY-PRODUCING AND INDUSTRIAL COUNTRIES,* 1953–58

	Exports in 1958			Change from 1953 to 1958		
	Primary produce	Manu-factures	Total †	Primary produce	Manu-factures	Total †
	$ billion, f.o.b.			Percentage		
Exports from primary-producing countries of which to :	26·5	5·1	31·6	+18	+37	+20
Industrial countries	18·9	2·7	21·6	+13	+30	+15
Intra-trade	7·6	2·4	10·0	+30	+46	+35
Exports from industrial countries of which to :	18·9	43·8	62·7	+26	+53	+44
Primary-producing countries	4·9	20·2	25·1	+26	+55	+43
Intra-trade	14·0	23·6	37·6	+25	+50	+44

* 'Industrial countries' are North America, EEC and EFTA countries and Japan. 'Primary-producing countries' are all other countries, including Soviet bloc. All figures exclude the intra-trade of Soviet countries.
† Excluding trade not classified by commodity group.

Source : *International Trade*, 1959, GATT, Geneva, 1960.

TABLE III

EXPORTS OF MAIN CATEGORIES OF PRIMARY PRODUCE FROM
PRIMARY-PRODUCING AND INDUSTRIAL COUNTRIES, 1953–58

	Exports in 1958			Change from 1953 to 1958		
	Food *	Materials	Fuels	Food *	Materials	Fuels
	$ billion f.o.b.			Percentage		
Exports from primary-producing countries of which to :	10·3	8·4	7·9	+ 10	+ 1	+ 64
Industrial countries	7·9	6·4	4·6	+ 8	− 8	+ 88
Intra-trade	2·4	1·9	3·3	+ 11	+ 46	+ 39
Exports from industrial countries of which to :	8·9	6·7	3·2	+ 24	+ 30	+ 24
Primary-producing countries	2·8	1·3	0·7	+ 17	+ 68	− 1
Intra-trade	6·1	5·4	2·5	+ 27	+ 24	+ 35

* Including beverages and tobacco.

Source : *International Trade*, 1959, GATT, Geneva, 1960.

TABLE IV

APPARENT CONSUMPTION AND NET IMPORTS OF MAJOR FOODSTUFFS
IN THE INDUSTRIAL AREAS,* 1948/52 TO 1957/59

Commodity group	Apparent consumption				Net imports			
	1957–59	Change from 1948–52			1957–59	Change from 1948–52		
		Volume	Unit value	Value		Volume	Unit value	Value
	$ billion	Percentage			$ billion	Percentage		
Cereals	10·87	+ 16	− 22	− 9	0·25 †	− 19	− 13	− 38
Meat	14·38	+ 36	+ 10	+ 49	0·56	+ 56	+ 20	+ 87
Dairy produce	4·11	+ 24	+ 7	+ 33	0·23	+ 10	+ 6	+ 12
Sugar	1·90	+ 31	− 9	+ 19	1·00	+ 21	− 9	+ 10
Tropical beverages	2·46	+ 18	− 18	− 4	2·37	+ 16	− 19	− 6
Bananas and citrus fruits	1·49	+ 31	− 12	+ 15	0·50	+ 72	− 12	+ 51
Tobacco	1·63	− 1	+ 8	+ 7	0·25	+ 50	+ 7	+ 9
Vegetable oils and oilseeds ‡	1·47	+ 13	− 9	+ 3	0·60	− 3	− 11	− 14
Total	38·31	+ 24	− 7	+ 16	5·76	+ 20	− 13	+ 6

* EEC and EFTA countries, North America and Japan.
† Net imports of wheat and wheat flour into EEC, EFTA and Japan, other than imports from North America.
‡ Five major oils and oilseeds (groundnut, soya bean, palm, palm kernel and coconut) accounting for about 70 per cent of world trade in this category. The figures relate only to the United States, EEC countries and the United Kingdom.

Sources : *Trade Yearbooks*, *Production Yearbooks* and *The State of Food and Agriculture* Food and Agriculture Organization, Rome ; *Vegetable Oils and Oilseeds*, *Dairy Produce* and *Grain Bulletin*, Commonwealth Economic Committee, London, 1959 ; national trade statistics

Table V

Apparent Consumption and Net Imports of Major Industrial Materials in the Industrial Areas,* 1950/52 to 1955/57

Commodity group	Apparent consumption				Net imports			
	1955–57	Change from 1950–52			1957–59	Change from 1950–52		
		Volume	Unit value	Value		Volume	Unit value	Value
	$ billion	Percentage			$ billion	Percentage		
Agricultural materials †	6·61	+3	−21	−19	3·94	+11	−24	−15
Traditional non-ferrous metals ‡	4·10	+17	+12	+31	1·60	+23	+9	+34
Forest products §	10·71	+21	+7	+29	0·60	+22	+11	+36
Steel (iron ore)	23·50	+31	+29	+68	0·54 ¶	+270	+90	+390
Processed materials ‖	7·34	+73	−2	+69	0·03 **	+150	+100	+200
Total	52·3	+27	+8	+38	6·71	+19	−14	+4

* United Kingdom, European Economic Community, North America and Japan.
† Cotton, wool, jute and natural rubber ; the figures for apparent consumption include reclaimed rubber. ‡ Copper, lead, zinc and tin. § Wood-pulp and softwood.
§ Aluminium, rayon and other man-made fibres, synthetic rubber and plastic materials.
¶ Exports of iron ore from countries outside Europe, North America and Japan.
** Bauxite only.

Sources : Adapted from J. A. Rowlatt and F. T. Blackaby, 'The Demand for Industrial Materials, 1950–57', *National Institute Economic Review*, No. 5, Sept. 1959.

Table VI

Apparent Consumption and Net Imports of Major Fuels in the Industrial Areas,* 1951/52 to 1957/58

Commodity group	Apparent consumption				Net imports			
	1957–58	Change from 1951–52			1957–58	Change from 1951–52		
		Volume	Unit value	Value		Volume	Unit value	Value
	$ billion	Percentage			$ billion	Percentage		
Solid fuel	13·71	−3	+23	+19	0·10	—	—	—
Petroleum	18·99	+34	+15	+53	5·06	+89	+17	+121
Gasoline	3·99†	+31	+12	+47	—‡	—	—	—
Kerosene	0·39†	+56	+9	+70	0·09	+125	+33	+200
Fuel oil	2·21†	+61	+1	+64	1·02	+117	+12	+143
Crude petroleum	12·40	+30	+18	+53	3·95	+83	+17	+115
Natural gas and hydro-electricity §	4·15	+42	+15	+63	—	—	—	—
Total	36·85	+18	+18	+39	5·16	+94	+17	+126

* EEC and EFTA countries, North America and Japan.
† Production valued at difference between market price and price of crude petroleum.
‡ Net export.
§ Very approximate valuations, based on figures for the U.S. and Canadian natural gas and electricity supply industries.

Sources : *World Energy Supplies*, 1951–54 and 1955–58, *Statistical Papers*, Series J, Nos. 2 and 3, United Nations, New York ; *International Financial Statistics*, May 1960 ; *Petroleum Press Service* ; *Minerals Year Book*, 1952, 1953 and 1960 ; *Canada Year Book*, 1953, 1954 and 1959.

TABLE VII

SUPPLIES * AND IMPORTS † OF MANUFACTURED GOODS IN PRIMARY-PRODUCING COUNTRIES, 1913–59

Year	Industrializing countries ‡			Other countries §		
	Supplies	Imports	Import-proportion	Supplies	Imports	Import-proportion
	$ billion at 1955 prices		%	$ billion at 1955 prices		%
1913	*c.* 8	4·5	*c.* 60	—	—	—
1929	14	5·7	42	—	—	—
1937	17	4·8	29	9	5·1	55–60
1950	28	6·5	23	12	7·3	60–65
1955	36	7·3	20	17	9·5	*c.* 55
1957	40	7·7	19	22	11·6	*c.* 55
1959	42	7·4	18	—	—	—

* Gross value of production of non-food manufactures, free of duplication, *plus* value of imports of 'finished' manufactures (i.e. goods not normally subject to further processing).
 † Imports from the industrial countries and India only. Major exclusion consists of non-ferrous metals imported from semi-industrial and non-industrial countries. Valuation is c.i.f., estimated from f.o.b. values of exporting countries.
 ‡ Australia, New Zealand, Union of South Africa ; India, including Pakistan ; Argentina, Brazil, Chile, Colombia, Mexico ; Palestine/Israel, Turkey ; Yugoslavia.
 § Countries outside Europe and the Soviet bloc.

Sources : Based on national trade and production statistics.

TABLE VIII

TRADE BETWEEN SOVIET COUNTRIES AND THE LESS-DEVELOPED PRIMARY-PRODUCING COUNTRIES,* 1950–59
($m. f.o.b.)

	1950	1953	1959
Exports to less-developed countries From :			
U.S.S.R. and Eastern Europe	131	151	670
China	213	229	365
Total	344	380	1,035
Exports from less-developed countries To :			
U.S.S.R. and Eastern Europe	227	138	697
China	336	172	201
Total	563	310	898

* Primary-producing countries outside Europe and North America, *except* Australia, New Zealand and the Union of South Africa.

Source : U.N. *Statistical Yearbook, 1960*, New York, 1961.

TABLE IX

EXPORTS OF MANUFACTURES AND PRIMARY PRODUCTS FROM THE INDUSTRIAL COUNTRIES,* 1913–59

	Exports in 1913	Change during period :				Exports in 1959
		1913–29	1929–37	1937–50	1950–59	
	$ billion†	Percentages				$ billion†
Manufactures ‡						
Intra-trade	8·6	+ 28	− 29	+ 28	+ 123	22·3
Exports to rest of world	8·3	+ 49	− 6	+ 23	+ 44	20·6
Total	16·9	+ 38	− 17	+ 25	+ 77	42·9
Primary products §						
Intra-trade	8·1	+ 15	− 14	+ 4	+ 54	12·8
Exports to rest of world	2·9	+ 17	− 18	+ 36	+ 45	5·5
Total	11·0	+ 15	− 15	+ 12	+ 51	18·3
TOTAL	27·9	+ 29	− 16	+ 21	+ 68	

* Exports from Belgium-Luxembourg, France, Germany (West Germany in 1950–59), Italy, Netherlands, Sweden, Switzerland, United Kingdom ; Canada, United States (excluding Special Category exports) ; Japan.
 † Valued f.o.b. at 1955 prices.   ‡ S.I.T.C. 5 to 8, inclusive.
 § Including shipments under various aid programmes.

Sources : Based on national trade statistics.

TABLE X

SUPPLIES * AND IMPORTS † OF MANUFACTURED GOODS IN INDUSTRIAL COUNTRIES, 1913–59

	Large countries ‡			Small countries §		
	Supplies	Imports	Import-proportion	Supplies	Imports	Import-proportion
	$ billion at 1955 prices		%	$ billion at 1955 prices		%
1913	80	6·6	8·4	—	2·8	—
1929	130	7·6	5·9	16	4·3	26
1937	140	5·4	3·9	17	3·1	18
1950	195	5·4	2·8	30	5·3	18
1955	270	9·1	3·4	38	7·9	21
1957	290	11·4	3·9	41	9·2	22
1959	320	14·2	4·4	45	9·4	21

* † See notes * and † to Table VII.
 ‡ France, Germany (West Germany in 1950–59), Italy United Kingdom United States and Japan.
 † Belgium-Luxembourg, Netherlands, Norway, Sweden and Canada.

Sources : Based on national trade and production statistics.

51

Chapter 3

TRENDS IN TERMS OF TRADE, AND THEIR REPERCUSSIONS ON PRIMARY PRODUCERS[1]

BY

T. MORGAN
University of Wisconsin

I. CONCEPTS OF THE TERMS OF TRADE

WITH one exception, we will in this paper use the simplest and most available concept of the terms of trade :

(1) The ratio between the prices of two commodities, or of two groups of commodities, that may be exchanged against each other. This is often called the *commodity terms of trade* ; Taussig called it the 'net barter terms of trade'.

(2) The classical concept is different. It looked to the real quantity of factors exchanged for each other through the inter-mediation of commodities — in Marshall, the labour in G-bales exchanged for the labour in E-bales. The classical concept is thus *the double factoral terms of trade*, or the commodity terms of trade times the reciprocal of changes in technical coefficients for exports and imports.

These two concepts amount to the same thing if there are con-stant proportions among the factors used in each of two countries trading, and constant returns to scale. Conversely, they diverge to the extent there are technological improvements and/or diminishing returns due to limited supply of one of the factors.

The classical concept therefore immediately indicates a limitation on the significance of the commodity terms of international trade : a change in the latter might be offset, in its effect on factor real earn-ings, by an inverse change in factor productivity. A further qualifica-tion lies in possible effects on distribution of income, including the remission abroad of earnings on foreign investment and for immigrant labour services, as an offset to export surpluses. Such surpluses may

---

[1] I am indebted to Mr. M. C. Madhavan for diligent and imaginative work far beyond the line of duty, in the preparation of the data and charts of this study.

be a fourth or more of the total value of exports, so that the question of the proportion in which export earnings are shared may be as important for local people as the terms of trade. A third qualification is that real prices received by primary producers can differ from export and import (border) prices to the extent that there are export or import tariffs, price divergences due to exchange control or quota restrictions on imports, and, of course, domestic transportation and handling costs.[1] Fourth and finally, the terms of trade ignore favourable or unfavourable effects from the check or stimulus they can give to growth and/or business cycle cumulative processes of expansion or contraction.[2]

At least five other terms-of-trade concepts have been suggested, of which three can be calculated, and may be useful for special purposes.

(3) One of these, *the income terms of trade*, is used below. It is the index of the value for exports divided by the index of the price for imports, and so shows the imports obtainable in exchange for the exports actually sent out.[3]

(4) A fourth terms-of-trade concept is Taussig's 'gross barter terms of trade', or the ratio of real values of exports to real values of imports (*International Trade*, New York, 1927, p. 113). This, he judges, should be used whenever a country's balance of payments contains unilateral payments, that is, more than goods and services only. (Cf. Haberler's criticism of the concept, *op. cit.* p. 164.)

(5) The 'single factoral terms of trade' is a modification of the classical double factoral concept ((2) above). It measures the quantity of imports bought by a unit of factors; that is, the commodity terms of trade corrected for changes in productivity in producing exports.

[1] Cf. H. Myint: 'The Gains from International Trade and the Backward Countries', *Rev. of Econ. Stud.*, Vol. XXII (2), 1954–55, pp. 131, 132.

[2] Haberler feels that the possible distribution and business cycle effects of trade and terms-of-trade changes give 'such an unreal air [to the basic analysis] that there is little point in pursuing [it] further'. *The Theory of International Trade*, New York, Macmillan, 1937, p. 166.

[3] Or, alternatively, the income terms of trade weights the commodity terms of trade in proportion to shifts in the volume of exports. The two statements are algebraically identical. The income terms of trade are, by definition,

$$\frac{Px_i}{Px_o}\frac{Qx_i}{Qx_o} \cdot \frac{1}{\dfrac{Pm_i}{Pm_o}},$$

where P is price, Q is quantity, x stands for exports, m for imports, and i for the given year, o for the base year. The formula can be presented instead as:

$$\frac{Px_i/Px_o}{Pm_i/Pm_o} \cdot \frac{Qx_i}{Qx_o}.$$

See G. S. Dorrance, 'The Income Terms of Trade', *Review of Economic Studies*, 1948–49, pp. 50-6.

(6) Viner suggests that a closer approximation to the real gain from trade can be obtained by multiplying (5), the single factoral terms of trade, by the 'disutility co-efficient' of the factor inputs used in the export commodities.

(7) A still closer approximation, Viner continues, is logically obtainable through multiplying (6) by an index of the average relative marginal utility per unit of imported commodities, and of home commodities that would have been produced had resources not been shifted to producing for exports.

Concepts (6) and (7) are hardly calculable, even given much statistical coverage, while (2) and (5) require almost as much coverage, as soon as we move away from a world in which there is only one factor. But (1), (3) and (4) are plain going.[1]

II. IMPORTANCE OF THE TERMS OF TRADE

A chorus of opinion from economists who in other respects have held very different views attests to the importance of the (commodity) terms of trade. In 1912, the late Lord Keynes estimated at £37 million the extent to which Britain was worse off because of falling terms of trade between 1900 and 1911.[2] D. H. Robertson in 1915 spoke of the trend of the terms of trade as 'perhaps the most significant economic fact in the world today'.[3] The UN Committee authors of *Commodity Trade and Economic Development* stressed the basic policy implications of terms-of-trade changes.[4] Ohlin and Kindleberger both draw from it central morals as to central economic policy.[5] So also does Raul Prebisch.[6] And recently a distinguished group of British economists, in a letter to *The Times*, worried over the terms of trade of under-developed areas : 'It is not always realized that a comparatively small fall in commodity prices is

[1] Cf. Viner, *Studies in the Theory of International Trade*, pp. 558-65; Haberler, *International Trade*, 159-66; C. Iversen, *International Capital Movements*, Copenhagen and London (Oxford Press), 1936, pp. 337-42; W. W. Rostow, 'The Terms of Trade in Theory and Practice', *The Economic History Review*, 2nd series, Vol. iii, No. 1, 1950, pp. 1-15.

[2] *Economic Journal*, 1912, 'Official Papers, "Return of Estimated Value of Foreign Trade of United Kingdom at Prices of 1900"', p. 630. Quoted in W. W. Rostow, 'The Terms of Trade in Theory and Practice', *The Economic History Review*, 2nd series, Vol. iii, No. 1, 1950, p. 14.

[3] *Industrial Fluctuations*, King, London, 1915 (reprinted London School of Economics, 1948), p. 169 n.

[4] New York, 1953, p. 13.

[5] *An International Economy*, Harper, New York, 1956, pp. 230 *et seq.*, and *The Terms of Trade, A European Case Study*, Technology Press and Wiley, New York, 1956, pp. 253-7.

[6] *The Economic Development of Latin America*, United Nations, New York, 1950, pp. 8 fol.

equivalent in its effect to a cut of billions of dollars in aid to under-developed countries.' [1]

III. CAUSES OF CHANGES IN THE TERMS OF TRADE

Analyses in this century have run in two channels. One is short-run monetary or cycle analysis, classical in inspiration, and once stimulated by a remarkable teacher, Taussig, and once again by a major problem, German reparations payments in the 1920s. The second is longer-run, emphasizing basic productivity and demand trends, and shifts of functions rather than movements along given functions. Some of these longer-run analyses are partial, arguing that some one influence or trend is dominant, at least for a given commodity, period and place. Others are 'complete', or macro-economic, attempting to include in logic, or even empirically, all the supply and demand influences on both the export and import sides, or primary and secondary production sides.

The following table attempts to present in an organized pattern the more conspicuous of these hypotheses. Unless there is explicit exception, the terms of trade are spoken of below with primary products or agricultural products in the numerator, and secondary products or manufactures in the denominator ; that is, a 'rise in the terms of trade' means that primary product prices are rising compared to secondary products.

Of the 18 entries below, 4 offer short-run monetary or cyclical explanations, specific to a particular country and time. Of the 14 longer-run interpretations, 10 are 'partial' approaches (as defined above). Among these 10, 3 accept (for their periods or for the 'long run') and explain improving terms of trade for agriculture as compared to manufacturing ; 3 more accept and explain hetero-geneous experience, and 4 assume and explain worsening terms of trade. Then there are the 4 remaining, whom I have classified as offering a macro-economic or 'complete' analysis : 1 predicts improving terms of trade for primary products, 1 deterioration, and 1 sees stability in its given time period, and 1 is agnostic.[2]

---

[1] October 29, 1957. I have found only one dissenting voice. Frank Graham was a sceptic on this as on other matters, and deprecates the terms of trade between two countries only, as 'irrelevant to almost any conceivable purpose, and probably not susceptible to any form of measurement'. *Theory of International Values*, Princeton, 1948, p. 249.

[2] Haberler generalizes from three of these studies in his Cairo lectures : *International Trade and Economic Development*, National Bank of Egypt, Cairo, 1959, p. 19. See also his 'The Terms of Trade and Economic Development', *Round Table*, Int. Econ. Assoc., Rio de Janeiro, August, 1957.

TABLE I

ANALYSIS OF CHANGES IN TERMS OF TRADE, 1912–60

	Short-run, monetary analysis	Long-run patterns of analysis	
		Partial	Complete
1. Keynes, 1912		Terms of trade are rising, due to diminishing returns in primary production	
2. Robertson, 1915		Terms of trade are rising, due to diminishing returns in primary production	
3. Beveridge, 1923			Approx. stability exists in terms of trade: productivity and demand in both industry and agriculture must be taken into account
4. Viner, 1924 (Also the 1920s discussions of German reparations effects)	Presumption terms of trade turn in favour of borrowing or reparations - receiving country		
5, 6, 7. Coates, 1915; Carr, 1931; Stovel, 1959	Contradiction to Viner's theory re Canadian 1900–13 experience: not borrowing, but cyclical boom and industrial growth explain terms of trade change		
8. Colin Clark, 1942			Prediction of rising terms of trade; macro - mathematical model
9. Kindleberger I, 1943, 1950			Terms of trade of primary - producing countries are falling, due to 'continuously increasing efficiency, and . . . Engel's law'
10. Kindleberger II, 1956		Falling terms of trade of under-developed countries (not of primary commodities), due to lack of flexibility in economic adjustments	
11. Prébisch, 1950		Falling terms of trade, due to wage rises of unionized workers in industrialized countries, and monopoly pricing	

56

TABLE I (contd.)

	Short-run, monetary analysis	Long-run patterns of analysis	
		Partial	Complete
12. U.N. experts, 1953			Agnostic judgement : no adequate ground for choosing among theories
13. Arthur Lewis, 1955		Poor terms-of-trade experience of under-developed countries due to wages in exports fixed by peasant - earnings' level	
14. Myrdal, 1956		'Under - developed countries have had rather bad luck', plus lack of flexibility	
15. Ellsworth, 1956		Trend from 1876 on, partly spurious, and partly explainable by successive *ad hoc* causes	
16. Aubrey, 1957		Rising terms of trade expected. Main basis : specific commodity studies	
17. Morgan, 1959		Heterogeneous experience since 1800. Diverse dominant influences for different commodities, countries, times	
18. Bernstein, 1960		Failing terms of trade. Chronic surplus of primary products, due to secular fall in raw material content of industrial output	

IV. WORLD EXPERIENCE OF THE TERMS OF TRADE

I will first try to summarize long-run experience up to about 1950 ; then to present in more detail estimates for the past ten to twenty-odd years.

(i) *The Long Run*

The frequent generalization that prices of primary products have been falling relative to prices of manufactures has as its substantial basis British terms-of-trade data stretching from 1876–80 to 1938 (and in one series, 1948).[1] The trend downward for primary product prices seems plain despite a wide fluctuation in the 1920s and 1930s.

In addition we have had more recently the major Kindleberger study of the terms of trade of European countries, in which he concludes that in the European context the terms of trade between primary products and manufactures do *not* run against primary products, though they 'favor the developed and run against the underdeveloped countries'.[2]

Any long series is subject to a fringe of uncertainty due to weighting, and qualitative changes, so that only major shifts are to be taken seriously. But in addition the British data have, as a number of economists have pointed out, two systematic sources of bias. (1) Qualitative improvements in products are inadequately accounted for in the data, and these improvements (I should like to assert here, without digressing into evidence) have taken place predominantly in manufacturing. Hence the British and all similar data systematically understate, over a period of time, the relative price position of primary producers. (2) In addition the British (or European or like data) cannot validly be used to measure the price position of primary producers of the world in their own regions and countries. The reason is that transportation costs have been falling over the past century and more; and primary producers have been receiving prices that fell short of British prices by a smaller and smaller amount, while at the same time they have been paying prices for manufactures that were larger than British prices by a smaller and smaller amount. Both distortions work in the same direction: producers of primary goods in the world have been doing much better than the British data indicate. It is readily possible to find commodities whose prices were at the same time falling in London and rising in Bombay, or falling in New York and rising in Minneapolis.

In addition, it is possible to obtain British data for a much longer period, back to 1801, and reliable domestic primary-manufactured products data for the United States back to 1787. I have found long-run data that I thought acceptably reliable for five other countries besides, three of them now 'under-developed' and two 'developed'.

The over-all impression from these seven series is that of the wide variety of experience of different nations. Primary products

[1] League of Nations: *Industrialization and Foreign Trade*, Geneva, 1945, pp. 154-7. The main author is Folke Hilgerdt. The data of this study were reproduced and added to in the United Nations' *Relative Prices of Exports and Imports of Underdeveloped Countries*, Lake Success, New York, 1949, pp. 21-4.
[2] *Op. cit.* pp. 239, 263-4.

had sharply *rising* relative prices in the United Kingdom up to the 1860s or 70s, when the UN series began. Primary producers in the United States have experienced a remarkably favourable trend pricewise since the 1790s — to over three times the relative price position then. The other five countries show extreme fluctuations, and various changes of trend. India, for example, shows amidst its fluctuations a rising relative price trend for primary products up to 1900–10, an irregular fall to the 1930s and a rise since.[1]

The data as a whole underline the prudence of *not* trying to predict, from the experience of one country or region, what is likely to be the experience for others.

(ii) *Recent Experience with Terms of Trade*

(1) *Terms of trade of developed and under-developed countries*, 1953 and 1937 compared with 1959 or 1960.[2] The following are median values for the terms of trade of 18 'developed' countries, and 29 'under-developed' countries for two periods, 1953 to 1960; and for 15 countries in each classification for 1937 to 1959:

TABLE II

MEDIAN VALUE OF TERMS OF TRADE

(1953=100)

	1954	1955	1956	1957	1958	1959	1960
Developed countries *	100	99	99	96	100	100	101
Under-developed countries *	108	106	110	98	90	88	89

(1937=100)

	1948	1950	1951	1952	1953	1954
Developed countries *	102	96	98	100	102	102
Under-developed countries *	108	130	160	126	125	128

	1955	1956	1957	1958	1959	1960
Developed countries *	100	97	97	99	101	102
Under-developed countries *	135	131	127	117	123	119

* For list of countries, and full data, see Appendix II, Tables *A*.1 and *A*.2, below, pp. 73 and 74.

Charts I*a* and I*b* reproduce the data of Table II. The greater stability of the developed countries is apparent throughout. For the under-developed countries, 1948 data show surprisingly little improvement over 1937 experience. The Korean War brought a

[1] T. Morgan, 'The Long-Run Terms of Trade Between Agriculture and Manufacturing', *Econ. Develop. and Cult. Change*, Oct. 1959, pp. 1-23.
[2] For Burma, the final year is 1958; for Ecuador, 1957; for Malaya, Sudan and Turkey, 1959.

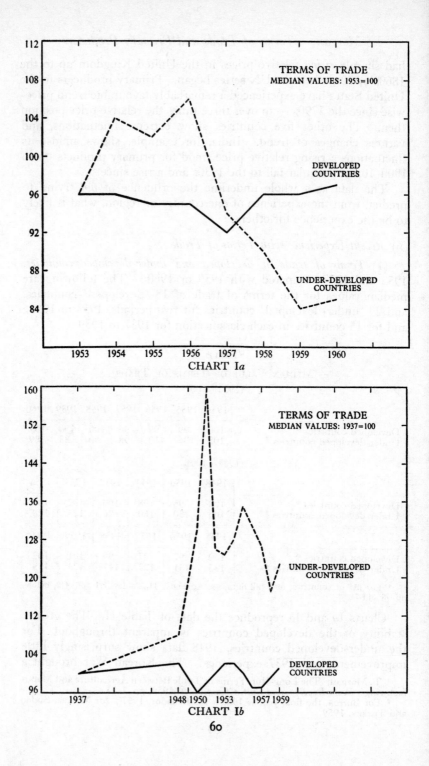

TERMS OF TRADE
MEDIAN VALUES: 1953=100

DEVELOPED
COUNTRIES

UNDER-DEVELOPED
COUNTRIES

1953 1954 1955 1956 1957 1958 1959 1960

CHART I*a*

TERMS OF TRADE
MEDIAN VALUES: 1937=100

UNDER-DEVELOPED
COUNTRIES

DEVELOPED
COUNTRIES

1937 1948 1950 1953 1957 1959

CHART I*b*

major boom to their terms of trade, from which they were receding in the 1950s. But by the end of our period, the terms of trade of four under-developed countries were above 1937 by over 70 per cent, and of two, by over 100 per cent. Among the developed countries, the maximum improvement of the terms of trade was 26 per cent.

We can present a frequency distribution for these same countries, in accord with the change in their terms of trade at the end of each period :

TABLE III

DISTRIBUTION OF CHANGES IN TERMS OF TRADE
(1953–60)

| | Total number | Terms of trade | | | | | |
| | | Improved | | | Worsened | | |
		+20% or better	+10% to 20%	0% to 10%	−10% to 0%	−20% to −10%	−20% or poorer
Developed countries	18	0	4	8	4	1	1
Under-developed countries	29	3	1	5	3	7	10
(1937–59)							
Developed countries	15	2	0	8	2	2	1
Under-developed countries	15	7	3	2	1	0	2

We may generalize that during the more recent period the under-developed countries include more extreme changes, and show more tendency to deterioration. Post-Korean War recession in prices of primary commodities has a relationship to this experience ; some relevant data will be given below. For the 1937 to 1959 group, under-developed countries demonstrate major improvement from depression levels for primary products ; they again show a tendency towards more extreme changes.

(2) *Terms of trade and aid* per capita *received*. There is some interest in inquiring into the empirical relationship between aid *per capita* to under-developed countries, which in some has attained relatively high levels, and the terms of trade. Here we are in the classical framework of thinking. The literature left some presumption that the terms of trade would shift in favour of a country receiving capital inflows. The simple presumption does not find support in 1950's data. We have calculated the average terms of

trade for a sample of 20 under-developed countries during 1954–1959, compared with their terms of trade in 1953. The 5 countries receiving the highest *per capita* aid show a terms of trade worsening at 2 per cent, the highest 2·5 per cent. The 5 countries receiving the least *per capita* aid show a terms of trade improvement of 2 per cent, the 10 lowest, improvement of 1 per cent. (Appendix II, Table *A*.4.)

The results are consistent with the effects of relative supply of *commodities* on domestic prices — but, of course, 'other things' were not equal.

(3) *Percentage of national export earnings from leading primary export commodity.* We have data for 6 developed countries and 21 under-developed countries :

TABLE IV

RATIO OF LEADING PRIMARY EXPORT TO
TOTAL NATIONAL EXPORTS

	1950	1957
	%	%
Developed countries :		
median	24	14
arithmetic mean	27	22
Under-developed countries :		
median	50	54
arithmetic mean	54	51

The contrast is interesting. The developed countries seem to be diversifying their exports as the 1950s wore on ; but the high dependence of under-developed countries on the chief export continued, despite the high price variability of primary products. (Data : Appendix II, Table *A*.3.)

(4) *Leading primary export commodity as percentage of world exports of that commodity.* We can apply this test of monopolistic or oligopolistic power, and crude index to the likelihood of price decline with increased exports to, once again, 6 developed countries and 21 under-developed countries.

A *prima facie* judgement from these figures is that the developed countries have more power to influence price to their advantage, among these products ; but that the under-developed have the advantage of weakness — they are less threatened from price declines as they expand these exports. (Data : Appendix II, Table *A*.3.)

62

TABLE V

RATIO OF LEADING PRIMARY EXPORT TO
WORLD EXPORT OF THAT COMMODITY

	1950	1957
	%	%
Developed countries :		
median	49	70
arithmetic mean	49	60
Under-developed countries :		
median	30	38
arithmetic mean	40	37

(5) *Prices of primary export commodities in the 1950s, by kinds.*
Since 1953, prices of primary product exports of developed countries
have fallen by exactly the same percentage as those prices in under-
developed countries (6 per cent). In prices of food exports, the
under-developed countries have done relatively badly, in agricultural
non-food products and in minerals, relatively well (Appendix II,
Table *A*.5).

Price variations for individual primary export commodities
typically vary widely. Moderate variations occur where there are
price stabilization schemes (e.g. tobacco and cotton in the U.S.A.),
or guaranteed purchase prices (Cuban sugar into the United States
before Castro). (See Appendix II, Charts *A*.1–*A*.8, Tables *A*.6, *A*.7,
A.8, *A*.9, *A*.10.)

(6) *Is there a correlation between a country's having agricultural
exports which form a large proportion of total value of exports, and the
trend of its terms of trade?* Developed countries show, by 1956–58
terms-of-trade data compared with those of 1936–38, no advantage from
having agricultural exports a large proportion of total export values ;
but under-developed countries have a wide advantage from relatively
large agricultural exports. Since 1953, there has been some advantage
for both groups of countries in *not* specializing in agricultural exports.
(Appendix II, Charts *A*.9 and *A*.10, Table *A*.11.)

(7) *Data on services.* Information on the relative prices of services
is remarkably scarce, refractory and heterogeneous. This is true
despite the fact that services make up a large part, some 28 per cent
in 1958, of total world trade.[1] Receipts from invisibles as a percentage
of total trade range for major trading countries normally from 18 per
cent to 44 per cent, but for some countries that rely heavily on aid

---

[1] From the International Monetary Fund's *Balance of Payments Yearbook*, 1958,
quoted in Ely Devons, 'World Trade in Invisibles'. *Lloyd's Bank Review*, April
1961, pp. 37 *et seq.*

TABLE VI

RELATION OF AGRICULTURAL EXPORTS TO TERMS OF TRADE

	1956–58 median terms of trade	
	1936–38 * = 100	1953 = 100
Out of a sample of 14 developed countries :		
the 5 countries with agricultural exports as the highest proportion of total exports	99	94
the 5 countries with agricultural exports as the lowest proportion of total exports	99	103
Out of a sample of 16 under-developed countries :		
the 5 countries † with agricultural exports as the highest proportion of total exports	242	87
the 5 countries † with agricultural exports as the lowest proportion of total exports	108	107

* 1937, and 1936 or 1938 data were taken as available, and averaged.
† Due to sparseness of data, only 2 under-developed countries are listed for the 1937 comparison.

or gifts, the percentage rises much higher. Trade in invisibles has grown smoothly during the 1950s, whereas in contrast there have been marked variations in merchandise trade.

In the United States at least, the price of services has risen spectacularly in recent years. In 1961 they were 52 per cent above their level in 1947–49, as compared to 21 per cent for non-durable commodities and for food, and 10 per cent for durable commodities — all measured at retail price levels. Wholesale commodities as a whole were meanwhile rising 20 per cent. The reasons for the services price rise are diverse : rising average costs in urban transport due to falling demand ; worsening unbalance between supply and demand with respect to medical care ; in rents, slow response of supply and rising construction costs ; and in repair services, wage rates rising as in more technically progressive manufacturing.

The rapidly rising prices of services, therefore — as under-developed countries should note — are no indication of either good social performance or of high incomes in that sector.[1]

Short-run data on maritime shipping charges show wide variations in flexible response to changes in demand. Secular declines in transportation costs have been drastic — see, for example, the

[1] Cf. analyses of causes of price changes for services in *Staff Report, Study of Employment, Growth, and Price Levels*, prepared for the Joint Economic Committee, Congress of the United States, U.S.G.P.O., Washington, Dec. 1959.

illustrations collected by Ellsworth [1]— and a major influence on commodity terms of trade of distant countries. European terms-of-trade data have negligible value towards indicating the terms of trade of primary producers in their own countries abroad.

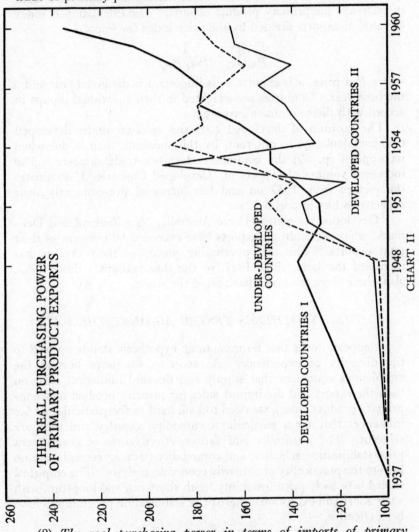

CHART II

THE REAL PURCHASING POWER OF PRIMARY PRODUCT EXPORTS

DEVELOPED COUNTRIES II

UNDER-DEVELOPED COUNTRIES

DEVELOPED COUNTRIES I

(8) *The real purchasing power in terms of imports of primary product exports.* This series, together with the commodity terms of

[1] 'The Terms of Trade between Primary Producing and Industrial Countries', *Inter-American Economics Affairs*, summer 1956, pp. 51-7. See also Douglass North, 'Ocean Freight Rates and Economic Development, 1750–1913', *Journal of Economic History*, Dec. 1958.

trade (see Table II, p. 59), seems to us the most significant of our data findings. Chart II (data in Table *A*.12 in the Appendix II) are Dorrance's 'Income Terms of Trade' [1] for the countries and years in question. The series measures in real terms what could be bought in exchange for primary product exports. The calculation is index of value of exports divided by the price index for imports :

$$\frac{Px_iQx_i}{Px_oQx_o} \cdot \frac{1}{Pm_i/Pm_o},$$

where P is price, x is exports, m is imports, i is the given year and o the base year. Countries are weighted in their individual groups in accord with their volume of exports.

The position of developed countries *vis-à-vis* under-developed countries looks quite different, by this measure, than it did when we applied (p. 59) the commodity terms-of-trade measure. The increased volume of exports of 'Developed Countries I' dominates the picture from 1937 on and has increased pre-eminently their capacity to buy imports.

'Developed countries II' are Australia, New Zealand and Denmark, whose agricultural exports have exceeded 60 per cent of their total exports. The real purchasing power of their exports has increased the least, since 1937, of the three groups. Since 1953, also, these three countries have fared the worst.

V. THE HYPOTHESES TESTED AGAINST THE DATE

It appears to us that no monotonic hypothesis stands up well to the diversity of experience. As soon as we move beyond the tautologous statement that supply and demand influences exist on both the export and the import sides (or primary product and non-primary product sides), we need to look hard to the particular *ad hoc* influences that for a particular commodity, country and time are relevant. The possibility and various effectiveness of government price stabilization schemes, and commodity trade agreements, are no help to the practicality of narrowly economic analysis. The empirical record is of wide price instability, both short-run and long-run, with a few short-run exceptions where price stabilization programmes have been effective.

VI. IMPLICATIONS FOR POLICY

Suppose that a careful prediction for future terms of trade — for example, like that of Aubrey's — turns out to be accurate. Even so,

[1] See p. 53.

past experience for all the nations for which we have data indicates we should expect sharp interim fluctuations. And flexibility is needed to cut production and one's losses, if the fluctuation is adverse ; or to expand and gain whatever possible, if the fluctuation is favourable.

But it is difficult to know which predictor one should rely on — whether Bernstein (poor terms of trade for primary producers) or Aubrey (sharply rising) ; or Myrdal or Lewis (poor terms of trade) or Colin Clark (rising) ; or Kindleberger I or Prébisch (falling) ; or the 1953 UN experts (agnostic). The policy-maker would find his bets shifting widely, depending on which soothsayer he relied on. The cautious, hedging implication for policy suggested by widely diverse empirical data *and* hypotheses, is reinforced by consideration of the general ill success of predictions in other areas of economics : a recent sample study of the fate of new products in the United States finds that some 23 out of 25 fail. In one period studied, the U.S. President's budget forecasts in January of each year for the fiscal year beginning July 1 were substantially wrong in 5 years out of 7, right in only 2. Department of Agriculture forecasts of the incomes of farm operators have fared only moderately better. It is easy to remember extreme blunders of prediction : for example, the 1929 President's Committee on Economic Trends who foresaw only continued prosperity ; and the nearly uniform predictions, in the United States, of deep depression following 1945.[1]

Officials will continue to try to forecast the terms of trade, by one or another of the patterns we have surveyed above, or by some combination ; and they will influence industrial and agricultural expansion accordingly. But the moral is plain, that the prudent policy-maker will hedge on even the most careful predictions, and that he should have as a main goal the attaining of a high degree of flexibility in his economy.

How can one secure adequate flexibility at minimum cost ; equating, that is, gain through flexibility to cost at the margin ? Clearly not through diversification for its own sake, which increases poverty for fear of poverty. Probably one main reliance should be on technical training and general education, in which concepts are inculcated of adaptiveness, experimentation, thinking for oneself, acceptance of the challenges of novelty and self-reliance. Such training might well include the history of sciences and of technology, with focus on problem-solving and the origins of innovations in their historical contexts. A pragmatic open-mindedness as to organization,

---

[1] Hansen summarizes several studies of forecasting results in *Business Cycles and National Income*, Norton, New York, 1951, pp. 583-7.

as well as technical possibilities, is desirable.[1] The skills taught should be those adaptable to new functions : increasingly our world is likely to have people at kinds of work that did not exist when they were in training ten or twenty, or more, years back.

Another likely policy is regularly to try out pilot projects in alternative attractive industries — to train people by doing, to obtain actual experience on costs and returns, and to lay the foundation for rapid expansion should the terms of trade and comparative advantage prove favourable in a given line. This follows the venerable counsel that we should aim at 'small mistakes and big successes'.

APPENDIX I

Hypotheses on the terms of trade : Sources, and amplification of the summary material on pp. 56-7.

(1) J. M. Keynes, *Official Papers*, 'Return of Estimated Value of Foreign Trade of the United Kingdom at prices of 1900', *Econ. Jour.*, 1912, pp. 630-1. 'The deterioration — from the point of view of this country — shown above is due, of course, to the operation of the law of diminishing returns for raw products which, after a temporary lull, has been setting in sharply in quite recent years. There is now again a steady tendency for a given unit of manufactured product to purchase year by year a diminishing quantity of raw product. The comparative advantage in trade is moving against industrial countries.' (Also in W. W. Rostow, 'The Terms of Trade in Theory and Practise', *Econ. Hist. Rev.*, 2nd series, 1950, p. 14.)

(2) D. H. Robertson, *A Study of Industrial Fluctuations*, King, London, 1915, reprinted by London School of Economics and Political Science, 1948, pp. 167-70, 169 n. 'The general conclusion to which [Bowley's figures on United Kingdom terms of trade, down to 1911] lead is that the normal tendency for the ratio of exchange to alter against the manufacturing and in favour of the agricultural communities was in force in the seventies, was suspended in the eighties and nineties, and is now once more on the whole triumphing. This is perhaps the most significant economic fact in the world today.' (Also in Rostow, *ibid.*)

---

[1] Malenbaum and Stolper think that the greater success in development that they judge West Germany and China to have experienced in recent years, as compared with East Germany and India, has originated not in ideology as to organization, but in that the two most successful runners 'demonstrated flexibility in selecting courses of action. Only those were finally adopted in which practice gave promise of the changes needed.' In 'Political Ideology and Economic Progress', *World Politics*, April 1960, p. 420.

Kindelberger also finds that favourable terms of trade experience is correlated with the capacity of a country to shift resources in accord with the changing pattern of advantage; *The Terms of Trade*, etc., pp. 253, 307-8.

(3) W. Beveridge, 'Population and Unemployment', *Econ. Jour.*, 1923, pp. 447-75 ; and 'Mr Keynes' Evidence on Over-Population', *Economica*, pp. 1-10.

(4) J. Viner, *Canada's Balance of International Indebtedness, 1900–1913*, Harvard Press, 1924, p. 295 : 'Prices during a period of capital borrowing rise in the borrowing country, fall in the lending country. . . . It is corollary of this reasoning that during a period of international borrowings the terms of international exchange shift in favor of the borrowing country and against the lending country — in other words, that the borrowing country obtains more foreign produce in exchange for each unit of its exports than it did prior to the borrowing. Adequate inductive verification of this proposition is supplied by the demonstration already made that export prices rose relatively to import prices [in Canada].' Cf. also Viner : *Studies in the Theory of International Trade*, Harper, New York, 1937, Chapter 67, pp. 568-9.

(5) (6) (7) R. H. Coates, Cost of Living Report : *Synopsis of Exhibit by the Statistical Branch*, Department of Labour, Canada, 1915 referred to in Viner, *Canada's Balance, etc.*, pp. 248-53.

R. M. Carr, 'The Role of Price in the International Trade Mechanisms', *Quar. Jour. of Econ.*, Vol. xlv, August 1931, pp. 710-19. 'Instead of finding that continuous heavy borrowing was the dominating factor in this period of Canadian history, one finds that change and industrial growth were the outstanding factors' (p. 719).

J. Stovel, *Canada in the World Economy*, Harvard, 1959, esp. pp. 193-197. 'Frequently there is not even a prima facie support for the Mill-Taussig theory regarding the terms of trade. Increasing capital exports to agricultural countries have on numerous occasions been associated with increasing demands for industrial products on such a scale that the terms of trade have shifted in favour of the capital exporting country. . . . The improvement in terms of trade enjoyed by Canada in the early years of the century could hardly be explained on the basis of capital imports, which remained relatively unimportant until the increase of 1904. . . . The altered terms of trade are probably best explained on the grounds of a world slump in the demand for investment and other manufactured goods in 1908, while the demand for agricultural commodities was only very slightly changed' (pp. 193-6).

(8) Colin Clark, *The Economics of 1960*, Macmillan, London, 1942, especially pp. 49-52. 'The primary cause is rising productivity in secondary and tertiary industries, — which determines the level of agricultural wages, — which determines the marginal productivity of agriculture (not vice versa) by determining the expansion or contraction of the industry. . . . The level of world prices for agricultural products must be high enough to hold in agriculture enough workers to produce the agricultural supplies required at the real incomes implied by the projected productivity trends in secondary and tertiary industries.'

(9) Kindleberger I : 'Planning for Foreign Investment', *Amer. Econ. Rev.*, March 1943, p. 349 : 'Inexorably the terms of trade move against

agricultural and raw material countries as the world's standard of living increases . . . and as Engel's law of consumption operates'. Similarly in *The Dollar Shortage*, Technology Press, Wiley, New York, 1950, p. 122 : 'The certainty of loss arises for agricultural and primary product countries from the assumption of continuously increasing efficiency of production in these and in manufactured products, and . . . the application in these circumstances of Engel's law on a national basis'. This argument raises three questions : (i) whether a modification of Engel's law, to make it apply to real expenditures over successive time periods, is valid ; (ii) whether the world's *per capita* income has been rising, or rising enough, so that such a modified Engel's law has had a chance to work ; and (iii) whether efficiency increase in the two areas has been sufficiently near the same rate, so that the redefined Engel's law effect dominates. Kindleberger has abandoned this reasoning in his later book on European terms of trade.

(10) Kindleberger II : *The Terms of Trade, a European Case Study*, Technology Press, Wiley, New York, 1956. The terms of trade are said to favour developed countries (but not their commodities as compared to those of under-developed countries) because of 'systematic differences in the capacity of the two types of countries to shift resources' (p. 253). 'Bad terms of trade are a result of bad luck and inflexibility, or incapacity to enter other industries or to withdraw resources from existing lines' (p. 306). The basic data for this exhaustive study are European, for commodities only, exclude qualitative changes in manufactures and the relevance for under-developed countries of falling transportation costs.

(11) Raul Prébisch, *The Economic Development of Latin America*, United Nations, New York, 1950. 'The advantages of technical progress have been mainly concentrated in the industrial centers and have not directly extended to the countries making up the periphery of the world's economic system.' The cause is that 'the characteristic lack of organization among the workers employed in primary production prevents them from obtaining wage increases (in the boom) comparable to those of the industrial countries and from maintaining the increases to the same extent (in depression)' (pp. 8, 13). Questions raised by this thesis are : (i) Are domestic money prices that rise freely and fall sluggishly either necessary, or sufficient, to cause relatively high prices in the world market ? (Balance of payments effects ; exchange depreciation.) (ii) Do higher money wages cause higher domestic prices ? (The productivity variable.) (iii) Do unions secure higher money wage rates, for labour of given quality, than the wage rates of non-union labour ?

(12) United Nations : *Commodity Trade and Economic Development*, New York, 1953. The Committee authors were C. F. Carter, Sumitro Djojohadikusumo, J. Goudriaan, Klaus Knorr and Francisco Garcia Olano. 'Some observers have interpreted . . . others have seen. . . . We see no adequate ground for discriminating between these (and other) theories, and we conclude that the evidence of the past offers no help in predicting the future secular movements of the terms of trade' (p. 12).

(13) W. Arthur Lewis, *The Theory of Economic Growth*, Allen and Unwin, London, 1955. 'So long as the peasant farms have low productivity, the temperate world can get the services of tropical labour for a very low price. The labour for producing [such export commodities as tea, cotton, sugar, oilseeds and various mineral products] can be had cheaply because its alternative is to stay on peasant farms growing food with very low productivity per man. Moreover, when productivity rises in the crops produced for export, there is no need to share the increase with labour, and practically the whole benefit goes in reducing the price to industrial consumers' (p. 281).

(14) Gunnar Myrdal, *An International Economy*, Harper, New York, 1956. Myrdal relies on the United Nations' *Relative Prices* study as an adequate basis for generalizing. He writes : 'With individual exceptions, the underdeveloped countries have had rather bad luck in the historical development of prices of their typical export articles, which have not, on the whole, been the dynamic industrial raw materials, essential to modern industrial development. . . . Rigidity and lack of enterprise . . . explains why they have been sticking so tenaciously to the bad risks in production and export. . . . (pp. 230-1).

(15) P. T. Ellsworth, 'The Terms of Trade between Primary Producing and Industrial Countries', *Inter-American Economic Affairs*, Vol. x, summer 1956, no. 1, pp. 47-65. For 1876–80 to 1901–05, falling transportation costs are seen as the dominant and perhaps complete explanation of the relative fall in primary product prices in British terms-of-trade data. For later periods (to 1933 in the UN data) causative elements are bargained higher real wages for British labour, excess capacity development and stocks accumulation during World War I, competition of synthetic nitrates and substitutes for silk with the natural products and (1929–33) the inverse response of agricultural output to falling demand and prices.

(16) Henry G. Aubrey, *United States Imports and World Trade*, Oxford, Clarendon Press, 1957. Specific commodity studies are made for about two-thirds of US import trade ; the residual one-third estimates are extrapolation of post-war import functions. Relative to US prices, the 'most likely' result is that in 1975 'a unit of the projected import commodities could . . . buy . . . about 60 per cent more American goods than in the base period 1937/40, and about 37 per cent more than in 1948' (p. 26). 'No matter how rough the method of computation, the trend here illustrated is so marked that it leaves little doubt about the reversal of an earlier unfavourable trend for primary products' (p. 27).

(17) Theodore Morgan, 'The Long-Run Terms of Trade Between Agriculture and Manufacturing', *Economic Development and Cultural Change*, Oct. 1959, pp. 1-23. British (UN) terms-of-trade data and European (Kindleberger) data are criticized as not being relevant to the experience of primary producers outside of Europe. Studies of terms-of-trade data for six other countries than the U.K., and for various periods produce, including U.K. data back to 1801, remarkably diverse results, in both the short and long run. 'The data of this paper suggest that

emphasis ought to be centred on the heterogeneity of price experience. Particular supply influences, and particular demand changes, for different commodities, countries, and times, have dominated the historical picture' (p. 20).

(18) E. M. Bernstein, 'International Effects of U.S. Economic Policy', prepared in connection with the Study of Employment, Growth, and Price Levels, for the Joint Economic Committee, Jan. 1960. '[There is a] chronic surplus of primary products. . . . The supply of primary products increases with the growth in population and the improvement in technology in the raw materials exporting countries. . . . As incomes rise in the high-income countries, the proportion of personal income spent on food declines. . . . The decline is greatest for . . . such staples as cereals, sugar, fats, and oils, and not inconsiderable for coffee and tea. . . . The demand for meat, dairy products, fruits, and similar foods does rise almost in proportion to the rise in personal incomes. . . . There are two reasons for the decline in the raw material content of industrial production. The first is technological : the development of synthetic materials, technological changes in the use of raw materials, and displacement of less highly fabricated by more highly fabricated raw materials. The second reason . . . is [that] the raw material content of nondurable manufactures, such as textiles, manufactured foodstuffs, etc., is considerably higher than the raw material content of durable manufactures ; and in the post-war period, durable goods output has risen relative to non-durable goods. Furthermore durable goods are becoming more intricate in their manufacture, so that the labor and capital content of output has grown much more than the raw material content' (pp. 50-1).

Notes to Table *A*.1 : (1) The terms of trade for Bolivia, the Dominican Republic, Ecuador and Uruguay have been calculated from their export price indices and the import price index for Latin America. (2) The terms of trade for Burma, Nigeria, Sudan, Morocco, Vietnam, Angola and Pakistan have been calculated from their unit value indices, while that of Turkey is based on Chamber of Commerce wholesale price index 'Series B'. (3) The letter (A) or (B) in the first column identifies the series in those cases in which the country has more than one index for import or export prices.

Sources: *International Financial Statistics*, June 1961, pp. 34-35; *U.N. Monthly Bulletin of Statistics*, June and Dec. 1960 and June 1961.

APPENDIX II : TABLES AND CHARTS

TABLE *A*.1

TERMS-OF-TRADE DATA

(1953 = 100)

Country	1954	1955	1956	1957	1958	1959	1960
Developed countries							
1. U.S.A.	96	96	98	102	106	109	108
2. Canada	97	98	100	95	96	99	98
3. Austria	102	109	107	108	113	113	114
4. Belgium (A)	98	101	104	104	104	102	104
5. Denmark (A)	102	102	102	96	102	109	104
6. France (A)	95	97	97	95	99	99	100
7. Germany (A)	100	98	99	100	108	110	111
8. Italy	101	97	92	90	97	96	101
9. Norway (B)	107	108	106	104	106	109	108
10. Portugal (A)	99	104	97	94	95	94	—
11. Spain (B)	103	96	94	97	99	100	94
12. Sweden (B)	99	101	99	96	101	100	101
13. Switzerland	100	99	95	95	99	100	—
14. U.K.	100	99	101	104	111	111	112
15. Japan (B)	100	100	104	101	103	111	115
16. Australia	92	81	80	82	64	69	66
17. New Zealand (A)	104	105	101	96	83	96	89
18. Ireland (A)	97	97	91	88	93	99	96
Median value	100	99	99	96	100	100	101
Under-developed countries							
1. Argentina	97	93	80	74	81	88	92
2. Bolivia	100	98	102	89	82	88	89
3. Brazil	136	106	99	96	93	79	—
4. Colombia (A)	130	105	116	103	88	78	76
5. Costa Rica	115	106	112	102	86	79	78
6. Dominican Republic	120	101	94	115	115	88	87
7. Ecuador	116	91	85	88	—	—	—
8. El Salvador	128	112	109	107	90	77	80
9. Guatemala (B)	120	111	121	107	84	88	76
10. Honduras	108	108	107	—	90	81	77
11. Nicaragua	128	108	109	94	82	71	71
12. Uruguay	104	93	82	85	69	67	83
13. Venezuela	106	106	100	108	107	98	95
14. Greece	103	113	116	110	118	106	108
15. Ceylon (A)	121	135	121	109	117	124	124
16. Ghana	148	132	101	95	135	121	100
17. India	108	108	107	98	103	103	115
18. Malaya	107	166	142	132	122	157	177
19. Indonesia (A)	104	120	110	113	97	126	124
20. Philippines (A)	93	84	86	84	85	90	88
21. Burma	83	70	76	63	63	—	—
22. Nigeria	119	107	99	98	102	109	—
23. Pakistan	109	99	88	85	72	70	—
24. Angola	108	90	80	80	82	73	—
25. Morocco	107	109	111	109	115	106	—
26. Vietnam	93	104	103	98	91	99	91
27. Chile	90	106	116	88	79	89	—
28. Sudan	126	114	125	113	107	104	—
29. Turkey	106	108	110	114	85	79	—
Median value	108	106	110	98	90	88	89

TABLE A.2
TERMS-OF-TRADE DATA
(1937=100)

Country	1937	1948	1950	1951	1952	1953	1954	1955	1956	1957	1958	1959	1960
Developed countries													
1. U.S.A.	100	88	76	70	73	76	74	75	76	78	81	83	83
2. Canada	100	96	93	92	104	102	99	100	102	97	98	101	100
3. Belgium (A)	100	118	107	116	118	105	103	106	109	109	109	107	109
4. Denmark (A)	100 **	90	83	73	79	83	85	85	85	80	85	91	—
5. France (A)	100 †	115	98	88	97	100	95	97	97	96	99	99	100
6. W. Germany (A)	100	135	80	77	88	93	93	92	93	93	101	103	104
7. Italy	100	88	90	83	80	84	85	81	77	75	82	80	85
8. Norway	100 **	103	96	108	106	100	107	108	106	104	106	109	108
9. Sweden (B)	100	111	96	118	111	105	104	106	104	101	106	105	106
10. Switzerland	100	100	112	98	100	102	102	101	97	97	101	102	—
11. U.K.	100 ‡	93	87	77	82	87	87	86	88	90	97	97	98
12. Japan (B)	100	—	101	115	105	110	110	110	114	111	114	122	126
13. Australia	100	103	139	137	103	114	106	93	92	95	73	79	76
14. New Zealand (A)	100	87	118	119	87	103	106	110	104	100	86	100	—
15. Ireland (A)	100	126	130	122	122	132	128	128	120	116	123	131	126
Median value	100	102	96	98	100	102	102	100	97	97	99	101	102

For notes and sources see p. 75.

TABLE *A.2* (*contd.*)

TERMS-OF-TRADE DATA

(1937=100)

Country	1937	1948	1950	1951	1952	1953	1954	1955	1956	1957	1958	1959	1960
Under-developed Countries													
1. Bolivia	100	115	128	164	155	128	128	126	131	114	105	113	114
2. Colombia (A)	100	136	198	207	205	227	295	239	264	234	200	177	173
3. Costa Rica	100	106	151	149	145	154	177	163	173	157	132	122	120
4. Dominican Republic	100	216	246	265	223	208	250	210	196	240	240	183	181
5. El Salvador	100	141	259	256	198	256	328	287	280	275	231	197	205
6. Honduras	100	76	93	87	97	94	—	102	101	—	85	76	73
7. Uruguay	100	109	140	183	118	122	127	113	100	104	84	82	101
8. Venezuela	100	100	129	118	119	125	133	133	125	135	134	123	119
9. Ceylon (A)	100*	87	125	126	91	100	121	135	121	111	117	124	124
10. India	100*	97	100	119	96	92	100	99	99	90	95	95	106
11. Malaya (incl. Singapore)	100	88	131	156	126	109	113	142	131	119	113	134	—
12. Philippines	100*	126	116	110	88	112	104	95	96	94	96	102	99
13. Burma	100	140	112	195	278	340	282	237	257	213	215	—	—
14. Sudan	100*	131	164	173	170	137	173	156	170	153	146	142	—
15. Turkey	100	—	—	—	81	80	84	86	88	91	68	64	—
Median value	100	108	130	160	126	125	128	135	131	127	117	123	119

* 1938.　† 1936.　‡ 1934–36.

Notes: (1) The terms of trade for Bolivia, the Dominican Republic and Uruguay have been calculated from their export price indices and the import price index for Latin America. (2) The terms of trade for Burma, Malaya and Sudan have been calculated from their unit value indices while that of Turkey is based on Chamber of Commerce wholesale price index 'series B'. (3) The letter (A) or (B) used in the stub identifies the series in those cases in which the country has more than one index for import or export prices.

Sources: *International Financial Statistics*, Oct. 1957, pp. 40–1 and June 1961, pp. 34–5; *U.N. Monthly Bulletin of Statistics*, Dec. 1953, June and Dec. 1960 and June 1961.

TABLE A.

MAJOR WORLD TRADE COMMODITIES : EXPORTS IN PERCENTAGE OF WORLD EXPORTS AND COUNTRY'S EXPORTS
(For selected commodities)

Country	Commodity	Percentage of world exports				Percentage of country's exports		
		1948	1950	1952	1957	1950	1952	1957
I. Developed countries								
1. U.S.A.	Coal	37	—	57	81	—	3	4
	Cotton	34	49	42	50	10	6	5
	Tobacco	44	47	48	32	—	2	2
	Wheat	51	40	52	52	5	6	4
	Rice	10	19	24	21	—	1	1
	Linseed oil	10	6	7	22	—	—	—
2. Canada	Pulp	34	46*	51*	48*	7	7	6
	Wheat	23	32	41	28	13	17	9
	Zinc	29	39	42	42	—	2	1
	Copper	8	18	11	17	—	2	3
	Lead	15	16	17	12	—	1	—
	Fish	—	34	29	25	—	2	2
3. Denmark	Bacon and ham	27	61	76	82	13	16	13
	Butter	13	33	30	31	20	13	8
4. Australia	Wheat	43	16	7	9	14	13	6
	Wool	21	49	58	62	51	48	50
	Butter	8	15	5	14	4	1	2
	Zinc	—	12	10	—	—	—	—
5. New Zealand	Mutton and lamb	17	72	93	77	13	20	16
	Wool	31	15	16	17	41	34	38
	Butter	9	25	41	34	19	23	14
6. Union of South Africa	Wool	11	12	14	11	28	20	15
II. Under-developed countries								
7. Turkey	Tobacco	11	11	11	21	23	17	40
8. Burma	Rice	31	27	26	29	88	74	74
9. Ceylon	Tea	36	45	41	41	48	48	61
	Rubber	6	7	7	6	26	25	18
	Coconut oil	43	16†	21†	12†	16	16	9
10. India	Tea	49	46	46	50	13	14	19
	Burlap	—	40‡	53‡	57‡	18	22	16

Country	Commodity							
11. Indonesia	Copra	21	18†	24†	16†	7	6	4
	Rubber	30	30	38	33	43	44	36
	Tin	58	44	35	38	—	22	16
12. Malaya	Rubber	47	53	40	38	—	58	57
	Coconut oil	27	8†	7†	6†	13	2	2
13. Philippines	Hemp	—	93	93	35	56	12	9
	Coconut oil	24	58†	48†	65†	14	33	41
	Sugar	—	6	10	6	46	26	19
14. Pakistan	Jute	87	60‡	47‡	43‡	38	40	49
	Cotton	8	7	13	3	49	49	21
15. Thailand	Rice	20	32	33	30	24	65	48
	Rubber	—	5	8	—	85	27	19
16. Egypt	Cotton	17	21	17	17	4	87	72
	Rice	9	5	1	—	—	1	7
17. Rhodesia (North)	Copper	18	26	26	23	16	87	54
18. Argentina	Wool	17	12	8	7	14	17	12
	Wheat	—	13	—	10	4	1	16
	Quebracho	—	—	91	85	8	5	3
	Beef	—	48	53	57	6	15	26
	Linseed oil	41	53	28	57	6	3	3
19. Brazil	Coffee	55	55	52	40	64	74	61
	Cacao	12	23	10	18	6	3	5
	Cotton	10	—	1	2	8	2	3
20. Chile	Nitrate	—	5	100	100	25	13	10
	Copper	33	34	67	47	52	85	81
21. Cuba	Sugar	49	71	6	6	89	50	55
22. Dominican Republic	Sugar	3	5	6	8	51	23	23
23. Mexico	Cotton	35	4	26	26	18	23	7
	Lead	10	26	20	19	13	13	6
	Zinc	6	18	5	26	5	8	50
24. Uruguay	Wool	21	11	18	9	60	33	5
	Linseed oil	—	15	37	—	—	4	6
25. Ghana	Cacao	39§	—	9	36	—	68	62
26. Greece	Tobacco	4	7	37	—	42	44	43
27. Bolivia	Tin	—	21	22	—	68	59	60

* Percentage of newsprint and pulp combined.
† Percentage of copra and coconut oil combined.
‡ Percentage of jute and burlap combined.
§ Including Togoland.

Sources: *International Financial Statistics*, Sept. and Nov. 1953, pp. 24-7; *International Financial Statistics*, April 1959, pp. 32-5; *International Financial Statistics*, June 1961, pp. 30-3; *International Financial Statistics*, July 1954, pp. 26-30.

TABLE A.4

AID PER CAPITA AND TERMS OF TRADE

Country	Per capita aid received during 1954–59 in $	Terms of trade (1953=100)						
		1954	1955	1956	1957	1958	1959	Average
1. Bolivia	38·8	100	98	102	89	82	88	93
2. Costa Rica	37·9	115	106	112	102	86	79	100
3. Peru	22·3	104	103	98	106	93	—	101
4. Haiti	15·8	—	—	—	—	—	—	—
5. Chile	15·2	90	106	116	88	79	89	93
6. Colombia	13·9	130	105	116	103	88	78	103
7. Uruguay	11·5	104	93	82	85	69	67	83
8. Honduras	11·1	108	108	107	—	90	81	99
9. Ecuador	10·4	116	91	85	88	—	—	95
10. Pakistan	8·4	109	99	88	85	72	70	87
11. Ceylon	8·0	121	135	121	109	117	124	121
12. Thailand	7·6	—	—	—	—	—	—	—
13. Brazil	7·3	136	106	99	96	93	79	102
14. El Salvador	7·2	128	112	109	107	90	77	104
15. Mexico	7·2	—	—	—	—	—	—	—
16. Philippines	6·5	93	84	86	84	85	90	87
17. Argentina	3·5	97	93	80	74	81	88	86
18. Ghana	3·1	148	132	101	95	135	121	122
19. Indonesia	2·9	104	120	110	113	97	126	112
20. Sudan	2·5	126	114	125	112	106	104	115
21. India	2·4	108	108	107	98	103	103	105
22. Burma	2·3	83	70	76	63	63	—	71
23. Dominican Republic	0·8	120	101	94	115	115	88	106

General Note : (1) *Per capita* aid received during 1954–59 is the sum of *per capita* aid calculated by IMF for the years 1954–57 (with mid-1956 population) and for the years 1958–59 (with mid-1958 population). (2) (*a*) Terms of trade for Bolivia, the Dominican Republic, Ecuador and Uruguay have been calculated from their export price indices and the import price index for Latin America. (*b*) Terms-of-trade data for Sudan, Chile and Burma are based on unit value indices. International Economic Aid is measured by the flow of grants and long-term loans between countries. This flow includes grants and loans in cash and in kind, including within the better category the provision of services as well as of commodities. Grants and loans specifically linked to the defence of the recipient country such as transfers of military equipment, direct military expenditure and financial contribution for the support of military forces are so far as possible excluded. Entries here refer to actual amounts expended rather than to commitments or authorizations. Repayments by under-developed countries of the principal of loans extended to them are considered as an offset to aid received.

Assistance extended to under-developed countries by Bulgaria, China (mainland), Czechoslovakia, East Germany, Hungary, Poland, Rumania and the U.S.S.R. are not included.

Sources : U.N. *Statistical Yearbook, 1958*, p. 439 ; U.N. *Statistical Yearbook, 1960*, p. 402 ; *U.N. Monthly Bulletin of Statistics*, March 1957, p. 108 ; *U.N. Monthly Bulletin of Statistics*, Dec. 1957, p. 114 ; *U.N. Monthly Bulletin of Statistics*, June 1960, p. 109 ; *International Financial Statistics*, June 1961, p. 35.

TABLE *A.5*

EXPORT PRICE INDICES BY KINDS OF PRIMARY COMMODITIES
(1953 = 100)

	Code	1951	1952	1953	1954	1955	1956	1957	1958	1959	1960
1. Primary commodities	D	116	104	100	98	96	98	99	93	94	94
	U	121	105	100	109	102	101	104	99	94	94
(a) Food	D	97	102	100	94	93	93	91	91	94	92
	U	105	101	100	117	98	97	102	97	85	83
(b) Agricultural (non-food)	D	145	108	100	101	99	99	101	89	90	91
	U	167	115	100	101	108	105	103	93	101	105
(c) Minerals	D	87	99	100	96	98	109	115	110	104	103
	U	103	102	100	103	104	105	108	110	105	103
2. Non-ferrous base metals	D	125	118	100	101	113	121	114	103	108	111
	U	102	110	100	98	124	125	90	80	93	96

Notes:
  D — Indices representing exports of developed areas (North America, Western Europe, Australia, New Zealand, Union of South Africa, Japan).
  U — Indices representing exports of under-developed areas (all other areas).
Source: *U.N. Monthly Bulletin of Statistics*, June 1961, p. ix.

TABLE A.6

PRICE INDICES OF BEVERAGE, MEAT, BUTTER AND SUGAR

(1937–38=100)

Commodity and country	1948	1949	1950	1951	1952	1953	1954	1955	1956	1957	1958	1959	1960
Tea													
1. India	252	247	193	181	167	177	251	264	233	239	231	229	242
2. Ceylon	208	230	191	187	161	178	242	229	215	190	183	189	182
Meat													
1. New Zealand (Base : 1938)	147	165	124	106	122	140	161	179	183	193	174	153	161
2. Argentina (Base : 1938)	159	158	205	202	205	255	258	242	192	183	213	240	253
3. Denmark	199	199	134	148	160	153	144	151	163	150	154	147	148
Butter													
1. Australia	176	194	153	159	171	180	180	183	160	140	108	171	150
2. N.Z.	162	202	154	165	178	189	193	219	197	178	150	218	191
3. Denmark	247	247	148	156	162	181	183	188	192	155	128	184	159
Sugar													
1. Philippines	174	176	184	175	184	196	192	178	180	190	197	192	—
2. Cuba	219	230	241	240	253	256	246	236	241	251	256	253	—
3. Dominican Republic	437	349	500	381	310	287	284	298	459	332	291	321	—

Notes :—

General Note :—Prices are expressed per 100 pounds for all but pulp and
coal (short ton), and burlap (100 yards).

Tea : India — unit value of exports adjusted to include tax and export duty through March 1951 : Ceylon–Colombo market price
including export duty and taxes.
Meat : New Zealand — mutton and lamb, unit value of exports. Argentina — beef, unit value of exports. Denmark — bacon
and ham, export price to U.K.
Butter : New Zealand — contract price with U.K. through July 1954. Beginning 1955, market price in London. Australian
contract price with U.K. through July 1954. Beginning 1955, wholesale price. Denmark — contract price with U.K. through Sept.
1955. Thereafter, export price to U.K.
Sugar : Cuba — F.o.b. for sugar sold to U.S.A. Philippines — Manila price. Dominican Republic — unit value of exports.

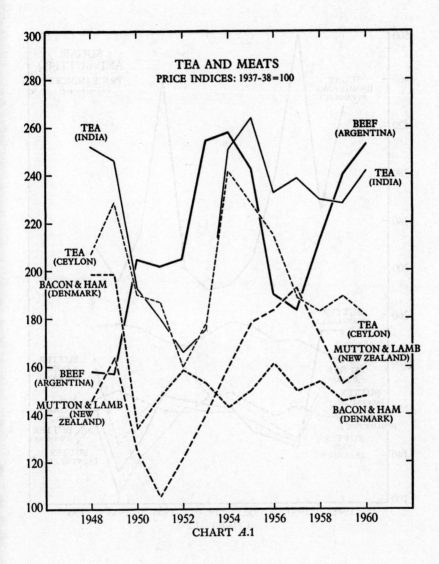

CHART *A*.1

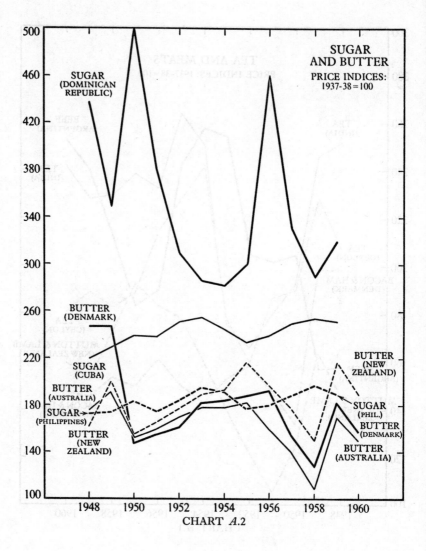

CHART *A*.2

SUGAR
AND BUTTER
PRICE INDICES:
1937-38=100

SUGAR
(DOMINICAN
REPUBLIC)

BUTTER
(DENMARK)

SUGAR
(CUBA)

BUTTER
(AUSTRALIA)

SUGAR→
(PHILIPPINES)

BUTTER
(NEW
ZEALAND)

BUTTER
(NEW
ZEALAND)

SUGAR
(PHIL.)

BUTTER
(DENMARK)

BUTTER
(AUSTRALIA)

TABLE A.7

PRICE INDICES OF CEREALS AND OILS
(1937–38=100)

Commodity and country	1948	1949	1950	1951	1952	1953	1954	1955	1956	1957	1958	1959	1960
Rice													
1. U.S.A.	346	257	249	284	304	311	254	287	241	264	281	255	235
2. Burma	537	537	392	406	515	607	456	362	333	323	332	314	297
Wheat													
1. Canada	222	185	163	183	197	179	155	151	150	147	143	149	146
2. U.S.A.	242	212	222	242	241	226	233	228	224	226	205	200	201
Oil													
1. U.S.A. (linseed)	299	269	186	210	—	152	147	130	142	137	139	131	132
2. Philippines (coconut)	500	327	342	357	237	351	290	245	234	240	331	408	357
3. Ceylon (coconut)	307	406	350	409	235	315	281	232	238	249	288	349	285

Notes :—

Rice : U.S.A. — New Orleans Zenith, extra fancy, miller to first distributor. Burma — Unit value of exports.

Wheat : U.S.A. — No. 2, hard, winter. Average of reported cash sales weighted by quantity sold, Kansas City. Canada — Manitoba Northern No. 1. F.o.b. Port William or Fort Arthur.

Oil : U.S.A. — 1953 to date, tank cars, f.o.b. Minneapolis. Philippines — Manila price. Ceylon — wharf delivery incl. duty and taxes.

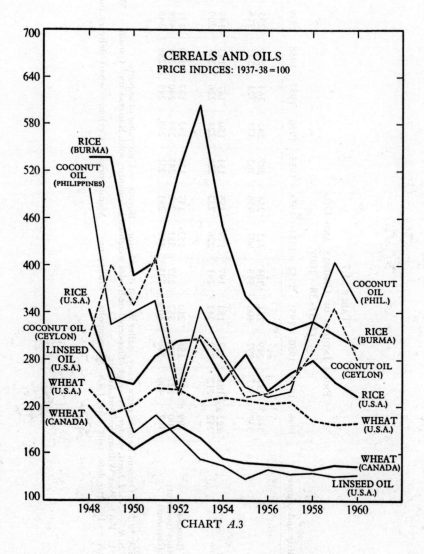

CEREALS AND OILS
PRICE INDICES: 1937-38 = 100

RICE
(BURMA)

COCONUT
OIL
(PHILIPPINES)

RICE
(U.S.A.)

COCONUT OIL
(CEYLON)

LINSEED
OIL
(U.S.A.)

WHEAT
(U.S.A.)

WHEAT
(CANADA)

COCONUT
OIL
(PHIL.)

RICE
(BURMA)

COCONUT OIL
(CEYLON)

RICE
(U.S.A.)

WHEAT
(U.S.A.)

WHEAT
(CANADA)

LINSEED OIL
(U.S.A.)

CHART *A*.3

84

TABLE *A.8*

PRICE INDICES OF WOOL, COTTON, HEMP AND JUTE
(1937–38 = 100)

Commodity and country	1948	1949	1950	1951	1952	1953	1954	1955	1956	1957	1958	1959	1960
Wool													
1. Australia	223	283	—	453	288	326	300	254	266	294	201	206	206
2. New Zealand	165	183	363	399	224	269	283	271	269	297	209	224	—
3. Union of South Africa	199	264	311	449	262	302	269	242	257	286	179	194	198
4. Uruguay	251	263	364	522	286	305	326	273	256	290	206	183	244
Cotton													
1. U.S.A.	325	319	348	400	372	316	327	323	326	325	334	319	302
2. Egypt (Ashmouni)	446	338	453	542	389	291	346	317	348	388	349	338	349
3. Mexico (Base : 1938)	—	—	—	491	321	299	323	296	284	274	257	228	242
Hemp													
1. Philippines	484	499	491	568	355	352	251	275	334	413	360	533	550
Burlap													
1. India	444	391	403	708	372	289	277	256	236	240	234	233	276

Notes :—

Wool : Australia — average price, greasy wool, Sydney auctions. New Zealand — auction prices, large sample greasy wool, selected grades. Union of South Africa — auction sales, average all types greasy wool. Uruguay — unit value of exports.

Cotton : U.S.A. — average corporation selling price, exports middling 1 inch, Houston. Egypt — unit value of exports. Mexico — Torreon middling $\frac{1}{16}$ inch through June 1953 ; afterward Mata'mores $1\frac{1}{32}$ inch, f.o.b. Texas.

Hemp : Philippines — Manila price.

Burlap : India — $10\frac{1}{2}$ oz., 40 inch, Calcutta. Incl. export duty.

85

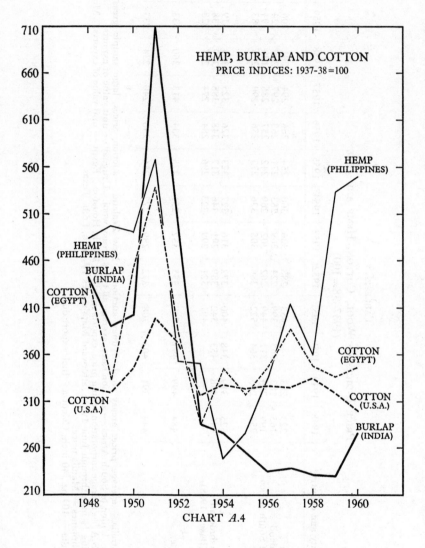

HEMP, BURLAP AND COTTON
PRICE INDICES: 1937-38=100

HEMP
(PHILIPPINES)

BURLAP
(INDIA)

COTTON
(EGYPT)

COTTON
(U.S.A.)

HEMP
(PHILIPPINES)

COTTON
(EGYPT)

COTTON
(U.S.A.)

BURLAP
(INDIA)

CHART *A*.4

86

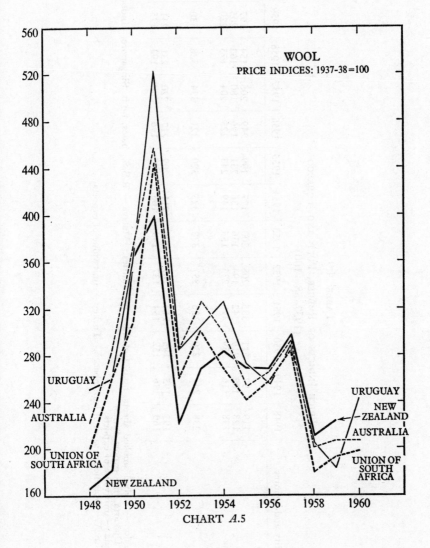

WOOL
PRICE INDICES: 1937-38=100

URUGUAY

AUSTRALIA

UNION OF
SOUTH AFRICA

NEW ZEALAND

URUGUAY

NEW
ZEALAND

AUSTRALIA

UNION OF
SOUTH
AFRICA

CHART *A*.5

87

TABLE *A.9*

PRICE INDICES OF RUBBER, PULP AND TOBACCO

(1937–38 = 100)

Commodity and country	1948	1949	1950	1951	1952	1953	1954	1955	1956	1957	1958	1959	1960
Rubber													
1. Ceylon	119	97	211	335	208	200	177	199	249	205	154	197	211
2. Malaya	123	102	219	342	194	136	136	231	196	180	162	205	219
3. Indonesia	138	116	259	378	233	155	149	243	225	204	175	220	—
Pulp													
1. Canada	238	247	230	336	357	328	325	320	321	334	328	330	325
Tobacco													
1. U.S.A.	195	195	195	214	207	206	211	209	217	220	231	241	237
2. Turkey	160	136	152	154	137	149	168	188	196	200	193	175	144

Notes:—

Rubber: Ceylon — ribbed smoked sheets, f.o.b. Colombo, incl. duties. Malaya — R.S.S., bales, f.o.b. Singapore. Indonesia — R.S.S. 1, f.o.b. Djakarta, incl. export duties.

Pulp: Canada — unit value of exports.

Tobacco: U.S.A. — warehouse sales of leaf tobacco. Turkey — unit value of exports.

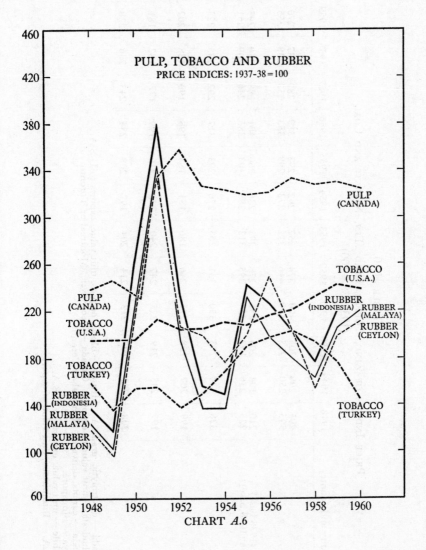

PULP, TOBACCO AND RUBBER
PRICE INDICES: 1937-38 = 100

PULP
(CANADA)

TOBACCO
(U.S.A.)

RUBBER
(INDONESIA)

RUBBER
(MALAYA)

RUBBER
(CEYLON)

TOBACCO
(TURKEY)

PULP
(CANADA)

TOBACCO
(U.S.A.)

TOBACCO
(TURKEY)

RUBBER
(INDONESIA)

RUBBER
(MALAYA)

RUBBER
(CEYLON)

CHART A.6

TABLE *A*.10

PRICE INDICES OF ZINC, COPPER, LEAD, TIN, NITRATE AND COAL
(1937–38=100)

Commodity and country	1948	1949	1950	1951	1952	1953	1954	1955	1956	1957	1958	1959	1960
Zinc													
1. Canada	295	299	305	400	374	257	262	293	319	281	237	270	291
2. Mexico	395	250	275	499	446	312	273	299	353	353	238	255	298
Copper													
1. Canada (1938 base)	210	194	204	251	278	291	286	360	401	288	250	295	298
2. Rhodesia (1938 base)	225	236	193	259	295	313	288	403	385	246	209	261	272
Lead													
1. Canada	328	324	263	350	331	263	276	293	317	292	235	223	221
Tin													
1. Malaya	199	207	188	271	246	186	181	188	198	190	188	202	201
Nitrate													
1. Chile	197	233	219	225	247	240	222	216	199	177	182	181	200
Coal													
1. U.S.A.	208	203	197	213	214	204	197	208	234	243	236	228	220

Notes:—
Zinc: Canada — electrolytic, grade A. Mexico — blocks or pigs, unit value, exports to U.S.A.
Copper: Rhodesia — unit value of exports. Canada — electrolytic, Montreal or Toronto.
Lead: Canada — carlots, delivered Montreal or Toronto.
Tin: Malaya — Singapore.
Nitrate: Chile — unit value, exports to U.S.A.
Coal: U.S.A. — Bituminous, unit value of exports.

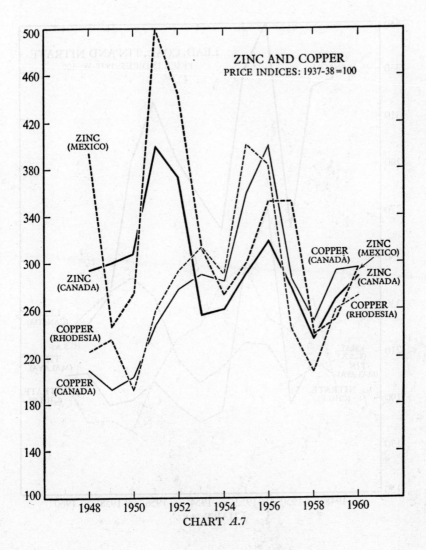

ZINC AND COPPER
PRICE INDICES: 1937-38=100

CHART A.7

91

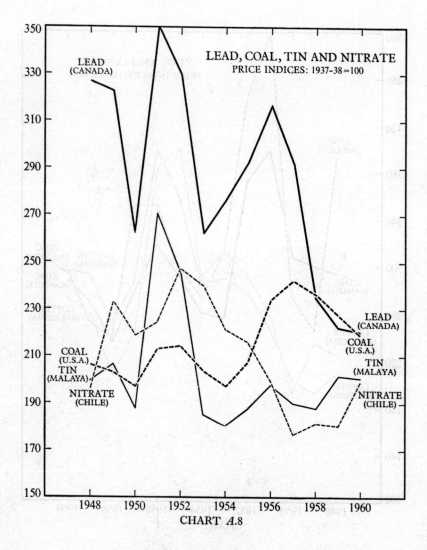

LEAD, COAL, TIN AND NITRATE
PRICE INDICES: 1937-38=100

LEAD
(CANADA)

COAL
(U.S.A.)
TIN
(MALAYA)

NITRATE
(CHILE)

LEAD
(CANADA)

COAL
(U.S.A.)

TIN
(MALAYA)

NITRATE
(CHILE)

CHART *A*.8

92

TABLE A.11

	Agricultural exports as a percentage of total exports (annual average for 1956–58)	Terms-of-trade index	
		1956–58	1956–58
		1953	1937 and 1938 or 1936
Developed countries			
1. West Germany	4	103	99
2. Belgium	10	104	110
3. U.K.	11	105	87
4. Japan	13	103	113 ¶
5. France	20	98	98 ‖
6. U.S.A.	24	103	77
7. Italy	25	93	85
8. Sweden	33	99	104 ‖
9. Canada	39	98	101
10. Norway	39	105	105 §
11. Denmark	68	100	83 ‖
12. Ireland	75	91	109
13. Australia	79	75	85
14. New Zealand	97	94	99
Under-developed countries			
15. India	45 *	103	94 §
16. Malaya (incl. Singapore)	63	112	121 ‖
17. Indonesia	61	107	—
18. Colombia	83	102	—
19. Ghana	83	110	—
20. Turkey	85	103	82 §
21. Greece	86	111	—
22. Dominican Republic	89	108	225
23. Nigeria	91	100	—
24. Brazil	92	96	—
25. Ceylon	92	116	116 ‖
26. Argentina	93	79	—
27. Burma	95	67	221
28. Ecuador	95 †	87 ‡	—
29. El Salvador	98	102	262
30. Nicaragua	98	95	—

* Average for the years 1957 and 1958.
† 1955–56 average.
‡ 1956–57 average.
§ Base year 1937.
‖ Base year 1938.
¶ Base year 1934–36.

Notes :—
Column 2 : Based on the figures given in *FAO Trade Year Book*, 1959, pp. 2-11.
Columns 3 and 4 : Terms-of-trade indices are calculated from the data given (1953=100) in *International Financial Statistics*, Oct. 1957 (p. 41) and June 1961 (p. 35) except for that of Burma, Malaya, Nigeria and Turkey. The indices of Burma, Malaya and Nigeria are based on the unit value index given in *U.N. Monthly Bulletin of Statistics* (Dec. 1953, June and Dec. 1960 and June 1961), while that of Turkey is derived from the Chamber of Commerce wholesale price index 'series B'.

93

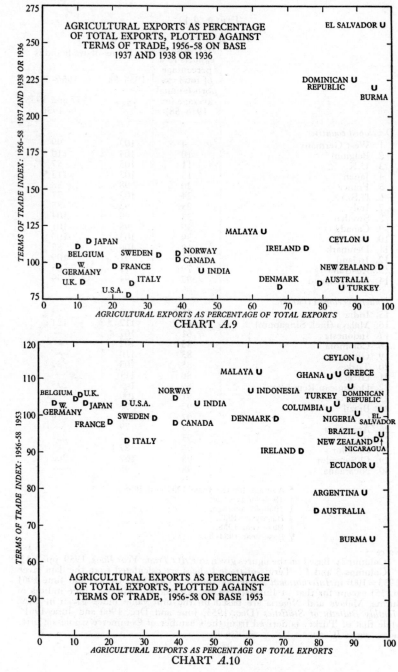

CHART *A.9*

CHART *A.10*

TABLE *A.*12
REAL EXPORT PURCHASING POWER INDEX
(1937=100)

Group	1937	1948	1950	1951	1952	1953	1954	1955	1956	1957	1958	1959	1960
1. Developed countries, I	100	138	128	129	138	149	149	162	178	177	189	206	236
2. Under-developed countries	100	104	143	151	140	161	190	177	179	169	159	172	179
3. Developed countries, II	100	105	133	136	118	194	130	137	143	154	140	163	165

Notes : Developed countries I include U.S.A., Canada, Belgium, France, West Germany, Italy, Norway, Sweden, U.K. and Japan. The base year used for calculating import price indices for France and Sweden, West Germany, and Japan respectively are 1938, 1936 and 1934–36. The value index for Belgium is based on the total value of exports for Belgium–Luxemburg.

Under-developed countries include Bolivia, Colombia, Dominican Republic, El Salvador, Uruguay, Turkey, India, Burma, Ceylon and Philippines. The base year for Ceylon's import price index is 1938. As the import price indices for Bolivia, Dominican Republic and Uruguay are not available the import price index for Latin America is used. The import price index of Burma is based on unit value import price index. The value index for India is based on the 1937 estimate made taking into consideration the 1948 proportion of total value of exports of India and Pakistan.

Developed countries II include Australia, New Zealand and Denmark, whose total value of agricultural exports as a percentage of total exports exceed 60 per cent. Ireland has been excluded for the lack of 1937 value data. In the case of Denmark, 1938 import price index is used.

Sources : *International Financial Statistics*, Oct. 1957, 28–31 and 40–1 ; *International Financial Statistics*, June 1961, 34–9 ; *U.N. Monthly Bulletin of Statistics*, Oct. 1953, June and Dec. 1960.

Chapter 4

EFFECTS OF CHANGES IN COMPARATIVE COSTS AS INFLUENCED BY TECHNICAL CHANGE

BY

H. G. JOHNSON
University of Chicago

I. INTRODUCTION

INTEREST in the effects of technical change on comparative cost, the volume and terms of trade, and the gains from international specialization is of relatively modern origin, a by-product of post-war concern with the 'dollar shortage' and the alleged long-run adverse trend of the terms of trade of the primary-producing or under-developed countries. More fundamentally, it reflects a growing awareness of the importance of technology among the causes of the wealth of nations, and of technical change among the causes of economic progress and economic change.

Technical change raises a variety of problems in the theory of international trade, according to the context in which it is considered. Thus there is the problem of the costs of adjustment to the new pattern of comparative cost conditions created by technical change, and the distribution of the adjustment costs between the country in which the change occurs and its trading partners; the problem of the effects of technical change on domestic employment levels and international monetary equilibrium under Keynesian conditions; the problem of the effects of technical change on the volume and terms of trade and the economic welfare of trading countries under long-run classical full employment conditions; and the problem of the effects of continuing technical change on the pattern of trade and the extent and distribution of the gains from international specialization.

In what follows I shall be concerned mainly with the last two problems, on the assumption that the costs of making adjustments to technical change are of less interest than the nature of the adjustments themselves, and that the monetary disturbances that may

96

result from technical changes call for the specification of appropriate monetary policies rather than analyses for their own sake. I shall, however, revert briefly to these problems later in the argument. The first section of the paper attempts a restatement and extension of the modern pure theory of the effects of technical change on trade. The second section goes on to a more general discussion of trade and technical change, and is concerned with the question of how technical change may be expected to affect international trade in a developing world.

II. THE FORMAL THEORY OF THE EFFECTS OF TECHNICAL CHANGE ON TRADE

(a) Historical Background

Classical analysis of the effects of technical change on trade begins and very nearly ends with J. S. Mill's analysis [1] of the effects of improvements in the method of production, according to which an improvement that results in the creation of a new branch of exports leads to a favourable movement of the improving country's terms of trade, foreign countries benefiting from the new product but losing through an increase in the prices of their other imports, while an improvement that lowers the cost of production of an existing export will give the foreign country less or more (and the improving country more or less) than the benefit of the cost reduction, depending on whether the foreign elasticity of demand for the improved product is greater or less than unity. From the latter part of this analysis, Edgeworth drew the obvious implication that under certain conditions 'the exporting country is damnified by the improvement; and by parity of reasoning may be benefited by a restriction of its exports'.[2]

The concentration of Mill and other classical writers on improvements in exporting industries gives the impression that technical

---

[1] J. S. Mill, *Principles of Political Economy*, Book III, Chapter XVIII, sec. 5.

[2] F. Y. Edgeworth, 'The Theory of International Values', *Economic Journal*, IV, No. 13, March 1894, p. 40. Mill, also Edgeworth following him, was aware that if the country consumed part of the improved export it would still gain even if the foreign demand for the export were of unit elasticity. Edgeworth criticized Mill for obscuring the subject by considering the effect of the improvement on the rate of exchange between exports and imports instead of on producers' and consumers' surplus. This was perhaps unfair, since Mill was concerned with how the benefit of the cost reduction was divided between domestic and foreign consumers, not with its effects on the welfare of the improving country. As Murray C. Kemp ('Technological Change, the Terms of Trade, and Welfare', *Economic Journal*, LXV, No. 259, September 1955) has shown rigorously, Mill's unit elasticity criterion is defective since it neglects the cross-effect on the improving country's demand for imports; Mill did in fact recognize the income part of this effect as a possible complication, but overlooked the substitution effect.

change in one country always tends to broaden the range of comparative cost differences and benefit the rest of the world, possibly to the detriment of the country in which change occurs.[1] Modern theory, which stems from J. R. Hicks' *Inaugural Lecture*, has tended to place the emphasis on the opposite possibility.[2] Hicks used a Ricardian-type constant-cost model in which each country produced exports and import-substitutes to argue that a general increase in productivity must, except in freak cases, turn the terms of trade against the country in which productivity increased; he then distinguished between productivity increases in the exporting industry ('export-biased' productivity change) and productivity increases in the import-competing industry ('import-biased' productivity change) and argued that export-biased productivity change must *a fortiori* turn the terms of trade in favour of the rest of the world, but that *per contra* import-biased productivity change must turn them against the rest of the world, damaging the latter's gains from trade and reducing its welfare. In this last possibility he found the explanation of the dollar shortage, suggesting that it was the result of the import-biased character of American technical progress.[3]

The empirical evidence fails to support Hicks' contention about the nature of American productivity increases, and the dollar shortage has dramatically ceased to be a problem; but his model has stimulated further theoretical research on the effects of technical change. One line of this research has concentrated on Hicks' four-good model, and shown that Hicks' conclusion about the effect of an import-biased improvement may be invalidated by the income-effect of the improvement on the demand for imports; [4] though this model is perhaps more realistic than that used in the other line of research, the results are less interesting since the authors in question start from a reduction in (constant) cost assumed to be brought about by a technical change without investigating the nature of that change.[5] The other, and to my mind more interesting, line of

---

[1] Mill's first case, of an improvement opening a new branch of exports, will improve foreign welfare unless cross-effects on the domestic demand for imports reduce that demand by a certain critical amount. The case is analogous to that of an improvement in a domestic substitute for imports analysed by Hicks, Asimakopulos and Kemp, and referred to below.

[2] This point has been made very succinctly in Richard Caves, *Trade and Economic Structure* (Cambridge, Mass.; Harvard University Press, 1960), pp. 153-4.

[3] J. R. Hicks, 'An Inaugural Lecture: the Long-Run Dollar Problem', *Oxford Economic Papers*, n.s., Vol. v, No. 2, June 1953, reprinted in his *Essays in World Economics* (Oxford: Oxford University Press, 1959).

[4] Murray C. Kemp, *op. cit.*; A. Asimakopulos, 'A Note on Productivity Changes and the Terms of Trade', *Oxford Economic Papers*, n.s. Vol. ix, No. 2, June 1957.

[5] The literature on this subject is in fact frequently marred by a failure to distinguish between 'productivity increase' and technical change; the former, as

research has concentrated on applying the simplified Heckscher-Ohlin model to Hicks' problem, and has gradually succeeded in working back into the theory the classification of inventions into neutral, capital-saving, and labour-saving developed in the 1930s.[1]

(b) Modern Theory

The broad outlines of the logic of the theory can be summarized as follows. (To avoid burdening the argument with mathematical and geometrical analysis, the exposition is confined to the logic and the key variables.) A technical change in one country will tend to benefit or harm the rest of the world according as it increases or decreases the progressing country's demand for imports at the initial terms of trade, so requiring an adverse or favourable shift of its terms of trade to restore equilibrium. The direction and extent of the required shift in the terms of trade is determined by the direction and magnitude of the change in the progressing country's demand for imports and the elasticities of the reciprocal demand curves, and the gain or loss of welfare to the rest of the world is roughly measured by the change in the cost of its initial volume of imports. If the restoration of equilibrium requires an adverse movement of the progressing country's terms of trade, this is an offset to the increased productive capacity resulting from the technical change, which may in the extreme more than wipe out the gain in productive capacity from the technical change. A rough approximation to the condition for the extreme case is that the reduction in the value of the progressing country's initial quantity of exports exceeds the increase in the value of its output (at the initial terms of trade) due to the technical change ; and it can be shown that such a loss of welfare as a result of technical change does not require the foreign demand for the country's exports to be inelastic.[2]

The results of the technical change, so far as the rest of the world is concerned, depend on its effects on the progressing country's demand for imports at the initial terms of trade. In the simplified Heckscher-Ohlin model, with two commodities produced by a fixed endowment of two factors in different constant-returns production

usually measured, can result from occupational shifts or capital accumulation, which have different effects on prices and distribution from a change in technique of production.

[1] E. J. Mishan, 'The Long-Run Dollar Problem : a Comment', *Oxford Economic Papers*, n.s., Vol. vii, No. 2, June 1955 ; W. M. Corden, 'Economic Expansion and International Trade : a Geometric Approach', *Oxford Economic Papers*, n.s., Vol. viii, No. 2, Sept. 1956 ; R. Findlay and H. Grubert, 'Factor Intensities, Technological Progress, and the Terms of Trade', *Oxford Economic Papers*, n.s., Vol. ix, No. 1, Feb. 1959.

[2] J. Bhagwati, 'Immiserizing Growth : a Geometrical Note', *Review of Economic Studies*, XXV (3), No. 68, June 1958.

functions under perfectly competitive conditions, this effect is the net outcome of the technical change on domestic demand for, and production of, the imported goods, and it turns out that, with certain exceptions to be noted shortly, the technical change will increase or decrease import demand according to whether it occurs in the exporting or the import-competing industry, as in the Hicks analysis.

In the simplified Heckscher-Ohlin model just described, the international price ratio between the two commodities in conjunction with the factor-endowment ratio uniquely determines the prices of factors and the factor ratios employed in the two industries (which must be such as to equate the relative production costs of the goods with the international price ratio), and the factor ratios together with the endowment ratio uniquely determine the allocation of the factor endowment and of total output between the two industries. A technical improvement in one industry must reduce the relative cost of production in that industry as compared with the other, at the initial relative factor-price ratio. To restore the equality of the relative cost ratio with the given international commodity price ratio, the relative price of the factor used relatively intensively in the industry whose technique has improved must rise, incidently inducing substitution of the other factor for it in both industries. The technical change and the associated alteration of relative factor prices determine new equilibrium factor ratios for the two industries, which together with the factor endowment determine the new allocation of factors and production between the two industries.

The change in relative factor prices implies that the factor used intensively in the industry whose technique has improved not only gains the whole of the increase in national product resulting from the improvement, but benefits by a redistribution of income from the other factor. Assuming neither good to be inferior, some part of the increase in national product will be spent on each of the commodities ; but the redistribution of income will reduce the demand for one of the goods if the marginal propensities to consume of the two factors differ, and this effect may be strong enough to outweigh the other and reduce the demand for one of the goods. Specifically, if factors have strong marginal preferences for the products of the industry in which they are used intensively, the demand for the product of the industry in which improvement occurs may increase by more than the increase in national product due to the improvement.

The effect of the technical change on the allocation of production depends on its effects on the equilibrium factor ratios in the two industries. At this point we define technical change in an industry as neutral, intensive-factor-saving, or intensive-factor-using, according as it would leave unchanged, reduce, or increase the ratio of the factor used intensively in that industry to the other, at the pre-technical-change factor-price ratio ; and we recall that the increase in the relative price of the factor used intensively in the improving industry required to restore equilibrium after the technical change leads to substitution against that factor in both industries, lowering the optimal ratio of that factor to the other in both industries. It follows that a neutral or intensive-factor-saving technical change must lower the optimal ratio of the factor used intensively in the industry where the change occurs to the other factor in both industries. To reconcile these lower factor ratios with employment of the factor endowment, some of both factors must be shifted to the industry with the higher ratio of this factor — the industry in which the change occurs. This implies an absolute reduction in the output of the other industry, in which no technical change has occurred, since the factor used intensively in that industry, of which less is now employed there, has a lower average product than before, owing to the reduced ratio in which the other factor is combined with it. In other words, a neutral or intensive-factor-saving technical change increases the output of the industry in which it occurs by more than the total increase in the output of the two industries combined.

An intensive-factor-using technical change, on the other hand, while it must still reduce the optimal ratio of the factor used intensively in the improving industry to the other factor in the industry in which change does not occur, owing to the substitution effect of the associated factor price change, may raise that ratio in the industry in which change occurs — and will do so if the intensive-factor-using bias of the change is stronger than the substitution effect of the associated factor price change. If the optimal ratio rises in the industry in which change occurs, while falling in the other industry, the reallocation of factors and production required to keep the total factor endowment employed may involve a decrease or an increase in the output of the unchanged industry, and production in the industry in which change occurs may rise by more or less than the increase in total output, or even fall absolutely, depending on the magnitudes of the relevant parameters (the extent of the cost reduction and the bias of the technical change, and the elasticities of substitution between the factors in the two industries).

It follows from the foregoing analysis that, the international price ratio being given, a technical change in an industry will increase the output of that industry by more than it increases the demand for that output except in two possible cases. The first is where a neutral or intensive-factor-saving technical change occurs, but the resulting reduction in the output of the other industry is more than offset by a reduction in the demand for that output due to the redistribution effect of the factor price change associated with the technical change ; this case requires that each factor prefers the product of the industry that uses it intensively, and for convenience can be described as the factor-preference exception. The second is where a technical change is sufficiently intensive-factor-using for the increase in output, in the industry where it occurs, to be smaller than the increase in demand for the product of that industry resulting from the increase in, and redistribution of, income due to the change ; for convenience, this case can be described as the intensive-factor-using exception.

The application of these results to the problem of the effects of technical change on trade is straightforward. The factor-preference and intensive-factor-using exceptions apart, a technical change in the exporting industry will increase the country's supply of exports (demand for imports) at the initial terms of trade, so tending to turn the terms of trade in favour of the rest of the world ; and a technical change in the industry producing importable goods will decrease the country's demand for imports, so tending to turn the terms of trade against the rest of the world. Apart from the exceptional cases, therefore, the direction of the effect of a technical change in one country on its trade with the rest of the world depends on whether the change occurs in the exporting or the import-competing industry. It may be noted in passing that in extreme cases technical change in the exporting industry may lead the country to specialize completely on its export industry, eliminating the domestic production of importables, and technical change in the industry producing importable goods may lead to a reversal of the direction of international specialization.[1]

(c) Some Extensions of the Analysis

The argument set out above can easily be extended to allow for relaxations of the restrictive assumptions of the simple Heckscher-Ohlin model, though such modifications are better handled by explicit mathematical analysis. Increasing or decreasing returns to scale respectively accentuate or mitigate the changes in relative factor prices and production pattern resulting from technical change.

[1] Where technical change in an industry results in complete specialization on it, it is possible that the relative price of the factor used intensively in that industry will fall rather than rise. This will happen if the technical change has an intensive-factor-saving bias so strong that the optimal ratio of the intensively-used factor to the other at the initial relative factor price ratio is less than the endowment ratio. This possibility is ignored in the subsequent argument.

Allowing for a third factor of production complicates the classification of technical change, and normally operates to reduce the extent of the required production shifts. An interesting extension is the introduction of a third commodity assumed not to be traded — a version of the Hicks model. A technical change in the method of producing this good will lower its relative price, given the international price ratio, with income and substitution effects on the demand for importable goods. Depending on whether demand for it is elastic or inelastic, the expansion of output required to supply the increased quantity demanded at the lower price will draw factors from or release factors to the exporting and import-competing industries. The production changes in these industries will be determined by the factor intensities in the three industries, it being possible for their outputs to be required to change in opposite directions to employ the economy's factor endowment.[1] Thus a technical change in a domestic goods industry may either increase or decrease the quantity of imports demanded, depending on the net result of its effects on demand for, and domestic supply of, importable goods. This analysis can be readily reinterpreted to show the possible effects of the introduction of a new commodity ; and it can be extended to include Mill's case of an improvement that opens up a new branch of exports, by adding a similar analysis of the effects of the availability of a new export on the foreign supply of imports. In Mill's case, however, the effects on foreign welfare cannot be identified with the movement of the terms of trade.

A more interesting extension of the Heckscher-Ohlin model, and one more relevant to the problems of trade in a developing world, is to relax the assumption of fixed factor supplies. Factor supplies may be variable either because factors are internationally mobile, or because a country's stock of factors is responsive to factor earnings, as will be the case with capital and may be the case with labour. As shown above, technical change raises the real price of the factor used intensively in the industry where the change occurs, and lowers the real price of the other factor, at the initial international price ratio. If factor supplies are perfectly elastic at the initial real prices, the new international equilibrium after the technical change must entail a reduction in the relative price of the commodity produced by the industry in which the change has occurred, by the amount of the cost saving due to the technical change. Abstracting from the complications that international factor mobility introduces into the

---

[1] It can readily be shown that the outputs of the exporting and import-competing industries must change in opposite directions if the domestic goods industry uses its intensive factor more intensively than the other two industries and the technical change is neutral.

concept of national economic welfare, this implies that the rest of the world must gain or lose according as the change occurs in the exporting or import-competing industry.

Perfect elasticity of factor supplies, national or international, is not a very interesting assumption — if it were, international trade theory would not be an interesting subject. A more interesting assumption, and one in line with the tradition of the subject, is that factors are internationally immobile but that national factor supplies may be responsive to price. Two extreme cases seem especially relevant to the problem of the influence of technical change on international trade in a developing world : perfect elasticity of domestic supply of capital at a given interest rate, and perfect elasticity of supply of labour at a given real wage. These may be taken as typifying the long-run characteristics of advanced and under-developed countries, as these have been treated in recent literature.[1]

Before considering these cases, it is advisable to notice that the Heckscher-Ohlin model, as generally used in international trade theory and as employed in the foregoing argument, is fundamentally incapable of dealing with the role of capital in production, and can only be used for this purpose on the basis of assumptions of a not obviously acceptable kind. The reason is that it treats factors as physically homogeneous permanent stocks, and the factor prices it determines are rental rates on units of these stocks. To apply it to capital, one must assume capital equipment to consist of physically quantifiable homogeneous units that can be continuously combined with labour in production processes, and to translate the rental rate on these units into a rate of interest requires assumptions about both the productive life of the units and the process by which they are produced.[2] To take account of the crux of the problem, the physical diversity of capital equipment in different industries requires an elaborate mathematical analysis. These complexities cannot be treated here ; instead, we simplify the problem by confining attention to the changes that would occur with a given international price ratio — which makes it unnecessary to specify how capital is produced — and assuming that the rate of interest is uniquely related to the price of (the services of) capital.

---

[1] See, on the one hand, the literature on dynamic economics stimulated by R. F. Harrod's *Towards a Dynamic Economics* (London, Macmillan, 1948) ; on the other, the literature on economic development typified by W. A. Lewis, 'Economic Development with Unlimited Supplies of Labour', *The Manchester School*, XXII, No. 2, May 1954.

[2] An exhaustive treatment of capital accumulation and technical change in a closed economy along these lines, which illustrates the restrictive assumptions necessary to make the problem manageable, may be found in James E. Meade, *A Model of Economic Growth* (London : Allen & Unwin, 1960).

On this assumption, it follows readily that if either capital is in perfectly elastic supply at a fixed rate of interest, or labour is in perfectly elastic supply at a given real wage rate, a technical change in one of the industries must lead the country to specialize completely in that industry (at the initial terms of trade). In the former case the real wage rate, and in the latter case the rate of profit, must rise, since the ratio of the factor in elastic supply to the other must rise to offset the effect of the change in raising the former's marginal productivity. It can also be shown that these latter effects cannot be offset by the fall in the price of the commodity in which the country specializes resulting from the adjustment of international trade to the technical change.

III. TECHNICAL CHANGE IN A DEVELOPING WORLD

(a) Preliminary Observations

The formal theory of the effects of technical change on trade indicates the effects that technical changes may have, and the nature of the parameters on which the effect of a particular type of change depends, but does not by itself throw any light on the likely actual effects of technical change in a developing world on the magnitude and distribution of the gains from trade and the volume of international trade. As has already been mentioned, Hicks (and others before and after him) attempted to explain the dollar shortage by reference to the alleged import-biased characteristics of progress in the United States; but there has been little satisfactory attempt to explain why technical progress there should have these characteristics. Similarly, Prébisch and Singer [1] have supported their contention that the long-run trend of the terms of trade between advanced industrial and primary-producing countries is adverse to the latter, by the assumption that increases in productivity in manufacturing are taken out in higher wages while in primary production they are taken out in lower prices, without explaining satisfactorily how this comes about or examining its consistency with trade equilibrium.

To approach this question properly, it is necessary to look into the forces making for technical change, to see what sorts of technical change are likely to occur. Unfortunately no convincing simple theory of technical change suggests itself, so that this section will consist mainly of an exploration of various mechanisms causing

[1] H. W. Singer, 'The Distribution of Gains between Investing and Borrowing Countries', *American Economic Review*, XL, No. 2, May 1950; United Nations (Raul Prébisch), *The Economic Development of Latin America and its Principal Problems* (United Nations, 1950).

or inducing technical change and their probable or possible consequences.

Before approaching the main question, some preliminary observations are worth making. First, regardless of whether technical change is export-biased or import-biased, in the sense of its effect on international trade equilibrium, it will give rise to a transitional international monetary disequilibrium if the adjustments of money incomes and prices that accompany it are inappropriate. Such monetary disequilibria, however, do not necessarily correspond to the underlying real disequilibrium; an export-biased change, for example, can lead to either a balance of payments surplus or a deficit for the country concerned, depending on whether money incomes rise too little or too much. Secondly, any technical change disturbing international equilibrium imposes short-run costs of adjusting resource utilization and trade patterns to the new pattern of beneficial international specialization; countries differ in their capacity to make these adjustments readily, with the result that changes from which a country would benefit in the long run may be extremely harmful to it in the short run, if the immediate response takes the form of lower incomes and unemployment. In this respect, as Kindleberger has argued,[1] undeveloped countries may suffer unduly from technical progress owing to the lack of adaptability of their resources.

Thirdly, a point which becomes important in considering technological progress in a growing world, the influence of technical change on trade is not confined to its direct effects on comparative cost ratios; instead, technical change may affect trade directly through its general contribution to the growth of one country or region, and changes in comparative costs may follow as an indirect response to the price changes that such sectional growth brings about. Fourthly, the influence of technical change in a context of growth depends on the response to it of the other variables that determine growth — broadly speaking, capital accumulation and population growth. An important illustration of the differential impact of the context in which change occurs may be the growing inequality between the advanced and under-developed nations, for which various economists (including Singer and Prébisch) have offered explanations based on assumed differences in the nature of technical change in the two types of countries, but which may be better explained in terms of

---

[1] C. P. Kindleberger, *The Terms of Trade : a European Case Study* (Cambridge, Mass. ; Harvard University Press, 1956), and 'The Terms of Trade and Economic Development', *Review of Economics and Statistics*, XL, No. 1, Part 2, Supplement, Feb. 1958 ; see also Thomas Balogh, 'The Dollar Crisis Revisited', *Oxford Economic Papers*, Vol. vi, No. 3, Sept. 1954.

the formal theory presented earlier by the assumption that advanced nations respond to technical change by accumulating capital, incidentally raising real wages, while under-developed nations respond by increasing the supply of labour.[1]

In what follows I shall ignore problems of monetary disequilibrium and short-run adjustment, and also confine the argument so far as possible to technical changes that operate differentially on comparative cost conditions. The main part of the argument will be concerned with factors influencing technical change and the likely direction of their effects on trade, on the assumption that technical changes are confined to the country in which they occur ; but I shall conclude with some remarks on the forces making for diffusion of technical change, and the likely effects of such diffusion on international trade.

(b) Two Approaches to Technical Change

Our main concern is with the question of whether technical change is likely to promote or inhibit international trade. At the outset, it must be observed that there are two crucial areas of economic activity in which technical change is likely to promote international trade, namely, transport and communications. It is one of the basic propositions of international trade theory that were it not for transport costs (and commercial policy) every commodity a country consumes would enter international trade as either an import or an export. Reductions in the cost of international transport must therefore tend to increase the range and value of commodities entering international trade ; similarly, improvements in international communications must have a trade-increasing effect. Nevertheless, even improvements in methods of transport and communication can have a trade-inhibiting effect by promoting internal trade at the expense of external trade. Further, as noted below, the fact of transport and communication barriers to trade, as distinct from the influence of technical change in them, may exert some pressure for import-biased technical improvements, by giving a form of protection to the profits resulting from such improvements.

Turning to technical change in general, one can look at the process of technical change in either of two ways — as the consequence of the inquisitive scientific spirit, or as a rational response to economic incentives. In the absence of reliable knowledge as to what motivates inquisitive and inventive minds, the former approach leads to no definite conclusions about the bias of inventions. 'There must be a better way of doing this' would tend to favour technical changes in existing activities, and so tend to be export-biased ; 'if

[1] See W. Arthur Lewis, *op. cit.*, especially pp. 181-4.

they can do it there, I don't see why we couldn't do it here' would tend to favour import-biased technical changes. In so far as these different motivations can be linked to other characteristics of the national economy, however, they can lead to conclusions about the bias of technical change in different circumstances ; Hicks in effect argues that developing countries go through a long cycle from export-biased to import-biased improvements because they switch from the first motivation to the second as they acquire international stature, and one could argue that countries leading in economic development will tend toward export-biased (or, if one prefers, import-biased) technical change and countries following in economic development towards import-biased technical change. But such arguments make a suspiciously rapid jump from national to individual psychology. In so far as technical change is motivated by the pure spirit of scientific inquiry or human curiosity, one would expect technical changes to be random, without over-all export- or import-bias. In that case, the effects of technical change in a country on its trade would be determined by its industrial structure in conjunction with its income-elasticities of demand.[1]

The alternative approach is to consider technical change as the result of a rational economic process, a deliberate or unconscious outcome of the play of economic incentives. It is natural, at least in an advanced industrial economy in which production is carried on by large corporate enterprise, to think of advances in technical knowledge as a form of capital that can be created by investment in organized research ; even where research is not organized as part of the productive process or conducted and marketed by specialized enterprises, it is likely to be motivated at least in part by considerations of potential profit. The question, then, is whether and in what circumstances profit-motivated research is likely to be biased towards export- or import-biased technical change.

Before going into this question, it would be as well to recognize the importance of technical change resulting from research carried on directly or indirectly by governments. The most important type of such research is defence-connected research, the primary intention of which is import-substituting, though it may result in exports to military allies and have indirect export- or import-biased effects on non-defence industries. Apart from government defence research, the possibility of war probably has some import-biasing influence on

---

[1] There is, however, one respect in which random technical change may have an inherent import-bias — through the replacement of natural products by synthetics more amenable to the strict control of characteristics important to the use of such products in advanced production processes ; but technological progress also permits stricter control of the characteristics of natural products.

technical change, while actual engagement in war almost certainly does. Another type of government research influencing trade is that conducted on behalf of small-scale producers, most usually farmers and other primary producers, though in some instances manufacturers, to improve their methods and therefore their competitive position. Such government assistance gives an export-bias or an import-bias to technical change according to whether the products of the favoured sector are marketed abroad or at home. In the past, such research has typically been conducted on behalf of agriculture and probably tended to be export-biased. But the policy of assisting domestic industries afflicted by foreign competition by means of subsidized research rather than tariff protection has been recommended increasingly in recent years, and if it becomes accepted practice will have an import-biasing effect on technical change.

On the assumption that private research leading to technical change is profit-motivated, the effects of technical change on trade will depend on whether the prospects of profit from changes favour import-biased or export-biased change, that is, favour technical change in exporting or import-competing industries. Prospective profit depends on the one hand on the cost of achieving the required advance in technical knowledge, on the other hand on the income that can be captured by applying it. There seems to be no obvious reason to expect the cost of successful research to be biased in favour of research on technical improvements in exportable or importable goods ; rather, one might expect the prospective costs of achieving an advance in knowledge to be low or high in a particular industry at various times, depending on whether or not advances in knowledge or technique achieved elsewhere could be readily applied to that industry or not.[1]

The returns from successful research are more amenable to analysis. The prospective profits from improving or cheapening a product are the more likely to be large, the larger and more certain the market for it and the greater the prospects of increasing demand. The size-of-market consideration would imply a tendency for technical change to be export-biased in small economies, and import-biased in large economies ; the rate-of-growth consideration would imply a tendency for technical change to be import-biased in relatively rapidly growing economies, and export-biased in relatively slowly growing economies. The prospective profits from technical

---

[1] Alternatively, some industries might acquire the tradition of and organization for continued technical progress ; if this were the case, these industries would ultimately become exporters, and progress in the economy as a whole export-biased.

change are also likely to be the greater, the more rapidly the prices of inputs are expected to rise; this would also imply a tendency for technical change to be import-biased in a rapidly growing economy and export-biased in a slowly growing economy (assuming that growth by itself tends to turn the terms of trade against the growing country, thus tending to raise the prices of factors used intensively in producing importables [1]). In general, in so far as technical change is guided by prospective trends in demand and cost, it will tend to counteract these trends, so exercising a restraining influence on trends in the terms of trade and tending to keep the growth of national real income in line with the average rate of technical change.

Two other elements may be noted as tending to foster import-biased technical changes. One is the influence of transport costs and communication difficulties in providing some degree of protection in the domestic market against foreign competition and rendering the domestic market less risky than the foreign, which might provide some incentive to direct research investment towards technical changes in import-competing rather than exporting industries; as mentioned above, the influence of technical change in transport and communications in promoting international trade may be much more important. The other element is the business cycle: in the recession phase, general uncertainty and marketing difficulties may bias technical change towards reducing costs in import-competing industries, and these influences may be encouraged by the greater protectionism into which governments tend to be led or forced in order to maintain domestic employment of labour and capital.

(c) *The Transmission of Knowledge*

Thus far the argument has been concerned with factors influencing the direction of technical change within a country, on the assumption that the advance in knowledge that makes technical change possible is generated in that country. Technical change may and often does also occur as a consequence of the transmission of knowledge from one country to another. According to the analysis of the previous section, such transmission is beneficial or harmful to the world outside the receiving country according as it has an export-biased or import-biased effect there — in general, according as it

---

[1] It might be expected that research in each industry would tend to aim at saving on the use of the factor used intensively in that industry, since this would maximize the ratio of proportional saving in total cost to proportional reduction in quantity of factor used per unit, so that technical change in an industry would tend to be intensive-factor-saving, thus reducing the likelihood of the intensive-factor-using exception to the theoretical conclusion that the bias of technical change corresponds to the industry in which it occurs.

reduces costs in the exporting or the importing industries [1] — and beneficial to the receiving country unless the export bias turns the terms of trade against it sufficiently to offset the gain from increased productive capacity.

Whether beneficial or harmful to the economic welfare of the countries involved, such transmissions may be profitable to the possessor of the knowledge. Indeed, the transmission of technical change to countries at lower stages of development may be profitable where the investment of capital without technical change would not be, since a low level of technology may make both real wages and the rate of profit lower than in advanced countries, giving both labour and capital an incentive to flow towards the advanced countries.[2] In these circumstances, the lower real wages in the countries at lower stages of development provide an incentive to the application of more advanced technology there by native businessmen or entrepreneurs from the advanced countries. The application of superior technology may have either an import-biased effect, as when an advanced-country corporation establishes a branch plant in a foreign market instead of exporting to it, or an export-biased effect, as when such a corporation establishes a foreign subsidiary to supply goods for the home market instead of expanding its domestic facilities. In either case, obviously, the transmission of technical knowledge benefits labour in the receiving country at the expense of labour in the transmitting country, though the benefit to the former may be through increased employment rather than higher real wages.

(d) *The Meaning of Comparative Advantage*

Consideration of the international transmission of technical change brings us to a final, fundamental problem, the meaning of comparative advantage in a world developing by means of capital accumulation and technical progress. In such a world, the sources of comparative advantage are to be found in the possession of particular natural resources, or in the possession of technology superior to the average corresponding to the economy's real wage level and the prevailing rate of profit, acquired by superior scientific or engineering research, or by exploitation of economies of scale

---

[1] The knowledge-transmitting country will gain, even though the rest of the outside world loses, from transmitting an import-biased technical change if its exports happen to be competitive with those of the receiving country, or if it imports in competition with the receiving country ; and vice versa. Also, the rest of the world may gain in the long run if the import-biased technical change sets off a process of economic development in the receiving country.

[2] Where labour is prevented from moving to the advanced country by restrictive immigration laws, the transmission of technical knowledge can be regarded as a form of compensation for damages.

and experience in particular lines of specialization. The gains from trade are the results of taking advantage of comparative cost differences by specialization and international exchange, as in classical analysis. But instead of being firmly grounded in stable and enduring characteristics of national economies — inherent cost differences, as in the Ricardian model, or differences in factor endowments, as in the Heckscher-Ohlin model — comparative advantage is the evolving consequence of the dynamics of technical progress, capital accumulation, and population increase, and their diffusion through the world economy.

As the argument of this section has shown, there is no reliable presumption as to whether continuing technical progress will tend over the long run to increase or decrease comparative cost differences and the advantages of international specialization. Various reasons have been suggested, however, for believing that in the long run no country is likely to enjoy increasing gains from trade at the expense of its trading partners, since such gains are likely to be undermined by the development or transmission of countervailing technical change. The possibilities of technological improvement as a substitute for natural advantages also suggest that international trade will become of relatively decreasing importance as a contributor to national real income levels.[1]

[1] Cf. J. G. Smith, 'Economic Nationalism and International Trade', *Economic Journal*, XLV, No. 180, Dec. 1935, pp. 619-48 ; D. H. Robertson, 'The Future of International Trade', *Economic Journal*, XLVIII, No. 189, March 1938, pp. 1-14, reprinted as Chapter 21 in American Economic Association, *Readings in the Theory of International Trade* (Philadelphia ; Blakiston Press, 1950).

Chapter 5

DESIRABLE INTERNATIONAL MOVEMENTS OF CAPITAL IN RELATION TO GROWTH OF BORROWERS AND LENDERS AND GROWTH OF MARKETS

BY

R. F. HARROD

Christ Church, Oxford

I. OPTIMUM RATE OF INTERNATIONAL CAPITAL FLOW

IT is expedient to spend a little time, if only to remove conceptual difficulties, in dwelling on the optimum rate of investment, since the optimum rate of foreign investment must depend partly on that. I take the main factor governing the optimum rate of investment to be the growth potential of the economy. This depends on the rate of increase of the working population and on the greatest feasible increase in output per head. In mature countries the latter is largely dependent on the occurrence of new ideas, including, but not consisting only of, the latest findings of technology. But in developing countries the latter depends mainly on the rate at which cadres of entrepreneurs, production engineers, managers, foremen, designers, draughtsmen, accountants *et hoc genus omne* can be made to grow. The maximum rates of increase of these impose, in my judgement, a far more important limitation on the growth of developing countries than the lack of availability of capital disposal, although that also has its place.

I define the optimum rate of saving (equals investment) as that required to implement the maximum growth of production rendered possible by the growth of factors other than capital disposal, subject to what will be said about the rate of interest. This is in conflict with views that have been much canvassed recently in the theoretical literature. In some of this writing it is implied that the growth of income depends primarily on the extent to which a community is prepared to sacrifice present consumption in favour of future consumption. It is even suggested that a sufficient willingness to make

E

present sacrifices could make the rate of advance to some ceiling-level of production as rapid as one wished. It would not follow that one ought to bring consumption down to a subsistence level. F. P. Ramsey's famous article [1] sought to trace the right path of advance towards the ceiling-level, called Bliss, which would maximize aggregate utility.

Once we recognize that the increase of future income obtainable by a sacrifice of consumption now is a function of the rate at which non-capital factors are growing, it appears that Ramsey's solution lacks a dimension. The rate at which future income can be raised by sacrificing present consumption depends essentially on the relation between the consequent rate of growth of the capital stock and that of the other factors, notably those of the kinds specified above. In most circumstances — not all — any attempt to increase capital stock considerably faster than the other factors will add little to the rate of growth of income. This is the dynamized version of the law of diminishing returns to one factor, which is familiar in static economics.

I believe that, usually, the relative valuation of present and future consumption will have little effect in determining the optimum rate of investment. But it should in principle be used to determine the optimum rate of interest. That in turn can, in cases, have a significant influence on the capital intensity (degree of round-aboutness) of the production process chosen. I hasten to add that the rate of interest is not likely to be the most important influence on optimum capital intensity. Of much greater importance will be the availability of other factors — the various kinds of technicians. If a more round-about process requires more skilled personnel of a type that is more scarce in country A than in country B, then it may be less economical in A than a simpler process, while being more economical in B, even if capital is equally available and the rate of interest the same in two countries. However, in certain cases the ruling (or notional) rate of interest may have some influence on the right choice of capital intensity.

So much for the optimum rate of saving. But then there is the actual rate, which may be quite different. I doubt if the rate of growth of the principal mature countries is now — post-war adjustments having been largely made — held up for lack of capital disposal. If saving is excessive, this may retard the rate of growth, in accordance with a dynamized version of Keynes' theorem that excessive saving causes unemployment. Excessive saving may indeed have been the cause of the rather poor growth rates shown recently

[1] *Economic Journal*, Dec. 1928.

by some countries. To the extent that saving is excessive in mature countries they can invest overseas without cost to themselves.

But in immature countries saving is often deficient. There, it is the deficiency that impedes growth. Any impediment to growth has a lasting effect, since the rate of increase of the non-capital factors depends on exercise and experience. If growth is held down for a time by lack of capital disposal, ground lost cannot be regained.

Thus, even if lack of capital disposal has for some time been the factor limiting growth in a certain country, and if capital disposal is then made more abundant (e.g. through foreign lending), it will not necessarily follow that the growth rate can be increased quickly. For the process of accelerating the growth of the non-capital factors may be a slow one. The optimum flow of international lending (from the point of view of the borrowing country) would be such as to deprive capital disposal of its role of being the limiting factor in it; there should be enough capital disposal to give the non-capital factors as much capital equipment as, given their own limited growth rates, they are able to use to the best effect. The rate of interest may have some relevance for the determination of this amount, but is not likely to have great influence (although it will be of paramount importance in relation to the external balance of payments).

Of course, if we suppose the flow of capital to be stimulated by some kind of international co-operation, it is reasonable to postulate special measures, adopted simultaneously, for expediting also the growth of the non-capital factors, in the receiving countries. A 'plan', set up by the government, or by a special agency, may supplement enterprise where that is short. I here use 'enterprise' in a more fundamental sense than that in which it has tended to be used, namely, as risk-taking or the co-ordination of the other factors of production, in recent theoretical work. By 'enterprise' I mean pure will power or initiative. There may be a potential production project, the risks of which can be demonstrated as negligible, which is not taken up because no one has the necessary will-power. By a 'plan' a governmental agency, supposed to be more enterprising than the main mass of individuals, takes on the role of supplying this basic will-power.[1]

Domestic cadres of experts in the various fields may be supplemented by the hiring of foreigners, both to do work themselves and

---

[1] A 'plan' may be useful in mature countries also, where enterprise is not lacking among the main mass of people, but for a slightly different purpose, namely, to reduce the influence of the monetary authorities and prevent their stunting growth by an unduly restrictive policy, actuated by fears of inflation or balance of payments difficulties.

to expedite the growth of these factors in the indigenous populations, by training them and giving them opportunities of experience. The cost of such hiring, to the extent that pay is remitted home, should be regarded as part of foreign borrowing. It may even be right so to regard pay spent *in situ*, since this draws upon domestic output (directly or through the need to export more in order to pay for the additional imports); such drafts can be ill-afforded owing to the other heavy claims upon domestic income in the early stages.

It is surely not too optimistic to suppose that, by programmes involving both more capital disposal and a supplementation to the non-capital factors required for growth, super-normal rates of growth could be achieved in some developing countries over a period.

In the limited space available I propose to dwell briefly on factors specifically related to the external balance as such, and more extensively on the possibilities of building up domestic saving to a level which renders sustained growth possible without insolvency. The latter topic also has a close relation to the external problem, since any deficiency of local saving spills over into an excess of imports or a curtailment in the supply of exportable commodities available for export.

II. FOREIGN BORROWING

In general, foreign borrowing should be regarded as a burden upon the balance of payments. In respect of any unit of foreign borrowing the amount subsequently remitted back, however generous the terms — short of outright gifts — over-tops the amount borrowed. It has been suggested that the rise in service charges on foreign borrowing could be offset (or more than offset) by an increase each year in the amount borrowed. After an initial period of stepped-up borrowing, during which the balance of payments of course benefits, we should not suppose the increase in borrowing from abroad each year to be more than in proportion to the country's increase in income and capital stock. For, if we did suppose a greater increase, foreigners would in due course approach the point of owning the whole capital of the borrowing country. That is not acceptable. Furthermore, what would happen after that?

Now suppose foreign borrowing to grow at no higher rate than national income — and even so great a rate as that would be undesirable. If in year r borrowing were £100 million, in year $r+1$ it would be £100 million $(1+g)$, where g is the percentage rate of growth of income. Thus the increase in borrowing would be g (£100 million). But the increase in outward payments by way of service charges would be s ($£100$ million), where s is the percentage rate of service charges on principal. We must assume that, except for a transitory period of expedited growth, $s > g$. Therefore even increased borrowing year by year, growing at the same rate as national income, would not prevent foreign borrowing and service charges together from being a net burden on the balance of payments.

If there is an element of planning in the direction of new investment, the propensities of private enterprise being corrected, if necessary, in order to get a suitable balance between uses, it is supposed that as between infra-structure and housing and welfare services on the one hand, and the production of tradeable goods on the other, the division will be in proportions that produce supplies of end-goods and -services in the proportion that consumers require of their own volition and also as governed by the routing of purchasing power through the use of taxes for the public provision of welfare. If this is successfully done, the aggregate increase in the production of tradeable goods will be equal to the aggregate increase in purchasing power directed to them, subject to what is to be said hereafter about the distribution of aggregate purchasing power between consumption and investment goods.

What tradeable goods should be produced? There is a *correct* answer to this question, although one which it may be difficult to ascertain either by market forecast or by experience. Prior to the programme for expediting the provision of capital disposal and the growth of non-capital factors, there will have been a certain distribution of productive resources between exported goods and import-competing goods, including a nul assignment to many types of imported goods. The provision of additional capital disposal and of non-capital factors should lower costs in the industries to which they are applied. The conjunction of more capital disposal and other high quality factors with a given quantum of common labour power will reduce costs over a certain range of increased output more in the production of some products than in that of others. The additional factors should be applied to the commodities of which the cost of production can be lowered more, over the range in which they can be lowered more. But that is just what it is difficult to prognosticate. The introduction of additional capital disposal and other highly qualified factors may be regarded as *fertilizing* the productivity of common labour.

I would suggest that it is *a priori* probable that the fertilizing effect of the increased supply of these factors will be greater (*a*) where there are certain specific natural resources that gave the pre-existing factors a comparative advantage, compared with other countries, and (*b*) in those lines of production to which pre-existing factors were habituated. If correct, this prior presumption suggests that further endeavour should be directed more strongly to industries producing exportable goods than to those making import-competing goods. This doctrine runs somewhat counter to prevailing pre-conceptions.

It is necessary to consider the question of the terms of trade. If a planned programme causes the output of the country in question to grow more rapidly than world output, there is an *a priori* presumption that the terms of trade will move against it. Furthermore, whatever its rate of growth, there is a prior presumption that the terms of trade will move against a country of which the income elasticity of world demand for the exports is less than one. It is probably the case that the income elasticity of the world demand for primary products, in which many immature countries specialize, is less than one. Thus in these cases a worsening in the terms of trade is to be foreseen.

There are instances of mono-culture countries that satisfy a substantial proportion of the world demand for their products. Then the case for diversification may be overwhelming. Furthermore, if we envisage a gathering momentum of foreign investment in a number of developing countries, national planning should be modified by international planning, to ensure that the production of the same commodity is not stimulated in a number of countries, which together contribute a substantial proportion of the world supply.

It need not be doubted that a wide-ranging plan for expedited investment should include import-competing industries. But, if we are confronted with the argument that higher production by exporting sectors may cause a worsening in the terms of trade, it is important to bear in mind weighty counter-considerations. The fertilizing effect of capital disposal, etc., is to reduce the cost of production. What if, despite this fertilizing effect, an import-competing industry requires 'protection', if it is to be viable ? If the increased output of an exported product leads to a worsening in the terms of trade in regard to that product of 10 per cent, its export representing, say, 5 per cent of the national effort, while an import industry, representing also, as built up from zero, or to the extent that it is increased, 5 per cent of the national effort, requires a 20 per cent tariff in order to be viable, the former is to be preferred.

It will be found below that it is tremendously important that any investment programme should lead to as great and early an increase in national income as possible. On the one hand incentives have to be provided in order to mobilize the best possible input of indigenous factors, and on the other a proportion of the increased output must be earmarked for saving, if long-run solvency is to be achieved. There is no room for any kind of wastage. But there is wastage if resources are directed away from an export commodity, their application to which would cause a 10 per cent deterioration in the terms of trade in respect of that commodity, to an import-competing commodity requiring 20 per cent protection. The income available for consumption by the indigenous population will thereby be lessened, and, if they insist none the less on a certain rate of increase of consumption, the chances of ultimate solvency will be lessened in proportion.

III. FROM FOREIGN BORROWING TO SELF-DEPENDENCE

I propose next to present certain tables illustrating the passage from foreign borrowing to self-dependence in what may be called an 'assisted take-off'. I have not ventured to try to give algebraic formulation to the relations involved. I believe that the more laborious arithmetical presentation can establish certain important points fairly securely, and that there are advantages in giving specific numerical values to the parameters throughout, particularly in order to keep assumptions in the full light of day. Furthermore, this method may be helpful to our weaker brethren, of whom I ought to pronounce myself one.

The underlying idea is that, if the shortage of capital disposal has been an important inhibiting factor, we can, by making it more abundant, fertilize latent non-capital productive capacities and enable a super-normal growth rate to be achieved for a period. It may well be that this can be done only if special measures are taken to secure a more adequate supply of non-capital factors also. The tables concentrate attention on the provision of capital disposal.

It is sometimes assumed that the process of capital build-up in a developing country does not alter the capital-output ratio, but only increases the capital-labour ratio, where 'labour' stands for all non-capital factors. Attention has been drawn to an apparent stationariness in the capital-output ratio, at some value in the neighbourhood of 3 : 1, in mature countries, even in periods when these are making strong increases in productivity. The problem for developing countries would be substantially easier if it could be assumed that no rise in the capital-output ratio was required. For that very reason it is a dangerous assumption to make, unless really good grounds for it can be shown. Of course, the expression 'developing country' covers a wide variety of different situations. I find it hard to believe that it is appropriate to assume that a really poor country has initially so high a capital-output ratio as 3 : 1. For the purpose of assessing this, the value of land should not, I submit, be included; rather we should revert to the old tripartite division of factors by the classical economists into land, labour and capital. Land includes any permanent improvements effected in the past, to the extent that they do not have to be followed up by equivalent replacement expenditures from time to time.

The various 'schemes' that follow represent what may be called crash programmes for making more capital disposal available over a twenty-year period. In most of them it is assumed that the crash programme succeeds in trebling national income in twenty years at the steady geometric rate of increase of 5·6 per cent p.a., and that, for this purpose, it is required that the capital-output ratio should stand at 3 : 1 at the *end* of the period, as in more advanced countries. Where the initial capital-output ratio is taken to be lower than this (it is 2 : 1 in Scheme *A*), the build-up of capital stock has to be greater than the increase of income. If a growing economy maintains a steady capital-output ratio of 3 : 1, the gross marginal product of capital is 1/3. If, on the other hand, the capital-output ratio is rising, the gross marginal product of capital must be less than this. In Scheme *A*, showing a rise in the capital-output ratio from 2 : 1 to 3 : 1, the gross marginal product of capital is 1/3·5.

SCHEME A

In the construction of Scheme *A* a number of assumptions have been made. These are in part arbitrary; but it is hoped that they are not unreasonable. The procedure allows the possibility of demonstrating the effects of varying the assumptions.

Of primary importance is the second column in the tables showing 'income not available for capital formation'. The amount there shown rises at a steady geometric rate throughout the period. The increment of income said to be not available for capital formation is intended to compound three elements, namely (i) the increase of income required to support the increase of population, (ii) the increase of domestic production lost through the deterioration in the terms of foreign trade and (iii) the section of the increase of income that it is necessary to earmark for increased consumption per head, in order to provide incentives for the superior efforts that will be required of the non-capital factors during the crash programme.

It need hardly be said that the population increase is a factor of vital importance. Although all closely concerned with development know this full well, I feel that the point is not sufficiently stressed in the open forum of international discussion. There may still be some old-fashioned (and out-moded) delicacy which inhibits forthright statements to the effect that the best laid plans will inevitably be frustrated if developing countries cannot keep population increases in check. Throughout I have intended to assume (and embody in column (ii) in all the tables) a population increase of 1·5 per cent p.a. It is to be feared that this, although high, falls short of the realized rate in many places. In Scheme *A* solvency is eventually achieved by a narrow margin. But if a further population increase of no more than 0·5 per cent had to be allowed, the scheme would lead to fairly hopeless insolvency. (See Scheme *B*.)

Earlier considerations have suggested that some deterioration in the terms of foreign trade is to be expected, mainly because the crash-programme countries are supposed to be growing at a greater rate than their trading partners, but also because many developing countries, as primary producers, may be producing tradeable commodities, the income elasticity of the world demand for which is below one. I have intended to allow a loss of 0·5 per cent p.a. consequent upon deterioration in the terms of foreign trade in column (ii) in all the tables except *H*. This may seem small in relation to the large deteriorations sometimes experienced in a single year. But the problem of *oscillations* and the well-known need to reduce them by buffer stocks or some such method lies quite outside my subject matter today. The allowance of 0·5 per cent p.a. of national income, amounting to 11 per cent over twenty years, is a fairly generous one, implying a much larger deterioration than 11 per cent in the terms of trade, since production for export is only part of total national income.

I take some allowance for increased consumption per head to be absolutely indispensable. A stern moralist might adjure a developing country to set about its task in the hard way and reduce consumption in order to build up its capital. In passing I may note that it would be difficult to assess the optimum depression of consumption. The dynamics of crash programmes is a sub-branch of general dynamics. It has been seen that in the case of a steadily growing economy it is possible to formulate the optimum rate of saving without reference to the whole journey to 'Bliss', which would make an assessment impossible in practice. But in crash-programme dynamics it would be difficult to avoid reintroducing Ramsey-type considerations, if a reduction in consumption were regarded as allowable. Fortunately any such approach should be disallowed. In a crash programme many members of the indigenous population will be required to do harder work, or more difficult work, or, anyhow, different work. This cannot be achieved unless an incentive is provided.

Column (ii) of Scheme *A* is intended to incorporate an increase in consumption per head of 2 per cent a year. This is a very narrow allowance for incentive. It may be supposed that some increase, say between 0 per cent and 1 per cent, was already occurring before the inception of the crash programme. Thus the extra incentive involved is small. In practice, no doubt, in the early stages only some sections, perhaps rather small sections, of the population would be drawn into new-type work; and these could be attracted by much higher incentives without causing a rise of average consumption per head of the population of more than 2 per cent p.a. But something must be allowed for the fact that the pay of those not drawn into the new-type work would be levered upwards by example or competition.

The incentive problem provides an additional reason for trying, within reasonable limits, to apply the fertilizing effect of increased capital disposal to occupations in which the population was already engaged, i.e. exporting industries rather than import-competing industries. A larger incentive is needed if people are to move to new occupations, but there will be all too little to spare for increased incentives in the early stages.

Column (ii) of Scheme *A* shows an annual increase of 4 per cent, which is intended to be compounded of 1·5 per cent for increase of population, 0·5 per cent worsened terms of trade and 2 per cent for incentive. A constant amount, representing 5 per cent of the *opening* national income, is deducted each year from the total amount said to be not available for saving, this being taken to be the amount that people were saving and will continue to save out of their old original income before the inception of the programme. All *other* domestic saving during the course of the programme is derived from subsequent increments of income.

The third column gives the contribution towards new net investment made by amortization funds; this is of substantial amount. Domar has shown how, in a steadily growing economy, amortization funds make their contribution to new net investment; this will be enhanced in the early stages of a crash programme.

Among the many evil effects of inflation upon a developing country, I take the reduction in the real value of amortization funds to be one worth stressing. There has been some confusion of thought about this. It is argued that, if a certain rate of capital formation is actually achieved, the maintenance of the real value of amortization funds merely serves to determine who *owns* the assets that have been created. But this is all important ! For the central problem in all this business is to prevent consumption increasing too much, which means drawing away a certain proportion of distributed incomes in the form of saving. The maintenance of amortization funds intact reduces the amount that has to be thus drawn away, in order to finance a given programme of capital formation.

The figures in column (iii) have been computed as follows. It is assumed that the basic stock of capital at the opening is being looked after by replacement and generating no excess of amortization over replacement expenditure. Of the new capital formation after year 0, it is assumed that one-sixth is circulating capital, giving rise to no amortization fund, and that the average length of life of the remaining five-sixths is twenty-five years. Accordingly, 0·033 of capital stock outstanding at the end of each year (less the opening stock in year 0) is credited to the amortization fund in the next. From this has to be subtracted expenditures on replacement. It is assumed that one-twentieth part of the five-sixths capital has to be replaced at the end of ten years, one-twentieth at the end of eleven years and so on up to twenty years (this representing roughly 'plant and equipment'), while the other ten-twentieths (representing 'construction') only have to be replaced at dates of more than thirty years after formation (and therefore do not enter our calculations). This mode of reckoning is retained in all the tables.

In Scheme *A* foreign service charges (column (iv)) are taken to be 7 per cent of total net foreign borrowing outstanding (viz. of figure shown in the previous line in column (ix)). This is taken to be an average figure. Private investment is supposed to play some part and get a high rate of return. Official loans may require amortization, which has to be included in the average figure. There may also be official loans at low rates with redemption postponed for a long period, and some outright grants. Taking the over-all average, even 7 per cent may be optimistic. But in Scheme *C* I have taken 4 per cent instead.

Funds domestically available for capital formation (column (v)) are national income (column (i)) minus that part of it which for reasons explained is deemed not available for capital formation (column (ii)) plus the net contribution of amortization funds minus foreign service charges.

Capital stock is related to national income on the basis of a two-year gestation period. The capital stock stated for each year is that outstanding at the *end* of the year. It is calculated from the increase in income postulated for the following year. Thus in Scheme *A*, in which the marginal gross product of capital is 1/3·5, the increase of capital outstanding at the end of year 1 is three and a half times the increase in national income postulated for year 2. The *saving* required in year 0 is, owing to the two-year gestation period, equal to the difference between the capital stock outstanding at the end of year 1 and the capital stock outstanding at the end of year 0. It is not, of course, assumed that all capital comes to fruition at the end of two years. Thus *some* of the saving stated as required in year 0 may not come to fruition until 4 or 5. *Per contra* some of the saving stated as required in year 1 may come to fruition at the end of year 1 — and so on throughout the table.

Required foreign borrowing (column (viii)) is simply saving required in any year less saving domestically available.

Year 21 is shown, although outside the crash programme. There it is assumed that growth in national income relapses, after the crash programme is finished, to a rate which may be taken to be nearer a normal rate, namely, 4 per cent a year. The capital-output ratio, having been jacked up to 3·1, is taken to remain at that level after year 20, and capital formation has accordingly a marginal gross product of 1/3.

It might be thought at the outset that it is not worth considering such a scheme even in the abstract, since the borrowing implied is unrealistically great. If we consider that more than 1000 million people in the 'free' world need crash programmes, borrowing on the scale implied in some of the tables might add up to upwards of £10,000 million a year. That would not be feasible. But we must have in mind that the insufficient potential growth rates of non-capital factors would anyhow make such schemes unfeasible in many cases, that there would necessarily be some staggering in the inception of crash programmes and that political obstacles must lead to postponements. An investment of, say, £5000 million a year, although much above the present rate, should not be beyond the combined capacities of the United States and Europe, especially if the productive capacity of the U.S. and the U.K. were more fully extended than they have been in recent years. In reality, I would guess, *viable* development projects are likely to be insufficient to use the lending capacity of the mature countries to the full.

TABLE I

SCHEME A

(One unit is one-hundredth of initial national income.)

Income trebles. Income not available for capital formation rises at 4 per cent p.a. Initial capital-output ratio: 2·1. Marginal gross product of capital: 1/3·5. Amortization: 0·033. Foreign service charges: 7 per cent.

Years	Income (i)	Income not available for capital formation (ii)	Amortization less replacement expenditures (iii)	Service charges on foreign borrowing (iv)	Domestically available for capital formation, viz. (i) − (ii) + (iii) − (iv) (v)	Capital stock (Excluding land) (vi)	Saving required (vii)	Foreign borrowing required, viz. (vii) − (v) (viii)	Accumulated foreign borrowing (ix)
0	—	—	—	—	—	200·0	19·6	− 19·6	− 19·6
1	100·0	104·0 less 5	0	1·4	− 0·4	219·6	21·0	− 21·4	− 41·0
2	105·6	108·1 less 5	0·6	2·9	+ 0·2	240·6	22·1	− 21·9	− 62·9
3	111·6	112·5 less 5	1·3	4·4	+ 1·0	262·7	23·4	− 22·4	− 85·3
4	117·9	116·9 less 5	2·1	6·0	+ 2·1	286·1	24·5	− 22·4	− 107·7
5	124·6	121·6 less 5	2·9	7·5	+ 3·4	310·6	25·9	− 22·5	− 130·2
6	131·6	126·5 less 5	3·7	9·1	+ 4·7	336·5	27·6	− 22·9	− 153·1
7	139·0	131·5 less 5	4·5	10·7	+ 6·3	364·1	29·0	− 22·7	− 175·8
8	146·9	136·8 less 5	5·4	12·3	+ 8·2	393·1	30·8	− 22·6	− 198·4
9	155·2	142·2 less 5	6·4	13·9	+ 10·5	423·9	32·2	− 21·7	− 220·1
10	164·0	147·9 less 5	7·4	15·4	+ 13·1	456·1	34·3	− 21·2	− 241·3
11	173·2	153·8 less 5	7·7	17·0	+ 15·1	490·4	36·1	− 21·0	− 262·3
12	183·0	160·0 less 5	7·9	18·4	+ 17·5	526·5	38·1	− 20·6	− 282·9
13	193·3	166·3 less 5	8·2	19·8	+ 20·4	564·6	40·6	− 20·2	− 303·1
14	204·2	173·0 less 5	8·4	21·2	+ 23·4	605·2	42·4	− 19·0	− 322·1
15	215·8	179·9 less 5	8·8	22·5	+ 27·2	647·6	45·1	− 17·9	− 340·1
16	227·9	187·1 less 5	9·1	23·8	+ 31·1	692·7	47·6	− 16·5	− 356·6
17	240·8	194·5 less 5	9·5	25·0	+ 35·8	740·3	50·0	− 14·2	− 370·8
18	254·4	202·3 less 5	9·8	26·0	+ 40·9	790·3	53·2	− 12·3	− 383·1
19	268·7	210·4 less 5	10·2	26·8	+ 46·7	843·5	56·5	− 9·8	− 392·9
20	283·9	218·8 less 5	10·5	27·5	+ 53·1	900·0	60·0 *	− 6·9	− 399·8
21	300·0	227·5 less 5	11·1	28·0	+ 60·6	960·0	36·0	+ 24·6	

* This figure is kept here (and in the other tables) at a level implying a high rate of capital expansion, so as to clear the figures for year 20 of all influence of the subsequent slowing down in capital expansion.

Note to Cols. viii and ix: Minus sign = borrowing; plus sign = repayment.

Scheme *A* may be regarded as just within the limit of achieving solvency. Dependence on foreign borrowing begins to fall notably in the last six years. When the requirement for capital formation is relaxed after year 20, a 3 : 1 ratio having been achieved, repayment can begin at a substantial rate. In practice there would be some tapering off towards the end, some relaxation in favour of better incentives being allowed. Even under the strict scheme, however, consumption doubles.

But the viability of this scheme, if that be allowed, depends on the strict observance of the rule that consumption per head must not increase by more than 2 per cent p.a. Let the increase be only $2\frac{1}{2}$ per cent and we have Scheme *B*, as follows, which is clearly unacceptable.

SCHEME *B*

The results shown in the succeeding tables, which are abbreviated to save space, have not been worked out by a short-hand method, but are simply extracts from full tables, worked out by the same method as in Scheme *A*, which are in my possession.

It is surely worthy of heavy stress what a vast difference the additional increase in consumption by no more than $\frac{1}{2}$ per cent p.a.

TABLE II
SCHEME *B*

(Assumptions the same as in Table I, except that column (ii) rises at 4·5 per cent p.a.)

Years	Income	Income not available for capital formation	Amortization less replacement expenditures	Service charges on foreign borrowing	Domestically available for capital formation, viz. (i) – (ii) + (iii) – (iv)	Capital stock (Excluding land)	Saving required	Foreign borrowing required, viz. (vii) – (v)	Accumulated foreign borrowing
	(i)	(ii)	(iii)	(iv)	(v)	(vi)	(vii)	(viii)	(ix)
0	—	—	—	—	—	200·0	19·6	− 19·6	− 19·6
1	100·0	100·4·5 less 5	0	1·4	− 0·9	219·6	21·0	− 21·9	− 41·5
10	164·0	155·2 less 5	7·4	17·8	+ 3·4	456·1	34·3	− 30·9	− 284·7
15	215·8	193·4 less 5	8·8	29·7	+ 6·5	647·6	45·1	− 38·6	− 462·6
20	283·9	241·0 less 5	10·5	44·1	+ 14·3	900·0	60·0	− 45·7	− 676·1
21	300·0	251·9 less 5	11·1	47·3	+ 16·9	960·0	36·0	− 19·1	

Note to Cols. viii and ix : Minus sign=borrowing ; plus sign=repayment.

makes. In Scheme *B* the foreign borrowing required even within the period is nearly seven times initial national income, as against four times in Scheme *A*. In Scheme *B* the dependence on foreign borrowing continues to grow until the end of the period, and even after the requirement for large capital formation is relaxed (in year 21), the dependence continues and is almost as great as in the early years of Scheme *A*. The foreign service charge is proportionally higher. Practical persons might view the result in rather a despairing way. Confronted with all the practical difficulties of a real situation, with lack of statistical information, with political vetoes against many types of measure, how in the world could they hope to maintain discipline within so fine a limit as $\frac{1}{2}$ per cent of consumption! On the other hand, looked at in the opposite way, the result may be regarded as cheering. 'You have only to reduce your increase of consumption by $\frac{1}{2}$ per cent to turn yourselves from being a nation sinking further and further into the abysm of debt into being one making fair way to solvency.' (A greater increase of population, viz. one of 2 per cent instead of $1\frac{1}{2}$ per cent would have an unfavourable effect of equal magnitude to that of allowing an increase of consumption per head by $\frac{1}{2}$ per cent more.)

SCHEME C

Scheme *C* has been prepared to show the effect of reducing average foreign service charges to 4 per cent of accumulated borrowing, including grants — a highly optimistic proposal.

It is to be observed that the reduction in average foreign service charges from 4 per cent to 7 per cent, while greatly improving the situation compared with that in Scheme B, does not fully offset the unfavourable effect of allowing an increase in consumption per head of $2\frac{1}{2}$ per cent instead of 2 per cent. Despite the reduction of foreign service charges, the foreign debt grows more in Scheme *C* than in Scheme *A*. Whereas in Scheme *A* dependence on foreign borrowing falls quite markedly after the thirteenth year, in Scheme *C* it does not fall until after the sixteenth year, and then only slightly. When the rate of capital formation is relaxed (in year 21), the rate at which repayment is possible is sizeably less in Scheme *C*. But Scheme *C*, although substantially inferior to Scheme *A*, is probably just acceptable, while Scheme *B* is decidedly not.

It should be stressed that a reduction in the rate of increase of consumption by $\frac{1}{2}$ per cent a year would do more to help a country to solvency than so spectacular a reduction in the average of foreign service charges as one from 7 per cent to 4 per cent. This would probably be the case even if certain other basic assumptions were varied. On the other hand, it may be the case that a 2 per cent

TABLE III

SCHEME *C*

(Assumptions the same as in Table II, except that services charges on foreign borrowing are set at 4 per cent instead of 7 per cent.)

Years	In-come	Income not avail-able for capital forma-tion	Amortiza-tion less replace-ment ex-penditures	Service charges on foreign borrow-ing	Domesti-cally avail-able for capital formation, viz. (i) − (ii) + (iii) − (iv)	Capital stock (Exclud-ing land)	Saving required	Foreign borrow-ing re-quired, viz. (vii) − (v)	Accumu-lated foreign borrowing
	(i)	(ii)	(iii)	(iv)	(v)	(vi)	(vii)	(viii)	(ix)
0	—	—	—	—	—	200·0	19·6	− 19·6	− 19·6
1	100·0	104·5 less 5	0	0·8	− 0·3	219·6	21·0	− 21·3	− 40·9
10	164·0	155·2 less 5	7·4	8·7	+ 12·5	456·1	34·3	− 21·8	− 239·3
15	215·8	193·4 less 5	8·8	13·1	+ 23·1	647·6	45·1	− 22·0	− 350·1
20	283·9	241·0 less 5	10·5	17·3	+ 41·1	900·0	60·0	− 18·9	− 452·3
21	300·0	251·9 less 5	11·1	18·1	+ 46·1	960·0	36·0	+ 16·1	

Note to Cols. viii and ix : Minus sign=borrowing ; plus sign=repayment.

incentive (as in Scheme *A*) is just not enough, so that any scheme which allows no more will founder ; but the reduction of foreign service charges might itself prove impracticable. It is hoped that the juxtaposition of these three schemes illustrates how narrow is the path that has to be trodden, and how precarious the success of an attempt at assisted take-off.

SCHEME D

We may now go over to the assumption that is sometimes made, although, in my judgement, with undue optimism, that the initial capital-output ratio is 3 : 1. If this is maintained (roughly) level during the period of super-normal growth, we have a marginal gross product of capital of 1/3. It seems reasonable to assume — but this is not a point of vital importance — that for so much capital to have been created before the plan, the pre-plan saving ratio was somewhat higher than in Scheme *A* ; I have taken 6 per cent of pre-plan income. This assumption of an initial 3 : 1 ratio gives a substantially better picture, since the build-up of capital required is smaller.

TABLE IV

SCHEME *D*

(Assumptions the same as in Scheme *A* except that the pre-plan capital-output ratio is 3 : 1 and the marginal gross product of capital is 1/3.)

Years	Income (i)	Income not available for capital formation (ii)	Amortization less replacement expenditures (iii)	Service charges on foreign borrowing (iv)	Domestically available for capital formation, viz. (i) – (ii) + (iii) – (iv) (v)	Capital stock (Excluding land) (vi)	Saving required (vii)	Foreign borrowing required, viz. (vii) – (v) (viii)	Accumulated foreign borrowing (ix)
0	—	—	—	—	—	300·0	16·8	− 16·8	− 16·8
1	100·0	104·0 less 6	0	1·2	+ 0·8	316·8	18·0	− 17·2	− 34·0
10	164·0	147·9 less 6	6·3	11·4	+ 17·0	519·6	29·4	− 12·4	− 175·4
15	215·8	179·9 less 6	7·5	14·8	+ 34·6	683·7	38·7	− 4·1	− 215·8
20	283·9	218·8 less 6	9·1	13·9	+ 66·3	900·0	52·0	+ 16·3	− 182·4
21	300·0	227·5 less 6	9·4	12·8	+ 75·1	952·0	36·0	+ 39·1	

Note to Cols. viii and ix : Minus sign = borrowing ; plus sign = repayment.

In this more cheerful picture the foreign borrowing required goes only slightly above twice initial national income. The amount begins to fall appreciably after the sixth year and self-dependence is achieved in the seventeenth year, when repayment can begin. It can be continued on a generous scale after the termination of the crash programme period ; in practice doubtless it would be expedient to taper off with a more generous allocation to incentive (consumption) towards the close of the period.

SCHEME E

But, as under the assumptions of Scheme *A*, the allocation of an extra 0·5 per cent p.a. increase to consumption transforms the situation. Scheme *E*, which embodies this, is substantially better than Scheme *B*, but can barely be regarded as a viable scheme.

Dependence on foreign borrowing continues to grow until the sixteenth year and declines only very slightly thereafter. More than four and a half times initial national income is required, and even after the crash programme some foreign borrowing is required. What is to be noted is the vast difference made by the assumption of 0·5 per cent, more or less, in the increase of domestic consumption.

TABLE V

SCHEME *E*

(Assumptions as in Table IV, except that an increase of 2·5 per cent per head p.a. in consumption is allowed. Income not available for capital formation therefore increases at 4·5 per cent p.a.

Years	Income (i)	Income not available for capital formation (ii)	Amortization less replacement expenditures (iii)	Service charges on foreign borrowing (iv)	Domestically available for capital formation, viz. (i) − (ii) + (iii) − (iv) (v)	Capital stock (Excluding land) (vi)	Saving required (vii)	Foreign borrowing required, viz. (vii) − (v) (viii)	Accumulated foreign borrowing (ix)
0	—	—	—	—	—	300·0	16·8	− 16·8	− 16·8
1	100·0	104·5 less 6	0	1·2	+ 0·3	316·8	18·0	− 17·7	− 34·5
10	164·0	155·2 less 6	6·3	13·8	+ 7·3	519·6	29·4	− 22·1	− 219·8
15	215·8	193·4 less 6	7·5	22·0	+ 13·9	683·7	38·7	− 24·8	− 364·6
20	283·9	241·0 less 6	9·1	30·7	+ 27·3	900·0	52·0	− 22·7	− 461·4
21	300·0	251·9 less 6	9·4	32·3	+ 31·2	952·0	36·0	− 4·8	

Note to Cols. viii and ix : Minus sign = borrowing ; plus sign = repayment.

This is clearly the crucial point in the whole programme. The assumption of a 3 per cent p.a. increase in consumption would lead to hopeless insolvency even if a gross marginal product of capital of 1/3 is assumed.

SCHEME F

It is possible that to hold an opening capital-output ratio of 2 : 1 (excluding land) is too optimistic. A scheme (*F*) has been drawn up showing an opening ratio of 1 : 1. If there is to be a build-up to the conventional ratio of 3 : 1 during the course of the plan, this implies a marginal gross product of capital of 1/4. In these conditions of capital poverty it may be appropriate to assume that only 3 per cent of pre-plan income is saved. The build-up is a hard task and in Scheme *F* it is assumed that income not available for capital formation increases at only 3½ per cent p.a. allowing only a 1½ per cent p.a. increase of consumption per head. As there would presumably have been some increase before the plan, this will probably allow less than 1 per cent p.a. for incentive which may be impractically low. This scheme is just viable.

TABLE VI

SCHEME *F*

(Assumptions as in Table I, except that initial capital output ratio is 1 : 1, marginal gross product capital is 1/4 and income not available for capital formation rises at 3·5 per cent p.a.)

Years	Income (i)	Income not available for capital formation (ii)	Amortization less replacement expenditures (iii)	Service charges on foreign borrowing (iv)	Domestically available for capital formation, viz. (i) – (ii) + (iii) – (iv) (v)	Capital stock (Excluding land) (vi)	Saving required (vii)	Foreign borrowing required, viz. (vii) – (v) (viii)	Accumulated foreign borrowing (ix)
0	—	—	—	—	—	100·0	22·4	– 22·4	– 22·4
1	100·0	103·5 less 3	0	1·6	– 2·1	122·4	24·0	– 26·2	– 48·5
10	164·0	140·9 less 3	8·4	17·9	+ 16·6	392·8	39·2	– 22·6	– 278·0
15	215·8	167·3 less 3	10·0	25·1	+ 36·4	611·6	51·6	– 15·2	– 373·5
20	283·9	198·6 less 3	12·1	28·1	+ 72·3	900·0	69·2	+ 3·1	– 399·0
21	300·0	205·5 less 3	12·6	27·9	+ 82·2	969·2	36·0	+ 46·2	

Note to Cols. viii and ix: Minus sign=borrowing ; plus sign=repayment.

Here foreign borrowing begins to fall off substantially after the twelfth year. Foreign dependence comes to an end only in the twentieth year. The total amount of borrowing required is four times income. Repayment can begin on a substantial scale after the scheme is over. But, although viable, it cannot be pronounced feasible, since the incentive is too low.

SCHEME G

Scheme *G* retains the initial low capital-output ratio of Scheme *F* but restores the incentive of Scheme *A* (withdrawal of 4 per cent from availability for capital disposal).

Foreign borrowing barely drops within the period. The total amount is over six and a half times initial income. But there is thereafter some prospect of slow repayment.

TABLE VII

SCHEME *G*

(Assumptions as in Table VI, except that income not available for capital formation rises a 4 per cent p.a.)

Years	Income (i)	Income not available for capital formation (ii)	Amortization less replacement expenditures (iii)	Service charges on foreign borrowing (iv)	Domestically available for capital formation, viz. (i) − (ii) + (iii) − (iv) (v)	Capital stock (Excluding land) (vi)	Saving required (vii)	Foreign borrowing required, viz. (vii) − (v) (viii)	Accumulated foreign borrowing (ix)
0	—	—	—	—	—	100·0	22·4	− 22·4	− 22·4
1	100·0	104·0 less 3	0	1·6	− 2·6	122·4	24·0	− 26·6	− 49·0
10	164·0	147·9 less 3	8·4	20·1	+ 7·4	392·8	39·2	− 31·8	− 318·9
15	215·8	179·9 less 3	10·0	31·6	+ 17·3	611·6	51·6	− 34·3	− 486·1
20	283·9	218·8 less 3	12·1	43·8	+ 36·4	900·0	69·2	− 32·8	− 653·6
21	300·0	227·5 less 3	12·6	45·7	+ 42·4	969·2	36·0	+ 6·4	

Note to Cols. viii and ix: Minus sign = borrowing; plus sign = repayment.

The moral of these last two schemes appears to be that in these conditions it would be mistaken to attempt to raise the capital (and national income) so much in a twenty-year period. Initial poverty necessitates a somewhat slower build-up.

A capital build-up may have to be moderated because the maximum possible increase in non-capital factors available for fertilization by capital disposal is insufficient. This may indeed often be the case. Any attempt in these conditions to increase capital disposal by more than a certain rate will be attended by diminishing returns to capital-disposal (see p. 115). If a marginal gross product of no more than 1/5 or 1/6 can be obtained, then we may be sure that the country will go deeply into insolvency, and indeed it is unlikely that utility will be maximized through time. (*Some* consideration must be given to utility in the mature countries!)

SCHEME H

But it might happen that the increase in capital-disposal was held down, not owing to the insufficiency of non-capital factors in the developing countries, but because the mature countries were unwilling to lend so much. Scheme *H* is intended to examine this situation. It is there supposed that, so far as the developing country is concerned, Scheme *A* would be feasible, but that, owing to the unwillingness of the mature countries to lend so much in the first instance, the capital-output ratio is raised to 3 : 1 and income trebled over a *thirty*-year period.

It is arguable that under this scheme of slower increase not so much 'withdrawal' (column (ii)) need be allowed. Thus if the total deterioration in the terms of trade (owing to the super-normal growth) is spread over thirty, instead of twenty, years, only 0·3 per cent a year need be allowed. And if income is to grow at 3·75 per cent, instead of 5·6 per cent, a year, the incentive of 2 per cent p.a. might be replaced by one of 1·2 per cent. It is on this basis that the total withdrawal of 4 per cent in Scheme *A* is replaced by one of 3 per cent. This is rigorous.

It is clear that, on the whole, Scheme *H* is inferior to Scheme *A*. It is true that the foreign borrowing required in earlier years is somewhat lower ; but it eventually rises to 17·3 (in year 19), and

TABLE VIII

SCHEME *H*

(Assumptions as in Table I, except that (*a*) the trebling of income, along with the required rise capital stock, is executed over thirty years, and (*b*) the income not available for capital disposal rises at 3 per cent p.a.)

ears	In-come	Income not avail-able for capital forma-tion	Amortiza-tion less replace-ment ex-penditures	Service charges on foreign borrow-ing	Domesti-cally avail-able for capital formation, viz. (i) − (ii) + (iii) − (iv)	Capital stock (Exclud-ing land)	Saving required	Foreign borrow-ing re-quired, viz. (vii) − (v)	Accumu-lated foreign borrowing
	(i)	(ii)	(iii)	(iv)	(v)	(vi)	(vii)	(viii)	(ix)
0	—	—	—	—	—	200·0	12·9	− 12·9	− 12·9
1	100·0	103·0 less 5	0	0·9	+ 1·1	212·9	13·6	− 12·5	− 25·4
10	139·0	134·3 less 5	4·5	9·3	+ 4·9	354·5	18·9	− 14·0	− 147·3
15	166·9	155·6 less 5	4·8	14·5	+ 6·6	455·9	22·7	− 16·1	− 223·2
20	200·4	180·3 less 5	5·2	20·2	+ 10·1	577·5	26·9	− 16·8	− 305·3
25	240·7	208·9 less 5	6·7	26·0	+ 17·5	723·6	33·2	− 15·4	− 386·3
30	289·2	242·1 less 5	9·2	30·3	+ 31·0	900·0	39·2	− 8·2	− 440·5
31	300·0	249·4 less 5	10·7	30·8	+ 35·5	939·6	36·0	− 0·5	

Note to Cols. viii and ix: Minus sign=borrowing ; plus sign=repayment.

only begins to drop by sizeable amounts after year 25. The aggregate amount of borrowing required is substantially greater in Scheme *H*, and in the thirty-first year the country is not in a position to begin repayment, while under Scheme *A* it can start repayment on a substantial scale (or otherwise raise its own incentives) in the twenty-first year. Thus, *if conditions are right* in the borrowing country, the more rapid take-off scheme is to be preferred to the slower one.

IV. POSSIBLE DIFFICULTIES OF APPLICATION

These are all macro-economic schemes. It will naturally be objected with some vigour that no such statistical information, even in rough approximation, would be obtainable during the progress of any scheme and that the discipline implied could not be enforced in practice. None the less it may be useful to have such schematic representations of what is *possible* present in the background of the minds of planners. The narrowness of the path in each case, given the need for *some* incentive, with $\frac{1}{2}$ per cent deviation causing hopeless insolvency, is determined by the arithmetical relations between capital formation and consumption. Planning can govern the choice of path, but it cannot make any of the paths broader.

The question may be raised whether the lessons derivable from the macro-economic schemes could be applied on a micro-economic scale, i.e. to specific capital projects. Would it be possible to regard the investments of each separate firm or project as an aliquot part of the total investment occurring and to require that conditions required for the whole are fulfilled on a proportionate scale in each? There are serious difficulties in this. The two fundamental points are (i) that the gross marginal product of capital must be sufficient and (ii) that not too much must be allowed for consumption increase.

(i) *Sufficiency of Gross Marginal Product of Capital*

The concept of gross marginal product is one not commonly used in micro-economics and presents accounting difficulties in relation to a particular capital project. The concept of value added is applicable in accountancy. But to get the gross product of capital we have to subtract from this the opportunity costs in *some* sense of the non-capital factors co-operating. And this is where the difficulty lies. In the computation of profit in the ordinary sense the cost of non-capital factors consists simply of the pay for which they can currently be hired. In a growing economy the rates of pay may be expected to rise year by year in accordance with the growth of productivity in the economy as a whole. (For simplicity, I take the case of constant prices and rising factor rewards rather than falling prices and constant factor rewards.) A particular firm rightly regards the increases in pay that it has to grant as coming upon it *ab extra* ; even if it undertook no operations, the increases in market pay-rates might occur just the same, owing to the activities of all the other firms. But from our point of view what is important is that each particular firm, or project, is contributing its aliquot part to the total increase in the productivity of the economy that renders the rise in pay rates possible.

It is often stated in relation to developing countries that there is a considerable amount of disguised unemployment, and it is argued consequently that the opportunity cost of labour in a new project, anyhow so far as unskilled labour is concerned, may be literally nil, since in its absence the labour in question would not be employed. It need not, of course, be supposed that the firm scours the country-side for some unemployed, presumably the least eligible, but only that, through a multi-lateral swapping of jobs, the end result of its activities is that some unskilled labour produces something instead of nothing. If this were indeed the case, it would be appropriate to debit nothing or only a small amount against value added in respect of the hiring of unskilled labour, in order to compute the gross product of its investment.

Then the firm may seek out personnel for foremanship, management, etc., and, in doing so, have to offer them higher pay than they would otherwise get. Only what they would otherwise get should be debited against net value added. Or, if rates for such people are being levered up by a number of simultaneous projects, the rates that they could obtain in their previous inferior occupations in year minus one should be debited. The essential point is the obvious one that part of the gross product of capital is distributed to the non-capital factors in the form of an increment of pay in excess of what they could otherwise have earned. The cost of hiring *foreign* factors of superior type should presumably be reckoned as part of foreign borrowing, as I have suggested above.

(ii) *Allowance for Increase of Consumption*

In computing what is distributed as additional disposable income, unfortunately we do not only have to reckon what the firm itself pays out, but also the pay increases in the rest of the economy that occur owing to its example or by competition. To the extent that other investments are simultaneously taking place, those outside increases may be debited to *them*. But increases of pay-rates may also occur in sectors of the economy which are not currently being fertilized by any additional capital disposal. This is a further reason for holding it desirable that, if only the availability of non-capital factors renders it feasible, any crash programme should be introduced as rapidly as possible and thus have as wide an ambit of fertilizing effect as possible.

(iii) *Criterion for Solvency*

It may be observed that under (i) and (ii) there are certain items not readily ascertainable by accountancy that in part at least cancel out, namely, under (i), that part of the gross product constituted by the excess of paid out rewards to non-capital factors over their opportunity costs in year minus one, and, under (ii), the increase in disposable income distributed. This suggests that it might be possible to find on a micro-economic scale some criterion, which was viable in accountancy, for determining whether the activities of a firm really constituted an aliquot part of a totality that was leading to eventual solvency. I cannot solve this problem, but will make a tentative suggestion.

I hasten, however, to interpose the point that no prescription for the aliquot parts can solve the general problem of an excessive rise of disposable incomes in sectors not being fertilized, or not much fertilized, by new capital disposal. If income-distributions are excessive, we shall have not only the general evils of inflationary pressure, but the specific evil, which must stab any plan for eventual solvency to the heart, of an overspill of purchasing power into the external balance of payments. For such an overspill will make still more foreign borrowing necessary, if the programme of investment is to go forward. The ideal remedy is, of course, for the government to syphon off by taxation any undue excess of income-distribution — but we are told that there are great difficulties in this in many developing countries. Less good, because it adds to internal inflationary pressure, is the familiar remedy of an extensive restriction of imports of consumer goods; but this may be better than no remedy. More important would be some method for curtailing the home consumption of exportable goods. If rationing is out of the question, much could be done by far-reaching official plans for long-term purchase contracts for *rising* amounts of exportable goods, so that they would be drawn away from the possibility of an excessive increase in the domestic consumption of them. Not that this would by itself be a substitute for the need to have expansion in *mature* countries, in order to secure rising demands for the products of developing countries.

V. A METHOD OF INCREASING SAVING

To return to capital formation. Some writers have been driven, under the *force majeure* of the relations shown in the preceding tables, to postulate a high marginal rate of saving in the growth period. But surely such a postulation is a pipe-dream, in so far as disposable personal incomes are concerned. It will have been noted from the tables that in the crucial period when the country is moving over from dependence on foreign borrowing to self-reliance, a very high rate of domestic saving has to be postulated.

So we may think of company saving. If we may be allowed to derive a general impression from the minutiae of the tables, it seems that company saving at the rate of 5 per cent a year on all capital formed after year zero would lead to an adequate accumulation over a twenty-year period. This is not a large proportion in relation to *industrial* capital, and many companies would of their own volition doubtless plough back more. But there are other forms of capital, e.g. housing, to which the principle would not so readily be applicable. It might be a good thing in the strenuous conditions of a developing country to make ploughing-back on at least this scale, viz. 5 per cent p.a. on the operating capital, mandatory (or on a higher scale, if some forms of capital would not be brought within the net). Amortization on the basis of replacement cost, or historic cost, whichever was higher, should also be legally required. If all or part of the 5 per cent withheld from distribution was redundant to the requirements of the company, it could be lent on revocable loan to a National Development Bank.

But this brings us to a cardinal difficulty. To the extent that there is a foreign equity in the company, the ploughing-back of profit is tantamount to fresh foreign borrowing and therefore contributes nothing to the objective of making the country able to rely, wholly or mainly, on domestic saving. This brings me to my specific proposal.

I suggest that a proportion of the minimum statutory amount of profit to be withheld from distribution, equal to the proportion that foreign-owned equity bears to the total capital of the company operating in the country in question, should be segregated from the foreign equity holding. No doubt various alternative technical methods could be devised for securing this. Any method would, it must be admitted, be in the nature of a levy on foreign investment. One method would be that the said proportion should be compulsorily paid into the national Development Bank and be recoverable, on request, for use in the company. But when thus lent back by the Bank, it should not be at a fixed rate of interest, but on an equity basis. For, if it were lent back at a fixed rate of interest, the excess of true profit on the said reborrowed capital over the rate of interest charged on it would accrue in part to the foreign equity holders and thus increase the country's foreign service charges.

The National Development Bank need not be given any 'control', or voting rights, a point on which foreign investors are sensitive. What is important is that it should be the agency for securing to the country the means of progressive domestic capital investment out of its own resources. Any portion of its funds not required by the company that had contributed them would be used by the National Development Bank for supplying other domestic capital requirements.

The foregoing must not be taken to imply that foreign owners would be debarred from ploughing back the profits of the enterprise to their own benefit — quite the contrary. During the period of dependence on foreign borrowing, and indeed afterwards, the ploughing-back of the profits of a (wholly or partly) foreign-owned company may be the most convenient way of getting fresh foreign capital. Subject to the payment of 5 per cent on their capital to the National Development Bank, the foreign owners would be allowed to plough back as much of their profit as they liked ; the more the better. There would be no prior requirement on the company to draw back from the National Development Bank any of the funds currently or previously contributed by it to that Bank. Having discharged its 5 per cent obligation in respect of foreign equity capital, the company could proceed to use all its opportunitites to make money for its own shareholders, foreign or otherwise. But the National Development Bank would have the funds (with no foreign service charge attached) to proceed with other developments needed by the country.

In no case could the National Development Bank use accruing revenue for any other purpose than further capital development. When domestic ownership of capital was sufficiently increased, the 'levy' could eventually be terminated. It might seem rather churlish for a country in the process of being assisted by a crash programme to impose a levy of this kind. Enlightened planners, such as international agencies, might not think so. There would be three main objectives. (i) It is needful to build up a locally held fund for the purpose of becoming self-reliant; it would be most imprudent to rely on a high rate of marginal personal saving for this purpose. (ii) It is desirable to have a sieve with which to sort foreign investments. If the 5 per cent levy prevented certain capitals coming in, that would probably be a good thing, since it would be a sign that the project in question was not likely to contribute to the ultimate solvency of the country. (iii) The 5 per cent requirement might be a brake upon distribution of pay for hired local services in excess of necessity. A foreign enterprise that has a large margin of profit may be carefree in the rates of pay at which it hires local services, regardless of the ill-effect of that on the general economy of the country through example and competition.

It might be argued that where 'official' loans require amortization to be remitted back, the country eventually has the benefit of itself owning the assets thus written off. But the value of these assets would be considerably less than the fund built up by the payments of 5 per cent a year, especially if the official agency, wishing to press only lightly on the country's balance of payments in early years, granted generous amortization terms. However, any amortization payments remitted home *in excess of the physical deterioration of the assets in question*, could well be allowed as deductible from the requirement of 5 per cent to be paid into the Development Bank.

VI. SUMMARY

(1) Shortage of capital disposal is only one among many factors, and may not be the most important factor, limiting growth in developing countries.

(2) Any attempt to increase capital disposal at a much greater rate than the co-operant factors can achieve would be subject to the law of diminishing returns (dynamized version), and likely to contribute little to the progress of developing countries, while imposing an unjustified burden on mature countries.

(3) Subject to not imposing substantial hardship on mature countries — a situation not likely to arise at present — it would be desirable to make capital disposal available in such quantities that its shortage would no longer be an independent factor impeding growth in developing countries, i.e. in quantities consistent with the maximum possible rate of growth of non-capital factors locally.

(4) The direction of development should be in accordance with the dynamized version of the law of comparative costs. Some considerations, of a very general nature it must be admitted, and

subject to exceptions, are offered for a prior presumption in favour of exportable goods as against import-competing goods.

(5) Borrowing from abroad should normally be regarded as imposing a net long-run burden on a country's balance of payments. It is a fallacy to suppose that this can be obviated by increasing the amount borrowed year by year.

(6) None the less it may be, practically speaking, impossible for a country with a poor capital equipment, to achieve the progress of which it is capable, except by heavy foreign borrowing. But because of proposition (5) it is important to contemplate that this will lead to a development enabling the country eventually to become self-sufficient (more or less) on capital account.

(7) Possibilities in this regard have been shown by conspectuses covering a twenty-year period. It is assumed that some incentive, in the form of rising consumption per head, must be allowed in order to elicit the co-operation of non-capital factors in the country.

(8) While the conspectuses show that excellent progress can be made with rising incentives, it is vitally important that the rise should not be too great. An excess rise of no more than a half of one per cent transforms a viable scheme into one leading to hopeless insolvency. This is true on a number of different hypotheses concerning initial capital endowment. An excess rise of consumption of $\frac{1}{2}$ per cent has a more damaging effect on the prospect of achieving independence from foreign borrowing than a reduction of average foreign service charges on foreign borrowing from 7 per cent to 4 per cent has good effect.

(9) Always provided that the growth potential of non-capital factors domestically available is sufficient, a larger supply of foreign capital at the outset and a more intensive crash programme will have more successful results than a slower plan and require a smaller cumulative amount of foreign borrowing at the peak.

(10) It is difficult to translate the lessons derivable from the macro-economic tables into criteria or precepts for application on a micro-economic scale, viz. to particular capital projects.

(11) However particular projects are sieved, there is likely to be an over-all problem of preventing an excess distribution of disposable incomes, through the example of, or competition with, those sectors that benefit in the first instance by additional capital disposal. Such remedies as taxation (for budget surplus) and the restriction of consumable imports may have to be considered. A suggestion is made for the (still more important) restriction of the consumption of exportables, by long-term official contracts for the purchase of exportable goods (for export) on a rising scale.

(12) Since voluntary marginal personal saving is not likely to be as high as is shown by the conspectuses to be necessary, it is proposed that a sufficient rate of company saving should be compulsorily secured. In particular it is proposed that a levy be made in respect of foreign-owned capital operating, to ensure that some part of the retained profit is made available for domestic expansion without increasing the amount of foreign indebtedness.

Chapter 6

INTERNAL STRUCTURAL CHANGES REQUIRED BY GROWTH AND CHANGES IN INTERNATIONAL TRADE[1]

BY

MAURICE BYÉ

Faculté de Droit et des Sciences Économiques, Paris

INTRODUCTORY

THE subject assigned to me directly involves two fields of economic research — namely, forecasting and development planning — and it requires to be shown how these are interrelated.

We have a mass of recent literature on this, of various kinds: theoretical studies on a number of different models; surveys of the history of thought on the subject; historical research on the emergence and development of industry in various countries; statistical investigations on the present state of specialization throughout the world; case studies of the problems of under-development; and interpretations and applications on a regional basis.[2]

In these circumstances, this paper should really attempt a synthesis over a very wide field. I shall have to limit myself to a few essentials. Being partial in the sense of being less than complete, this report will also have to be partial in the other meaning of the word, in so far as I shall use concepts and methods which, through my long association with the Paris Institute of Applied Economics (I.S.E.A.), I owe to François Perroux.

The paper will be in three parts:

(1) In the first part the problem will be posed in precise terms.
(2) The second part will be devoted to a definition of certain characteristics of the sectors of production, the relative

---

[1] Translated from the original French by Elizabeth Henderson.
[2] See, in particular, J. M. Letiche, *Balance of Payments and Economic Growth*, New York, 1959; H. B. Chenery, 'Comparative advantage and development policy', *American Economic Review*, March 1961, pp. 18-51. A good account of the theories about international specialization in general and its relationship with dynamic analysis is given by R. E. Caves in *Trade and Economic Structure*, Cambridge, Mass., 1960.

weight of which in an economy is determinant for its specialization.

(3) The third part will be more directly concerned with relations between different countries.

I. THE PROBLEM

(i) *Definitions*

By 'internal structural changes' I mean changes concerning a country's characteristic economic proportions and relationships.

International trade and economic growth may, of course, well 'require' all kinds of structural change. Both, for example, have a direct bearing on the distribution of incomes, wealth, rights and powers. This is fundamental.

I shall make a distinction between the economy of a 'country', that is, the territory bounded by the national frontiers, and the economy of a 'nation', which may have economic dependencies outside the national frontiers.

The 'specialization of a country' is characterized by the proportions between 'sectors of production'. These proportions may be expressed in terms either of the composition of the national product or of the distribution of factors, or one factor, of production. Each of these definitions is meaningful in its own way, but the former is generally more useful.

The title of this paper suggests a comparison between two families of analysis : those which we may group together under the heading of 'traditional theory of international specialization', and those which we shall call 'growth theories'.

By traditional theory I mean the whole body of work which, starting out from Ricardo, is today generally based on indifference systems. There is, it is true, the theory of comparative statics — but, though in saying this we do less than justice to some of its proponents, it remains a fact that strictly speaking this theory excludes all dynamics and assumes absolute factor immobility within each country. What I call traditional theory will, therefore, be described as a static approach, or an approach of comparative statics.

By growth I mean an increase in gross domestic product per head, the development and structural transformation which accompanies positive growth and indeed enables it to take place.

I shall have to confront, on the one hand, the traditional theory of specialization, and on the other hand the consequences which come about when two countries, each producing in an open economy, undergo structural changes involving changes in specialization.

This is how I interpret my subject.

(ii) *The Principles of a Comparison between the Traditional Theory of Specialization and the Theory of Growth*

Traditional theory provides an answer to three questions :

(1) It explains how, when trade is opened, a certain specialization results from the free play of decisions by autonomous decision units in various countries, each with its own resources and conditions.

(2) It shows that when trade is free, and even in the presence of complete factor immobility, the resulting specialization is the most advantageous in the given circumstances. I shall speak in this case of 'short-term advantage'.

(3) It justifies free trade policy — but this justification pre-supposes not only the validity of the conclusions under (1) and (2) above, but also the additional assumption that there is a 'long-term advantage' corresponding to the short-term one.[1]

Without this additional assumption, there would, for example, be no point at all in comparing the advantages accruing to England in 1845 and in 1847. I believe, incidentally, that there is not much point in these discussions anyway, because, if we want to appreciate the beneficial effects of the repeal of the Corn Laws in 1846, we should look not only at what England gained in 1847, but at her whole development since 1846 to our days and beyond.

I take it for granted that there is general agreement on points (1) and (2) ; that is to say, given the assumptions of the traditional theory, we accept its short-term interpretation of international specialization in an open economy, and we accept that this specialization is advantageous in the short period under consideration.

The last point, on the other hand, has been controversial ever since the origins of protectionism, right up to the present-day debate on development policies. Being static, traditional theory has never been able to make the transition between points (1) and (2), on the one hand, and point (3) on the other.

Nor can the transition be made by some device of comparative statics. Yet it has to be made.

The only means of doing so is a dynamic analysis, such as the traditional theory never even mentions. What policy is then judged best is a matter which comes only afterwards — so much so that we can leave it aside here and concentrate mainly on the requirements of dynamic analysis itself.

[1] Various papers published by the North Holland Publishing Co.

Now, if we are to analyse the long-term increase in gross domestic product per head, we can do this only with reference to a time series of production within a certain system defined by structural and behavioural coefficients (the propensity to save, the propensity to consume certain products, etc.), as well as by the nature of the inducements capable of calling forth the autonomous decisions which are determinant for the system. In a private-enterprise system, these inducements are, in the first place, profit rates and, at a higher level, the internal and external causes which, by modifying the rates of profit, affect investment decisions.

The aggregate models of even a closed economy show up one of the fundamental dynamic relationships, namely, the necessary equality — in the long period — of the increase in national product, the increase in the sum of additional incomes and additional aggregate demand.

But if we want to know something about 'additional' specialization in the open economy we must work with at least two sectors. The more sectors we consider, the greater will be the explanatory value of the model.

Following this line of thought, we have research work of two kinds :

(*a*) the work done mainly by the group around J. Tinbergen — that is to say, multi-sector models on the plane of what I have called a nation, and working with input-output tables ; [1]

(*b*) the adaptation of traditional theory for purposes of economic growth in the models of, say, H. G. Johnson, M. Corden, J. Black and Paul Streeten.[2]

In any event, to admit that several sectors have to be considered implies also a recognition of the need to take account of the heterogeneous characteristics of the different sectors in any kind of explanation. It is these characteristics which determine the bias of economic development.

But what particular characteristics are important in this analysis? Obviously, we need all those characteristics upon which depend, on the one hand, each sector's reactions to international equilibrium and, on the other hand, its reactions to growth.

[1] Various papers published by the North Holland Publishing Co.
[2] H. G. Johnson, *International Trade and Economic Growth*, London, 1958 ; M. Corden, 'Economic Expansion and International Trade : a geometric approach', *Oxford Economic Papers*, June 1956 ; J. Black and P. Streeten : 'La balance commerciale, les termes de l'échange et la croissance économique', *Économie Appliquée*, 1957, pp. 299-322.

(iii) *The Problem of Long-term Comparative Advantage*

How are we to formulate the problem of 'long-term comparative advantage' — a problem which has long worried the advocates of free trade, just because it is implied in the transition between the points (2) and (3) of our schematic outline of traditional theory above.

Any short-term comparative advantage would necessarily have to give rise to a long-term one. This presupposes that if a nation specializes, at t_0, in accordance with that moment's short-term comparative advantage, it can be sure of reaping in the final period, t_n, greater advantages than would have resulted at t_n if the nation had made any other choice at t_0.

There are, *a priori*, two ways of proving such a proposition.

(1) From the point of view of *effective* factor and demand creation we can argue as follows. Thanks to (short-term) comparative advantage, a country maximizes its product at t_0. This product will, according to the marginal propensity to save, give rise to additional capital, which in turn will raise the country's productive capacity, modify its factor proportions and satisfy additional demand. In the new conditions of t_1 the principle of comparative advantage will again come into play, new factors of production and new demand will again be generated, and so on. In every separate period short-term comparative advantage prevails.

But if comparative advantage is to be assured in the long period between t_0 and t_n, the creation of factors of production in the interval has to be optimized. Suppose for the sake of argument, and without entering into the substance of the matter, that specialization on agriculture generates no saving, but that specialization on industry does. It is then not certain *a priori* that specialization on agriculture in accordance with the comparative advantage in the given conditions of t_0 and subsequent specialization according to the same principle will also maximize long-term comparative advantage by the time t_n.

(2) To reason instead in terms of *potential* factor and demand creation might seem to avoid this difficulty. If we apply the rule of 'potential advantage' assumed in comparative statics, we might say that the largest product will, by way of taxation, yield the largest saving.

But does this assumption not contradict the hypothesis of spontaneous entrepreneurial decisions? If the sectoral characteristics are modified by what I shall call here a macro-decision, can we still expect the same chain of events?

I might add that the dynamization of traditional theory makes it still more difficult than it is in static presentation to make welfare comparisons over time. Apart from all the well-known difficulties, we then have the additional one of reducing to a common denominator the sacrifices of savers between the initial and the final period — not to speak of how hard it is to know what period to choose. In a nation's life through time, the costs incumbent upon successive generations and the advantages accruing to them are not comparable. We need even more ethical and political judgements than the critics of welfare economics assumed.

(iv) *The Growth Relationships*

We can, of course, build any model we like, so long as it is coherent, but if it is to have some sort of explanatory value, it must take account of observed correlations.

From this point of view the most useful piece of work, to my knowledge, is H. B. Chenery's recent study.[1] Surveying some fifty countries at different stages of development at one and the same time, Chenery finds a strong correlation between industrialization and the level of *per caput* income. Differences in the level of income alone explain 70 per cent of the differences in industrialization. There is a similar correlation between level of income and type of industry : at a *per caput* income level of 100 dollars 68 per cent of manufacturing industry produce consumer goods and 12 per cent of it capital goods ; at an income level of 600 dollars the corresponding proportions are 43 and 35 per cent.

The relation between increase in sectoral production and increase in *per caput* income is, furthermore, characterized by an elasticity of growth. This coefficient of elasticity diminishes from 2·16 for investment goods through 1·50 for intermediary goods to 1·31 for consumer goods. The elasticity is very high for the production of machines (2·80) and transport equipment (2·33), and very low for the food industry (1·13) and the tobacco industry (0·93).

Naturally, we shall not here summarize an article which everyone knows. We have quoted it merely to show just what kind of relationships need to be explained. To state the facts alone is not yet a solution ; indeed, as Chenery himself writes : 'the association between industrialisation and growing income does not tell us much about the factors determining the income growth itself'.[2]

But in attempting a theoretical explanation, we should, surely, at least give prominence to all the factors which create a relationship between industrialization and wealth, in complete *ex post* conformity, over the short period, with the law of (short-term) comparative advantage. The question is only which is cause and which is effect.

---

[1] H. B. Chenery, 'Patterns of Industrial Growth', *American Economic Review*, Sept. 1960, pp. 624-53.   [2] *Ibid.* p. 650.

(v) *Conditions to be included in any 'Specialization-Development' Model*

My reference to a statistical investigation and to some of its conclusions was intended to show what may, and what may not, rightly be assumed as a working hypothesis in a model serving our particular purposes.

Nobody contests, of course, that in any kind of deductive analysis one has to make up one's mind to leave out some considerations which the simplest observation of facts might suggest. One might prefer, for instance, to choose as a first approximation a system without monopoly, or without transport costs.

Nevertheless, it has to be recognized — as H. G. Johnson, for one, does recognize — that certain simplifications, while admissible at a first stage, have to be dropped very quickly in an explanatory approach. This applies in particular to the assumption of (absolute or relative) factor immobility, since it is common knowledge that whether specialization develops or not throughout the world depends upon the existence, or non-existence, of international capital flows. Similarly, a simplifying hypothesis might at first leave out innovation, but it would have to be reintroduced sooner or later.

On the other hand, there are some simplifications which are not admissible even at a first stage of analysis, in so far as they would prevent the model from coming anywhere near the desired explanation. No simplification must be adopted which is incompatible with any of the other fundamental conditions of the model. Let me give some examples.

(1) If we have a dynamic system — increase in product, factors (mainly capital), demand — can we still assume an unchanged composition of demand? Such an assumption would, of course, enable us to enter into the consumption indifference map of the initial period any shift to the right of the production possibility curve which, now intersecting higher consumption indifference curves, would indicate certain effects on the terms of trade. But this would correspond only to coincidences entirely devoid of theoretical or practical interest, for two sufficient reasons :

   (*a*) according to well-known laws and observations the composition of demand for consumer goods changes with an increase in income ;

   (*b*) according to other laws and observations demand for producer goods changes even more and its share in total value added grows continuously.

The indifference curves of demand (which, incidentally, are preferable in this kind of analysis to those of consumption) cannot be the same at t_0 and at $t_1 \ldots t_n$. We have to make new indifference maps and move the production possibility curve on a modified map. Quite a number of models seem to neglect this.

What we would have to do is to draw for t_n a demand indifference map which is different from that at t_0 in so far as the t_n curves would reflect different marginal rates of substitution. This would allow us to treat in a precise manner the fundamental problem, which is this : if, in a country specialized at t_0 on capitalistic production, the nature of specialization itself leads to sizeable capital increases (comparatively to the rest of the world), in what conditions

(a) will new industries settle in that country rather than elsewhere?

(b) will intermediary demand be propagated?

(c) will the country's pre-existing industries displace themselves or maintain themselves (by capital deepening, for instance) on the spot?

(2) Other assumptions which are ruled out are all those which, while admissible in static analysis, are impossible in dynamic analysis where any change in any one element, say, product, factor supply or the volume and composition of total demand, is necessarily accompanied by changes in all the others. This applies in particular to assumptions such as absence of external economies or economies of scale : the increase in diversification or in the size of the market is an inherent part of any particular type of growth or of growth in general. It applies also to the assumption of equal power among competitive firms, since firms have different dynamic capacities in different sectors according to the latters' characteristics, especially as regards the amount of saving. It applies to the assumption of equal planning periods, because this compromises one of the essential growth factors, namely, the formation and use of the firms' gross income. It applies, finally, to the assumption of absence of integration, because the dynamism of operations of this kind provides important investment opportunities for the capital so employed. To sum up, it is inadmissible to assume what is known as pure and perfect competition.

(vi) *Consequences for the Traditional Theory*

It follows that if traditional theory is to be used to provide a base of reference, or a series of bases of reference, for dynamic analysis, certain assumptions of traditional theory, in any of its forms, have to be dropped.

Traditional theory may be taken at three levels.

(1) *At the level of money costs and prices.* If one merely wants to explain the reaction of individual entrepreneurs to international trade, it can always be stated that they tend towards those productions where, at internationally determined prices, their cost position is least bad.

(2) *At the level of opportunity cost.* In a situation of full employment and perfect competition the opportunity cost of a product, that is to say, the value of the factors which would have to be used to supply that product in the best alternative way, equals that product's market price.[1] In the conditions indicated specialization according to opportunity cost maximizes (short-term) comparative advantage and the spontaneous behaviour of economic units achieves that advantage for the country.

(3) *At the level of cost determinants.* There is general agreement that opportunity cost depends partly on natural, partly on man-made data. The question is whether these data can be made to fit into a calculation of the numerical relations between factors of production. In the literature, the law of factor proportions does not always have the same content. In Leontief's interpretation, this law does achieve very general validity, but only with the help of a concept of 'abundance' of factors of production which deprives the analysis at factor level of much of its usefulness.

On the other hand, if we take the law of factor proportions in Ohlin's sense, it becomes a very convenient tool. It gives us much more general results than does the definition of collective advantage 'at the level of products', because we can drop the assumption of competition.[2] It is particularly tempting for dynamic applications, because modifications in factor proportions are of the essence in that case.

But just because it is so tempting, this law also has its dangers. In statics, the expression factor of production is badly defined and becomes meaningless when we begin to speak of specific factors, as we often feel we have to nowadays. Furthermore, if it is difficult enough to imagine in static terms that production functions are internationally homogeneous, it becomes quite impossible in dynamic analysis. Finally, just because changing factor proportions are so congenial to dynamic analysis, there is a danger of forgetting that these changes are not isolated but are connected, above all, with changes in demand.

I am not suggesting that we should do without the Heckscher-

---

[1] H. B. Chenery, 'Comparative Advantage and Development Policy', *American Economic Review*, March 1961, p. 19.　　　　[2] *Ibid.* p. 20.

Ohlin principle, but I think we have to be rather careful in using it for dynamic analysis.

In any event, whatever the level at which we consider comparative advantage, we have to remember to take into account the effects of a large number of factors not considered in static theory. We should not forget, as T. Balogh puts it, that 'scarcity of factors of production is not a concept of disequilibrium'.

II. THE HETEROGENEITY OF PRODUCTION SECTORS

If the key to the determination of long-term comparative advantage lies in the heterogeneity of production sectors, we must, in this part of the report, consider the production sectors themselves in so far as they are heterogeneous. We shall have to try and identify the growth characteristics of separate sectors.

That different sectors grow at unequal rates is a primary fact, empirically proved, for example, in I. Svennilson's work. By way of illustration, Table I shows growth differentials in France over a ten-year period of rapid structural change.

The inequalities of growth in the various sectors are due to the latters' own peculiarities and also, of course, to the effects on each sector of changes in the economy as a whole.

Since it is the essential task of dynamic analysis to link two aspects of one and the same aggregate quantity, such as 'increase of product and demand', we shall, successively, examine the conditions generating growth and the incentives stimulating growth in heterogeneous sectors.

(i) *The Conditions of Sectoral Growth*

The basic relationship in this context is that between objective profit and instrument of growth. There are other possible relationships, not all of which are measurable in quantitative terms and not all of which are symmetrical.

(1) *Sectoral capital formation.* The specific influence of any one production sector on national capital formation may be more or less diffuse. One may say, for example, that the preponderance of the agricultural sector, in certain historical and geographical conditions, gives rise to a type of society having certain institutions and, with these institutions, certain habits of saving and investment.

The concept of sectoral capital formation is more precise. It means the part of capital formation directly imputable to productive activity as such, and therefore includes the undistributed profits of companies and entrepreneurs.

TABLE I

INDICES OF INDUSTRIAL PRODUCTION IN FRANCE, 1949–59

Sectors	1959 index (1949=100)
Fats	106
Solid mineral fuels	113
Leather	123
Textile industry	129
Construction and public works	136
Tobacco and matches	144
Ceramics and manufacture of construction materials	169
Mining and processing of miscellaneous minerals	175
Glass	177
General index including construction	180
Metallurgy	181
Mining of metallic minerals	189
General index without construction	191
Printing and publishing	198
Rubber	200
Paper and board	210
Transformation of metals	211
Electricity	213
Mining and quarrying of construction materials	224
Gas	290
Chemical industry	291
Petroleum and liquid motor fuels	318

Source: *Annuaire Statistique de la France*, 1961, p. 121.

Table II shows the importance of self-financing by companies, which, in 1956 in France, furnished on the average 56 per cent of financial resources. For the rest, it should be remembered that part of the remainder comes not from the capital market but from public funds.

It will be seen that there is no clear relation between a sector's saving and its value added. Investment decisions are governed by the profit rate, capital/output ratio, propensity not to consume or not to distribute dividends, and by the general attitude to investment.

Even if the savings of firms were to lose their identity on a perfect capital market, their inequality as between one nation and another, due to the heterogeneity of sectors and to their different weight in the originating economy, would compromise the relationship between short-term and long-term comparative advantage.

VALUE ADDED AND CAPITAL ACCOUNT BY SECTORS IN FRANCE, 1956
(million new francs)

Sectors	Value added	Uses			Resources			Total 2+3+7 or 5+6+7
		Gross fixed capital formation	Inventory changes	Investable funds	Gross saving a	Financing by entrepreneurs	Financing requirements	
	(1)	(2)	(3)	(4)	(5)	(6)	(7)	
1. Agriculture, forestry and fisheries	18,371	2,883	−476	—	104	1365	938	2,407
2. Agricultural and food industries	14,992	926	39	253	799	225	194	1,218
3. Solid mineral fuels	2,977	981	−15	—	649	1	316	966
4. Petroleum, liquid motor fuels	5,702	865	160	93	1,104	4	10	1,118
5. Electricity, gas, water	3,163	2,808	105	24	1,361	—	1576	2,937
6. Mining and quarrying of ores, construction materials and other minerals	1,290	254	45	11	271	17	22	310
7. Production of glass, ceramics and construction materials	2,082	286	58	1	257	16	72	345
8. Chemical and rubber industries	5,286	790	220	2	961	7	44	1,012
9. Metallurgy	3,999	978	309	—	918	5	365	1,288
10. Engineering	12,334	1,277	581	141	1,284	29	686	1,999
11. Construction of power plants	3,428	318	374	—	312	2	378	692
12. Motor vehicles	3,692	655	234	2	529	8	354	891
13. Shipbuilding and aircraft	1,592	268	421	—	204	5	480	689
14. Textile industries	5,867	558	284	135	866	96	15	977
15. Clothing	2,884	63	71	—	64	4	66	134
16. Leather and hides	1,653	69	50	—	41	—	78	119
17. Timber and furniture	2,606	132	68	—	123	—	17	200
18. Paper and board	1,403	170	98	1	235	60	27	269
19. Printing and publishing	2,207	252	43	—	167	7	95	295
20. Miscellaneous industries	1,109	61	55	—	75	33	41	116
21. Construction and public works	11,738	739	266	—	391	—	307	1,005
22. Transport and communications	11,154	3,587	15	63	2,704	307	838	3,665
23. Miscellaneous commerce	20,371	1,144	952	—	1,057	123	862	2,096
24. Hotels, catering	4,171	752	40	12	29	177	81	372
25. Miscellaneous services	5,710	320	62	4	486	262	269	818
26. Finance and property companies	1,179	1,157	40	158	579	63	737	1,355
27. Liberal professions	5,764	255	−10	43	122	39	—	288
Balancing item in the transition to semi-aggregate accounts	2,966	+258	−336	—	—	166	−78	−78
Total	159,690	22,806	3753	944	15,692	3021	8790	27,503

a Companies' undistributed gross income.

Source: *Les Comptes de la Nation*, Ministry of Finance, 1960, pp. 136-9.

However, the very low figures for 'investable funds' in Table II suggest that any one sector's profits are hardly employed outside that sector. There are two possible uses that have to be considered, though, use abroad (in the rest of the world, which is to be discussed in Part III of this paper), and use in other sectors through vertical or horizontal integration. Even though the relevant figures in Table II are so small, a sector which saves much may use resources in 'additional integration' as a means of sectoral imperialism or of rationalization, according to the widely differing position of strongly expanding industries or industries acutely threatened with decline.

But, on the whole, the savings of companies are predominantly used in self-financing. In the broad sense, sectoral self-financing includes firms gaining control over other firms in the same sector; in the narrow and more current meaning, it is reinvestment in the firm itself.

Table III shows the proportion of self-financing in sectoral investment in two different periods. It will be seen that this proportion differs widely as between sectors, types of firms and periods. It is lower in nationalized industries (coal mining, Electricité de France, Gaz de France, and similarly in the Compagnie Nationale du Rhône) than in private companies; high in acutely threatened industries (textiles : 93 per cent in 1959) and low in very prosperous ones (chemicals : 48 per cent in 1959); generally low in a period of reconstruction (First Plan) and high when capital equipment is better. While a sector's self-financing capacity is not necessarily the condition of the sector's growth (chemical industry), it does appear to be connected with all its growth characteristics.

(2) *The supply of labour and entrepreneurs; research.* To begin with, some sectors may be more philoprogenitive than others. It is often said, for example, that in agriculture people tend to have larger families than in industry.

Secondly, different sectors definitely turn out different kinds of people. Railway construction in the United States created a class of mechanics who later transferred to industry; extensive cattle farming, on the other hand, has always had a poor reputation as a source of skilled labour. This is, of course, one of the reasons which push young nations towards big industry, and also one of the reasons why big industry is rightly regarded as a 'development pole'.[1]

Finally, big industry is more capable of research than others and is also in a better position to take advantage of the opportunities of innovation offered by an expanding market.

---

[1] On this point, cf. the work by J. M. Letiche (*op. cit.*). During a number of meetings held in Paris our colleague, Mr. Kindleberger, made several pertinent remarks on the subject.

TABLE III

PROPORTION OF SELF-FINANCING IN INVESTMENT IN DIFFERENT
SECTORS IN FRANCE, 1947–52 (FIRST PLAN) AND 1959

Sectors	1947–52 %	1959 %
Agriculture	45*	48
Energy	24	31
of which :		
Coal mining	18	10
Electricité de France	15	21
Cie Nationale du Rhône	8	15
Gaz de France	5	39
Carburants	81	65
Energie atomique	—	0
Industry	34	70
of which :		
Iron and steel industry and iron-ore mining	31	67
Non-ferrous minerals and metals		24
Construction materials		74
Chemicals	41†	48
Engineering and electrical industry		80
Textile and miscellaneous industries		93
Communications	8	48
of which :		
State railways	6	59
Air France	12	27
Inland Water Transport	24	89
Merchant fleet	0	56
Tourism	—	67

* Including food industry, nitrogen and agricultural machinery.
† Including tourism.

Sources : *Rapport sur la réalisation du Plan de Modernisation et d'Equipement de l'Union Française*, 1952, Paris, 1953, Table 31, p. 80 ; *Rapport annuel sur l'exécution du Plan de Modernisation et d'Equipement*, 1960, Vol. i, Table II, p. 11.

(3) *Expectations.* The most important, perhaps, of all the differences between sectors has to do with the length of the planning period. The time horizon of the dominant firms in one sector is different from the time horizon of the dominant firms in another, for a number of reasons among which the outstanding one is that technological requirements and the conditions of the economic struggle in each sector impose a different size on the leading firms.

Each large firm calculates its 'advantage' in terms of current values concerning the whole of its activities (its own and that of integrated firms within or outside the country itself). Depending on technological conditions, the firm therefore has to plan, say, for some five years ahead in the motor-car industry or some ten years in the oil industry.

It follows that anticipated demand varies, which rules out any summation of demand on collective indifference curves and makes nonsense of such concepts as an optimum with respect to all firms, current effective demand or the nation as a whole.

It also follows that the principle of equalization of marginal productivities has to be qualified and cannot be expressed in the form it takes in the traditional theory of international specialization.

(ii) *Sectoral Investment Incentives: the Role of Profits*

In an economic system governed by entrepreneurial decisions such as traditional theory envisages, the allocation of resources is directly influenced by the rate of profit.

As Jean Weiller says : 'In this as in other fields, the traditional view assumed a general correspondence between the Schumpeterian world of recurring profit and the Ricardian world without profit accumulation, between the conditions of trade governed by the law of maximum monetary gain for firms setting out to conquer the world market and those governed by maximum real gain, calculated, on the national scale, in the wholly static terms of comparative cost.' [1]

This implies a link between the comparative advantage of the initial period and that of all subsequent periods, provided

- (*a*) the ratio of profit rates in two industries reflects the ratio of their comparative advantage in the same period, and
- (*b*) the allocation of capital resources is really governed by the ratio of profit rates.

If, in addition, there obtained also the above-mentioned condition of equal factor increase from one period to another, then long-term comparative advantage would be maximized by the same process which maximizes short-term comparative advantage in each period.

A bias may be introduced either (1) by the non-coincidence of the ratios of profits and real advantage, or (2) by the type of investment.

(1) The *ratio of profit* rates may differ from the *ratio of real advantage* for two main reasons :

(*a*) *Imperfect competition as between national economies.* The

---

[1] J. Weiller, 'Échanges, profits d'entreprise et gains', *Économie Appliquée*, 1957, p. 327.

principal among many causes of this type of bias is, as A. Lamfalussy has noted, the long-term inflationary or deflationary character of an economy.

It may be argued that in certain conditions which may be regarded as connected with an economy's structure and specialization, certain national systems tend towards either inflation or deflation. If a country like Belgium has a permanent deflationary climate and at the same time the formation of saving continues to be large, an abnormally low interest rate will cause certain activities to be financed which, in the same real conditions, would not be financed elsewhere in the world.

(*b*) *Anomalies in the conditions of the economic struggle within the national economy.* We know that some of these anomalies are traditionally excluded from the data of growth models or models of international trade. I have in mind especially anomalies due to government intervention. Farmers in Western Europe and the United States, for example, certainly operate in other conditions than are the rule in the great primary-producing countries ; similarly, Belgian coal mining has enjoyed privileged conditions during these last ten years.

Under the same heading we have to note monopolistic agreements and concentration, as well as more generally any 'revolutionary' structural change such as a change in the property order, in the distribution of power or in the distribution of planning periods of different length.

(2) *Investment trends* in relation to *profit rates*.

It would be useful in any specialization-development analysis to make certain distinctions regarding investment, as H. G. Johnson and P. Streeten, for example, well appreciate. I should classify investment at least from the following points of view.

A. *According to structural effect* :

    (*a*) capital widening ;

    (*b*) capital deepening ;

    (*c*) innovation.

The first type of investment directly increases output. The second type may not increase output at all, or may increase it in accordance with price elasticities, the length of expectations or the market form relevant for the investing firm. The third type of investment may either modify the production function or meet new demand.

Type (*a*) always increases production, types (*b*) and (*c*) do so sometimes.

Type (*b*) always, and type (*c*) sometimes, improves productivity, while type (*a*) is neutral with respect to productivity unless there is an indirect improvement through the effects of economies of scale.

B. *According to the origin of the demand to which investment responds.* From this point of view the most important distinctions are between domestic and foreign demand, and between demand for consumer and producer goods.

On the assumption of the driving power of consumer demand, we have indeed to speak of the acceleration principle. But nothing authorizes a national economy to discount a change in consumer demand in advance, in so far as it may increase the demand for producer goods either within the country, or abroad, or yet in some economic dependency of the country elsewhere (some foreign branch set up specially by a firm, for example).

C. *According to the ultimate effect on the national economy.* There is a difference between what we might call 'aggressive' and 'defensive' investment. Any economy is, from the point of view which interests us here, a combination of threatened and advancing sectors, the co-existence of which determines the very character of the economy and has to be explained, alongside the latter, by any theory of specialization development.

Only a careful analysis of the different types of sectors and types of investment incentives can explain how a national economy, assumed to be initially characterized by a certain pattern of specialization in accordance with short-term comparative advantage, will in effect react from one period to the next.

III. TYPES OF NATIONAL DEVELOPMENT

A nation must be considered as a unit through a long period of time, and it is, at any particular moment, characterized by an established structural pattern. To describe it adequately, we must go beyond the mere enumeration of the sectors which go towards its composition. The size of each national unit and its particular conditions of development confer upon it specific characteristics, which we shall call 'national' characteristics.

In their turn, these national characteristics are reflected in the development conditions of each separate 'national sector', and these have a direct bearing on the study of international specialization.

National sectors may be heterogeneous in several respects; we shall here examine the relationship between the national economy as such and sectors which are heterogeneous with respect to :

(1) growth ;
(2) economic space ;
(3) external economic relations.

(i) *Inequalities in Sectoral Growth : Defensive Investment*

At first sight, the principle of (short-term) comparative advantage would seem to imply :

(*a*) that countries (as distinct from nations — see the *Definitions* at the beginning of this paper) with growing capital accumulation should specialize on capital-rich products, while less capital-intensive industries develop spontaneously in other countries, with less capital accumulation ;

(*b*) consequently, that, as the less capital-intensive industries are gradually set up elsewhere, they should disappear from the capital-accumulating countries.

However, this second conclusion is not confirmed in practice. H. B. Chenery's cross-section analysis through a world of nations of unequal wealth clearly shows that, while the share of certain industries in the domestic product declines with growing national wealth, there is never any actual contraction in absolute terms. On the contrary, in all industries without exception we find some increase in output accompanying the rise of *per caput* income, and none of them was shown to have a zero elasticity of growth. Agricultural products, textiles, fats — to mention only a few which are commonly held to be most likely to be dislodged from richer countries and to move to those less well endowed with capital — are all produced in greater quantities when *per caput* income rises.

The actual course of events suggests that, if there is, as Chenery says, a primary connection between types of production and levels of income, it corresponds to the pattern of demand rather than to the traditional theory's pattern of factor endowment. Expanding demand calls forth an increase in local supply ; however, if demand expands less than proportionately with income, supply also increases less than proportionately with income.

Now, this could be explained in various ways without invalidating the traditional theory. It might be said, for instance, that transport cost, which traditional theory neglects, is in fact not negligible ; or that the threatened sectors, such as agriculture in Europe and the United States or the textile industry in some countries, demand and receive some kind of protection, under the umbrella of which they manage to survive. It might also be said that high external economies, which, too, are absent from the classical model, work out to the benefit of the more advanced countries. All this is no doubt true, but it is not the whole explanation. The roots of what Jean Weiller calls 'structural preference', expressed in 'structural inertia', seem to go much deeper.

In order to seek out these roots, let us make the simplifying assumption that growth has no effect on labour skills. We assume, therefore, that so far as factors of production are concerned, the only effect of growth is the successive formation of additional (financial) capital. According to the rationale of the system under consideration, this capital must tend to find its way into those sectors where the highest relative profit is to be expected. The directly relevant element, in dynamic analysis, is, therefore, the ratio of profit rates, and neither relative factor costs nor the relative volume of factor supply. But if the principle of (short-term) comparative advantage is to prevail, all these different explanations must coincide.

The *sequence of events* we should expect would, then, be one roughly corresponding to the following pattern.

Let us say that at t_0 England produces mainly cloth (a capital-rich product) and, as a secondary product, some wine (less capital-rich). England's capital endowment increases between t_0 and t_i. The 'price' of capital tends to fall relatively to the 'price' of labour. From the point of view of costs, therefore, England is at t_i even better placed than before to produce cloth. Admittedly, this trend could be counteracted by movements in the terms of trade. If the increase in wealth from t_0 to t_i were to be accompanied by a more than proportional increase in the demand for wine, the pattern of specialization at t_i might conceivably be the same as it was at t_0, or England's wine-growers might even expand their production in both absolute and relative terms. But this is a rather remote possibility if our model is meant to apply to the growth of an industrial country. As a rule, both the terms of trade and cost trends must be expected to favour the production of cloth. What, then, are the actual conditions needed to attract new capital to that industry? They are :

(*a*) that profit rates rise more in the 'favoured' than in the 'less favoured' branch of production, and

(*b*) that investment responds to the profit ratio.

There can hardly be any doubt about the first condition, given our assumptions. The real problem resides in the second condition.

As regards the profit rate, three considerations may help to explain the considerable and lasting *differences among sectoral profit rates* within one and the same country and at one and the same time.

(1) As soon as the firms in a sector exceed the very smallest size, or, on the assumption of a different market form, as soon as such firms dominate a sector, the relevant profit is the profit expected

over a more or less lengthy period. The economic horizon is not the same in all industries, but varies from sector to sector. Current costs and demand are, therefore, less relevant for investment decisions than expected costs and demand. It follows that if an industry established in a 'developed' country considers that the advantages of its new competitor in a 'young country' will be only temporary in that they depend on cheap land and labour, that industry will have no reason to contract. Generally, it succeeds in obtaining some protection from the government, but, failing that, it may even accept a cut in its current profits. This kind of argument is often heard from spokesmen of European agriculture.

(2) Successful defence is often possible by means of a reinforcement of the capital base and/or innovation — assuming that production functions are not required to remain unchanged in the play of (short-term) advantages. Either method may enable an industry not only to defend itself, but ultimately to beat its competitors, if it should prove possible to restore a profit rate compatible with normal capital returns. An industry can strengthen its position through mergers and rationalization, such as are familiar, for instance, from the history of the steel, textile and shipbuilding industries in France. It is an observed fact that often agricultural productivity tends to rise with industrial productivity (speaking not only of marginal, but also of average productivity) and that growing output may very well be combined with growing productivity. This happened in Japan during the industrial revolution and is happening in France today.

(3) Whatever may be its possible wider meaning, the term *defensive investment*, as used by A. Lamfalussy in contrast to investment in new ventures or innovations, covers rather a narrow concept. It means investment in contracting industries where the profit rate is abnormally low.[1] Table IV reproduces some of the statistics on the basis of which this young Belgian economist of Hungarian origin developed his interesting and original theory and applied it to the case of the Belgian economy.

To explain the relative stagnation of the Belgian economy, we must bear in mind that the bulk of Belgian industry earned rather low profit rates during the period considered and that the branches with a high profit rate accounted for only a small share in total industrial output (cols. 1 and 2). In some branches profit rates declined over the nine-year period (col. 3). Yet, far from disinvesting, all branches increased their gross fixed assets over the

---

[1] A. Lamfalussy, *Investment and Growth in Mature Economics : the Case of Belgium.* London, 1961.

TABLE IV
TYPES OF INVESTMENT IN BELGIUM

Industries	Distribution of Belgian industrial output in 1953	Average rates of profits in Belgian industries, 1948-56	Real net profits in 1956 as percentage of 1948	Real gross fixed assets in Belgian industry in 1957 as percentage of 1948	Output in Belgian industry in 1957 as percentage of 1948	Productivity of labour in Belgian industry in 1957 as percentage of 1948	Capital/Output ratios in Belgian industries in 1957 as percentage of 1948	Capital intensity in Belgian industry in 1957 as percentage of 1948
	(1)	(2)	(3)	(4)	(5)	(6)	(7)	(8)
	%	%						
Chemicals	4·8	11·3	200	178	167	159	107	170
Cement	2·0	11·3	260	188	160 (142)	169	118	225
Electrical engineering and electronics	1·8	10·0	270	210	170	133	123	164
Electricity and gas	4·6	8·7	198	163	154	143	106	155
Steel	6·1	7·0	250	143	170 (150)	140	84	134
Food and beverages	16·7	6·3	220	146	141	135	104	140
Textiles	10·0	3·7	66	125	136 (142)	152	92	133
Rolling stock and railway equipment	1·0	3·2	Losses	149	—	—	—	455
Coal mining	13·1	- 3·1	Losses	144	111	130	130	170
Others	39·9	—	—	—	—	—	—	—

Source: A. Lamfalussy, *Investment and Growth in Mature Economics — The Case of Belgium*, London, Macmillan, 1961. Various tables have been regrouped.

(1) Table XIV, p. 124; (2) Table IV, p. 9; (3) *Ibid.*; (4) Table XVII, p. 140; (5) Table XVIII, p. 142; (6) Table XXIII, p. 150; (7) Table XIX, p. 143; (8) Table XXII, p. 149. The intensity of capital is the ratio capital/work in input.

same period (col. 4). The reason probably was that, as we shall see, new investment makes it possible to raise the productivity of labour (col. 6) in the most vulnerable branches or, what comes to the same thing, to increase their capital intensity (col. 8). In column 5 we see that some of the weakest sectors considerably raised not only their productivity, but also their output.

All this can largely be explained in terms of defensive investment. Instead of taking the short-term view, the entrepreneur is guided by the profit rate he expects to be able to earn at some future date. He owns certain real assets ; if he goes out of business now, the only compensation he gets for a certain loss of profit are the proceeds from the sale of his plant and equipment. If the profit rate he expects is not too small, if the price at which he can sell his real assets is very low, and if the date by which he expects to make a profit is not too far ahead, he might feel it to be worth his while to stay in business and even to proceed to further investment and minor innovations, such as merging with other companies or rationalizing production methods. If this enables him to reduce costs and thus to bring down prices, he may even be able to reach new classes of consumers.

The fact that, financially speaking, the various branches usually operate in fairly water-tight compartments accentuates the process we have described. Unwillingness both of lenders and of borrowers impedes the flow of funds from, say, textiles to electronics. Furthermore, a generally deflationary market like the Belgian one would tend to make a large volume of savings accessible to less than first-class borrowers.

(ii) *Inequalities in Economic Space*

So much for the apparent paradox of the aggressive defence of threatened sectors in economically advanced countries. But the explanation of historical situations in terms of the principle of (short-term) comparative advantages immediately comes up against a second paradox, namely, the premature appearance of advanced sectors in under-developed countries. In the Arab countries, in Bolivia, in the Cameroons and in Guinea we have examples of oil fields, mining enterprises and electric power schemes requiring very large amounts of capital. It would surely be unreasonable to try and salvage the law of factor proportions by pointing out that, on the other hand, natural resources are cheap. In any case, neither the law of factor proportions nor the Ricardian tradition is really involved. We are, in fact, stepping out of the framework of the traditional model as soon as capital proves to be as mobile as products and as soon as the concepts of 'nation' and 'country' cease to mean the same thing.[1]

In dynamic analysis, we simply cannot assume immobility of capital. We have to explain the (spontaneous) movements of capital and of capital income, in other words, the financial transfers which govern the movement of goods in one or the other direction.

No dynamic theory of international specialization is, to my mind, conceivable without reference to three elements, as follows :

(1) *The generation of demand.* The 'spontaneous' progress made by the older countries in complete conformity with the principle of (short-term) advantages gave rise in the first place to a local consumer industry and later to local investment industry. A cumulative process led to the creation of additional demand for intermediary goods as well as of additional financial resources.

Once a country has progressed that far, (short-term) advantage may dictate the use of savings and other disposable resources abroad — but surely, the advantages accruing from such movements of national factors, both to the factors themselves and to the nation, have nothing but a name in common with the comparative advantages of the Ricardian model.

Instead of saying that in the nineteenth century it was to England's advantage to produce cloth and to Canada's (or the Canadians') advantage to produce wheat, we should say : in the nineteenth century the people living in England (that is, England) found it to their advantage to divide their resources between England and Canada in such a manner that, due regard being paid to the risks and the disutility of migration, the marginal productivity of these resources in the two territories was equalized.

It would, in any event, be inadmissible to deal with factor movements on the assumption of constant demand or with the help of models devised for the static analysis of welfare maximization.

(2) *Non-communicating sectors.* We know that self-financing is the rule in most industries, though to varying degrees. Barring revolutionary changes or major innovations, for instance, the American oil industry, threatened with the imminent exhaustion of its local resources, will more readily use its corporate savings to prospect for oil in Venezuela than to finance a chain of grocery stores in Chicago. As a result, the equipment used in oil wells all over the world will have much the same capital/output ratio. By the same token, the unity of the oil industry as a whole makes it far

---

[1] On these points, cf. my article on 'La Grande Unité Interterritoriale' in Vol. ix of the *Encyclopédie française* (published under the supervision of François Perroux).

more likely that the undistributed profits of Venezuelan oil companies will be used to build a refinery in Texas or to prospect for more oil in Iraq than to be invested in a textile mill in Venezuela. The same often applies to profits distributed to the host government or to local shareholders. Kuwait, for instance, does not appear to have developed any large-scale capital-intensive industry, although it seemed well placed to do so. If, elsewhere, events have taken a different course, it was always as a result of the government's macro-decision to 'sow the oil', and macro-decisions of this kind would seem to run counter to the existing mechanisms rather than to fit into them.

(3) *Sectoral time horizons.* Every one of what I have elsewhere called closed investment sectors [1] has its own peculiar planning period. A sector which makes its investment plans for a long time ahead, may well retain funds which, in the shorter view, could more profitably be invested in other sectors. Conversely, a sector with a short time-horizon may employ savings which could be put to better use elsewhere in the long run.

These kind of 'incompatibilities of temperament' obviously escape notice in a short-period analysis; yet they go a long way towards explaining why countries where speculative crops are traditional offer so much resistance to industrialization.

(iii) *Inequalities in External Economic Relations*

There is yet a third paradox to be explained. This can be expressed in various ways, but all formulations eventually come to the same thing.

First formulation. The principle of (short-term) comparative advantages implies that there should be increasingly intensive specialization in two countries with asymmetrical rates of growth as far as capital and skilled labour are concerned. Both countries should concentrate on production for export and in both of them any industries competing with imported goods should disappear. The volume of foreign trade in relation to national income should therefore tend to increase.

In actual fact, the exact contrary tends to happen in the most highly developed countries, as all the arguments about the dollar shortage have shown beyond doubt. Furthermore, Chenery's investigations made it abundantly clear that in developing countries the industries which develop first and fastest are precisely those whose products compete with imported goods.

[1] On 'self-financing sectors', cf. my paper, 'The Rôle of Capital in Economic Development', to the Conference of the International Economic Association held in Rio de Janeiro; published in *Economic Development for Latin America* (ed. by Howard S. Ellis), 1961. See also my article in *Économie Appliquée*, 1958.

Second formulation. With reference to the specific case of the United States, the Leontief paradox shows up the particularly capital-intensive nature of industries competing with imports. If, like most observers but unlike Leontief, I assume that in the United States comparative advantages lie with the capital-intensive industries, the 'strongest' industries are again not those which produce for export, but those which compete with imports.

In both cases the explanation seems to be as follows:

In the course of a dynamic process, capital — and possibly labour — tends to be attracted towards those industries where both the rate of profit and the rate of increase of profit are expected to be highest. The industries possessing this characteristic are most often those which can look forward to a long-run expansion of demand for their products.

At each stage of the dynamic process, therefore, and in each national economy, capital and labour will tend to move towards those sectors where demand expands most.

Let us take one or two hypothetical cases.

(*a*) Suppose that additional demand arises within the country itself and is for a product which that country is best (or least badly) suited to produce. For instance, if the country is highly developed, the additional demand is for a capital-rich product.

In such a case the new industry which, at the time, will be best suited to the country's potentialities will be an industry catering for the home market and not for export. If this market is attractive enough to stimulate the production of the same good abroad, that is, if specialization is partial and not total, the new, highly capital-intensive domestic industry will compete with imported goods.

The process may be accentuated by capital movements. The 'strong' sector may set up subsidiaries abroad to supply the home market, and thus create rival 'foreign' industries (e.g. American oil installations outside the United States).

If the process I have described takes place after the country has already acquired an industrial structure, and if that industrial structure remains as it was, we shall find that a whole set of industries seen, *ex post*, to be competing with imported goods are better suited to the country's potentialities than export industries. Leontief's paradox ceases to be paradoxical in a dynamic context, when demand, structural inertia and the import-biased character of certain forms of growth are taken into account.

(*b*) Now take the case of the so-called poor countries. We encounter a symmetrical paradox there, and it is astonishing that none of Leontief's followers should ever have discovered it. Many of the countries which are least well endowed with capital in fact export not their least, but their most capital-rich products.

In tropical regions export crops are invariably more capital-intensive than subsistence crops. More and more frequently, tropical countries import staple foods such as wheat or rice, thus exposing to the competition of imports precisely those products which it should be to the advantage of a poor country to produce.

Here again, the explanation lies in profits. In an export-biased economy, it is the export sectors which have the highest profit expectations and therefore attract both domestic and foreign capital. It is also, again, additional demand — though this time, foreign demand — which creates additional advantages and which distorts an existing structure in apparent contradiction with traditional theory.

To what extent is the contradiction real or merely apparent?

In actual fact, traditional theory does apply in both our examples at all levels of analysis, but in conditions proper to dynamic analysis.

Additional — domestic or foreign — demand generated by a growing — domestic or foreign — national product between t_0 and t_i leads to a location pattern of additional industries which is in strict accordance with the (short-term) comparative advantage during that period. By raising profit rates in the industries producing goods A and B, the additional demand leads to additional production of A in country I, if I is comparatively better (or less badly) suited to produce A, and to additional production of B in country II, if II is comparatively better (or less badly) suited to produce B. In one country good A, and in the other good B, absorbs the new factors of production generated during the same period, and probably also diverts some factors previously used in C or D.

But there is nothing to suggest that, as a general rule,

— additional demand will stimulate export industries in both countries (on the contrary, this would be an absurd assumption);

— the industries stimulated will be those which, prior to t_0, had the greatest comparative advantage in each country;

— equilibrium can be achieved only thanks to the new production. On the contrary, if the production of A in country I induces or entails additional (but less than proportionate) imports of B, and also of C and D, into country I, then equilibrium comes about because country II imports, not the product A, but the goods E and F, which it already imported previously and which country I produces in less 'progressive' conditions than the good A.

To sum up, the confusion between comparative advantage and comparative cost, which is acceptable in static analysis, when demand is given, is no longer acceptable in dynamic analysis, when demand varies with the factor proportions. It follows that, in the absence of structural change, the industries stimulated by the new demand, whatever their markets, may be either more or less in line with the original comparative advantages of each country and with the law of factor proportions.

Since any structure incorporates a series of legacies inherited from different periods, there is no reason why it should correspond to what an observer might consider rational at any particular moment.

Suppose that the new demand, being domestic, does not alter the structure of exports but calls forth a new domestic industry or one competing with imports, or that the new demand, being foreign, alters the structure of exports but does not affect domestic industries or those competing with imports. In these circumstances, there seems to be no reason why in any given year international specialization should correspond to the static model.

IV. CONCLUSIONS

Let us, finally, see what conclusions, or at least outlines of conclusions, we may draw from some of the points discussed in this paper.

Traditional theory was meant to be both explanatory and normative, and any dynamic theory of long-term specialization could hardly rest content with being less.

(i) *The Explanatory Aspect*

What features must a model possess if it is to explain the spontaneous course of international specialization?

(1) *Simplifying assumptions.* The model may neglect government and monopoly, and it may be limited to only a few nations and only a few sectors.

We may not, on the other hand, make any simplifying assumptions which would remove from the model any of the growth variables, including economies of scale, external economies and, above all, the relationships between aggregates, any change in one of which necessarily affects the other, such as the relationship between the volume of factor supply and the composition of aggregate demand, or between aggregate profits and sectoral saving.

(2) *Scope*. The model must record reactions both within the country and outside it. It must also be dated. Charts prepared for the short period are useless unless corrected in successive periods for the intervening changes in the indifference maps of consumers and producers. We must therefore establish a conventional time-lag between successive corrections.

(3) *Exogenous variables*. Exogenous variables in the form of, say, autonomous changes in the anticipated demand for a sector's products or of innovations, must always be specified with respect to the location of the autonomous change (within or outside the country, in what sector).

(4) *Structural and behavioural coefficients*. The model needs, for each sector and each country, such coefficients as the income elasticity and the price elasticity of demand ; the capital/output and the labour/output ratio and, more generally, the production functions ; the sectoral propensities to save and the sensitivity of investment to profit rates ; the relation between the length of expectation periods and amortization ; the input/output coefficients which govern induced demand for investment goods (acceleration) and inter-mediary goods ; and so on and so forth.

(5) *Endogenous variables*. The most important endogenous variables in the model must be the volume of output, the productivity of the various factors of production (especially labour), the amounts of factors used in the various sectors, product and factor prices, and intersectoral and international flows.

This is, of course, a far from exhaustive list. Furthermore, a number of essential considerations cannot be quantified at all.

(ii) *The Normative Aspect*

To assess the short- and the long-term advantages of current specialization, we can compare its immediate results with the results it engenders from period to period over a certain time.

If even static analysis found it almost impossible to compare two collective situations, it is even more difficult to do so in dynamic analysis. Some prior moral or political choice will, in particular, always govern the length of the nation's anticipation period and the dating of the final period.

If, abstaining from value judgements, we merely draw up a list, we see that the national product and its composition depend jointly upon

      initial specialization,
      the data governing factor creation in each sector,
      the data governing demand creation, by types of demand,

the data governing the movement of factors from country to country,

external economies and economies of scale,

each sector's and each national economy's 'propensity to innovate'.

We have to start out, therefore, from a choice not between two or several products in which to specialize, but between two or several types of specialization and growth patterns.[1]

If the analysis is to lead to policy recommendations, we shall also have to examine to what extent the government, acting within its own time-horizon and within the limits of its powers of compulsion, may be able to withdraw resources from the economy, to re-allocate them, and to redistribute income.

In any event, we would be wise to distrust any summary prescription purporting to be valid for all countries and all products and, more particularly, for all under-developed economies, if that prescription speaks of nothing else except factor proportions and balanced sectoral growth.

The theory of international specialization must be more than just a theory of the balance of trade between countries, however neat and satisfactory that may be. It must take account of nations in their historical setting, with everything that this implies about their inequalities, asymmetries, preferences, structural inertia, types of growth and each nation's past and its future prospects.

V. RECAPITULATION

To facilitate discussion, it may be convenient to recapitulate briefly some of the main propositions of this paper.

(1) A specialization/development analysis may use the law of (short-term) comparative advantage and its several variants, provided certain assumptions are discarded as being incompatible with a dynamic process and provided specific allowance is made for the consequences of the rejection of these assumptions.

(2) The law of (short-term) comparative advantage compares cost and demand. Growth alters, jointly and simultaneously, factor supply and costs, on the one hand, and the volume and composition

---

[1] R. Nurkse, 'Patterns of Trade and Development', 1959 Wicksell lecture; Stockholm, 1959. H. B. Chenery, 'Comparative Advantage and Development Policy': '. . . In short, we are forced to compare alternative patterns of growth rather than separate sectors, and we cannot expect to find simple generalisation of the Heckscher-Ohlin type concerning the characteristics of individual lines of production'; *American Economic Review*, March 1961, p. 23.

of demand, on the other. It is not admissible to consider the first set of changes without the second.

(3) Sectors of production are heterogeneous. Their capacity to create factors of production differs, and so does their propensity to demand new — final or intermediary — goods. Initial specialization is, therefore, a determinant of future specialization and of the rate of growth.

(4) Not all sectors are equally capable of attracting capital and labour from outside or to release them for outside use. Factor movements have a bearing on the type of specialization and may not be neglected. The assumption of factor immobility is incompatible with dynamic analysis.

(5) Additional demand created by any one country's additional produce may, depending upon the type of specialization/development, call forth a new line of production in the same or in another country, and may thus make the economy either marginally export-biased, or self- or import-biased. This proposition is not in contradiction with the traditional theory of short-term advantage.

However, while traditional theory shows how trade tends to increase, in absolute terms, in the transition from a closed economy without specialization to an open economy with specialization, it does not, and cannot, show that additional domestic or foreign demand and the related creation of new factors of production necessarily increase the import/income ratio in all the countries concerned.

Everything depends on the nature and the location of the additional demand, on the nature and location of the additional factors of production, and on the type of growth.

(6) It is possible to construct an abstract model in which a new industry might, through the complex network of effects on the country's foreign trade arrangements, displace some existing industries.

In the real world, the existing industries defend and adapt themselves by methods which traditional theory neglects by definition. To be valid, any explanation has to be based on an historical situation, and the theory of comparative advantages cannot be either proved or disproved by statistics.

(7) Long-term advantages cannot be deduced from short-term advantages, because short-term advantages are defined in terms of the traditional theory of international equilibrium (over a short period) and long-term advantages depend on dynamic data related to the specific nature of types of specialization/development.

We need a multi-sector model in which due account is taken of sectoral factor formation, the possibility of macro-decisions and the differential effects of heterogeneous impulse sectors.

It follows that the law of (short-term) comparative advantage alone, in any of its forms, cannot justify any long-term policy choice, such as free trade, protectionism or the promotion of particular industries, whether these do or do not conform to the law of factor proportions in the initial period.

Chapter 7

INFANT INDUSTRY ARGUMENTS FOR ASSISTANCE TO INDUSTRIES IN THE SETTING OF DYNAMIC TRADE THEORY

BY

H. MYINT
University of Oxford

I. INTRODUCTORY

THE aim of this paper is to survey the protectionist arguments which have been commonly put forward in relation to the economic development of the under-developed countries. I shall begin in Section II with a brief account of the traditional 'infant industry' and kindred arguments for protection. In Sections III and IV I shall consider a number of more recent arguments for protection, first on the cost side and next on the demand side of the question, which claim to deal with the broader structural and dynamic problems of economic development of the under-developed countries. In Section V we shall consider some of the difficulties of pursuing an effective protectionist policy in the setting of the present-day under-developed countries, which suggest a conflict, *at the practical level*, between such a policy and the commonly adopted form of over-all economic development planning involving an all-round restriction of imports.

II. THE TRADITIONAL INFANT INDUSTRY ARGUMENT

The theory of comparative costs is a branch of welfare economics and, in so far as the free trade argument is based on it, the logically acceptable cases for protection may be regarded as the deviations from the optimum due to a divergence between social and private costs. This is how free trade theorists like Professor Haberler would regard both the infant industry case and the related case of external economies and diseconomies which need not be associated with decreasing costs. 'Social as well as private costs may be increasing, and the underlying situation may therefore be quite stable and still there may be a deviation between social and private

173

costs due to external economies or diseconomies, i.e., due to certain cost-raising or cost-reducing factors which would come into play if one industry expanded and another industry contracted — factors which for some reason or other are not, or not sufficiently, allowed for in private cost calculations.' [1]   Given a wide enough divergence between the two, private comparative costs may lead a country into a 'wrong' pattern of international specialization, say exporting commodity *B* and importing commodity *A*, while the true social transformation ratio between the two commodities would require the opposite pattern with the given international price ratio.   This can happen even if both *B* and *A* are working under conditions of increasing costs.   Thus the 'infant industry' argument, which further postulates that the neglected industry *A* may enjoy decreasing costs as its output expands, can therefore be regarded as a particular case (although a highly dramatic one) of the divergence between social and private costs.[2]

Having conceded the logical possibility of this divergence, the free trade theorists would, however, maintain that 'as a rule the ratios of private money costs do reflect the true social real cost ratios', and that 'the burden of proof is on those who maintain that the exceptions are numerous, persistent, large and, last but not least, practically recognizable and calculable'.[3]   They would also stress that in order to make a valid case for protecting an 'infant industry' with potential decreasing costs, the following rather restrictive conditions have to be fulfilled.   (*a*) The economies should

[1] G. Haberler, 'Some Problems in the Pure Theory of International Trade', *Economic Journal*, June 1950, pp. 236 *et seq.*

[2] Diagrammatically, it is possible to have two variants of the 'infant industry' argument.   Firstly, we may depict increasing returns in industry *A* as in Figure I, by a shift in the production possibility from *BA* to *BA₁* as the output of *A* is increased.   This is the version adopted by Haberler (*loc. cit.* p. 239).

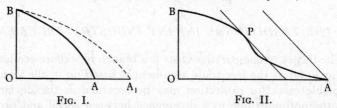

FIG. I.   FIG. II.

Secondly, we may depict increasing returns in industry *A* on the same production possibility curve by a change in the curvature as in Figure II.   Here, if at a given international price ratio specialization takes place at point *P*, the country has not attained a full optimum position, because although the marginal conditions are fulfilled, what Professor Hicks described as 'total conditions' are not fulfilled. Full optimum will be attained only by complete specialization at point *A*.   This is Tinbergen's suggested version of the Graham argument (J. Tinbergen, *International Economic Co-operation*, Amsterdam, 1945, Appendix I).

[3] Haberler, *loc. cit.* pp. 237-8.

be external to the firm : if they are internal to the firm output will be expanded automatically and there is no need of protection. (*b*) On the other hand, the economies should be internal to the industry. If the industry is not the true source of the economies but derives them from somewhere outside, then there is no case for protecting the particular industry in question. Professor Knight in his criticism of the Graham case expressed doubts concerning the existence of these economies which are external to the firm and internal to the industry and their compatibility with the assumption of competition.[1] Even Professor Viner, who would not go so far as to deny their existence, concluded that 'the scope for the application of the argument is extremely limited'.[2] Murray C. Kemp, in a recent review of the Mill-Bastable version of the 'infant industry' argument making the 'learning process' of new methods of production the essential cause of decreasing costs, also drew a parallel distinction between a firm learning internally from its own experience only and learning externally from the experiences of other firms and again stressed the special nature of the assumptions required to justify complete protection.[3]

If the free traders are lukewarm, the present-day protectionists are definitely cool towards the accepted version of the 'infant industry' argument — but for different reasons. Their position is that all the notable protectionist writers from Hamilton, List to Manoilesco have meant their arguments to be applied to the industrially under-developed countries of their times ; that, in tearing the protectionist argument from its original context and applying it to minor deviations from the static optimum on the basis of a very narrow concept of 'infant industry', the orthodox economists have, not surprisingly, reduced it to the status of a theoretical curiosity ; and that it is only when the protectionist argument is reconsidered in its proper setting of the present-day under-developed countries that it can be restored to its full stature having important applications to the broader structural and dynamic problems of the economic development of these countries.

III. COST ASPECT OF CURRENT ARGUMENTS

We can most conveniently consider the current trend in protectionist theory in terms of two main groups of arguments for

[1] F. H. Knight, 'Some Fallacies in the Interpretation of Social Cost', *Quarterly Journal of Economics*, 1924.
[2] J. Viner, *Studies in the Theory of International Trade*, pp. 478-9.
[3] M. C. Kemp, 'The Mill-Bastable Infant Industry Dogma', *Journal of Political Economy*, Feb. 1960.

protection, both of which claim to have a much broader scope than the infant industry argument and both of which are closely related to the leading theories on the economic development of the under-developed countries.

On the cost side of the question, we have a revival of the 'Manoilesco' type of argument for protection which has been stimulated by the widespread adoption of the concept of 'disguised unemployment' among the writers on the under-developed countries. This argument accepts the basis of the static optimum analysis, but maintains that social and private costs will diverge significantly over large areas of the under-developed economies due to various market imperfections and structural rigidities, particularly those affecting the allocation of labour between rural and urban sectors.

The starting-point of the argument is the assumption that in the rural sectors of the under-developed countries there is a vast surplus of labourers whose marginal product in agriculture is zero, but who are maintained by their relatives at a subsistence level approximately equal to the average product of labour in agriculture. This labour cannot, however, be attracted to industry at this sub-sistence wage although this already exceeds its marginal product in agriculture. To overcome inertia and immobility, a considerable premium would have to be added to this subsistence wage before the rural surplus labour would become available to the urban industrial sector. Thus the private transfer wage of rural surplus labour to industrial employment far exceeds its true social opportunity cost which is determined by its marginal product in agriculture which is equal to zero. In formulating the argument, some writers stress the zero marginal product of the surplus labour in agriculture while others stress the observed gap between the industrial and agricultural wages which, they maintain, may be larger than can be accounted for in terms of 'net advantages'. In any case, the con-clusion is that labour is systematically over-valued for the urban industrial sector and this should be corrected by protecting manu-facturing industry.

(*a*) Professor W. A. Lewis has given a clear formulation of the first version of the argument based on the zero marginal product of labour. 'We assume that two countries can produce the same things and trade with each other. *A* is the country where labour is scarce, *B* the country where unlimited supply of labour is available in the subsistence (food) sector. Using the classical framework for comparative costs, we write that one day's labour,

in *A*, produces 3 food or 3 cotton manufactures ;
in *B*, produces 2 food or 1 cotton manufacture.

This, of course, gives the wrong answer to the question, "Who should specialize in which?" since we have written the average instead of the marginal products. We can assume that these coincide in A and also in cotton manufacture in B. Then we should write in marginal terms that one day's labour,

in A, produces 3 food or 3 cotton manufactures;
in B, produces 0 food or 1 cotton manufacture.

B should specialize in cotton manufacture and import food. In practice, however, wages will be 2 food in B and between 3 food and 6 food in A, at which levels it will be "cheaper" for B to export food and import cotton.' [1] Thus, to correct this difference between private money costs and true social marginal costs, B should protect its textile industry.

(*b*) There are many exponents of the second version of the argument stressing the gap between wages in agriculture and industry. In so far as this gap is explained in terms of rural surplus population,[2] this is not really very different from the first version. But it is also possible to formulate the argument on the basis of an empirically observed gap between agricultural and industrial wages which may or may not be due to rural over-population. Professor E. E. Hagen has recently put forward an interesting variant of this, which seems to be based simply on 'the empirically observed fact that in any economy in which *per capita* income is rising secularly, the output of manufacturing and mining grows secularly relative to agriculture. . . . As a result of this secular trend, except in the unreal case of perfect geographic and occupational mobility of labour, wages in manufacturing industry must be higher than in agriculture. This is true even in the long run and even assuming complete absence of monopoly in all markets. . . . As a result of this wage disparity, manufacturing industry having a real comparative advantage will be undersold by imports when foreign exchanges are in equilibrium. Protection which permits such industry to exist will increase real income in the economy.' [3]

In appraising this 'Manoilesco' type of argument, we may start with a number of qualifications which reduce its range of application. Firstly, in so far as it is based on the concept of rural surplus population, it will not be applicable to the thinly populated under-developed countries such as those in Latin America, South-east Asia and

[1] W. A. Lewis, 'Economic Development with Unlimited Supplies of Labour', *Manchester School*, May 1954, p. 185.
[2] Cf. for example G. Myrdal, *An International Economy*, pp. 277-8.
[3] E. E. Hagen, 'An Economic Justification for Protection', *Quarterly Journal of Economics*, 1958, pp. 497-8.

West Africa. It is necessary to point this out, partly because of the frequent assumption that surplus labour exists in *all* under-developed countries [1] and partly because these thinly populated under-developed countries, many of which are 'export economies', are themselves very anxious to protect their manufacturing industries to reduce the ratio of their primary exports to national income. In these thinly populated countries, there may be a considerable degree of urban exploitation of the agricultural sector due to the widespread pattern of using the proceeds from Government Marketing Boards and taxation on primary exports to subsidize industry.[2] Secondly, even in the thickly populated under-developed countries, quantitative estimates of the extent of the 'surplus' population are by no means reliable and may be frequently subject to considerable exaggeration,[3] and the observed gap between agricultural and urban wages may be in part due to rational considerations and 'net advantages' which have not been fully taken into account.[4]

Next, let us accept that there is a genuine over-valuation of labour for the manufacturing sector due to surplus population, or to Professor Hagen's growth mechanism or to any other cause. However, this by itself does not provide a conclusive argument for protection. Labour is merely one of the factors of production and in particular it is widely recognized that rates of interest are much higher and capital is more 'over-valued' in the rural sectors of the under-developed countries than in the urban industrial sectors. Thus the question whether manufacturing costs as a whole are over-valued relatively to agricultural costs will depend on the relative capital-labour ratios in the two sectors and the relative sizes of the wage and the interest gaps. The effects in the opposite direction of the higher rate of interest in the rural sector and the higher capital-labour ratio in the urban industrial sector (not to speak of other advantages such as better transport and public utility services) may more than counterbalance the handicap which the latter may suffer due to 'over-valued' labour. In so far as the champions of the under-developed countries recognize these opposite effects, their remedy would seem to be to recommend both protection for the industrial sector and cheaper loans for the rural sector, thus having the best of both worlds, but adding to the pressure of inflation and rising prices which these countries are already suffering.[5]

[1] E.g. Myrdal, *op. cit.* p. 278.
[2] See Viner's trenchant remarks on the urban exploitation of the rural sectors in such countries, *International Trade and Economic Development*, p. 51.
[3] Cf. Doreen Warriner, *Land Reform and Economic Development*, Cairo, 1955, pp. 25-6.   [4] Viner, *op. cit.* pp. 47-9.
[5] It is sometimes alleged that, even in the urban industrial sectors, it is only the *foreign* entrepreneurs who enjoy cheap credit facilities from the banks, while

Finally, we may question how far the complex historical and dynamic factors which enter into the movement of labour from the subsistence agricultural sector to the urban industrial sector can be satisfactorily analysed in terms of a rather simplified static analysis. First, it is not realistic at all to speak of the two types of labour in the two sectors as though they were a homogeneous factor, when complex changes involving the way of life, attitudes, rhythm of work, etc., have to take place before an agricultural worker from the traditional rural society can become even an unskilled worker in an urban industrial sector.[1] Next we may refer to the only large-scale historical experience which the tropical under-developed countries had of transferring labour from subsistence agriculture to wage employment — viz. to the plantations and mines in the export sectors. Here, leaving aside the complication of the introduction of cheap immigrant labour from abroad, the existence of an indigenous subsistence agricultural sector seems to have worked, at least in the transition stage, for the *lowering* of the wage in the mines and plantations. The migrant labourers who still had a foothold in the rural society and were therefore willing to accept low money wages which they regarded merely as a subsidiary source of income ; the freezing of 'customary' wage rates at the initial level ; and the persistence of the 'cheap labour' policy are familiar experiences of these under-developed countries.[2] Here no one has suggested that the mines and plantations should be subsidized because labour was 'over-valued', although the mine and plantation owners in fact complained that the raw labour was 'dear' even at the low wage. On the contrary, many writers on the under-developed countries, including the leading exponents of the protectionist argument,[3] have complained that the colonial powers have been able to maintain low wages in the mines and plantations by neglecting and impoverishing the subsistence agricultural sector. Yet within the framework of the static optimum analysis, the essential situation governing the structure of money wages and productivities in the under-developed countries is exactly the same whether we are

indigenous entrepreneurs have to pay higher rates of interest. Whatever the truth of this allegation, it does not affect the point that even an indigenous industrial entrepreneur is likely to be able to borrow at a lower rate of interest than the indigenous peasant.

[1] This is not to deny the possibility or desirability of training rural labour for industrial employment. In fact the creation of a trained labour force is the most important type of external economy to be claimed by manufacturing industries. But this gets us back to the 'infant industry' argument proper and we do not need a separate 'Manoilesco' argument to stress this point.

[2] For a fuller treatment at this point see H. Myint, 'The Gains from International Trade and the Backward Countries', *Review of Economic Studies*, Vol. xxii, No. 2, pp. 134-6.   [3] Cf. Lewis, *loc. cit.* pp. 149-50.

thinking of the transfer of agricultural labour from the subsistence sector to the manufacturing sector or to the mines and plantations. In terms of the static analysis we are indifferent whether labour is employed in peasant agriculture, or in mines or plantations or in urban manufacturing industry, provided the static social productivities are equated to wages in these occupations. Thus the divergence between social and private marginal costs due to the 'over-valuation' of labour in wage employment would apply both to manufacturing industry and to mines and plantations : [1] and in both cases it may be corrected either by protecting (or subsidizing) the sectors in which labour is employed on a money wage basis or by subsidizing various policies to raise the productivity of labour in the non-wage subsistence agricultural sector so that it is no longer 'over-valued' in the money wage sector. Therefore, in order to argue that this wage-productivity gap between the subsistence agricultural sector and the urban industrial sector should be corrected only by subsidising or protecting the latter, we need to go beyond the static optimum analysis and postulate that the manufacturing sector is more desirable than agriculture on some other grounds, e.g. its broader dynamic effects in stimulating economic development.

IV. DEMAND ASPECTS OF CURRENT ARGUMENTS

We may now turn to the second group of protectionist arguments which are concerned with the demand aspect of the question and with the enlargement of the domestic markets of the under-developed countries. Many of these arguments are amorphous and are concerned only indirectly or implicitly with protection. But it is worth trying to piece them together as they exert a pervasive influence on current protectionist thinking in relation to the under-developed countries. The starting-point of these arguments is stated in general terms by Professor Myrdal as follows : 'One of the difficulties of industrial development in under-developed countries, and one of the great hindrances to giving real momentum to a development policy, is that internal demand must be built up simultaneously with supply. The unlikelihood or, anyhow, the exasperating slowness of any self-engendered process of "natural growth" offers a main explanation why sustained stagnation becomes a sort of natural equilibrium and why policy interventions are called for. Indeed the entire idea of a policy of economic development is to break away

---

[1] Professor Hagen explicitly includes mines under the heading of 'industry', *loc. cit.* p. 490.

from this low-level equilibrium. Now import restrictions afford a means of by-passing altogether the process of "natural growth" and creating at once the necessary demand for a particular domestic industry. They create a sizeable internal demand for a specific commodity, without the necessity of waiting for the slow and difficult growth of the entire economy.' [1]

For the further development of this idea of imports as the creator of potential domestic markets, we may turn to Professor Hirschman. 'But imports still provide the safest, most incontrovertible proof that the market is there. Moreover, they condition the consumer to the product, breaking down his initial resistance. Imports thus reconnoitre and map out the country's demand ; they reduce uncertainty and reduce selling costs at the same time, thereby bringing perceptibly closer the point at which domestic production can be economically started.' [2] Professor Hirschman uses a somewhat different frame of reference from Professor Myrdal. He starts, not from a 'low-level equilibrium', but from a situation where there is already some autonomous growth of income and exports and is interested in protection only in so far as it enlarges the size of the domestic market for a particular import, thereby inducing further investment in the setting-up of an import-substitute industry. Professor Hirschman's argument may be best summarized in terms of his input-output model with fixed coefficients which is 'dis-aggregated' for imports so that the total direct and indirect imports at a given income level are clearly shown as $M_1, M_2 \ldots M_k$. As income automatically expands the M's will expand so that sooner or later the domestic market for one of the exports, say M_1, crosses its threshold T_1 which is determined by the minimum economic size of domestic production for it and so on along the line. Now under ideal conditions, as soon as the demand for a particular import crosses the threshold of its domestic production it will cease to be imported, as private entrepreneurs will now find it worth their while to set up the import-substitute industry. But in the realistic conditions of the under-developed countries, this induced-investment mechanism is not likely to work smoothly. Further, at any given moment of time we may not find any import which has actually crossed the threshold but only those which are approaching it and are expected to cross it in the near future. In a slow-moving economy, Professor Hirschman is willing to consider protection to help those industries which are on or near the threshold, provided protection is given to one industry at a time.

[1] G. Myrdal, *An International Economy*, p. 276.
[2] A. O. Hirschman, *The Strategy of Economic Development*, p. 121.

The first difficulty in this argument is the concept of the 'threshold' to be determined by the minimum economic size of production. This involves assumptions made to give a preponderant weight to technical factors, viz. (1) that it is possible to determine the minimum economic size of a new industry (which is in fact a single factory) by studying the conditions governing it in other countries where the general economic conditions, relative factor supplies, etc., may be quite different; and (2) that once this minimum size is attained, the domestic producer of the import-substitute commodity can compete with foreign producers whose scale of production is likely to be much larger. At first sight, this amounts to a denial of the comparative costs doctrine that the cost of producing a given product is likely to differ in different countries due to differences in factor endowments or factor productivities. But it is not too implausible when we remember that in many under-developed countries, setting up new industries frequently means importing from a common source not only all the equipment, but also foreign managers and many of the semi-finished materials and parts. Thus the concept of a 'threshold' may have a greater degree of validity than an economist is normally inclined to believe; at least, for the range of light consumers' goods industries which are likely to be set up in the under-developed countries. As for the second question, whether a fairly small-sized domestic industry is likely to be able to compete with its large-scale foreign competitors, there is some support for the view that the cost curves in manufacturing industries, at least in the U.S., are shaped like either a very flat U (‿‿‿‿) or a J on its side (‿‿‿‿).[1] Here again the argument comes out much better than at first sight.

The second difficulty is somewhat more serious from the point of view of many writers on the under-developed countries. They would say that Hirschman's model works on the assumption that there is already some autonomous expansion in incomes and exports whereas the real problem facing the under-developed countries is the 'low-level equilibrium' with small domestic markets, and low incomes, combined with a world demand for their primary exports which (with a few exceptions like petroleum) is *not* autonomously expanding. Here Professor Nurkse in particular reiterated the view that while in the nineteenth century the industrial centres of the world transmitted their economic growth to the periphery of the under-developed countries by a vigorous expansion in demand for primary products, this is no longer true at present, and that this relative decline in world trade in primary products may be attributed

[1] Joe S. Bain, *Industrial Organization*, pp. 153-5.

to various factors, mainly on the demand side, such as the special position of the United States as the world's dominant economy, the low income elasticity of demand for primary exports, the shift in the industrial centres from light to heavy engineering and to chemical industries with a lower raw material content, the invention of synthetic substitutes for raw materials, etc.[1]

It is to meet this problem of trying to find a substitute for the nineteenth-century dynamic mechanism of growth through an expansion in primary exports that Professor Nurkse put forward his version of the doctrine of 'balanced growth'. 'Now domestic markets are limited because of mass poverty due to low productivity. Private investment in any single industry considered by itself is discouraged by the smallness of the existing market . . . the solution seems to be a balanced pattern of investment in a number of different industries so that people working more productively with more capital and improved techniques become each other's customers. In the absence of vigorous upward shifts in the world demand for exports of primary products, a low-income country through a process of diversified growth can seek to bring upward shifts in domestic demand schedules by means of increased productivity and therefore increased real purchasing power. In this way, a pattern of mutually supporting investments in different lines of production can enlarge the size of the market and help fill the vacuum in the domestic economy.' [2]

This doctrine of 'balanced growth' designed for the 'closed' economy has somewhat equivocal implications for the protectionist argument. In the version expounded particularly by Professor Nurkse and Professor Lewis, agriculture is explicitly included as one of the 'industries'; and the export sector, the domestic agricultural sector and the domestic manufacturing sector are to be expanded in balanced proportions according to the relative expansion in demand expected in each sector.[3] Stated in this way, the 'balanced growth' doctrine can be used as a criticism of those pro-trade economists who mistake the special dynamic or growth-transmitting aspect of the nineteenth-century international trade for the general static gains from international specialization and continue

[1] R. Nurkse, 'Some International Aspects of Economic Development', *American Economic Review*, May 1952; and 'The Conflict between "Balanced Growth" and International Specialisation', published by Istanbul and Ankara Universities (to be referred to hereafter as the 'Istanbul Lecture'); and 'The Trade of Poor Countries and the International Economics of Growth', a lecture given at the Institut de Science Économique Appliqué, Paris, 1958.

[2] R. Nurkse, Istanbul Lecture, pp. 8-10.

[3] R. Nurkse, *ibid.* pp. 12 and 16; W. A. Lewis, *Theory of Economic Growth*, pp. 277-83.

to urge the under-developed countries to concentrate on their export of primary products in the face of a passive or declining world demand for these products. On the other hand, the same doctrine can also be used as a criticism of one-sided concentration or industrialization : for, in order to create the demand for domestic manufactures, domestic agriculture should also be expanded in a balanced proportion. But this only deals with the allocation of resources on the production side. What about the imports and the possible inflation and balance of payments pressure of a 'balanced-growth' programme ? Here Professor Nurkse reluctantly admitted that 'while it is not to be denied that import restriction can help a policy of domestic balanced investment', it should be used very sparingly because of its tendency to encourage costly and inefficient production of import substitutes. 'Import restrictions imposed in spite of such unfavourable effects can be justified only on the grounds of future benefits, which is the infant industry argument for protection.'[1] Professor Lewis also prefers to use either the 'infant industry' argument or the 'disguised unemployment' argument rather than the 'balanced growth' argument for protection, but has a keener appreciation of the possibility that a balanced growth programme might lead to inflationary pressure on balance of payments requiring import controls to economize foreign exchange rather than to protect domestic industry.[2]

But there is, however, a narrower and incidentally older version of the 'balanced growth' doctrine which is meant to be regarded as a method of industrialization to be applied *inside* the manufacturing sector only.[3] This version is favoured by those who believe that the under-developed countries are currently starting from a position not of balance, but of extreme imbalance amounting to a 'structural disequilibrium' which has to be corrected by a concentrated effort to expand the manufacturing sector before we can proceed along the path of inter-sectoral balanced growth. Some of them would argue that this 'structural disequilibrium' exists not only in over-populated countries with rural 'disguised unemployment' but also in thinly populated 'export economies', as the result of the 'export-bias' of the nineteenth-century pattern of international trade and investment.

The export-bias argument may be summarized as follows. The expanding world market for primary products contrasted with the very small domestic markets for manufactures in the under-developed

---

[1] R. Nurkse, Istanbul Lecture, pp. 17-18.
[2] W. A. Lewis, *op. cit.* pp. 348-9 ; pp. 282-3 ; pp. 387-8.
[3] Cf. P. N. Rosenstein-Rodan, 'Problems of Industrialisation of E. and S.E. Europe', *Economic Journal*, 1943.

countries first attracted foreign capital and enterprise into their export sectors, entirely by passing their domestic sectors. But this very process aggravated the initial disparity in the productivity of resources between the two sectors and further served to divert, not only foreign, but also indigenous, capital and enterprise from the domestic to the export sector. As the result of this cumulative bias in development, the export economies now have a high rate of export to national income and a 'dualistic economic structure' with the highly specialized and technically advanced export sector existing side by side with the backward domestic sector. This means that they not only suffer from a high degree of instability through their fluctuating and frequently deteriorating terms of trade but also are unable to shift resources easily from the export to the domestic sectors to adjust to the changing terms of trade.[1] Thus in order to correct this cumulative export-bias, it may be necessary to protect, not one or two industries, but a fairly large group of industries which would form a sort of 'infant' manufacturing sector.

It may be noted that although this argument uses the disparity in the sizes of the domestic and the export markets of the under-developed countries to trigger off the process of cumulative bias, the essential mechanism which is supposed to cause the bias is the 'wrong' allocation of the flow of resources over a period of time between the export and the domestic sectors. Thus this 'export bias' thesis turns out to be a species of the familiar argument based on the divergence between social and private products. At first sight, therefore, it seems that the purely demand type of protectionist argument has not been strengthened by the shift from the broader inter-sectoral version of 'balanced growth' to the narrower version of the doctrine confining it within the manufacturing sector. We do not seem to have progressed beyond the propositions conceded by Professor Nurkse : viz. (i) that the taking over of ready-made markets for imports by domestic import-substitute industries will undoubtedly help a 'balanced growth' programme (of either version) ; (ii) that, nevertheless, we cannot entirely rely on the balanced-growth principle (in its narrower version) to show convincingly that instead of protecting one industry at a time it is better to protect a group of industries simultaneously because of the external economies and complementarities arising only from the demand side ; and (iii) that therefore, in order to justify the protection of a group of in-dustries, we shall have to fall back on the 'infant industry' argument

[1] The most articulate exponent of this argument is H. W. Singer, 'The Dis-tribution of Gains between Investing and Borrowing Countries', *American Economic Review*, Papers and Proceedings, May 1950, pp. 473 *et seq.* Dr. Singer, however, is rather silent on the protection issue.

to show that there are substantial external economies on the cost side likely to accrue to the group as a whole.

But on further examination, the demand side of the protectionist argument has in fact made some progress. This can be seen by having a closer look at the type of industries which balanced-growth theorists choose to set up simultaneously as a group. They would advocate that the group should be selected on a horizontal basis to consist of light consumers' goods industries for two reasons. (1) Firstly, these industries most readily create a market for each others' products and lighten the burden of the sacrifice required by the in-dustrialization process. (2) Secondly, the under-developed countries can still enjoy the advantages of international division of labour by producing, and even exporting, the simpler manufactured goods and importing heavy capital goods which require more complicated and capital-intensive methods of manufacture.[1] But given the horizontal grouping of light consumers' goods industries, we can say two things about the type of external economies on the cost side which they are likely to generate for each other. Firstly, the types of economies (though not necessarily their quantitative magnitude) are much the same as those recognized by the traditional 'infant industry' argument such as the creation of a growing pool of skilled industrial labour, the overcoming of the 'indivisibilities' in the pro-vision of various 'social overhead' facilities such as power, transport, etc. Secondly, and what is more important for our argument, these external economies are not likely to be specific but may be generated without glaring quantitative differences by almost any type of light industries. Thus in trying to select a sub-set of industries for pro-tection, we shall have to put a greater weight on the demand factors, and select that group which contains those commodities with the highest income elasticities and cross elasticities (or complementarities) of demand.

But for a more radical development of the demand approach to industrialization, we shall have to go to critics of the balanced-growth approach such as Professor Marcus Fleming and Professor Hirschman. Professor Marcus Fleming in his critique of the balanced-growth doctrine has argued that in any realistic situation where the supplies of labour, capital and other resources are not perfectly elastic, the simultaneous setting-up of a group of light consumers' goods industries is likely to result in the external dis-economies for each other through their competition for the limited

---

[1] On this basis, Professor Myrdal has emphasized that protection adopted by the under-developed countries will not reduce the world volume of trade, but merely shift the pattern of the advanced countries exports from light consumers' goods to heavy capital goods.

supplies of resources and that these diseconomies are likely to outweigh the external economies which such a horizontally selected group of industries is likely to generate for itself. He suggests that more substantial economies might be obtained by a *vertical group* of industries at different stages of production, each of which is the other's supplier or customer.[1] This concept of vertical linkages between different industries has been systematically developed by Professor Hirschman and used as the basis of his unbalanced-growth approach to economic development.[2] Professor Hirschman argues that the balanced-growth approach is unsatisfactory not only because of the inelastic supply of certain factors, notably entrepreneurs required to run a whole flock of new industries, but also because its concept of the nature of economic development is basically wrong. Economic development, according to him, is not a once-over shift from 'low-level equilibrium' to a 'balanced growth' equilibrium and then coming to a stop at this plateau of a higher level of income. Rather it should be a continuous process, generated and sustained by a chain of disequilibria and it should be the aim of economic development policy to try to prolong and keep alive this disequilibrium process by a series of autonomous investments injected into strategic places in the economic structure which will lead to the maximum amount of imbalances inducing further investments. An autonomous investment in a given industry can induce further investments through the pressure of excess demand on the industries which are its suppliers. It can also induce investment through the pressure of excess supply on the industries who are its customers. Ideally, we should start with an autonomous investment in an industry which is capable of generating induced investments in both directions on its suppliers and on its customers ; but if that is not available we should start by generating the pressure of *excess demand* which is to be regarded as a more powerful and reliable force.[3]

Applying this approach to international trade, Professor Hirschman points out that the typical light consumers' goods industries of the under-developed countries are what may be described as the 'finishing-touches' industries, importing not only machinery, but also materials which are semi-processed or frequently very nearly completely processed. Thus the domestic net value added consists mainly of the wages of the workers engaged in giving the 'finishing touches' to the imported materials so that a large proportion of

[1] J. M. Fleming, 'External Economies and the Doctrine of Balanced Growth', *Economic Journal*, June 1955.

[2] A. O. Hirschman, *Strategy of Economic Development*, especially Chapter 3, etc.

[3] Hirschman, *ibid.* pp. 116-17.

the expansion in the demand for the product of these 'domestic' industries leaks out in the form of further imports of materials and machinery from abroad.   In many under-developed countries the normal process of economic development in fact consists in industrialization working its way backward from the 'finishing-touches' stage to the domestic production of intermediate, and finally to that of basic industrial materials.   But this process of introducing industry by small successive bits of domestic value-added may be too slow to pay off and the under-developed country may try to bite off a somewhat larger piece of value — added by jumping a few stages backwards from the 'finishing-touches' stage to some intermediate stage which may also open out a wider network of linkage effects with other industries.

In so far as Professor Hirschman's approach can be used in support of the protectionist case, it is notable on two counts. Firstly, if we accept the Fleming-Hirschman view that the *vertical* transmission of external economies between different stages of industries is likely to be more powerful than the horizontal transmission of external economies between a group of light consumers' goods industries, we are led to consider a protectionist policy 'in depth' as contrasted with a protectionist policy 'in breadth' suggested by the balanced-growth approach. A policy of protection 'in depth' cannot be dismissed particularly for a large under-developed country like India with a population pressure requiring heroic methods of economic development. Secondly, and more generally, Professor Hirschman's approach has the merit of putting forward, explicitly and at a formal level, a basic proposition which has been implied in very general terms in most protectionist arguments : viz. that manufacturing industry is to be preferred to agriculture, not because it is supposed to be more 'productive', not because there are 'divergences' from the optimum and deviations from the balanced-growth path, but simply because it is likely to be a more powerful generator of induced investment through the vertical linkage effects.[1] Now, one may challenge Professor Hirschman's generalizations at the empirical level by pointing out various exceptions : for instance, why should not an improved method of agriculture using fertilizers and machinery generate as much induced investment, say in the chemical and engineering industries, as any manufacturing industry ? But logically, it is a notable step to strike out boldly to the position that manufacturing industry is to be preferred to agriculture because of its dynamic (but not conclusively demonstrable) effects in stimulating economic development. This is perhaps as far as we can usefully

[1] Hirschman, *Strategy of Economic Development*, pp. 109-10.

go at the present stage of development of economic analysis.[1] Looking back, we can now appreciate the difference between Professor Hirschman's approach and many of the other arguments on protection which fail to live up to their claim to be based on 'dynamic' considerations of economic growth because, at some stage or other, they fall back on the extended applications of concepts such as the deviation from the optimum or the balanced-growth equilibrium which essentially belong to the framework of static analysis.

V. PROTECTION VERSUS OVER-ALL BALANCE-GROWTH DEVELOPMENT PLANNING

Let us now turn to the practical difficulties of pursuing an effective protectionist policy in the setting of the present-day under-developed countries. The orthodox economists considered the question of protection in a situation where free trade conditions prevailed in the other parts of the economy and where the balance of payments is in equilibrium. In contrast, in the present-day under-developed countries we start from a situation which is already rife with all types of control on international trade, particularly with direct quantitative restrictions of imports. Typically, these quantitative restrictions have been imposed on an *ad hoc* basis and allowed to spread over the whole range of imports to ease foreign exchange difficulties. These foreign exchange difficulties in their turn arise from the inflationary pressure exerted by investment programmes for economic development. The characteristic results are not only a rising general price level and an all-round premium on all imported goods, but also distorted price differentials between different types of imports haphazardly reflecting short run and speculative factors.

There are a number of difficulties in trying to pursue an effective protectionist policy in such a setting. (1) Firstly, however broadly we may choose to define the area for protection, a protectionist policy remains essentially a method of selective encouragement of a given sector of the economy by conferring on it a sectional price increase. Thus in order to make protection effective, the price-differential in the protected sector must be maintained in sharp

[1] Beyond this we get into the broader sociological generalizations concerning the 'educative' effects of manufacturing industry and its superiority in providing 'the growing points for increased technical knowledge, urban education, the dynamism and resilience that goes with urban civilization', etc. Cf. H. W. Singer, 'The Distribution of Gains between Investing and Borrowing Countries', *American Economic Review*, Papers and Proceedings, May 1950, pp. 476-7.

relief for some time and not allowed to be neutralized by random price rises in the non-protected sectors. It is difficult to fulfil this condition when the inflationary pressure is continually threatening to boil over with a further round of import restrictions. (2) Secondly, in order to protect a given sector effectively, it is necessary to be able to import the non-protected items freely and easily. This is fairly obvious where these non-protected items happen to be machinery and materials needed by the protected industries. But this requirement stands even when the non-protected items are other consumer goods, because an unintended rise in their prices might weaken the stimulus to the protected industries and might also possibly draw away the scarce resources from them. Thus, for instance, the restrictions on imported luxuries frequently lead to the setting-up of import substitute industries for these luxuries where non-luxury goods with a wider domestic market might have been a more suitable candidate for protection. But again this liberalization of the import of the non-protected items is not possible where a large balance of payments deficit cannot be met except by an all-round restriction of imports. (3) Thirdly, even assuming the existence of 'disguised unemployment', the protected sector cannot expand without attracting the scarce capital and entrepreneurial resources from the rest of the economy. But, given inflation and a general shortage of imported goods, capital and enterprise tend to be attracted into trading and speculation in these scarce imports, particularly so when, due to the inefficiency or corruption in import controls, large monopoly profits can be made in these activities.[1]

Some under-developed countries have attempted to meet these difficulties by imbedding permanent tariffs on some selected industries amongst the quantitative controls over all imports. The idea here is to try to induce the more far-sighted entrepreneurs into the selected industries by offering a permanent tariff shelter as distinct from the quantitative controls which are supposed to be temporary. The success of such a policy depends on how far the balance of payments pressure and the general premium on imports can be kept under reasonable control. During an export boom which expands the foreign exchange receipts of the under-developed countries, such a policy can claim a double advantage. Firstly, the

---

[1] In many under-developed countries such as in South-east Asia, where the export-import trade has been in the hands of foreigners, the governments use import control and licensing as a weapon to replace the foreign merchants by indigenous merchants. Thus the scarce import licences are not auctioned to the highest bidders for fear that they would go into the hands of the more efficient foreign merchants, but are rationed out somewhat haphazardly to a privileged class of indigenous merchants who frequently make their monopoly profits not so much by selling the imports as by selling the import licences.

protected industries will enjoy an increase in price differential because the prices of the non-protected imports will be lowered as the authorities feel able to relax the temporary restrictions on them. Secondly, the increase in foreign exchange earnings will ease the supply of investible funds for the protected industries. Unfortunately, given the passive trend in the world demand for primary products, what tends to happen more frequently is that due to severity of the quantitative restrictions, the rise in the prices of the 'non-protected' imports soon outstrips the height of the fixed tariff in the 'protected' industries, so that quantitative restrictions have to be clamped down on the latter also on top of formal tariffs. Since these restrictions look like being continued indefinitely, it becomes somewhat academic to draw a distinction between 'permanent' and 'temporary' shelter against foreign competition. Even if things do not reach such a pass, it is still rather doubtful whether the somewhat reduced price differential which can be offered even by a high permanent tariff imbedded amongst quantitative restrictions is sufficient to overcome the difficulties we have listed.[1]

Now the basic and continuing cause of inflation and balance of payments difficulties in the under-developed countries must be attributed directly or indirectly to their economic development plans along 'balanced-growth' lines requiring an all-out drive for a high percentage ratio of aggregate investment to national income. Theoretically, of course, the balance of payments difficulties can be kept under reasonable control by stricter fiscal and monetary policy. But in practice, in many under-developed countries, investment programmes for economic development tend to outstrip the amount of savings which can be mobilized with the existing administrative machinery so that recurring foreign exchange crises seem unavoidable. We are then faced with an important practical question : How far is an effective protectionist policy compatible with the type of over-all economic development planning attempted in most under-developed countries ?

---

[1] It may be asked whether all-round quantitative restrictions on imports even if they do not give special encouragement to any particular branch of industry might nevertheless encourage resources to move generally from export production to domestic import-substitute industries. If what is desired is a uniform height of protection in all imports, it would be more satisfactory to impose an *ad valorem* tax on all imports or adopt multiple foreign exchange rates, or simply devalue. The imposition of all-round quantitative restrictions, although it has the same general effect, tends to be accompanied by considerable short-run fluctuations between the relative prices of different imports and thus increases the risks to an entrepreneur contemplating the setting up of an import-substitute industry. But however broadly we define the 'infant' manufacturing sector, an effective protectionist policy would have to be more selective than a uniform *ad valorem* tax on all imports.

To a large extent this is really a conflict between the 'balanced-growth' and the 'unbalanced-growth' approach to economic development in another form. If we believe that economic development can be achieved only by a critical minimum amount of investment to break away from the 'low-level equilibrium' and to push ahead simultaneously on all fronts, then we should be prepared to accept a considerable amount of inflationary pressure and quantitative restrictions of imports. This should be regarded as a necessary consequence of the 'big push' when the indivisible critical minimum amount of investment required happens to exceed total savings, including the savings potential from the use of disguised unemployment. Here our main hope is that the inflation will be 'self-destroying' when the forced investment dramatically expands the national output, and the 'infant economy' as a whole gets over the hump. If we seriously believe in this approach to economic development, then we should be prepared to give up pursuing a serious protectionist policy rather than forgo the quantitative restrictions on imports which offer the most important and flexible instrument of control over the foreign exchange accounts of the developing economy. If, on the other hand, we believe that economic development can be more effectively pursued by concentrating on certain strategic sectors instead of trying to push ahead on all fronts, a protectionist policy would appear to be the most promising instrument of such an approach. If inflationary pressure and quantitative restrictions on imports interfere with an effective pursuit of a protectionist policy, then we should be prepared to cut down the attempted rate of over-all investment and pursue a fairly conservative monetary policy. We should then be in a position to liberalize the imports in non-protected sectors and confine trade restrictions and tariffs to certain selected sectors, thus giving them a maximum stimulus. Behind this conflict between the balanced- and the unbalanced-growth approach there is also the important further conflict between the reliance on the market mechanism implied by the protectionist policy, and its replacement by direct controls implied by the over-all type of planning.

The existence of this conflict at the practical level between an effective protectionist policy and the over-all economic development planning of the type favoured by many under-developed countries has been obscured by writers who are firmly attached to both types of policies and try to compromise between their conflicting pulls. But there is no doubt that this conflict is more important and more immediate in the setting of the present-day under-developed countries than the traditional conflict between protection and free trade.

To round off our argument, let us conclude with a very brief comment on the traditional free-trade-protection issue. Starting from the typical situation of the under-developed countries in which all types of controls, including quantitative controls, have been allowed to spread promiscuously over all international transactions, it is difficult to imagine wiping the slate clean and returning to the free traders' basic point of reference, viz. the ideal free trade equilibrium. Further, if we are concerned not only with static allocative efficiency but with promoting economic development, it is difficult not to share Professor Nurkse's doubts whether the advantages of international specialization by itself (whatever its static gains) are sufficient to provide a powerful enough dynamic mechanism in the existing passive condition of world demand for primary products. Thus we are led to view with some leniency the traditional evils of protection emphasized by the orthodox economists. Firstly the difficulties of selecting singly the right industry to protect are reduced when we are prepared to experiment with a fairly large group among which we may have a greater chance of picking some winners. The free traders may reply that the chance of picking the losers will also be increased and thus the wastage from misallocation of resources will be correspondingly greater. But if we use as our point of reference the existing situation in the under-developed countries, such wastages already exist so that the net cost of a protectionist policy is small. It may therefore be worth the gamble when the winners may bring us a very considerable dynamic impetus for the further development of the economy. Next, the evils of the tariff-sheltered monopolies are not too frightening when we start from a situation where pure monopoly profits are already reaped in merchandise trading in imports and where the continuance of the haphazard and indiscriminate import controls perpetuates these large trading profits. From a dynamic point of view, a monopolistic class of manufacturers may be preferable to a monopolistic class of traders, particularly for its more favourable effect on the rate of investment. While profits in trading are likely to trickle only slowly into manufacturing industry, profits made inside the manufacturing sector are likely to be more easily reinvested. This process may perhaps also encourage a new and vigorous class of entrepreneurs with an entirely different outlook from the traditional mentality of the traders. There finally remains the difficulty of ever removing the tariffs when these have outgrown their use. This evil cannot be avoided and our only consolation is that a protectionist policy is merely replacing the 'temporary' quantitative controls on imports which are, in practice, equally likely to be permanent.

Chapter 8

REGIONAL FREE TRADE: TRADE-CREATING AND TRADE-DIVERTING EFFECTS OF POLITICAL, COMMERCIAL AND MONETARY AREAS

BY

H. H. LIESNER
University of Cambridge

I. INTRODUCTION

THE analysis of economic unions should rightly be regarded as a relatively new branch of the science. Its existence is a response to the post-war popularity of the concept of regionalism; this in turn was both a defence mechanism against adverse economic conditions, and a practical manifestation of changed political aims and ideas.

The issues raised by the formation of an economic union may be conveniently grouped under two broad headings, (i) the welfare effects of the union in the partner countries as well as in the rest of the world, and (ii) the practical problems of creating conditions conducive to the attainment of these welfare ends. The two main sections of this paper will deal briefly with each of these groups of issues in turn. It may be added at this early stage that the discussion will confine itself to the issues arising in connection with 'commercial areas', for this itself is a subject which can hardly be dealt with adequately within the confines of a single paper. In other words, the special problems which a political or monetary area may raise will not be discussed.

II. WELFARE EFFECTS OF ECONOMIC UNION

The theory of customs unions has been defined as 'that branch of tariff theory which deals with the (welfare) effects of geographically discriminatory changes in trade barriers'.[1] The point of departure

[1] R. G. Lipsey, 'The Theory of Customs Unions: a General Survey', *Economic Journal*, Vol. lxx, No. 279 (Sept. 1960), p. 496. This article has been the natural starting-point for section II of the present paper.

of the analysis was Viner's rejection of the apparently self-evident argument that a customs union — a move towards free trade — would necessarily also imply a move towards an improved distribution of world resources.[1] Viner coined the terms 'trade creation' and 'trade diversion' in order to classify the possible effects of the formation of an economic union into two groups. In the first case the union leads to a greater degree of division of labour between the partner countries, each specializing on those commodities in which it is at a comparative cost advantage and substituting imports for those domestic goods in the production of which it is relatively inefficient; in other words, the partner countries will come to rely more heavily upon foreign supplies. This is the case of trade creation. In the case of trade diversion the discriminatory reduction of tariffs encourages the member countries to buy from each other the goods which they had hitherto purchased from third countries outside the union. As third-country commodities were preferred at the old non-discriminatory trade barriers, this diversion of trade represents a shift towards higher-cost sources of supply; from this Viner deduced that a trade-creating customs union will increase world welfare, whereas a trade-diverting one will decrease it.

Viner implicitly assumed that supply elasticities were infinite and demand elasticities zero. His concentration on inter-country substitution and the complete neglect of inter-commodity substitution provided the starting-point for a further development of the theory. This was undertaken independently by J. E. Meade,[2] F. Gehrels[3] and R. G. Lipsey[4] and in essence consisted of the recognition of the fact that the lowering of consumers' prices which takes place with trade diversion as well as with trade creation would permit an expanded consumption of commodities which the tariff had previously made artificially scarce. This means, in the case of trade diversion, that a favourable consumption effect has to be placed against the loss due to the switch to higher-cost sources of supply and that trade diversion will not necessarily lead to a decrease of welfare, though a full appreciation of welfare gains and losses must also include the unfavourable effect of a possible decrease in the consumption of commodities still subject to tariff restriction (i.e. of imports from third countries).[5] One might add that in the Viner

[1] J. Viner, *The Customs Union Issue*, New York and London, 1950, Chapter 4.
[2] *The Theory of Customs Unions*, Amsterdam, 1956.
[3] 'Customs Unions from a Single Country Viewpoint', *Review of Economic Studies*, Vol. xxiv (1), No. 63, pp. 61-4.
[4] 'The Theory of Customs Unions : Trade Diversion and Welfare', *Economica*, Vol. xxiv, No. 93 (Feb. 1957), pp. 40-6.
[5] In other words, the full consumption effect is made up of two elements — the gain from larger consumption of (previously taxed) imports from the partner

case (supply elasticities = infinity, demand elasticities = zero) the increase of consumers' surplus will be entirely at the expense of lower government revenue [1] and will therefore be offset either by a reduction in government services or by higher taxes elsewhere. Given Viner's restrictive assumptions, therefore, his conclusions stand.

Once this level of sophistication is reached, the theory becomes more and more refined, and, as usually happens, the price of refinement is the sacrifice of general conclusions which will hold in every case.[2] However, the original Viner criteria are still useful in so far as a customs union which mainly creates trade is more likely to lead to an increase of economic welfare than a customs union which has large trade-diverting effects. Whether trade creation rather than trade diversion will take place depends in turn upon a number of factors; perhaps the most important of them is the 'degree of rivalry of the member countries with respect to *protected* industries prior to customs union'.[3] The wider is the range of industries producing similar goods under tariff protection, the greater the elements of trade creation and the smaller the element of trade diversion, and vice versa.

Although it can rightly be claimed that the formal theory of customs unions as developed over the last twelve years has added considerably to our appreciation of the problems and issues involved, there can also be no doubt that at least two major defects remain: (i) the theory rests on unsatisfactory premises, and, in particular, upon the assumption that other optimum conditions are satisfied, and (ii) the theory is almost entirely confined to a consideration of static welfare effects and has little to say on such important questions as the effect of the formation of a customs union upon the rate of economic growth in the member countries (combined as well as taken separately). Both defects reflect, of course, similar shortcomings in the general body of international trade theory and thus do not occasion any surprise. However, attempts have been made to deal in a rough-and-ready sort of way with some of the points

country and the loss from reduced consumption of third country imports which are still subject to duty. On balance, the consumption effect may therefore be negative, in which case the Viner-type trade-diversion loss understates the unfavourable effect of the customs union.

[1] The loss of government revenue will in fact always be greater than the gain in consumers' surplus.

[2] Examples of such refinements can be found in R. G. Lipsey, *The Theory of Customs Unions : a General Equilibrium Analysis*, unpublished University of London Ph.D. thesis ; J. E. Meade, *op. cit.* ; and H. G. Johnson, 'Discriminatory Tariff Reduction : a Marshallian Analysis', *Indian Journal of Economics*, Vol. xxxviii, No. 148 (July 1957), pp. 39-47, and 'Marshallian Analysis of Discriminatory Tariff Reduction : an Extension', *Indian Journal of Economics*, Vol. xxxix, No. 153 (Oct. 1958), pp. 177-81.   [3] J. Viner, *op. cit.* p. 51.

which formal theory has neglected ; one simple example will indicate the kind of argument put forward.

In discussing the arguments in favour of European economic integration many observers have *inter alia* distinguished between the effects upon the allocation of resources and upon what may loosely be called 'internal economic efficiency'.[1] The first issue, of course, corresponds to the subject matter of customs union theory, but the second problem has not been the object of any detailed formal analysis ; indeed, it is hard to see how traditional theory could cope with it. Briefly, the argument is that protection permits firms to use methods of production which are not the most efficient ones available ; in other words, the profit motive alone is not enough to ensure that each producer operates along the lowest of all possible cost curves. The opening of frontiers increases competitive pressure and thus forces firms to increase efficiency, i.e. to obtain lower input/output ratios. The upshot is that an economic union may bring benefits not only because an actual reallocation of resources between different uses takes place, but also because resources are employed more efficiently in their existing uses (and at given scales of production). It might be added that such improvements in efficiency do not depend upon migration of factors and will therefore not give rise to the same adjustment problems as the ordinary reallocation of resources. On the other hand, the precondition for resource allocation to result from the union — that before the union the member countries produce similar goods though at different costs — also applies in the case of improved efficiency, for unless the partner country produces substitutes, the possibility of domestic firms having to face increased competition does not arise.

Finally, in this section a word must be said about applications of the theory and about the results obtained. Many of the discussions of the regional free trade schemes undertaken or proposed in the recent past have implicitly or explicitly been based upon analytical reasoning of the type outlined above, though there have been few attempts to provide a statistical measure of the gains and losses involved. The two best-known estimates, both referring to the effects of free trade within Western Europe, are probably those put forward by Professors Verdoorn and Johnson. The methods used by both writers are basically similar ; calculations are made of the net expansion of trade resulting from the union, and the figures obtained are weighted with the tariffs in force before the union

---

[1] See, for instance, T. Scitovsky, *Economic Theory and Western European Integration*, London, 1958, pp. 19-44 ; and H. G. Johnson, 'The Economic Gains from Freer Trade with Europe', *Three Banks Review*, Sept. 1958, pp. 6-10.

(expressed as a fraction of the purchase price). The result, when compared to annual national incomes, showed the gains from freer trade to be exceedingly small; Verdoorn's calculations yielded a figure of 0·05 per cent of national income, while Johnson arrived at a *maximum* figure of 1·0 per cent of national income.[1]

Mention should also be made of a recent study by J. Wemelsfelder of the gains obtained by Germany from lower import duties.[2] Using a model similar to that underlying Verdoorn's and Johnson's work, Wemelsfelder reaches the result that the reduction of duties unilaterally undertaken by Western Germany between 1956 and 1957 resulted in a gain amounting to 0·18 per cent of German G.N.P. Although Wemelsfelder was only concerned with part of the effect caused by a customs union, this conclusion clearly supports the results obtained by Verdoorn and Johnson.

It is not difficult to find fault with the details of the statistical measurements undertaken by these writers — many of the estimates are very crude and subject to a considerable margin of error — but the results are such that even major changes in the figures would not alter the general conclusion. Moreover, common-sense reasoning also supports the contention that the economic benefits from free intra-European trade are likely to be limited.[3]

In a country such as the United Kingdom, for example, the proportion of national output which could theoretically become subject to foreign competition is of the order of 27 per cent,[4] and as the U.K. tariff on the average amounts to something like 20 per cent, the *greatest* reduction in costs and prices one can expect to result from free trade would likewise be 20 per cent. However, it would clearly be unrealistic to maintain that all commodities which are not exported are *ipso facto* more expensive than potential imports by the full amount of the tariff. Rather, one should imagine that these goods are arranged along a scale of relative competitiveness with potential imports; at one end of the scale there would be commodities identical in kind and price with those exported, and at the other end there would be goods which face strong competition on

[1] In other words, gains arising as a result of new economies of scale becoming available or as a result of firms being forced to become more efficient are excluded. For fuller details of the Verdoorn and Johnson estimates, see R. G. Lipsey, 'The Theory of Customs Unions: a General Survey', *loc. cit.* pp. 509-10.

[2] J. Wemelsfelder, 'The Short-term Effect of the Lowering of Import Duties in Germany', *Economic Journal*, Vol. lxx, No. 277 (March 1960), pp. 94-104.

[3] The subsequent paragraph has benefited from discussion with R. G. Lipsey (who uses a similar type of reasoning in his article, *loc. cit.* pp. 510-11).

[4] Industries producing goods — defined as agriculture, mining and quarrying, and manufacturing — contributed about £8800 million to G.N.P. in 1958–59. If we subtract the value of exports of goods on the grounds that export production must by definition be competitive, we obtain a figure of £5500 million, 27 per cent of G.N.P.

the domestic market despite the pressure of tariff protection. It would therefore be nearer the mark to estimate the average excess of the prices of retained (i.e. non-exported) products at 10 per cent ; the freeing of trade could thus be expected to lead to a 10 per cent reduction in the costs and prices of 27 per cent of G.N.P. — a gain of 2·7 per cent, equivalent to about eighteen months' growth in G.N.P. Moreover, in one way at least this must be regarded as a maximum estimate, for free trade with Europe is not the same as free trade with the world as a whole.

There is no need to dwell on the crudity of this kind of back-of-an-envelope calculation, but one point must be emphasized. The lowering of costs in question can be obtained either through an actual substitution of imports for domestic production or through producers increasing efficiency. This means that an 'estimate' of this kind includes the 'forced-efficiency effect' which was discussed earlier on and which some people regard as the most important source of gain from free trade.[1] On the other hand, gains obtained from positive consumption effects as well as through further economies of scale becoming available would be additional to those discussed. There is little one can say regarding the probable significance of any consumption effects (which may, of course, be negative) ; as to the importance of economies of scale, there has been a good deal of discussion but little factual evidence.

In the last resort it is not surprising that the static gains from free trade in Western Europe should appear rather small. True, the economies are fairly similar and there should therefore be fair scope for trade creation, but on the other hand there is little reason to believe that differences in comparative cost ratios which do not already reflect themselves in trade are very large. There may be other sources of gain, for instance, through greater stimuli being given to economic growth, but as already indicated, this is as yet uncharted territory.

III. CREATION OF CONDITIONS CONDUCIVE TO WELFARE ENDS

The final part of this paper is concerned with the conditions which must be created in order to ensure that a given economic union achieves the welfare ends which its founders aimed at. The problem in essence arises because the member countries of a union do not

---

[1] T. Scitovsky, *op. cit.* p. 68 ; and R. G. Lipsey, *loc. cit.* pp. 512-13.

constitute economic systems which are perfectly competitive all round and which are free from government interference of any kind. As a result, the building of a common market is not just a matter of abolishing the obvious trade barriers such as tariffs and quotas, and it may be necessary to inquire into business practices, government policies and the pricing of public utilities, to mention but a few examples, before one can be reasonably certain that the purposes of freer trade are not being frustrated.

However, the problem is not merely one of making the minimum changes in economic policies in line with the requirements of the union. Regional free trade is often embarked upon primarily for political ends, and the countries in question may therefore wish to carry 'integration' further than the realization of welfare gains may require.[1] However, given the ends it is up to the economist to indicate the problems which a particular plan raises and to suggest possible ways of dealing with these.

It is difficult — and not particularly illuminating — to enter into a general discussion of the obstacles which arise in the course of building economic unions, and it is therefore proposed briefly to draw on the experience of two economic unions which now have some history behind them — namely, the European Coal and Steel Community and Benelux — in order to illustrate the kind of issue which one may have to face.[2]

The problems of building the ECSC which are of particular interest at this juncture may be divided into two broad groups, (i) the problems encountered as a result of the Community's attempt to create a free and competitive market for the integrated commodities, and (ii) the problems caused by differences, as between the Community countries, with respect to the nature and height of various charges imposed upon commodities and factor earnings.

The outstanding features of the markets for coal and steel at the time of the Community's creation were the existence of far-reaching government control measures over prices and distribution, of private cartels and monopolistic arrangements and of large and even dominant nationalized undertakings. The task of the High Authority (the executive organ of the Community) was to obtain the abolition of government control and to create conditions in which enterprises —

[1] This argument shirks the issue as to what these minimum changes are, a matter which is almost bound to be controversial. Further on in this paper, for instance, the unification of indirect taxes in Benelux will be cited as a case of a change which goes further than is essential, but some experts would no doubt disagree with this view.

[2] The subsequent discussion is based upon a book entitled *Case Studies in European Economic Union* (by J. E. Meade, S. J. Wells and H. H. Liesner), London, 1962.

whether publicly or privately owned — would act independently of one another and compete for custom on level terms.

This task proved to be an exceedingly difficult one. Price controls, for example, did not necessarily become superfluous in the eyes of governments as a result of the establishment of the common market, and the lifting of controls was therefore frequently in conflict with national economic policy objectives. A possible alternative to a free market — the adoption of common control measures in all member countries — was provided for in the treaty which established the Community, but this solution does not in fact avoid problems of incompatibility with national economic policies, and the need for such measures may in any case vary from country to country.

A more specific account of one particular issue may illustrate the point. At the time of the Community's establishment coal prices were government controlled in all six countries, for the authorities generally regarded a relatively low price for coal as an important factor in over-all price stability ; any problem of excess demand was taken care of by official or unofficial rationing. As the cost of producing coal varied substantially between the different countries, the prices fixed likewise varied. The setting-up of the Community brought about little change : control measures, first officially imposed by the High Authority, then unofficially by the member governments, remained in existence, and the price structure never became what one would expect it to be in a common market, i.e. a system of prices which allows the low-cost producer to obtain a higher-than-average margin of profit, thus giving him both the incentive and the means to expand at the expense of his higher-cost rivals. The appearance in 1958 of a surplus of coal permitted this issue to recede into the background, though in the steel market a very similar problem has continued to exist.

The difficulties raised by the existence of producers' associations, of collusion and of public ownership have been no less serious, but lack of space forbids further discussion.

The other interesting issues are those connected with the existence of different outside charges in the member countries of the Community. The charges which have proved most difficult to deal with have primarily been of two kinds, indirect taxes and differences between the cost of transporting goods and the rates payable.

When the Community was formed, the indirect taxes affecting both coal and steel differed both as regards their nature and their height, and there was a sharp cleavage of opinion between the member countries as to how these differences influenced the working of the common market. In particular, the problem arose as to whether the existing fiscal treatment of internationally traded goods — to exempt exports from the payment of indirect taxes and impose on imports taxes equivalent to those paid by domestic substitutes — could be retained in a common market. One school of thought maintained that the taxing of imports at the frontier was incompatible with free trade even if these taxes were the same as those paid by domestic producers ; it was therefore demanded that indirect taxes should be imposed on all goods produced in a country, whether these were intended for export or for home consumption, and that no tax should be imposed on imports. Others held that the existing system — which in effect meant that goods were taxed at the point of consumption — was the only appropriate one.

The general solution to this problem is that one should choose that fiscal treatment which least distorts comparative costs. From this point of view there is no advantage in either system, given *that the whole of a country's international trade is treated in the same way.* In other words, it does not matter whether traded goods are taxed in the country of origin or of destination as long as all trade is subject to the same practice.[1] As the six countries had no intention of altering the fiscal treatment of their remaining trade, the only course of action open to them was to retain the existing system in their common market for coal and steel. However, this conclusion was reached only after a period of acrimonious controversy which threatened to do serious damage to the relations between the member states.

The problem of transport rates stems from two factors — the bulky nature of the common market products (which means that transport charges form a high proportion of the final price unless a consumer is situated in the immediate vicinity of the producing unit) and the widely varying differences between transport costs and charges. Moreover, there frequently existed more than one per ton rate for the same commodity within a single country, the rate actually applied depending upon particular circumstances such as the location or nationality of producer and/or consumer. In quantitative terms the effects of these conditions upon relative prices were frequently very substantial, but the Community has found it exceedingly difficult to achieve more than a limited measure of progress. This has ultimately been due to a wide divergence of views between the member countries as to the proper basis of transport charges and to

---

[1] This conclusion holds, whether or not there is a uniform rate of tax within a single country ; however, if tax rates are not uniform, a distortion is unavoidable, and the fiscal treatment will only shift the distortion wholly either on to the production or to the consumption side.

the role of transport in the national economy. Some governments have held, for instance, that the structure of transport charges should be such as to assist in the pursuit of certain economic policies and, in particular, of a policy of industrial decentralization, but this view has not been shared by all of them ; moreover, there exists a conflict between such a policy and the aims of a common market.

One particular aspect of the transport problem which in a way really belongs to Section II of this paper might be mentioned in passing. One of the common market products, coal, was relatively scarce during the first five years of the Community's existence. It was therefore unlikely that free trade would bring about significant shifts of production from high-cost to low-cost basins. However, free trade and the ensuing measures in the field of transport could achieve (though the available statistics are inadequate for a reliable check) a more efficient distribution of the coal produced, in the sense that the average journey travelled by a ton of coal could be reduced now that each consumer was faced with greater number of basins to choose from. In other words, any saving of resources was likely to occur in the transport industry — not itself one of the integrated sectors — rather than within the common market itself.

In general one can probably say that the difficulties encountered in the course of building a common market for coal and steel arose in spite of the fact that the Community did not try to go further than to create some of the minimum conditions compatible with free trade. Benelux, on the other hand, provides an example of a union which at least in some respects attempted to push 'integration' further than the realization of welfare gains required. A brief account of one of the problems which arose as a result will conclude this paper.

When Benelux was negotiated in the middle 'forties it was decided to unify the rates of indirect tax in the three member countries. This plan encountered two difficulties of substance. (i) The contribution made by indirect taxes to total government revenue differed substantially from country to country. As things stood, a unification of indirect taxes would have meant a shift away from direct and towards indirect taxation in Holland and perhaps also in Luxembourg and/or a shift away from indirect and towards direct taxation in Belgium or a combination of these shifts. Such changes were not easy to accept for a variety of reasons, prominent among which were the effect of indirect taxes upon the cost of living and technical problems connected with the tax systems used. (ii) There was considerable divergence of opinion among the member countries as to which products were the proper sources of revenue. For instance, in Belgium both brewers and consumers were unwilling to see higher taxes imposed on beer, the national drink, whereas in Holland corresponding opinions were held with respect to spirits, which the Dutch consume in relatively large quantities ; before the union Belgian duty on beer had been relatively low and that on spirits high, whereas in Holland the opposite had been the case. Similar difficulties existed with respect to many other taxed products. As a result of this type of problem little progress has been made with respect to the unification of indirect taxes and the customs official has not yet become redundant.

By now the discussion seems far removed from the initial issues of trade creation and trade diversion. However, adequate solutions of the kind of problem briefly looked at are no less important from the welfare angle than the reduction of trade barriers which appears to constitute the decisive step, and very frequently the difficulties involved are much more formidable.

Chapter 9

THE THEORY OF COMMON MARKETS AS APPLIED TO REGIONAL ARRANGE-MENTS AMONG DEVELOPING COUNTRIES

R. F. MIKESELL
University of Oregon, Eugene, Oregon

I. INTRODUCTION

BY and large the theory of customs unions has been confined to considerations of welfare gains or losses arising from a disturbance of the existing pattern of trade which is assumed to reflect comparative advantages in the commodities traded as determined by existing factor endowments. Some attention has been paid to the realization of gains from the economies of scale and from increased competition. However, the effects of the creation of regional markets on the more fundamental problems of developing countries such as increasing opportunities for profitable foreign and domestic investment, broadening the export base, achieving balance of payments equilibrium, mobilizing unemployed resources and avoiding economic dualism, have been largely neglected. Some of these problems, which are concerned with the dynamics of economic growth, are of interest to under-developed and to industrially advanced countries alike. I doubt, for example, if the most significant gains from the creation of the European Economic Community are to be discovered through a comparison of trade-diverting and trade-creating effects on welfare, even if we could measure them. Rather, the major impact will occur as a consequence of the effects on entrepreneurial decisions arising out of the new market structure and out of the acute awareness of the continual generation of new products, new processes and new methods of distribution on the part of competitors within the broad regional market. In other words, broadening of the area of unfettered activity of competitive enterprise creates opportunities for innovations and forces changes in investment patterns which constitute the dynamic elements of growth. These intangible factors, which are basic to business

205

decisions and expectations, often lie outside the economist's analytical framework.

But the fact that analytical work on common markets has been largely directed to problems of welfare under somewhat static assumptions which permit the employment of the analytical tools at our disposal, does not mean that the conclusions reached have no relevance for economic growth or for developing countries generally. I believe, however, that the theoretical analysis of customs unions or of regional preference arrangements generally should be directed more towards the problem of their impact on the direction of investment in the developing countries for future output rather than limited to an analysis of the welfare implications of shifting existing trade patterns. There are two general reasons for this conclusion, the first of which also has applicability for regional markets among industrially advanced countries. One is that plans for the creation of a customs union or free trade area usually involve relatively long time-periods for fruition so that the initial impact, and perhaps the most important one, is on expectations regarding future market opportunities rather than on existing trade patterns arising directly out of changes in intra-regional trade restrictions. Thus what is most relevant are the effects on investments which will determine trade and production patterns a decade in the future, as compared with what they might have been in the absence of the creation of the regional trading arrangements. The second factor, which is related to the first, is that developing countries are undergoing rapid and far-reaching changes in the structure of their production and trade. Very often there is relatively little trade among the members of regional trading blocs to begin with and virtually no exports of manufactures either between members or to the rest of the world. Hence, while the European Common Market and the European Free Trade Area are striving to achieve an expansion of intra-regional trade within the framework of an existing economic structure, developing countries, such as the members of the Latin American Free Trade Area, are seeking to bring about within the next decade or two a fundamental change in the structure of their production and trade and have sought to fashion a regional trade mechanism which will help to orient their economies in the direction of regional specialization.

Although no two economic regions or groups of countries which regard themselves as a region capable of economic integration are alike, we might begin by setting forth certain characteristics, some if not all of which under-developed regions tend to have in common. These characteristics are frankly based on those of the countries making up the Latin American Free Trade Area or Montevideo Treaty Association. I have chosen this group as a model because it constitutes the most important group of under-developed countries that have formulated, and are actually in initial stages of carrying out, a free trade area plan. The only other group where significant progress has been made is the Central American group, the countries of which are in a much less advanced stage of development and whose domestic markets are smaller. The Central American group also differs from the Montevideo group in that a much larger proportion of the total income of the Central American countries is derived from foreign trade, and for most of them, at least, balance of payments problems have been less acute.

The characteristics of our model group of countries contemplating the formation of a customs union or free trade area are as follows :

(1) Intra-regional trade in primary commodities is not likely to be affected immediately by the regional trading arrangements either because (*a*) the countries are complementary and do not have significant restrictions if they are not substantial producers of these commodities, or (*b*) they are competitive and sell the same commodities in world markets. In addition, the agriculture escape clauses in the agreement may take agricultural products out of the regional trading arrangement.

It should also be noted that in Latin America, bilateral agreements and multiple exchange rates which favour exports to convertible currency areas (to say nothing of the U.S. dumping of surplus agricultural commodities) have tended to put trade within the region at a disadvantage compared with trade with the outside. Hence we begin with a system of trade restrictions which discriminates against trade among countries forming the free trade area or customs union.

(2) Trade in industrial products is virtually non-existent. Production for the domestic market is being initiated in more and more commodities and industrialization is moving into intermediate products and investment goods, especially in the more advanced members of the regional group. The expansion of output takes over a larger share of the market from imports in commodity after commodity, mainly as a consequence of trade restrictions, although in many cases domestic costs may be competitive with imports. Frequently former suppliers of imports from abroad with well-established distribution channels will have undertaken domestic production either directly or under licensing arrangements, perhaps including the provision of management and technical services. The same foreign firms may be suppliers of imports or may be producing

locally in other members of the region. Domestically owned firms usually lack marketing outlets in other members of the region even if they were permitted to compete on a cost basis in the markets of their regional partners.

(3) Slowly growing, if not stagnating, export proceeds from primary commodities, together with rapidly expanding import requirements and debt service plus the necessity of finding employment for unemployed workers, have directed national policies towards the promotion of rapid industrialization with special emphasis on the production of substitutes for imported commodities. The policy of directing or influencing production on the basis of achieving direct savings in foreign exchange, rather than on the basis of relative efficiency, usually leads to substantial cost and price disparities for the same products produced within the region and also to overcapacity sometimes for the same commodities in more than one country in the region. For example, there is substantial overcapacity in Argentina, Brazil, Mexico and certain other Latin-American countries for the production of consumers' durable goods such as refrigerators.

(4) Members of the regional trade group include relatively advanced countries with well-developed industrial sectors, such as Argentina, Brazil and Mexico, and less advanced and little-industrialized countries such as Paraguay and Uruguay. This creates the problem of assuring a balanced distribution of the welfare gains from regional trading arrangements or at least of preventing certain countries from gaining at the expense of others.

On the basis of the foregoing characteristics of our model regional trade group encompassing several developing countries, we shall examine the relevance of certain generalizations formulated by recent contributions to the theory of customs unions.

II. THE BALANCE BETWEEN TRADE-DIVERTING AND TRADE-CREATING EFFECTS

We may begin with the well-known argument of Professor Jacob Viner that trade diversion tends to be harmful to welfare while trade creation is beneficial, and the net effects of a customs union on welfare will depend upon the balance of these opposing forces.[1] By and large the traditional primary exports of developing countries to the rest of the world will not be significantly affected by the

---

[1] Jacob Viner, *The Customs Union Issue*, Carnegie Endowment for International Peace, New York, 1950, Chapter 4.

creation of a regional trading arrangement. Moreover, their total purchases from the rest of the world will continue to depend very largely upon the growth of their primary commodity exports. However, the improved competitive position of their manufactures and semi-manufactures as a consequence of the creation of the competitive regional market may very well enable them to increase their total exports to the rest of the world. Also, if the regional market creates trade in other primary products not previously sold abroad, members may be able to broaden their primary commodity export base with respect to both regional and extra-regional trade. Hence, the long-run impact of a regional trading arrangement is not to decrease trade with the rest of the world but rather to change its pattern and possibly to enlarge it. In this sense, therefore, there is no over-all trade diversion, only trade creation. Thus, the basic questions which we must examine are : (i) whether the new regional pattern of trade with the rest of the world will become more economical as a consequence of the trading arrangements than would have otherwise have been the case ; and (ii) whether the newly created trade is economical or increases economic welfare.

As regards the first question, imports from the rest of the world will be determined by the effects of the regional trading arrangement on the pattern of production and trade within the region. In the absence of intra-regional trade in manufactures, each member will seek to produce as many commodities as possible for sale in the domestic market and import the rest from abroad. In order to save exchange, many commodities that cannot be produced domestically (because of limitations on investment capital and foreign exchange or otherwise) will be subjected to heavy duties or restrictive quotas or prohibitions. The creation of a regional market, however, will enable individual countries to obtain many of these goods from regional markets and to expand their own output for sale to the region. This will not only change the pattern of investment but will increase the total volume of investment. The additional foreign exchange required for the larger imports of capital goods, raw materials and fuel not produced by the regional partners will become available as a consequence of the reduced demand for consumers' goods and other commodities (including some capital goods) from outside the region. Thus, the new pattern of imports from the rest of the world will contribute to the process of greater specialization within the region.

There seems little doubt that a pattern of industrialization based on greater specialization within the region will be more economical than one based on production by each country for its own domestic

H

market. To the extent that greater specialization is permitted in agricultural commodities, there will also be gains from the removal of intra-regional trade barriers. The welfare gains will arise from the availability of a greater variety of goods at lower average cost, but substantial changes in price relationships may occur. Recent discussions of customs union theory which have emphasized *inter-commodity substitution* as against *inter-country substitution* have special relevance for the case of developing countries.[1] While a customs union will not establish the optimum relations between internal prices of domestic and internationally traded goods for maximizing welfare, intra-regional trade and specialization will change relative prices and consumption patterns toward optimum conditions. The increased consumption of commodity x in country A resulting from a lowering of the tariff on commodity x supplied from regional partner B as a consequence of increased investment and production for exploiting the larger regional market, will change consumption patterns in country A in the direction of increased welfare. In turn, investment in country A can be diverted to expanding output of commodity y rather than towards the production of more commodity x in which it is relatively less efficient.

It might be objected that resources will be transferred from production for the world market to production for the regional market and that this would result, in effect, in a reduction in the terms of trade since imports will be acquired from a higher-cost source. However, for reasons noted earlier, this is not likely to take place as a consequence of the creation of the regional market *per se*, although the urge to industrialize as a means of finding employment for labour has undoubtedly shifted capital resources out of primary production for world markets.[2] Of course, as incomes within the regional market grow, Chile and Peru may sell somewhat more copper to Argentina, Brazil and Mexico, and Brazil may sell more coffee to her southern neighbours. These exports will not be displacing the exports of copper and coffee from other areas of the world, and depending upon long-run supply conditions, they may not even be at the expense of exports of Chilean copper or Brazilian coffee to the rest of the world. Certainly it could not be argued that greater production and income promoted by the existence of a regional market, which in turn expands the demand for primary

[1] See R. G. Lipsey, 'The Theory of Customs Unions: a General Survey" *The Economic Journal*, Sept. 1960, p. 504, and J. E. Meade, *The Theory of Customs Unions*, North Holland Publishing Co., Amsterdam, 1955, pp. 34-41.

[2] Whether or not this is desirable for primary-producing countries as a whole depends upon the demand elasticities for primary goods and effects on their terms of trade. However, one can easily cite examples, e.g. Argentina, where this has been disastrous for the particular economy.

products from relatively efficient producers for the world market — which happen to be members of the regional trading area — are harmful to economic welfare.

All that we have said on this point with reference to developing economies reinforces the view of Professor Meade and others that there is a gain in welfare if there is a net expansion of trade. This point seems to be particularly evident when we consider that the alternative to directing investment to the production of those commodities in which countries have a relative competitive advantage within the regional market, is a haphazard directing of investment into production for the domestic market of those commodities which can most readily displace imports from the rest of the world.

III. COMPLEMENTARY VERSUS COMPETITIVE PARTNERS AND THE PATTERN OF EXISTING TRADE

Recent contributions to customs union theory have evolved certain hypotheses with respect to the potential welfare gains from discriminatory regional trade arrangements which relate to the existing patterns of production in the member countries and to the proportion which trade among regional partners bears to their total trade. We shall present these generalizations without necessarily taking a position as to their correctness within the context of the assumptions under which they are made, and then seek to determine their relevance for our typical developing regional group.

(*a*) A regional trading arrangement is more likely to increase economic welfare if the economies of the members are very competitive but potentially very complementary.[1]

(*b*) Welfare is likely to be the greater, the higher the proportion of trade among the partners relative to their total trade.

(*c*) Welfare is likely to be the greater, the lower the proportion of the foreign trade of each member to purchases of domestic commodities.[2]

In our typical case of a regional group encompassing developing countries, members at the same stage of industrialization tend to be

[1] See Meade, *op. cit.* p. 107.

[2] See Lipsey, *op. cit.* pp. 508-9. Professor Meade concludes that 'a customs union between two countries will be the more likely to raise economic welfare, if each is the principal supplier to the other of the products which it exports to the other and if each is the principal market for the other of the products which it imports from the other'. He also concludes that 'the formation of a customs union is more likely to raise economic welfare the greater is the proportion of the world's production, consumption, and trade which is covered by the members of the union'. See Meade, *op. cit.* pp. 108-9.

producing many of the same manufactured goods, but there is little or no trade between them. So far as primary commodities are concerned, they may in some cases be highly competitive in the sense that both are producing the same commodities for world markets. For example, both Brazil and Mexico, which are members of the Montevideo group, produce both coffee and cotton for world markets. On the other hand, they may be quite complementary with respect to some primary commodities which each sells in world markets. The creation of a regional market is not likely to have much effect on trade in either of these two groups of primary commodities. Where they are competitive in primary commodities which they do not export on world markets, but each maintains import restrictions in order to support domestic output and prices, the elimination of trade restrictions within the group is likely to bring about a much more efficient utilization of resources and result in some displacement of imports from outside the group; the reduced prices and production costs for total regional output are likely to outweigh any loss from trade diversion for the region as a whole.

As regards developing countries, it might be said that because of the emphasis on industrialization, all members are actually or potentially competitive and certainly all members of a regional group are potentially complementary. Thus it would not be correct to say that the outlook for achieving economic welfare gains through a customs union of Central American states is poor because the members are at such a low stage of industrialization that they are actually not competitive at the present time ; nor would it make much sense to argue that because they all produce coffee and bananas and hence are actually competitive, this augurs well for a net increase in welfare from the creation of a customs union. They are not going to trade in coffee and bananas anyway, except possibly for some border trade. As industrialization proceeds, they are going to be more competitive ; but what these countries should strive for is a pattern of investment which will introduce a substantial degree of complementarity for the future.

When we come to consider the generalization noted in paragraph (*b*) above regarding the proportion of intra-regional to total trade, it might be concluded that there is little prospect for increasing welfare through a customs union or free trade area for our typical regional group. This conclusion would be wrong, however, because the alternative to increased intra-regional trade is not reduced trade with the outside world but, rather, the production of a larger proportion of each country's requirements within its borders, thus inevitably leading to a less efficient utilization of resources as compared with regional specialization. Nor can we accept the implication in paragraph (*c*) above, that because the proportion of foreign trade to domestic expenditures is quite high for many developing countries, their chances for achieving welfare gains from the formation of regional trading groups is severely limited. The reason is that if the countries are going to develop on the basis of a rather slow growth of export proceeds (and perhaps a large part of these going to pay for debt service), the ratio of foreign trade to domestic expenditures will decline rapidly in the future. Welfare gains will be achieved through the creation of regional markets because they will tend to retard the rate of decline in the ratio of foreign trade (including intra-regional trade) to domestic expenditures.

It is for these reasons that I seriously question the applicability of the generalizations of the theory of customs unions which relate to complementarity, competitiveness and trade patterns, to the potential gains from regional trading arrangements for developing countries. It is necessary to look beyond the existing patterns of production and trade to those which are likely to emerge in the absence of the formation of a customs union or a free trade area.

IV. *PARTIAL* VERSUS *COMPLETE REMOVAL OF RESTRICTIONS ON INTRA-REGIONAL TRADE*

Contrary to the traditional approach to customs unions and that which is embodied in the General Agreement on Tariffs and Trade,[1] recent theories of customs unions have suggested that a *partial* reduction of duties on imports from regional trading partners is more likely to increase welfare than is a *complete* removal of restrictions on trade within the preference area.[2] The basis for this generalization is that each successive reduction of duties within the preference area will contribute less to the gains from the expansion of trade between the partners, but the loss from trade diversion will continue as the degree of discrimination within the preference trade area continues to increase. This generalization is usually made on the assumption of an all-round reduction of tariffs affecting all commodities.[3]

---

[1] See Article XXIV of the General Agreement on Tariffs and Trade.
[2] See Meade, *op. cit.* pp. 110-11 ; see also Lipsey, *op. cit.* pp. 506-7.
[3] Closely related to this generalization is the one which states that the formation of regional preference arrangements is the more likely to increase welfare, 'the higher are the initial rates of duty on imports into the partner countries'. See Meade, *op. cit.* p. 108.

From the standpoint of the long-run effects on investment decisions within the regional trading bloc, and again considering the fact that individual countries will, over time, seek a maximum displacement of imports with domestic production in the absence of a regional arrangement, I seriously doubt the validity of the above generalization. I do not believe that a preferential trading arrangement can possibly have the same impact on resource distribution as one which looks towards the removal of *all* barriers to trade within a given time-period. Again, we are not concerned simply with the readjustment of existing trade patterns, but rather with alternative principles for the direction of investment which will establish the trade and production patterns a decade or so hence.

In this connection mention might be made of another generalization of Professor Meade's to the effect that 'a customs union is less likely to have adverse secondary repercussions upon economic welfare in a world in which trade barriers take the form of fixed quantitative restrictions rather than of taxes on imports'.[1] The reasoning here, of course, is that the removal of quantitative restrictions on trade among the partners, while maintaining the same quantitative restrictions against imports from the outside world, is likely not to affect the imports within the quotas from the outside world and hence there would be no trade diversion. On the other hand, the use of quantitative restrictions as against tariffs and discriminatory tariff treatment favouring imports from regional partners removes the necessity of competing for markets on a price and quality basis. In short, I would favour the use of tariffs over quantitative restrictions as a means of providing a discriminatory advantage to intra-regional trade.

To a considerable degree import restrictions of developing countries have taken the form of quotas or outright prohibitions on imports. Moreover, as developing countries become relatively self-sufficient in additional commodities in the future, they will, in the absence of a regional trade arrangement, restrict or eliminate foreign competition one way or the other. It might also be said that there has been a tendency to maintain the most restrictive import measures on the very commodities which might have been imported from neighbouring countries, since it is in these commodities — at least in the industrial field — that developing countries tend to be most competitive with their neighbours. Again, so far as the future is concerned, it is not so much a matter of trade diversion as between the outside world and the regional group, but rather whether policies will be adopted which favour regional specialization as against those

[1] *See* Meade, *op. cit.* p. 110.

which favour the maximum degree of self-sufficiency at whatever cost on the basis of domestic markets alone.

V. THE ECONOMIES OF SCALE

While the gains from economies of scale are usually mentioned as a significant argument for the formation of customs unions or free trade areas, there is considerable difference of opinion as to its importance and some are frankly sceptical regarding its significance for Western Europe.[1] First of all, the possibilities of realizing economies of scale differ greatly for different types of commodities for the same market, and for the same commodity for countries of varying market size. For countries like Brazil and Argentina, the domestic market may be large enough to permit realization of economies of scale for a wide range of consumers' goods and even intermediate goods ; this is certainly not true for the countries of Central America, most of which could not support an economically sized soap factory or fertilizer plant on the basis of the domestic market alone. On the other hand, the domestic market even in the largest and most industrially advanced of less-developed countries is not large enough to justify a plant of economical size for a large number of items, such as specialized machinery, transport equipment, certain chemicals, and electronics.

In a recent study on 'Patterns of Industrial Growth',[2] Professor Chenery has shown that as *per capita* income rises from $100 to $600, the percentage of production of investment goods to total manufacturing output approximately triples according to the normal pattern based on a sample of some fifty countries, including both industrialized and under-developed. When allowance is made for variations in the size of the country, deviations from the normal pattern are 'smallest for services, agriculture, and most manufactured consumer goods', while the greatest variation from the normal is found in 'industries producing machinery, transport equipment, and intermediate goods, where economies of scale are important'.[3] Chenery points out that in modern developing countries, the leading sectors of the economies — or those which provide the impetus to growth — are 'likely to be the industries in which import substitution becomes profitable as markets expand and capital and skills

[1] See, for example, H. G. Johnson, 'The Criteria of Economic Advantage', *Bulletin of the Oxford University Institute of Statistics*, Feb. 1957, p. 35 ; see also 'The Economic Gains from Free Trade with Europe', *Three Banks Review*, Sept. 1958.

[2] See Hollis B. Chenery, 'Patterns of Industrial Growth', *American Economic Review*, Sept. 1960, pp. 624-54.   [3] *Ibid.* pp. 650-1.

are acquired'.[1] Hence he concludes that limitations on market size are an important factor in preventing normal growth of developing countries by their being unable to move into the production of investment and intermediate goods where economies of scale are especially important. Thus he lays special emphasis on the creation of regional trading arrangements which will increase market size as a means of promoting development in accordance with the normal pattern of industrial growth.[2]

Any realistic discussion of the advantages to be derived from economies of scale must take into account the nature of the market in which producers are operating. Outside of Communist countries, few manufacturing industries are complete monopolies and in most cases the existence of several producers, some or all of which may already have excess capacity, prevents the realization of potential economies of scale on the basis of the domestic market alone. Imperfect competition, government restraints and private collusion of various kinds prevent individual producers from establishing new low-cost plants which would force competitors out of business by taking over a larger share of the market, or prevent new foreign enterprises from doing so. Hence the impetus for the establishment of new low-cost plants may need to come from the opening up of an external market where conditions of competition, either with firms in the export market or from third countries, may be such as to require lower-cost production achieved through economies of scale. Moreover, if production is in the hands of a foreign firm which has established distribution facilities throughout the regional market, the foreign firm may be able to supply its entire regional market by expanding the output of one country, or the foreign firm may be able to lower costs by producing certain components in individual countries while continuing to assemble the finished product in the plants of several individual countries within the common market. Finally, this same firm may as a consequence of reduced costs of the finished product or, more likely, of components, be able to supply markets outside the regional group, thereby broadening the export base of the regional group.

The contribution of Professor Tibor Scitovsky to the economies of scale which might be realized from economic integration is especially relevant for developing countries.[3] The high degrees of market imperfection, the factor of risk and uncertainty arising from political instability, and the tendency on the part of domestically

[1] See Hollis B. Chenery, 'Patterns of Industrial Growth', *American Economic Review*, Sept. 1960, pp. 624-54.   [2] *Ibid.*

[3] See Tibor Scitovsky, *Economic Theory and Western European Integration*, Stanford University Press, 1958, Chapter 3.

owned firms to favour high margins and low output, greatly limit the willingness of firms to build plants which will be optimal for the level of domestic demand, say, five or ten years hence. Therefore, accretions in demand tend to be supplied by the addition of sub-optimal equipment. On the other hand, an expansion of the market area to other countries in the region may lead some firms to establish plants with equipment permitting substantial economies of scale. Unfortunately, several of the countries in the Montevideo group are already highly competitive in a number of industries, such as durable consumers' goods and steel, in which significant economies of scale could probably be realized. Therefore, reductions in trade barriers affecting these commodities are likely to proceed very slowly if indeed much progress is made at all in the next few years. Greater progress will be made in the reduction of barriers to trade in goods, the domestic production of which is not yet substantial and imports still supply the vast bulk of the region's requirements. However, in the absence of a regional trade arrangement, relatively high-cost plants for the production of these commodities will eventually be established in some of the countries as the process of substitution continues. On the other hand, more economically sized plants might be established if production for a regional market could be assured. The reduction of intra-regional barriers on new goods, such as specialized capital equipment, will be determined on the basis of intra-regional bargaining, since the first interest of each country will be to preserve the potential domestic market for its own production of a given commodity, an interest that it will compromise only if each country is assured the opportunity of exploiting the regional market for other commodities. Tariff negotiations among the members of the Montevideo Free Trade Area are therefore likely to lead to agreements or understandings regarding the establishment of plants, and this will not always mean production in the most efficient country. It can be argued, of course, that this will increase the extent of trade diversion, but it should be kept in mind that trade diversion will take place in any case and that *total* trade with the outside world is not likely to be greatly affected.

VI. THE EFFECTS OF COMPETITION

As we have already noted, any discussion of the gains from the economies of scale cannot be separated from the nature of the markets and the degree of competition within countries and competition between members of the regional group. Most discussions of the benefits of customs unions have tended to emphasize the gains from competition that are likely to result from the more impersonal competitive forces arising from the creation of the regional market, impinging upon the imperfect or oligopolistic structure of domestic markets. This argument undoubtedly has significance for Western Europe and perhaps should apply with even greater force with respect to developing countries which are characterized by monopolistic elements of all kinds.[1] However, competition is by no means a popular principle in developing countries, and in Latin America regional trading arrangements are viewed more as mechanisms for development planning on a regional basis than as providing the basis for intra-regional competition. In fact, the term competition is not found in the text of the Montevideo Treaty and has been virtually absent from discussions of the gains from regional integration. The emphasis is on the principles of 'reciprocity' and of 'planned complementarity'.[2] Hence, we may find, initially at least, that the intra-regional trade liberalization measures within the Montevideo group will emphasize reductions in barriers on industrial commodities in which members are not currently competitive, while avoiding those in which they are competitive. In other words, the arrangements would seem to favour trade diversion over net trade expansion. However, as we have already indicated, we must look beyond the shorter-run impacts on the existing pattern of trade to the effects on future patterns of production and trade as determined by alternative policies affecting investment and resource allocation. If the Montevideo Treaty programme moves toward its long-term goal of complete free trade — at least in industrial commodities — members must begin undertaking reductions in barriers which will affect the commodities in which they are competitive. This will be easier to do if the reductions take place gradually so that, given the general accretion of demand, serious damage will not be done to existing firms, but, rather, there will be a gradual increase in the proportion of the market represented by intra-regional trade. Such a development cannot help but have an impact on breaking down internal market rigidities. In fact, the major gains in this respect may occur in the countries which become important exporters of certain commodities, since in order to compete abroad, these firms

[1] See Tibor Scitovsky, 'International Trade and Economic Integration as a Means of Overcoming the Disadvantages of a Small Nation', *Economic Consequences of the Size of Nations* (Proceedings of a Conference held by the International Economic Association), Macmillan, London, 1960, pp. 282-90.

[2] See Raymond F. Mikesell, 'The Movement Toward Regional Trading Groups in Latin America', *Latin America Issues : Essays and Comments* (edited by Albert O. Hirschman), Twentieth Century Fund, New York, 1961, pp. 125-51.

will inevitably undertake cost-reducing measures and introduce optimal equipment which will result in lower prices and perhaps the forcing out of marginal firms in the exporting country. The political repercussions of such developments will be less severe than in cases where marginal firms are forced out as a consequence of import competition.

Even the threat of eventual competition from abroad or a stepped-up pace of competitive activity for exporting abroad will shake a number of Latin American industries out of their lethargy and stagnation. They will see that sooner or later they must adopt new methods in both production and distribution. Moreover, the creation of a regional trading area will lead to greater contacts among business men with the consequent increase in the exchange of ideas. Finally, as a spur to a competitive activity within the region, competing foreign firms will enter on the expectation of being able to exploit a larger regional market, either directly with their own subsidiaries or through joint ventures. Such firms are accustomed to competing with one another in markets throughout the world and will spread the arena of their competitive activities to Latin America.

As has already been mentioned, Latin American policy-makers are hoping to work out complementary agreements in certain industries as a basis for trade, rather than simply lowering the barriers and letting competition take its course. In Central America this principle has been formalized in the General Treaty on Central American Integration, which, among other things, provides for joint planning and certification of manufacturing firms in particular industries which would be given free access to the Central American market under conditions which would avoid over-capacity and unrestricted competition. Although formal provisions for the certification of industries are not included under the Montevideo Treaty, the idea of special complementarity agreements is well established.

In a recent article Professor Jan Tinbergen [1] argues for regional planning as opposed to competition in the heavy industry field on grounds that free entry and competition in these industries are not likely to produce optimal development. Tinbergen favours planned production with the aid of economic models by means of which the optimum pattern of heavy industry development, including plant size and location, could be determined for the region as a whole.

[1] See Jan Tinbergen, 'Heavy Industry in the Latin American Common Market', *Economic Bulletin for Latin America*, United Nations Economic Commission for Latin America, Santiago, Chile, March 1960, pp. 1-5.

He gives several reasons why free entry and competition would not achieve these conditions, including: (1) the long construction period required for the individual projects, which would reduce the accuracy of decisions arising out of the market mechanism; (2) the large amount of capital required to establish plants of optimum size which would not be forthcoming except under conditions of planning and assured demand; and (3) the failure of free enterprise to establish heavy industry in optimum locations.[1]

It is undoubtedly true that regional planning of heavy industry based on Professor Tinbergen's economic models would provide a closer approximation to the optimal size and location of heavy industry than that which would be achieved under the operation of completely unfettered competition. However, freely competitive conditions in this field may be ruled out as unrealistic in any case because of the oligopolistic nature of heavy industry and of the role played by governments as providers of credits or of direct participants in the enterprises. Moreover, I do see a danger in leaving the planning of heavy industry to government negotiators. Agreements in this field are likely to be negotiated by political representatives with a view to achieving a kind of 'balance of industrialization' among the countries within the regional group, rather than on the basis of optimal size and location of plants in accordance with a rational programme. Also, I can think of few processes more stifling to growth than to leave the development of heavy industry to the almost interminable deliberations of government negotiators. This problem might be dealt with by the creation of an independent or supra-governmental authority such as the European Coal and Steel Community, which would have the power to control investments in heavy industry, but such an institution, so far as I am aware, has not been contemplated for the Latin American Free Trade Area. The price of achieving or attempting to achieve optimal solutions may be a considerably slower rate of investment and a prevention of the full operation of the inducement mechanisms. For countries in a hurry to develop, this is far too great a price to pay. However, the formulation of long-range economic programmes prepared by ECLA or other regional groups, which would serve as a guide to domestic and foreign private investors, to governments, and to external lending institutions, together with arrangements for regional consultations on plans for major investment expenditures in the heavy industry field, would be of immense value.

[1] See Jan Tinbergen, 'Heavy Industry in the Latin American Common Market', *Economic Bulletin for Latin America*, United Nations Economic Commission for Latin America, Santiago, Chile, March 1960, pp. 2-4.

VII. UNEQUAL WELFARE EFFECTS AND
ECONOMIC DUALISM

Customs union theory has recognized that some members of a customs union or free trade area may gain in terms of economic welfare while others may lose. For example, if one of the members does not appreciably increase its exports but simply shifts its imports from lower- to higher-cost sources, membership in a preferential trading area may mean little more than a deterioration in its terms of trade. An extreme case would be one in which a country, as a consequence of joining a customs union, would have to raise its import duties on commodities from the outside world in order to provide a market for higher-cost imports from its partners, while at the same time there was no offsetting export gain. Even if it did not raise its duties, and consumers were able to import at somewhat lower prices or at least no higher prices, from partner countries, the government would lose the tariff revenue on imports diverted from external sources and presumably would have to make up the revenue by taxing its citizens in some other way.

Looked at from the standpoint of the longer-run impact on developing countries, a customs union or other regional preference arrangement might have an even more adverse impact upon certain members. Capital, skills and entrepreneurs, both from within the preference region and from abroad, might be drawn to the major industrial centres of the more advanced partners in order to take advantage of external economies in these areas, and to locate their plants closer to the major markets. In his study of the *Strategy of Economic Development* Professor Hirschman warns against what he calls the *polarization* effects which operate in developing countries to create a situation in which progress in certain areas, mainly the rapidly industrializing regions, is accompanied by, and even contributes to, stagnation in other regions.[1] The creation of free trade areas or customs unions which include countries encompassing less advanced regions and partners representing the more industrially advanced regions may well reinforce these polarization effects. While there are some offsetting forces resulting from the increase in demand for primary commodities from the less advanced regions, these may not be strong enough to offset the polarization effects.

The problem of dualism can be handled by a single country or

[1] Albert O. Hirschman, *The Strategy of Economic Development*, Yale University Press, New Haven, 1958, Chapter 10.

an economic union with a strong central government and centralized fiscal system. Special encouragements can be given to the location of industries outside the metropolitan centres by means of tax inducements, and by heavy expenditures for transportation, power and other overhead facilities in advance of immediate industrial needs. Loan capital can be distributed in a way which favours the development of the hinterland. However, if economic integration programmes do not include some mechanism by means of which the less advanced countries are given somewhat more favourable treatment in the distribution of capital expenditures for economic overhead projects or possibly special measures for attracting direct private investment, the net results of combining less advanced and more advanced countries in a regional trade arrangement may very well be to increase the degree of dualism with its attendant political and social frictions and frustrations. This problem has been recognized in the EEC by the creation of special financial institutions such as the European Investment Bank and the European Social Fund, but it is likely to be much more serious among the developing countries forming common markets and free trade areas.

Although the Central American integration plan provides for the establishment of a Central American Integration Bank, the Montevideo Treaty has thus far not established financial facilities which would help to balance the advantages as between the less advanced and the more advanced partners. Provision is made in the Montevideo Treaty for the less advanced members to proceed more slowly with import liberalization than the more advanced members, but what is needed is something more positive which will help the less advanced members to broaden their export markets within the region, particularly in industrial commodities, rather than simply retard the impact of regional competition on their own markets. It would seem highly desirable, therefore, that either there be established a special long-term financing institution to operate as a part of the Montevideo Treaty Organization, or the Inter-American Development Bank play a special role in dealing with this problem in close co-operation with the Montevideo Organization.

There is little doubt that the less advanced members of the Latin American Free Trade Area have an actual or potential cost advantage in a number of industrial and agricultural products with respect to other members of the regional group. But for these advantages to be exploited there must be enterprise, capital, better transportation facilities, and perhaps distribution facilities in other members in addition to reduced trade barriers. Disadvantages arising from high transportation costs and location relative to the major markets may well outweigh the cost advantages of producing in the less advanced members.

The fact that the Montevideo Treaty takes the form of a free trade area rather than a customs union undoubtedly reduces the extent of welfare loss on the part of the less advanced members, while at the same time it reduces the possibilities for trade expansion within the area. Countries like Uruguay and Paraguay, which cannot expect to produce their own tractors or capital equipment for a long time to come, tend to have low rates of duty on these commodities so that they can provide little margin of preference for imports of these goods from Brazil and Argentina even though they abolish all of their restrictions on industrial imports from partner countries. On the other hand, such industrial goods as they are likely to be able to export successfully in competition with producers in other members of the regional group are likely to have a high margin of preference. The tendency for countries to have low tariffs or few restrictions (except for balance of payments or revenue purposes) on commodities which they do not produce or expect to produce in the near future themselves, but a high degree of restriction on commodities they are producing for the domestic market, has led many Latin American economists to the position that the Montevideo Treaty Organization must be converted into a customs union if it is to be successful in expanding intra-regional trade. In other words, there is a fear that countries will not be willing to afford to partner members a discriminatory wall of protection on the commodities they are willing to import from them; while they are not willing to make concessions to their partners on the commodities on which they are maintaining a high level of protection as a means of securing the market for their domestic producers.

This position seems to arise from a view that a Latin American preference area should be mainly trade-diverting and that intra-regional trade is possible only if a high and fairly uniform tariff wall around the entire region is maintained. I think this is a rather static and short-sighted view of the potential benefits from a regional free market. I suspect that the principal incentive to the expansion of investment in one country in order to market a portion of its output in neighbouring countries is the assurance or expectation that it will have free access to those markets with low or non-existent restrictions, rather than the expectation that it will have a substantial margin of preference over exports from third countries. Moreover, I do not believe that it is possible to create a successful regional trading area on a basis of raising prices to consumers in one country in order to provide a market for the goods of partner countries.

Finally, there is reason to believe that given equilibrium rates of exchange and adequate transportation facilities which will permit the realization of locational advantages, costs of production in developing countries will not be significantly higher (in fact, they might well be lower) for the goods which they are exporting within the region than those from industrially advanced countries outside of the preference region.

While admitting that a free trade area can and will provide a considerable degree of regional preference over external goods, the deliberate creation of a common high wall of protection against outside competition for all goods sold within the region does not appear to be either feasible or desirable from the standpoint of the long-run development of the region. In fact, the long-run aim of the region should be a gradual reduction of barriers on imports from outside as well as within the region itself.

VIII. THE PAYMENTS PROBLEM

So much has been written regarding the payments problem in relation to common markets and free trade areas, and the subject has so many ramifications, that an adequate discussion of this problem for developing countries would require a separate paper in itself. Students of customs unions have evolved sharply conflicting positions with respect to the payments problem and the means of dealing with it. Dr. Thomas Balogh and Dr. Raul Prebisch (and his colleagues in the United Nations Economic Commission for Latin America) tend to favour a multilateral compensation system for financing trade among members of a regional preference area which would avoid, or largely avoid, the necessity for settlements in convertible exchange or gold.[1] At the other extreme are those who believe that a successful customs union or free trade area is not possible except under conditions of financing with freely convertible currencies and the maintenance of over-all balance of payments equilibrium by individual members without restrictions. According to this view, the attempt to achieve freedom of payments internally, while at the same time permitting individual countries to maintain balance of payments restrictions on trade and payments with the

[1] See T. Balogh, 'The Dollar Crisis Revisited', *Oxford Review Economic Papers*, Sept. 1954, and 'The Dollar Shortage Once More, a Reply', *Scottish Journal of Political Economy*, June 1955 ; for a discussion of the position of Dr. Prébisch and of the ECLA Secretariat, see *The Latin American Common Market*, United Nations Economic Commission for Latin America, Mexico, July 1959, pp. 17-22 ; see also Victor L. Urquidi, *Trayectoria del Mercado Comun Latino-americano*, Centro de Estudios Monetarios Latinoamericanos, Mexico City, 1960.

outside world, is unworkable since such an arrangement would lead to large imbalances within the preferential system. Even a common policy with regard to trade and payments relations with third countries is difficult to maintain in the absence of a full economic union.[1] Professor Meade favours a system of fluctuating exchange rates as perhaps the best means of maintaining balance of payments equilibrium and freedom from restrictions, while others, including myself, believe that the uncertainties resulting from frequent changes in exchange rates would greatly reduce the benefits from the formation of customs unions.

As regards developing countries which meet the conditions for our model, those who favour a multilateral compensation system involving no settlements in external currencies are usually identified with the position that it is necessary to establish a highly discriminatory system in which each member country's trade is balanced over time with the group, and no country is permitted to earn convertible exchange by increasing its exports to the group. This view is based in turn upon the conviction that manufactured exports from one partner to another simply cannot be competitive with external goods or, more generally, that there exists within the group a shortage of convertible currency which would lead members to avoid using their convertible exchange for purchases within the area. There is really little basis for this approach, which reflects adherence to a 'dollar shortage' philosophy long after there is any justification for it. There is no general shortage of convertible means of payment in the world today. Nearly all Latin American countries have adopted realistic exchange rates for the bulk of their trade with the outside world and they urgently need to remove existing price and cost disparities among themselves artificially created by subsidies, bilateral trade agreements and import controls of various kinds. If the problem is one of providing additional liquidity for financing an expanded volume of trade among themselves by means of convertible currencies rather than bilateral agreements, this can and should be handled by special assistance from external sources such as the International Monetary Fund.

Apart from this, the attempt to create a multilateral compensation scheme among countries whose existing intra-regional trade is relatively small is fraught with difficulties, since anything approaching a regional balance would be little short of a miracle. If the desire for a balanced expansion of trade is an important aspect of the

---

[1] For a discussion of the balance of payments problems of customs unions, see Scitovsky, *Economic Theory and Western European Integration, op. cit.* pp. 95-100 ; and Meade, *op. cit.* pp. 14-28 and pp. 116-19.

regional trading scheme, it should be achieved by means other than through a payments scheme. In fact, the results of the operation of a payments scheme is only a reflection of the operation of the fundamental trade liberalization programme, and if the payments positions cannot be compensated multilaterally over time, it will be necessary to change the basis of the trade liberalization programme. Hence all that is really needed is some means of keeping track of the intra-regional balances on current account, and an elaborate payments mechanism is unnecessary for this purpose.

A more fundamental question is whether the *trade* arrangements should be such as to achieve an approximate balance of each member with the group. Personally, I do not believe that this should be a fundamental aim since the existence of a surplus or a deficit of an individual member with the group does not measure the welfare gain or loss from membership. As the economies of partners progressively grow, the pattern of their production and trade will change and the determination of the long-run benefits of individual partners from membership in the preference area will require far more subtle means of measurement. For some countries, for example, there may be no loss whatsoever involved in increasing the share of imports from regional sources in their total imports, while at the same time they are enjoying the gains from a broader market for their export. Indeed, they may find their terms of trade improving even though they develop with their regional partners which they must finance with convertible currencies. Likewise, the achievement of a surplus on intra-regional account by one partner country is not a necessary measure of its relative benefits from membership in the regional preference area. Conceivably it could be paying too much in terms of a deterioration in its terms of trade from the intra-regional surplus that it is achieving.

All of this is not to say that there is not a problem in making sure that the benefits and losses from the creation of a regional preference area are equitably shared, but this must be done by means much more fundamental than setting up a multilateral compensation scheme.

IX. THE INDUCEMENT EFFECTS ON INVESTMENT FROM BROADENING THE MARKET AREA

Development literature is full of examples of the impact of market growth upon investment and productivity and on the revitalization of stagnating industries serving a local market. As a rule this has come about through the development of transportation within a country, through improved marketing methods and the expansion of incomes. For modern developing countries the expansion of external demand has not provided the basis for the growth of investment in manufacturing, and for many countries exports of primary commodities have been growing slowly or stagnating and have provided little inducement for increased investment. Also, the surplus of labour in the agricultural regions has provided little inducement for increasing productivity. Inducements to investment based solely on internal developments have certain limitations. First, for a large number of industries, income elasticities may be rather low and production of new goods as substitutes for imports depends upon whether or not the internal market has grown to the point where plants of an economical size can be established. Such substitution can be forced by high or prohibitive import restrictions, but this may mean an uneconomical use of capital through the creation of excess capacity or of very high-cost productive facilities. Once these industries are established, they tend to stagnate for lack of dynamic growth of demand.

A second difficulty with internally induced investment is that it does not provide any additional foreign exchange to meet import costs of investment goods, intermediate goods, raw materials and fuel, unless, of course, the industries are established by foreign capital. But even here, the actual foreign exchange contribution of foreign manufacturing enterprises is likely to be small since they depend for their growth upon reinvested profits and perhaps for a part of the capital for their initial establishment on domestic sources. There is, of course, an offset against these additional foreign exchange expenditures from increased supplies of the import-competing goods, but this does not occur fast enough for the country to maintain a high level of investment with slowly rising or stagnating export receipts. Hence, domestically induced investment is hampered by exchange shortages which result in the imposition of import restrictions and/or exchange depreciation. The import restrictions or steadily depreciating exchange rates in the face of growing domestic demand creates a condition of chronic inflation which brings about a misdirection of investment and a tendency for savings to flow into less productive uses or to find their way to foreign capital markets.

Investment induced by an expansion of external demand for export goods avoids these disadvantages. Export demand does not depend upon slowly growing domestic income and provides the foreign exchange for the increase in investment in productive facilities. The opening-up of markets in neighbouring countries adds a new dimension to market growth. Demand and supply elasticities will increase substantially, particularly because they tend to be rather low in countries of limited industrial development. This will increase economic flexibility and open up new opportunities for investment, both foreign and domestic.

The literature dealing with the importance of broadening the export base for regional economic growth is of particular relevance for the creation of regional trading arrangements among developing countries.[1] Successful regional growth cannot be a 'bootstrap operation', but depends upon the creation of an export base which permits specialization in the production of those goods and services for which the region's resources are best suited and the creation of external economies. Of course, successful regional centres of economic growth soon develop local industries producing mainly for local consumption, but it is the exports to other regions that provide the external impetus which then has a multiplier effect. By analogy, the same reasoning can be applied to nations: for maximum growth they need the stimulus of an external demand for their products and the possibility of broadening their export base to include new export industries as the old ones lose their earlier vitality.

X. CONCLUSION

In concluding this paper I would say that the principal way in which customs union theory needs to be modified for application to the problems of developing countries is by taking into account the likely long-term changes in the pattern of production. This is especially important for those countries where the export industries do not constitute the leading sector, but rather as a consequence of the slow growth of export proceeds there is a strong drive towards substitution. Growth is inhibited by the fact that (*a*) substitution cannot take place fast enough to keep import requirements within the limits of exchange availabilities; and (*b*) efforts to create new industries on the basis of supplying the domestic market alone result in high-cost production and misdirected resources. Because countries cannot or do not specialize in their industrial production, they either produce with sub-optimal equipment or create over-capacity, or both. In addition, they cannot take advantage of the opportunities to specialize in the production of commodities in which they have peculiar advantages resulting from access to raw

[1] See Douglass C. North, 'Location Theory and Regional Economic Growth', *Journal of Political Economy*, June 1955, pp. 243-58.

materials, location, etc. Moreover, the problem is not so much that countries may be producing the wrong things, since in time, and given broad enough markets and access to skills, techniques and know-how from abroad, they might become reasonably productive in any one of a very large range of industrial commodities. Rather, the problem stems from the fact that they are unable to specialize, and in trying to grow on the basis of limited exchange resources, they are seeking to produce too many things, including finished commodities, intermediate goods and, to an increasing extent, capital goods as well.

The creation of regional trading arrangements provides an opportunity for specialization and increased trade, thereby broadening the export base of individual countries and increasing the productivity of the trading region as a whole. It might, of course, be argued that the gains would be greater if each country broadened its export base by expanding its export of both primary commodities and of manufactures to the rest of the world. This is a good doctrine to preach, but it has not happened and it is not likely to happen until developing countries learn to trade and compete with one another on a regional basis. At a later stage, just as the countries of Western Europe soon began to compete actively in a wide range of commodities with the United States once they had learned to compete with one another, so also, I believe, trade and competition in industrial products among developing countries will provide the experience and discipline for them to sell their industrial products on world markets, thereby broadening the export base of the entire region. This process, of course, will be assisted by the operations of international corporations with distribution facilities throughout the world. Moreover, increased investment by foreign enterprise in developing countries will be greatly encouraged if they can produce finished products or components for sale throughout the preference region.

There is, of course, another pattern by which development can and will take place, at least for some countries: that is, for the export sectors to be the leading sectors and industrialization to develop, first for supplying the local market, and later for sale to world markets. Such countries may be able to develop along the same lines as the United States, Canada and Japan and certain Western European countries developed during the nineteenth century. However, I fear that this pattern of development may be the exception to the rule in the twentieth century.

Chapter 10

FORMS OF INTERNATIONAL ECONOMIC RELATIONS WHICH INFLUENCE DEVELOPMENT OF WORLD TRADE

BY

A. BECHIN

Institute of World Economics and International Relations, Moscow

I. INTRODUCTION

THE world economy of today presents an aspect of coexistence and peaceful economic competition between two different social systems. This is a self-evident and fundamental fact. Another feature of contemporary economic relations is the number of young sovereign states which are entering the world arena after having achieved the political conditions necessary for independent economic development.

The necessity for a special analysis of international economic relations arises in the first place by reason of this diversity of social and economic conditions and of existing social structures, together with the great differences in the levels of material production in the various countries and regions of the world.

And indeed, whether we are studying the individual problems of classical economic theory or some of the more significant practical problems of trade — the movement of capital, economic collaboration, payment balances — we must in all cases first answer the following questions : Who are the protagonists in the process ? What form of economic relations has caused one phenomenon or another to arise or to predominate ? Furthermore, the sceptical mind of the scientist inquires : 'Could things not have been done differently ? Are there not alternative forms of development which could have brought about different results ?'

Many of the characteristics of present international economic relations were already determined during the industrial revolution in England and other countries of Western Europe. Factory production of cheap goods ruined the handicraft industries in many countries with the result that these countries became the primary-producing

230

dependencies of the industrially developed countries. Other lines of development in the world economy have been determined by colonial conquest and by the export of capital. Specific forms of foreign investments in the economies of colonial and dependent countries have exerted a tremendous influence on the structure of the world economy and on the whole trend of its development. At the turn of the century, the world was already divided into a small group of creditor states and an overwhelming majority of debtor states.

As a general result the number of industrially developed countries has remained rather small, and the established forms of international economic relations, having resisted changes appropriate to progress, have tended increasingly to come into conflict with the real demands of economic growth in individual countries and in the world economy as a whole. This has resulted in the creation of powerful explosive forces which have made themselves felt in world wars, social revolutions and the disintegration of the colonial system.

The subject of my paper deserves all the more attention in view of the fact that the process of renovation of economic forms of life — a process which has so radically changed the face of the world in the last few decades — may be expected to accelerate increasingly in the near future.

The great principle of universal progress which the Soviet Union seeks to uphold is based on the acceptance of peaceful coexistence between countries with different social and economic systems and of non-interference in the internal life of their peoples. The maintenance of this principle in the field of world economic relations requires the development of trade to be on terms of equality and mutual benefit, with disinterested assistance to the economies of other countries in the promotion of world peace and prosperity. The vital force and excellence of this principle in international relations is strikingly demonstrated not only within the world socialist system, but in other systems as well.

Significant advances through modernization of the forms of economic relations have also taken place in capitalist states. The disintegration of the colonial system has brought with it great changes in international trade, in the movement of capital, and in the sphere of currency, payments and the settlement of accounts, all of which have already speeded up the economic development of many countries and have favourably affected the world market. There still remain, however, a number of forms of association characterized by inequality and dependence which are obsolete and only hamper the development of world trade and individual economic growth.

II. FORMS OF CAPITAL EXPORT

In practice the various forms of capital export and the methods of employing it by the importing countries often lead to very diverse results. For instance, so-called direct investments in the economies of primary-producing countries, which up to recent times have predominated in international movements of private capital, have in almost all cases proved ineffective. Here no distinction is made between ownership of capital and its employment in production, trade or banking : capital is simply transferred into another country and continues to be under the control of its owner and is used in his interests. The business enterprises of foreign monopolies act like colossal siphons extracting wealth from the primary-producing countries and pouring it into the capital-exporting countries. And this is not limited to the remittance of profits, the size of which is often so much greater than that of the capital originally invested. Even more harmful is the influence of direct investments on the economies of capital-importing countries and on international trade owing to the fact that the capital-exporting countries remove large quantities of material assets, and export earnings appropriated primarily by foreign monopolies. On the other hand, when capital is exported as a loan, and placed at the disposal of a national government or of the business men of a capital-importing country and used in production, the export receipts enter directly into the national economy. Returns to the creditors are only a part of the profits and take the form of interest on the loan capital, the rate of which is regulated by the market mechanism.

It is not possible to estimate the exact amount of wealth which is inequitably exported from capital-importing countries, but some idea may be obtained from the following data : during the twelve-year period from 1946 to 1958 the export of new capital by the United States amounted to $11·4 billion, while remittances of profits alone during the same period reached the enormous sum of $19·6 billion. Thus, total profits received were considerably greater than the amount of capital originally exported. During the period 1957–1959 alone, the net export of capital in terms of direct investment totalled $5·1 billion, and profits $9·8 billion. In this connection one cannot but agree with an important point made by Sir Roy Harrod in his paper, namely, that 'borrowing from abroad should normally be regarded as imposing a net long-run burden on a country's balance of payments. It is a fallacy to suppose that this can be obviated by increasing the amount borrowed year by year' (p. 140).

But profits received represent only a portion of the wealth exported with equivalent repayment. Perhaps even more significant is the fact that a considerable share of the total remaining value, for example of oil, metallic ores and other kinds of export goods which are produced by foreign-owned enterprises, is withdrawn completely, and without any compensatory return, from the economies of under-developed countries because these countries receive only a part of the declared profits. To this we should add that foreign firms engaged in trade, insurance, banking and shipping appropriate a considerable part of the value of goods produced by national enterprises. Without risk of error, we may assume that up to 40 per cent of the value of the exports of many countries is appropriated, in one way or another, by the owners of foreign capital. On the other hand, it is easy to imagine what great advantages would accrue in the development of the economies of dependent countries and in the expansion of world trade if this form of employment of foreign capital were abolished.

To avoid misunderstanding, I would point out that foreign capital directly invested in industrially developed countries, or in those branches of the economy which serve the needs of the internal market of a capital-importing country, is essentially different in character. Even in these cases, however, the negative consequences of direct investments are obvious. Unfortunately, lack of space prevents me from giving a more detailed analysis of this important problem. I should, nevertheless, like to stress one essential point : direct investments, even in the economies of industrially developed countries, can create conditions of dependence and heavily overburden the balance of payments ; and in many cases these direct investments compete with the national production of a capital-exporting country, just as in capital-importing countries. Such facts are well known and need not be dwelt upon at greater length.

For these reasons, the Soviet Union and other socialist countries do not make direct investments in the economies of foreign countries.

In regard to changes in other forms of capital export during recent years, we should note that these have been of a dual and contradictory nature. On the one hand, it is a cause for satisfaction that the problems of financial assistance for the economic development of primary-producing countries are widely discussed and that definite measures are being taken to solve them, including some of international scope. At the same time we should also note that government loans, which now predominate in the export of loan-capital, are quite often used for non-productive purposes — for the preparation of war, for the waging of colonial wars against nationalist movements, and, in a number of countries, for the maintenance of police and military forces in support of reactionary regimes. As a rule, only a small part of these loan resources go into the national economy for the development of national industry.

It is far from my purpose here to make captious criticisms of the shortcomings of the capitalist system. There are other reasons for bringing up these matters — reasons which touch the very principle of peaceful coexistence and the livelihood of entire peoples. It is the task of economists to provide an objective evaluation of the inner nature of various economic phenomena ; in this endeavour, many facts are encountered which require the most careful attention.

Economists, in analysing a country's balance of payments, for example, cannot help raising certain questions. It can hardly be considered that government loans and subsidies have been used productively if the amount of money coming from abroad is found to be many times greater than the annual value of its exports — as is the case in South Korea and several other countries. It can only be disquieting to find a situation in which debt repayments amount to from one-third to one-half of the total value of a country's annual exports.

In addition to the unproductive use made of the lion's share of capital received in the form of government loans, one notes also the extremely high rates of interest paid on these loans. Profits must be large, and revenue from exports vast, in order to be able to repay in gold or foreign currency both principal and 6-8 per cent interest on loans received. It must be clear to all that this is extremely difficult to accomplish, even when all the money received in the form of a loan is utilized for the development of production, and favourable export conditions exist.

As is well known, the Soviet Union, taking into consideration a country's actual economic conditions, provides loans and credits at low interest, with arrangements for repayment in local currency or goods. Moreover, though this policy is not altogether philanthropic, its sole aim is to accelerate the economic development of the trade partners of the U.S.S.R. Soviet policy is based on a sober appreciation of a simple and manifest truth, namely, that normal economic relations cannot exist in the world if one state grows rich at the expense of another. One can promote the economic development of one's own country through foreign trade only by mutually advantageous co-operation and a complete appreciation of the economic conditions of other countries. Only through such an approach can international economic relations bring forth a rich harvest for all nations.

III. FORMS OF INTERNATIONAL TRADE

It must always be remembered that trade between countries is a road with two-way traffic. In order to buy it is necessary to sell, and vice versa. Undoubtedly there may be temporary deviations from this rule, but, all in all, continuous and steady trade growth is possible only on this basis.

The new situation in the world market provides an opportunity of verifying the validity of different conceptions of foreign trade. It is one of the manifestations of the general law of science and reality that truth is always concrete. Can the principles of the classical theory of foreign trade be applied to present conditions, when participants in international trade represent groups of countries which differ so greatly? And if they can be applied, then to what extent? In what actual forms of trade relations between states, with such different social and economic characters and levels of development, is it possible to apply the principles of classical theory and free trade? Or do the new conditions in which foreign trade now develops perhaps call for new forms of organization? Without answers to these questions, it is difficult to discuss the problems which are the subject of most of the papers at this conference.

The basic fact (empirically established) that characterizes the state of the world market is the dangerously rapid and substantial decrease in the share of primary-producing countries in export and import trade. While in 1950 their share in the exports of the capitalist world was 34 per cent (by value), in 1960 it dropped to 24 per cent, while their share in the export growth was less than 16 per cent. It must also be remembered that about 70 per cent of the population of the capitalist world lives in these countries. The same tendency is observed in the dynamics of export.

Furthermore, we must take into consideration the fact that the exports of these countries consist of the products not only of national enterprises, but also of those owned by foreign capital. We may cite as an example the export of oil, ores of non-ferrous metals, etc. In many cases even the products of national enterprises are exported by foreign companies, on foreign ships, financed and insured by foreign banks and insurance companies, as, for example, in the case of Australia. In the last eighteen months, expenditure on freight and insurance amounted to about 15 per cent of the value of Australian exports, to which must be added profit remittances, loan payments, etc. As a result there is a lack of foreign currency resources to pay for imports. And this, incidentally, is a country which is economically developed.

If these characteristic conditions of the agrarian and primary-producing countries are taken into consideration, then it becomes apparent that the real situation on the world capitalist market is more difficult than appears from foreign trade statistics. However, statistics concerning the distribution of gold reserves are quite significant. The share of the U.S.A., the countries of Continental Europe and Great Britain at present amounts to about 90 per cent of the gold reserves of all capitalist countries (excluding the international organizations). In 1950 this share was 88 per cent. The ratio of gold reserves to foreign currency reserves has decreased sharply. A substantial increase in foreign currency reserves in many countries reflects nothing but the growth of international indebtedness, and, foremost, that of the U.S.A. and Great Britain.[1]

These are some of the main facts and it is in the light of these facts, in my opinion, that the more concrete problems of international trade should be discussed. Using the colourful expression of Professor Rueff, we may say that 'the secret of a deficit without tears' has not yet been discovered. As to the present deficits in payments balances which make it possible to give without taking, to lend without contracting a loan and to get without paying — such chronic and growing deficits, which, moreover, have no prospect of adjustment, will lead to no good. In this we may entirely agree with Professor Rueff.

The great changes in the dynamics and pattern of trade which have taken place in the world capitalist market in recent years give enough ground for a more practical and more realistic reconsideration of some of the theories and principles of the organization of international trade under present-day conditions.

The first problem which seems to us particularly urgent concerns the formation of closed economic groups, uniting the countries of Western Europe. There is no doubt that the decrease in the share of primary-producing countries in exports and imports is one of the primary results of the organization of the Common Market in Western Europe. In fact the value of exports in the period 1957–1960 showed practically no increase in the U.S.A., and even a decrease in the countries of Latin America, Asia (excluding Japan), Africa and Oceania. The total value of exports in the entire capitalist market actually increased in the same period by \$12·5 billion and that of the countries of Western Europe by \$14 billion. It seems, therefore, that the increase in the value of exports must be attributed

---

[1] In this connection I do not intend to discuss the contents of the series of articles by the well-known French economist, Professor Jacques Rueff, published in *Le Monde* in June 1961 ; but in passing it may be noted that the views of this prominent specialist deserve very serious attention.

to a small group of industrially developed countries of Western Europe. The remaining countries, with the exception of the U.S.A. and Japan, reduced their exports in terms of current prices.

The growing anxiety felt in most countries of the capitalist world concerning further measures taken to increase the separation of the Common Market countries from the other regions of the world is fully understandable. Such anxiety is all the more justified as the strong link between this closed economic grouping and the military and political measures of NATO becomes increasingly evident. It is worth noting that about one-third of the total increase in value of world exports in the period from 1957 to 1960 fell to the share of Western Germany. This country now has at its disposal a third of the total foreign currency reserves of the capitalist countries of Continental Europe, and its share alone amounts to 22 per cent of the exports of this group of countries.

It must be pointed out that there is nothing more incompatible with the balanced development of world trade than this closed economic grouping. The introduction of uniform tariffs and the pursuance of a joint foreign trade policy in relation to third countries cannot but result in still more dangerous instability for the world capitalist market. It would seem advisable to give some thought to other ways of increasing foreign trade without discrimination against third countries, particularly when they happen to be countries of Asia and Latin America whose exports consist chiefly of raw materials.

Another question of trade policy, which is of great importance at present, is the problem of safeguarding the national economies of the less developed countries which only recently started upon the road of independent development. As a result of the special conditions of their economic development in the period of colonial rule and economic dependence, the production and export trade of these countries acquired a monocultural character. Their manufacturing capacity is too weak to withstand competition from the industrially developed states ; therefore measures to safeguard their national economies from the destructive competition of developed capitalist powers are natural and absolutely indispensable. Safeguards are necessary in the sphere of tariff policy and quota restrictions, as well as that of currency control.

The experience gained from the so-called stabilization plans, realized in a number of countries under the auspices of the International Monetary Fund, demonstrated how dangerous it is not to take into consideration the economic interests of such states. The 'open door' policy, the policy of complete 'freedom of trade', the right of the foreign investor to transmit profits without limitation, equal investment rights for foreign and national capital — all these schemes can, and do, provide great benefits to investors from the wealthy capitalist countries; but at the same time it is highly improbable that they have assisted the balanced growth of the local economy and the balanced development of international trade.

The safeguarding of international interests (as opposed to the selfish preferment of individual states or corporations) requires forms of intra-national trade organization and a foreign trade policy that can be adjusted to the specific conditions prevailing in states which have recently embarked on the road of independent economic development. The most valuable aid that could be given to these states would be the opportunity to accelerate the development of their national economies and bring about the expansion of international trade. Such a policy does not in fact call for any sacrifice on the part of the developed and wealthy capitalist states, unless the abstention from harming another state with which one intends to do business can be considered a sacrifice. Without these safeguards, the slogans of 'free trade' and 'equal opportunity' will, in fact, only be a cover for inequitable economic relationships with the most harmful consequences.

The third problem of the new sovereign states in the sphere of international trade is that of the balance of their economic development. The economies of these countries suffer from frequent fluctuations in raw material prices. The one-sidedness of their exports, the frequent predominance of a single raw material in production and export, the domination of foreign capital in the production of these goods and in foreign trade, the absence of a national merchant fleet, etc., are all legacies of colonialism which are responsible for the continuance of the semi-colonial character of their economic relations with the rest of the world.

Although there is no dearth of scientific works devoted to the problems of international integration, balanced development, etc., in general their authors, when dealing with questions of international economic relations, in the final analysis come to pessimistic conclusions which are not justified if the problems are looked at from a broad historical viewpoint. A closer examination of their arguments reveals that these authors see the problems as insoluble in the setting of the prevailing forms of economic relations. A solution, however, can be found: experience in recent years has shown that the liquidation of colonialism — of the most pernicious and anti-social type — has not led a single country to disaster. On the contrary, improvements in the forms of social life have only served to accelerate economic and social progress.

In the long run the economy of the United States could only benefit if American corporations were to buy at world prices the raw materials, oil and metals produced in the countries of Latin America, Asia and Africa, instead of appropriating them as their own property, as at present, and thereby undermining the economies of a number of countries and, consequently, international trade. Therefore only the total abolition of all vestiges of colonialism in the sphere of international economic relations can open up opportunities for the balanced development of the national economies of those countries which are the most populous of the capitalist world.

The only way to end the unequal position of these countries in the world economy is industrialization. The division of countries, into agrarian and industrial, can no longer be made on the basis of the international division of labour and of international economic co-operation. As historical experience and economic theory demonstrate, the division of labour by means of greater specialization of industrial production in different countries is a powerful force in accelerating the expansion of international trade, as exemplified by the development of the world socialist system. The experience of the West European countries also reveals, though in a different way, that greater specialization in the industrially developed countries speeds up economic development as a whole, including the expansion of foreign trade.

IV. THE NEED TO END THE ARMAMENTS RACE

Of the greatest importance and urgency in the sphere of international economic relations is the need for disarmament. Historians will in the years to come be astonished at some of the evidence of today. Enormous sums are expended to work out new means of human destruction, while it is not found possible to devote even a tenth of such sums to further the economic development of states in dire need.

The benefits of disarmament have been so much emphasized by the press and by economists and statesmen of various political views that it may seem pointless to say anything further. It is, however, our duty to do so, given the immense dangers inherent in the accumulation of means of mass destruction, and the equally grave consequences of the armaments race.

Much has been written in recent months to the effect that the outbreak of a crisis in the U.S.A. has been checked by increasing military expenditure. Nothing could be more erroneous, for the same magazines and newspapers also contain reports about the vast requirements of municipal services, public education and health, and the huge sums of money and the effort needed for the development of areas within the U.S.A., not to mention the demands for capital equipment of industry, agriculture and transport in many other countries of the world.

Now if the enormous resources at present being wasted in preparation for war were used to satisfy the requirements of peaceful development, mankind would be saved not only from the danger of destruction but also from the economic breakdowns that are the inevitable result of the armaments race.

To sum up, we may draw the following conclusions : first, that a change in the forms of international economic relations was brought about by the disintegration and abolition of the obsolete forms of relations which originated in the period of industrial capitalism ; and secondly, that the complexity of the modern world makes urgent the establishment and strengthening of relations of equality between nations, based on principles of mutual advantage and of non-interference in the domestic affairs of other countries. This will go a long way in the promotion of universal peace and the acceleration of economic and social progress throughout the world.

Chapter 11

INTERNATIONAL TRADE AND TRADE CYCLES, 1950–60

A. LAMFALUSSY
Banque de Bruxelles

I. INTRODUCTION

THIS essay in applied economics is not concerned to advance new theories. Its purpose is to contribute in a small way to the understanding of the working of the international economy between 1950 and 1960. More specifically, I shall try to provide part of the answer to an ambitious question : How does it happen that there has been no major trade cycle in the world economy during the last decade ?

The scope of a paper, as well as the limitations of the statistical evidence, seriously restricts analysis. After some (unsuccessful) attempts to work out a complete, though simplified, model of the world economy which would fit past history, I resigned myself to answering the question by applying a semi-historical, semi-analytical method. This consists in concentrating upon periods of recession in Western Europe and North America, and in trying to find out the reasons why the international multiplier had been too weak to induce a cumulative process leading to world-wide depression. In other words, I shall stop short of building a formal model and limit myself to preliminary work on some of the elements, leaving it for someone else to fit them together as a whole.

II. WORLD TRADE CYCLES FROM 1949 TO 1960

It might be convenient to start off by showing the cyclical fluctuations between 1950 and 1960. This is done in Graph I.

The United States has experienced three recessions : the first in 1954, the second in 1957–58 and the third in the second half of 1960 and the first quarter of 1961. This pattern does not come out quite clearly in the yearly averages. The index of industrial production has been more sensitive to the trade cycle than that of the gross

241

national product; but both indicators show that in no cases have there been actual drops in two successive years, and that recessions were followed both in 1955 and in 1959 by a period of short but sharp up-turn.

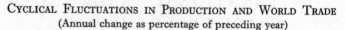

GRAPH I

CYCLICAL FLUCTUATIONS IN PRODUCTION AND WORLD TRADE
(Annual change as percentage of preceding year)

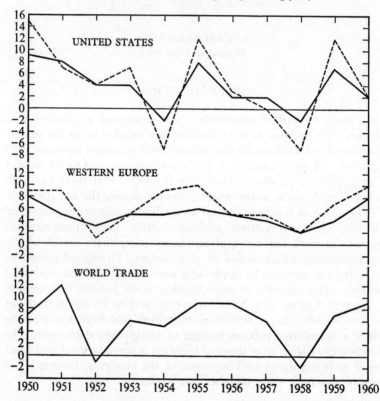

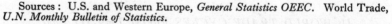

Sources : U.S. and Western Europe, *General Statistics OEEC*. World Trade, *U.N. Monthly Bulletin of Statistics*.

Notes : U.S. and Western Europe ————: GNP at constant (1954) market prices.
U.S. and Western Europe — — —: Index of General Industrial Production.
World Trade : volume index.

Western Europe's story runs on somewhat different lines. There has not been a single year between 1950 and 1960 during which the OEEC figures would have shown a decline. The worst years were 1952 and 1958 ; but in both cases the 'recession' became apparent only in a substantial slackening of the rate of growth. Slight absolute fluctuations could be detected in the over-all *quarterly* index of industrial production, and also in some individual countries, such as the United Kingdom and Belgium ; but if we look at Western Europe as a whole, and if we do not go beyond yearly indices, the trade cycle appears only in the changes in the rate of growth of output. It is worth noticing that the recession coincided, in the United States and in Western Europe, only in 1958 ; [1] there was a lag of somewhat more than a year between the European pause in 1952 and the American down-turn in 1954, while the U.S. recession in 1960–61 took place at a time when Western Europe as a whole was booming ahead at a very rapid pace.

With the exception of two years (1952 and 1958), when there was a slight fall, the volume of world trade has been progressing rapidly, at an average rate nearly as rapid as that achieved by industrial production in Western Europe.

Lack of statistics makes it impossible to work out a reliable indicator of over-all economic activity for the non-industrial areas. But even without this piece of information, three points stand out fairly clearly :

(a) Trade cycles have been apparent in changing rates of growth rather than in the fluctuations of absolute levels. This applies especially to Western Europe.

(b) The degree of synchronization between the cycles in the two main industrial areas and in International trade has been remarkably weak. Only 1958 seems to be a major exception to this rule ; this is the only year when the recession in the United States and the pause in Europe took place at the same time as an absolute fall in the volume of world trade.

(c) Recessions, whether defined as a fall in rates of growth or as a decline in levels of activity, have been short-lived. There has been no world depression — if this phrase is defined as a synchronized, cumulative and long-lasting fall in activity and trade all over the world.

The happy development of the 'fifties is the more surprising as it has been running against the expectations of most economists. Since 1944 we have, in fact, been expecting a depression every other year. It may not be too disrespectful to remind you that the tone underlying the discussions of the IEA.'s Oxford Conference in 1952 was

[1] Strictly speaking, even this is not completely true. The U.S. recession took place in the fourth quarter of 1957 and in the first half of 1958, while the European pause started roughly at the beginning of 1958 and lasted until the first months of 1959.

definitely pessimistic about our ability to prevent the international transmission of a depression which might originate in an autonomous recession in the United States.[1]

Looking back over economic events since 1950, one would be tempted to suggest that the reasons for the high degree of stability of the 'fifties should be sought in the strong upward trend displayed by the greater part of the world. Since we have been living in a period of rapid expansion, it is only too natural that cyclical disturbances should have been influencing rates of growth rather than absolute levels, or should have been producing only short-lived recessions located mainly in the United States. Western Europe has been growing more rapidly than the United States ; hence it is normal that absolute declines in activity should have occurred in America rather than in Europe.[2]

A statement of this kind, however, would amount to little more than begging the question. For even if we assume (as I shall do) that there has been a rising stream of 'autonomous' investment, or deliberate government policy acting as a stimulus to rapid growth *within* each country or area, we are still left wondering about the actual ways and means by which this *primum mobile* prevented the recessions in the United States or the pauses in Europe from spreading out to other parts of the world and developing into a full-scale depression. This boils down to saying that we still have to find out why the 'international floor' has been so resistant in 1952, 1954, 1958 and 1960–61. My paper concentrates upon this floor-searching activity by examining the history of the recessionary or quasi-recessionary years, mainly from the point of view of the international transmission of the trade cycle.

III. A DIGRESSION ON THEORY

(i) *A Distinction*

Before getting down to history, it will, however, prove useful to have a short look at theory.

Any area may affect the level of activity of the rest of the world — *via* international trade — in two distinct ways : by producing autonomous cyclical disturbances, and transmitting them to the

---

[1] *The Business Cycle in the Post-War World,* edited by Erik Lundberg, London, 1955 ; especially pp. xv, 246-82, 326-7, 342-51.

[2] This reasoning can be carried even further by calling attention to the fact that the two main European countries where cyclical disturbances have actually taken place — the United Kingdom and Belgium — have also experienced the lowest rate of growth among European countries.

rest of the world, or by being sensitive to shocks coming from abroad, and reflecting them back into the world. The practical importance of this distinction is fairly obvious. The United States have often been regarded as an autonomous source of cyclical disturbances; yet it has also been often asserted that they are not very sensitive to cyclical disturbances coming from the rest of the world. Hence it does not seem possible to say (without making precise assumptions about both sides of the medal) whether a change in the share of the United States in world trade would have a stabilizing or a de-stabilizing effect on the world economy.[1]

(ii) *The External Impact of Autonomous Cyclical Disturbances*

Let us first examine, shortly, the channels through which autonomous cyclical disturbances can be transmitted to the rest of the world. The first of these channels is the area's marginal propensity to import, i.e. the change of imports (ΔM) relative to a change in the area's income (ΔY). The second channel, which is often neglected in theoretical writings (but closely watched by policy-makers), is the response of exports (ΔX) to an (autonomous) change in the area's income (ΔY).

If the area's imports consisted exclusively of goods not produced by the home industry, if exports consisted exclusively of goods which could not be sold on the home market, and if there were no competition on the factor level either, it would be relatively easy to deal with these propensities. The marginal propensity to import would depend on the pattern of home expenditure and on the production functions of the home industry. As for the 'marginal propensity to export', it would clearly be nil: a change in Y could induce no change in X this latter being determined exclusively by the intensity of external demand.

Once we admit that there are possibilities of substitution, either on the commodity or on the factor levels, or on both, the analysis becomes much more complicated; indeed so complicated that an arbitrary simplification seems to be unavoidable. Let us assume, to begin with, that it is possible to talk of a general level of prices in the area relative to those in the rest of the world. Acting on this assumption, the influence of the relative price level on the two marginal propensities may be outlined as follows:

(a) In the case of an *increase* in Y, the rise in M and the fall in X will be the greater, the higher the relative price level in the

[1] The implications of this have been most usefully stressed by W. Beckerman, 'The World Trade Multiplier and the Stability of World Trade, 1938 to 1953', *Econometrica*, July 1956.

area. In other words, the marginal propensity to import (which is positive) and the marginal propensity to export (which is negative) will be the greater, the higher the area's relative price level. This amounts to saying that, if the competitive position of a country is weak, its expansion will exert (all other things being equal) a strong stimulating influence on the activity of the rest of the world, both through increased imports and through falling exports.

(*b*) In the case of a *decrease* in Y, the reverse holds. The fall of imports and the rise in exports — and therefore the recessionary impact on the rest of the world — will be the greater, the lower the relative price level of the area. Low relative prices will tend to amplify the impact of a falling income on imports ; moreover, they are likely to induce a 'perverse' increase in exports. This latter may happen on the assumption that in a fully employed economy, firms prefer to sell to the home market, even if their prices allow them to invade foreign markets ; once, however, they start working below capacity, they will be prepared to undertake the necessary selling effort in the export markets. Conversely, if relative prices are high, a fall in home expenditure may leave imports little affected, the burden of the reduction falling on home production ; and exports will not rise in this case.

The conclusion is that relative prices will have an asymmetrical influence on the international transmission of cyclical disturbances. If what we fear is world depression, a country which produces autonomous disturbances is apt to be a much greater nuisance if its price level is low ; while, if there is a danger of world inflation, an expanding high-cost country will have a greater de-stabilizing influence. Or, to put things in a slightly different way : a high-cost country will exert a strong upward influence on the world when its income is rising, and a weak downward pressure when its income is falling. Bearing in mind that this conclusion applies only if (and when) there are possibilities of substitution between commodities and/or factors of production, we see that the asymmetrical nature of the area's impact on the rest of the world will increase along with the expansion of the range of goods or factors which are adequate substitutes for each other.

(iii) *The Reflection Ratio*

Turning now to the other side of the medal, it seems advisable to approach the problem in three different ways.

First, let us assume that the area, which receives an impulse from abroad through its foreign trade, pays no attention to its exchange reserves and has no government policy at all. In this case, the area's reflection ratio, i.e. the change in its imports in response to a change in its exports, will depend on its marginal propensity 'not to spend' and on its marginal propensity to import. If g stands for the international reflection ratio, s for the marginal propensity not to spend (which is the combination of the marginal propensity to save and of an investment coefficient) and m for the marginal propensity to import, then [1]

$$g = \frac{m}{s+m}.$$

Secondly, let us assume that exchange reserves are adequate. This enables the government to carry out an internal policy of stabilization, without having to pay attention to the balance of payments. If exports rise, the government will cut its own expenditure or try to curb private spending ; if exports fall, it will follow the opposite line of policy. Now it is of course quite possible that a policy of this kind may fail to achieve greater stability. This can happen if it is implemented with undue delay, in which case it may even lead to greater instability. But if it is carried out with luck, speed and ability, it will result in offsetting, partly at least, the working of the area's international reflection ratio.

The third possibility is that exchange reserves are not what they ought to be : they can be too high. Although we are unlikely to meet very frequently national governments genuinely believing that they own excessive reserves, the rest of the world may, in a few outstanding cases at least, exert some political pressure on a high-reserve country, the government of which will then have to behave as if it were really convinced of possessing too much gold. If this happens to be the case, the result will again be asymmetrical. When its exports are rising, the high-reserve country will be compelled to adopt a policy resulting in an increase in imports at least equal to the rise in exports ; this would occur in the absence of a deliberate policy only if the propensity 'not to spend' were nil. Government policy might take various forms : internal expansion (if there is no danger of inflation), or tariff reductions (if there is already excess demand), or even capital exports or grants if the government wishes to avoid a deterioration of the external balance on current account or is under the influence of local pressure groups. This will in any

[1] For a full discussion and proof, see J. J. Polak, *An International Economic System*, London, 1954, p. 42.

case amplify the expansionary effect induced by rising exports. But if exports are falling, too-high reserves are apt to lead to the dampening of the recessionary impact : first, because the government will feel free to carry out a counter-cyclical policy ; secondly, because external pressure will be put upon national authorities to maintan imports or the outflow of capital funds. Thus a high-reserve country is likely to weaken its own reflection ratio when the outside impulse is a recessionary one, and amplify it when it receives an inflationary shock.

The reverse holds, *mutatis mutandis*, for a low-reserve country, with the slight difference that maintaining the reserves *above* a certain minimum level is more binding than keeping them *below* an ill-defined maximum. A low-reserve country will, in any case, strengthen a recessionary impact and weaken an expansionary one.[1]

IV. THE HISTORY OF THE LOWER TURNING-POINTS

(i) *Tools and Assumptions*

I shall concentrate upon the history of four recessionary or quasi-recessionary years : 1952 (pause in Western Europe), 1954 (recession in the United States), 1958 (recession in the United States and pause in Western Europe) and 1960–61 (recession in the United States).

The main statistical tools are given in the statistical appendices (below, pp. 271–6). They consist of yearly international trade statistics between three areas,[2] covering the eleven-year period from 1950 to 1960, of yearly statistics of national product and expenditure and of the balance of payments for Western Europe and the United

---

[1] It is the asymmetrical role of low-reserve countries which throws some doubt on the validity of Dr. Polak's analysis at the IEA's Oxford Conference in 1952 (see his paper on 'The Post-War International Cycle' in *The Business Cycle in the Post-War World*, London, 1955, pp. 246-65). He argues that in order to take into account the inadequate level of reserves in the post-war world, imports have to be made a function of the level of reserves rather than of the national income and of relative prices : a procedure more appropriate to the analysis of the inter-war period. As a result, he works out a model in which imports are assumed to be a linear function of reserves two periods before ; and his model leads to cyclical fluctuations which, on the whole, are of a more unstable nature than cycles resulting from the inter-war mechanism. My objection to this way of thinking is that if reserves are really too low, as Dr. Polak assumes they are, their *increase* will *not* induce higher imports, or at least not by the same amount as the reduction in imports which is induced by a *fall* in reserves. According to the *Proceedings* of the Conference, Mr. Champernowne criticized Dr. Polak's paper for a similar reason (p. 344).

[2] Namely, Western Europe (often called just Europe, which is a convenient short-hand for the member countries of the defunct OEEC), North America (comprising the United States and Canada), and a rather heterogeneous group of Non-Industrial Areas (NIA, which is the rest of the world with the exception of Japan, China, the Soviet Union and Eastern Europe).

States, and of the official gold and foreign exchange holdings for all three areas. These figures have two obvious defects : first, they are yearly, whilst quarterly figures would have been much more useful ; secondly, they are dollar values at current prices (with the exception of the data on national product and expenditure). Although these are handicaps, little can be done about them in the present state of our statistical information. Quarterly trade returns would only be really useful if they were adjusted for seasonal variations ; and such statistics are not readily available.[1] There are no integrated quarterly national product statistics for Western Europe. Volume and price indices for inter-area trade, to the best of my knowledge, are not available, and the aggregation of scattered national indices seems to be a hopeless task. So we have to accept the appendices as a starting-point ; but I shall try to supplement them with fragmentary information whenever this seems possible and desirable. Some of the material is supplied in Appendix V (p. 276).

When summing up ten years' history in a dozen pages, a high degree of simplification is unavoidable. I shall proceed on the assumption that both the United States and Western Europe are capable of producing autonomous recessions, and that both of them are open to external influences. The Non-Industrial Areas, on the other hand, are assumed to have no cyclical autonomy and to behave therefore only passively. Moreover, I shall deal with the internal mechanics of autonomous recessions only in so far as this is necessary for the understanding of their international impact. Finally I shall assume that in all three areas there have been forces at work (government policy, private investment, etc.) producing a general upward trend ; in other words, it will be assumed that, had all three areas been closed economies, they would have experienced only short-lived recessions. International trade, however, might have changed this state of affairs : either by inducing cumulative down-turns through the working of the (spontaneous) international multiplier, or by imposing upon the governments policies leading to the aggravation of recessions. This did not happen. Why ?

(ii) *1952 : Pause in Western Europe* [2]

Although the decline in the rate of growth of Western Europe in 1952 was sharper than that of the United States (see Graph I),

---

[1] There are OEEC statistics of this kind from 1952 ; but the areas covered are not the same as those used by the yearly GATT reports ; moreover, imports are computed at c.i.f., while exports are computed at f.o.b. values. The adjustments required are beyond the means of a solitary research worker.

[2] Unless otherwise stated, the figures quoted throughout the paper are taken from the statistical appendices, below, pp. 271-6.

especially if growth is measured by changes in industrial production, there was also a slackening in the pace of the American expansion. In both areas, the outbreak of the Korean war had been followed in 1951 by the resurgence of inflationary pressures. Restrictive measures, both monetary and fiscal, had been adopted by the end of 1951 and this, jointly with a more or less spontaneous exhaustion of the inventory boom, resulted in 1952 in a lower rate of growth. The slack was very unevenly distributed both geographically and by industry. Europe was more affected than North America, and within Europe, the United Kingdom, Belgium, the Scandinavian countries and France registered absolute falls in their industrial production. The textile industry suffered severely in all countries ; the OEEC index of textile production shows a decline of 10 per cent from 1951 to 1952. There was a fall of about 4 per cent in the output of chemicals, while production in other branches of industry continued growing, howbeit more slowly than in 1951.[1] Thus there is some justification in calling the 1952 pause a textile recession, occurring as a 'natural' consequence to the stock-piling of textile goods which took place at all stages of trade and production in 1950–51.

Although the decline in inventory accumulation and the recession in the textile industry were common both to Western Europe and the United States, it is interesting to note also the differences between the two areas. The steel strike in the United States in the summer of 1952 has a somewhat disturbing effect on the comparison ; it is nevertheless plausible to assume that, without the strike, industrial production in the United States would have grown faster in 1952 than it did. Thus the divergence between the two areas is even greater than that suggested by Graph I. The difference in demand came, to a large extent, from the rapid increase in military spending. The gross national product of the United States increased by \$12·5 billion in 1952, in spite of a \$4 billion drop in inventory investment, of a fall in net exports, of the near-stability of fixed capital investment and of a rise of only about \$6 billion in private consumption. The upward stimulus came from a \$13·7 billion increase in public consumption, equivalent to 4 per cent of the gross national product in 1951. Meanwhile, in Western Europe, the same factors were at work with two notable exceptions : net exports did not fall ; on the other hand, public consumption rose only by \$2·9 billion, i.e. 1·6 per cent of the gross national product in 1951.

Let us now turn to the international implications of this development. The current value of Western Europe's imports from the Non-Industrial Areas fell from \$12·1 to \$10·5 billion, while European

[1] *General Statistics*, OEEC, Jan. 1961.

purchases in North America declined from $4·8 to $4·4 billion. There is some evidence suggesting that in both cases volumes changed only very little.[1] North America's imports from the Non-Industrial Areas went down from $6·7 to $6·2 billion, but imports from Europe slightly rose from $2·3 to $2·4 billion. This involved, in the first instance, a near-stability of volumes, and in the second, an increase.

It thus appears that both Western Europe and the United States emitted a recessionary impulse towards the Non-Industrial Areas; since in both industrial areas there was a decline in the rate of accumulation of stocks, this is not an unexpected result. There are also good *a priori* reasons for believing that this deflationary disturbance ought to have been reflected back into the industrial world with some vigour. True, there seems to have been no decline in the *volume* of the exports of the primary producing countries;[2] but one may argue that the fall in export prices is apt to produce in these countries a deflationary effect — *via* the profit margins and the investment programmes of the exporting firms — which may be as strong as a deflation induced by a fall in the physical volume of exports. It is even more important that the foreign exchange receipts of the Non-Industrial Areas derived from their exports to industrial countries fell by $2·1 billion, i.e. by more than 11 per cent. If one adds to this the strong deterioration in the terms of trade of the primary-producing countries — of the order of 15 per cent — one should have expected a rather high reflection ratio, i.e. a substantial fall in the imports of the Non-Industrial Areas from the industrial countries. This ought to have taken place in the current value, and even more in the volume, of imports. Table I sums up the argument.

It is therefore surprising that *actual* imports from the industrial areas fell by only $0·4 billion in 1952, i.e. by about 2 per cent, while the decline in volume was only 4 per cent. The reason for this lies, first, in the other items of the Non-Industrial Areas' balance of payments. The strong deterioration in the balance on current account was to some extent offset by the increase in the surplus on capital account.[3] As a result, the fall in gold and foreign

[1] The price index of imported food and raw materials by the OEEC countries shows a fall of about 12 per cent between 1951 and 1952; this points to a probably unchanged quantum of imports from the Non-Industrial Areas. On the other hand, the *total* volume of OEEC imports fell by only 1 per cent in 1952; hence the suggestion that the volume of imports from North America did not change noticeably (*General Statistics*, OEEC, Jan. 1961).

[2] *World Economic Report* 1953–54, UN, New York, 1955, p. 132.

[3] This is not shown by the balance of payments of Europe and North America as given in Appendix IV, but by an independent estimate prepared by the GATT Secretariat (*Le Commerce international en 1959*, Geneva, 1960, p. 47), and is also

exchange reserves was less than one would have expected on the basis of the trade returns. This, however, is not the only explanation. For the compensation was *not* complete ; and the gold and foreign exchange reserves *did* fall by $0·3 billion. The second factor at work was a one-year time-lag : the major drop in imports from the industrial areas took place only in 1953. Fortunately enough, as is argued in subsection (iii), below, on the 1954 recession in the United States, this 'reflective' recessionary impact came too late to disturb Western Europe whose exchange reserves and activity were already expanding by that time.

TABLE I

EXPORT AND IMPORT CAPACITY OF THE NON-INDUSTRIAL AREAS
(Changes from 1951 to 1952)

	As percentage of 1951
(1) Current value of exports to industrial areas	− 11
(2) Unit value of exports to industrial areas	−12
(3) Volume of exports to industrial areas	+ 1
(4) Unit value of imports from industrial areas	+ 2
(5) Import *capacity* :	
(a) current value of import capacity	− 12
(b) volume of import capacity	− 14

Note : (5)(a) is given on the assumption that the exchange reserves of the NIA were at a minimum at the end of 1951, so that a fall of gold and foreign exchange receipts of $2·1 billion should have been offset by a fall of the same magnitude in imports. (5)(b) is obtained by dividing the decline in the current value of import capacity by the rise in the unit value of imports.

Sources : Appendix I (below) and *World Economic Report 1953–54*, UN, New York, 1955.

What happened meanwhile in the industrial areas ? There is no need to go into details about the development in the United States and Canada. In spite of the stability of its trade surplus (but because of an increased outflow of invisibles), North America experienced a reduction in its current external surplus ; however, capital exports and grants declined heavily (mainly those going to Western Europe), so that the over-all balance registered a small surplus. This trend was reversed in 1953. Anyway, this did not really matter. The level of the United States gold reserves (in comparison with the dollar balances held by other countries) was at that time so high that the big deficit in 1953 was greeted with satisfaction by all concerned, including the United States. On the other hand, the internal

supported by a comparison of the strong increase in the trade deficit (Appendix I) with the fall of only $0·3 billion in the NIA's exchange reserves (Appendix III).

upward trend was strong enough to offset the depressing impact of the heavy decline in the net exports of goods and services. Between 1952 and 1953, the gross national product rose again by about as much as in the previous year, under the joint influence of rising private consumption and of fixed capital formation. Defence expenditure also increased, though much less than the year before. Under the impact of the rising level of activity in the United States, North American imports from Europe expanded by more than 10 per cent in 1953, while imports from the Non-Industrial Areas remained unchanged. Looking exclusively at the current balance, Appendix IV clearly shows that North America's current balance with Western Europe had deteriorated already in 1952, and continued to drop even more disastrously in 1953 ; while its balance with the rest of the world, after a slight improvement in 1952, worsened substantially in 1953.

It is not so easy to sum up further developments in Western Europe, although the main factor responsible for the area's resilience to the contraction in world trade brought about by its own 'pause' seems to be the rapid and substantial improvement of its balance of payments. The deficit of $1·9 billion on current account in 1951 turned into a surplus of $0·7 billion in 1952, and the distribution of the over-all balance by area shows that this improvement took place at the expense both of North America and the Non-Industrial Areas. We shall examine in a concluding section whether the improvement of the current balance with North America may be attributed to some general trend ; but it already appears at this stage that some special factors were at work in 1952 : the smaller decline in North America's rate of growth, the steel strike in the United States, and the increase of the inflow of invisibles. As for the current balance with the Non-Industrial Areas, its improvement is due very largely to that of the trade balance, and this, in turn, may be attributed to the change of the terms of trade in favour of Western Europe, and to a smaller extent to the one-year lag mentioned above.

The appearance of a surplus in Western Europe's external balance in 1952, and its increase in 1953, enabled various European governments to relax step by step the restrictive measures taken in 1951. The revival which set in slowly at the beginning of 1953, however, owes something to the fact that exports to North America continued growing, while the fall of exports to the Non-Industrial Areas started only when the internal expansion was already on the way.

One last point should be mentioned at this stage. Trade *within* Western Europe remained on the same level in 1952 (at current dollars) as in 1951. In 1953 intra-trade increased both in volume and in value. This development played the role of an undoubted stimulus ; and it could take place only because of the establishment of the EPU. The years 1951 and 1952 witnessed a growing imbalance within Europe : without the mechanics of the EPU, the major debtor countries (the United Kingdom and France) would have been compelled to restrict their imports from other members of the OEEC more drastically, and this could have had a cumulatively adverse effect on the balance of payments of the surplus countries.

(iii) *1954 : Recession in the United States*

There can be little doubt that the 1954 recession in the United States was of purely internal origin. From 1953 to 1954, net exports of goods and services rose by $1·6 billion, while the gross national product fell by $4·1 billion. Both private consumption and fixed investment increased, but this was more than offset by the heavy cut in public (mainly military) spending which unhappily coincided with a fall in inventory investment.

The external impact of the recession took the form one might have expected. North American imports from Western Europe fell from $2·7 to $2·4 billion, those from the Non-Industrial Areas declined from $6·2 to $5·9 billion and the intra-area trade also dropped from $5·5 to $5·2 billion. Thus the recession was duly transmitted to the rest of the world ; yet neither Europe nor the Non-Industrial Areas suffered the slightest set-back from this impulse. Indeed the reverse seems to have happened. Western Europe's economic growth became faster in 1954, and even faster in 1955 ; its total imports from North America and from the Non-Industrial Areas went up from $14·8 to $16 billion in 1954, and then to $17·4 billion in 1955. Similarly, the Non-Industrial Areas' imports (from Western Europe and North America) rose from $16 billion in 1953 to $17 billion in 1954 and $18·5 billion in 1955.

The sources of Western Europe's resilience are likely to be found in two facts : first, in the rapid increase of its exports towards the Non-Industrial Areas (+ $0·9 billion offsetting largely the − $0·3 for the exports going to North America) and in the even more rapid expansion of the intra-European trade (+ $1·5 billion) ; secondly, in the vanishing of the imbalance within Europe and in the rise of European gold and dollar reserves.

The first of these facts suggests that while North America properly emitted a recessionary impulse towards Western Europe, the latter did not *receive* it. Since total European exports, even after eliminating intra-European trade, actually increased in 1954, the foreign trade multiplier acted as a stimulus to expansion. Some individual countries or industries may have experienced local difficulties in switching resources from sales in America to exports to the Non-Industrial Areas ; but there have been no difficulties for Europe as a whole. As for the increase in intra-European trade, it is, of course, impossible to know to what extent it created an addition to total demand and to what extent it merely reflected a substitution of foreign goods to home-produced ones ; but it is reasonable to believe that at least part of the increase contributed to European expansion.

The favourable balance of payments position influenced Europe's resilience in face of the American recession in two ways. First, by stimulating intra-European trade. The two deficits and surpluses *within* Europe which gave so great a headache to the EPU in 1951–52 gave way to a fair degree of internal balance during the years 1953–1955 ; although Germany was already well on the way to becoming the biggest creditor of the Union, the position of the other member countries had become more or less stabilized.[1] As a result, considerable progress was made in relaxing quantitative restrictions and in liberalizing intra-OEEC trade ; it is this process of liberalization which seems to have been the decisive factor in promoting the rapid growth of the intra-European trade.

The other facet of the favourable balance of payments position of Europe was the steady increase in the OEEC countries' exchange reserves. Gold and dollar holdings of Western Europe, which stood at \$8·3 billion at the end of 1952, reached \$10·5 billion one year later and \$12·5 billion at the end of 1954. As shown in Appendix IV, Western Europe earned both in 1953 and in 1954 a surplus of around \$2 billion on its over-all balance of payments. The strong exchange position, which was shared by most individual countries, enabled national governments to pursue a fairly liberal import policy not only towards the rest of Europe, but also towards the United States ; moreover, it made it possible to relax the restrictive internal policies adopted in 1951. Official discount rates are good indicators of government policy : between the beginning of 1952 and the end of 1954, almost all OEEC member countries[2] reduced their discount rates. The more important reductions occurred in Germany (from 6 to 3 per cent), in the Netherlands (from 4 to 2·5 per cent), in France and in the United Kingdom (from 4 to 3 per cent).

---

[1] R. Triffin, *Europe and the Money Muddle*, New Haven, 1957, especially p. 184.

[2] The exceptions were Italy, Iceland, Portugal, Switzerland and Turkey.

Owing to the lack of adequate statistics, it is more difficult to get a clear picture of the factors which enabled the Non-Industrial Areas to remain unaffected by the American recession. The trade statistics by themselves, however, provide a good starting-point for the analysis. Table II tells an interesting story. After the rather sharp drop in 1952, exports to North America remained unchanged in 1953, and fell by about 5 per cent in 1954, while sales to Western Europe were picking up already in 1953 and continued to rise in 1954; therefore the *total* currency receipts of the Non-Industrial Areas derived from their trade with the two main industrial areas have been rising steadily between 1952 and 1955. Imports followed the same pattern, though with a certain time-lag. They fell slightly in 1952, and then sharply in 1953, but they picked up in 1954 (especially those from Western Europe) and continued to rise in 1955.

TABLE II

TRADE OF THE NON-INDUSTRIAL AREAS WITH WESTERN EUROPE
AND THE UNITED STATES
(Thousand million dollars, f.o.b. values)

	1951	1952	1953	1954	1955
Exports to					
Western Europe	12·1	10·5	11·0	11·8	12·4
North America	6·7	6·2	6·2	5·9	6·3
Total	18·8	16·7	17·2	17·7	18·7
Imports from					
Western Europe	10·8	10·7	10·1	11·0	12·0
North America	6·9	6·6	5·9	6·0	6·5
Total	17·7	17·3	16·0	17·0	18·5

Source : Appendix I.

There seem to be two possible ways for explaining the pattern of development of imports. First, one might assume that there has been some sort of lagged 'spontaneous' multiplier at work ; secondly, one might point to the recovery of the foreign exchange receipts in 1953–54 which may have induced the governments of the Non-Industrial Areas to relax import restrictions. Since we have no consolidated national accounts for the Non-Industrial Areas, it would be very difficult to make an empirical inquiry into the workings of a 'spontaneous' reflection ratio. We are more lucky with the second assumption ; for there is ample empirical evidence showing that a change actually took place in import policy during 1953.[1] That the substantial improvement in the trade balance of the Non-Industrial Areas in 1953 (as shown in Table II) did in fact result in an over-all surplus in the balance of payments of these areas is clearly shown in Table III. The comparison of the variations in the foreign exchange reserves with the change in the trade balance suggests that the improvement in the trade balance in 1953 was partly (but fortunately not completely) offset by adverse changes in other items of the balance of payments ; this is consistent with what we know about the combined balance of payments of Western Europe and of North America with the rest of the world (see Appendix IV).

TABLE III

OFFICIAL GOLD AND FOREIGN EXCHANGE HOLDINGS
(End of period, thousand million dollars)

	1951	1952	1953	1954	1955
Overseas Sterling Area	7·4	7·2	7·7	7·9	7·7
Latin America	3·0	3·0	3·3	3·2	3·2
Other non-industrial countries (i.e. the rest of the world, excluding North America, Europe and Japan)	3·0	2·9	3·0	3·0	3·2
Total	13·4	13·1	14·0	14·2	14·1

Source : *International Financial Statistics*, May 1961.

Thus it appears that Europe's favourable balance of payments position played a vital role in checking the diffusion of the American recession over the rest of the world. I am even tempted to argue that it played the decisive role. For it is the disappearance of the major imbalance within Europe that made it possible to relax internal restrictions and to encourage the intra-European trade ; and it is the growth of its gold and dollar reserves that enabled Western Europe to resume its expansion and to develop its imports from the Non-Industrial Areas. This, in turn, improved the exchange position of the primary-producing countries already in 1953 and continued to support it in 1954 despite the stagnation (and then the fall) of North American imports and the decline of the capital inflow in 1953. As a result, the Non-Industrial Areas were able to increase their own imports from Western Europe quite sharply in 1954, and thus contributed to keeping Europe immune from the depressing influence of the United States recession. Whether this spectacular phenomenon of external balances would have provided the world with

[1] *World Economic Report 1953–54*, UN, New York, 1955, pp. 138–42.

enough resistance in the case of a prolonged depression in the United States, is a different matter ; but it so happened that the strong revival in North America at the end of 1954 spared the world this experience. The revival, just as the recession, was dominated by internal influences ; but the rising exports both to Europe and to the primary-producing countries had obviously a welcome effect.

(iv) *1958 : Recession in the United States and Pause in Western Europe*

The recession in the United States preceded the pause in Europe ; it took place in 1957–58 rather than in 1958. Hence the yearly national product figures give a somewhat distorted picture of what happened during the recession. They underestimate the decline in the gross national product and do not show the decisive role played by the fall in inventory investment for the very reason that the rate of accumulation of stocks already started rising in the third quarter of 1958. According to the yearly data, the somewhat less than 2 per cent decline in the gross national product took place under the joint influence of three components of total expenditure : a slight fall in inventory investment, a rather severe contraction in fixed capital formation and a substantial decline in net exports of goods and services. The fall in (gross) exports (12 per cent of their 1957 value and somewhat less than 1 per cent of the gross national product) conveys the impression that the decline in foreign demand may have had something to do with the recession. This, however, would be a misleading impression. Both fixed and inventory investments had reached their maximum rate already in 1955–56 ; it was their decline in 1957 and in 1958 which had the main depressing influence. All one can say is that it is not impossible that the sudden rise of North American exports in the winter of 1956–57 — under the impact of the Suez crisis, of the bad harvest in Europe and of the boom in Western Europe — *delayed* the pending recession until the autumn of 1957.

The recession in the United States had a remarkably odd impact on the trade flows between North America and the rest of the world. North American imports from the Non-Industrial Areas declined only very slightly from $6·8 to $6·7 billion ; since prices of primary products fell by about 6 per cent, this may have involved a 4-5 per cent rise in the volume of imports. The oddity was even more obvious in the case of Europe. Imports from Western Europe rose in 1958, both in value and in quantum. Thus the United States, despite their recession, emitted no deflationary impulse ; indeed their foreign trade encouraged expansion in the two other areas. North America's surplus in its trade balance with Europe was lower in 1958 than in any of the years from 1955 to 1957 ; and its surplus over the Non-Industrial Areas was in 1958 lower than in 1957. At the same time, the other items of the balance of payments of the United States did not offset the worsening of the trade balance ; in fact, there was a rise in the outflow of invisibles and in private capital exports. Hence the conclusion that neither Western Europe nor the Non-Industrial Areas received any recessionary impact from North America in 1958. On the contrary, both areas' exchange position towards the United States improved, giving their governments greater scope for expansionist policies.

Western Europe's pause can therefore by no means be regarded as induced by the American recession. The rising exports continued to support Western Europe's activity, while the slackening of the rate of growth was the combined result of a minor inventory recession and of restrictive government policy tending to put a brake on residential construction and on fixed capital formation. The emergence of an excess supply in coal played a particularly conspicuous role in some countries. The restrictive government policy aimed in all countries at preserving internal balance ; in France and in the United Kingdom it aimed also at restoring the balance of payments. Individual surpluses, however, offset individual deficits, so that Western Europe as a whole was earning a small over-all surplus already in 1957, and then a very large one in 1958.

Although they occurred independently from each other, the joint appearance of the recession in the United States and the pause in Europe had a depressing effect on the main international markets. The prices of primary products fell by 6 per cent from 1957 to 1958.[1] The combined exports of the Non-Industrial Areas to Western Europe and to North America fell by $0·7 billion in 1958. This must have had an obviously depressing influence on the area (*via* the profit margins and the investment projects of exporting firms and by influencing government policies), despite the fact that the volume of exports remained more or less unchanged. The 'reflection' of this on imports developed in two stages. Imports from North America fell by $1·0 billion in 1958,[2] while those from Western Europe slightly increased that year. These latter fell, however, by 0·4 billion in 1959, alongside a further decrease in imports of $0·5 billion from North America.

[1] *Le Commerce international en 1959*, GATT, Geneva, 1960, p. 89.
[2] The *whole* of the $1·0 billion fall cannot, of course, be regarded as a reflection of the decline in export earnings. Part of the United States exports to the Non-Industrial Areas are primary products, and these were affected by the fall in prices as much as were the exports of the Non-Industrial Areas. The share of these products in the total fall of $1·0 billion is, however, no more than $0·3 billion. (See *Le Commerce international en 1959*, GATT, Geneva, 1960, p. 76.)

This pattern of reflection had a happy influence on the further development in the industrial areas. The burden of the reflection fell on North America ; and in the early part of 1958, there was no talk about a dollar 'crisis'. Indeed fears of a dollar shortage revived again during the Suez crisis in 1956–57 and the reappearance of a heavy United States external deficit in 1958 was greeted by most governments, for a few months at least, as a welcome change. There was no internal pressure either on the United States government to restrain home activity in order to re-establish the external balance. On the contrary, expansionist monetary measures were adopted in the spring of 1958 which, together with the end of the inventory recession, contributed to the revival that took place in the second quarter of 1958. The rapid increase in the United States' activity in 1958–59 brought about a substantial increase in North American imports in 1959. Western Europe's shipments to North America went up by $1·3 billion and those of the Non-Industrial Areas rose by a more modest $0·4 billion.

Thanks to this, when European exports to the Non-Industrial Areas declined in 1959, their depressing effect was more than offset by the export boom to North America. Western Europe's balance of payments on current account registered a surplus of $4·0 billion in 1959 — an increase of $0·4 billion over the preceding year. Thus, while there was an increase in the outflow of official grants and public capital, there was no concern about the balance of payments. France started earning surpluses and the United Kingdom's exchange reserves grew satisfactorily, at least until the last quarter of 1959. Restrictive measures had been gradually relaxed in all countries by the beginning of 1959 ; the external convertibility of the European currencies was established at the end of 1958 ; on January 1, 1959, the first tariff reductions and quota increases took place within the Common Market. All this gave a strong stimulus to intra-European trade, which increased by $2·3 billion during 1959. Western Europe started booming in the spring of 1959.

(v) *1960–61 : Recession in the United States* [1]

Another recession occurred in the United States in 1960–61. The gross national product of the United States [2] reached a peak level at $506 billion in the second quarter of 1960; it fell to $496 billion — i.e. by 2 per cent — in the first quarter of 1961. There is no doubt about the internal origin of the recession. Net exports of

---

[1] The following analysis can, of course, be nothing but a preliminary assessment of the international implications of the recession.

[2] *Economic Indicators*, June 1961.

goods and services rose, during the same period, from $2·0 to $5·3 billion. The deflation was produced by an inventory recession : inventory investment fell from $11·4 billion in the first quarter of 1960 to − $4·5 billion in the first quarter of 1961.

This recession differed from the previous one in so far as it *did* emit a deflationary impulse. North American imports from Europe fell by $0·3 billion in 1960 (i.e. by about 6 per cent), and there was also a slight decline of the Non-Industrial Areas' exports to North America. The external impact has, in fact, been much heavier. Western Europe's exports to North America reached a maximum of $5·8 billion (at a seasonally adjusted yearly rate) in the first quarter of 1960 ; they fell by 19 per cent to $4·7 billion in the last quarter of 1960.[1] Moreover, we have to keep also in mind the substantial increase in North American exports especially to Europe and to some extent also to the Non-Industrial Areas. As a result, the deficit of the United States on current account in 1959 turned into a rapidly growing surplus in 1960. In the first quarter of 1961, the current surplus reached the annual rate of $6·5 billion, which is close to the maximum quarterly surplus earned during the Suez crisis.

Western Europe, as a whole, has not suffered from this development until now. The deflationary effect of the fall of its exports to North America has been more than offset by the rise in its sales to the Non-Industrial Areas. At the same time, the spectacular increase in intra-European trade has no doubt resulted in a substantial net addition to total demand. As for the balance of payments situation, the heavy deterioration of its trade balance with North America (which does not seem to have been offset by any improvement in its trade balance with the Non-Industrial Areas) did not affect, at least until the end of 1960, its exchange reserves. Indeed rather the reverse happened. Western Europe's gold and foreign exchange reserves rose from $22·7 billion at the end of 1959 to $25·1 billion at the end of 1960. This suggests a very heavy increase in capital inflow, reflecting probably both rising long-term capital imports from the United States and an influx of short-term capital attracted by interest rate differentials as well as by fears about the dollar. It is a strange thing that these speculative capital movements gathered momentum at the very time when the current balance of the United States was displaying a startling recovery. With the major exception of the United Kingdom, whose current balance worsened more than that of the other European countries, and which was the first to suffer from a return of the confidence in the dollar in February 1961,

[1] *General Statistics*, OEEC, May 1961.

no European countries have adopted until now policy measures aiming at the restriction of imports. The restrictive monetary measures which were adopted in some countries (for instance, in Germany) were devised in order to weaken internal inflationary pressures. The revaluation of the D. Mark and the Dutch Guilder in March 1961 clearly shows the lack of worry about external balances. As a result, the boom in Western Europe, which started in 1959, has shown no signs of exhaustion until now — again with the exception of the United Kingdom.

The Non-Industrial Areas' current balance deteriorated as a result of the recession in the United States, and this was not offset (as in Europe's case) by a compensating inflow of capital. This, at least, is what is suggested by the statistics on external assets. Official gold and foreign exchange holdings of the Non-Industrial Areas fell during 1960 from $13·5 to $13·1 billion. It is, of course, too early to know whether this will, or will not, induce a decline in their imports. We know, however, that a recovery has already started in the United States ; this makes it likely that the world economy will soon get some support from North America.

V. POSSIBLE INTERPRETATIONS

This, then, is the abridged history of the lower turning-points during the period from 1950 to 1960. I shall now try to sort out whatever pattern seems detectable in the preceding confusion of description and *ad hoc* explanations. There seem to be three possible lines of approach.

To begin with, I have to point out a certain number of 'exogenous' chance occurrences which are unlikely to repeat themselves and can therefore hardly be subject to generalization. The year 1952 was particularly rich in these happy coincidences. The steel strike in the United States in 1952 had a stimulating effect on the European steel industry at a time when internal European demand was slackening. The strong increase in military expenditure in the United States, which had by no means been devised as a counter-cyclical measure (indeed it was rather viewed with some apprehension as adding to the inflationary pressure), gave at the same time a welcome encouragement to the American economy. The recently established EPU performed an exceedingly useful role in 1951–52. It is fairly obvious that without the liquidity-creating ability of this new organization, both France and the United Kingdom would have been compelled to take more heavily restrictive measures, and the German recovery would have been delayed by a few years ; it is quite possible that in these circumstances the 1952 pause in Europe would have turned into a genuine recession.

Another chance occurrence was the very rapid rise of United States exports in 1956–57, due to the Suez crisis. The reappearance of the normal sources of raw-material supply in 1957–58 provided both Western Europe and the Non-Industrial Areas with a 'hidden' source of dollar reserves.[1] Last, but not least, we must bear in mind the stimulating effects of the rapidly rising intra-European trade. In 1953 and especially in 1959, the expansion of intra-European trade made it much easier for Western Europe to recover from the pause — not, of course, by increasing the integrated exchange reserves of the area, but by putting a brake on internal deflationary pressures. However, the various steps of European integration (ECSC, EEC, EFTA), the growing degree of trade liberalization and convertibility, which all contributed to this development, should not be regarded exclusively as 'exogenous' factors. As I shall point out below, their emergence is closely linked to the steady growth of the gold and foreign exchange holdings of Western Europe as a whole, and this fact has played (also for other reasons) a strategic role in preventing pauses and recessions from turning into a world-wide depression.

The second line of approach would insist on the actual mechanics of the fluctuations in imports and exports. Various formal models could be built, taking as data some of the observed characteristics of post-war cycles. The starting-point could be outlined as follows.

The American recessions in 1954 and 1960 took place at a time when Western Europe was booming; this lack of synchronization played in both instances an important part in checking deflationary developments. The American recessions called forth both in 1954 and in 1960 a decline in Western Europe's exports to North America; however, in both cases, this decline was more than offset by the increase in European shipments to the Non-Industrial Areas, so that total European exports actually *increased*. Now the ability of the primary-producing countries to raise their purchases in Europe (in a year when their own exports to North America suffered a setback) might be attributed to the fact that Western Europe's activity had been expanding both in 1953–54 and in 1959–60, resulting in a substantial rise of European imports from the Non-Industrial Areas. Thus the total export receipts of the Non-Industrial Areas, just as those of Western Europe, were *not* affected by the American recessions in 1954 and in 1960.

[1] Sir Donald MacDougall, '*The Dollar Problem : a Reappraisal*', *Essays in International Finance*, Princeton, Nov. 1960, p. 30.

In 1952 and in 1958, a different kind of mechanism was at work. Although there was no complete synchronization in the autonomous cycles of the two industrial areas, the trends were not diverging as clearly as in 1954 and 1960; as a result, the total export receipts of the Non-Industrial Areas fell in both years. The 'reflection' of this worked, however, in an odd way. The imports of the Non-Industrial Areas from North America were declining already in 1952 and in 1958, and continued to fall in the following years. Western Europe's exports to the Non-Industrial Areas were affected, on the other hand, only with a time-lag of one year: in 1953 and in 1959. Now this time-lag may be regarded as a most fortunate event; for both in 1953 and in 1959, recovery in Europe was already sufficiently advanced to be able to go on in spite of a fall in exports to the Non-Industrial Areas.

Thus it seems that we could build several models based on the combination of a few simple assumptions, such as the lack of synchronization in the emergence of recessions in the two industrial areas, short inventory cycles in both of these areas, various lags in the reflection ratio in the Non-Industrial Areas and so on, and examine the conditions on which the fluctuations would remain damped or become explosive. This line of research is worth being (and ought to be) pursued in order to get a complete explanation of the high degree of stability in the 'fifties. But a model-building of this kind falls outside the self-imposed scope of my paper, and I believe anyway that before going into the mechanics of a formal model, it might be advisable to have a closer look at its components on the lines suggested in the theoretical section of this paper. This third method of approach is adopted in what follows.

As on pp. 245-8, we shall examine (i) the extent to which autonomous recessions in North America and Western Europe have been transmitted to the rest of the world, and (ii) the way the three areas reflected back into the world cyclical disturbances coming from abroad.

VI. THE TRANSMISSION TO OTHER COUNTRIES OF RECESSIONS IN NORTH AMERICA OR EUROPE

Owing to the shortcomings of the statistical evidence and to the difficulty of making a *ceteris paribus* analysis when other things are not equal, it is far from being easy to make valid generalizations regarding the first point.

If it were possible to look exclusively at the trade statistics of Appendix I (and to forget all about the role of 'exogenous' factors), it would be quite easy to establish a general rule, which could be summed up as follows. While the United States have proved to be the more unstable of the two industrial areas, it also appears that the external impact of the American recessions has been much weaker than that of the milder and less frequent European pauses. The 1958 recession in the United States had no deflationary impact at all on Europe and only a negligible one on the Non-Industrial Areas.[1] In 1954, North American imports from Western Europe fell by somewhat more than 10 per cent, while those from the Non-Industrial Areas declined only by 5 per cent. In 1960 European sales to North America fell by about 6 per cent, while exports by the Non-Industrial Areas suffered only a very slight set-back. On the other hand, Western European imports from North America fell by about 20 per cent from 1951 to 1953, and imports from the Non-Industrial declined by 13 per cent in 1952. In 1958 North American exports to Western Europe declined by 17 per cent, and those of the Non-Industrial Areas by 5 per cent. If one adds to this that there was no absolute fall in Europe's activity in either of these years, while the United States' output fell both in 1954 and in 1958, it is fairly clear that the marginal propensity to import in periods of recession was lower in North America than in Western Europe.

A conclusion of this kind would be a welcome starting-point for interesting theorizing. One would be at once tempted to put forward the assumption that North America's lower marginal propensity to import during recessions ought to be explained in terms of the weak (or worsening) competitive position of those U.S. industries which are competing with the rest of the world. This would fit in with the theoretical analyses of pp. 245-8 and is also in agreement with some recent academic writings,[2] as well as with what is a widely held view in the business community on both sides of the Atlantic. The 'loss of the competitive power of the American industry' has become since 1958–59 one of the most often quoted phrases in business news-letters. If this were a valid assumption, we could conclude that the world economy has been until now in a lucky position : the more unstable of the two industrial areas, having had higher costs and prices, emitted weaker deflationary disturbances ; its greater autonomous instability has therefore been offset by its unfavourable competitive position.

[1] This remains true even if we regard exclusively the development of U.S. *imports*, and disregard the fall of *exports*, which may be attributed to the after-effects of the Suez crisis.
[2] R. Triffin, *Gold and the Dollar Crisis*, New Haven, 1960, p. 6 ; and E. Benoit, *Europe at Sixes and Sevens*, New York, 1961, pp. 137-70.

The trouble is, however, that the empirical foundations on which the reasoning is built are not absolutely firm. To begin with, a closer examination of the statistical evidence does not confirm unequivocally that the marginal propensity to import of the United States (during cyclical down-turns) has in all cases been lower than that of Western Europe. First, the more adequate quarterly figures of Appendix V show that in 1960–61 American imports from Western Europe have been much more sensitive to the decline in United States industrial output than in 1954 or in 1957–58 (although their sensitiveness has still been less than that of Western Europe's imports from North America during the European pauses in 1952 and 1958). Secondly, one has to bring into the picture the *volume* of imports as well as their current value. Unfortunately, I have been unable to discover quantum indices for inter-area trade. However, assuming that the changes of import prices have been similar both for North America and for Western Europe, it seems that in 1952 the relation between the fall in the volume of imports from the Non-Industrial Areas and the decline in industrial activity had been very much the same for the two industrial areas. Admittedly, things became different in 1957–58 when (assuming again identical changes in import prices) Western European imports from the Non-Industrial Areas fell (relatively to changes in industrial production) more than those of the United States. Thirdly, as regards the trade flows between Western Europe and North America, we have to take into account the fact that European imports had been exceptionally inflated in 1956–57 by the Suez crisis and by food imports ; hence their sharp decline in 1958–59 cannot be explained exclusively in terms of the trade cycle. It would require a special study to sort out the respective roles of the pause and of the two chance occurrences mentioned above.

Thus it does not seem justified, in the present state of our statistical information, to conclude that North America's marginal propensity to import has been persistently weaker in periods of cyclical down-turns than that of Europe. We have to remain also somewhat sceptical about the assumption that the competitive position of the United States has been declining during the 'fifties. The available evidence may be briefly summed up as follows. There is no clear statistical evidence suggesting that there has been a rise in the labour costs per unit of output in the United States industry, relatively to labour costs in Western Europe as a whole. There is some evidence, however, supporting the view that United States costs and prices have risen more rapidly than in the main competing countries in such important exporting industries as steel and engineering.[1] There is also ample evidence showing that the price *level* of producers' equipment is higher in the United States than in most European countries.[2]

Our present empirical information relies unfortunately either on too general statistics or on too fragmentary sampling ; much has to be done before really convincing evidence can be produced. I suggest, however, that this does not really matter ; for a moderate worsening in the competitive position of the main exporting industries of the United States need not be regarded as incompatible with the strong improvement of the trade balance of North America in 1960 with Western Europe. A number of restrictions on dollar goods had been maintained both in the United Kingdom and in some Continental countries until 1959 ; assuming that no adequate substitutes are available in Europe for *all* dollar goods, the disappearance of restrictions may have had a stimulating effect on imports from the dollar area, even if the relative costs of these goods had risen between 1953 and 1960.[3] Moreover, it may have been possible for some European producers to enter the North American market so long as their invasion remained marginal ; once, however, their share in the market reached a certain level, American producers decided to react. The resulting technological changes in American products may have more than offset the possible cost-advantages favouring European exporters. This is the likely explanation for the rapid increase, and then the decline, in European automobile exports to the United States. Last, but not least, the boom in Western Europe created labour shortages in 1960–61 in some of the Continental countries (especially in Germany) which were much more acute than those which had been experienced in 1954 and 1958.

VII. REFLECTION BACK OF EXTERNAL DISTURBANCES

Fortunately enough, it seems possible to reach a somewhat more vigorous conclusion as regards the reflection ratio of the three areas. As expected, the reflection ratio of North America has been nil : there is no evidence that drops in the area's imports have had anything to do with declines in its exports. Western Europe has had but one occasion to show — in 1953 — that a fall in its exports did not induce a fall in its imports ; for the rest of the period, one

[1] Sir Donald MacDougall, *op. cit*. pp. 17-20.
[2] E. Benoit, *op. cit*. pp. 154-5.
[3] The increase of the share of dollar countries in selected manufacturing imports to the United Kingdom is shown in a recent study by the National Institute (*Economic Review*, May 1961, p. 37).

can only guess that (owing to the steadily rising volume of its exchange reserves) it would have required quite a large fall in exports to offset the accrual of foreign exchange holdings resulting from non-commercial operations, and to induce in this way import restrictions. As for the Non-Industrial Areas, their reflection ratios proved to be rather high both in 1952–53 and 1958–59, even if we disregard the disturbing effect of the Suez crisis.

Now this pattern has to be looked upon in the light of the development of the external balances of the three areas. The high reflection ratio of the Non-Industrial Areas should clearly be attributed to the inadequately low exchange reserves of the primary-producing countries. The resilience of the United States to recessionary influences coming from abroad can, on the other hand, be explained in terms of more than adequate gold reserves during the greater part of the period. These *high* exchange reserves, however, have been *falling* ; [1] and, as counterpart to this development, the gold and foreign exchange reserves of Western Europe, which were relatively *low* during the greater part of the period, have been steadily *growing*.[2] Thus, while the level of Western Europe's foreign assets may have been unsatisfactory, the trend was upwards ; while the reverse was true of the United States. The happy outcome of this development was that neither Western Europe nor North America had to worry about their external balances ; both could therefore apply counter-recessionary measures whenever this seemed necessary.[3]

But it is also clear that this need not be an endless process, and that the redistribution of reserves may sooner or later reach a point where the United States will *no longer* have enough reserves and Western Europe will *not yet* have enough of them. Whether this will, or will not, happen depends on the total amount of international liquidity available for the trading nations ; and a discussion of this would fall beyond the scope of my paper. I may, however, point out that public opinion clearly does not regard any longer the United States' gold reserves as being excessive, while it is by no

[1] As shown in Appendix III, the net exchange position of the United States (column 3) worsened every year between 1951 and 1960, with the single exception of 1957. [2] See Appendix III.

[3] The spectacular increase in Europe's gold and foreign exchange reserves has also played an effective role in the relaxation of controls within Europe and, hence, in stimulating intra-European trade. Ever since 1951–52, Germany has been earning substantial surpluses on her balance of payments, independently of what has been happening to the balance of payments of Europe as a whole. As a result, there were periods (in 1956–57, for instance) when the German surplus had its 'counterpart' in a deficit of European countries. Europe as a whole needed very large total surpluses in order to be able to afford the German imbalance without having to accept import restrictions on behalf of its own deficit countries. Such a favourable change occurred in 1958–59, when the 'counterpart' of the German surplus was 'shifted' to the United States.

means obvious that Western Europe's reserves are now more than adequate.[1]

The channels through which the world gold and exchange reserves have been redistributed during the 'fifties are given in the balance of payments statistics of Appendix IV. North America has been losing reserves (– $10·5 billion for the nine-year period from 1951 to 1959) to the benefit of both Western Europe (– $3·6) and the rest of the world (– $6·9). None of these losses occurred through deficits in the trade balances. The over-all deficit with Europe took place because of the big deficit in invisibles ; and more than two-thirds of this was due to non-commercial military payments. As for the rest of the world, its gold and dollar gains from North America arose out of the substantial public capital outflow from the United States (and also out of 'invisible' military payments which completely offset the United States' investment income).

Western Europe, which already earned a surplus in its transactions with North America, added to this an even bigger surplus coming from the rest of the world. The size of this surplus ($+$6·1) was just about the same as that of the gold and dollar transfers from North America to the rest of the world ; this explains the stagnation of the Non-Industrial Areas' gold and foreign exchange reserves. Western Europe earned the over-all surplus through its positive current account which more than offset the outflow of public capital.

It would, of course, be unjustified to draw too many conclusions from this triangular pattern of external balances. The commercial items are not independent of the non-commercial ones, and nobody can tell whether the absence of United States' military expenditure in Europe and the rest of the world, or the lack of public capital exports from Europe and the United States to the rest of the world, would, or would not, have altered the size and the direction of international trade and of private capital movements. But it is perhaps not unjustified to say that the redistribution of international reserves, which played such a decisive role in the stabilization of world trade, could hardly have taken place without the actual pattern of the non-commercial money flows. Without this pattern, import restrictions by Europe would have proved from time to time unavoidable, while the reflection ratio of the Non-Industrial Areas

[1] At the end of 1960, the official gold and foreign exchange holdings of Western Europe ($25·1 billion) amounted to 43 per cent of Western Europe's total imports in 1960. As for continental Western Europe alone, the coverage was 50 per cent. The coverage is of course much higher — 74 per cent — if we cut out intra-European trade ; but this latter figure has little significance so long as the balance of payments policy falls within the competence of individual countries (*International Financial Statistics*, June 1961).

would have been surely greater. In other words, more violent cyclical fluctuations would have occurred in a more slowly expanding world trade.

VIII. A GENERAL CONCLUSION

I should like to draw one major conclusion from this paper. While there are many ways for explaining the resilience of the world economy to deflationary pressures — chance occurrences, the mechanics of international cycles, the rather weak emissions of cyclical disturbances by the United States, the redistribution of gold and foreign exchange reserves — I have been unable to find a built-in stabilizer working on the level of international transactions. I see no reason for being complacent about the likely course of future events.

APPENDIX I

NETWORK AND DEVELOPMENT OF WORLD TRADE, 1950–60
(Thousand million dollars, f.o.b. values)

Exporting Areas	Importing Areas		
	North America	Western Europe	Non-Industrial Areas *
North America			
1950	3·9	3·4	4·6
1951	4·8	4·8	6·9
1952	5·2	4·4	6·6
1953	5·5	3·8	5·9
1954	5·2	4·2	6·0
1955	5·9	5·0	6·5
1956	7·0	6·1	7·6
1957	7·0	6·6	8·8
1958	6·4	5·5	7·8
1959	7·1	5·5	7·3
1960	6·9	7·5	7·9
Western Europe			
1950	1·7	9·7	7·5
1951	2·3	13·0	10·8
1952	2·4	12·9	10·7
1953	2·7	13·3	10·1
1954	2·4	14·8	11·0
1955	2·8	17·1	12·0
1956	3·5	18·8	12·5
1957	3·7	20·5	13·7
1958	4·0	19·9	13·8
1959	5·3	22·2	13·4
1960	5·0	26·7	14·8
Non-Industrial Areas			
1950	5·7	9·2	6·5
1951	6·7	12·1	8·3
1952	6·2	10·5	7·0
1953	6·2	11·0	6·7
1954	5·9	11·8	7·1
1955	6·3	12·4	7·7
1956	6·7	13·1	7·9
1957	6·8	13·1	8·4
1958	6·7	12·5	7·8
1959	7·1	13·3	7·8
1960	7·0	14·8	(?)

* i.e. rest of the world, excluding Japan, Eastern Europe, China, U.S.S.R.

Sources : *International Trade in 1959*, Geneva, 1960, for 1950–59 ; *National Statistics and OEEC and Economic Survey of Europe* 1960, Geneva, 1961, for 1960.

APPENDIX II

NATIONAL PRODUCT AND EXPENDITURE

(Billion dollars — at 1954 prices and 1954 exchange rates)

	(1)	(2)	(3)	(4)	(5)	(6)
A. Western Europe						
1950	117·4	24·0	28·7	2·2	0·0	172·2
1951	121·2	25·9	29·8	4·5	0·3	181·6
1952	124·2	28·8	30·4	2·6	0·7	186·5
1953	131·3	29·6	33·2	1·2	1·3	196·5
1954	136·3	29·7	36·6	2·0	1·9	206·4
1955	144·0	29·8	40·6	3·5	1·0	219·0
1956	150·9	31·2	43·3	3·6	− 0·3	228·7
1957	156·7	31·8	45·6	3·9	0·4	238·3
1958	160·0	32·4	46·5	2·3	1·4	242·7
1959	165·9	33·8	49·5	2·1	1·3	252·5
B. United States						
1950	214·5	39·7	56·6	7·1	1·6	319·7
1951	216·4	58·4	56·7	9·1	3·4	344·0
1952	221·7	72·1	56·5	4·0	2·1	356·5
1953	232·0	75·9	58·9	4·5	− 0·3	370·9
1954	234·7	68·4	60·1	0·4	1·3	364·8
1955	252·3	66·9	66·2	7·5	1·1	394·0
1956	260·0	66·8	67·4	4·0	3·2	401·5
1957	266·7	68·4	67·2	1·4	4·5	408·2
1958	269·1	69·8	62·4	0·0	0·6	401·9
1959	284·5	72·9	67·9	6·2	− 1·6	429·9

(1) Private consumption.
(2) Public consumption.
(3) Gross domestic fixed capital formation.
(4) Change in stocks.
(5) Net exports of goods and services.
(6) Gross National Product at market prices.

Source : *General Statistics*, OEEC, Jan. 1961.

APPENDIX III

GOLD AND FOREIGN EXCHANGE RESERVES
(Billion dollars, end of period)

	United States			Western Europe			Non-Industrial Areas
	(1)	(2)	(3)	(4)	(5)	(6)	(7)
1950	23·7	7·1	16·6	5·5	2·9	8·4	12·9
1951	23·8	7·2	16·6	5·9	2·2	8·1	13·4
1952	24·3	9·0	15·3	6·7	1·5	8·3	13·1
1953	23·0	10·0	13·0	8·2	2·3	10·5	14·0
1954	23·2	11·2	12·0	9·9	2·6	12·5	14·2
1955	23·3	11·7	11·6	11·4	2·1	13·5	14·1
1956	24·0	13·5	10·5	11·9	1·8	13·7	14·6
1957	25·1	13·6	11·5	12·5	1·6	14·1	13·9
1958	23·1	14·6	8·5	16·1	2·8	18·9	12·9
1959	22·1	16·2	5·9	17·0	2·5	19·5	13·5
1960	21·4	17·4	4·0	19·5	2·8	22·3	13·1

(1) Gold and short-term foreign assets.

(2) Short-term foreign liabilities, excluding, however, the international organizations.

(3) (1) − (2). This net exchange position is somewhat over-optimistic, as (1) includes the reputedly unliquid short-term foreign assets, while (2) excludes dollars held by international organizations.

(4) Continental Europe : gold and dollar balances held by official organizations ; both sterling and EPU balances are excluded in order to avoid double counting when added to (5), and to ensure comparability with Appendix IV.

(5) United Kingdom : only gold.

(6) Total : (4) + (5).

(7) Rest of the IMF world, less Canada, Japan, Eastern Europe and China : official gold and foreign exchange holdings.

Source : *International Financial Statistics*, IMF, March 1958 and May 1961.

BALANCE OF PAYMENTS

A. Western Europe	(1)	(2)	(3)	(4)	(5)	(6)
	(billion dollars)					
(a) With the world						
1951	− 3·0	+ 1·1	− 1·9	+ 1·5	− 0·1	− 0·5
1952	− 0·7	+ 1·4	+ 0·7	+ 0·5	− 0·6	+ 0·6
1953	− 0·9	+ 2·4	+ 1·5	+ 0·2	+ 0·6	+ 2·3
1954	− 1·3	+ 3·2	+ 1·9	− 0·4	+ 0·4	+ 1·9
1955	− 1·9	+ 3·3	+ 1·4	− 1·0	+ 0·1	+ 0·5
1956	− 1·5	+ 2·4	+ 0·9	− 0·9	+ 0·1	+ 0·1
1957	− 1·2	+ 2·6	+ 1·4	− 1·3	+ 0·6	+ 0·7
1958	+ 0·6	+ 3·0	+ 3·6	− 1·3	+ 1·4	+ 3·7
1959	+ 1·2	+ 2·8	+ 4·0	− 3·8	+ 0·2	+ 0·4
Cumulative 1951 to 1959	− 8·7	+ 22·2	+ 13·5	− 6·5	+ 2·7	+ 9·7
(b) With North America						
1951	− 2·5	+ 0·2	− 2·3	+ 2·1	+ 0·5	− 0·3
1952	− 2·2	+ 0·9	− 1·3	+ 1·3	+ 0·4	+ 0·4
1953	− 0·8	+ 1·4	+ 0·6	+ 0·5	0·0	+ 1·1
1954	− 1·5	+ 2·0	+ 0·5	+ 0·2	+ 0·3	+ 1·0
1955	− 2·3	+ 2·4	+ 0·1	− 0·1	+ 0·1	+ 0·1
1956	− 2·4	+ 2·0	− 0·4	0·0	+ 0·3	− 0·1
1957	− 3·2	+ 2·1	− 1·1	− 0·1	+ 0·8	− 0·4
1958	− 1·9	+ 2·3	+ 0·4	+ 0·1	+ 1·7	+ 2·2
1959	− 0·4	+ 2·3	+ 1·9	− 1·0	− 0·8	+ 0·1
Cumulative 1951 to 1959	− 17·2	+ 15·6	− 1·6	+ 3·0	+ 2·7	+ 4·1
(c) With third countries						
1951	− 0·5	+ 0·9	+ 0·4	− 0·6	0·0	− 0·2
1952	+ 1·5	+ 0·5	+ 2·0	− 0·8	− 1·0	+ 0·2
1953	0·0	+ 0·9	+ 0·9	− 0·3	+ 0·6	+ 1·2
1954	+ 0·3	+ 1·1	+ 1·4	− 0·5	+ 0·1	+ 1·0
1955	+ 0·4	+ 1·0	+ 1·4	− 1·0	0·0	+ 0·4
1956	+ 1·0	+ 0·3	+ 1·3	− 0·9	− 0·2	+ 0·2
1957	+ 1·9	+ 0·6	+ 2·5	− 1·2	− 0·3	+ 1·0
1958	+ 2·5	+ 0·7	+ 3·2	− 1·3	− 0·2	+ 1·7
1959	+ 1·7	+ 0·5	+ 2·2	− 1·8	+ 0·2	+ 0·6
Cumulative 1951 to 1959	+ 8·8	+ 6·5	+ 15·3	− 8·4	− 0·8	+ 6·1

(1) Trade balance. The trade balances given in these balance of payments statistics are not comparable to those resulting from the foreign trade statistics in Appendix I. The differences are the greatest for the trade balance between Western Europe and the third countries ; they are due mainly to the fact that the GATT statistics overestimate the value of Western European imports from the NIA (relatively to the OEEC balance of payments figures) by 1·2 to 1·5 billion dollars. The year-to-year changes, however, are of the same direction and of comparable size in both sets of statistics. The differences in the area coverage play a negligible role.   (2) Invisibles ; comprising private donations.
(3) Current balance : (3)=(1)+(2).   (4) Official grants and capital.
(5) Private capital : a residual item, which includes errors and omissions as well as changes in the assets of commercial banks.
(6) Over-all balance : (6)=(3)+(4)+(5). Over-all balance is supposed to represent the changes in the gold and exchange holdings of official organizations.

BALANCE OF PAYMENTS

B. North America	(1)	(2)	(3)	(4)	(5)	(6)
	(billion dollars)					
(a) With the world						
1951	+3·0	0·0	+3·0	−2·7	−0·4	−0·1
1952	+2·9	−0·9	+2·0	−1·5	+0·2	+0·7
1953	+1·4	−2·0	−0·6	−2·1	+0·5	−2·2
1954	+2·6	−2·2	+0·4	−1·3	0·0	−0·9
1955	+2·6	−2·5	+0·1	−1·3	+0·6	−0·6
1956	+4·0	−2·3	+1·7	−2·5	+0·2	−0·6
1957	+5·7	−2·0	+3·7	−2·8	−0·2	+0·7
1958	+3·3	−2·8	+1·1	−2·6	−1·5	−3·0
1959	+0·6	−2·9	−2·3	−2·6	+0·4	−4·5
Cumulative 1951 to 1959	+26·1	−17·6	+8·5	−19·4	+0·4	−10·5
(b) With Western Europe						
1951	+2·5	−0·2	+2·3	−2·1	+1·2	+0·4
1952	+2·2	−1·2	+1·3	−1·3	−0·5	−0·5
1953	+1·0	−1·6	−0·6	−0·7	0·0	−1·3
1954	+1·8	−2·3	−0·5	−0·2	+0·1	−0·6
1955	+2·2	−2·6	−0·4	+0·1	+0·4	+0·1
1956	+2·6	−2·4	+0·2	0·0	0·0	+0·2
1957	+3·0	−2·2	+0·8	+0·1	−0·5	+0·4
1958	+1·6	−2·4	−0·8	−0·1	−1·5	−2·4
1959	+0·4	−2·4	−2·0	+1·0	+1·1	+0·1
Cumulative 1951 to 1959	+17·3	−17·3	0·0	−3·2	−0·4	−3·6
(c) With third countries						
1951	+0·5	+0·2	+0·7	−0·6	−0·6	−0·5
1952	+0·7	+0·3	+1·0	−0·2	+0·4	+1·2
1953	+0·4	−0·4	0·0	−1·4	+0·5	−0·9
1954	+0·8	+0·1	+0·9	−1·1	−0·3	−0·3
1955	+0·4	+0·1	+0·5	−1·4	+0·4	−0·5
1956	+1·4	+0·1	+1·5	−2·5	+0·2	−0·8
1957	+2·7	+0·2	+2·9	−2·9	+0·3	+0·3
1958	+1·7	−0·4	+1·3	−2·5	+0·6	−0·6
1959	+0·2	−0·5	−0·3	−3·6	−0·7	−4·6
Cumulative 1951 to 1959	+8·8	−0·3	+8·5	−16·2	+0·8	−6·9

(1) Trade balance. (2) Invisibles.
(3) Current balance : (3) = (1) + (2).
(4) Official grants and capital. (5) Private capital.
(6) Over-all balance : (6) = (3) + (4) + (5) ; i.e. the over-all balance represents changes in official gold reserves, plus the liquid foreign assets and liabilities held by banks. Thus this is not comparable with the over-all balance given for Western Europe. Since the exchange reserves given in Appendix III for Western Europe comprise only official holdings (the others not being available for all countries), this ensures a measure of comparability between Appendices III and IV.

Note : As a result of errors and omissions (*b*) and (*c*) do not add up necessarily to (*a*).

Sources : 1951–53 : *Balance of Payments Yearbook*, IMF. 1953–59 : *General Statistics*, OEEC.

APPENDIX V

INDUSTRIAL PRODUCTION AND FOREIGN TRADE DURING RECESSIONS
(Quarterly indices, 100 = previous cyclical peak)

A. Western Europe	Industrial production (seasonally adjusted)	Import (current value) (seasonally adjusted) * from	
		North America	Third Countries
The 1952 pause			
1951	100	100	100
1952 I	104	119	97
II	97	104	90
III	98	87	86
IV	105	81	89
1953 I	102	78	88
II	105	76	90
III	107	75	91
The 1958 pause			
1957 III and IV	100	100	100
1958 I	101	89	97
II	101	86	94
III	101	85	96
IV	102	85	98
1959 I	103	77	97
II	106	77	97
III	107	81	99
B. United States		**from**	
		Western Europe	Third Countries
The 1954 recession			
1953 III and IV	100	100	100
1954 I	94	78	108
II	94	91	95
III	93	85	97
IV	97	100	107
1955 I	101	96	108
II	104	97	108
III	106	102	108
The 1957–58 recession			
1957 I and II	100	100	100
III	100	95	96
IV	96	107	94
1958 I	90	98	93
II	89	98	94
III	94	104	90
IV	997	127	99
The 1960–61 recession			
1960 I and II	100	100	100
III	99	81	97
IV	96	88	92
1961 I	93	83	91

* Except for the United States.

Sources: Western Europe: *General Statistics*, OEEC; United States: *Survey of Current Business*.

Chapter 12

ECONOMIC PRINCIPLES OF THE FOREIGN TRADE OF SOCIALIST STATES

BY

V. P. SERGEYEV
U.S.S.R.

I. INTRODUCTION

To the ancient world, the antithesis of the sword — the symbol of war — was the balance — symbolizing trade — the relationship between nations that fostered peace and friendship. And today, too, it is foreign trade that knits together in peaceful coexistence states with contrasting socio-economic systems.

With the emergence of the world socialist system, foreign trade has brought socialist countries into closer economic co-operation and mutual assistance. Its purpose is not to make profit, but to pave the way for the expansion of socialism, the growth of socialist industry and the continual improvement of the living standards of working people; it puts into practice the theories of international socialist division of labour.

The rapid development of foreign trade by the socialist states and the rational modification of its structure testify to the successes achieved by them in the sphere of material production and in the spread of the benefits of international socialist division of labour; the business of foreign trade also serves as an expression of mutually advantageous division of labour between socialist and non-socialist countries.

II. RAPID GROWTH OF FOREIGN TRADE

The development of new relations through the socialist international market is characterized by constant and rapid growth of foreign trade. A high rate of progress, which is a feature common to socialist economies, as proved by the experience of all socialist countries, is manifested both in the sphere of production and in the sphere of commodity circulation within the world socialist system.

277

In a space of time that has been short in terms of the scales of history, the foreign trade of the U.S.S.R. and the People's Democracies has developed vigorously ; and trade between countries practising socialism is developing much faster than that between capitalist countries.

TABLE I

TOTAL TRADE OF THE SOCIALIST COUNTRIES

	1950	1956	1958	1960
Total foreign trade of the socialist countries				
$m.	9·9	20·0	24·9	31·5
1950 = 100	100	203	252	320
Trade within the socialist system				
$m.	6·6	14·5	18·0	22·0
1950 = 100	100	220	273	340

While the socialist states grow steadily and increase economic co-operation within their own circle they do not isolate themselves ; autarky is no part of their policy. Quite the contrary : loyal to the principle of peaceful co-existence, they constantly strive to broaden and strengthen economic contacts, including trade, with non-socialist countries.

Division of labour between different owners of means of production both creates and requires the development of international commodity-currency relations. Thus different owners of means of production are linked economically in a uniform commodity and money scale.

The extent to which the socialist countries have increased their share in international trade is seen, for instance, from the growing number of countries with which they do business. Whereas in 1921 the Soviet Union traded with 25 countries, in 1946 this number rose to 40, in 1953 to 51 and at present it exceeds 80. At the beginning of 1961, China had commercial contacts with 94 countries and regions of the world. The G.D.R., Czechoslovakia and Hungary maintain trade with more than 100 countries. There has been a similar increase in the number of trading partners of the other socialist countries.

Moreover, between 1950 and 1960, commodity exchange between the members of the two world social systems nearly trebled, growing from $3·3 billion to $9·5 billion. During the same period rapid progress was also made in trade between socialist and economically

278

under-developed countries. For instance, in the last seven years Soviet trade with countries that have lately gained their independence has shown an eightfold increase with the result that these countries themselves have simultaneously benefited by a share in the foreign trade of the socialist system.

In the immediate future, the foreign trade of the socialist countries has good prospects of further growth ; between 1958 and 1965 commodity exchange between socialist countries should go up by more than 70 per cent. In the same period the foreign trade of Albania may increase by 170 per cent, that of Bulgaria by 200 per cent, of Hungary by 100 per cent, of the G.D.R. by 70 per cent, of Poland by 80 per cent, of Rumania by 120 per cent and of Czechoslovakia by 90 per cent. In the seven-year period (1959–65) the foreign trade of the U.S.S.R. is planned to rise by at least 100 per cent. There should also be a considerable increase in the foreign trade of the socialist countries of Asia. A specially high rate of increase in trade should be achieved by those countries whose industrial development under capitalism was inadequate ; this will reflect the higher rate of growth of their industrial production.

While pooling their efforts in the building of a new society, the socialist states are continuing to broaden trade and other forms of economic co-operation with countries that have cast off the shackles of colonialism. At the same time, they are prepared to engage in large-scale, mutually advantageous trade with capitalist countries.

III. SOCIALIST DIVISION OF LABOUR

The systematic modification of the commodity structure of exports and imports of each country in accordance with its own and other countries' potentialities and needs is a characteristic feature of the development of foreign trade among the socialist group. The changing structure of trade in the international socialist market is a manifestation of the development and extension of a new, socialist division of labour. In particular it represents a rejection of such barren principles of the old international division of labour as the sharp classification into agrarian and industrial states, into manufacturers of finished industrial products and primary producers. There are no countries with a lop-sided economy, or with an excessively narrow range of exported goods in the world system of socialism.

Socialist industrialization has been accompanied by an increase in the proportion of industrial goods among the exports of the

U.S.S.R. and the People's Democracies. Before the Great October Socialist Revolution, farm products accounted for 70 per cent of Russia's exports ; industrial goods for 30 per cent. In 1959 industrial goods made up 89·4 per cent, and unprocessed farm products 10·6 per cent of Soviet exports. The proportion of these goods in the exports of China grew from 9·3 per cent in 1950 to 40 per cent in 1959. The other socialist states also show a rise in industrial exports since the war.

The successful development of the engineering industries in the socialist countries and their progressive specialization in the manufacture of machinery has resulted in an increase in the share of machinery exports.

TABLE II

THE PROPORTION OF MACHINERY AND EQUIPMENT
IN TOTAL EXPORTS

(Percentages of total exports)

	1937–38	1959–60
U.S.S.R.	5	>21
Hungary	11	38
Poland	1	28
Rumania	<1	18
Czechoslovakia	6	42

At the present time the Soviet Union is recognized in the world market as one of the principal exporters of machinery and equipment : in fact she supplies 3500 types of machinery and equipment ; and in the last five years about 4 billion new roubles' worth has been exported to at least 40 countries. The export of machinery and equipment from other socialist countries has also increased.

At the same time, machinery figures prominently in the imports of socialist countries : in the last five years the U.S.S.R. has imported machinery, equipment and vehicles at a total cost of 5·3 billion new roubles.

Raw materials form an important part of the foreign trade of socialist countries. In recent years, moreover, as a result of the great increase of industrial capacity, there has been a greatly increased output of consumer goods and, consequently, of their sales both at home and abroad.

Rational adjustment of the structures of exports and imports of the socialist countries will continue to be studied in the future. A characteristic feature is the abnormally rapid expansion of trade in machinery and equipment. For example, by 1965 reciprocal deliveries of machinery and equipment within the socialist system are expected to have grown by more than 130 per cent, representing a much greater increase than the total volume of trade. In consequence the share of machinery and equipment in total commodity exchange within the socialist system will grow. For instance, in the total exports of the member countries of the Council for Mutual Economic Assistance the proportion should rise from 29 per cent in 1958 to 36 per cent in 1965, that of fuel and of raw and semi-manufactured materials will drop from 50 to 39 per cent. This relative decrease in the share of raw materials in the exports of these countries testifies to the expansion of their processing activities, and a fuller utilization of local resources. In general terms, the exports and imports of socialist countries will increase in all commodity groups. At the same time, the quality of goods exported by the U.S.S.R. and the People's Democracies is improving and their range widening, while they are also increasing their imports of a variety of goods.

IV. PLANNED DEVELOPMENT

The rapid and rational development of international socialist trade is the result of applying definite principles on planning. *Planning* is a decisive factor for both the uninterrupted growth of socialized production and the steady development of foreign trade within the world socialist system. There is no doubt that *planned development* is the most characteristic feature of the foreign trade of every socialist country — wherein lies the fundamental difference between socialist and capitalist trade. In socialist states, plans for exports and imports, forming, as they do, an essential component of the national economic plans, are based on long-term trade agreements. On the other hand, the foreign trade plans are taken into account in the preparation of the national economic plans themselves.

In the preparation and implementation of export and import plans, account is taken of the economic principles of socialism — and especially of the law of planned proportionate development — which operate throughout the whole world socialist system.

In contrast to the chaotic and haphazard market fluctuations inherent in the foreign trade of capitalist states, commodity exchange between socialist countries develops in accordance with the demands of their planned economies and serves as an important means of coordinating their national economic plans. Demand and supply in the world socialist market are likewise deliberately and consciously regulated by long-term trade agreements. Thus trade between socialist countries does not suffer from market fluctuations. Plans for trade between socialist countries, based as they are on long-term agreements, provide a firm basis of expectations, of the organization of the production and of stable trade relations. The planned character of their commodity exchanges eliminates cyclical fluctuations in the levels of their trade and ensures a steady growth.

Foreign trade in the U.S.S.R. and the People's Democracies is conducted on the basis of a state monopoly. This is a necessary corollary of a system in which the main export resources as well as the imported commodities constitute public property. Under present conditions the concentration of all external trade in the hands of the government greatly facilitates the expansion of trade contacts with other socialist countries, since a state monopoly ensures the punctual and exact fulfilment of all commitments. Even under conditions of state monopoly, all foreign trade corporations in the U.S.S.R. are given separate legal status and operate with full independence.

Long-term trade agreements serve to co-ordinate the economic development of socialist countries and promote a rapid and continuous increase in the exchange of goods. At the present time trade between these countries is conducted on the basis of agreements covering the period 1961–65. In extension of this, the member countries of the Council for Mutual Economic Assistance are in the course of drafting long-term economic development plans for the period ending in 1980, and preliminary consultations and joint discussions have already commenced between them concerning the main problems of this period.

A long-term agreement between the U.S.S.R. and Italy (1958–61) has been largely responsible for the increase of 80 per cent in the trade in 1959 and more than 40 per cent in 1960. In 1961 trade between the U.S.S.R. and Italy will total approximately 240 million dollars, as against 200 million dollars in 1960. Last June (1961) N. S. Patolichev and M. Martinelli, Foreign Trade Ministers of the U.S.S.R. and Italy respectively, signed a Soviet-Italian trade agreement for the period 1962–65. This agreement provides for a considerable increase in trade between both countries and a broader range of goods to be delivered.

Thanks to these long-term trade agreements concluded with socialist countries, non-socialist countries are guaranteed for long periods of time the steady import and export of various goods. The world socialist market, being free from crises and enjoying a smooth and constant expansion, has many benefits to offer to some capitalist economies. Increase in employment is guaranteed and a more efficient use of their productive capacities. Above all their trade is bound to expand and to be consolidated through contact with the steady planned development of socialist countries and through the assurances given by a foreign trade, conducted as it is by a state monopoly. Both industrial capitalist states and under-developed countries in fact find in socialist countries reliable trade partners with stable markets for their exports, and large potential supplies of a wide range of manufactured goods and raw materials.

The experience of the socialist countries testifies convincingly to the decisive *role of the new, socialist international system of production* in rapidly and steadily developing both the foreign trade and the entire economies of these countries. Only when a country is administered according to socialist principles can its foreign trade be sure of rapid and rational growth without abrupt booms and depressions.

The great importance of the new *socialist international social relations* in respect of the development of the foreign trade of any socialist country is typically exemplified by the experience of the Soviet Union. When it was the only socialist country in the world, rapid and steady growth (which is a characteristic feature of socialist economy) marked its progress from the state's very inception, but only as regards its national productive forces and domestic trade. In its foreign trade, where partners with different interests and aims were encountered, this was not the case. The Soviet Union's constant efforts to promote mutually advantageous trade on equitable terms with capitalist countries were rendered nugatory by a policy of discrimination on the part of imperialist powers. In this early period, its foreign trade, unlike its national economy, failed to expand either steadily or rapidly.

Things changed after the establishment of the world socialist market. The formation and consolidation of international market relations of the socialist type opened the way for remarkable advances in foreign trade for the U.S.S.R. and other countries that had pioneered in the practice of socialism. Since the Second World War Soviet foreign trade has developed steadily and rapidly. In 1960 the volume of Soviet foreign trade was 9·3 times greater than it had been in 1938, and its turnover totalled 10·1 billion roubles as against 2·9 billion roubles in 1950 (at world prices calculated at the rouble exchange rate of January 1, 1961).

The essential feature of the international market relations of socialist countries is the community of interests and aims of the partners to the trade. A second important factor is the development of the foreign trade in a planned and systematic increase of the purchasing capacity of the population. Indeed in the socialist countries the purpose of the manufacture and marketing of machinery and other means of production, in the final count, is not so much to provide a source of profit but to increase the output of consumer goods and thus improve the well-being of the population. Thus, thanks to the constant growth of the purchasing capacity of the nation, a socialist state experiences no difficulties in marketing goods at home. In the last three years, with the substantial rise in *per capita* cash incomes, the total volume of retail trade in the Soviet Union has grown by 26 per cent, by 15 per cent in Czechoslovakia, by 28 per cent in the G.D.R. and by 47 per cent in Bulgaria. The structure of retail trade has also improved qualitatively and the range of goods marketed has been broadened. Such an increase in the effective demand of the population is a prerequisite for the greater import of both consumer goods and means of production for their manufacture.

Rapid growth of the foreign trade and modification of the structure of exports and imports of the socialist countries are promoted by the constant development of productive forces, by increase in the output of goods, and by sectoral structure planning in the national economies of these countries. In this way both export capabilities and import requirements are raised.

In 1960 the industrial output of the socialist system showed an almost sevenfold increase over the pre-war period, whereas the equivalent improvement for the capitalist world was in a ratio of less than 2·5 : 1. Between 1959 and 1965 industrial production in all socialist countries is planned to go up by 130 per cent and to account for more than 50 per cent of total industrial output in the world.

The modification of the sectoral structure of the economy of the socialist countries implies, as a consequence of industrialization and the introduction and expansion of new activities, a modification also of the commodity structure of their exports and imports.

The growing contribution of industry to the aggregate national product has also been reflected in the growth of the share of industry in the exports of socialist countries. With the extension of old, and the creation of new, branches of industry, the relative proportions of individual branches are continually changing, in accordance with their essential irrelations. Priority is given to the engineering industry, upon which depends the technical re-equipment of all branches of the national economy. On the eve of the Second World War the engineering industry accounted for 7 per cent of gross industrial output in Poland ; 24 per cent in Czechoslovakia ; and 4·5 per cent in Bulgaria. In 1960, twenty years later, the shares reached 22, 33·7 and 15 per cent respectively in these three countries. In 1960 about 2500 new types of machinery, appliances, apparatus and other equipment and more than 500 new types of instruments for production control and automation had been designed and were being built in the U.S.S.R. Inevitably the growth of the share of engineering industry in total industrial production and the increasing manufacture of new machinery led to an increase in the export of these commodities by socialist countries.

The wider extension of the socialist international division of labour, together with systematic specialization and co-operation between socialist countries in the production of the most important goods, as noted above, must also be counted among the necessary conditions for our economic progress, since the potential size of the market is intimately connected with the extent of specialization of social labour which had been achieved.

International economic co-operation of this kind is becoming increasingly important. Equally important is the direct co-ordination of the long-term national economic plans of the various socialist countries. This co-ordination makes possible the systematic planning of specialization and co-operation and ensures the fullest development of the productive forces of each country and the most effective use of its natural and economic advantages for the benefit of all the countries of the world socialist system.

Specialization of production between these countries is effected in two ways : (i) by priority development of those branches or types of production in each country for which the most favourable natural and economic conditions already exist, and (ii) by planned specialization in the manufacture of defined products.

International specialization of production in the socialist system is always combined with the creation in each country of a national economic complex best suited to its interests. A lop-sided structure of the national economy, dominated by one or two branches of production operating exclusively for export, such as is typical of many dependent countries of the capitalist world, is unacceptable to the socialist states, for it restricts the possibilities of economic growth, it increases unrealistic transportation costs, and reduces, in the final count, the efficiency of the national economy. In contrast to this, socialist international division of labour, far from precluding a diversified national economy, presupposes its development with a range of activities including the production and processing of raw materials, and the manufacture both of consumer goods and of means of production.

International specialization is planned and organized for the purpose of making a fuller and more rational use of production capacities, so as to increase labour productivity and the volume of production, improve the quality of products, and satisfy more fully the requirements of each individual country and of its fellow socialist states generally for certain goods.

The establishment of the most rational and scientifically based structure of activities is still in progress in the socialist countries; proposals, based on the principles of the socialist international division of labour, take account of the actual conditions of development of the countries involved. An important part in drafting recommendations is played by permanent commissions of the Council for Mutual Economic Assistance. For example, in 1960 the commission for the engineering industry adopted a recommendation for further specialization of production of the principal types of machinery and equipment for the power, metallurgical, building materials, oil and food industries, which will make possible large-scale production and improved efficiency, and increase the volume of this equipment exchanged between the member countries of the CMEA.

Thus between 1961 and 1965, production of the principal types of power equipment is expected to represent 71 per cent of power equipment in total for the specialization of which recommendations were adopted; by 1965 its export in trade between member countries of the Council should approximately treble as compared with 1960.

For the chemical industries, the implementation of recommendations for specialization in the manufacture of equipment over the period 1959–65 will raise mutual deliveries by about 45 per cent as compared with the total prior to specialization.

Evidence of the growth of similar co-operation in the engineering industries is provided by figures of the recent increases in the shares of machinery and equipment in the imports of countries with an already well-developed engineering industry: from 23·9 to 26·6 per cent in the U.S.S.R. (1957–59), from 13·3 to 21·6 per cent in Czechoslovakia (1955–60), from 12 to 27 per cent in Hungary (1955–60). Between 1955 and 1958 the share of engineering products imported from the G.D.R. rose from 5 to 12 per cent.

V. PRINCIPLES OF EQUALITY, MUTUAL ASSISTANCE AND POLITICAL NON-INTERFERENCE

The foreign trade of the socialist countries also involves other forms of co-operation between them: co-ordination of long-range economic plans, programmes of international specialization and co-operation of production, joint construction projects, credits and so on. Nearly all of these involve an exchange of products and a mutual settling of accounts, which is in one way or another reflected in foreign trade.

One of the reasons for the constant development and consolidation of economic contacts between socialist countries is that they are founded on the most progressive principles of international relations. The principles on which trade between them develops are those of friendship and close collaboration, unselfish reciprocity of assistance, mutual trust and the harmonious reconciliation of the national interests of each country with the collective interests of the socialist system as a whole.

In all their trade relations, whether among themselves or with capitalist countries, the socialist states are guided by the principles of complete equality of large and small nations, equal benefit for both partners, respect for territorial sovereignty and non-interference in each other's internal affairs. Although these general democratic principles were proclaimed in the days when the bourgeois nations were in their infancy, it is to be observed that in relations between the capitalist countries of today no more than lip-service is paid to these principles, without any attempt to put them into practice. The U.S.S.R. and the People's Democracies work tirelessly for the realization of these principles in all the steps they take to promote trade with capitalist countries.

The application of these general democratic principles is most manifest in the trade relations of socialist countries with economically under-developed countries, where the national bourgeoisie recognizes the benefit and willingly supports these principles. In contrast, imperialist states have at various times violated these general democratic principles of international trade and have organized economic blockades and discrimination against the U.S.S.R. and the People's Democracies.

All socialist countries base their foreign policy on the principle of the peaceful coexistence of states with differing social systems, the only correct and reasonable principle of international relations in a world divided into two social systems.

The principle of mutual assistance governs the economic relations between states of the socialist system. It finds expression in the growing exchange of essential goods and in the delivery of these goods on credit or on easy terms. Thus, trade with the Soviet Union enables the People's Democracies to satisfy the import requirements of goods needed for the development of key branches of their economies. In recent years the People's Democracies have received from the U.S.S.R. the following proportions of their imports : approximately 27 per cent of their machinery and equipment, nearly 75 per cent of their iron ore, 84 per cent of their pig iron, almost 60 per cent of their non-ferrous metals, 97 per cent of their oil, nearly 59 per cent of their oil products, more than 60 per cent of their sawn timber, about 67 per cent of their cotton and nearly 84 per cent of their grain. Reciprocally, the Soviet Union is a big importer of various goods produced by the People's Democracies.

In the world socialist system *the more developed countries render all-round assistance to economically weaker countries*. As an example, the delivery of Soviet goods on credit and on the basis of planned exchange has been one of the principal factors in speeding up the pace of the industrialization of these countries. The industrial states, such as the U.S.S.R., the G.D.R. and Czechoslovakia, by encouraging co-operation over the whole range of activities with other socialist countries, have helped them gradually to overcome traditional differences in the levels of economic development and at the same time have made practicable a more or less simultaneous transition of all the peoples of the socialist system to communism.

At certain periods, and for certain socialist countries, particularly those formerly lagging in economic development, the sum of their imports is bound to exceed that of their exports in trade with other socialist countries. But this is not a chronic state (as is frequently found among capitalist countries), and is not allowed to have an adverse effect on the development of a socialist economy. For a socialist country, an adverse balance of trade does not imply a position of dependence and does not entail the drain of gold reserves or a chronic foreign currency deficit. Indeed, as their economies develop, these countries increase the rate of growth of their exports and gradually eliminate their adverse trade balance.

The credits granted by the Soviet Union to other socialist countries serve as a form of economic assistance to help them to strengthen socialism, to carry out industrialization and to raise the welfare of the working people. These credits encourage division of labour and specialization and co-operation in production between socialist countries : they thus benefit both the debtor and creditor.

Credits are defrayed by the delivery of goods — usually specified under trade agreements — within specified time-limits, and thus no currency problem arises for the debtor country. The rate of interest is low, being usually 2 per cent ; but this low rate serves to offset in part the withdrawal of a fraction of production from the turn-over of the creditor country. Soviet loans and credits granted to People's Democracies total more than 7·8 billion new roubles.

On the other hand, a regular excess of exports over imports (such as is specially characteristic of the United States and Western Germany) is not common among socialist countries ; and it is avoided because it adversely affects the development of international trade. The Soviet Union, like the other socialist countries, never aims to sell without buying or vice versa ; it favours mutually advantageous and equally balanced international exchange of goods. Thus the foreign trade of socialist countries grows in terms both of exports and imports.

Large-scale financial and technical assistance is being provided by the Soviet Union for the People's Democracies for the construction of industrial establishments and other projects : there are in all 758 enterprises which the Soviet Union is helping to construct, 382 of which have already been completely or partially brought into operation. The share of equipment and complete installations of machinery that go to furnish these assisted projects grew from 11 per cent of the total export of such Soviet products in 1950, to 50 per cent in 1960. Technical specifications are exchanged between socialist countries gratuitously, the only change made being for the expenses involved in the actual preparation of the designs : to such lengths is the principle of unselfish mutual assistance carried in actual practice. Rough estimates suggest that the value of the technical designs supplied free by the Soviet Union to the People's Democracies (if reckoned according to prices prevailing in capitalist practice) is more than 40 billion 'old' roubles, while those received in their turn by the Soviet Union are similarly estimated at 6 billion 'old' roubles.

Peoples who are struggling for independence, or who have succeeded in freeing themselves from imperialist oppression, find sincere and loyal friends among socialist states. The support they can offer covers every field in which assistance is needed to ensure progress and to build up and consolidate the national economy. The Soviet Union alone is providing technical assistance in the erection of 149 large industrial establishments in under-developed countries, besides helping to construct 198 other projects of various kinds. More than 40 of these enterprises are already operating.

The Soviet Union has made available to industrially backward countries 2·4 billion roubles in loans on easy terms (as a rule, at 2·5 per cent interest, to be repaid in twelve years). The loans are repaid by delivery of the debtor country's traditional exports.

Trade relations between socialist countries are based upon a comprehensive study of mutual interests, special needs and potentialities. Almost all commercial treaties between them contain a provision whereby the parties undertake to conclude agreements, both long-term and short-term, which specify goods for delivery on both sides and set out other conditions designed to ensure the development of trade to meet the particular needs of the national economies concerned. And since new activities in the economy are bound to appear and modify requirements for imported goods, agreements are never limited to the traditional commodity composition, opportunities are left for trade to develop parallel with the growth of industry and agriculture and in accordance with changes in their structure. Similar opportunities for adjustment are provided in drafting agreements with non-socialist states.

The three principles of voluntary agreement, non-interference in each other's internal affairs and genuine equality can be seen at work in all the activities of the Council for Mutual Economic Assistance. Their realization is ensured by the fact that all recommendations and decisions are adopted by the Council only with the consent of the countries concerned. Its committees can only make final decisions on matters relating to organization and to procedural questions : on all issues concerned with economic, scientific and technical co-operation, they agree recommendations which have to be submitted for the approval of the member countries themselves. Those recommendations which are approved by countries are implemented by decisions of the governments concerned or by other competent bodies, as laid down by legislation. In this respect, incidentally, is to be found one of the fundamental differences between the CMEA and the 'Common Market', the latter being a supra-governmental organization vested with the power to work out and approve 'regulations' binding upon all the members of this association.

The application of the principle of complete equality to the trade between socialist and non-socialist countries has been prevented by the policy of discrimination and restrictions pursued by some capitalist countries with respect to the U.S.S.R. and the People's Democracies. This policy had the unfortunate effect of considerably decreasing from time to time the share of capitalist countries in the foreign trade of socialist countries. The abandonment of discriminatory measures by capitalist countries could soon lead to an increase in their share in the exports and imports of socialist countries.

A respect for the principle of mutual benefit, like the principle of equality, governs the trade dealings of every socialist country with other countries, and is usually embodied in the economic agreements with under-developed countries of Asia and Africa.

The socialist countries base their treaties and agreements with one another and with capitalist countries on *the principle of the most-favoured-nation treatment*. The favourable effect of this treatment on the development of trade between a socialist and a capitalist country may be judged from the following instance. It was only when the Union of Soviet Socialist Republics and Japan adopted, in October 1956, their Joint Declaration and signed the Protocol on the Promotion of Trade and the Mutual Granting of the Most Favoured Nation Treatment and later, at the end of 1957, signed the Soviet-Japanese trade treaty, that the two nations created the necessary legal arrangements for the development of trade between them. Immediately Soviet-Japanese trade began to grow rapidly : from a total of 15 million roubles in 1956, it rose to 68 million roubles in 1957, 151 million roubles in 1958 and 227 million roubles in 1959. By 1960 the trade exceeded 500,000 million 'old' roubles.

VI. PRICES AND CLEARING ARRANGEMENTS

The fact that the expansion of the trade between socialist countries is planned eliminates any unregulated price increases. The world socialist market is unaffected by the 'free' play of prices or by the spirit of profit-seeking and speculation. Although trade is conducted on the basis of world prices existing on the chief markets for a particular commodity, these prices are not applied automatically in trade between socialist countries. The prices of goods exchanged between them are agreed for a definite period by the foreign trade organizations of the governments concerned ; thus profiteering margins and violent market fluctuations are absent. The agreed prices remain unchanged as a rule for at least a year, and in the case of many goods they are fixed for several years. This principle of stable prices in the world socialist market makes it possible to safeguard the economies of the socialist countries against the consequences of fluctuations in the world capitalist markets due to profit-seeking motives. But the fact that prices in the trade between socialist countries are stabilized does not mean that they are incapable of change. The prices of certain commodities exchanged on the world socialist market are revised regularly, in accordance with the main trends in the world values of these commodities.

A major advantage of these methods of pricing between the socialist countries is the opportunity it offers for *uniform prices*. In contrast to the plurality of prices on the world capitalist market, a characteristic of price formation on the world socialist market is the uniformity of price at which a commodity is sold by socialist countries to each other. Price differences are limited, as a rule, to the difference in transport and insurance costs due to different terms of delivery.

Planning has been introduced into the accounting arrangements between the socialist countries, as into all other forms of their economic associations. The methods employed in the international settlement of accounts is designed to encourage economic links between socialist countries and to ensure prompt and timely payment for commodities as well as for other services. The balance of payments is adjusted according to plan, and reflects the friendly economic relations among these countries, grounded upon equality, mutual benefit and assistance.

Three special features are to be found in trade agreements between socialist countries :

(i) As a result of the currency monopoly of the state, all currency operations are concentrated in central banks of issue.

(ii) Agreements for reciprocal deliveries are concluded on the basis of a balance of deliveries over a period of a year, the schedules of reciprocal deliveries being drawn up each year.

(iii) The socialist countries settle accounts between themselves without payment in gold or foreign currency but by a process of clearing. All clearing accounts are settled in roubles. The prices of commodities and payments to be made for them under the contracts made between the foreign trade agencies are fixed in roubles.

There are two kinds of clearing accounts : one for trade, and one for non-trade operations. The bulk of international accounts are settled under the former type of clearing system. These are the accounts which are opened by the central banks, reflect foreign trade operations and register the receipts and payments for these operations over a definite period. The sums in roubles transferred to these clearing accounts reflect the value of reciprocal deliveries at prices established on the basis of world market prices.

The clearing accounts include all accounts for exports and imports, for complete-plant deliveries (except for deliveries on credit, the accounts for which are settled separately), as well as for technical aid and transport and other operations involved in foreign trade.

The clearing account turnover in roubles reflects the actual movement of commodity production in trade between socialist countries and is equivalent to the value of the contracts that have been completed.

Accounts in national currencies are settled between the central banks and foreign trade agencies of the respective countries after changing the roubles paid to the clearing accounts, into the currency of the country concerned (in export operations) or, conversely (in import operations), by changing the foreign currency into roubles. The official exchange rates are used in all these transfers.

There are no risks of exchange fluctuations in the trade relations between socialist countries. Payments to export organizations are made by a bank of the exporting country without regard to the balance in the clearing accounts. Those accounts are audited only at the end of the financial year. If there are not sufficient funds standing to the account of the bank of an importing country, settlement will involve a debt by the importing country. This has to be paid off by future deliveries in accordance with the provisions of the trade agreements.

Besides the accounts for trade and credit, there are accounts to be settled for non-trade operations, including all kinds of payments not directly concerned with trade. Socialist countries settle their non-trade accounts on the non-trade payment-clearing basis. The latter is also used for the clearance of inter-governmental grants and subsidies.

Bilateral clearing is used for the bulk of commodities. This is partly to be explained by the fact that trade between socialist countries is based on bilateral trade agreements. But accounts can also be settled in the form of multilateral clearing. It may happen that in practice country *A* is prepared to purchase goods in excess of the planned bilateral trade with country *B*, though the latter is not in need of anything further that *A* can supply. At the same time, *B* is anxious to buy an additional amount of what *C* is offering, and *C* in turn wishes to buy goods from *A*. This combination of interests provides a basis for three-party clearing.

Multilateral clearing obviates the need for exact bilateral balancing of the sums involved in deliveries of goods. All that is needed is to secure that equality exists between the export and import of goods by any given country in its relations with all others participating in the multilateral clearing system. This system, based on planning of the structures of the economies concerned, simplifies the balancing of mutual obligations over a long period.

For multilateral clearing, two prerequisites are necessary : a country must have an active balance in trade with some countries and a passive balance in trade with others, since it is essential that each of the member countries of a multilateral clearing arrangement shall be able to settle its over-all balance with all the other participants in combination ; secondly, there must be a uniform base of prices for goods the accounts for which are to be settled multilaterally. Both these conditions are to be found in trade between socialist countries. To provide a suitable basis for multilateral clearing the member countries of the Council for Mutual Economic Assistance concluded an agreement on this subject in June 1957.

A country having roubles on the clearing account can use them in the four following ways :

(i) they can be transferred to the clearing account of a third country, i.e. by payment in roubles for goods received from it (such transfers need the consent both of the debtor country and of the third country) ;

(ii) they can be transferred to the multilateral clearing account (with the consent of the debtor country) and the sum so transferred can be spent on the purchase of goods in any country participating in this clearing system ;

(iii) they can be used to obtain the currency of the debtor country to cover any expenditure by the creditor country in the territory of the debtor country (e.g. for payments on non-trade operations involving expenditure to be made in the currency of the country and within the territory of the country concerned) ;

(iv) they can be used to grant credit to the debtor country of a third country.

The socialist countries have entered into multilateral trade relations where a non-socialist country has been one of the parties. For instance, the Soviet Union has three-party clearing agreements between the U.S.S.R., Poland and Finland ; between the U.S.S.R., Czechoslovakia and Finland ; and between the U.S.S.R., Finland and the G.D.R. By an agreement between the U.S.S.R., Burma and Czechoslovakia, a definite sum was transferred in 1956 from Burma's account with the State Bank of the U.S.S.R. to the account of Czechoslovakia. As a result, Burma acquired a credit balance on account with Czechoslovakia and was able to buy Czechoslovakian goods with the funds it had acquired from the U.S.S.R. by the sale of rice. Thus it is clear that the socialist countries favour mutually advantageous international trade both on a *bilateral and a multilateral basis*.

Bilateral agreements, whether between socialist countries or between a socialist and a non-socialist country, lead to an increase of trade. At the same time they do nothing to affect the interests of the third countries. The editors of the *Economic Bulletin for Europe* in 1960 noted very rightly that those West European countries which experience difficulties in trade with other capitalist countries and do not possess sufficient amounts of freely convertible currency have a sure way of increasing their exports through the development of bilateral trade with socialist countries.

VII. COUNCIL FOR MUTUAL ECONOMIC ASSISTANCE

The Council for Mutual Economic Assistance has a role in the organization of economic co-operation between socialist countries which is becoming yearly more important. This body is an inter-governmental economic organization of sovereign socialist states of Europe and represents an international institution of a new type. Its purposes are

   (i) to promote the uninterrupted economic development of the member countries, through the pooling and co-ordination of their efforts ;

  (ii) to speed up economic and technical progress in them ;

 (iii) to raise the level of industrialization in countries where industry is backward ;

 (iv) to achieve a steady increase of labour productivity ;

  (v) to improve at a steady rate the living standards of the peoples associated in the Council.

The CMEA is open to other European countries which agree with its objectives and principles and which are prepared to assume the obligations contained in its Charter. One of its more important practical functions is to bring about the co-operation of its members in the co-ordinated planning of their national economies. This does not mean that the Council acts as a kind of joint-planning body for these countries. Each drafts its own economic plans independently. The co-ordination of the various plans, drawn up in the light of the actual characteristics of each country concerned, is designed to promote the rational division of labour between them. The Council pays great attention to the development of the foreign trade of the socialist countries. On recommendations from the Council, its member countries conclude long-term agreements with one another and carry them out successfully. The Council's aim is not the establishment of a closed market or bloc, nor the creation of a self-contained economy. But in the Charter of the Council, its member countries reaffirm their readiness to develop economic contacts with all countries — regardless of their social and political systems — on the principles of equality, mutual benefit and non-interference in domestic affairs. Unlike the capitalist countries, which have formed closed markets and blocs in Europe, the member countries of the Council adhere to the principle of the most-favoured-nation treatment in trade and economic relations with all countries. Their agreements on customs and other trade privileges are the same for all the countries of the world. Under Article XI of the CMEA Charter, the Council can establish and maintain relations with the economic agencies of the UNO and other international agencies.

The principles on which the CMEA was founded accord with the spirit of the UN Charter, since it strives to strengthen the unity and solidarity of the socialist countries and to promote in every way the peaceful co-operation and friendship of these countries both among themselves and with all other countries.

The development of trade, establishment of business relations and the extension of contacts between countries is of great economic importance. Closer economic contacts, in turn, help to create favourable conditions for the improvement of political relations between countries. The widening of trade serves to strengthen mutual trust between nations and to ease international tensions. Thus the development of trade contributes to the maintenance of peace throughout the world.

Chapter 13

ECONOMIC GROWTH AND BALANCE OF PAYMENTS PROBLEMS

BY

K. M. SAVOSNICK

University of Manchester

I. AN ANALYSIS OF THE PROBLEMS

THE approach to political economic planning for growth that is now almost traditional is to assume that import requirements will take such and such a course and that consequently the planners must provide for investment in export production to balance the future external accounts. There are, however, no particular reasons why investment in export production should improve the future balance of payments, unless it can be assumed that export investments are more profitable than other investments and that therefore savings will turn out larger as a result of export investment than as a result of other investment.

Any increase in production tends to improve the balance of payments, but any accompanying increase in incomes tends to worsen it, so far as the income increases are spent on domestic consumption or investment. If incomes are a function of output and are spent to one hundred per cent on the margin on consumption and domestic investment, no amount of economic growth will improve a country's balance of payments. In such conditions the case for investment in export production must rest on the assumption that exports are more *productive* and *profitable* than other forms of production, raising the level of real national income more than it otherwise could be raised.[1] Another case for investment in exports — i.e. as a means of improving the balance of payments — may be made if it can be assumed that this would alter the *income-distribution* in such a manner as to encourage savings relatively to what otherwise would be the case and relatively to induced investment. Even if exports were *less* productive and profitable than other forms of activity, it could be argued that an emphasis on exports would

[1] The reference to 'profitability' means that long-term price changes induced by changes in the production structure must be taken into account.

produce greater aggregate savings relative to aggregate investment than other production and income-distribution structure. This would lead to an improvement in the balance of payments.

Obviously, this kind of approach to the balance of payments which would result from growth is rather futile ; on the whole it can more reasonably be argued that the structure of investment should be keyed to expectations of productivity and profitability rather than to expectations as to the balance of payments outcome. Balance of payments problems should be dealt with by means of monetary and fiscal policy, possibly combined with exchange rate policy, and not by an emphasis on this or that kind of production structure — this is at least the conclusion one is led to draw if one believes that the balance of payments is a net resultant of changes in aggregate demand and aggregate supply.

There are many reasons why a process of economic growth may produce a more or less continuous disequilibrium between aggregate demand and aggregate supply. What I am going to deal with here is the case of a laggard country which finds itself in continuous balance of payments problems, not as a result of its own rate of growth, but as a result of more rapid growth in a competing economy. I assume that growth abroad necessitates adjustments in the laggard country which its economy tries to resist.

Let us assume two countries, which we will call, arbitrarily, Germany and Great Britain, which both compete in exports to third markets, U-country. Germany is assumed to be a country of rapid economic growth, while Great Britain and U-country are, for the sake of simplicity, assumed to be more or less stagnant. The pattern of growth in Germany is assumed to be neutral or biased in favour of exports, so that its growth in any case results in an increase in its export supply and a more or less parallel increase in its import demand. This would lead us to expect some worsening of Germany's commodity terms of trade with U-country — Germany can only sell more exports to stagnant or near stagnant U-country at some reduction in export prices, paying relatively more per unit of imports from U. (This does not necessarily mean that money costs of imports from U have to increase per unit. On the whole, money prices in U may tend to fall rather than rise if they get imports cheaper.)

Growth in Germany need not produce balance of payments problems in U if we assume that the U-economy is so flexible as to be able to absorb more imports and produce more exports and enjoy the improvement in its commodity terms of trade. The problem of adjustment and the balance of payments problem may instead arise in Great Britain which is competing with Germany in U-country. Great Britain does not grow but will nevertheless suffer a worsening in its commodity terms of trade with U, as a result of Germany's export drive. A loss of export markets to the German competitors will occur even if British export prices are always perfectly competitive, so that Great Britain and Germany always keep the same price — but the loss will be even greater if British export pricing is sticky.

Thus, Great Britain suffers a fall in export income as a result of growth in Germany. *Ultimately* we would expect this reduction in export income to lead to a readjustment of the British production structure and to a reduction in British import expenditure so that the external account would be balanced. Market forces would be expected to lead to a release of productive resources from the export sector. They would find their way to British import-competing production and this would have the effect of reducing imports. In addition to that, the fall in British real income would lead to a reduction in demand for importables.

However, in a continuous process, where Germany all the time gains in U-markets, Great Britain will be lagging behind in the adjustment and suffer a continuous balance of payments deficit.

U-country may not be disposed to accumulate surpluses corresponding to Great Britain's deficit. Therefore, to the extent that U-country manages to spend all their current export earnings abroad, the surplus will accumulate somewhere else. By definition it cannot accumulate in Great Britain, and it must therefore find its way to Germany (if we deal with a three-country model). Germany will get a surplus even if it is not *actively* trying to accumulate one.

As long as this process continues we would expect some visible unemployment in British export production. But in a slightly more dynamic model this unemployment may become disguised. If we assume that Germany is growing fast, and modify our assumptions about Great Britain and U-country so that they are also assumed to be growing, but slowly compared to Germany, the effect of Germany's faster growth on the British economy may show itself as a *stagnation* of exports rather than as an actual *reduction* on British exports. As a result of this there will be a tendency for net resource flows in the British economy to become diverted to production for the home market rather than exports.

Assuming a constant total labour supply in the British economy, employment in export production may be maintained if labour is sticky and unwilling to move, while other sectors instead will be more rapidly capitalized than otherwise. (I assume here that new capital is more mobile and flexible in its 'choice of employment' than labour.) Again, we would ultimately expect Great Britain to be able to reach external equilibrium by increasing its domestic import-competing production, but this may take a long time. In the meantime there may be a persistent surplus capacity in the economy as a whole, which cannot be eliminated until British costs and prices fall relatively to the rest of the world. Efforts to eliminate domestic surplus capacity in sectors producing for the home market by means of demand *creation* are likely to worsen the balance of payments problem, unless imports can be positively discouraged, for example by devaluation. The trouble is that a continuous process of rapid growth in Germany may necessitate repeated devaluations.

The result of a fast neutral or export-promoting growth in the competing German economy may thus, as far as the slow-growing British economy is concerned, be a reduction in the British ratio of foreign trade to GNP (even if British productivity-increase and the British demand structure are neutral). This is the consequence of the worsening in commodity terms of trade imposed by the German rapid growth. The more rapidly the British economy can adjust itself to this imposed change in comparative cost conditions, the better. Economic policy should therefore aim at canalizing net additional productive resources into directly import-competing production. This can be done either the painful way, by policy action to reduce aggregate domestic demand, causing a reduction in demand for importables and at the same time causing sufficiently great unemployment of resources in the home market to stimulate a drift of productive resources into directly import-competing production. Or the authorities could take the easy way of making directly import-competing production more profitable, e.g. by devaluation.

It is tempting to believe that Germany could do something to lessen Great Britain's problem; for example, it could lend its surplus to U-country. This would undoubtedly lead to an increase in Germany's and Great Britain's combined exports to U-country — but U-country would in all probability tend to use the funds on loan to buy from Germany rather than from Great Britain, so that Germany again would tend to end up with a surplus, even if not so great as before, while Great Britain would benefit only to a limited degree. Germany could also actively try to increase imports from U-country (for example, by appreciation of the German currency). To the extent that U has a fully employed economy, any increase in U exports to Germany would necessitate an increase in U imports, especially of U imports from Great Britain, if the Germans have appreciated. In a continuous process of rapid German growth, the Germans would have to appreciate repeatedly. Alternatively, Germany could export capital and technique to Great Britain in order to speed up the rate of economic growth there and thus reduce the difference in growth rates between the two economies.

The following is an attempt to explain some of the reasoning presented above.

II. GROWTH, STAGNATION AND TERMS OF TRADE

In a two-country, two-commodity model, some of the benefits of economic growth in one country will be transmitted to a stagnant or slowly growing economy by way of a change in commodity terms of trade in favour of the stagnant country. This is the general and well-known rule except in extreme cases where combinations of output expansion and demand expansion in the growth economy will lead to a reduction in its supply of exports. Thus as a general rule the non-growing or slowly growing economy will experience an improvement in its commodity terms of trade with its growing partner. This will tend to raise the level of real income in the stagnant economy.

The effect of growth abroad on the stagnant country will tend to be a stimulus to expansion of its export sector and increased competition in its import-competing sector. On the whole there are no particular reasons to expect this process to lead to balance of payments difficulties in the stagnant economy. A tendency to spend more on the now cheaper imports will be counterbalanced by increased foreign demand for its exports and increased export prices. Even if, temporarily, some unemployment of factors arises in the import-competing sector, and even if these factors are slow to move over to the export-producing sector, a moderate increase in export production will tend to maintain equilibrium in the balance of payments because of the rise in export prices.

In a *three-country*, two-commodity model, the balance of payments situation is likely to be more of a problem for a stagnant country competing with a growing country in a stagnant third market. Let us assume that the growth economy is not trading with its competitor but only with the third country. Benefits of growth will be transmitted to the third country as before, *via* a change in commodity terms of trade. But our non-growing country, competing with the growing country in third markets, will experience a worsening of its commodity terms of trade.

In Figure I, offer curve 1 represents our stagnant economy's long-term equilibrium reciprocal export supply of commodity X and import demand for commodity M at different relative commodity prices. Offer curve 2 represents its competitor's original reciprocal

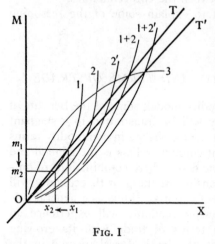

FIG. I

offer curve (supplying X and demanding M). By adding the two offer curves along radii from O we arrive at a joint offer curve $(1+2)$. We now assume trade-promoting economic growth in one country, so that its long-term offer curve shifts from 2 to 2'. This leads to a corresponding shift in the joint offer curve from $(1+2)$ to $(1+2')$.

Offer curve 3 represents third market long-term export supply of commodity M and import demand for commodity X. In an original equilibrium situation the joint offer curve $(1+2)$ intersects curve 3 at commodity terms of Trade T. As a result of the shift of the joint offer curve to $(1+2')$ the new long-term equilibrium price will be T'. For our stagnant economy this means a reduction in the equilibrium volumes of exports and imports. Because of the worsening in commodity terms of trade, imports have to fall relatively more (from $m1$ to $m2$) than exports (from $x1$ to $x2$).

III. SHORT-TERM BALANCE OF PAYMENTS PROBLEMS

The movement from one equilibrium situation to another is much more likely to be accompanied by a phase of disequilibrium in the stagnant economy's balance of payments than when we deal with a simple two-country model. In the two-country model we can expect the enforced contraction of one sector of the economy to be accompanied by external stimulus of another sector. In addition we find that the two-country model involves an improvement in commodity terms of trade for the stagnant economy which tends to facilitate the balancing of the balance of payments. But in the three-country model the enforced contraction of one sector in the stagnant economy, the export sector, is not really accompanied by

external stimulus of the other sector. True, the worsening of commodity terms of trade should in the long run lead to a stimulus to
increase domestic import-competing production. But the process
of adjustment is only partly working *via* the price system : final
external equilibrium will not be achieved until the effects of the fall
in real incomes have worked through the system, resulting in
sufficiently great reduction in aggregate domestic demand.

The worsening in commodity terms of trade means that imports
have to be reduced proportionally more than exports. This means
that all resources made redundant in the export sector have to be
reabsorbed elsewhere in the system, or short-run external equilibrium
will have to be achieved at less than full-employment levels. Therefore, the stagnant economy can be expected to have to go through
a painful phase of achieving short-term external equilibrium while
some of its productive resources are unemployed or employed in
combinations which, from a long-term point of view, are sub-
optimal.

IV. LONG-TERM AND SHORT-TERM PRODUCTION POSSIBILITIES

In Figure II our stagnant economy is in initial output equilibrium
at point *a* on the long-term production possibility curve *AB*. Relative
commodity prices are represented
by the slope of *T* which is tangential
to the curve at *a*. As a result of
growth in the competing country,
long-term equilibrium commodity
prices will change to *T′* and the
new long-term equilibrium output
combination will be point *b* on the
curve *AB*.

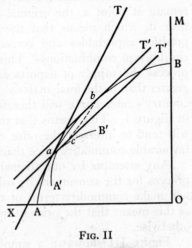

Due to assumed short-term
rigidity of the productive system,
the short-term production possibility curve is assumed to be *A′B′*.
Factors of production are assumed
to be imperfectly mobile in the
short run. (Structural change
therefore means some unemploy-

Fig. II

ment and some suboptimal combinations in the short run.) For a
while, therefore, the production structure will remain at point *a*,

even if price T' is ruling. ($A'B'$ may be thought of as being initially very sharply kinked at point a.) As $A'B'$ gradually becomes more smooth the production structure will change towards point b, following a path a-c-b which lies inside the long-term production possibility curve AB. Thus real income is reduced, not only because of the effects of worsened commodity terms of trade on the final equilibrium situation (the final budget line lying inside the original budget line in relevant parts), but also because the path towards final equilibrium lies inside AB. If growth in the competing economy is a continuous process instead of a once-for-all affair, our stagnant economy may spend a long time moving inside its long-term production possibility curve towards a steadily receding long-term equilibrium position.

V. COMMODITY TERMS OF TRADE DURING THE PERIOD OF ADJUSTMENT

During the process of adjustment, commodity terms of trade will tend to be worse for the stagnant country than in the final equilibrium situation (assuming that we are analysing a once-for-all growth situation). This follows because our stagnant economy's short-term export supply and import demand will tend to be less elastic than the long-term schedules.

We have seen that the output structure *for a while* will tend to remain at point a, the original output combination, or stay rather near it, which means that the economy will tend to continue to produce exportables and consume importables in excess of final equilibrium combinations. This means that during the adjustment process the supply of exports and the demand for imports will be greater than in the final analysis ; the short-term path of the stagnant country's offer curve will therefore lie to the right of offer curve 1 in Figure I. This means that the joint offer curve in the short run will tend to intersect the offer curve of the third country at a less favourable commodity price than T'.

Any attempts by our stagnant economy to ease the adjustment process for the consumers by using up reserves of foreign currency will make commodity terms of trade even worse — at least as long as this means that the price of imports is being boosted higher than otherwise.

Figure III shows in a simple way that the stagnant country's export supply and import demand will be greater during the adjustment process than in the final equilibrium. AB is the production possibility curve ; *T* is the initial commodity price ; *a* is the initial output and *b* is the initial consumption. Therefore, initial exports are *a* – *c* and initial imports *b* – *c*. The final commodity price is *T'*. Final output equilibrium is *f*, which also, for the sake of simplicity, is assumed to be the final consumption equilibrium. (Thus, in the final situation there is no trade at all.)

But, during the early phases of the adjustment process, production will remain at or near point *a*, and the country's budget line will be represented by a line parallel to *T'* passing through *a*. Assuming, again for the sake of simplicity, that income elasticity of demand for each commodity is near unity, we find that short-term consumption equilibrium will be at point *d*. Short-term export supply will therefore be (*a* – *e*) and short-term import demand will be (*d* – *e*), meaning

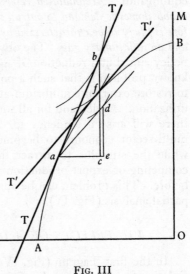

Fig. III

that in the short run our economy will have a greater equilibrium export supply and import demand at price *T'* than in the final analysis. Therefore intermediary commodity terms of trade will tend to be worse than final. This conclusion can be drawn even if final equilibrium results in *some* trade and not in *no* trade. (The exception would be if the final equilibrium situation is one where the stagnant country optimally would be exporting its former imports and importing its former exports.)

VI. THE ADJUSTMENT PROCESS AND THE TENDENCY TO BALANCE OF PAYMENTS DISEQUILIBRIUM

The worsening of commodity terms of trade for our stagnant country occurs in its trade with third markets. In a three-country, *multi-commodity* model, we may assume that some trade also takes place directly between our stagnant country and its growing competitor and that this trade concerns other commodities than those traded with the third country. In this case some of the worsening of commodity terms of trade already described may be offset by an improvement in commodity terms of direct trade with the competitor. But as long as it is only partly offset we can assume that the income reductions and price changes will only slowly take effect so as to move our stagnant economy to final internal and external equilibrium. *Accumulated reserves and consumption credits, etc. will enable domestic demand to outrun supply during the process which therefore is likely to be characterized by a combination of falling real incomes and an inflationary gap.* The obvious policy remedy is a deflationary policy aimed at a reduction of aggregate domestic demand. A well-known problem is that such a policy, if it is of a general kind, tends to restore external equilibrium at the cost of a sub-optimal resource utilization. As demand for all sorts of commodities is being reduced, there will arise a tendency for resources in the home sector in a multi-sector economy to become unemployed or under-employed, while the stimulus to attract these released resources to import-competing or export production will be only very little greater than before. This problem can be analysed in terms of a simplified static partial analysis (Fig. IV).

VII. EFFECTS OF A DEFLATIONARY POLICY

In the first diagram (Fig. IVa) we represent the 'typical' export situation for commodity X. Supply of X is S, the domestic demand for exportables is D, the export price is P_0, and for the sake of simplicity foreign demand for exports is now assumed to be infinitely price elastic. A deflationary policy *via* fiscal or monetary measures or both, is expected to result in a negative shift of the domestic demand curve to D'. Therefore the volume of exports at export Price P_0 increases from x to x'. But as long as factor prices remain constant there is no incentive to expand production of exportables.

In the next diagram (Fig. IVb) we represent a typical commodity for the home market which is neither exported nor sold in direct competition with imports. The initial equilibrium price is P_0. Deflationary policy leads again to a negative shift of domestic demand from D to D'. Production for the home market therefore falls from h to h'. Prices fall from P_0 to P_1. This reduction in output entails some unemployment of domestic productive resources.

In the third diagram (Fig. IVc) we represent the import-competing sector. Import prices are P_0 and, for the sake of simplicity, foreign supply of imports is assumed to be infinitely elastic. Domestic supply of import-competing products is S. Deflationary measures reduce domestic demand from D to D', as a result of which imports shrink from m to m'.

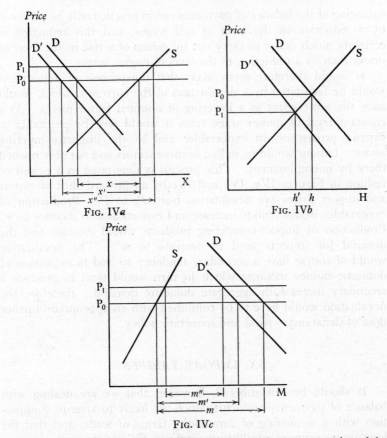

FIG. IVa

FIG. IVb

FIG. IVc

So far the policy is successful and unemployment produced in the home sector may ultimately cause a push of resources towards the other two sectors. *If* factor prices are adjustable downwards, we will ultimately have some lowering of the cost (supply) schedules in all three sectors, leading to increases in export production and exports and also leading to increases in domestic production of importables and reduction in imports. If and when factor prices fall there will also be some re-employment of previously released factors in production for the home market again.

VIII. DEVALUATION A REMEDY AGAINST STICKY WAGES

However, the stickiness of factor prices, especially the stickiness of wages with regard to downward adjustments, is well known. The balancing of the balance of payments can in practice only be achieved by a reduction in the level of real wages, and this reduction is certainly much easier to carry out by means of a rise in the level of prices than by a reduction in the level of money wages.

It would therefore seem likely that the process of adjustment would be facilitated by a devaluation of the currency, which would have the same effect as a lowering of nominal factor prices. At a constant level of money wage rates it would now be profitable to expand production in exportables and in the import-competing sector. Labour would be pulled to these sectors and not only pushed there by unemployment. This process is illustrated in a primitive fashion in Figures IVa, IVb and IVc by an upward shift of export and import prices *via* devaluation from P_0 to P_I. Production of exportables would tend to increase and exports also to increase to x'' Production of import-competing products would increase and the demand for imports tend to decrease to m''. The devaluation would of course have a secondary tendency to lead to expansion of domestic money incomes which in turn would tend to produce a secondary increase in aggregate domestic demand : therefore the devaluation would have to be combined with an appropriate further dose of deflationary fiscal and monetary policy.

IX. IMPORT TARIFFS

It should be remembered, however, that we are dealing with balance of payments problems which are likely to arise in conjunction with a worsening of commodity terms of trade, and that the long-term optimum equilibrium situation for our stagnant economy is one of less trade than in the original situation. In this optimum our economy is assumed to produce less for export and more for home use than originally. It is desirable that short-run balance of payments policy should be working in the same direction as long-term structural tendencies. The movement towards long-term structural equilibrium will therefore be speeded up if the stagnant country uses a combination of devaluation, *tariff policy* and general deflationary measures, rather than devaluation and deflationary measures alone. A rise in import tariffs would stimulate greater movement of productive resources towards import-competing production, and would ease the country on the way towards greater economic self-sufficiency. And the revenue from the raising of tariffs would facilitate the deflationary policy.

Chapter 14

TRADE AND PAYMENTS POLICY FOR A DEVELOPING ECONOMY[1]

BY

I. G. PATEL

Delhi, India

I. INTRODUCTION

A GREAT deal of attention has been devoted in recent years to the problems of the so-called less-developed countries. While economic growth is by no means the exclusive concern of any particular group of countries, there can be little doubt that the task of developing the poorer societies is particularly urgent and difficult. Partly as a recognition of the urgent and difficult nature of the task and partly in response to world-wide trends, the opinion seems to be crystallizing that the economic development of the less-developed countries must be attempted on the basis of consciously directed plans or programmes and within a framework of international co-operation. Problems of trade and payments as they emerge in the process of growth among the less-developed countries cannot, therefore, be divorced from the broader strategy of development as such ; nor is it necessary to study them without reference to the present and potential forms of co-operation among nations for dealing with these problems. Accordingly, the present paper seeks to explore the ingredients of a rational trade and payments policy in a developing economy on the assumption that such a policy would be part and parcel of a general programme of development which could or actually does command active international support in a greater or smaller degree.

While the discussion aims at a measure of generality, it is clear that the problems and prospects of different developing countries would differ greatly. This is all the more so when the focus is on international trade where the 'specifics' of a given situation are of the essence of the matter. It may, therefore, be made clear at the

[1] I am extremely grateful to Dr. Subimal Mookerjee for his valuable comments and suggestions for improvement of this paper. Dr. Mookerjee, of course, is not responsible for the views expressed here or for the errors and omissions that may remain.

outset that the distribution of emphasis in this paper is derived largely from the experience and circumstances of countries such as India.

II. THE SETTING

The basic task in a developing economy is that of initiating a progressive spiral of growing productivity, savings and external viability so as to achieve and sustain a satisfactory rate of growth in *per capita* incomes. Whatever view one takes of the relative importance of the technological, managerial, sociological, psychological, educational or biological attributes which endow a human being with productive efficiency, it is clear that economic progress requires a continuing increase in such efficiency ; and more often than not — most certainly over the long pull — the fullest development and exploitation of human productivity would require a growing capital base and rising savings to sustain such a base. To a certain extent, the deficiency in productivity and savings in the initial stages of growth can be overcome by external assistance ; but for practical, if not moral, reasons, there is much to be said for achieving as soon as possible a rate of saving and an environment of efficiency which would permit a satisfactory rate of growth without extraordinary forms of external assistance. Thus understood, the objective of external viability would be subsumed under the other two objectives of higher savings and productivity.

There is, however, a real sense in which it is important to speak of external viability as a separate or distinct objective. Most of the poor nations of the world suffer from the lack of a diversified economic structure. Economic growth sets up demands for imports which are too large for the small export sector to meet, especially when this export sector is confined to a range of goods for which world demand is not particularly responsive. To put it differently, internal resources cannot always be converted into the required machines or materials or consumer goods in adequate quantities either directly by internal production or indirectly by providing large enough export receipts. The balance of payments barrier, to use an expression of Mrs. Robinson's, generally appears before the inflation barrier so that the balance of payments difficulties of developing countries are not necessarily a reflection of inadequate savings or of inflationary fiscal and monetary policies. This is not to say that inadequate savings are not a factor in the situation or that many if not most cases of balance of payments difficulties are not generally aggravated by inflationary policies. Nor does it deny that there are obvious cases among the less developed countries where even a single export product can earn more than sufficient foreign exchange to sustain all the development that is otherwise possible. Nevertheless, as a general rule, the less developed countries suffer from such a limited degree of manœuvrability in their balance of payments that it is meaningful to refer to their balance of payments problems as something distinct from a mere manifestation of inadequate savings or inappropriate fiscal and monetary policies.

In any *ex post* reckoning, of course, the level of investment will exceed domestic savings exactly by the deficit in the balance of payments so that the actual deficit in external accounts may reasonably be referred to as signifying a net claim on resources from abroad. What is contended here is simply that, in such a situation, an effort to increase domestic savings by the relevant amount, while feasible, would not eliminate — though it would in all probability reduce — the deficit in payments.

Perhaps a simplified example might serve to define the scope of the argument attempted here. Let us assume that a poor country has attained equilibrium at a low rate of growth with savings equal to investment and with its single export product, tea, earning enough to pay for the machines and the motor-cars it imports. Assume further that it decides to increase the level of productivity of its farmers by importing additional fertilizers for free distribution by the use, in the first instance, of its foreign exchange reserves which it hopes to recover by the improvement in the balance of payments resulting from an additional tax on its rich people. The tax is expected to produce a revenue equal to the cost of the additional import of fertilizers so that there is no deterioration in the budgetary position of the government. If the response of the rich to higher taxation were to be an equivalent cut in the demand for imported motor-cars, all would be well. But they may just as well respond by dismissing their chauffeurs or by curtailing somewhat their demand for personal service in many directions. If the fertilizers were applied immediately to raise production and if the persons employed in services were in one way or another related to the farming community, the consumption of the 'poor' might even increase despite visible unemployment for some of them. The higher 'savings' of the rich — or more appropriately, their lower consumption — would be reflected in a disappearance of a part of the services from the national income stream; and the initial dissaving in the form of a loss of foreign exchange reserves would remain with its counterpart in the availability of additional fertilizers.

The foregoing example, while tailored to provide an extreme

illustration, is not altogether unrealistic. The general point it seeks to make, viz. the difficulty of creating or releasing specific resources by over-all financial policies, is one which has a relevance to the entire process of development. When we are dealing with 'advanced' countries with a diversified economic structure and when the changes in question are small, it is a valid procedure to assume that real resources are easily interchangeable. But the real or physical aspects of the situation will require specific attention in a developing economy if neglect or inappropriate action at one point of time is not to create crippling bottlenecks at subsequent periods of time. In the context of balance of payments, two conclusions would seem to follow from the consideration under discussion. At any given time, it may be necessary to take direct or specific action to reduce the pressure on balance of payments so as to exploit to the full the available savings potential. More important, the pattern of investment and of resource allocation in general over a period should be such as to remove progressively the balance of payments constraint on further progress.

An investment pattern of the kind just suggested does not imply a disregard of the productivity criterion and its substitution entirely by some balance of payments criterion. Apart from the logical difficulty of trying to segregate those elements of growth which enter, in the long run, into the balance of payments potential and those which do not, the ultimate objective of achieving higher production *per capita* cannot be sacrificed in favour of what is after all a means to growth. What we need to emphasize is simply that it is not so much the immediate contribution to production as the consequences over a period which should be relevant to investment priorities at any given time. And, given the balance of payments constraint that generally operates in developing countries, a course of action designed to strengthen progressively the balance of payments may be preferable to any available alternative even if the immediate consequences of such preference imply a smaller increase in production. Whether this is the case or not is not, of course, a matter for *a priori* judgement but for a detailed consideration of the likely consequences of alternative actions. And it is precisely the function of a proper development strategy to unravel the future patterns of alternative sets of consequences so as to give an advance warning, so to speak, to policy-makers.

Reference may be made in this connection to an argument which is often advanced, viz. that the exchange rate is generally overvalued in most developing countries in the sense that it does not reflect the 'true' value of imports and exports. The presumption in favour of this contention is based on the fact that the current exchange rate does not equate supply and demand for foreign exchange without the help of foreign aid or import restrictions. Given the over-valuation of the exchange rate in this sense, it is further argued that correct investment decisions require the assumption of a 'true' or 'equilibrium' exchange rate. This would clearly give to 'import substitution' and 'export promotion' a considerable weightage in relation to their direct contribution to production when valued at the current exchange rate. The significance of this argument, how-ever, is difficult to see despite the air of plausibility given to it by the use of familiar concepts such as supply and demand and equilibrium. Even if one could arrive at an exchange rate which would equate the supply and demand for foreign exchange at any given time without foreign aid or import restrictions, there is no *a priori* reason why invest-ment decisions based on this exchange rate would produce the most satisfactory result in the long run. The only sensible meaning one can assign to an equilibrium or accounting exchange rate would be a rate which, if used as a basis for investment decisions, would produce the optimum long-term result. But in this sense, the accounting rate will itself have to be determined on the basis of a comparison of the long-term consequences of alternative actions and there can be no presump-tion about the level of this rate of its deviation from the current rate except on the basis of a comparison of alternative concrete possibilities.

In actual practice, of course, decisions about an appropriate development strategy may have to be based not so much on a detailed consideration of likely long-term consequences as on broad judge-ments based on past experience or on such light as one might gather from over-all models which must of necessity incorporate a number of assumptions. But given the outlines of a broad strategy, the question that arises in relation to international trade and payments is that of defining a policy which would be consistent with the development strategy and its objectives and which would, in fact, reinforce the development strategy over time. While the search for a rational trade and payments policy raises many related issues which must be taken into account in framing the developmental strategy as such, it may be convenient to group the discussion mainly around import and export policy with a few remarks on exchange rate policy as well as on foreign aid and private foreign investment.

III. IMPORT POLICY

The process of development inevitably sets in motion a growing demand for imports. A rising level of production and investment cannot be sustained without a steady increase in the demand for machinery, raw materials and consumer goods ; and while some of these growing needs can be satisfied by growing domestic production and by imports financed by exports or foreign aid, the question naturally arises whether the demand for imports should not be kept in check with a view to supplying a somewhat larger part of total demand from domestic production. The case for developing such industries or activities as would reduce the potential demand for imports, if necessary by 'protection' while the industries or activities to be developed achieve the necessary level of efficiency, has long been generally accepted by economists of all persuasions. But, in a sense, the familiar 'infant industries' argument is both too narrow and too broad. It is too narrow in the sense that the industries or activities that may have to be developed from the point of view of 'import-saving' [1] are not necessarily those where demand is already established (e.g. imported food or textiles) or where it can be curbed at least temporarily without affecting growth. In many cases, if not in most, it may be just as important to focus attention on potential domestic supply to meet a potential demand which cannot be curtailed without retarding growth (e.g. for fertilizers or oil) ; and in such cases, it is not the familiar protection of tariffs or quotas but protection in the form of priority in investment and training which should receive attention.

The 'infant industries' argument is also too broad in the context of development planning in so far as it says very little about how many 'infants' should begin to be artificially nourished and how soon and in what sequence. For a country like India, for example, a case can be well made out that practically every conceivable industry or activity would qualify for 'infant industries' protection since there is no *a priori* reason why sooner or later India cannot develop any of these industries on efficient lines. Nor can the inevitable choice among the 'infants' to be protected or promoted be made with reference simply to the pace at which protection could be dispensed with. As already indicated, a whole set of considerations involving alternative uses of resources and their implications over time would be relevant.

In particular, it must be emphasized that what needs to be economized (given judgements about potential export opportunities)

---

[1] The term 'import-saving' is rather misleading in the context of a developing economy where total imports and even the imports of particular categories of goods would increase in all probability and where all production, in a sense, is import-saving. Nevertheless, satisfaction of potential demand by domestic production rather than by exports and imports is a sufficiently distinct process to deserve a name.

is the level of imports over time and not just immediately. One cannot, therefore, just pick out the current import list and start encouraging import-substitution in proportion to the importance of different items in current imports. Equally, the development of import-substituting industries in itself would set up additional demands for imports both for investment goods and for raw materials and components. And while this additional import demand is a relevant part of the total picture which should determine the choice of action, it cannot be assumed that a course of action which swells imports more for a while may yet not be the most import-saving in the long run. A clear instance in point is the development of heavy and basic industries such as those producing steel or machinery in situations where the resource pattern of the country and the amenability to training of its people would establish the presumption that those industries could be efficiently established. Despite the fact that the development of basic industries is likely initially to set up large demands for imports, it may still make sense to try and develop such industries comparatively early rather than late in the process of development. Whether such a course is feasible or not, even where the underlying comparative cost advantages exist, is of course a different matter — for prospective saving of imports does nothing to relieve present or immediate shortage of foreign exchange. In actual practice where most developing countries depend on foreign capital to supplement their resources, the feasibility of the course of action which is heavy on current imports and light on future imports would turn on the decisions of those who supply the capital from abroad as much as on the decisions of the developing country. But the fact remains that even from the point of view of minimizing foreign assistance over the whole period, there might be a case for an intensive administration of such assistance over a limited period.

Needless to say, the drive for import-saving cannot be carried to the point at which it defeats its purpose by cutting too deeply into efforts to promote exports. From the point of view of balance of payments strength, export promotion is just as important as saving on imports. Even the familiar argument that there is a greater degree of uncertainty in any assessment of chances for larger exports than in an estimate of potential import-saving has, at best, a limited validity when we speak of a comparatively long period of time where mistakes are as likely to be made in estimating domestic demand and supply as in gauging foreign demand and supply, where at least the law of averages would apply with somewhat greater force. Similarly, the superiority of import-substitution over export-promotion cannot be established merely by reference to the fact that at any given time existing exports face a somewhat unresponsive international market. In the context of long-term growth, the resources that go into import-substitution can equally be diverted to the creation of new export opportunities where domestic supply conditions or world market conditions are more favourable than in the case of existing exports. Whatever judgement, therefore, one arrives at about the balance to be struck between import-substitution and export-promotion in the light of long-term possibilities and potential would still be a relative judgement; and it certainly would not be divorced from considerations of comparative cost.

What is perhaps less obvious but equally valid is that, beyond a point, import-substitution or -saving would be harmful when it is at the expense of domestically produced and consumed goods. Any undue retardation of the growth of the purely 'domestic' sector — if there is such a sector — would have a repercussion on the growth of savings and productivity in general and, therefore, on the balance of payments to some extent.

The discussion so far has centred on the 'infant industries' argument about which there is little disagreement in economic literature. Nevertheless, this argument gives only a limited clue to the policy that ought to be pursued in any given situation.[1] There are, however, two other arguments in favour of some restrictions on import demand in a developing economy to which we may now turn. It is often argued that a developing country which urgently needs to increase investment should curtail the demand for in-essential or luxury imports so as to allow for a larger import of machinery and other developmental goods. The argument is again reinforced by reference to the so-called demonstration-effect. The availability of imported luxuries creates new demands and reduces the saving-potential of poorer societies especially where the consumption of imported goods enjoys an altogether unusual social prestige.

[1] Partly in response to this consideration and partly in view of the difficulty of making over-all judgements of the kind suggested by a logically integrated policy, investment priorities in actual practice are often decided by rules of thumb which derive vague comfort from the familiar jargon of economics. Thus quite often investment priorities proceed from the necessity of having to allocate available foreign exchange. Once certain 'inescapable' or 'obviously preferred' demands are met, the rest of the foreign exchange available is allocated among competing claimants for expansion of capacity on the basis of how soon and how surely any particular line of investment would recoup its initial foreign exchange cost after allowing for the recurrent need for foreign exchange to employ fully the capacity created. Quite apart from considerations of validity, it is clear that a conscientious application of even a simple rule of thumb such as that just mentioned would raise the same kind of general questions of alternative uses and their consequences that it seeks to avoid.

In their simple or naïve versions the arguments for import restrictions just advanced are, of course, easy to demolish. It does not take much knowledge of economics — or even of simple logic — to show that, by increasing the imports of machinery and reducing the imports of cars or refrigerators or air-conditioners, we do not necessarily produce the additional savings which alone can sustain additional investment. And terms such as demonstration-effect can be countered by reference to inducement-goods. Nevertheless, the arguments under consideration contain an essential core of truth.

If the basic thesis advanced earlier, viz. that the balance of payments barrier often comes before the inflation barrier, is right, it is clear that a reduction in 'luxury' or 'inessential' imports would make it possible to raise both savings and investment beyond what would be otherwise possible. That measures to economize on less essential imports must be supplemented by conscious measures to raise savings is axiomatic ; but that does not mean that it would be impossible to raise savings. What may not be (and often is not) possible is to ensure that measures to promote savings get automatically reflected in a requisite improvement in balance of payments. Under the circumstances, direct measures to curtail the demand for luxury imports would be a necessary, if not a sufficient, part of an optimum developmental strategy. Similarly, the availability of inducement-goods has a definite place in any development strategy in so far as willingness to work, to take risks and to accept technical changes depends on what one can do with the rewards of such willingness. But that does not mean that the demonstration-effect also does not operate or that the totally free exercise of demand is at all a feasible proposition where the essence of developmental planning lies in moderating and modifying the pattern of demand even when it may have nothing to do with imports. A conscious environment of austerity is as vital to economic progress in less developed countries as some evidence of the fact that such progress is worth while. And where status-conscious consumption is involved, a situation where the lure of imported commodities is less prevalent (as in early Japan) would make for greater growth potential. While it may be difficult to strike a precise balance in matters such as these, a correct balance is certainly not struck by a policy of free imports.

Notwithstanding the controversy that often surrounds this issue, the importance of import restrictions in a developing economy is recognized both by common custom and international sanction. Import restrictions for so-called balance of payments reasons are recognized by the GATT, which also provides that these reasons apply with special force to the developing countries. The Articles of Agreement of the International Monetary Fund do not recognize the need for a similar differential regime as between the advanced and the poorer countries. The special dispensation of Article XIV of the IMF is not supposed to apply with special reference to the developing countries. But in actual practice, the shelter of Article XIV of the Fund's Agreement is now sought mainly by the developing countries; and the jurisdictional difference between exchange restrictions and import restrictions is of little substantive significance in any case.

The argument against import restrictions often takes the form of advocating that such restrictions should be exercised by tariffs and general fiscal measures rather than by direct import quotas. In a sense, such an argument accepts the fundamental case for a restraint on less essential imports, for an argument about proper means to implement a policy does not deny the validity of the policy in question. As far as the choice between tariffs and quotas is concerned, there is no doubt that tariffs are generally to be preferred and that this point is not often fully appreciated by the less-developed countries. The administrative complications of quotas and the corruption they give rise to may not be a significant factor in some countries. But there is no justification for import quotas unsupported by higher tariffs when the benefit of such quotas in terms of higher domestic prices and profits goes to a few quota holders. Even if it is desired to make things doubly sure, the proper prescription would be a combination of higher tariffs and quotas.

The difficulty in levying high enough tariffs sometimes arises from earlier hasty and unwarranted binding of tariffs under the GATT; and in such cases a rectification of such a situation would represent a sensible form of international co-operation. The idea that in matters such as tariffs the notion of strict parity or *quid pro quo* ought to prevail even as between advanced and developing countries can only contribute to the proliferation of quotas with all their baneful effects on distribution of income in the poorer countries. Sometimes the preference for quotas arises from the legislative difficulty in making frequent changes in tariffs to suit changing circumstances. But it should not be impossible to obtain greater executive or administrative freedom in regard to tariffs. It is also arguable that far too frequent changes in quotas have themselves been a source of much instability and undesirable speculation in developing countries so that a regime of more or less stable restrictions which rides out minor fluctuations in the payments position has much to recommend itself.

The basic objection to the policy of import restrictions in developing economies is not against the policy as such but against the way in which this policy is often applied without a clear conception of the objective in view. If the rationale for restrictions against luxury imports is that such restrictions widen the balance of payments bottleneck and encourage savings by moderating the demonstration-effect and thus permit a higher rate of growth than would be otherwise possible, it is clear that there should be no attempt to substitute the import of less essential items by greater domestic production of the same commodities. And yet, far too often restrictions on the import of cars or refrigerators or air-conditioners are allowed to be followed by greater domestic production of the same items. Even where domestic production of luxuries is not deliberately encouraged, it is certainly not discouraged ; and the taxes that domestically produced luxuries bear are generally only a fraction of the duties to which they might have been subject when imported. More often than not, the domestic production is undertaken by the foreign suppliers of erstwhile imports ; and the general clamour for encouraging private foreign investment, supported by foreign governments providing assistance, obscures the fact that 'investment' of this kind represents a wasteful diversion of resources which prevents any dampening of the demonstration-effect and nullifies directly or indirectly the original import-saving that was intended. Often, the domestic production of erstwhile luxury imports is manufacture only in name, in the sense that the bulk of the components are imported and the easy profits made in a sheltered market represent an additional burden on the balance of payments. Even if care is taken to ensure that the cost of imported components and profits sent abroad is less than the cost of importing the commodity in a fully manufactured form, it does not follow that the course of action chosen is not worse than the alternative of cutting down imports and not permitting their domestic production at the same time.

It may be argued that the domestic production of erstwhile luxury imports would be desirable in view of the unemployment which prevails in most developing countries. In so far as domestic luxury production depends on the employment of domestic savings, the existence of unemployment is totally irrelevant since the same savings could be employed in a more worth-while investment to produce the same or even larger improvement in employment. Even where luxury production is established by private foreign investment, one will still have to demonstrate that the investment in question could not have been induced to flow in a different direction ; and even then, the undesirable consequences on the flow of savings in view of the continuance of the demonstration-effect would remain.

Nor is it clear that all the resources of skill and materials that foreign producers would employ represent no diversion of scarce resources. Once established, domestic luxury industries become vested interests claiming a share in growing production and investment opportunities so that their direct and indirect claims on the balance of payments and on available savings tend to grow. What starts out, therefore, as an import-saving and employment-giving activity often develops into a voracious trap for scarce resources. At any rate, it is evident that if there is a case for allowing domestic production to take the place of imported luxuries, it is a case that can be established only after much careful and detailed consideration of the likely chain of events over time. But in actual practice, high-cost domestic luxury industries are generally allowed to grow without question, in the wake of restrictions on luxury imports.

The accent of the discussion so far has been on the development of import-saving industries and activities and on the suppression or curtailment of less essential imports. But if the balance of payments acts as a special or distinct brake on development and if the circumstances are such as to warrant a margin of priority [1] for activities that improve the balance of payments, it would follow that the current exchange rate would not restrain imports in general as much as it should. It would, therefore, be necessary to restrain the demand for imports in general by a tariff on all imports. From this point of view, the normal tendency to exempt from tariff duties items such as machinery or raw materials or essential consumer goods is not appropriate. In so far as the objective here is not so much protection or a specific restraint on demand, but a general incentive to economize on imports, the generalized duty need not be high. How high it should be is difficult to say *a priori*. But the contention that all imports need to be taxed may be very relevant though generally ignored. Apart from the consideration here in mind and the much needed gain to public revenues, a general tax on imports including those of machinery would also correct what is sometimes referred to as the artificial relative cheapness of capital in most developing countries. The normal prescription for correcting the phenomenon of under valuation of capital is a rise in interest rates which is seldom acceptable to the harassed fiscal authorities. An increase in the price of imported capital goods would serve the same purpose to some extent.

The policy of import restriction we have recommended so far takes no account of the repercussions on other countries and their

[1] Over and above what would be indicated by considerations of immediate productivity.

reaction thereto. The general presumption in this field seems to be that the repercussions of restrictions on luxury imports would be mainly on the richer countries. The examples of motor-cars, refrigerators and air-conditioners would support such a presumption. And it may be argued that for philosophical, if not moral, reasons the richer countries would not retaliate and that at any rate they should not retaliate. The double standard of morality that Professor Myrdal has been preaching in this regard is certainly not without an obvious appeal. But there are several developing countries and the policies of any one of these countries cannot be deemed rational if they fail to take account of the interests of other countries similarly struggling with their own balance of payments weakness. Iraqi dates, or Zanzibar cloves or Burmese high-quality timber would be luxuries for most Indian consumers and therefore good targets for import restrictions in India. If similar restrictions existed in Iraq and Zanzibar and Burma on exports of luxuries such as carpets or fine cloth or cashew nuts from India, a simple and logical way out of the dilemma would be a mutual liberalization of restrictions. But in practice such a course may not prove so simple. For one thing, the mutual liberalization of imports may have to be on a bilateral or discriminatory basis if the baby is not to be thrown out with the bath water. Wine is produced both in France and Tunisia ; and if liberal imports of wine are to be permitted from Tunisia, there is no point in giving up restrictions on the import of wine altogether. If the current international dogma of non-discrimination were strictly adhered to, the only alternative before most developing countries would be to maintain restrictions against each others' imports to the detriment of all of them. At the same time, if the principle of some marginal discrimination, whether through bilateral and barter deals or otherwise, is accepted, it would be extremely difficult to apply such a principle rationally or equitably. The markets that different developing countries can provide to the products of other developing countries would vary so much in size and scope that it would be difficult to establish even an approximate degree of reciprocity ; and it may well be that the discrimination implicit in any bilateral arrangement is against some other developing country rather than against those who can well take it in their stride. The dilemma that is posed in these conflicting considerations is difficult to resolve, and in actual practice it is likely to be resolved more by pressures and counter-pressures than by the application of any rational principle.

One way of resolving the dilemma which has become a practical reality in some areas is that of forming units of regional co-operation.

But apart from the difficulty of forming such regional co-operation units in some areas, there would still remain the question of relations between different regional groups among the developing countries. The logical thing to do, if one follows this line of thought, would be for all developing countries to adopt a liberal import policy towards each other except in so far as considerations of 'infant industries' argument apply. The exception just noted is clearly important in view of the fact that different developing countries are not at the same stage of development. Even so, a considerable part of the trade among developing countries could still be brought within the purview of liberal import policy to the mutual benefit of all of them. A general principle of this sort may produce better results all round than a congeries of bilateral arrangements arrived at after much bickering and bargaining. The implicit discrimination against advanced countries could also be justified as being not without precedent in recent history ; and, unlike the discrimination still practised in parts of Europe against non-dollar non-OEEC countries, it would certainly not be perverse in the sense of being applied against weaker nations.

IV. EXPORT POLICY

There can be no doubt that with all the emphasis on potential import saving, the total import bill of the developing countries will continue to grow if development itself is to be a continuing process. Sooner or later, therefore, the developing countries must increase their exports substantially. The magnitude of the problem that faces the developing countries in this regard may be illustrated with reference to Indian experience. During the last ten years while a vigorous development programme has been under way, India's total imports have increased steadily from some $1·5 billion a year to about $2·5 billion. During the same period, exports have increased only marginally and are running currently at about $1·4 billion a year. In the meanwhile, the draft on reserves and the growth in foreign indebtedness has led to the disappearance of the sizeable surplus on invisible account and there may well be a sizeable deficit on this account in the years to come. While it is reasonable to expect that imports may not grow as fast as they have in the past, it would be surprising if they do not reach the level of $3 to 3·5 billion in another ten years. India's exports, therefore, must be at least doubled over the next ten years if reliance on external assistance is to be reduced. Even a more heroic effort to increase exports would not be out of place considering that the very emphasis on exports would underline to some extent the need to increase imports since export markets must be nourished even if it requires the import of more and more sophisticated components, materials and machinery. A similar order of export performance would be required sooner or later on the part of other developing countries as well. Given these magnitudes, what kind of export policy would produce the necessary results?

Basically, of course, the first and foremost requirement for a rational export policy would be sufficient attention to the development of export industries in the allocation of investment and other scarce resources. Judgement as to the kind of industries and activities which are more likely to emerge as significant export industries or activities would vary from case to case. About the only generalization one can make is that the problem is sufficiently large to warrant the fullest exploitation of all the avenues for export — whether old or new, whether those relating to primary production or secondary production or invisible income. No developing country which refuses to forfeit its ambitions for continuing development can afford, for example, to neglect such natural advantages as it possesses in the supply of primary products. Much less can it withdraw from the growing sectors of world trade in manufactures and semi-manufactures unless it enjoys superabundance of some natural resources for which world demand promises to grow rapidly. Equally clearly, the policy of adequate investment in export industries must be buttressed by a policy of restraint in domestic consumption of exportable items, by vigorous market promotion and by a scrupulous regard for efficiency and standards. There should also be a determined effort to avoid inflation which cannot but hurt the export drive ; and when a general price rise becomes unavoidable, there should be a prompt adjustment in the exchange-rate. While so much would be — or should be — common ground among most economists, it is doubtful if a rational and adequate export policy for the developing countries can stop at the principles just outlined.

For one thing, vigorous and efficient export industries cannot be created overnight. At the same time, export markets must begin to be tapped and cultivated as soon as possible if they are to be fully exploited in due course. A deliberate policy of giving incentives to the export industries in the initial stages is, therefore, imperative. The case for export incentives is essentially the same as that for 'infant industries' protection or for import restrictions with a view to widening the balance of payments bottleneck.

Unfortunately, while the 'infant industries' argument is generally accepted, its application is generally supposed to affect only import policy and the equally valid case for export incentives often gets branded with the emotive term 'dumping'. Here is one field where economic analysis and economic statesmanship have much to offer by way of a clarification of the basic issues involved. Without such a clarification, there is every danger that the export efforts of the developing countries would founder, with the consequent perpetuation of economic stagnation or of foreign aid. More likely, there would be the alternative danger of a surreptitious growth of export incentives such as would ill serve the interest of the developing as well as the developed parts of the world. If the case of export incentives is generally accepted, the debate could shift to the more fruitful plane of the proper form that such incentives should take.

The developing countries cannot obviously compete with the richer countries as regards export incentives in the form of cheap credits and the like. The general practice among the developing countries is to offer a variety of incentives such as remission of taxes, subsidized transport or power facilities, or cheaper supply of raw materials, or easier access to import licences for replacement of imported components. Some of these incentives, such as remission of customs and excise duties and licences for the import of machinery and components, are not really 'incentives' in the strict sense of the term. In some cases, a system of retention quotas whereby exporters can retain a part of their earnings and import therewith goods which are in scarce supply has been in force. The profits made on imports subsidize the exports. From the point of view of equity as well as efficiency, indirect forms of export subsidization leave much to be desired. It would be far simpler and rational to give a straightforward subsidy to exports ; and the main reason why this is not done as often as it might be is the one already referred to, viz. a lack of international appreciation of the legitimate case for export incentives in a developing economy.

A closely related but more complex issue arises in connection with bilateral arrangements for export-promotion. The issue here is posed mainly but not entirely by the need to develop trade with state-trading economies, i.e. with Eastern Europe, the Soviet Union and China. The growing desire on the part of the Soviet Union and other allied countries to develop trade with the outside world presents a valuable opportunity to the developing (as well as the developed) countries. It is as if a new continent had suddenly been discovered, a continent not virgin and unexploited but with a well-developed economic structure. Many of the developing countries, and particularly those which find that the traditional markets for their limited exports (e.g. Ghana and cocoa, India and tea, Ceylon and rubber) are not growing sufficiently rapidly, have been anxious to exploit the opportunity thus presented. Traditionally, the growing trade with state-trading countries has developed on bilateral lines. This is true to some extent even where the trade has been ostensibly on the basis of multilateral clearing of bilateral balances, since by administrative and other methods net clearings in third currencies are often minimized.

The conventional attitude to such bilateral trade is that it might distort trade patterns : sooner or later one partner would find that it has sold more than it was able or willing to buy from the other partner so that it would be inclined to divert normal imports from other sources to the bilateral trading partner or to import more with a view to re-export. What might appear as a net gain to exports may be much less so and may be offset by higher prices for imports. Notwithstanding the need for caution dictated by the kind of considerations just mentioned, it is doubtful if they destroy totally the validity of growing trade with state-trading countries on a bilateral basis. If Ghana can produce cocoa beyond what the non-Soviet world could conceivably consume and if the Soviet authorities wish to permit an increase in cocoa consumption in the Soviet Union, it would make sense for Ghana to sell the cocoa to the Soviet Union in return for Soviet goods even if these goods were more expensive than similar goods that can be obtained from elsewhere. In actual practice, the normal vigilance of trading partners and the desire to establish enduring and mutually profitable trading relations will ensure that fears about unreasonable pricing and trade diversion do not materialize so that the hypothetical arguments against bilateralism in relations with state-trading countries may not be valid at all (except perhaps where the motivation is predominantly non-economic). In time, when the Soviet Union and allied countries trade with the rest of the world on a general rather than selective basis, as at present, it may well be that strictly bilateral trading will appear superfluous and even unduly complex. But in the meanwhile, profitable and growing bilateral trade with the state-trading countries cannot be eschewed by the developing countries on purely hypothetical grounds.

In the nature of things, however, the bulk of the trade of the developing countries would be with the industrialized and richer countries of the West and it is to these countries that one must largely look for the expanding export markets which are such a vital necessity for the developing countries if they are to cease to rely on external assistance. Practically the whole of the current (and prospective) deficit in the balance of payments of the developing countries is with the industrialized countries of the West; and the present lop-sided trade relationship cannot continue unless one is to become reconciled to a continuing transfer of capital from the richer to the poorer nations. The problem that is inherent in the present pattern of world trade is perhaps the toughest one that international economic statesmanship has yet to face.

As it is, the industrialized nations discourage imports from the developing countries in a variety of ways, including tariffs that discriminate against imports of semi-manufactures and manufactures, quotas, administrative action, high internal excises and the like. Much attention has been focused on this problem in recent years. But the actual progress in freeing and encouraging imports from the developing countries has been only of minute proportions. As a matter of fact, there are grave possibilities of a set-back — possibilities which are underlined by the formation of regional units of co-operation, by the frequent and open use of the oft-exploded 'cheap labour' argument, and by the recent tendency to 'regulate' the exports of textiles from the poorer countries.

And yet, it should be obvious to anyone who looks at the orders of magnitude involved in the problem at hand that what is required is not merely a removal of the obstacles in the advanced countries to imports from the developing countries but a positive and sustained act of co-operation in this regard. Any reference to integration of investment policies or to a deliberate programme in the advanced countries to provide growing room for the products of developing countries runs the risk nowadays of being summarily dismissed out of hand. But this is the direction in which we will inevitably have to move if international economic co-operation is to have any real meaning.

To a certain extent, the export problem of the developing countries would be rendered easier if the so-called advanced countries themselves were to continue to enjoy a significant rate of growth. Apart from the normal growth of demand consequent upon rising levels of income, the task of adjusting the economic structure of the advanced countries so as to lean more heavily on the developing countries would become that much easier. From this point of view, what the world needs is not so much progress towards some abstract concept of equality among nations as rapid progress all round. A 5 per cent per annum growth in the United States, for example, would be all the more desirable if it facilitated a 5 per cent per annum rate of growth in India and if the consequence of, say, a 3 per cent rate of growth in the United States were to hold the Indian rate of growth to 4 per cent per annum.[1]

It may be argued that the developing countries need not look mainly to the advanced countries for their growing markets. If the suggestion is that the developing countries can develop surpluses with countries still not quite developed in order to meet their deficits with more advanced countries, it is hardly likely to square with the present mood and shape of the world. In the past, the triangular kind of exchange envisaged here has played an important part; and, in view of the inevitable differences in the stage of development among the poorer countries, it may still have a part to play. But the hinterland of undeveloped virgin lands ready to take the place of those that have graduated from that stage is fast disappearing, if it has not already disappeared altogether. And today, the surge for development has enveloped all nations. This is not to say that the developing nations cannot trade more and more among themselves; whether they do so only absolutely or in relation to total world trade is as irrelevant as it is difficult to predict. But given the ubiquitous urge to develop and the inevitable growth in imports in order to satisfy this urge, there is no likelihood of a decline in the imports of the developing countries from those already advanced economically. There can consequently be no escape from the task of finding some way whereby the advanced countries may increase fairly rapidly their absorption of the products of the developing countries.

V. EXCHANGE RATE POLICY

Reference has been made in the earlier pages to the fact that a developing country may need to impose general import duties to act as a damper on import demand and at the same time to subsidize exports till such time as export industries attain their maximum efficiency. The question naturally arises why the same results should not be achieved by a straightforward devaluation. To the extent that imports are generally taxed and exports are subsidized across the board, there is, of course, no substantive difference between a

---

[1] In passing, it may be mentioned that, from the point of view of the problem we are considering, it might be desirable for the current discussions on a suitable international monetary and payments system to be resolved in favour of a more liberal system allowing more automatic settlement of international credits and debits. The fear of irresponsible behaviour on the part of deficit countries has imparted a bias which often acts to the detriment of truly forward-looking and imaginative policies on the part of surplus countries. One has also the suspicion that a measure of bilateralism in foreign assistance — through tied loans — might contribute, albeit rudely, to the kind of awakening that is needed among the richer countries in respect of their trade relations with the poorer countries.

regime of import-duties-cum-export-subsidies and a devaluation of the exchange rate. Perhaps the only difference would be in terms of government revenues in so far as uniform rates of import duties and export subsidies would produce a net revenue where imports generally exceed exports. There may, however, be other considerations which argue against the alternative of devaluation. Apart from the psychological repercussions of devaluation, it should be remembered that a rational policy may well require a gradual reduction in import duties and export subsidies. Small and frequent upward revisions in exchange rates are not as convenient as modifications in import duties and export subsidies.

Again, the arguments we have advanced so far in favour of import duties and export subsidies would not dictate a uniform rate of duty or subsidy on all imports and exports. That being the case, devaluation will not be a complete substitute for a regime of import duties combined with export subsidies. Given the degree and pattern of restraint on imports and encouragement of exports, there would, of course, still be room for choice as to the level of exchange rate around which the additional restraints or incentives should be organized. If the exchange rate were kept rather low, there would be comparatively little scope for import duties or export subsidies and perhaps a need for taxation of some exports and subsidization of some imports. With a somewhat higher rate, there would be no need for export taxes or import subsidies and a correspondingly greater range over which import duties and export subsidies should apply. There might be a net fiscal advantage in one or the other alternative course. But in actual practice, the choice is more likely to be a matter of historical accident, with the exchange rate within the lower range of the permissible spectrum whenever past inflation necessitated a devaluation, and within the higher range on other occasions.

It cannot be gainsaid that the continuing balance of payments weakness of the developing countries carries within it the dangers of competitive devaluations of the beggar-my-neighbour variety among the developing countries. Each hard-pressed country may find it difficult to resist the temptation to attract a larger share of the existing market for the traditional and narrow range of exports as well as for some of the newer exports. Sooner or later, the competing countries will follow suit and the net advantage may belong mainly to the developed countries in the form of improved terms of trade. Whether the competition through depreciation takes the form of devaluations or unreasonable proliferation of export incentives makes little difference to the economics of the situation.

Unfortunately, international co-operation in matters of this kind is exceedingly difficult ; and the general presumption in favour of devaluation — engendered by the continuous history of inflation in most developing countries — deters any serious examination of the competitive and mutually destructive aspects of any particular act of devaluation.

VI. EXTERNAL ASSISTANCE AND PRIVATE FOREIGN CAPITAL

A detailed discussion of external assistance and private foreign capital is not germane to the present discussion. Where appropriate, I have already referred to them incidentally. I may, however, refer here to some aspects of external assistance and private capital movements which have a bearing on trade and payments problems. The first point relates to tied assistance. From a general point of view, tied loans and grants represent an unwholesome departure from the principle of international division of labour. At the same time, when assisting countries suffer from acute balance of payments or unemployment problems, the desire to tie assistance becomes understandable. In a sense, the principle of international division of labour can also hardly be applied rationally when the international responsibility for external assistance is not rationally divided. At the same time, the case for tied assistance is being accepted a little too uncritically nowadays.

For one thing, if the rationale for tied assistance is to bring about a more rational distribution of the responsibility for aid, the latter objective can and must be approached more directly. At any rate, as progress is made in that direction — while, indeed, it is being made — the scope of tied assistance must be progressively reduced. Again, even if a measure of tying or discrimination is deemed justifiable in cases of payments difficulties, such discrimination cannot be without discrimination itself. While aid from countries temporarily in deficit may not be utilized for purchases in surplus countries, there is no reason for a similar bar on purchases from deficit countries. As a rule, the tying of aid need not and should not apply to purchases from the developing countries who are themselves the recipients of aid unless one is to make good with one hand what the other destroys. Lastly, the waste implicit in tied aid is often increased by further insisting on tying the use of the aid funds to certain kinds of purchases, mostly machinery or capital goods. The fallacy of misplaced concreteness, which assumes that capital formation is assisted only by the importation of capital goods, has often led to the creation of additional capacity when existing capacity cannot be fully utilized for want of raw materials and components. It often accentuates the bias against the import of consumer goods which cannot or need not all be dispensed with. In the context of tied aid, limiting the use of aid to purchase of capital equipment has the added disadvantage of not allowing the most competitive — or least non-competitive — purchases within the assisting country itself. If the object of tied aid is to subsidize or boost domestic production, there is no reason why producers of machinery ought to be subsidized more than the producers of drugs or metals or lubricants.

Throughout the preceding discussion we have assumed that, sooner or later, the developing countries should eliminate their dependence on external assistance. The reasons for this are practical rather than moral. But this does not mean that sooner or later the developing countries should cease to be net importers of capital and much less that they should reverse the earlier capital inflow. There is no reason why private capital and even international capital mobilized through agencies such as the World Bank should not continue to flow to the developing countries till kingdom-come. How sanguine one can be about the prospects of a continuing and substantial availability of international capital through normal private channels and through accepted international institutions is a matter of taste and mood. But to the extent that one can be so sanguine, the urgency of the task of developing balanced trade relations would be that much less acute and the consequent claims on economic statesmanship that much less baffling.

VII. SOME CONCLUDING REMARKS

The general drift of the argument developed in this paper may be noted briefly. The balance of payments position of the developing countries acts as a special and distinct constraint on the continuing growth of their economies. The policy implications of this phenomenon and the truly gigantic nature of the task of overcoming this bottleneck within a reasonable period are not generally appreciated. Many of the concrete measures required in this connection run counter to accepted norms of international trade and payments behaviour. Some would appear as establishing a double standard of morality among nations. But the double standard is more apparent than real. Problems of international trade in the world as we find it cannot, after all, be approached in terms of some abstract model which seeks to maximize some abstract concept of world welfare in which each nation has an equal claim to share. There exists already a will to co-operate in the development of the less developed countries ; and while an extension of this co-operation in the field of international trade would not be at all easy, especially as it cannot be expressed through simple rules, the need for such co-operation is none the less vital. All this, however, does not amount to throwing overboard all the accepted norms in the field of commercial and payments policy — much less a retreat from economics in the planning and programming of development. The fact that there are more developing countries than one would also dictate that the policies of any one developing country cannot be divorced from the interest of others equally beset with difficulties ; and this consideration would tend to restore the validity of many of the liberal principles of trade and payments, at least so far as relations between the developing countries are concerned.

Chapter 15

EXISTING INTERNATIONAL PAYMENTS AND EXCHANGE SYSTEMS IN RELATION TO PROBLEMS OF GROWTH: I

BY

J. WEILLER
University of Paris

I. INTRODUCTION

IT seems hardly possible to discuss certain essential aspects of the relationship between existing international payments and exchange systems and problems of growth without at least touching upon the origin of these systems. Fortunately we can assume as known the many other important aspects of the question, such as those relating to each country's monetary system and to the attempts of national economic policies to combine the two purposes of keeping up economic growth and re-establishing monetary stability. Particular interest attaches, in this context, to the courses followed by the major European currencies during the years 1951–58 in the direction of convertibility, after a period in which non-convertibility appeared as a necessary evil.

The first thing to note about the international payments systems is their dissimilarity of origin and functioning. Some can be classed as institutions in the legal sense of the word ; and foremost in this category stands the International Monetary Fund, which dates from the Bretton Woods agreements of July 1944. And now, ever since the introduction of transferability — a form of limited, or so-called external, convertibility — for the principal currencies at the end of 1958 raised a new set of problems, the opinion has been gaining ground that the Fund's possibilities of action should be strengthened. Nothing could be better proof of the potential importance of a truly world-wide institution.

However, the difficulties encountered in trying to modify the IMF rules according to the Triffin, Bernstein, Stamp or Zolotas proposals in fact show up the reasons why it has so far proved impossible to allow such an institution a really decisive part in international payments. Nevertheless, with judicious manipulation of the 'rules of the game' and the escape clauses under Article XIV, the IMF has shown what might be done by an international authority, or an advisory council on a world scale.

As regards the two others in this category, the European Payments Union, which functioned between the summer of 1950 and the end of 1958, was a very different sort of institution ; the European Fund (which was to have replaced it in 1956 and eventually did so under such different conditions) can hardly be put on the same level and its potential role can safely be ignored in this discussion.

Whatever classification scheme is adopted for the sake of simplicity, it is always difficult to draw dividing lines in practice. During the 'fifties, certain currency areas, and especially the franc area, had what we all took to be a well-defined (and perhaps too well-defined) institutional character, but it tended to get blurred when the system moved up to the international plane, where the dangers grow together with the opportunities of better currency management. In other words, as negotiations with the governments of newly independent nations modify and soften the original rigidity of the principles of a currency area, the latter becomes more fluid and in many ways more empirical. Under the simultaneous effects of emancipation from colonial practices and of external convertibility, the franc area began to assume the well-known characteristics of the sterling area.

If, again, we look from the angle of empirical evolution at the functioning of what is, in terms of the dollar since the end of the last war, often called the gold exchange standard, we have to take into account a whole series of elements which combined in an extraordinarily complex way during the period 1945–58. But right through these vicissitudes we note a common feature which this system shares with the currency areas of the fluid type and which the developments of recent years have made more and more obvious. In point of fact, the dollar system never could be called institutional in any but an extremely vague and debatable sense which is nowadays repudiated by most sociologists.

I should perhaps speak, not of the role, but of the several different roles, which the dollar has played for more than fifteen years. It was, above all, an accounting unit or even accounting money (in the traditional sense which antedates the very brief phase of metallic standards and the even briefer one of the gold standard). We should have to distinguish the rules of 'settlement in gold or dollars', of exchange reserves in gold, in dollars or in 'other convertible currencies'. If we were to stick strictly to institutional aspects we would probably end up in the absurd position of limiting the discussion to what has sometimes been called the dollar area and we might even be led to deny, as others have done, that the dollar area ever existed as a consistent system. In any event, we would have to take a very close look at the significance attaching, for instance, not only to the accumulation of dollar reserves but also to the conditions governing the settlement of deficits about 1947, or to the play of compensatory finance in the relations of any European country with, say, Canada, the Philippines, Mexico, Venezuela or, for that matter, Japan. What was much more important at the time, from the practical point of view, was that the dollar became the centre of a much wider system of revived trade, which was presently to acquire new substance from the Marshall Plan. Equally important was the system of indirect and conditional aid which prepared the ground for inter-European payments agreements, in so far as its multilateralism, partial and lop-sided though it was, became a precursor of the European Payments Union. This is how the countries of Western Europe started on their road to convertibility, and might well repay further close analysis.

In the meantime, I should like to recall the conditions in which certain trade and payments patterns came to be established and to acquire a more or less lasting equilibrium. This amounts to an exercise in classifying the dollar problem : the extreme cases, that is to say, on the one hand, the so-called dollar area countries, and on the other those which had the greatest difficulty in getting hold of any hard currencies at all, are easy enough to distinguish.

The former group of countries, by their insistence on payment in dollars, were destined to follow a particular type of growth process based on the widest possible multilateralism in trade flows, subject to whatever discriminatory restrictions or exchange controls the rest of the world imposed against them.

The other countries were for ever clamouring for a currency like the dollar and the dollar shortage alone was the declared obstacle standing in the way of the immediate adoption of an equally wide multilateralism no less than of the accumulation of dollar reserves. These countries felt constrained to try and re-establish the conditions of balanced economic growth by a series of what are usually termed unorthodox measures. In particular, they developed international trade patterns and payments systems which were certainly less than fully multilateral, but which held out the prospect of greater internal balance, together with the possibility of stimulating growth through trade liberalization. At the same time, by virtue of the very structure of their external trade and of the system of compensatory finance for their deficits, these countries still took part fairly extensively in a series of nationally and internationally controlled monetary flows within the wider international system governed by the dollar.

Between these two types of participation in the dollar system, which occupied a central place that might fittingly have belonged to the International Monetary Fund, we find a whole range of international payments and exchange practices which sometimes had a recognizable institutional character but most often did not. More dynamically, we might say that international systems of this kind owe their emergence (or their disappearance) to the more or less lasting convergence (or divergence) of decisions taken by more or less numerous countries. For one reason or another some countries may regard it as necessary (at least temporarily), and others as distinctly advantageous, to hold large balances in a currency considered as sufficiently hard. In these circumstances certain international payments flows will tend to fall into permanent and 'privileged' patterns and this tendency will be reinforced by the policies usually associated with developments of this kind.

It is interesting to consider what will happen to these balances, once the institutional framework or, for that matter, the mere rules of the game are seen to be extremely precarious. Depending on the circumstances and the period, we might, in the absence of sufficiently flexible economic policies, witness the alternate weakening and strengthening of the role played within some system of international transactions by its key or reserve currency or, ultimately, of the role played by a currency of an international payments centre.

But I regret that I cannot proceed further with my description of how certain payments systems, which put some order into international monetary relations, came into being within a fairly short span of time, or at any rate managed to function during the 'fifties. This discussion necessarily had to be as short as possible, if only because it is the background that matters and the permanent characteristics of these systems, rather than fortuitous historical factors of transitory effect; but certain limitations of space and time also force my list to be incomplete.

I cannot here compare — let alone combine — the study of the past and possible future of various international payment systems among the western economies with an analysis of the type of international settlements within the rouble area (as it is sometimes called, although this has never meant the same thing as 'sterling area' or 'franc area').[1]

[1] Considering the very definite historical break between the two blocs of countries there is perhaps little point in a comparative study of the past problems

In the rest of the world, the widest of the existing payments systems centred on the dollar as its principal currency — paradoxically, but necessarily, just because of the difficulties of settlement in hard currencies. Other international key currencies, the main function of which was to mitigate these difficulties, appeared in the 'fifties as secondary payments and exchange centres.

I need not recall, in this context, the kind of dialectical somersaults at the turn of the years 1957 and 1958. The discussions of the 'new' dollar problem were conducted with much heat at the time, but I had better not reopen them here.[1]

It will no doubt be appreciated that I must limit the scope of my paper to a subject which, notwithstanding its wide implications, is at any rate somewhat different. Supposing we really have solved the problems of equilibrium that were with us in the period 1945–58 and that the principal European currencies' return to convertibility has put the seal on this solution, two questions remain to be answered next :

(1) To what extent do the systems examined satisfy the conditions of economic growth in the most advanced countries ?

(2) How far can we be sure that these international payments and exchange systems will not again be upset by the requirements of other participating countries' development plans or programmes ?[2]

There is no simple answer to these questions. However, I shall try, in the next section of this paper, to indicate the rudiments of a reply with respect to the tasks of the most advanced countries, and in the third section I shall concentrate more particularly on the second of the above questions.

within each group. This may not necessarily be so in the future. In considering the growth problems of a fairly large number of developing countries the attraction of the rouble area may merit no less attention than that, say, of the dollar area.

[1] Once the serious disequilibria that affected the relations of the various currency centres earlier were removed, did not everything seem possible again — a general extension of the dollar payments system and the constitution of dollar reserves no less than the total disappearance of any system of this kind ? Other papers have already thrown light on various aspects of this question.

[2] I am well aware that I shall be dealing with only a few topical problems of economic growth or development (without dwelling too much on the semantic differences in the interpretation of these two terms). This will, alas, not satisfy the expectations aroused by the inclusion of so wide a subject in the Round Table programme, even if two reports are to be devoted to the subject. I should have been well content if I could have developed a whole series of replies to the questions implied in this title, but it seemed wiser to discard most of what I was tempted to say in favour of the more far-reaching theoretical aspects of the problems to be treated.

II. THE GREAT INTERNATIONAL CURRENCY CENTRES AND THE RETURN TO CONVERTIBILITY (RULES AND PROCEDURES)

So far as concerns most of the principal European countries whose currencies have again become largely convertible, the role of the International Monetary Fund in the past (until 1957) has not been so much to make any practical contributions through bringing its machinery into play (the European Payments Union being obviously much more effective from this point of view), but rather to lay down the 'rules of the game', and, more important still, the transitional exceptions permissible in the application of these rules.

At the same time, the other great international centres — London and Paris no less than the EPU — worked in a manner contrary in many ways to what they can be expected to do from now on. Their currencies were not convertible. After an interruption of growth due to the discontinuity imposed by the Second World War and its effects, the chances of renewed growth depended upon the solution of the problems arising from a kind of disequilibrium which we thought (and still think) was structural. Only the solution of these problems, it seemed, could again create conditions of balanced growth.

In retrospect, everything that has ultimately happened, sometimes by long and devious routes, seems to correspond well enough with the predictions of the International experts who met at Bretton Woods in July 1944. When it was said at the time that the war-ravaged developed countries needed to return to international economic equilibrium, this was much the same as what came to be known as external convertibility in 1958. Some preliminary observations need to be made in this connection.

(i) It is easy enough to sympathize with the glow of satisfaction following the achievement of an aim which may be described as orthodox, albeit in a somewhat broad and superficial sense. This applies more especially to the countries which for one reason or another have managed to improve their balance of payments position. In spite of some asymmetry in the very definition of desirable equilibrium for reputedly deficit or surplus countries, plain common sense suggests that over-all balance in any system will always afford satisfaction of this kind to some countries and there is a presumption, right or wrong, that their economic, monetary or budgetary policy may have counted for something in the process.

(ii) It is equally easy to understand that, once the return to convertibility had become an accomplished fact, the international experts deflected their attention for a while from the partial disequilibria which for ever threaten to appear in international payments and turned instead to the danger of general disequilibrium due to international liquidity shortage in relation to the needs of a global expansion of world trade. This question has been treated in the final paper to the Round Table and I have to leave it in suspense. But to state a personal opinion, I should say that quite serious partial disequilibria are bound to persist or to reappear and that their control conditions the solution of the general problem.

Disequilibria of this kind may on occasion slow down economic growth in the countries concerned, at least unless judicious countermeasures are taken. They may also accelerate growth; in that case we speak of them as one of the aspects of intersectoral linkages in a type of unbalanced growth which is sometimes theoretically recommendable, provided the required financial resources are actually at hand.

From the point of view of economic growth it is surely wrong to limit the discussion of partial disequilibria of this kind to developing countries. It may be well to recall that the experts who drafted the Bretton Woods agreements had no hesitation in putting industrialized countries with post-war reconstruction problems on the same plane. At the time, the intention was to insert the payments system of the International Monetary Fund into the wider context defined in the very title of the second creation of Bretton Woods, the International Bank of *Reconstruction and Development*.

What was explicitly intended and 'institutionalized' in July 1944 had, from the theoretical point of view, much wider scope. While it is essential to keep in mind the reasons why the principles of the International Clearing Union and Keynes's Bancor were rejected, it is a good deal less important that it was the EPU rather than the IMF to which the European countries had to turn from 1950 onwards. Nor is it really important that in 1948 it was the Marshall Plan which carried out the purposes of the International Bank. In considering here the functioning of international payments and exchange systems, we must put them back into a context which they may occasionally have helped to shape or alter or put in order, but on which they are ultimately dependent.

A true international payments and exchange system presupposes much more than (*a*) certain procedures or drawing rights, by which a country can raise resources to sustain an expansion which might otherwise be checked prematurely by the effects of external disequilibrium, and (*b*) certain rules by which member countries are obliged, sooner or later, to check expansion whenever there appears to be a danger that inflationary tendencies might lead to a lasting combination of internal and external disequilibrium.

Some of the Fund's rules, e.g. Article XIV, which provides for transitional arrangements and for periodic consultations with countries availing themselves of these arrangements, have had, and will no doubt continue to have, rather more influence than might have been thought. (A more topical example than the European countries' path to convertibility is, today, that of the Latin American countries which use not only exchange control but multiple currency practices — which, incidentally, are not contrary to the Fund's Articles of Agreement.) Another very important point is that member governments are obliged to provide full details of their balance of payments, which has helped and to some extent still ought to help to redress the above-mentioned asymmetry in the assessment of what constitutes external disequilibrium.

However, the lesson to be learnt from a careful study of the period 1951–58 (as, indeed, of the actual working of the gold standard on the world scale, to which we shall refer later) is that what counted most in the event was not the set of rules devised and codified on the occasion of the creation of an institution like the International Monetary Fund but its influence on the conduct of member governments. It is worth stressing again the Fund's forbearance with countries which, in spite of persistent imbalance, pursued certain economic, monetary, budgetary or commercial policies designed to ensure steady growth, besides the Fund's systematic efforts, once certain partial disequilibria seemed on the point of clearing up, to guide all national and international policies towards the reintroduction of external convertibility.

While it is true that the profound disequilibrium of the post-war years had its own very specific features, there is certainly no reason at all to discard everything that was learnt during that period about the effective functioning of a wide international payments and exchange system, especially as regards its complexity and the sort of diagnostic grading of the practices employed by various countries and currency areas pending an improvement in their situation. *Ex posteriori*, one might well attempt to reconcile the point of view of those who advocated a speedy return to more rigorously orthodox principles in the application of the rules with the point of view of those who defended exceptional means and methods with a view to the re-establishment of balanced patterns of trade. It was perhaps doctrinaire rigidity more than anything else which so long prevented a meeting of minds on this subject.[1]

---

[1] Incidentally, to advocate a speedy return to the application of the rules, implied somewhat paradoxically much more far-reaching adjustments, since a

Be that as it may, it fits in well with my present context to discuss rather briefly this type of disequilibrium ; for it implies that when a country's former structural links with the rest of the world are seriously impaired, it should not be expected to start on the road to renewed expansion from too low a level of international balance and hence of domestic economic activity. In any event, such an explanation made — and will make — it easier to define the contribution to economic growth which can, in certain circumstances, be made by efforts to restore previous international economic patterns (subject, of course, to such changes as may be judged necessary in the light of events). It is an essential contribution to economic growth that countries be exempted from the strict application of the rules and be assured of finance for their deficits for a more or less extended period : it saves time to reactivate blocks of development which might have to be abandoned if external equilibrium were achieved at much too low a level.

As the situation approaches the normal, regular recourse to the machinery of an international system will become a sort of routine for many member countries, provided it is possible to avoid new threats to equilibrium, such as insufficient liquidity creation by all the existing monetary centres together or, conversely, the use of liquid funds for speculative purposes.

Again, the problems are set in the widest possible institutional framework, which alone can make the agreed rules fully effective ; and much will depend on the judicious exercise of influence on national and international policies. These latter will have a decisive effect on structural readjustment within each monetary system's pattern of international flows.

Today, the link between these two propositions seems obvious enough. Suppose that there are certain centrifugal structural tendencies within a currency area, so much so that eventually the trade flows are attracted towards another international monetary centre ; the payments system concerned does not, for that reason, necessarily lose its justification, but it will have to revise its working and its rules. If, on the other hand, we return to the background of the creation and efficient functioning of such a payments system, we always find the need to face the common danger of balance of payments disequilibrium between the members of one system and those of another — or of several others.

At an early stage, the remedy is sought in the simple alignment

balance achieved in a system of exchange control and quantitative restrictions could not necessarily be expected to continue in the absence of such restrictions. This is what makes the concept of structural disequilibrium so precarious, once there is a marked improvement in the position of the deficit countries.

of currencies. What used to be called the 'sterling bloc' during the years of the great depression affords the simplest and most familiar example : the coalition did not, on the whole, concern anything more than exchange fluctuations and it was not always strengthened by preferential tariffs, as was to be the rule, later, in the sterling area.

Exchange alignment — but in another form and combined with a joint payments system — was still in evidence in the currency areas which came into being after the Second World War and continued to function until the introduction of external convertibility. Neither the sterling area nor the franc area, incidentally, commanded universal solidarity in currency devaluations.

But what came to count more as time went on was the application of common quantitative restrictions *vis-à-vis* other countries or other currency areas. The main elements of cohesion in the 'fifties were not so much the institutional conditions of central currency management or a common foreign exchange pool, but a common interest in maintaining quantitative restrictions.

By maintaining joint import restrictions the currency areas strengthened the 'monetary' protectionism, notwithstanding free transferability among a large number of countries. But import restrictions perforce discriminated against hard-currency countries and for that reason were, rightly or wrongly, held to be incompatible with the principles of convertibility — quite apart from the fact that they already stood condemned in the light of the principles of international trade embodied in GATT.

If, in theory, the concepts and decisions of monetary policy (convertibility) and commercial policy (non-discrimination) converge at this point, there is, in practice, room for the appearance of leads and lags in the course of structural readjustment on the international level. The divergence may be considerable if we abandon the idea of a return to the traditional rule of stable equilibrium and think instead in terms of an optimum rate of balanced and harmonized growth.

But a discussion of the requirements of an optimum rate of growth is not relevant here. As regards the functioning of an international payments system, it would seem hardly possible to establish any direct connection between such requirements and the rules governing the use of certain monetary facilities ; however, a few conditions can be identified, difficult as they may be to find in combination.

Fundamentally, no truly international payments system has ever come into being or can be expected to develop unless (i) it displays a sufficient ability to promote, safeguard or re-establish a multilateral and reciprocally advantageous network of trade, and (ii) it is resilient enough to survive such occasional disturbances or speculative attacks to which it is exposed, precisely by reason of the multilateral character of the payments involved. This latter condition comes to mind in connection with the problem of currency reserves and with the danger of their more or less rapid exhaustion in the case of cyclical balance of payments difficulties.

Now, the fear of persistent disequilibrium may, as I have noted, help to strengthen the cohesion of a currency area, especially in the phase of non-convertibility, when member countries adopt common attitudes. But the strengthening effect of this fear cannot be durable, especially when once convertibility is restored, unless there is also a permanent base of mutual confidence — and if there is confidence, one would hope to see it more patently displayed in the development of trade relations within the currency area or indeed within any other international payments system (except, of course, in the case of institutions like the International Monetary Fund, which is immune from dangers of this kind).

Symptoms such as the flight of hot money may sometimes presage the disruption of the system, but on the other hand they may be merely speculative and temporary. One can never be quite sure either about the real reasons or about the lasting consequences of monetary movements of this kind, especially with regard to the conditions of economic growth in the member countries of the payments system from which the funds are withdrawn.

In the limiting case of a temporary flight of hot money, the upheaval in the relations between two systems may call forth the hasty and premature introduction of deflationary measures and may thereby slow down the long-term rate of growth of those groups of countries which, in one way or another, suffer the repercussions of a monetary contraction not otherwise justified. On the other hand, the transitory accumulation of international liquidities in the temporary home of the hot money in no way helps the growth of the economies depending upon this particular reserve currency : on the contrary it is very likely that measures will be taken to counteract the effects of imported inflation.

A series of prolonged or repeated pathological reactions will eventually entail a structural alteration of the results achieved on the basis of a sounder and more stable multilateralism. Capital flight will be responsible, to a greater or lesser degree, for the accumulation of balances in the payments and exchange system at the receiving end. Apart from changes in the distribution of reserves and in the hierarchy of the world's monetary centres, we may therefore witness also certain trade-diverting effects and, as a result, changes in the international pattern of trade, the solid base of the multilateral compensation system which was upset by the flight of hot money in the first place.

These changes are not necessarily irreversible. Confidence can return and more than one European currency has made a remarkable recovery in the course of the last forty years. But whenever some international payments system allows itself to become unduly impressed with the more or less transitory manifestations of distrust in certain currencies which might otherwise attain to some degree of autonomy, then the situation really becomes highly unstable. When the holders of the suspect currency lose confidence in it, and especially when one or more member countries of the system fail or are slow to repatriate their export proceeds, a number of mistaken or exaggerated notions usually aggravate the situation and at the same time set off artificial oscillations which are bound to be harmful for the economic growth of all countries concerned. For instance, faced with a flight of capital, a country tends to take an exaggeratedly pessimistic view of its own export capacity and so may overestimate its trade deficit consistently. As a result, imports which may be necessary for continued growth appear excessive.

Again apparent miracles happen when exports eventually pick up after a structural renewal of industry that has been going on for a long time, in spite of and partly because of the imports as well as because of prior investment.

It cannot be stressed too often and too forcefully how important it is not to make the slightest mistake in distinguishing between what is due to current deficit and what to speculative exaggeration. Since the decisions taken may involve either the encouragement of economic expansion or its restriction with a view to a more staid and steady rate of growth, capital flight may unleash a whole sequence of repercussions of which only a few are foreseen in the limited perspective of the classical theories of the re-establishment of equilibrium.

It may seem right from an ethical point of view that what was built on lack of confidence should collapse when confidence returns, but this is deceptive and we should be at pains to avoid any emotional connotations connected with the kind of speculative exaggeration I have just discussed. The payments system where balances from the most diverse sources accumulate is, in its turn, also subject to quasi-mythical delusions of a psychological or sociological character (such as are hardly ever absent from the commonplace interpretation of balance of payments vicissitudes). There is a tendency to neglect the accounting significance of a money stock, especially if it happens to be a gold bullion stock, and to forget about the national and international capital flows to which this money stock corresponds.

To be sure, this phenomenon is accompanied by a number of practical consequences for the evolution of the system itself. I cannot, here, dwell at length on the complex factors which brought down the gold exchange standard between 1928 and 1931, nor can I repeat everything that has been said about the dollar problem in the last three years. But a clear distinction must be made between the collapse of a financial myth (the delusory interpretation of a monetary system) and the survival of the real elements, only partly vitiated by these delusions : trade flows and patterns of trade requiring a volume of international liquidity which cannot easily be compressed.

With external convertibility of all reserve currencies there is, certainly, a temptation to focus attention on the global aspect of the operational conditions of a very wide system — the system, that is, which we have so far called the dollar system and the rules of which seem once more to be very strictly those of Bretton Woods. But, tomorrow as yesterday, we shall have to pay attention to the separate and particular structural aspects of the movement of goods and the movement of capital. From the point of view of any single country affiliated to one or the other international payments centre these aspects are more important than global considerations which tend to overshadow the problems of economic growth.

A few more points remain to be made. The multilateralism inherent in any international payments system always involves a danger of sudden change. A country which already has at its disposal large international liquidity reserves may still claim more from another, debtor, country provided this latter possesses such reserves itself or can get some from the international centre to which it belongs. There can be no conceivable opposition to rules which translate the very spirit of multilateralism, but it does seem possible to eliminate the speculative aggravation of the alternation of distrust and confidence often reinforced, in democratic countries, by the effects of political change. International monetary co-operation has already made some progress in this direction and should make more if only we can manage to substitute some notion of common economic growth for the traditional devices by which each member country looks after its own external equilibrium, without a common standard and without any thought for others. Similarly, co-operation between major international centres may help to counteract the harmful consequences of growth-restricting policies applied in the fear of inflationary pressures. Surplus countries accepting the precepts of a brand of neo-liberalism and intent above all on internal equilibrium should surely be the first to recognize the importance of such co-operation. And as regards the application of the IMF rules, it should always be remembered that in the intention of the Bretton Woods experts governments should have some power of control over the movements of hot money.

III. ECONOMIC POLICY AND INTERNATIONAL PAYMENTS AT VARIOUS LEVELS OF DEVELOPMENT (MERCHANDISE AND CAPITAL FLOWS)

When, in December 1958, ten countries simultaneously accepted external currency convertibility, it seemed that the last word had been spoken. But we all know how relative, in historical terms, such an expression can be. Certain problems subsist, as we have seen, even with respect to the relations between major international centres ; others arise from the new easements or difficulties introduced by the economic policy of the individual countries which, in one way or another, play a part in the working of international payments systems.

Is it, in international payments, always an advantage to renounce certain weapons of restrictive trade policy ? Are we to take an entirely negative view of the use of these weapons resorted to by certain countries in an effort to mitigate the balance of payments difficulties attendant upon a process of readjustment ?

It is a hard question to answer. As it is, the rules which rightly or wrongly surround convertibility, as it is currently understood, demand the abolition of quantitative restrictions. Other commitments tend to eliminate also the manœuvring space which many countries had traditionally in the field of tariff changes. The main idea seems to be to hamstring commercial policy — and yet no international agreement is without its escape clauses. Leaving aside all the more or less durable reasons which may militate in favour of a higher or a lower tariff, the fact remains that if governments retained for so long the right to vary tariffs either autonomously or within the framework of trade agreements, this was generally not unconnected with a certain balance of payments situation.

We cannot, without detailed historical investigation, explain precisely how, in the nineteenth century and again in the inter-war period, protectionism ultimately helped to introduce some harmony into international economic relations. Historically speaking, it would seem that at least in the case of the economically developed countries, which were for ever engaged in the negotiation of commercial agreements, there was a certain continuity of tendencies, expectations and preferences as regards internal economic structure and international patterns of trade. However, while the participating countries kept for more or less prolonged periods to one and the same line of structural development, they were led to revise their tariffs (and the tariff concessions embodied in the agreements) whenever cyclical fluctuations caused their imports or exports to vary beyond certain limits.[1]

Like all historical interpretations, this one no doubt needs to be qualified by a great many reservations. The point I wish to make is simply that it is quite wrong to belittle the extent and frequency of variations in commercial policy, except perhaps in the limiting case of outright free-trade countries or of autonomously determined tariffs which tended to be relatively rigid in between major cyclical turning-points. If the point of view here expounded is acceptable, I shall be led to conclude that, while the governments' commercial policies were, on the whole, tendentially steady enough to promote long-term growth, they were also apt to lighten the task of national and international payments systems — which is just what France, for example, seems to have done quite recently, between 1952 and 1958, with her alternate policies of trade liberalization and restriction within the OEEC group of countries.

If in many countries commercial policy is losing its cyclical flexibility, it becomes all the more important to assure strict coordination through old or new international payments systems — except perhaps for those countries which have at long last learnt to use other instruments of economic policy. This necessity of coordination is one to which the International Monetary Fund is very much alive, especially in its relations with Latin America. All the large international payments centres will have to accept their re-

---

[1] It would no doubt be useful to make a number of case studies of economically advanced countries in this intermediary situation. France, for example, was, ever since 1880, clearly wedded to a policy of slow structural evolution, and this did not change until the Rome Treaty of 1957. Whether we speak of 'structural preference' (within which there is room for changes in tariffs, preferential tariffs and quotas) or whether we use some other operational concept, the point is that we must not allow ourselves to be misled by superficial variations in commercial policy which reflect no fundamental change in the network of international trade.

For all their complexity, such reactions to balance of payments difficulties were not in the least infrequent. See 'The Problem of Long-term International Balance', Proceedings of a Round Table held by the International Economic Association, *Unesco International Social Science Bulletin*, Vol. iii, No. 1, Spring 1951 ; and, for the more detailed background, papers on various countries, including my own on France, 'Balances commerciales en longue période', *Revue Économique*, May 1950. Cf. also *Cahiers de l'I.S.E.A.*, Série P, Nos. 2 and 4.

sponsibilities in this matter if they are to survive in a new form, and this goes more particularly for the centres of the existing currency areas. To say this is only another way of acknowledging the current difficulties encountered by policies envisaging direct action to adjust international payments, especially if the optimum rate of growth is to be maintained, so far as possible, for each participating country.

There is a possibility, of course, of choosing a type of common growth. So far as most of the industrial countries of Western Europe are concerned, there is at the moment the additional complication that some of them have simultaneously plunged into what is, in spite of all precautions, still a risky venture, whether it be the Common Market or the Free Trade Area. A policy of growth through economies of scale, no doubt. But what the old commercial policies did was to make determined efforts to prevent cyclical fluctuations from producing undue distortions in the domestic economy, even though more rapid change in periods of expansion might accord better with the general spirit of these policies. On the other hand, the current acceleration of structural economic change (which has been discussed in Professor Byé's paper) is really a leap into the unknown. It may well be that we shall have more need in the future for closer monetary co-operation if we want to avoid abusive recourse to the escape clauses. And it is easy enough to understand the recurring temptation to set up a new monetary system for this purpose, which would go much further along the line of integration.

Somewhat similar problems arise for the developing countries in reconciling general economic policy and their adherence to a currency area or international payments centre. However, the difficulties vary according to the stage of development. It is hard to say what, initially, governs the decision to remain in a currency area or to withdraw from it, or the decision to link up with some other international payments centre. Political motives may be predominant, but there is every reason to believe that the desire to maintain or refashion certain patterns of foreign trade is often of the essence.

Another immediately important consideration is how to finance the deficit in the current balance. From this point of view external aid and the certainty of regular long-term capital flows may assume prime importance and relegate to second place the sort of short-term monetary problems which nowadays beset all the economically advanced countries.

This, at any rate, seems to be the rationale of the present policies of newly independent countries; but it does not follow that this was historically the reason why dependent or independent, but in any event economically less developed, countries originally tied their currencies to some stronger currency (which was certainly convertible if we go back to the years before the First World War, but need not have been since).

From the strictly monetary point of view one would no doubt have to look for the earliest applications of the gold exchange standard in the relations between a country possessing strong gold reserves and another which, having just given up the silver standard, was unable to tie its currency directly to gold or for some reason did not manage to escape from a regime of paper money. It was a situation very different from that described by the old textbooks, which concentrated exclusively on a few Western countries and neglected the fact that as late as the eighteen-eighties, and even towards the turn of the century, the rest of the world had the greatest difficulty in establishing national currency systems linked to the gold standard. Stabilization loans and the upsurge of private foreign investment created only at a very late stage the basic conditions of an institutional framework which, from the purely monetary point of view, had seemed so satisfactory.

From the point of view of growth, or rather of economic development, the achievements of the system do not look so impressive in retrospect. The idea that the leading country at the centre of an international payments system might also assume the responsibilities of a growth-leader simply did not exist at the time. There was strict separation of duties in this type of pairing of countries at different stages of development, and the duties were few. Was it enough to fulfil them to the letter? What use could it be to a country whose domestic credit system was rudimentary to tie its currency either directly to gold or to a convertible currency, above all, as we would say today, when its gold coverage was 100 per cent ? [1] Is it necessary to say any more ? Surely, the modern theory of economic development tells us enough about the pre-conditions of growth according to type of country or world region.

However, there remains one point of monetary theory which is still very controversial. What dose of inflation — or, if preferred, what dose of monetary expansion not conducive to undue inflationary

---

[1] No doubt it escaped notice that the conditions of growth at different stages of economic development have very little in common. The severe restrictions imposed upon the Bank of England's issue department were perhaps the best possible stimulus for the development of bank money after 1844 and they were certainly instrumental in the creation of institutions best suited to promote England's domestic and international expansion (although economic historians still have their doubts about the achievement of an optimum rate of growth even in this remarkable case).

pressure — should have been or should now be tolerated or indeed encouraged at different stages of development? A country having the ways and means neither of voluntary saving nor of total planning may well need a much stronger dose than used to be thought. On the basis of a recent interpretation of the most reliable calculations made so far with respect to this question, I should, personally, feel inclined to suppose that the dose needs to be all the stronger the more primitive the stage of development and the more pressing the difficult transition from one type of society to another.

In its turn, the part that international payments systems can play in stabilization policy also varies greatly according to the stage of development. Before 1914, the lender countries' efforts to exercise a stabilizing influence on the currencies of the 'new countries' were not very determined so long as the latter could always look forward to receiving further long-term capital resources from foreign investors; nor was there, in the long run, any lack of short-term credit facilities, and in any event the task of monetary stabilization was not taken very seriously. This is, incidentally, the reason why there are so many examples of economic growth accompanied by fairly strong inflationary pressures.[1]

Many searching questions could be asked, on the other hand, about the success of the efforts made within the framework of an international payments system like the IMF to induce numerous Latin American countries to refashion their financial and exchange policy with a view to restoring conditions of convertibility more in keeping with the rigorous principles of the IMF statute (Article VIII).

Some developing countries, which had put into effect complicated and selective import and export regulations within the framework of exchange control (e.g. selling licences to the highest bidder, multiple exchange rates, etc.), seem to be reaching a new stage. Liberalization accompanied by credit facilities such as may be granted under stand-by agreements clearly offers many advantages, in so far as it makes economic strategy much more flexible in the choice of the ways and means of structural development.

A second set of considerations concerns the still somewhat chaotic forms and conditions of aid to developing countries. Even though international loans and grants may have only secondary importance in the formulation of national programmes and plans, they

---

[1] In our time, development programmes or plans try to avoid the sort of distortions in the domestic economy which were the rule so long as foreign investment concentrated predominantly on export products. Considering the additional monetary distortions due to inflationary pressures, it is easy enough to appreciate the many reasons why, in spite of the surviving glamour of payments equilibrium before the First World War, these examples no longer seem so convincing.

are of prime importance from the point of view of the readaptation of international patterns of trade and payments and take precedence, in particular, over all questions relating to the reorganization of existing international payments and exchange systems, especially currency areas, the creation of new international monetary centres and a possible reform of the International Monetary Fund.

I am obliged to confine this discussion to essentials, otherwise it might transgress all reasonable limits. The present currency-area type of payments systems were associated with certain forms of protectionism which they would now often wish to discard, but only to adopt other forms of protectionism. For countries in the early stages of economic development, currency-area protectionism has as yet introduced only the rudiments of an open economy and in spite of a multilateralism of principle at the level of the currency area, trade and capital flows are often still bilateral, in the sense of an exchange of primary products against manufactures and capital goods. Nowadays, the desire to get rid of the last vestiges of the colonial past by means of a development plan is often predominant.

However, if the development plan itself is to escape as far as possible from the principle of comparative advantage (contrary to a no doubt mistaken, but sometimes still accepted, interpretation of classical thought), the pattern of external trade cannot change rapidly because it is conditioned by domestic structural differences which are not likely to have diminished very much.

Each individual country affiliated to one centre tends to protect its own national economy, and within the protected currency area new regional protectionism tends to make its appearance. In practice, the chances of continued growth often depend upon the maintenance of existing tendencies, or at least upon the adoption of some formula limiting the proposed changes to gradual adjustments compatible, without a major upheaval, with certain rates of global investment.

Take the concrete example of primary producers with assured markets among a group of countries linked not only to a common international payments centre but to a protected network of international trade. Some of these primary-producing countries may wish to expand their outlets quickly in the world at large, whereas others, whose export products are already in plentiful supply, cannot hope to gain access to new foreign markets without prior structural readaptation. Whichever way the decision ultimately goes, the new problems have to be weighed in the light of the effective chances of making the necessary structural adjustment. The attractions of belonging to a more or less limited payments system or to a more or less advantageous foreign exchange pool will recede behind these prospects of structural development.

As in the case of all allegedly expansionary protectionism the argument has to be stated in terms of a comparison between potential growth and effective growth and the answer need not necessarily be the same in all cases, either in the short or, still less, in the long run.

To what extent, incidentally, is it to be expected that coalition cemented by past difficulties will be disrupted? Tariff preferences will be maintained or loosened for reasons which in large part have nothing to do with purely monetary decisions. The attraction of other international trading systems will weaken or grow whatever these decisions may be. Some of the rules which characterized the currency area are no longer so strict, certain countries being already free to keep their hard-currency balances in separate accounts ; while sterling or the franc were not convertible, this was an obvious advantage so far as dollar balances were concerned, but it may now still be desirable for other reasons.

In accordance with the new tendencies of international monetary co-operation, it might now seem preferable for countries at different stages of economic development not to devalue their currencies at the same time and to the same extent. It might be better to calculate separately for each affiliated country what change in the exchange rate is best suited to satisfy the conditions of more balanced growth (from the point of view of the country's external balance).

Generally speaking, in the rebuilt framework of international payments centres of all kinds the tactics will have to change. From now on, the tactics will have to be flexibly adaptable to the participating countries' varying stages of development. The principles of the currency area, which were suitable for conditions of widespread inconvertibility, will have to be transformed into the principles of an 'economic co-operation area'.[1]

An international payments and exchange system so conceived leaves ample room for international aid, whatever its modality and amount. By helping to finance large deficits, international aid facilitates the task of the international payments system, and, therefore, can be expected to increase its effectiveness. In this connection

---

[1] These principles might well mitigate the danger of new forms of protectionism, even though intervention and controls may still be necessary. In any event, 'co-operation area' principles could surely preside over the formulation of development programmes or plans.

It may be argued that matters are often complicated by the sort of zigzag path of unbalanced growth under protectionism, in so far as protectionism would tend to eliminate the excess imports necessarily resulting from a high rate of growth as soon as it is actually achieved. Differences in the pace of technical progress may, of course, also work in either sense.

I must forestall a misunderstanding. What concerns us here is to define a type of equilibrium which maximizes the participating countries' individual rates of economic growth. Structural distortions can be avoided by following a well-defined line of development. Certain rules enforced by the International Monetary Fund and other international institutions could, no doubt, bring short-term capital flows more into line with long-term objectives, but no payments system can, by itself, determine the conditions of balanced growth either on the national or on the international scale. In the future as in the past, such a system can function or indeed come into being only in an environment of spontaneous adjustments or in response to long-term economic policies. Nowadays, the policies concerned are far more diversified, from the international point of view no less than from that of the separate participating countries, and policy co-ordination is increasingly becoming a matter of over-all strategy.

However, we must not close our eyes to the resurgence of a myth which is not to be rejected out of hand, provided all the necessary corrections are applied to its traditional interpretation. The question is not what many generations of economists may have seen in the gold standard, conceived as the foundation of full convertible national currencies; the dangers of a certain brand of gold-bar fetishism are only too apparent even today. But the question is what should be our attitude with respect to the current proposals to set up again a very wide international payments system rather like the one which established itself towards the end of the nineteenth century in the name of the gold standard. This is a matter in which scrupulous historical truth is of the utmost importance. It is important in assessing the type of growth achieved at the time in various countries according to the stage of development of each, and important even for the definition of balance of payments equilibrium. It seems impossible to overlook in this context the kind of prior harmonization implied by larger international capital flows — the essential point being not the adjustment of short-term money flows but the systematic pattern of long-term investment.

It may not be too much to hope that this kind of historical reinterpretation will command fairly general agreement today. If this is so, we may conclude that a large part of the deficits which, according to classical theory, were to be covered through the working of the monetary system, was in fact evened out by capital flows — which, incidentally, were called forth by profitable investment opportunities. Far more than national monetary policies in the countries with the most advanced institutions, and far more, also, than commercial policies in many other countries, it was those large investment flows which played the leading part in this prior harmonization and which eventually fell into a pattern in which the intervention of monetary systems as such was considerably limited during the thirty or forty years preceding the First World War. It is true that we now have another type of growth in mind ; but there is much to say for the idea of a systematic reduction of external deficits. The effectiveness of international payments systems can only be enhanced by a strict delimitation of their scope.

There is general agreement to the effect that external aid should contribute in some measure to relieve balance of payments pressure in countries where long-term deficit is the counterpart of a universally accepted development policy. External aid must find its place in the context of a well-defined concept of development planning which we might, under some aspects, call a concept of unbalanced growth. But we must be careful not to confuse the manifestations of external disequilibrium (subject to all the reservations implied in this expression) with the requirements of domestic structural change (which are also controversial).

Resolutely discarding everything which historical investigation has shown to be questionable in the models of international equilibrium built upon the experience of the past, we must, today, focus our attention on the means of sparing the developing countries a whole set of noxious oscillations. There is assuredly a danger that the development of payments within each of the existing international systems will, alternately, enhance and encroach upon the generosity with which external aid is forthcoming. This might be avoided by closer co-operation among the different payments centres, whereby the contribution of each might be allowed to vary without detriment to the over-all result. In the past, the major financial centres could correct by short-term capital movements any difficulties resulting from excessive long-term investment. Nowadays monetary co-operation (as already envisaged at the end of the first section of this report) might alleviate such difficulties as arise in the relations between the major centres, while at the same time safeguarding the rate of growth of each member country. It would not appear to be beyond human wit to devise a distribution of development aid without impairing its continuity.

Chapter 16

EXISTING INTERNATIONAL PAYMENTS AND EXCHANGE SYSTEMS IN RELATION TO PROBLEMS OF GROWTH: II

BY

D. J. DELIVANIS
University of Thessaloniki

I. INTRODUCTORY

MY paper deals with a subject which is also being examined, though from a different angle, by Professor Weiller.[1] I have not had the opportunity of seeing his paper before writing my own. But I propose to assume that the Conference has already had before it an analysis of the external monetary problems facing an individual country as a consequence of growth. The problems are connected with the equilibrium of the balance of payments. May I begin by pointing out that disequilibrium in the balance of payments is only to be found when the rate of growth in one country differs substantially from that of its trading partners, when this difference of growth rate is not neutralized by other counterbalancing factors, and when the country in question has exhausted its foreign exchange reserves and its borrowing possibilities? In these days economic growth is undoubtedly affected — certainly in a majority of cases — by governmental activities and macro-economic decisions, not influenced exclusively by market factors. Thus it is frequently to be found that there are differences in growth rates, and that these lead to balance of payments disequilibria in those countries in which growth is highest, unless the countries concerned take steps to reduce or neutralize their deficits.

Exchange control or quota restrictions seem to be preferable for this purpose to devaluation, in so far as they can give the government the opportunity to use foreign exchange, gold reserves and foreign earnings in the most effective way to achieve the objectives of the country's development policy. Moreover, if the country can avoid the need for devaluation, and the consequential deterioration of the

[1] See pp. 332-53 above.

354

barter terms of trade,[1] there is less danger — particularly if there has been no experience of monetary collapse in the past — that individuals will be tempted to hoard gold or to transfer capital abroad, with the likelihood of creating a black market. There is an added risk of this when invisible receipts from abroad are important. By avoiding devaluation, there is more chance that savings will continue to be placed at the disposal of investors in the normal way and that the need to raise loans from the central bank will be diminished. But while exchange controls and quota restrictions may solve the external monetary problems encountered by each individual country as a consequence of growth if they are efficiently applied, and if foreign exchange reserves are substantial,[2] the same cannot be said if they are badly administered or if the country has exhausted its foreign reserves. This is very often forgotten in all parts of the world when devaluation is considered inadvisable.

Quite apart from this disequilibrium of the balance of payments arising from differences in the rates of growth of trading partners, there is a likelihood that the internal monetary equilibrium will also be upset when growth is abnormally fast. In effect, in these circumstances monetary incomes increase and are generally spent, even though prices start rising, as a result of the reduced elasticity of demand caused by the increase of money incomes. The flows of goods available for consumption and for investment will begin to increase only when the investments which are responsible for the economic growth begin to be productive. In the meantime domestic supplies are likely to fall because the export flow has to be not only maintained but even increased in order to procure from abroad those commodities needed for the implementation of investment plans.[3] Internal monetary disequilibrium will be aggravated, firstly, if credits are allowed by the central bank, whenever other loans are not available to investors carrying out the policy of economic developments ; secondly, if there is dishoarding of paper money ; thirdly, if there is stock-piling of goods by those who observe the price rise and foresee its continuance.

In view of the difficulty of guarding against such dangers in an expanding economy, the curtailment of imports should, if possible, be avoided, since a smooth rate of growth cannot be maintained once prices begin to rise with any speed or to any serious extent.

[1] Cf. R. F. Harrod, 'Foreign exchange rate and monopolistic competition. Comment', *Economic Journal*, 1953, pp. 294-8.
[2] Cf. M. Fleming, 'On making the best of balance of payments restrictions on imports', *Economic Journal*, 1951, pp. 48-69.
[3] As to the reasons for the increase of imports in a period of growth, cf. D. Delivanis, 'Croissance et importations d'une région sous-développée', *Cahiers de l'I.S.E.A.*, Série P, No. 3, Paris 1959, pp. 49-73.

Moreover, when an expansion of exports cannot be achieved by sub-stitution and without an increase of total foreign demand, a country may have to try to get imports on a credit basis ; this is particularly likely to be the case in a depression, even though mild. Where credit is secured through normal commercial channels, when repay-ment becomes due there will be increased demands to exchange holdings of the currency of the borrowing country, with the result that the currency concerned will become 'softer' or, if already 'soft', it will become still 'softer'. This was more or less the predicament of France in the years 1945–58, first during the post-war reconstruc-tion, and later because of rapid expansion, not only in metropolitan France, but also in the overseas territories within the French franc area.[1] Similar results occur when private traders and corporations with their headquarters in one country start investing abroad on a substantial scale with a view to securing the growth of their invest-ments, loans or balances abroad for any of the usual reasons that lead to such micro-economic decisions.

After this short introduction I shall present my comments under three headings : firstly, in Section II, I shall examine and analyse problems of growth so far as they concern international economic relations. Secondly, in Section III, I shall discuss the working of current international payments and exchange systems in relation to the problems analysed in Section II. Thirdly, in Section IV, I shall examine the ways in which these systems can operate to assist in the solution of the problems concerned and their adequacy to meet the needs that arise.

II. INTERNATIONAL ASPECTS OF GROWTH

For the proper development of an economy, as far as inter-national trade is concerned, there are four basic requirements :

(a) an adequate supply of foreign exchange ;
(b) the chance of securing increased capital from abroad whenever it is not available at home ;
(c) freedom to adjust exchange rates when this seems advisable ;
(d) a means of coping with any disequilibrium that may arise if exchange rates are not permitted to fluctuate, and with the declining internal purchasing power of the monetary

---

[1] The trade balance of France proper with its overseas territories is always active, since French loans, grants and direct investments are transferred in both consumer and capital goods, except when compensated with interest and redemp-tion funds.

unit in consequence of inflationary pressures intensified by growth.

(a) Adequate Supply of Foreign Exchange

Economic growth may be accelerated, and is certainly assisted, by a satisfactory supply of foreign exchange, though not necessarily of foreign capital. As to this latter point, the argument in Kenneth Berrill's excellent paper, read at the IEA Conference at Konstanz in 1960, went far to prove that foreign capital has never made any substantial contribution to 'take-off', even in those cases (e.g. Canada) which are usually cited as classical examples of 'take-off' financed by foreign capital. Though there were some who insisted, during the subsequent discussion on the paper, that in more recent periods, at least, a distinction must be drawn between foreign capital and mere foreign exchange, Berrill replied that in the nineteenth century the distinction was irrelevant since the countries proceeding to 'take-off' were in need of both. In my own opinion, however, based especially on experience since World War II, the distinction is vital, inasmuch as capital may to a certain extent be provided within a country through compulsory saving whenever voluntary saving is inadequate for the planned investments. The latter help to raise economic activity and to increase incomes, a process which leads in turn to a greater propensity to consume, reinforced by the demonstration effect.

The increase of payments abroad that results from increased investment and increased consumption has led many economists (W. A. Lewis, for example) to maintain that the total cost of any investment has to be met from abroad whenever there is a threat of inflation to be countered. This view is, I think, untenable. The success of the policy of the International Bank which lends only the amounts to be spent abroad for purposes directly connected with the proposed investment project, seems to be a strong argument in favour of distinguishing between foreign capital and foreign exchange. In fact the latter ceases to be available to any country after the exhaustion of its official foreign reserves which, by virtue of the law (given means to enforce it), have been declared and surrendered to the Treasury or central bank. By the use of efficient exchange control and quota restrictions, combined with a sufficiently deflationary monetary policy, some foreign exchange may be saved ; but it can never be created. When inflation is caused by growth, however, the difficulties of acquiring foreign exchange are enormous ; these can be illustrated by the attempts of the Bank of France in 1950–58 to sell French banknotes in Switzerland to tourists leaving for France and to use the proceeds to buy the gold needed for the only open market policy that is possible in such a situation.

(b) Means of Securing Foreign Capital

Even if it is admitted that a country whose growth rate exceeds that of other countries can cover its capital requirements from internal resources, it still remains true that extra capital from abroad with which to develop any idle land or labour within her territories is to be welcomed, if a still higher growth rate is desired. While obviously such a policy increases foreign liabilities and raises the cost of some existing investment projects by draining away available labour, the greater speed of development and the creation of external economics may lead to such an increase of national income and foreign earnings that reimbursement of foreign capital will not be difficult. The same satisfactory result may be attained if the additional growth takes the form of additional output of agricultural or manufactured products either for the home market or for export. In the former case this presupposes that consumers either buy these products to improve their standard of life or that they replace other commodities produced at higher cost or of a lower quality.

(c) Adjustment of Exchange Rates

The adjustment of exchange rates, whenever this may be called for by conditions resulting from rapid growth, constitutes a serious issue of international economic relations. But it is of importance only when the objective is to reduce imports or increase exports and when the relevant elasticities of demand are comparatively high. Manipulation of exchange rates cannot succeed if elasticity of demand is low, or is made low. The latter is likely to occur wherever incomes increase substantially as a result of growth. At the same time elasticity of supply may be low in a period of growth, at least until the new investments begin to give a return. This fact must be borne in mind in a period of full employment and partly explains the general reluctance to proceed to devaluation, except under pressure of necessity.

The repercussions of any adjustment of exchange rates — or even of rumours of one — upon movements of capital and trade flows can be substantial even though exchange control is in force : a mere advancement or postponement of the date for payment of debts due abroad or for the settlement of foreign claims may lead to big fluctuations of gold and foreign exchange reserves. Similar fluctuations may be caused, at a time when the market is nervous about future exchange-rate policy, merely by advancement or postponement of the dates on which orders are placed or met. Such reactions cannot be wholly prevented by those responsible for exchange control, so long as foreign trade is conducted along the lines adopted by the western nations in the 'forties. Apart from these repercussions attending any adjustment of exchange rates, there are certain institutional complications that will be discussed in Section IV.[1]

(d) Disequilibrium Consequent on Stable Exchange Rates and a Declining Purchasing Power of a Country's Currency

This tendency to disequilibrium is to be found only where exchange rates are pegged, as is common today and as they were, within the limits of the goldpoints, under the gold standard. The problem is that of coping with the normal difficulties caused by a high growth rate and more rapid inflation. Under such conditions it becomes more profitable to import than to export, since the demand on the home market is intensified. This trend need cause no anxiety so long as foreign reserves are adequate.[2] But usually the necessary change of policy is made too late. For the time being, while the effects on external equilibrium are adverse, the internal equilibrium is improved by the increased imports made possible by the gradual running down of foreign reserves. If these same goods permit the creation of capital, the deficit of the balance of payments may be ascribed to an increased stock of capital instead of to an increased flow of consumption expenditure.[3] This euphemistic interpretation is tenable, providing that the investments made possible by the running down of the foreign balance begin to yield an output before it has either completely run out or has reached such a low level as to demand a radical change of policy.

No such justification is to be discovered in the alternative case in which the foreign reserves are spent on consumer goods or on investments abroad. An exception can be made in the latter case when the incomes earned are transferred home and in this way help to diminish the deficit of the balance of payments. This may be expected so long as the foreign investment does not result from attempts to avoid the unfavourable consequences of unpopular

---

[1] One of the merits of the Radcliffe report is that it stressed the dangers of frequent exchange manipulations and showed that the 1931 devaluation of sterling was more effective than the 1949.

[2] Professor E. Lunberg considers this as undesirable, as in this way those responsible for the equilibrium of the balance of payments are not allowed to take the necessary steps. Cf. *Stability and Progress in the World Economy*, the first congress of the I.E.A., edited by D. Hague, London, 1958, p. 221.

[3] Cf. H. G. Johnson, 'Increasing productivity, income price trends and the trade balance', *Economic Journal*, 1954, pp. 462-85, and J. R. Hicks, *Essays in World Economy*, Oxford 1959, pp. 66-84.

economic policies at home.[1] In any case, income from foreign investments is not likely to flow back until some time after the out-flow of capital and, unless swelled by windfall profits, will be only a fraction of the capital invested. A recent illustration of this is pro-vided by the United States of America whose balance of payments deficit for the years 1958–60 was huge without affecting its gold reserve to an appreciable extent.[2] The reverse of this is to be seen when private firms or individuals liquidate their foreign assets and reinvest them at home.

III. THE WORKING OF THE PRESENT INTERNATIONAL PAYMENTS AND EXCHANGE SYSTEMS

In consequence of developments in Indonesia and the Congo, the guilder and the Belgian franc areas lost their importance, and in January 1959 the EPU ceased to exist. Thus at the moment there remain seven international payments and exchange systems :

   (i) the IMF ;
   (ii) the EMA (by virtue of which the EMF operates) ;
   (iii) the sterling area ;
   (iv) the French franc area ;
   (v) the Portuguese escudo area ;
   (vi) the rouble area ;
   (vii) the dollar area.[3]

(a) The Dollar Area

I shall not deal with the dollar gap of the years 1945–53, but shall merely note the more recent weaknesses of the system. Let me preface my remarks with a short description of its organization. To begin with, the countries concerned cannot be said to have any formally devised links between them, but they all have this in common, that they insist upon payment of claims against foreign debtor countries in freely convertible U.S. dollars. While they differ in their economic structures and their institutions, and considerable inequality of development, they resemble one another merely in

[1] At least undesirable from the micro-economic point of view of those suffering loss.

[2] This did not prevent a crisis in the foreign exchange markets in the autumn of 1960 despite the support for the dollar from the most important central banks of Western Europe.

[3] The European Common Market has no exchange and payments system of its own, otherwise J. E. Meade's article, 'The balance of payments problem of a European free trade area', *Economic Journal*, 1957, pp. 380-96, would have been relevant.

their adherence to a rule that settlement of debts due to them shall be made by credit at one of the banks operating in the United States. Among themselves there are no special reciprocal arrangements for granting or securing credits, short- or long-term ; there is not the slightest co-ordination of economic or monetary policy. But free convertibility of their respective currencies implies that there is absence of any exchange control : the central banks and commercial banks in the dollar area are free to grant one another credits, although the Import and Export Bank of the United States of America may intervene whenever risks are excessive for the private banks.[1]

Hence it may be seen that within the dollar area a satisfactory supply of foreign exchange is maintained without difficulty. On the other hand problems might well have arisen, if the United States had been in the position of needing foreign capital or foreign exchange, regarding its inflow. In reverse, the remaining countries of the dollar area have no difficulties in raising the capital they need in the United States (and especially New York), apart from those involved in political risks. The adjustment of exchange parities is carried out under the statutes of the International Monetary Fund as may be required to reduce a deficit in the balance of payments, or to eliminate a discrepancy between the internal purchasing power of the monetary unit and its foreign exchange value.

(b) Other Areas

In areas other than the dollar area, exchange control combined with quotas represents an additional instrument. It is effective only so far as it makes possible the isolation of the economy of the country concerned and the fullest use of the credit of the central bank to utilize the potential volume of available saving. Clearly, when full employment has been achieved and no increase of productivity is possible, excessive credits will lead to intensified inflationary pressure such as to make exports, foreign loans and foreign investments impossible without payment of subsidies by the taxpayer.

In consequence of the isolating effect of exchange control on the economy, a country would find it practically impossible to secure foreign exchange on a loan basis, except where for political reasons foreign governments or international institutions are induced to grant credits.[2] The difficulties are even greater if foreign capital is needed in order to increase investment within the framework of planned economic growth. In all these areas, change of foreign exchange rates — either in order to reduce a deficit of the balance of

---

And no political reasons prevent this activity.

[2] This was so, e.g., with Turkey, 1958–59.

payments or to eliminate a difference between the internal purchasing power of a currency unit and its foreign exchange value — is not difficult, provided that the International Monetary Fund is agreeable.

(c) External Convertibility

Since the end of 1958 external convertibility has been practised by all Western European countries except Turkey. External convertibility implies that foreigners are allowed to effect the free transfer of proceeds accruing to them from current transactions in the country concerned, though as a rule capital transfers are not included. In February 1961 ten countries [1] took the further step of declaring in accordance with Article XIX of the statutes of the International Monetary Fund, that they bound themselves not to revert to exchange control, affecting external convertibility, without its agreement.

The countries that have adopted external convertibility have been in a position to earn with reasonable ease the foreign exchange they might need for this purpose; but in practice they have possessed substantial foreign balances that have made it possible for them to make all their payments without strain. But the supply of capital has not in all cases been so adequate and on numerous occasions either their Treasuries or their public or private corporations have borrowed abroad. In many instances they have borrowed in Switzerland, since that is the one European country that has never applied exchange control for any purposes other than to protect Swiss creditors of foreign countries from a discriminatory use of exchange control against themselves. In spite of the fact that the right of convertibility does not ordinarily extend to capital transfers, this system of external convertibility has made it easier to secure loans abroad and has encouraged foreigners to invest in the countries adopting it. Any change of the parity of the currencies of such countries is governed by the statutes of the International Monetary Fund.

(d) The International Monetary Fund

Members of the International Monetary Fund are allowed to draw to a limit of 25 per cent of their quotas to purchase a balance with any fellow member of the Fund.[2] Hence in the ordinary way a supply of foreign exchange is easily secured. But it is a precondition of any drawing on its quota that the country concerned shall have

---

[1] Belgium, France, Germany (Western), Ireland, Italy, Luxembourg, Netherlands, Peru, Sweden and the United Kingdom.
[2] All the countries of the western world, with the exception of Switzerland, are members.

satisfied the Fund authorities that the deficit is not due to a structural weakness in the economy of the borrowing country but to some unforeseeable and temporary development. In practice, so far as I know this condition has never been enforced against any member country that has been seeking a stand-by or a full credit from the Fund. To show that the IMF interprets and administers its statutes with reasonable liberality, I may mention here that it made substantial contributions to ease the strains put upon the balances of payments of certain countries during the winter of 1956–57, and the following autumn. In the former case the reasons for the strain were of a political nature and in the latter case they were connected with capital transfers in expectation of the appreciation of a Western European currency. The same impression of liberal interpretation is gained from an examination of the credits granted in 1947–48 to certain members in order to ease strains on their balances of payments caused by attempts to accelerate the rate of recovery. And, since no clear-cut line can be drawn between the process of recovery and that of growth, it may be inferred that the Fund would not refuse credits to any member whose balance of payments was strained by growth.

But though this may be true it cannot be said that the International Monetary Fund is available to finance the growth of its members. The central banks themselves are not supposed to finance growth, either directly or indirectly,[1] and the IMF is in effect their banker. The body to which the financing of growth properly belongs is the International Bank for Reconstruction and Development. Where there is good evidence that the project to be financed will yield a satisfactory profit and, as far as experts may foresee the outcome, that transfer of the accruing interest and sinking fund can be made, it is the function of the Bank of Reconstruction and Development to make a loan. Hitherto there have been no cases of default ; the Bank has judged well the capacity and determination of borrowers to meet punctually their obligations and interest payments. But this success has depended on three vital factors : strict insistence by the Bank on its policy of lending only the amount needed by the borrower for payment abroad ; almost continuous world prosperity since the Bank started its operations ; great care in the choice of projects to be financed. If any one of these conditions were removed, the servicing and repayment of the outstanding loans of the Bank would be more difficult. Similar

[1] Though they are known to do so, especially for under-developed countries unable to secure other sources of savings ; in very abnormal conditions, e.g. in the first years after World War II, also for advanced countries.

difficulties might arise if a country in debt to the Bank were refused a further loan because of uncertainty about its power to transfer, borrowed elsewhere, and then found it impossible to maintain punctual transfer of amounts falling due.

As mentioned above, members of the IMF are not allowed to change the parity of their currencies without its permission; in practice there is, so far as I am aware, no record of such a request — usually for a devaluation — having been refused. Permission is always dependent on conditions that it is within the power of the applicant country to perform; the country concerned still retains its sovereignty despite the obligations and limitations on its freedom assumed under the terms of its membership. It is the policy of the IMF to persuade member countries to follow a policy which does not endanger their international liquidity or involve frequent devaluations or differential exchange rates, but at the same time permits the economy to develop at a satisfactory rate without intensifying the international pressures consequent on growth. So long as such a policy is reasonably followed, members can count on the assistance of the IMF whenever needed.

It would seem that the IMF places more emphasis on external than on internal equilibrium in the belief that monetary policy may be trusted to secure the latter so long as it is not neutralized by budget deficits or excessive price support of agricultural commodities.[1] The contribution of the Fund to the general liquidity of the world economy and thus to its capacity for growth must not be underestimated; in particular it has made bilateral agreements unnecessary and has relieved its members of the necessity of putting an excessive emphasis on the avoidance of a deficit in the balance of payments.

(e) The European Monetary Agreement

The European Monetary Agreement has replaced the European Payments Union as the organ for multilateral settlement of international claims. Credits, however, are not granted automatically to its members, whenever their current balance shows a deficit, as under its predecessor; the Council of Ministers in charge of its operations makes the necessary decision, which is then implemented by the European Monetary Fund. Hitherto (May 1961) the only countries to receive loans have been Spain and Turkey, both of whom needed them to meet deficits in their respective balances of payments on current account, in neither case the direct consequence of growth. The remaining members have not as yet had to face

---

[1] For the implications in general, cf. J. E. Meade, *The Balance of Payments*, Oxford, 1951, pp. 99-124.

any such deficit seriously affecting their foreign reserves. We have no means of knowing how the EMA Council would handle a case in which a loan was sought to meet a deficit consequent on growth.

In the near-normal conditions that have prevailed in the foreign exchange markets of practically all member countries since the EMF replaced the EPU, the central banks concerned have had an incentive to settle all their claims without their having recourses to the Fund, since they thus save the commission charged by the EMF. Clearly, then, the European Monetary Agreement has made hitherto no contribution to the promotion of growth. But it should be stressed that the European Monetary Agreement and the Fund do not exist to supply capital or to cure international disequilibria caused, or even aggravated, by growth.

(f) The Sterling Area

The sterling area is an important factor in international trade and international economic relations in general.[1] The participant countries pool their receipts of dollars, other hard currencies and gold. When the reserve is adequate, they are allowed to draw on the accumulated pool according to their needs; when reserves are not considered adequate, they draw according to fixed quotas negotiated between the United Kingdom and each separate country. The mechanism thus created permits the member countries to secure, within the above limits and as long as they have sterling balances in London to draw upon, all the foreign exchange they need for transferring their payments outside the sterling area. Whenever a country's sterling balance is low or exhausted, the system gives the members the opportunity to borrow for its needs, on the terms ruling currently on the London money and capital markets.

Thanks to the differing economic structures of the various member countries, the trends of their barter terms of trade tend to cancel out, and to stabilize in some degree the profits and losses due to price fluctuations for the sterling area as a whole. Thus when the barter terms of trade move unfavourably for those members whose external equilibrium depends upon the export of raw materials and agricultural products, the other countries which export manufactured goods will be better off. They can thus more easily help those in difficulties, if they need to draw on a larger scale from the common pool. On the other hand, when the terms of trade move adversely to the importers of raw materials and agricultural products,

---

[1] This is sometimes forgotten, cf. R. F. Harrod, 'Europe and the money muddle', *Economic Journal*, 1958, pp. 534-8.

the primary-exporting countries of the sterling area have increased receipts in foreign currencies and can, partially at least, offset any potential loss of gold from the area.

The system built up in the sterling area seems to be most effective in ensuring to its members the foreign currencies they need to support their own growth, so long as sterling is convertible. At the same time it ensures to any member country that is credit-worthy the capital needed for growth where this is more than can be raised on the home market. The achievements of the system can best be appreciated if it is remembered that, even during the severe depression of the 'thirties, no member country of the sterling area was obliged to suspend payments abroad.

If it should become necessary for any member country of the area to change the parity of its currency, it is a simple matter to fix the new valuation in terms of sterling and announce the change to the rest of the members.[1] If, however, the country contemplating a change is also a member of the IMF, it must, of course, comply also with the statutory requirements mentioned above.

The smooth functioning of the sterling area presupposes the convertibility of sterling. Convertibility, however, can only be maintained

(a) so long as no deficit of the balance of payments of the area as a whole seriously affects its gold and dollar reserve ;

(b) so long as the banker of the area, the United Kingdom, is able to lend to those wanting to borrow ;

(c) so long as a sufficient supply of manufactured goods and services can be obtained from the United Kingdom at reasonable prices and with no more than reasonable delay.

But even when these three conditions are not completely fulfilled, the problems of growth of the sterling area countries are better solved for them in their position as members than they would be outside. This explains why countries which decided for political reasons to abandon the sterling area found themselves facing serious difficulties that completely upset their mechanism of foreign payments and forced them to treat sterling as a hard currency — even in the years 1945–52 when it was *par excellence* a soft currency.[2]

---

[1] New Zealand, for example, re-established the parity with sterling 1 : 1 in 1948.

[2] For example, Egypt. The softness of a currency may be attributed to imperfect international competition ; cf. Delivanis, 'L'Effet de la concurrence imparfaite dans les relations économiques internationales sur le plan monétaire', *Revue d'Économie Politique*, 1957, p. 313.

(g) French Franc and Portuguese Escudo Areas

The great achievement of the sterling area is its solution of those problems of growth which affect international economic relations.[1] Following its example other Western European countries with closely related overseas territories have been led to use a similar mechanism to provide their associated countries with an appropriate means of payment abroad and with the capital needed for reconstruction or development, and to help them to fix suitable exchange rates. The French franc area and the Portuguese escudo area have thus developed on the basis of similar concepts. Within this framework the overseas territories of France — most of which have meantime become independent states — and of Portugal have been treated as overseas provinces enjoying the same rights as provinces of the metropolitan country, enjoying the advantages of a smooth system of payments in France or Portugal, and the rapid transfer of capital needed for growth. The most astonishing thing has been that, in the case of France, capital transfer to her overseas territories was unobstructed even when France was facing the most serious financial difficulties, and over the years 1945–58 the transfers *per capita* were on a scale higher than those of the United States in the same period.[2] The transfers from Portugal to her overseas provinces were also considerable ; these were facilitated by the fact that during the same period 1945–58, the financial problems of Portugal were much less acute than those of France.

(h) The Rouble Area

As I have emphasized above, the systems of the sterling, French franc and escudo areas were devised to solve the problems of payments and growth of overseas countries which, quite apart from their political relations with a 'mother country', have strong economic relations with it. The rouble area, on the other hand, was developed chiefly with the purpose of strengthening the economy of the Soviet Union, first by accelerating reconstruction, and secondly by fostering growth, both in general and in particular in those sectors considered essential to defence. The growth of the Soviet economy was of paramount importance to the whole communist group, since if the Soviet Union were strong, she would be in a position to help her allies.[3]

---

[1] Two other merits of the system are the fostering of foreign trade and multilateral settlement of claims ; cf. A. Conan, *The Sterling Area*, London, 1952.

[2] Cf. P. Moussa, 'Fonctionnement et équilibre de la zone Franc', *Revue d'Économie Politique*, 1959, pp. 351-61.

[3] Cf. J. Marczewski, *Planification et croissance économique des démocraties populaires*, 2 volumes, Paris, 1956.

(i) Payments Systems and Growth

This analysis of existing international payments and exchange systems leads one to the conclusion that the sterling area system gives the best solution of the twofold problem of providing for growth and for a growth of external economic relations.[1] The comparatively liberal foreign trade policy of the United Kingdom itself, at least in respect of its trade with the sterling area countries, is an added reason for reaching that conclusion. The French franc and the escudo areas are not far behind in the success of their methods. It must be added that, thanks to the activities of GATT, EEC and EFTA, it is certain that the progressive reduction of foreign trade barriers in Northern America and Western Europe will make further contributions to solving the external difficulties associated with growth, by expanding markets and thus facilitating the servicing of foreign investments and foreign loans.

IV. THE EFFECTS OF INTERNATIONAL PAYMENTS AND EXCHANGE SYSTEMS ON THE FACTORS INFLUENCING ECONOMIC GROWTH

In the last section I have tried to show that the sterling area system and, to a point, those also of the French franc and Portuguese escudo areas have operated in the way most appropriate to solve the external problems of economic growth. I shall now consider whether the same is true regarding their effects upon such factors in the theory of growth as the widening of markets, capital formation,[2] innovation and foreign trade.

(i) Widening of Markets

The widening of markets under the three systems depends upon a relatively liberal import policy on the part of the country which acts as banker and as pivot of the area concerned. It is only in this way that growth can be promoted or accentuated, since they depend on export to the 'mother' country. In practice, this arrangement is doubly beneficial, since the expansion of their activities leads both to an increase in their own national product and also in the real national product of the 'mother' country. This arises because the metropolitan country's inhabitants get at reduced prices increased

---

[1] And up to a certain degree those of the French franc area and of the Portuguese escudo area.

[2] But not the evolution of capital-output ratio, diminution of which makes for increase in the national income.

supplies of commodities for which demand has not yet reached saturation ; at the same time they can use the factors released from the home production of those commodities for other purposes — provided always that the transfer of resources is feasible both economically and technically and does not create social problems. If a transfer is not practicable in the short period, it will occur in the long period when replacement or heavy overhaul of plant is required. Provided that the proceeds of these imports are used by member countries for the purchase of goods and services from the 'mother' country, the latter's markets are also widened. The rate of growth would unquestionably have been lower if a protectionist trade policy had been followed within each of the areas concerned.

It is true that the IMF, the EMA, the working of the dollar area, and convertibility all confer substantial advantages on a country through the widening of its markets. But in my opinion they are less valuable than the advantages available through membership of the sterling, the French franc and the Portuguese escudo areas. The advantages of these other systems lie in the promotion of general international liquidity, which contributes to the widening of markets by enabling consumers to search out the best and cheapest supplier — a consideration of importance wherever elasticity of demand is high. Exchange control, on the other hand, can be effective only for relatively short periods in expanding the home market for certain commodities without spoiling the foreign market.

(ii) *Capital Formation*

Capital formation requires that $Y > C$, either in the country concerned or in foreign countries prepared to invest or lend abroad. Now, any widening of markets, arising through the operations of such exchange and payments as have been described above, leads to increase of profits, disregarding any unfavourable effects on windfall and monopolistic profits, particularly such as may have arisen from lack of transportation, insufficient stocks and trade barriers. Thus provided that employment increases or remains constant, so that the increased profits are not offset by diminished wage incomes, it may legitimately be argued that existing international and payments systems make some contribution to capital formation. Capital formation in turn stimulates growth in all sectors where demand has not reached saturation, provided that the other factors of production are available in the required quantities and qualities.

We must next ask under what system capital formation can make the greatest contribution to growth. If we consider the conditions that prevail in the sterling area and the French and Portuguese areas it is clear that it is under these conditions that capital formation can make the greatest contribution to growth. The other systems promote growth only indirectly, by eliminating the possible need to obstruct it by protectionist trade policies. The contribution of these systems consists in increasing international liquidity and the opportunity for multilateral settlements. These are important prerequisites but they do not provide a certainty of investment where it is most needed and where the marginal yield will be highest.

(iii) *Innovations*

Existing international payments and exchange systems obviously cannot influence innovations. They can, however, provide the facilities needed for their application where this is justified by a prospective increase of profits, reduction of costs, or increased opportunity to shorten the working day, where this is desirable. It seems clear that innovations have been introduced on a more extensive scale than would have been possible, had all countries been completely isolated from each other. Thus it is right to give some attention to them, though they should more properly be considered as one aspect of capital formation. It is clear that any system which increases the level of capital formation increases also the level of innovation. Where innovations are successful, they lead to still further growth of capital formation, up to the point where a particular sector of the market is saturated. Here again it seems that the contribution of the sterling area is greatest.

(iv) *Foreign Trade*

Finally it is necessary to consider the possible contributions of existing systems of international payments and exchange to increasing foreign trade. An increase of this will increase growth, provided that any labour displaced by imports is absorbed into other activities. The existing international payments and exchange systems make possible an increase of foreign trade except where deliberate obstacles are created by the commercial policies of individual countries. But protectionist tendencies are very effectively curbed by the regulations of GATT which work to the general satisfaction of those who favour expansion of international trade. So long as trade can expand without inhibiting growth, particularly in under-developed countries, the countries concerned can expand production either in industry or in agriculture, provided that costs can be made competitive. Competitive costs require efficient organization, wages properly adjusted to productivity, adequate supplies of materials, energy and transport facilities. Judging by the experience of Austria and Italy [1] as well as other countries, there are some advantages in a low ratio of exports to total production in a country or trading area. This appears to be an additional argument in favour of large customs unions and large free trade areas, which can offer a single large market and absorb a substantial part of their members' produce — always provided that the external tariff is not too high. If the competition provided by foreign trade is removed, there is a real danger that the world may be creating unions of cartels rather than unions of countries. This must always be remembered in judging the rival merits of different international payments and exchange systems.

[1] As described at the Lisbon Round Table Conference of the IEA in 1957. Cf. *The Economic Consequences of the Size of Nations*, edited by Austin Robinson for the IEA, London, 1960, pp. 151-81.

Chapter 17

THE PROSPECTS FOR INTERNATIONAL LIQUIDITY AND THE FUTURE EVOLUTION OF THE INTERNATIONAL PAYMENTS SYSTEM

BY

C. P. KINDLEBERGER

Massachusetts Institute of Technology

I. INTRODUCTION

It is now more than three years since the Suez monetary crisis came to an end, and economists and financiers have turned their attention to the so-called problem of international monetary liquidity. Interest was drawn to the question by Sir Oliver Franks in his report as chairman of Lloyds Bank in February 1958. It was sustained by an issue of *The Economist* at the end of May in the same year, balance of payments difficulties of the United States on trade account in 1959, and owing to an outflow short-term capital in the last half of 1960 did nothing to change the subject, partly as a result of the important contribution of Robert Triffin in his various articles of 1959 and his book, *Gold and the Dollar Crisis*, of 1960. Today world monetary liquidity is 'Hit Tune Number One' in the repertoire of the international trade and monetary economist, and a host of bankers, journalists and men of affairs.

This is perhaps not curious. Economics, like female dress and much else, moves in waves of fashion, continuously discarding the old for the 'New Look'. And like female dress, the new styles seldom involve much change in basic matter. I am reluctantly prepared to recognize that there may be a world liquidity problem. But I would claim that it is rather unimportant compared with the issues with which it is currently confused.

Analytically, one can separate out perhaps five distinct questions : obdurate or massive balance of payments difficulties of individual countries ; simultaneous world deflation of all industrial countries ; hot-money or short-term capital flows on a large scale ; the international reserve positions of individual countries ; and world liquidity.

I propose in this paper to devote attention to each of these in turn, and to demonstrate that :

(a) persistent or massive balance of payments deficits and surpluses remain a matter for continuous world concern and action by a variety of means in separate countries ;

(b) simultaneous world industrial deflation, which I shall call the Balogh problem, is not a current question, nor is it likely in my judgement to be; but it is important potentially, and thought, if not action, is now required to meet it should it arise ; it is unwise, however, to act as if it were certain to arise, or had arisen ;

(c) the instability of the gold exchange standard — hot-money or the Triffin problem — is real, and requires action, but the steps needed are much less drastic than the Triffin proposal, which runs the risk of rendering more difficult the solution to persistent balance of payments deficits ;

(d) there may be merit in increasing the reserves of individual countries, whose persistent balance of payments deficits have been cured ; the qualification makes clear, however, that no general or across-the-board measure is called for.

(e) if any world liquidity problem remains — as seen, for example, by the quantity theorists who want to enlarge the volume of international reserves annually by a percentage determined by some projected growth rate of world trade — it can readily be dealt with when and if it arises ; again, it is dangerous to anticipate.

It is clear, I hope, that there is work to be done. The world system for resolving international payments difficulties is not perfect. But progress has been made in recent years ; and future progress is possible, in separate, discreet steps, meeting specific needs as they arise, rather than attempting to solve all with one sovereign remedy. It is especially desirable not to subject the present system to the strain on confidence of a prolonged spate of constitution writing for an entirely new system. Constitutions, in my judgement, should be written, if at all, only after the system has evolved into satisfactory form, not in advance, to anticipate and meet all forms of possible disaster.

There is work to be done because the world has moved, and in directions which, however satisfactory from many points of view, require adjustments.

(i) Persistent or Massive Balance of Payments Difficulties

On balance of payments account, the persistent dollar surplus on current account in excess of its long-term lendings and compensatory transfers has been corrected. Transfers have changed from a compensatory item to an autonomous one. Some claim that such a persistent surplus never existed, or existed only because of erroneous monetary policies in the United States or abroad. This may be so, but I doubt it. The record of lend-lease, post-war economic assistance, the British loan and Marshall Plan, to say nothing of the early operations of the Bretton Woods institutions, suggest that a gap existed to be filled. There have since been changes : the technological lead of the United States over foreign industrial countries has been narrowed, and in some commodities closed or reversed. Reluctance to lend abroad has been overcome. The United States has replaced earlier under-investment, under-consumption and under-importing with overspending on defence, relative to the rest of the world, and accepting an unduly large share of responsibility for economic development. Consumption has also increased. Keynes' analysis of 1946 has proved to be only fifteen years and $50 billion premature. Whether he was right or wrong depends upon one's intellectual rate of interest.

But by no means all persistent balance of payments problems have been solved. Eliminating the biggest one is a long step forward, but it does not dispose of the issue intellectually, as many economists seem to think. The German persistent surplus remains, and underlying British weakness. French, Italian and Japanese surpluses correct themselves but slowly. Under-developed countries like India, Turkey, Brazil, Argentina have deficits which correct themselves hardly at all.

(ii) *Hot Money*

Hot money, which raged from 1925 to 1939 but subsided after World War II, has taken a new lease of life. This is where Triffin has made his most penetrating analysis. Prior to World War I there was no hot money because the world was willing to hold uncovered only one foreign currency apart from the national one, sterling. With stable exchange rates it was useless, too, to speculate between sterling and gold, although gold transfers took place between Britain and the sterling area on the one hand, and gold reserve countries on the other. It is also worth noting that the system was stable from 1945 to 1959 when, apart from limited sums held in Switzerland, Germany and the sterling area, the world held only dollars on an uncovered basis.

The asymmetry between dollars and other currencies has now gone, or in some cases opened up in the other direction, with speculators covering their dollar holdings and maintaining open positions in sterling, marks or Swiss francs. Speculation also takes place between national currencies and gold. Willingness to speculate in more than one currency brings short-term capital movements back into play, whether as a destabilizing element, or, potentially, as stabilizing. Rediscovery of money on the internal front, the need felt to manipulate short-term rates of interest for domestic monetary stabilization, and renewed responsiveness of international short-term capital movements to interest rate differentials open up a conflict between internal and foreign monetary policy which, however celebrated in textbooks, has been virtually dormant in practice, for the last fifteen years, save for a few centres like Germany.

(iii) *International Reserve Positions of Individual Countries*

Liquidity problems of individual countries have been affected since 1914 by two major changes : the cutting of the links between the money supply and international reserves, on the one hand, and on the other the limitation of long-term borrowing to specific investment projects. The first is familiar in developed countries ; bit by bit, however, the system has altered so that under-developed countries, including former colonies, with their high marginal propensity to import, have now established central banks to replace currency boards, and issue fiduciary currency in contrast to the former system of either using foreign currency in domestic payments, or maintaining a 1 : 1 relationship between local means of payments and international reserves. This is true not only of Malaya, Indonesia, Ghana and the British colonies, but also of Cuba and Haiti which had previously operated respectively with parity with the United States' dollar and 100 per cent reserves in French francs.

One hundred per cent reserves have been attacked in an interesting and relatively neglected series of exchanges in the *Economic Journal* in the early 1950s as lending from poor countries to rich, and hand exploitation. But, as Ida Greaves points out, the system included not only short-term lending by colony to currency centre, but also long-term borrowing. The money supply of the colony could be expanded by long-term foreign borrowing, and selling bonds abroad for local expenditure, which had the effect of adding to reserves and expanding the domestic monetary supply, was a normal operating procedure. Insistence that long-term loans be made for fixed capital only, and limited to their foreign exchange content, apart from a few exceptional loans designed to finance general balance of payments deficits arising from particular investment spending, has greatly altered the pre-1914 system when foreign borrowing was undertaken for the same purposes as domestic borrowing — whether local investment, deficit spending, or specific projects — with temporary or even permanent changes in the international reserve position and the domestic money supply.

These changes are relevant to the widely held view that the supply of the world's major currencies can only be expanded by deficits, or contracted by surpluses. The answer turns on the definition of 'deficit', to which we recur below ; but if deficit and surplus be limited to the net of the balance of payments on current account, transfers and long-term loans for real investment, the claim is invalid. Countries can add to their reserves through borrowing, as well as through export surpluses, and major currencies can be lent for stabilization purposes as well as for spending.

(iv) *World Liquidity*

Finally, there are those who claim that the world liquidity problem has been altered in ways which call for action by (*a*) the threat of a new world depression in the industrial countries ; and (*b*) the doubling in the world price level when the price of gold remained unchanged. On the first score one can accept the importance of the issue, but doubt the facts ; on the second, one can admit the facts, but reject the analysis which attributes significance to them.

In the foregoing real changes, it is worth underlining that the position of the United States has altered from a highly asymmetrical one in which it held a persistent surplus, and operated the only currency in which the world was willing to hold long positions. The passing of these asymmetries requires modification of some of the distortions in the system, which had grown up to match them : the fact, for example, that the United States was unwilling to hold other currencies, but only gold among its reserves. Or that other countries left to the United States the responsibility for managing and underwriting the payments system, and persistent deficits where they occur — the role played by Britain in the period before 1914. The system must evolve into one in which responsibility for world payments, and the burden of the world's load of defence and development expense are more widely shared. There are difficulties of sharing. The process requires a deep-seated sense of social and political cohesion. But it is a necessity. The necessity for a sense of cohesion does not produce it, of course ; but it is permissible to cite it as an argument in favour of efforts to operate the system on the basis of widely diffused participation in shared responsibilities, as opposed to strict contractual obligations.

The fact that the 'world liquidity problem' is best analysed as four separate problems does not imply that these problems are unrelated.

(i) Persistent disequilibrium in the single key currency or in one of two or more key currencies on the gold exchange standard leads to an acceleration of hot-money flows. A deficit both feeds liquidity to the market and attacks the confidence in the key currency needed to make it acceptable. Heilperin goes further and thinks that the gold exchange standard, even with a single key currency, leads inexorably to persistent deficits, as the country issuing the key currency fails to take the necessary corrective steps when the deficit is financed by an increase in liabilities.[1]

(ii) Speculation in exchange can alter slightly and become speculation in primary commodities or in foreign company shares, disguising what is a problem of speculation as a trade problem or as long-term capital flow. When a country's merchants switch out of cash into imported primary products, or the reverse, this appears to be a balance of payments imbalance, or camouflages one that already exists.

(iii) The adequacy of reserves of different countries is related to the adequacy of world reserves. But the relationship is not simply additive. World reserves may be badly distributed, so that an adequate over-all amount leaves many individual countries inadequately provided for, or adequate provision for all countries requires an excessive total. In addition, a solution of the hot-money problem will, it is claimed, eliminate most of the 'world problem' but still leave national problems which really exist.

(iv) One connection stressed by Triffin and Lamfalussy[2] does not appeal to me, the attempt to relate the problem of liquidity to the economic development of under-developed countries by using long-term loans for development as the backing for short-term liabilities which serve as international reserves. But this requires detailed discussion.

[1] There is, of course, the possibility that the monetary authorities will pay attention only to the gross reserve position, and not to the net; but there is no inevitable reason why they should. The question is one of interpretation of fact, and I see no reason to believe that monetary authorities are less sophisticated than, say, small businessmen who have learned to distinguish between, say, income and changes in cash. If, of course, there exists an asymmetry of response to decreases in assets and increases in liabilities, in the nature of human myopia and self-delusion, the case for 100 per cent reserves in domestic banking is irresistible, as many economists, the writer excluded, have convinced themselves.

[2] See Alexandre Lamfalussy, 'La Liquidité du système monétaire internationale', mimeographed paper prepared for the Colloquium of the Société Royale d'Économie Politique de Belgique, held in Brussels, April 22 and 23, 1961. While my paper was outlined and partly written in rough draft before this Colloquium, it has benefited greatly in revision from this paper and its discussion.

II. THE PERSISTENT BALANCE OF PAYMENTS PROBLEM

There is a balance of payments problem, in the sense in which we use the term, when the balance on current account, plus transfers, plus long-term capital movements — appropriate account being taken of algebraic sign — departs from zero. A current-account surplus requires outward transfers or capital exports. And the reserve is required for current-account deficits. Any net payments or net receipts we can call a persistent 'deficit' or 'surplus', which is distinguished from the current-account deficit or surplus.

The definition relates to extended periods of time, and not to seasonal or cyclical fluctuations around a balanced position. This means, of course, that there are difficulties of recognition and identification.

And there will be occasions when it is desirable to omit 'compensatory' transfers or long-term capital movements from counting in the deficit or surplus. Rescue operations, for example, whether from international institutions and the key currencies to India or Turkey, or in the form of pre-payment of debts by Germany to the United States or Berlin, should not be subtracted from the deficit or surplus, no matter what specific form they take. There is no unique criterion for measuring the 'deficit', under all circumstances, just as the International Monetary Fund learned that there was no reliable measure of 'compensatory' movements in the balance of payments. To recognize the problem occasionally, and to measure it, always calls for the application of art, after the scientific criteria have taken observers as far as they can go.

This definition leaves out short-term capital movements and gold, which, in equilibrium, and apart from the theoretical qualifications of the last paragraph, by definition are zero. It also ignores the practical question, whether Errors and Omissions, if its size is significant, is really long-term capital, short-term, or trade.

The normal definition includes all long-term capital. But some long-term capital in form — like speculation in shares — is short-term in intention, and some changes in short-term deposits are permanent. It might be desirable under particular conditions to count permanent additions to liquid reserves, acquired by long-term borrowing, as a long-term loan, with no long-term net movements to this extent. This supposes, of course, from the side of the long-term lender, that the currency borrowed is the currency added to reserves, such as would be true in a two-country model. Where one currency is borrowed, and another held as reserves, the reserve centres cannot net the movements. It is not a sin against the canons of finance to lend long and borrow short from the same party, when the latter understands that the short-term borrowing is for a permanent increase in reserves, and if drawn down will be quickly reconstituted. But it is dangerous to lend long and borrow short, when the short-term borrowing is undertaken from a third party who does not share that understanding.

Balance of payments problems of under-developed countries may be persistent and serious, but they have almost nothing to do with the world liquidity problem as it is generally formulated. More or less deliberately, these countries have chosen to convert liquid reserves into real investment. In so choosing, they have possibly underestimated the negative but real value of foreign exchange reserves, much as they underrate the importance of real liquid capital in inventories in their preference for fixed assets. Like insurance, foreign exchange reserves have a cost, but like insurance, they pay their way. Reserves enable a country subject to short-term fluctuations in export proceeds or long-term borrowing, around some average rate, to import at a continuous rate without interruptions, which are expensive, whether in rendering unfinished capital projects temporarily useless, even though their capital cost continues, or in encouraging destabilizing speculation in inventories of consumers' goods and raw materials against such interruptions.

Apart from the insurance value of reserves, however, the existence of persistent debtors running balance of payments deficits on current account in excess of long-term loans renders any system of international payments unworkable. The brilliant success of the European Payments Union should not delude us into thinking that the system could have solved the payments problems of 1950 had it not been (i) for the readiness of the United States to finance the persistent debit positions of Austria, Turkey and Greece for years ; (ii) for the readiness of the members to enlarge first the German quota on the debtor side, and then on the creditor side the quotas of both Belgium and Germany ; and (iii) for the financing, outside the payments system, of the lumpy mass of debits accumulated by France.

It is equally true that a new multilateral payments system, contrived or evolved, will break down if persistent debtors and persistent creditors exist. The Triffin view that deficits and surpluses are needed to enlarge reserves analytically overlooks the possibilities of enlarging reserves by swapping short-term liabilities, on the one hand, and adding to reserves through long-term loans on the other. But even apart from the analytical point here, it is a weakness of the

Triffin scheme that he expects to use it to finance persistent deficits of under-developed countries with rising reserves of an international payments medium held by the developed countries.

Quantities will be discussed shortly. Here the point is merely that the reconstituted International Monetary Fund would become increasingly saturated with 'phoney' assets — claims on the under-developed countries which no one expected them to require — and the International Monetary Fund would increasingly become frozen. It can be argued that this would be unimportant, for its liabilities would be required to be accepted. But under the Triffin scheme, and every other propounded, countries which do not like to acquire the liabilities of a frozen institution which may not for ever remain acceptable, have the option of insisting on gold. Then this system, too, could break down. Aside from Senator Monroney and the World Bank which has responded to him on political grounds, practically no one takes seriously the view that the local currencies accumulated by the United States in its Point IV programme are an appropriate basis for international monetary operations.

Lamfalussy suggests that in a world of under-employment it is appropriate to finance investment through money creation, exactly as deficit spending financed by a central bank is appropriate in an under-employed economy. There are, however, these differences : central banks create spending power for governments with power to convert debts into legal tender — within their own borders to be sure — and power to tax as well. In addition there is likely to be some mobility of resources within a country, so that an excess of spending in one area will spill over elsewhere or attract under-employed resources from other areas. In a multi-country world, these features are lacking. An international central bank creating new means of payment because of under-employment in the United States might find under-developed countries more disposed to spend in Germany, itself with relatively full employment and subjectively adequate reserves. This could be regarded as persistent dis-equilibrium in the balance of payments of the United States, or of Germany, if you like, but it suggests that Lamfalussy's analysis is better suited to a two-country model than the multilateral world. In the case cited, it would create less disturbance if Germany were to provide new loans out of savings, whether spent in Germany or the United States, or if the United States were to undertake loans or transfers abroad on a tied basis.

Persistent balance of payments deficits are serious, and I see no easy solution or sovereign remedy for them. In support of ex-panding markets, as free as possible, and the best possible allocation of resources, one must rule out foreign-exchange controls, trade restrictions, restrictions over foreign lending, unilateral cuts in military spending or aid. Balance of payments difficulties may none the less attract attention to an obsolete basis of dividing the world's burdens, which should be distributed according to some approximation of capacity to pay. Exchange rate changes around a given average price of gold may be desirable from time to time — one or more countries raising the price of gold and others lowering it, so as not to distort the money-gold relation. But these call for skill and nerve, more of both perhaps than was shown by Germany in the 5 per cent revaluation of February 1961 which was interpreted by the market as a first bite of the cherry. And they call for co-operation. A country's foreign exchange rate, like the composition of a country's reserve holdings, is more and more an international rather than a national question.

Moreover, discrete foreign exchange changes may not be open to all key currencies. If the dollar had been devalued as some foreign exchange markets thought likely in 1960, most of the other key currencies of the world would have followed suit, and gold would have been the only gainer — in the short run.

It is not my place to discuss flexible exchange rates, but I cannot forbear from offering the conclusion of other occasions that, however attractive or unattractive this may appear to the single country, it cannot constitute a world system of payments. Perhaps if no country interfered with its rate and all let markets clear themselves without recourse to intervention — or for that matter reserves — the system might work without interference. The instability of rates under these conditions seems to me a major depressant of trade and productive capital movements although I concede that there is room for debate. But, with reserves and market intervention, there is a need to concert moves, or monetary authorities might find themselves working at cross purposes, each of two currencies seeking to be depreciated against the other at the same time. It is of great help to a flexible exchange rate system to have a standard to work against; one key currency should be fixed in terms of gold to enable exchange rates and gold prices to be determinate at a given instant in time. If this is so, the system has to be managed at least to the extent of preventing all currencies from being depreciated or appreciated against the key currency when such a move is contrary to its authorities' view of interest. Other arguments against the adoption of a flexible exchange rate by a single country seem to me on balance, and for most countries, to have the edge. My present concern is rather with the system.

I have admitted the possibility of tied aid. It is a better-than-nothing solution and one which should be avoided if at all possible. This applies as well to redividing aid each time the balance of payments changes and much more strongly to foreign exchange control. But I can imagine circumstances in which it would seem appropriate to make use of these devices and none of them can be ruled out rigorously, no matter how much we would want to.

In short, there is no way, in my judgement, in which we can claim to dispose of balance of payments problems of separate countries, whether because they are inconsequential or because the adoption of a special brand of patent medicine would eliminate them. Different kinds of disequilibria require different sorts of treatment, and the same for qualitatively different troubles in the fields of merchandise, services, long-term lending and transfers. I see no reason to be discouraged ; on the contrary. We have come a long way. And the adjustment mechanism is by no means deprived of all effectiveness. The balance of payments deficit of the United States in 1959 has been corrected, although the speculative market was late in recognizing it. Persistent German, Italian, French and Japanese surpluses have diminished, although more by expedients than by action which goes to the root of the problem. Yet we are a long way from solving the balance of payments problems of developing countries.

But what distresses me about many of the proposals made which are basically designed to meet other problems, whether the instability of the gold exchange standard with two or more key currencies, or a quantitative shortage of world liquidity, is that they are likely to subvert the balance of payments discipline which is so needed and so hard to provide. More liquidity for all countries created before persistent balance of payments deficits have been corrected is virtually certain to be inflationary and to delay the achievement of responsible policies. Persistent balance of payments difficulties do not arise from lack of liquidity ; on the contrary.

III. THE CYCLICAL BALANCE OF PAYMENTS PROBLEM

We come now to what is a world problem, rather than separate problems of different countries, and one which I choose to call the Balogh, rather than the Triffin, view of world liquidity. In a series of articles and books,[1] Thomas Balogh of the University of Oxford

[1] The earliest major statement was *The Dollar Crisis* (Oxford, 1949) ; the most recent is in the *Economic Journal* for June 1960.

has held that the major concern in international trade should be to guard against the consequences of a simultaneous and deep depression in industrial countries which would cut imports of primary products and wreck both the balances of payments and the development programmes of a long list of countries. His reason for concern is that he expects depression in one industrial country to communicate itself to others in a deflationary spiral, rather than recession in one industrial country being corrected by buoyancy in others.

Mr. Balogh may well be right for the future, despite the fact that he has been wrong over the period since 1949. Repeated cries of 'wolf' should not blind us to the possibility that real wolves may materialize and do serious damage.

At the present time, however, it is sufficient to note that the question is hypothetical, and there are enough stop-gap measures of real value — the World Bank, the International Monetary Fund, the machinery of the Economic and Social Council of the United Nations and the Organization for Economic Co-operation and Development — to permit an orderly attack on the problem should it arise. There is no crisis here, whether of liquidity or anything else. To take measures to construct a world central bank now to meet a critical problem which does not exist does not recommend itself.

IV. THE HOT-MONEY PROBLEM

Triffin has performed a valuable service in calling attention to the instability of the gold exchange standard with two or three major currency centres. With one centre, or fifty, the system would be stable. But like the balance of power system in political theory, bipolarity breeds instability, except under particular circumstances.

Triffin goes too far, however, and Lamfalussy still further when he says that the gold exchange standard is ridiculous. It may be possible to stabilize it by simple adjustments. It is not totally irrational to hold national currencies in international reserves, as Triffin says.[1] In fact it is hard to imagine a cheaper, more convenient, or more useful form for reserves.

It is possible that the measures about to be suggested may reduce hot-money flows, or render them stabilizing, which would greatly reduce the need for reserves, whether under a fixed, occasionally adjusted, or flexible exchange rate standard — or they might not.

[1] Robert Triffin, *Gold and the Dollar Crisis*, New Haven, Yale University Press, 1960, p. 90.

There is the respectable view that with all major currencies more or less in line under the fixed exchange standard, and holders of liquid assets relatively indifferent as to which currency they hold, and therefore ready to speculate by taking open positions, the major money markets have become one market, and small differences in interest rates, such as one or another country may wish to support by reason of domestic monetary policy, will lead to large-scale out-flows and inflows of liquid funds.

This difference is not critical to the system in operation, though it would be if it became necessary to liquidate it. The device is one which underlay the Tripartite Monetary Agreement of September 1936, which, however, had a fatal flaw which made it ineffectual ; it is the essence of Alan Day's scheme in *The Observer* for uniting the dollar and sterling into a single reserve currency — though he makes his proposal too narrow — and it is the logical extension of the steps taken by the central banks of Europe in supporting the dollar during its troubles of 1959 and 1960, and extended by them to sterling somewhat more formally in February 1961, buying foreign currencies when they were dumped on the market by private speculators and not converting them into gold. The scheme, in short, is that the central banks of the major currencies, with treasury support, undertake to buy and hold each others' currencies during crises of confidence, when they are under speculative attack.[1]

The Tripartite Monetary Agreement was an absurdity because it provided that the Federal Reserve Bank of New York hold sterling for only twenty-four hours before converting it to gold. The Reserve System has the power, as I understand it, to hold foreign currencies longer than twenty-four hours, though it has never done so, and would probably be well advised not to undertake such a step without the precaution of consulting Congressional leaders. It is also desirable to have the Basle agreement broadened to include the politically responsible treasuries as well as the technically competent and detached central banks. But the essence is simple : as their defence departments collaborate for defence, so should central banks and treasuries of the responsible countries — the key currencies — collaborate on a flexible basis — and without the necessity for spelling out contractually all possible eventualities — to preserve monetary stability in the face of de-stabilizing speculation.

Formal and detailed agreements have an attraction. Suppose

---

[1] I find somewhat naïve the action (or the account of it in the press of April 28, 1961) of the United States Treasury in taking some of the German pre-payment of debts to the United States in Deutschemarks to hold against possible speculative attack. It does represent, however, a marked change in the United States attitude towards foreign currencies, and permits an increase in world liquidity.

the system fails to work, and one country or more gets stuck with a large supply of a currency which is devalued as the Netherlands Bank was with sterling in 1931, and as the Bank of France almost did when it pulled down sterling by converting its holdings into gold in 1930. Such agreements would be desirable if their prices were not too high — a protracted effort to imagine and provide for every possible disastrous contingency, and to write an international set of bankruptcy laws — an unnerving experience for foreign exchange markets. Far better, in my judgement, to have it understood that each country involved would do everything in its power, by appropriate means, to see that other countries did not suffer loss by any steps taken in its aid. In a world where all recognize the interdependence of the trading powers, and the peacetime principle of aid for reconstruction and economic development has been accepted, specific obligations do not seem vital, and a diffuse commitment, while somewhat uncomfortable, is better than any alternative.

It would be possible to insist on exchange or gold guarantees. Such insistence, however, calls for examination of which claims are covered and which not, what happens in the case of a country whose gold and foreign exchange assets were less than its liabilities, whether Congresses and Parliaments can bind their successors to vote such funds, and so on. It is necessary for mortal man to contemplate death and to dispose of his estate with precision and clarity, envisaging all possible contingencies. This is a secret proceeding. The state is presumptively immortal and the deliberation public. The gold clause in its bonds was repudiated by the United States under the claim of *force majeure*, and war debts to the United States by European powers. A diffuse obligation may be as valuable as a contractual one in an historical view, and is much more effectively put into operation.

What countries should join such an informal and loose agreement ? Those that experience hot-money movements in and out of their currencies — probably no more, to begin, than Belgium, Canada, France, Germany, Italy, the Netherlands, Switzerland, the United Kingdom and the United States. If hot money began to move in substantial quantities to Stockholm or Tokyo, Sweden and Japan would presumably become members. And the same for other countries. The central banks of these countries would undertake commitments to the international community which extended beyond their national obligations refraining from acting to save their own skins first, as central banks did, for example, in the events leading to 1931, and again in the gold scare of April 1937. Other smaller central banks and countries would be encouraged to act with moderation and restraint, but, given the limited nature of both their responsibilities and resources, would be forgiven if they acted in their short-run interests.

Even if central banks did not draw gold when their nationals brought home funds from overseas, the system would not be proof against a world run into gold by means of the London gold market—speculators buying first sterling, with dollars, francs or marks, and then gold, and forcing central banks to provide gold to the sterling authorities to enable them to keep the gold premium down. For the Bank of England to sell gold while acquiring foreign currencies would quickly run its stock through.

This weakness of the system, however, exists under all the other proposals for stabilizing the gold exchange standard or adding to world liquidity. If private speculators have ready access to gold, they are in a position to bring about a substantial shrinkage of the world credit base whether the International Monetary Fund or national central banks provide the metal. In the long run, therefore, it would be desirable to restrict the use of gold to international payments, and to stop feeding supplies to private hoarders through organized facilities like those in London, Canada or South Africa.

The issue is not an important one, nor pressing, however. Speculation in gold has been a losing game since February 1934, as compared with speculation in foreign exchange, even when the hoarders have not been so foolish as to pay a premium for it. Interest forgone and storage charges make indulgence in the atavistic impulse to hold gold expensive. To the extent that speculators are rational, it seems unlikely that they will continue long to speculate in this medium.

It would none the less tidy up the payments system, and add a bastion of defence against this possible irrationality, gradually to reduce facilities for private gold hoarding. It will probably be impossible to eliminate them : the determined speculator can buy gold in Bombay or other exchange markets off the beaten track, paying a premium and taking substantial risks. But there is no need to hand speculators a weapon with which they can discipline the monetary authorities, in these days when these authorities are fully aware of the importance of appropriate policies ; and it is silly to run unnecessary risks.

This view holds that central banks and treasuries of a limited number of countries, working presumably in Basle or Paris (alongside the OECD), are a better method of rendering the gold exchange standard stable than the Triffin plan, M. Bernstein's proposals for reserve stand-by credits at the Fund,[1] a similar scheme of Governor Zolotas of the Bank of Greece,[2] enlarging the Fund quotas for the second time,[3] Alan Day's 'Goldbuckquid'.[4] We cannot give these alternatives the attention they deserve, but a quick summary, in reverse order, can be given.

(i) The 'Goldbuckquid', linking only gold, dollars and sterling, is too narrow. The scheme is roughly the same as that above, though perhaps more formal and less flexible. It has the advantage of being limited to only two countries, which might make it easier to operate, but the two countries no longer are the only ones that count.

(ii) Merely enlarging the Fund again is insufficient, given the Triffin problem, and runs the risk of weakening balance of payments discipline of countries with no interest or concern for hot money by according them enlarged facilities. The International Monetary Fund is best suited to meeting the liquidity needs of individual countries — apart from hot money. Its limited utility for hot money has been fully demonstrated first by the fact that it was unused through every British crisis except for that in 1957 ; and secondly that no role was found for it in the troubles of the dollar in 1959 or 1960. A key currency cannot effectively turn to the Fund to meet attacks based on confidence. For the dollar to have done so would have been to weaken confidence in it. The pound could do so in the fall of 1957 only as one of a series of measures, including a Reconstruction Finance Corporation loan. The essential difficulty is that the rules of the Fund are designed to meet problems of balance of payments deficits arising from monetary, fiscal or exchange rate maladjustment, rather than short-run crises of confidence. In fitting it for the first task, its amounts, rules, methods of operations are necessarily made inadequate to the second.

(iii) The reverse stand-by credit schemes of Bernstein and Zolotas would amend the rules of the Fund by providing that countries requiring extraordinary assistance should obtain it from the Fund, and that the Fund should obtain the funds needed by arranging lines of credit in advance, from surplus countries. This is broadly similar to the central bank proposal, except that operations would go through the Fund, and would be subject to formal guarantees on exchange rates. It is flexible, unlimited in amounts, and would require very little legislation, all of which constitute distinct advances over the Triffin plan. It has the disadvantage of giving

[1] See his paper before the American Economic Association meeting at St. Louis, Dec. 1960.
[2] Letter to Per Jacobsson, Feb. 24, 1961, mimeographed.
[3] As proposed by Managing Director Jacobsson in April 1961.
[4] *The Observer*, Feb. 12, 1961.

the Fund two separate tasks to perform — the financing of individual country deficits and the maintenance of confidence; it involves a number of countries without responsibility in the affairs of the key currencies; and it provides rather more rigid exchange guarantees than the system may be able to withstand in the long run. But it is a major improvement over the Triffin proposal.

(iv) The Triffin plan suffers the weaknesses of the reverse-standby-credit scheme and from the further flaw of muddling up the balance of payments deficits of separate countries with the hot-money problem. Under-developed countries would have no basis for seeing that the credit arrangements needed for hot money should not be extended to their overdrafts to finance persistent deficits. In fact Professor Triffin's book encourages them in this view, by recommending enlargement of the international credit base at a rate of 3 to 5 per cent a year by loans to under-developed countries.[1] The Triffin scheme has the further serious disadvantage as compared with other schemes, that there is no incentive system for correcting persistent balance of payments disequilibrium.

Many questions arise as to how such a system of central bank co-operation would work, and especially what would happen if persistent balance of payments disequilibrium gave rise to a crisis of confidence and a hot-money outflow. This, of course, is the problem that puts any system to the test. All one can say is that the central bank and treasury authorities of the countries concerned — the key currency under attack and the other key currencies — would have to decide what the long-run prospects for the currency were, and whether or not to render short-run support at existing exchange rates. No system can evade such a decision, however. Each merely establishes a locus where it is taken. In my judgement it is for a superior system to decide in principle that the other key currencies will render short-run support if they believe the long-term prospects are strong. If all agree, the burden is distributed among them in accordance with the amount of capital inflow to each. Strong pressure would be exerted to reach a consensus, but if one country did not concur it could withhold compliance, a strong source of pressure for correcting persistent deficits. And group pressure would be exercised against the persistent creditors.

Note how effectively the system has operated in the last two years when many observers claimed we were moving rapidly towards a crisis. Pressure on the United States to correct its deficit was substantial; but while this was being felt, the central banks of Europe held the dollars that private holders dumped on the market.

[1] See pp. 97, 100, 101, 117.

And pressure was exerted by the group on the German balance of payments surplus.

If large-scale short-term capital movements come about, not because of crises of confidence, but because of attempts to maintain international differences in interest rates when all countries have virtually perfect confidence in each others' rates, central bank support of forward exchange rates might be used to separate international money markets. If New York wants a 2 per cent rate, for example, when Frankfurt has 4, rather than have the Bundesbank hold all the dollars which private holders want to transfer to the market with the higher rate, the Federal Reserve Bank of New York might buy forward dollars at a premium equivalent to 2 per cent per annum. This would enable holders of short-term funds to earn 2 per cent in the New York money market, and 2 per cent through a forward sale, or the same amount as in Frankfurt while holding their spot funds in New York.

I am not enthusiastic about the proposal in the President's balance of payments message of February 6, 1961, to establish special high rates for central bank funds in New York. The policies of central banks of key currencies should not be dictated by considerations of return, in international questions any more than in domestic. For the central banks of smaller countries, the issue does not matter. They will either try to earn the highest possible return in one of a number of currencies of equal safety and utility to them, or they will keep their funds in the currency in which they are needed for normal transactions.

For private holders, however, there may be point in separating the rate of return to foreigners from that accorded to domestic holders, and the use of intervention in the forward market is accordingly worth studying.[1]

V. THE LIQUIDITY PROBLEMS OF INDIVIDUAL COUNTRIES

An individual country without a persistent balance of payments deficit may have a liquidity problem in so far as its quick assets

---

[1] This proposal assumes, of course, that the number of domestic holders of dollars who will sell dollars forward to earn the premium is limited, or in any event no greater than the number who would be willing to open up accounts earning 4 per cent in Frankfurt — to use the same illustration. If it either is unlimited, or greater than the spot flow of domestic funds, the forward proposal gains nothing, except perhaps the change of an actual liability to a future one, and its non-appearance in the weekly central bank statement.

are insufficient to enable it to face the future with the confident assurance that it can meet any unlikely short-run variation in its requirement for foreign exchange. This is the problem which the International Monetary Fund and the Anglo-American Financial Agreement of 1946 (the British loan) were designed to solve. This liquidity problem cannot be met so long as a persistent deficit remains in a country's balance of payments — as the experience of both the fund and the British loan prior to the Marshall Plan amply proved. It is a real problem and, for a few countries, particularly Britain, a serious one. It is the sort of problem which used to be solved by stabilization loans — borrowed for adding to liquidity, not for spending. In retrospect, it appears that the United States made a mistake in undertaking the British loan first and the Marshall Plan second, or regarding the British loan as an amount needed for financing deficits.

Apart from Britain, and countries with persistent balance of payments deficits, this problem is in good shape. It may arise as a number of countries with persistent deficits manages to cure them and move towards convertibility and balance around a long-run level. Where IMF quotas are too small, if such cases exist, there may be room for new stabilization loans. This does not mean 'rescue operations' undertaken to provide exchange for current payments in sharp deficit.

The adequacy of reserves of individual countries has been thoroughly discussed in the literature, and I do not wish to summarize that discussion, or extend it. It is useful, however, to indicate opposition to the support of Triffin for a figure of 35 per cent of annual imports, which, however admirably qualified, none the less remains as the conclusion of his discussion. The adequate level for every country differs, depending upon its circumstances, and upon those of the countries with which it trades.

There is one possible device worth considering to rectify a possible shortfall of reserves of *pairs* of countries (or larger numbers) and that is a swap of foreign exchange. In present circumstances, for example, the Bank of England and the Federal Reserve System could strengthen their reserve positions by each establishing a deposit on its books in favour of the other : say $560 million at the Federal Reserve Bank of New York in favour of the Bank of England and £200 million at the Bank of England on behalf of the Federal Reserve System. The net reserve position of neither would be helped ; and this would in no way help them *vis-à-vis* the moderate persistent surplus countries of the Continent — Belgium, France, Germany, Italy and the Netherlands. But it would ease their position against one another. The same device could be used among all key currencies, assuming that all were in broad balance, to correct any alleged shortfall of world liquid resources. In the United States this action would ultimately require legislation to relax the ratio of gold to Federal Reserve liabilities, in preference to a change which would include foreign currencies along with gold. But by such a system, bilaterally or on a wide multilateral basis among key currencies with a fair degree of over-all balance, reserves can be created much more cheaply in terms of real resources than by mining gold.

VI. THE WORLD LIQUIDITY PROBLEM

While individual countries have a liquidity problem, I doubt that the world has one, apart from persistent balance of payments deficits and surpluses and hot money. I doubt further that any quantitative statement concerning such a problem can be made, either in terms of the need to expand reserves 3 to 5 per cent a year to take account of the needed expansion in trade ; or as a shortfall from new gold production ; or in terms of world gold stock (said by Harrod to fall $76 billion short of present needs). The quantity theory of money has no greater validity internationally than domestically, and in the latter connection I regard its validity as small. Moreover, to the extent that it is useful to add to world liquidity, whether for all countries or for key currencies, the methods of an increase in IMF quotas, or a swap of central bank funds can be adopted, without changing the gold price or establishing an international central bank.

I choose not to argue the case against raising the gold price : its arbitrariness, waste of real resources, the political difficulty of favouring South Africa and the Soviet Union, the spur to gold hoarding and speculation. It is hard to see what profound difference it makes in the world, apart from miners and speculators, whether one takes a given amount of gold and adds national moneys to it (appropriately stabilized among each other) or takes the same amount of gold and calls it the sum of the foregoing. The differences for miners and speculators argue strongly against revaluation.

Creation of formal world central banking institutions, or even an international currency as Jean Monnet suggests, is a worthy long-run objective. But effective progress is better made towards it empirically, than by constitution-writing, handling real problems as they emerge, and with the basis of such international consensus as is required and can be mustered, rather than by obtaining agreement in advance to all possible contingent problems. Ultimately if desirable, the rules of the game can be codified and even improved, when there is a sure consensus. To spend time now looking for such a consensus, examining attractive panaceas, seems to me to divert attention from real problems, run the risk of creating new problems where none now exist. A physicist acquaintance has observed that all games break down, as virtuosity in playing and interest in winning (called Gamesmanship by Stephen Potter) triumph over the initial purpose of enjoyment. Beanballs, offside bowling, the two-platoon system or the Queen's Gambit Declined come close to destroying their respective games. To the philosopher this can be generalized into the proposition that all order decays.

There is then little hope for fixing up the international payments mechanism in a way that will be eternally proof against the ravages of time and national gamesmanship, whether with rules of the game that emerge out of evolving practice, or with promulgated statutes of new or revised international organizations. I am disposed to believe, however, that more lasting progress and surer is achieved by solving problems one by one as they emerge, rather than undertaking the grand design of a new system of international payments.

SUMMARY RECORD OF THE DEBATE

BY

DOUGLAS C. HAGUE

THE DISCUSSION OF MR. BHAGWATI'S PAPER

Sir Roy Harrod introduced Mr. Bhagwati's paper saying that while everyone regretted that Professor Samuelson could not be here to present the first paper because of the illness of his son, all were most grateful that Mr. Bhagwati had been able to produce this paper at short notice. Sir Roy wanted to make some general remarks, especially on the first section of Mr. Bhagwati's paper, and he hoped that participants would not think these unduly revolutionary. The first section of the Bhagwati paper was built round Professor Ohlin's reconstruction of the classical theory of comparative cost, which was based on relative factor endowments. Economists agreed that Professor Ohlin's contribution represented an important and lasting reconstruction of the whole theory of comparative costs, but he thought that this particular formulation of it had caused international trade theory to take a wrong turn. Largely because of a pedagogic accident, teachers found it easiest to work in terms of two factors and two products, and the factors considered were usually capital and labour. Yet Sir Roy thought that relative endowments of capital and labour had a very small gravitation impact on the pattern of foreign trade.

Sir Roy said that he wanted to make it clear that he was not criticizing the theory, but merely putting the view that the ratio of the capital/labour endowment had a relatively small effect on the pattern of foreign trade, though it was undoubtedly a big factor for the standard of living and for productivity. He regarded the important thing as being the endowment of other factors of production, and especially the natural and human resources of the country in question. For example, Britain exported much wool, while being a still larger importer, mainly because some particular kinds of sheep could be most easily reared in Britain. A second example was that since the war there had been a big shift in the world's textile trade caused, he thought, by the increased importance of design. With a higher standard of living, people were not interested merely in warmth, and those countries which showed most talent in designing had been able to increase their share of world trade.

Relative factor endowments entered economic theory *via* prices. The relative cost of employing capital came in through the rate of interest alone, the cost represented in the principal being truly wages and other factor costs. Now interest was not a heavy item in cost and he doubted whether differences in rates of interest between countries had much effect on the pattern of trade. In the United States, capital endowment per head was high, and the famous Leontief finding had therefore been pronounced paradoxical. Sir Roy said that he was not surprised that Leontief had discovered this so-called paradox, because, as he had already explained, he did not think the capital endowment important in determining the pattern of trade.

While it was true that the United States' industry used much capital throughout, this could cause relatively capital-intensive commodities to have advantages only if it showed up in the pricing of capital, i.e. in the rate of interest (or profit); yet, during the century when the United States had developed, capital there had not been cheap. Nor was lending more readily available there. The United Kingdom had a better capital market — and in any case most investment took place in both countries through the ploughing back of profits. This naturally led one to the question of what had caused the United States' industry to become so capital-intensive, despite capital not being particularly cheap there, and in this connection he thought one could make a substantial point with a wide bearing. The reason was that the United States had a different endowment of *other* factors. If one provisionally worked with the assumption that raw material represented a factor in its own right, labour in the U.S. could be regarded as scarce relatively to materials (ultimately to land and natural resources). This meant that it was necessary to use as little labour as possible relatively to materials, and that could be done only by providing each man with more tools. Thus the more intensive use of capital in the U.S. had originally been the result, not of the cheapness of capital there — capital was not cheap there — but of the expensiveness of labour relatively to materials. The same situation would have arisen in the United Kingdom, had labour been so scarce relatively to materials. Since capital was not a cheap factor in the U.S.A., Sir Roy did not consider the Leontief finding as in any way paradoxical. If Leontief had considered the relative amount of labour and materials going into particular products, he might have obtained better results.

Sir Roy therefore feared that we might be giving wrong advice to under-developed countries when we told them to concentrate on industries which used little capital. There might be some capital-intensive industries or services which these countries *should* develop, for example, certain highly capital-intensive items of infrastructure. Similarly, it might be worth while to invest in capital assets with high productivity, even if this meant starving the rest of industry of capital.

Mr. Bhagwati had given an extremely good summary of the whole of recent international trade theory and fairly clear conclusions emerged. However, Sir Roy found it depressing that these were so agnostic. Perhaps other participants would be able to remove part of his depression. Mr. Bhagwati made a helpful point for world, as distinct from national, welfare when he said on page 24 that 'free trade (no restriction) is superior to no trade (total prohibition); and restricted trade is superior to no trade;

and free trade is superior to restricted trade'. But Sir Roy was not quite sure from the text if this was still subject to a 'first-best' condition.

If one had distortions, and these were inevitable, did that destroy the whole value of welfare analysis for the rest of the economy? If one had immovable distortions, the ideal solution would be to put in counter-distortions in order to achieve an optimum position. If this was impossible, could we not be saved from frustration by Pigou's doctrine of unverified probability? What if the distortions were small? Would one tiny distortion make so much difference as to render it immaterial whether we had free trade or a mass of interferences? If not, how big would a distortion have to be in order to make sensible analysis impossible?

Towards the end of his paper Mr. Bhagwati dealt with the question of expansion and suggested that the case for free trade might become worse if one took it into account. Sir Roy Harrod did not think one could deal with expansion along these lines at all; one would need a new structure. Sir Roy said that he would like someone to formulate in dynamic terms the conditions in which an optimum tariff would alter. It should be possible to state in what conditions the tariff would grow and grow, or, alternatively, in what conditions it would decline.

Professor Haberler said that while he admired the paper tremendously, especially in view of the very short time available for its preparation, he would concentrate on points of disagreement. First, on a point of methodology, Professor Haberler recalled that Mr. Bhagwati said that the pure theory of international trade was a matter of logic alone and therefore not verifiable. He would like to disagree with this. Mr. Bhagwati rightly pointed out that trade theory, like general economic theory, was largely based on the assumptions of maximization of utility and profits and stability of equilibrium. These were surely empirical propositions which were subject to verification or falsification. Mr. Bhagwati mentioned only one type of method of verification, namely, by macro-economic (econometric and statistical) methods. However, these assumptions could also be checked by micro-economic methods. For example, everyday knowledge of the world and human behaviour taught us that those assumptions were correct on the whole and in the majority of cases. (It was not necessary that they should hold in every single case.) If this was correct, it went a long way to verifying empirically the statements of general economic theory and of international trade theory without the use of any macro-economic or statistical methods.

Professor Haberler thought one ought to be careful when using the two-factor models of which much of our present trade theory consisted. While such models were useful or even indispensable, they were also dangerous. Professor Haberler suggested that Sir Roy Harrod's difficulties with the Heckscher-Ohlin theory resulted from the inadequacies of a two-factor representation, especially one which used capital and labour. If one considered a model using labour and land (natural resources), the Heckscher-Ohlin theory would look more plausible, since no one could deny that natural resources had much to do with the pattern of trade.

International Trade Theory in a Developing World

In appraising the Leontief paradox, the issue of two- versus many-factor models was very important. While Leontief measured only the labour and capital intensity of various industries, his underlying theory was *not* of the two-factor type. Capital, for him, was *not* merely a catchall for all factors other than labour but meant 'produced means of production' — machinery, equipment, buildings, inventories. In addition to labour and capital, there were other factors in Leontief's theoretical scheme such as land, natural resources and 'entrepreneurship'. This made interpretation much more complicated, but at the same time deprived his results of their paradoxical flavour. Professor Ohlin, for his part, had used a many-factor model from the beginning in his classical *Interregional and International Trade*.

Professor Haberler noted that in the second part of his paper, Mr. Bhagwati took up the celebrated Stolper-Samuelson theory on Protection and Real Wages. Here, too, the limitations imposed by the use of a two-factor model must be kept in mind. In such a model it could be shown, as the authors elegantly demonstrated, that the 'scarce factor' lost by trade and, by the same token, was benefited by protection in an absolute sense. The authors carefully qualified their results even in the two-factor case and admitted that their theory broke down if more than two factors were introduced.

Professor Haberler suggested that more useful results could be obtained if one operated with a model using two specific factors, one attached to the export industries, the other (say natural resources) to the import-competing industries in addition to one or two factors (say labour and capital) that were used in both industries, though in different proportions. Under these assumptions, which were often very realistic, especially in the short run, it was possible to reach definite conclusions at least for the immobile specific factors. He thought that this type of model was favoured by Sir Roy Harrod.

Sir Roy had asked for some comfort on the benefits of free trade in view of the seemingly protectionist conclusions of modern theories. Professor Haberler said that he, too, wanted to be comforted but that this was difficult on the high level of abstraction of Mr. Bhagwati's paper. But it might be comforting to reflect that free trade led — at least under the ordinary assumptions of free competition and the absence of external economies — to a Pareto optimum for the world as a whole. And the demonstration that any one country — in the absence of infinite elasticities of demand and of retaliation — could always improve its own situation, at the expense of others, by certain specific measures of protection, did not establish a presumption that protection in general was better than free trade, even from a purely nationalistic standpoint.

Professor Weiller wanted to revert to the Leontief paradox and asked why it was considered so. An important fact was that in the real world there was a great deal of protection of particular industries. We were far from free trade, and what we needed to deal with was not pure theory but structural evolution. We had to accept the fact that there was protectionism in the U.S.A. and that it had existed even in the United States of 1890–1910, when the country was in an evolutionary period; this was in a supposedly non-protectionist country. Professor Weiller suggested that we needed to think of the problem in terms of a very long period; for example, sixty years ago it had been normal for the U.S.A. to export cotton and wheat as normal and economic goods. There was no doubt that since then there had been a structural evolution of U.S. policy, but one nevertheless found that cotton and wheat were still exported. These were not genuine exports, but exports upheld by an economic policy which was so arranged that the U.S.A. could get rid of surplus products. We should not, therefore, make the statistical verification of our theory lead to the conclusion that there was no protectionism. Protectionism was a deliberate policy in all countries.

Professor Weiller thought it was a very false idea to suggest that profit gave more stimulus to the production of exports than of domestic goods. In the U.S.A., most profits were made on domestic output and he could not understand why anyone should think that the profit rate was lowest at home. One could find a number of cases where the U.S.A. earned less profit on exports; this was not a paradox but was based on facts. Professor Haberler had spoken of the relative prices of labour and capital and their place in the theory of comparative advantage. If we interpreted this theory intelligently, it would fit easily into classical analysis of the Heckscher-Ohlin type.

Sir Donald MacDougall was puzzled by Sir Roy Harrod's argument that, because the rate of interest was not very different in the U.S.A. and in the U.K. in the nineteenth century, capital was not relatively cheap in the U.S.A. compared with labour. It *was*, because Americans could get capital goods in Britain, so that the annual cost of capital equipment was about the same in the two countries, while labour was more expensive in the U.S.A.

As for attempts to verify theories, Sir Donald suggested that, in the first place, the simple, two-good models might first be extended by introducing non-traded goods, but he feared that this would lead to considerable theoretical difficulties. In working on the transfer problem he had found that bringing in non-traded goods made a large difference. (Incidentally, how would Mr. Bhagwati define internationally traded goods? Would they, for example, include all the services of a hotel where one foreign tourist spent one night?)

Secondly, one should allow for differences in factor rewards and marginal productivities between different sectors within a country. These could be large in practice, especially as between industry and agriculture — witness the difference between the marginal productivities of Swiss peasants and industrial workers. In an under-developed country, the rate of return in capital might be, say, 4-5 per cent in public utilities and 15 per cent in private organized industry, while the rural money-lender might charge 50 per cent or even 100 per cent per annum. We ought to look carefully at such big differences in any empirical test.

Thirdly, the pattern of trade in manufactures was worth investigating. Such trade between the major industrial nations had become much more free since before the war as a result of a lowering of the U.S. tariff, GATT, the effects of inflation on specific import duties, and now the European Common Market. This helped to explain the large rise that had taken place. It would be interesting to know how far the pattern of this trade was based on innovations, which would mean that it changed rather rapidly. Sir Donald said that in bringing up to date his study of the manufactured exports of the U.S.A. and the U.K., he had found that the pattern of trade had remained comparatively stable.

Professor Ohlin said that the basis of any theory of factor proportions was a mutual equilibrium position founded on money costs. One had to start from the money cost account, and introduce all the elements affecting it. He had always stressed the importance of bringing in many factors of production, but evidently it had not been made clear to others that he had been fighting against the two-factor model for as long as twenty-five years. He was glad that Professor Haberler had helped to clarify the position ; he usually agreed with Professor Haberler, especially when he criticized his (Professor Ohlin's) own work. There was nothing in the factor proportions model which forced one to concentrate on capital and labour, and capital was of many kinds. It did not contradict the theory of factor proportions if a country specialized in a product using much of a scarce factor. The product might need two or more other factors which were very abundant. He did not think it at all surprising that if one had eight or nine factors producing a product, one of them might be very scarce.

Professor Ohlin pointed out that there were about ten simplifying assumptions underlying the theory of factor proportions, and it was not surprising that it was difficult to prove such a simple theorem statistically, because so many conditions were not fulfilled in the real world. All Mr. Bhagwati's ingenious attempts to modify the theory were not sufficient to produce a reliable theory which was worth testing. We must allow for various costs of highly skilled labour and many different production functions. We must also consider economies of scale, the size of markets, monopolies (especially on the labour market) and transport costs. Sir Donald's non-traded goods were merely one extreme result of transport costs, but of course these also existed within countries.

Internal transport costs figured in two ways. First, a good and cheap transport system throughout a particular country meant that one factor was particularly cheap. For example, Switzerland, Italy and Belgium must benefit in this way. Secondly, one had to remember that the process of production could be divided up between countries. *A* might produce raw materials, *B* semi-finished manufactures and *C* final products. In this situation relative transport costs were obviously very important.

Professor Ohlin was very worried that 98 per cent of reasoning in international trade theory was based on the assumption that the whole of a good was produced in one country. Countries did import raw materials and export semi-manufactured goods. Any model which ignored transport costs might be useful at an elementary level, but would not be sophisticated enough to be tested statistically. He thought that the Leontief paradox might perhaps be a paradox because it did not take all these other elements, ignored in the factor proportions model, into account. One thing which was important for the use of capital was the amount of shift work. For example, a machine used 8 hours a day in Europe might be used 24 hours in the U.S.A., or perhaps a machine might be used faster in the U.S.A. Such factors as the rhythm of work ought to play a greater role in international comparisons.

Despite all his admiration for Mr. Bhagwati's first section, Professor Ohlin felt it might lead further if we first tried to develop short models and then to combine these when comparing our theories with the statistics. Nobody now presented a single theory of business cycles, but combined different models according to the situation. Perhaps we had been over-conservative in the theory of international trade in stressing a few basic models too much. Professor Ohlin felt that we needed factor proportions, economies of large-scale production, transport costs and other elements. At a later stage in the conference, we might discuss which of those types of model that had not yet been developed we needed most.

Dr. Savosnick thought that a simple model might elaborate the point made by Sir Donald MacDougall. He would assume that in the U.S.A. of year 1900 a man was using a lump of capital worth $5000 to produce $1000 worth of a commodity. The labour share of output could be assumed to be $750 and the return on capital $250, or 5 per cent on $5000. He would assume that at that time the same level of technology applied in the U.K. so that an Englishman working with a lump of capital worth $5000 would get exactly the same result.

Ignoring the possibility of importing capital from the U.K., he would now assume that a 'factor neutral' productivity increase took place in the U.S.A. but not in the U.K. The American, still working with $5000 worth of capital, would now be able to produce an output worth $2000 of which the share going to labour was $1500 and the share going to capital $500, or 10 per cent on $5000. Thus, with the same factor proportions as originally, output in the U.S.A. would be double what it was in the U.K. and, while American labour would get double its original income, so would capital. The fact that the real return on capital now was 10 per cent in the U.S.A. while it remained 5 per cent in the U.K. did not mean that one ought to say that capital in the U.S.A. was now scarcer than in the U.K. What one *could* say was that *both* capital and labour were scarcer relatively to income than they were in Britain — but not that capital was scarcer in relation to labour. This was in fact the kind of situation which would stimulate a migration of both labour and capital from the U.K. to the U.S.A. or, alternatively, an export of production technique from the U.S.A. to the U.K.

Professor Kindleberger wondered whether Mr. Bhagwati was right in stressing the need to construct verifiable theorems in international trade theory. In these days when verification needed more and more complex correlation techniques, it became less and less possible to prove theorems positively. For the most part one could only use data to dismiss simple explanations of trade. The Leontief paradox, for example, was useful both in disproving the generality of the Heckscher-Ohlin theorem and in stimulating a great deal of theoretical discussion, but it produced new data which in turn required new explanation. In Professor Kindleberger's view, the United States had so much capital that it could use it freely in producing import substitutes. This explained Leontief's results, but it was very difficult to prove that it was the explanation. How could measurement prove whether production functions were the same in the United States as elsewhere, and factor intensities unambiguous in different commodities, so that factor proportions determined trade? Or how could it prove that production functions differed between countries, or factor intensities changed at various factor proportions, so that the Heckscher-Ohlin theorem could not operate?

Professor Kindleberger found the Heckscher-Ohlin theorem useful in interpreting the history of international trade and commercial policy. Perhaps Professor Ohlin had dismissed his own theory too readily. Finally, he hoped that Mr. Bhagwati would not insist that theorists who did not use high-powered statistics were all obsolete, but leave room for some economists to continue to work with geometry in discussing the case of two countries, two commodities and two factors.

Mr. Lamfalussy was unhappy over Sir Roy Harrod's suggestion that we should include the use of human resources in explaining comparative advantages. This was exactly the kind of resource which one could not easily measure and there was a danger that we should introduce it as a final explanation when we found some comparative advantage that we were unable to account for in any other way. Perhaps it would be better to assume that skill and ability both developed parallel with the stock of capital. For example, the Belgian steel industry accounted for something like 25 per cent of Belgium's total exports, so that it obviously had a comparative advantage. If one asked why, the answer seemed to be mainly historical. Belgium had a high proportion of savings to income, and could therefore afford a highly capital-intensive industry; at the same time, both entrepreneurs and workers developed skills to produce and also to sell steel. It therefore seemed to him that it did not matter whether natural resources and capital came first, and skill second, or *vice versa.*

Professor Johnson wanted to redress the balance of the discussion. He wished to commend Mr. Bhagwati for producing his paper at such short notice and to stress that Mr. Bhagwati had been specifically asked to write a survey of current international trade theory and not a critique of it. Participants seemed to be criticizing Mr. Bhagwati for not having written either a critique or a programme for action.

Professor Johnson wanted to defend Mr. Bhagwati's concentration on empirical studies, and especially on that by Leontief, in the first part of the paper. Until one tested theories, one did not know whether they represented more than a mere list of factors or a description. It was useful if Leontief showed the existence of a paradox, because then economists worked to refute Leontief and to produce new explanations. While Leontief's work and work in Japan suggested that there *was* a paradox, work on Canadian trade seemed to give the opposite result. Professor Johnson stressed that we wanted a simple theory, not least because we had to explain it to others. Being able to say that a particular result depended on a large number of circumstances merely meant that we were wise men who happened to know what we did happen to know. Professor Johnson did not think there was any need to agree with Professor Kindleberger that geometers were becoming obsolete. The fact that some people were testing theories was a good check on the geometry as well.

Professor Johnson thought that, so far, international trade theory had paid too little attention to what capital was. This partially explained the difference between Sir Roy Harrod and Sir Donald MacDougall. Sir Roy assumed that capital was produced within a country. Therefore, if wages increased, the cost of capital goods rose and the rate of return could be constant, even though income was rising. Sir Donald MacDougall assumed that capital goods were imported, which allowed the owners of capital to earn rent and meant that a rise in wages led to a fall in rents.

Since capital was a produced means of production, it was very difficult to measure its quantity and Leontief had not investigated what capital was. If one was thinking of capital as a produced means of production, then one found that human ability was also a form of capital and that it paid us to invest in that too. Those who argued that we needed both to accumulate capital and to develop new skills were treating as different two things which were very similar. However, the introduction of capital theory into international trade theory made it much harder, as the writings of Joan Robinson and Paul Samuelson had shown.

On the questions of welfare and second-best policies, Sir Roy and Professor Haberler wanted reassuring. He would remind them that in international trade theory one had long had a very clear recognition of the applicability of second-best analysis in one specific context. This was the recognition by Mill and other classical writers that if one had an excise tax, an offsetting tariff was desirable. An excise tax without a tariff distorted the price of imports relatively to home-produced goods.

Professor Morgan said that intangible input factors seem to have affected output much more than had changes in the quantity of capital relative to that of labour. In the U.S.A., Fabricant (in N.B.E.R. studies), Schultz and Solow had agreed in their findings that between one-eighth and one-half of increased output resulted from increases in physical factors of production. The remainder was due to intangible factors — 'changes in productivity'. So far as labour itself was concerned, there were awkward issues in trying to apply *any* one theory to such a huge and heterogeneous factor.

With an historically increasing rate of innovation, the influence on output of changes in non-physical inputs was apt to become progressively more important as time passed. One supporting reason for this trend was that consumers in all countries, developed and undeveloped, had a sharp bias — an 'unreasonably strong' bias — in favour of products that seemed novel and modern. Something of the same bias existed for governmental choice of productive equipment and techniques in under-developed areas.

Professor Delivanis pointed out that in footnote three on page 12 Mr. Bhagwati insisted that it was the use and not the ownership of factors of production which we should stress. If this were done, it meant that something which looked like a paradox turned out not to be one. Professor Delivanis also said that in studying this excellent paper he could see how dangerous it was if we tried to simplify when solving economic problems. A scientific solution to each of the problems which the world's governments had to solve every day would take an extremely long time to discover and this was probably why the solutions they actually found often turned out to be wrong.

Dr. Myint wanted to apply what Sir Roy Harrod had said to under-developed areas. If one took the four factors, capital, labour, natural resources and human resources, it seemed at first sight that one had an unwieldy set to deal with. Then one discovered that it was possible to break them up quite easily. In a country where there were many natural resources relatively to labour, as in the U.S.A., this would raise wages. On the other hand, one might have a country like India where the reverse was true. On this basis, one could proceed to a fairly testable theory.

Dr. Myint thought this was relevant for those who advised under-developed areas not to use too much capital. Such advisers thought not only in terms of crude capital scarcity, but also of a country's ability to absorb capital. If a country was short of people rather than capital, it would install new machines, because skilled craftsmen were not available and capital relatively cheaper.

Professor Giersch drew attention to Professor Ohlin's remark in his book *Interregional and International Trade* that the theory of international trade was only a part of a general theory of the localization of economic activity. When Professor Ohlin now said that for an explanation of international trade we needed as many different theories as we did to explain the trade cycle, he was also correct. The features of reality from which we could or could not abstract varied with time and space and with the problem to be solved. The classical theory of international trade, abstracting from transportation costs within the countries and thus considering countries as points, could well explain trade between the British Isles and the rest of the world in the nineteenth century, for there was no difficulty in taking account of the transportation costs between the countries. But the classical theory was not very useful in explaining trade between neighbouring continental countries. Here transportation costs within the countries were very important, while transportation costs between them fell to zero. This had some bearing on how to explain trade within the European Common Market. In solving such problems one needed a location theory rather than a trade theory of the classical type.

Professor Sohmen referred to a remark in footnote one on page 15 of Mr. Bhagwati's paper, namely, 'there is nothing in the traditional literature on what happens to the *rate of interest* under trade'. He did not agree with this special treatment of capital. Every completed capital good had a rate of return per unit of time which would in pure theory, be equalized by trade under the usual assumptions. On the other hand, as Mr. Bhagwati said, labour embodied a certain amount of capital in the form of time and effort devoted to training. This meant that there was no intrinsic difference between labour and capital as factors of production. Indeed, he thought perhaps capital was more homogeneous than labour. Though *finished* capital goods could not be transformed into other finished capital goods, it was easier to transfer resources from one industry to another in order to change the pattern of a country's capital equipment than to transfer labour between industries. One was perhaps more justified in speaking of *newly created* capital at least as being homogeneous.

Mr. Liesner agreed that transport costs had not been taken sufficiently into account. If one looked at the European Coal and Steel Community, it was not very meaningful to talk of Germany or France having a comparative cost advantage in producing coal or steel. It was more realistic to consider particular areas of Germany where either France or Germany might be better placed to supply a particular product. With other goods, however, he doubted whether this kind of argument was so realistic. Motor-cars, for example, could be transported quite cheaply from France to Germany and even raw cotton sent by rail cost only, say, 1 per cent more than before transported. This was true with most manufactured goods and not merely for special products. The more traditional trade theory therefore became important once again.

Professor Tsuru expanded on Sir Roy Harrod's comments about natural resources being immobile. Before the war, both Japan and Germany had been countries claiming to lack natural resources and both had reacted by aggression. The economic solution would be to stress the need for new techniques and for innovation; that was, by a specific unbalance inducing efforts to innovate. This was similar to the suggestion put forward by Hirschman in his *Strategy of Economic Development*. Instead of resorting to aggression, Japan and West Germany were adjusting to the situation by trade and the development of science. Japan, for example, was producing industrial salt from sea water and synthetic fibres from limestone.

Professor Tsuru said the suggestion had been made that there was increasing trade between manufacturing nations. Japan, however, found growing restrictions on her exports, both tariffs and, more especially, quantitative controls. The way in which Japan's exports fared in the world market would provide a test for modern under-developed countries when, in future, they tried to expand trade as they became industrialized.

International Trade Theory in a Developing World

Dr. Savosnick wanted to support Sir Roy Harrod over his view that the factor proportions theorem was not relevant for trade between industrial nations. He thought the theorem was relevant for trade between Europe and the rest of the world (except the U.S.A.), but that trade within Europe might well develop on a haphazard basis. One could not easily explain the existing trade pattern in terms of differing factor endowments. The endowments of the U.K., Germany, France, etc., were quite similar; the precise line of development which each country was pursuing was largely a matter of historical accident, each country finding its own niche. A theory to explain intra-European trade needed to be different from the kind of theory we now stressed.

Professor Weiller did not agree that one could readily apply the factor proportions theory to actual trade between industrial and under-developed countries although it remained a starting-point for fundamental teaching. He would be more inclined to agree with Professor Ohlin that the products which developed countries sold to under-developed ones were largely the result of particular countries being accustomed to employing their factors in a particular way, and to following economic policies which kept them on the same line of structural developments while adjusting their pattern of trade more or less slowly to economic change. He was reminded in this connection of the Leontief paradox. It was true that under-developed countries generally lacked capital, but it was possible for them to acquire the capital they needed for particular projects. They could also lack specialized labour, and they could import that, too, in specific cases.

Professor Mikesell agreed with Dr. Savosnick's remark that the theory of factor proportions did not apply to trade within Europe, but thought that it also had relatively little to say about trade with overseas countries. Mr. Liesner on the other hand said that the factor proportions theorem did apply if sufficient factors were considered. This brought Professor Mikesell to one of his own worries; namely, what was a factor and how far could one go in defining it? If one defined a factor to include all external economies, labour attitudes, entrepreneurship, the social attitudes of labour and entrepreneurs, etc., where would one end? Moreover, trade itself tended to create productive factors. We could never be sure whether we were explaining the basis for, or the consequence of, trade.

Mr. Bhagwati said that he would deal with two minor and two major questions considered in the debate. Sir Roy Harrod had touched on the argument that the Heckscher-Ohlin theorem had welfare implications; Mr. Bhagwati described this as the 'Chenery fallacy'. The theorem was designed to explain the pattern of trade and had nothing to do with welfare.

Mr. Bhagwati's second minor point was that Professor Sohmen had misunderstood his footnote, which said that the Samuelson model had no equation for the rate of interest. All he meant was that if one wanted to discuss the equalization of interest rates internationally, one would have to build a new model.

Mr. Bhagwati's first major point was on testing. In the first section of his paper he had gone into the major tests concerning comparative advantage. It was all very well for people to complain that a particular theory ignored transport costs, etc., but this was precisely what theories did. One did not want to try to bring in all conceivable factors, but merely to discover whether some particular simplifications worked. A theory which attempted to explain everything would not be a theory but a catalogue or a description. One had to proceed from simple to more complex hypotheses if the simple hypotheses were refuted. The testing of simple hypotheses was thus a necessary step in the approach to empirical verification.

As for Professor Kindleberger's remarks about geometry, he would light-heartedly retort that the development of a science was more important than the bread of particular scientists. Besides, as he had remarked in his paper, surely deductive analysis was essential. Much deductive work had suggested new concepts and so long as new theorems were not actually operationally meaningless, one could go on producing useful deductive analysis.

Finally, on the presumption for free trade in welfare economics, Mr. Bhagwati stressed that there were second-best complications. We all knew that there *were* distortions so that there was a presumption in favour of intervention, if anything. We needed to sit down and work out what was the optimum policy in particular situations. Mr. Bhagwati also agreed with Professor Haberler that being in favour of intervention did not mean that the intervention should take the form of protection. He had dealt with the methods of reaching the second-best optimum in the third part of his paper. Once one agreed what the major distortions were, one could develop calculations for saying whether a change was desirable or not. The problem could be handled systematically, and free trade might well be the best policy.

THE DISCUSSION OF THE PAPERS BY
MR. MAIZELS AND PROFESSOR MORGAN

Sir Donald MacDougall said that these papers dealt with some hard facts but were not unrelated to the morning's discussion. Dealing first with Professor Morgan's paper on the terms of trade, Sir Donald said that this was clearly concerned with hard facts, although he was not quite sure how hard the facts given were. He became more and more sceptical of index numbers of the average prices of exports and imports. Paasche and Laspeyre indices could give very divergent results and he recalled a difference of something like 30 per cent in one case he had studied. There were other statistical problems too. The export price indices of many countries had large gaps, especially where engineering products were concerned. Difficulties also arose because of changes in quality (and these were not necessarily in an upward direction over time). All these factors added to the scepticism expressed by Professor Morgan over whether there was any long-run trend either in favour of or against primary products or under-developed areas.

Perhaps one had to explain instead an apparent long-run *stability* of the terms of trade between manufactures and primary products. Sir Donald did not think one would get very far by arguing in terms of models of factor proportions. Perhaps one could not get further than concluding that, with a large number of products in the two major categories, and with many influences working on each of these individual products, differences would tend to cancel out and lead to stability in the ratio between the two indices. In Professor Morgan's paper, tables $A.1$ and $A.2$ showed that fluctuations in the terms of trade over the period considered were smaller for developed than for under-developed areas. Perhaps this merely reflected the fact that while, so far as imports were concerned, both the developed and the under-developed countries had equally diverse trade patterns, the exports of under-developed areas were more specialized.)

What method of analysis ought one to use in attempting to predict the future of the terms of trade? Should one use the model of Professor Johnson in his *Manchester School* article, or Marshallian supply and demand analysis? He had found himself that, if one were trying to expound the problems of the terms of trade to non-experts, this could be done rather simply in terms of demand and supply. One could show that both the demand and supply curves of manufactured goods would tend to move to the right more quickly than those of primary products. Although this kind of analysis might not be satisfactory for professional economists, there was something to be said for it.

So far as the events of the next ten years were concerned, he thought that an important question would be the possible effects of greater Russian participation in world trade. It had been suggested that, since the cost of primary products relatively to manufactures appeared to be much greater in Russia than it was in world markets, it might pay the U.S.S.R. to export manufactures and import primary products on a much larger scale. This could have an important effect in improving the terms of trade of primary producers.

Turning to Mr. Maizels' paper, Sir Donald said that he would concentrate on two points: the growing trade in manufactures between manufacturing countries, and trade between under - developed and developed areas. On the first question Mr. Maizels asked whether the recent rapid increase in the ratio of imports to consumption was or was not a once-for-all occurrence. He concluded that it was, mainly because it had merely brought the ratio back to its longer-run trend line. Sir Donald was not entirely convinced by this argument partly because he was not certain that the figures showed any clear trend. Nevertheless, Mr. Maizels' conclusion that the trend was downward was consistent with the results of a cross-section analysis. If one plotted the ratio of imports of manufactures to manufacturing production against manufacturing production for the various countries of the world, the result turned out to be a straight line on a double logarithmic scale, with the ratio falling as manufacturing production increased. It did not necessarily follow, however, that one could use such cross-section results to project the ratio of trade in manufactures to manufacturing production in the future.

The recent upsurge in imports of manufactures might have been of a once-for-all nature in so far as it had taken producers in countries such as the U.S.A. and the U.K. by surprise, after many years of insulation from foreign competition, so that they had been rather slow to react. This was one example of the difference between a temporary and a permanent trade pattern. Mr. Lamfalussy had already suggested that, to some extent, the pattern of trade was accidental and it might well be that a pattern resulting from the accident of which country happened to develop a particular type of manufacture first would persist for ever where one had trade between countries with roughly equal standards of living and wage rates. However, he thought that if one were dealing with trade between the U.S.A. and Europe or between Europe and the under-developed areas one could only look on this kind of accidental trade pattern as something temporary, since the wage differences were so large.

On trade between under-developed and developed countries, Sir Donald agreed with Mr. Maizels that the rise in the former group's exports of primary produce was likely to be slow (provided one allowed for the possibility that this might be upset if Russia became a major trading country). This implied difficulties for the balance of payments of under-developed countries, and he had reached this conclusion in his own study of India. The Economic Commission for Europe had reached the same conclusion for under-developed areas as a whole. It was unlikely that their extra exports of primary products would be sufficient to pay for their imports. He very much agreed that developed countries should do all they could to encourage imports of primary products, but it would also be necessary for the under-developed countries substantially to increase their exports of manufactured goods in order to fill the gap. This did not seem impossible since wages were so much lower in under-developed countries, and productivity, in at least some industries, was not correspondingly lower. Indeed in India there were some new types of manufacturing where productivity was not far short of that in Europe.

This was a trend which should be encouraged by developed countries, who should embark on *import* drives from under-developed countries, and by the latter countries themselves, who should if necessary offer export subsidies on new types of manufactures. These could be justified by the infant industry argument which did not only imply import-replacement and protection. It could be applied to selling as well as to production, since time and experience were required to establish new export markets for manufactures. He wondered why economists and politicians always seemed to regard export subsidies as so much worse than import duties. Export subsidies would turn the terms of trade against rather than in favour of the country imposing them; they would tend to expand rather than to contract trade; and, given the existence of import duties they would bring the country nearer to the free trade position.

Professor Lundberg said he would suggest some points for discussion. A major question was, what were the facts? Export and import price indices and resulting calculations of the terms of trade were among the most dangerous of all the statistical manipulations we carried out. The structural changes in trade over time were very big, which made the use of these indices dangerous. Therefore there had to be alternative interpretations of the facts and not just one unambiguous set. However, the paper showed that over time, changes in the terms of trade did not appear to be very large. Over ten years a change of 1 per cent per annum in the terms of trade was big and yet an error of 10 per cent in the figure for the terms of trade was quite possible. The prices of engineering products were very hard to measure and it was precisely these products whose trade was growing most rapidly. Services, on the other hand, were not all included in the index.

The second question was how one should interpret the terms of trade. Sir Donald MacDougall had gone rapidly from saying how hard it was to measure the terms of trade and how little one could say about them over time, to making forecasts of how the terms of trade would vary in the future. A major problem was how much micro-economic and macro-economic research we needed in order to interpret terms-of-trade changes adequately. One also needed some integration between the papers by Mr. Maizels and Professor Morgan. Professor Morgan had argued persuasively about changes in demand and substitution effects in consuming groups. A major question was how far these were shown in changes in relative price and volume. This was an important question and needed some kind of synthesis. Professor Lundberg suggested that there was probably a bigger gap in international trade between pure theory and the facts than elsewhere in economics, the reason being that we were tied by so much traditional classical theory.

Turning to policy implications, Professor Lundberg said that it was easy enough to say that countries should adapt their pattern of trade and allow the under-developed countries to export more, but this meant that we had to discuss the thorny problem of how to increase flexibility in the economies of developed countries. Professor Morgan had pointed to all kinds of tax interference with trade in primary products. When it came to allowing the under-developed countries to expand their export markets for manufactured goods, this was bound to lead to serious problems in developed countries. Many of these would complain about competition with countries which had lower wages, and the situation would be even worse if Sir Donald had his way and export subsidies were also introduced.

In the U.S.A. in 1961 there was much pressure from unemployed or potentially unemployed workers which indirectly represented an obstacle to encouraging the rapid industrialization of backward areas. Even where there was less unemployment than in the United States, the immobility of resources became a major problem when one was trying to find export markets for the industries of under-developed countries. The U.K., for example, had experienced great difficulty in transferring resources from textiles to engineering. If similar shifts were needed over the whole developed world in order to allow under-developed countries to industrialize, the reactions were not likely to be easy or pleasant. Yet this was only a part of a necessary flexibility in economic policy in developed countries.

Dr. Olano said that he had been a member of the United Nations Committee on Commodity Trade to which Professor Morgan referred on page 57. He thought it important to remember that it was difficult to reach agreement among a group of people from very different countries and he was rather surprised that a unanimous report had been produced at all. On pages 66-8 of Professor Morgan's paper, he agreed that there were many factors to be dealt with and if any economist could tell him how the ten or twenty relevant factors would move he could fairly easily predict the future changes in the terms of trade. For all practical problems he thought that an important criterion was what the Americans called 'reasonably stable prices', which came to the same thing as the 'just' or 'fair prices' described in the United Nations report. He would be grateful if some of the participants from the U.S.A. could explain what reasonably stable prices were.

Dr. Olano said he agreed with every word in Professor Kindleberger's recent book. In particular he thought that there would be no change in the terms of trade between primary and industrial products, but that there might be a move against the products of under-developed areas relatively to those of developed areas. Dr. Olano added that he preferred the terms developing and advanced countries to the terms under-developed and developed countries. He thought it was clear that one reason why the terms of trade had moved against the developing countries was that resources were so immobile. He thought that the policy of the Kennedy administration was moving in the right direction on this point. Finally, he stressed that it was absolutely essential for the developing countries to export manufactured products unless they were to be faced with very serious problems.

Professor Gudin said that he would like to underline a point made in Table 2 of Mr. Maizels' paper. This showed that the exports of primary produce from industrialized countries had risen 26 per cent since 1953, while those from primary producers to industrialized countries had risen by only 13 per cent. One reason for this was that developed countries imposed barriers to trade, such as tariffs to protect beet sugar, price support schemes for soya beans, consumption taxes on coffee, etc. Naturally, the development of synthetic replacements for primary products made trading more difficult, but this was one more reason not to create difficulties for other countries.

Professor Gudin asked how long the developing countries would continue to need aid if such man-made barriers were raised against their exports? To revert to a British slogan of the early 1950s, what the developing countries wanted was trade not aid. The Haberler Committee set up by GATT showed that, so far as tropical produce sent to temperate countries was concerned, there had been an increase of 53 per cent during a period when trade in primary products between temperate countries increased only 15 per cent. The movement of tropical produce had not so far suffered very greatly from industrialization in developed countries.

Professor Gudin thought that Professor Morgan somewhat exaggerated the fluctuations in the terms of trade of primary producing countries. In a depression the primary producers suffered from falling prices while developed countries suffered unemployment. Although one showed in the price indices the other did not. Nor did Professor Gudin agree with what Professor Morgan said on pages 52-3 of his paper, where he implied that the question of who earned the profits on exports was as important as the problem of the terms of trade. Brazilian experience showed that a good deal of the profits of foreign enterprise was reinvested in the country where the profits were made. In Brazil, over eight recent years, 52 per cent of the earnings of U.S. investments were reinvested.

The important thing was not the effects of foreign investment on the balance of payments, but on the national income. He thought that if there was no inflation the balance of payments could take care of itself. He was not afraid of foreign investment because the earnings might go to foreigners. One had to remember the importance of backward and forward linkages. As for the views of ECLA, he felt that one could show almost anything about terms of trade depending on the choice of the base year. Furthermore, the ECLA comparisons were based on f.o.b. prices in the U.K. and one got different results if transport costs were included. One also had to realize that, as Sir Donald MacDougall had pointed out, quality changed over time and if one were comparing 1876 with 1930 it would be difficult to find any article which was common to both years.

Dr. Patel said that it was important to assess the significance of the fact that trade amongst primary producers had not risen as much as trade amongst industrialized countries. In the nature of things, the import requirements of developing countries would increase as they pushed ahead with plans of development. If these countries had to increase their exports rapidly in the short run to meet their growing import requirements they would inevitably have to try and increase exports along traditional lines. This approach, however, seemed to imply the acceptance on their part of worsening terms of trade. If, on the other hand, these countries were given sufficient time to diversify their economies, they would ultimately be able to export a wide variety of goods, and thereby avoid seriously harming their terms of trade. In this sense, the availability of foreign aid had the additional advantage of sustaining the terms of trade of weaker countries.

Dr. Patel added that in view of the general drift of the discussion it seemed that sooner or later under-developed countries must become manufacturing countries to some extent. This meant that in the long run the problem of the terms of trade should ease, since then the trade patterns of different countries would be much more similar. Both primary products and manufactures would figure to a similar extent in the imports and the exports of most countries and the big differences between the developed and under-developed countries in this respect would vanish. If this view were correct, it meant that we should not worry too much about the future of the terms of trade but concentrate instead on industrializing backward countries.

Professor Tsuru said that on pages 63-5 of his paper Professor Morgan discussed some data about services, suggesting that one might put invisible items in international trade on the same footing as service items in the national income. He thought that Professor Morgan was taking a dangerous step when he proceeded to draw policy conclusions from this. The prices of services in the internal economy were much affected by their slow rate of growth of productivity. If labour were mobile, workers could move from those sectors where the rise in productivity was slow. Differences in productivity change were bound to exist between various parts of the economy and in classical economic theory these should reflect themselves in changes in relative prices. Classical theory only allowed for differences in wages to cancel out other net advantages in particular jobs. Differences in wages resting on differences in productivity could only exist because of labour immobility. He therefore thought it was important to look at changes in productivity along with changes in the prices of imports and exports. If this were done many of the problems might be solved.

Professor Tsuru commented on Sir Donald MacDougall's reference to Russia, saying that looking at differences in productivity in the terms he had just suggested might help to solve the apparent enigma of the U.S.S.R. Russia held to a classical Marxist interpretation of wage rates, so that where productivity rose slowly prices rose a great deal. In these terms it was easy to understand why primary produce could have a high relative price.

Professor Kitamura said that so far as trade in manufactured goods between developed areas was concerned, Mr. Maizels' conclusions were based only on what happened in the 1950s. If one carried out a broader analysis one might show that trade in manufactured goods between manufacturing countries had increased in the twentieth century as compared with the nineteenth. This was brought home both by Professor Nurkse in his Wicksell lectures, and by the 1959 GATT Report mentioned in earlier discussions. He shared Sir Donald MacDougall's doubts in not being convinced that there really was a large once-for-all movement in the 1950s.

So far as exports of manufactured goods from primary-producing countries were concerned, Table 2 of Mr. Maizels' paper showed that exports of these goods to other primary producers had risen more than had any other type of trade. Professor Kitamura said that he had a complete breakdown of manufactured exports of some selected countries in Asia by region and commodity group (SITC section) and had tried to find where the exports of particular countries had gone. He had found that in all cases but one the primary-producing regions' share of the market was more than 50 per cent. If one wanted to export manufactured goods from a primary-producing country, one could not count on the industrialized countries to provide one with a market, but had to rely on other primary-producing countries. If one took a more specific case and looked at Indian exports of textiles one found that countries like the U.K. and the U.S.A. took a surprisingly low percentage. Perhaps this should lead under-developed countries to consider regional arrangements to expand trade in manufactured goods.

Sir Roy Harrod said he would like to ask Professor Kitamura how he thought his conclusion was related to the major problem that, as they developed, under-developed areas needed to increase their exports. The market for primary products was not rising as fast as the need of the under-developed countries for more imports. Therefore under-developed countries needed to export manufactured goods too. But he wondered whether an increase in trade in manufactured goods between primary-producing countries could do anything to solve their need to import capital goods. The real problem was how high-grade capital goods could be obtained by the under-developed countries through their own exports.

Professor Kitamura suggested that part of the answer was that, as they developed, backward countries would need to import more industrial raw materials and that some of these could be obtained from other primary-producing countries. In what he had just been saying he had only been considering exports ; when it came to imports he thought there was a big difference between the large and the small country. A large primary-producing country like India might be able to reduce the ratio of its imports to national income while a smaller country might not. Basically, he agreed that Sir Roy Harrod was right in saying that these countries needed to import capital goods from developed areas. Nevertheless he thought that, if the primary-producing countries could keep their imports from each other fairly high and if therefore they were relieved of the necessity to economize on foreign exchange, this would enable them at the same time to sustain their imports from developed countries.

Mr. Maizels said that, when under-developed countries were industrializing, the pattern of their industrialization was likely to be much more similar than it was if one compared all the developing countries with the older, developed areas. As a result, one could argue that all the under-developed countries would be introducing the same industries at the same time and would therefore find it necessary to protect these industries against competition from each other. This would clearly tend to hinder the development of trade between the under-developed countries while there would probably be no corresponding increase in barriers to trade with developed countries.

Mr. Lamfalussy asked Mr. Maizels what was the share of capital goods in the total exports of industrialized countries to the under-developed world. This was an important question because, if there was a high proportion of consumer goods among exports, it meant that trade between primary-producing countries could be substituted for trade with developed countries.

So far as trade between the industrialized countries was concerned, Mr. Lamfalussy suggested that an additional reason for the increase in the 1950s was probably that some countries, such as the Netherlands and Italy, had been industrializing very rapidly. In looking to the future one ought to remember the trivial fact that with a rise in the G.N.P. the number of different goods produced in a country would increase. This would lead to the possibility of greater specialization and, therefore, greater scope for international trade. However, this could only happen if protection was weak or disappearing.

Mr. Lamfalussy therefore concluded that the growing possibilities for specialization might well have been hidden by the protectionism of the 1930s, and he was not sure that Mr. Maizels' trend really was a trend at all. Turning to the rise in productivity in manufactured goods and primary products, Mr. Lamfalussy doubted whether there was any basis for Professor Tsuru's contention that productivity was rising more slowly in primary products. He thought, for example, of the rapid increases in productivity in the oil industry or even in coal mining.

Professor Delivanis agreed with Professor Morgan's warning about the dangers of predicting the terms of trade, though he thought that if one always allowed a margin of error the dangers of making wrong conclusions could be reduced. However, he did *not* agree with Dr. Patel that the terms of trade would become less important when the under-developed countries had industrialized. The degree of industrialization and the parts of the economy where industrialization had gone furthest would always differ.

Professor Delivanis thought Professor Morgan was right to say that countries exporting agricultural products and raw materials enjoyed both a rising volume and rising prices for their exports. He also thought Professor Morgan right to favour the flexibility of the economy in order that products which would help to improve or sustain the terms of trade might be introduced. However, he wondered how this could be done and whether Professor Morgan could make any suggestions.

Sir Donald MacDougall had supported the necessity of increasing the industrial exports of under-developed countries by export subsidies, even though the IMF prohibited these. But neither Sir Donald nor Mr. Maizels appeared to have thought about the possibility of selling more services abroad if one had an economy which was able to do this. Professor Delivanis did not think that Mr. Maizels was right when he expected that industrialization would reduce the volume or the value of imported manufactured goods. Greek export experience suggested that this happened with only some commodities, while imports of others increased with a rising level of incomes. Finally, he pointed out that Soviet imports from under-developed countries increased by a very large percentage because they started from near zero, as compared with a rather high initial level for Western countries.

Professor Robinson said that when participants were discussing the terms of trade and their measurement it was important to ask whose terms of trade one was concerned with. The U.K. was interested in exporting processes of manufacturing goods rather than the goods themselves. Part of the considerable variation in Britain's terms of trade could be explained by changes in the prices of imported raw materials which were sent out in British export goods. If one took a residual export figure, having allowed for the fact that some part of the price of an export good would be the price of imported raw materials, one got a very different result.

In the IEA conference at Addis Ababa it had been pointed out that there was a big difference in the terms of trade measured at, say, Lagos, and the terms of trade between exporting countries measured on the assumption that the trading houses were British and one was concerned with the terms on which raw materials were exchanged for manufactures up-country in Nigeria or Uganda. Again, one would get very different answers. The percentage of the landed cost of a primary commodity in London which went to the original producer varied from 20 per cent to 40 per cent. Profits and other margins differed a great deal and if one was interested in the terms on which the African himself sold as compared with the price he paid for his imports, one could clearly get very many different answers according to the place where one made the comparison.

Professor Robinson said that when economists in industrialized countries discussed the terms of trade they all expected their terms of trade to deteriorate. The economists in under-developed countries were equally pessimistic about their own terms of trade. He would therefore like to put the case for the terms of trade moving *against* manufacturing countries. If one looked at exports of food to advanced countries, everyone agreed that the ratio of expenditure on food, especially that produced in under-developed countries, to total expenditure would fall as income rose. However, within food if one looked at some goods, such as grain, one found that these had a low income-elasticity of demand while others, like certain kinds of meat and tropical fruit, had high income-elasticities. With a high standard of living such luxuries might well become important and offset part or all of the loss which exporters of low-elasticity products could reasonably expect to suffer. Similarly, if one looked at the demand of developed areas for industrial raw materials, while it was agreed that the import content of output as a whole was falling with increased income per head, the supplies of some raw materials could be scarce. If one turned to the under-developed countries, one found a higher income-elasticity of demand for food, which could, in exceptional cases, even exceed one — in some special areas where rents to the poorest families were very high. There might also be a high income-elasticity of demand for industrial goods so that import-elasticities of industrial raw materials might be greater than one. This gave one some indication of the potential growth of demand for primary products as a whole. In total, he was not convinced that there were no expanding markets for primary produce. However, one also had to distinguish between primary products from tropical and those from temperate countries. It was possible that since tropical countries produced only a very narrow range of industrial primary products and foods, there might be an excess of demand for the products of temperate countries, and at the same time a shortage of demand for products of tropical countries. Perhaps one type of flexibility would be achieved through an attempt by tropical countries to develop substitutes for the products of temperate countries.

Professor Sohmen did not think Sir Donald MacDougall was right in deducing from the difference between prices of primary products and manufactured goods in the Soviet Union that the U.S.S.R. should concentrate on imports of primary products. In the West we were used to the idea that prices bore some relation to marginal cost. In the U.S.S.R. prices were fixed centrally and there was no necessity for them to bear any particular relationship to marginal cost. Prices were used instead to direct consumption and as a means of taxation. While he believed that the socialist bloc could benefit materially from increased trading with the rest of the world, he did not think that relative prices could be used as indicators of which goods the socialist bloc ought to export and import.

Professor Nakayama was discouraged by the view of various participants that the terms of trade were very hard to compute. In the light of Japanese experience he would like to stress the importance of changes in the terms of trade for economic growth. After 1945, there had been rapid growth for ten years, supported mainly by an increase in exports. These had risen much more rapidly than industrial production as a whole. The role of the terms of trade had been important because this rapid expansion had been supported by a serious worsening in the terms of trade. This was similar in some ways to the position in the 1930s when export prices had fallen by 70 per cent, but export volume had risen by 68 per cent. However, Japan had been able to expand the volume of her export trade and this had enabled her to increase employment and to take advantage of a profitable international division of labour. For this reason he thought that the terms of trade and economic growth were connected.

Dr. Myint wanted to elaborate on what Professor Robinson had said about the unsatisfactory nature of calculations of the aggregate terms of trade. While he agreed with this, he thought that studying the position commodity by commodity represented a counsel of perfection. Perhaps a reasonable compromise was to distinguish between consumer and capital goods in the imports of under-developed areas, and between food and raw materials in their exports. Where food was concerned, population changes were important; with industrial raw materials a major factor was innovation in developed areas. He also thought it should be remembered that, apart from the fact that as standards of living rose some types of food might become luxuries, one ought to remember that food grains could always be diverted from human beings to animals. So far as Russia was concerned, he thought that the most important aspect of Russian trading so far was her impact on the supply of capital goods. The way the Russian economy was developing might well make it easiest for her to export such goods.

Mr. Maizels replied to those parts of the discussion directed towards his paper. He agreed that one got different results for the terms of trade according to the time period one considered. In the short run, changes in the terms of trade could lead to serious balance of payments problems, but there was no evidence that anything worse happened in the long run than that there was a series of cycles. Taking periods as long as fifty years, one found no obvious movement either upwards or downwards and he thought that this was a real result and not mere illusion. The result would be illusory if over a long period the structure of world trade had changed so much that no statistics were reliable. Perhaps one needed to calculate margins of error in the indices that were used and to decide whether the differences that one found lay between these margins of error. All the evidence he had seen showed that whatever series or whatever weights one used the results were much the same. He therefore assumed that in the long run the terms of trade would be constant, and in the present state of knowledge this seemed much the best assumption. The ECLA series, showing an adverse trend in the terms of trade, was heavily influenced by the export prices of the U.K. Since British export prices had risen over the past fifty years relatively to export prices in other countries this gave a misleading result. If an index was constructed for other countries than the U.K. one got quite different results.

Mr. Maizels said that one point of criticism was what he had said about trade between industrial countries. From an analytical rather than a policy point of view it was hard to assess how far the rise in this kind of trade had been genuine and in what direction the trend was. His own view was that the rise in trade within Europe had been an important factor leading to Britain's decision to try to join the EEC. However crude one's studies of trade between industrial countries were, he thought that some kind of analysis was necessary. What he had done had been not to compare the trend over the past fifty years with the position in the nineteenth century, but to compare trade with the consumption of manufactured goods. This showed a rise in the percentage of imports which was sharper than could be accounted for by some of the factors mentioned in the discussion. He agreed that as the number of products being produced increased this was likely to raise the proportion of trade to national income, but he did not think it could explain the kind of rise which he had actually discovered. The consensus of opinion seemed to be that, although the figures overestimated the size of the rise, there must have been a big one ; he did not feel that this was out of line with the theoretical discussions.

So far as the pattern of trade between industrial countries was concerned, Mr. Lamfalussy had suggested that particular countries specialized in given manufactured goods largely for reasons of historical accident; but there was also specialization by firms which made fully manufactured goods and firms which produced semi-manufactures. Looking at Western Europe today one found that there was greater diversity in the bigger countries. He therefore thought that size was the most important factor determining the pattern of trade. For example, smaller countries like Belgium and the Netherlands depended heavily on imports. He thought that the trade structure of Europe was determined by the activities of bigger countries.

Turning finally to the exports of under-developed areas, Mr. Maizels said that most participants seemed to agree that there was a need to change the fiscal and tariff policies of developed countries. He did not see the relevance of export subsidies, however, because the goods of under-developed countries were already cheap. Rather than cheapening them still further, the need was to give these countries markets in developed countries. This was the key problem and he did not want participants to avoid it.

Professor Morgan replied to the discussion of his paper. He said that he had a vested interest in defending the use of the terms of trade. Both Sir Donald MacDougall and Professor Lundberg were worried about the significance of this concept, but it was better to rely — cautiously — on terms-of-trade calculations, interpreted reasonably, than to talk vaguely only of 'more' or 'less'. Some criticism could be met by disaggregation; by taking separately individual commodities and groups of homogeneous commodities. This was in part done in his paper.

One should take only fairly large changes seriously; a change of, say, 10 per cent in ten years was hardly significant. One should also be conscious of cyclical changes. Over the cycle prices of primary products varied widely and some of the discussion of recent years had been dominated by events since 1953. Eight years was too short a period to generalize from.

Professor Morgan suggested that one should be aware of, and allow for, two kinds of bias in longer-run terms of trade. First, there was the effect of falling transport costs. Prices of U.K. imports from India had fallen in London while they were rising in Bombay. Similarly, there had been rising farm prices in Minnesota and falling ones in New York. This effect meant that one could not assume that a terms-of-trade pattern for one part of the world also held for trading partners elsewhere. Data for England or France need not hold for India or Madagascar. A second problem was that quality changes were more important for manufactured goods than for primary products, so that a long-run statistical series over-stated the prices of manufactured goods relatively to those of primary products.

Commenting on Mr. Maizels' suggestion that the terms of trade might be fairly constant, Professor Morgan argued that this was not borne out by the statistics. There had been extreme volatility in the short run;

in the long run, there were often major shifts or long waves. The data relied on by the 1950 ECLA study (*Economic Development of Latin America*) showed a fall in the terms of trade for primary producers between 1876 and the 1930s. But 1876 was a major peak in the still longer run series ! If one took data from 1801 to 1876, one got opposite results. In the U.S.A., long-run data from 1787 to the early 1900s showed continued improvement in the relative position of primary producers, whose price position improved roughly threefold over the whole period.

Sir Donald MacDougall had suggested that the under-developed countries should move into manufacturing because of the slow prospective increase in the demand for primary products. Like Professor Nurkse, Sir Donald was implying that the terms of trade were going to shift in favour of manufactures. Should under-developed areas with a broad comparative advantage in agriculture nevertheless shift to manufacturing ? Countries with resources adapted to manufacturing, perhaps Russia and China, might find it economically advantageous to have considerable concentrations of major manufacturing industries.

Professor Lundberg had stressed the need for flexibility in the policies of developed areas. He warmly agreed with this. The developed countries had a special responsibility because of their higher incomes and the flexibility which their advanced techniques and adaptable skills implied. There was a moral here for the foreign policy of the U.S.A. and of other countries.

Professor Delivanis had asked how a country could attain the flexibility that Professor Lundberg advocated. This was an important question. One possibility was by expanding the right kind of training. The more traditional our training, the more we were tied to continuing past techniques and types of production. Nowadays we needed increasingly to train people for jobs that did not yet exist and to stress the importance of experimentation and adventure. One way of developing new lines of activity was to set up pilot projects for making particular goods. These projects would show the true facts about costs and other difficulties, and therefore the potential prices for particular goods. They would also make it possible to train technicians and administrators. Better communications and transportation helped and adaptation could proceed more easily if workers and other resources could readily be transferred from declining to expanding parts of the economy.

Professor Delivanis had also asked about the proportion of world trade supplied by the developed and under-developed countries' leading export commodities. What was done was to compare the leading primary export of given countries with total world exports of that commodity. The median calculation showed that a much greater percentage of world output was typically accounted for by the leading export commodities of developed countries. *Ceteris paribus*, developed countries were most threatened by falling prices as their exports rose. Hence, it seemed right to claim for under-developed countries, in this respect, the 'advantage of weakness'.

Professor Robinson had given reasons why the terms of trade might turn against manufactured goods. Before being completely convinced, one should look at all the relevant arguments. First, there was the statistical projection by Henry Aubrey. Using U.S. data, commodity by commodity, he estimated future supply and demand and concluded that, in the next decade or so, primary-product prices would rise relative to manufactures. Second, on the issue of income-elasticity of demand for foodstuffs, U.S. data showed that from the 1940s on there had been a rise in the percentage of income going on food. This trend might be illusory, because when one bought food in the U.S.A. one bought more services with it and in it than previously. Still, it was possible that in under-developed countries, the income-elasticity of demand for food was greater than one in special cases and areas. Third, there was the problem of the technical revolution that was leading manufacturers to produce synthetic substitutes for raw materials. The question was whether this kind of change would be sufficiently large, compared with the increase demand resulting from greater world industrialization, to force a fall in the relative price of primary products. Perhaps the latter influence would dominate.

Professor Morgan said that none of this was proof that the terms of trade would necessarily turn against manufactures, but merely to provide some evidence to counterbalance the frequent assumption that the terms of trade were bound to turn against primary producers.

THE DISCUSSION OF PROFESSOR
JOHNSON'S PAPER

Professor Ohlin opened the discussion, saying that he had already stressed that one could not have just one model of international trade, and that if one had several, this would give a basic understanding. One could then study variations in things like trade policy or look at changes in demand and in supply. Professor Johnson studied an important type of supply when he analysed the influence of technical change on the commodity terms of trade. In doing so, he used many simplifying assumptions. One could, of course, take many other cases and Professor Ohlin would particularly have liked to see the analysis of a very small country making only a small proportion of the world's exports of a particular product. In this case, a country could increase its productivity through technical change and yet retain much of the advantage for itself, even though technical progress occurred entirely in the export industry. The same would be true for a small enough country, even if innovations took place everywhere. These remarks were not intended as criticisms of Professor Johnson for the cases he had chosen to consider. Professor Johnson had decided to concern himself with technological improvement in only one industry, and given that initial choice, this was a sound paper in which the reasoning was both lucid and accurat. The main conclusions were acceptable and valuable.

Having set out his two simple models in the first part of his paper, Professor Johnson turned to relax the assumption of a fixed factor supply. He thought his conclusions were out of the ordinary, but Professor Ohlin disagreed, having considered this problem himself thirty years earlier. Professor Johnson was doubtless right that capital had not been satisfactorily treated in factor proportions theory. One reason was that if one began from a money-cost account, as Professor Ohlin himself had, one avoided most of the difficulties.

In the second part of his paper, Professor Johnson went on to consider where technical improvement occurred. While this part of the paper contained many valuable observations, Professor Ohlin was surprised that Professor Johnson went over from his theoretical analysis to rather loose philosophizing. He himself would emphasize that the financing of research was an important element in technical progress. In particular, large firms and industries were in a very good position to encourage technical progress through research. They had money, large numbers of technicians and the interest of the public, since the man in the street was much more likely to know about the activities of the larger firms. He would emphasize more than Professor Johnson that when there was a spurt in innovation there was likely to be a rise in rates of profit. Firms felt that, having financed research, they deserved to recoup their expenditure from profits, and prices were likely to be higher relatively to costs than usual. If such a standard attitude existed among business men, prices could be raised without any need for monopoly.

Finally, Professor Johnson seemed to make an impressive attempt to analyse the reasons for differences in comparative advantage. However, on re-reading this part of the paper, he felt that Professor Johnson was saying little more than that technology did change. He wondered especially what Professor Johnson meant when he said on page 111 that the sources of comparative advantage were to be found in 'the possession of technology superior to the average corresponding to the economy's real wage level and the prevailing rate of profit'. There had been long discussions twenty-five years ago in Denmark from which it emerged that it was hard to define higher and low states of technology. Professor Johnson spoke of a technique which was superior to the average, but was such a statement really clear and precise enough to be important? He wondered whether Professor Johnson could not have used the factor proportions theorem assuming different production functions in different countries. On page 112, Professor Johnson said 'instead of being firmly grounded in stable and enduring characteristics of national economies — inherent cost differences, as in the Ricardian model, or differences in factor endowments, as in the Heckscher-Ohlin model — comparative advantage is the evolving consequence of the dynamics of technical progress'. There was nothing in the factor proportions theory which assumed a given factor supply or a given factor endowment. That part of technical progress which was the result of an increase in the supply of highly skilled labour had taken a place in his reasoning thirty years ago.

Professor Ohlin said that since he had little to quarrel with in Professor Johnson's paper, he would like to make some general remarks. He had emphasized the need for many different models and wondered which models we should use in order to economize in time and energy. The classical theory of comparative cost was superior for many purposes, but the factor proportions model was often useful as an introduction to a problem. Perhaps we needed statistics of whether the exports of different countries were made by large, medium or small firms. Such figures did exist and it would be a simple test of a theory to set them out. Similarly, we needed some models of large-scale production and of trade between markets of different size. We also needed studies of high protection which to some extent we had. To him one of the more neglected models should be central : namely, one that included transport costs. Some models of this kind already existed in location theory, where we considered internal transport costs in countries where travel was easy. What Marshall had said in 1923 in *Money, Credit and Commerce*, and some of Hawtrey's comments, had not received sufficient attention. Were there not some commodities requiring much transport and others requiring less, and could this not lead one to a reasoning parallel to that in the factor proportions theory ? Perhaps one could find out to what extent the need for transport and technical requirements were important. One should look at statistics on the price of transport per ton mile in particular cases, and then at the special transportation problem of raw materials and markets. Classical location theory could help in considering this problem.

If one wanted to explain international trade within Europe, he thought one would have to look at transport costs, economies of scale and the fact that technological change, once it began in particular industries, tended to become cumulative. We needed models to determine the reaction of factor supplies, and a theory of factor movements combined with a theory of capital movements which would deal with the lack of factor movements within countries. It went without saying that we also needed an analysis of monopolistic situations. Much attention had been given to the important problem of dumping, but other kinds of monopoly occurred too, including monopoly on the labour market.

There were many kinds of tariff which had to be paid by producers and a traditional trade theory dealt only with import and export duties. Tax systems developed within countries had been little considered, apart from a casual remark by Professor Meade and others. It was not only a question of taxation as a cost, but also of the effect of taxes on savings. Depreciation rules, which had been virtually ignored, were very important indeed. Another model we needed was one studying risk in factor and commodity movements. Political risks made investors reluctant to invest abroad ; risk also affected saving and was therefore much too important to ignore. Finally, there was the influence of chance. As Dr. Savosnick had said in an earlier discussion, some Swedish goods were exported largely by accident, for example, ball-bearings or telephones. Some people did not believe that the location of firms was entirely rational. He would prefer to say that chance elements came in.

Which particular combination of models would be required in a particular situation would depend on the character of the problem to be studied. However, he thought that the marginal utility of our efforts would be greater if we discussed some of the models he had just suggested, rather than continuing to discuss the comparative cost and factor proportions models. They had now been discussed at such length that the marginal return had fallen considerably — in some cases even below zero. He thought that one reason why Professor Johnson's paper was important was that it demonstrated a method by which we could deal with the very important problems of taxation.

Sir Roy Harrod thought there was still a good deal of work to be done on the factor proportions analysis. That theory was not yet in its perfect state, though he agreed that work should be done on the other models mentioned by Professor Ohlin as well. He felt that the great weakness in factor proportions models was the general reliance on the two-factor, two-commodity approach. It was absolutely essential to use at least three factors, one of which should be a specific factor. The two-factor, two-commodity model should have been struck a fatal blow by Paul Samuelson's demonstration that it led either to factor price equalization or to total specialization. Both were unacceptable conclusions, and he did not think that one got round them by introducing monopoly or transport costs. A third factor was needed. He submitted that Professor Johnson's analysis was marred by the two-commodity approach and would like to make some specific additions to the Johnson paper which would show what he meant.

First, on page 100, line 19, he would add after the words 'the relative price of the factor used relatively intensively in the industry whose technique has improved must rise' the words 'unless the improvement saved the intensive factor, in which case the price of the other factor *might* rise'. Since we were economizing on one factor, it seemed logical to argue that this would result in that factor becoming more abundant and in its price falling. Yet in Professor Johnson's model the price of this factor must rise, in order that relative costs should return to equality with the international price ratio. This implied a rise in the price of the good made with the intensively used factor.

He would then proceed to add on page 101, line 6, after the words 'substitution against that factor in both industries' the words 'unless the improvement saves on the intensive factor, in which case there *may* be substitution of the saved factor in the other industries', and in line 8 omit the words 'or intensive-factor-saving'. He would argue that because the amount of factor used had been reduced, its price would fall and therefore more of it could be employed in *both* industries. Professor Johnson, however, had to hold that the price could not fall, because if it did, one could never return to the international price ratio. Professor Johnson had to allow for a rise in the price of the saved factor, not because supply and demand analysis called for a rise, but because the inevitable end result that Professor Johnson had to achieve required it.

The whole analysis would be transformed, however, if a third factor were introduced. One could adapt the price relationship fairly easily between the three factors. He would therefore add in respect of page 101, that the previous amendment entailed that the propositions in the last eleven lines of the first paragraph held only if the improvement was neutral, or, in the event of its being intensive-factor-saving, if the price of that factor was none the less rising. In other words, the price of the factor *could* rise but need not. The words 'may be' were important because whether or not the price rose depended on the production function and on the third factor. He would not carry his amendments any further. The point was that if one proceeded on the lines he had suggested, considerable changes in the ensuing argument would be required.

Professor Johnson agreed with Sir Roy that the introduction of a third specific factor would lead to different results. Nevertheless, it would also introduce relationships of complementarity and substitution, and one would have to make specific assumptions about the production function, because different combinations of relationships among the three factors would be possible. He agreed with Sir Roy's general point, but insisted that a third factor analysis would require explicit mathematical treatment.

Nevertheless, he was still puzzled. Was Sir Roy's third factor limitational? For example, was a quantity of raw material necessarily required for each unit of product? Or could it be substituted for other factors; and could it be employed in the other industry? He had previously used an analysis introducing a specific factor, but one then really needed to use mathematics.

Sir Roy Harrod agreed on the need for mathematics, but stressed that in his suggested amendments he had only used the word 'may' in contrast to Professor Johnson's 'must'.

Professor Johnson agreed with this but pointed out that there was nothing to prevent the innovation being intensive factor using.

Sir Roy Harrod did not agree, holding that one had to get rid of the idea that whether the innovation was factor-saving or factor-using, one could measure factor intensity in terms of two general factors, regardless of the nature of the third. He had assumed that this third factor was specific, but not fixed in quantity.

Professor Johnson contended that once one introduced a third factor, Sir Roy's statement might not be accurate. Even if the innovation used more of the intensive factor, the price of the other factor might rise. He wanted to quarrel with the phrase 'unless the improvement saves the intensive factor'. The form of Sir Roy's argument implied that the fact that the improvement saved the intensive factor was crucial, but once one had three factors one could not base the argument on this one characteristic. Professor Johnson challenged Sir Roy to produce the mathematical analysis which even Sir Roy agreed was necessary in dealing with the three-factor case.

Professor Byé admired the precision of both parts of the paper, but did not think Professor Johnson's method of analysis was the best for our particular objective. We needed a theory of international specialization to explain facts such as those set out by Chenery in the recent *American Economic Review* article. He wanted to show how some of the hypotheses which were essential for Professor Johnson's results reduced the practical application of the paper very considerably.

Because he used comparative statics, Professor Johnson had to compare the situation before and after technical change occurred. Discussions of welfare economics had shown that comparative statics could not show the collective benefit accruing from such a change purely from an economic point of view. For Professor Johnson, improvements in the productivity of factors were only a complication to be added after the main analysis had been completed.

Professor Byé suggested that in dynamics such things were not separate complications, but essential parts of the theory. It was true that we now all knew that all innovations required additional capital. It was only *ex post facto* that we could say whether they were capital-saving or not. He therefore thought that there was an ambiguity in the notion of capital-saving or capital-using innovation. One could not say that, say, an innovation was capital-saving or capital-using if it required more or less capital. All innovations required more capital when they were introduced and only afterwards could one see whether or not they had saved capital. If one took a developing country like the U.K. in 1800, capital in textiles was provided out of profits earned from Indian sales. Innovation was only possible because of this capital. Even inventions like the spinning jenny would have remained unused if such capital had not been available. In new countries where innovation was mainly in export crops, much rather than little capital would be needed. In Brazil, for example, one had the cycle moving from the production of gold to wool to cotton to rubber to coffee. The production of each succeeding commodity was financed by profits from the preceding one.

As for the theory of factor proportions, unless one applied the Leontief form, which seemed to lead to paradoxical results, the factor proportions theory required homogeneous production functions in each country. If one assumed that production functions changed within the country in question, but not in other countries, then the theory would be modified. In the absence of a change in production functions, one would always have to allow for a change in demand. There was not just one pattern of innovation. Innovations could be major or minor, autonomous or induced, creative or defensive. With major innovations involving a new product like automobiles or man-made fibres, one could not base one's argument on existing diagrams, indifference maps and so on, since these had been established to deal with an unchanged situation.

In a dynamic situation where the production possibilities curve shifted, this meant a change in demand. For example, we knew quite well that at different levels of income one would get a different pattern of expenditure. An innovation would first change demand; later induce further changes in demand. All innovations not only changed technical production conditions, but also demand. For example, the development of automobiles in the U.S. brought a demand for petrol; the development of man-made fibres diminished the demand for cotton. This led to a point of terminology. Professor Byé pointed out that a new product could only lead to a change in the commodity terms of trade and not to one in the factorial terms of trade. Professor Byé also thought that innovation was incompatible with unchanged conditions of competition, since it either created rents for some producers or led to monopoly. He also thought that innovation was incompatible with unchanging time-horizons: the horizon of the small firm would be very different from that of a big one. He did not think that one could talk of an innovation being biased towards exports or imports. What did happen would depend on demand conditions and not on a forecast of an increase or decrease of imports. It was impossible to forecast, for example, a permanent dollar gap, because one must allow for some mobility of capital. He recalled all Machlup had said on the foreign trade multiplier, namely that, if such a gap occurred, it must be because foreign currency had been sterilized.

Professor Haberler thought this was a brilliant exercise in taxonomy which Professor Meade would be happy to read. Professor Johnson needed defending from Professor Byé, who said that traditional economic theory was pure analysis, not testable or capable of disproof. He would repeat what he had said on Mr. Bhagwati's paper, stressing that this criticism of economic theory was unjustified. Any theory that was not pure logic or mathematics started from empirical premises — 'behaviour equations', parameters, etc. — from which it derived its conclusions. The derivation of the conclusions from the premises was a logical process not subject to empirical tests or refutation, although it must obey the canons of logical reasoning. But the assumptions as well as the conclusions derived from the assumptions could, in principle though not always in actual practice, be confronted with observed facts, and were thus subject to refutation if not verification.

The content of Professor Johnson's paper was difficult to discuss, because his was an essay in verbal mathematics. Professor Johnson had said that the difference between Sir Roy Harrod's theory and Professor Ohlin's was that the former assumed a perfectly elastic factor supply while the latter assumed an inelastic one. Was that correct? In his classic book, Professor Ohlin did discuss modifications of the theory which were necessary if the supply of some factors was more or less elastic. We should use both types of models. But broadly speaking — except perhaps in the very long run with respect to some factors — a model which assumed zero elasticity of supply of factors was much more realistic than one which assumed an infinitely elastic supply either of capital in developed countries or of labour in under-developed countries.

Mr Bhagwati was right to say that very little real dynamics existed in international trade theory. It was often said that static analysis was of no use where one was considering under-developed countries, while it might be quite useful where developed countries were concerned. This criticism of trade theory was not valid. Developed countries, too, grew and developed — often faster than under-developed countries which were now often called, euphemistically, developing countries. Fortunately, one could achieve a great deal, in analysing problems of growth and development, merely by using comparative statics.

Professor Mahr did not quite agree with Professor Johnson's analysis, which was mainly concerned with the terms of trade and factor proportions. He regarded the important effects of technical progress as being those on national income. He would distinguish here between export-biased and import-biased changes. If one had an import-biased change, imports would decline and the balance of payments improve. One should also take into account the favourable multiplier effects. However, if the change was export-biased, technical progress would mainly be in manufacturing industries, where elasticity of demand was usually more than one. This was even more true of the demand for factors. If export prices were lowered, demand would rise and the elasticity of demand was likely to be greater than one, not least because there would be greater competition in foreign markets. This was one reason why a single country reducing its prices would get a big increase in its share of foreign trade. This would improve the balance of payments. He therefore thought that Professor Johnson overstressed effects on the terms of trade, and that, if technical progress occurred, the gain of the country where the technical progress took place would be greater than the loss of any one other country.

Professor Johnson said he assumed that multiplier effects and unemployment were dealt with by fiscal or monetary policy and that the government could offset any change in demand caused by technical progress. On the other hand, he agreed with Professor Mahr that, if world income rose because of technical progress, there would be a net gain to the world as a whole on any compensation test. The question was whether this would be enjoyed by foreign countries, and whether the loss to the one country would be considered greater than the gain of those countries which did gain.

Professor Mahr contended that, while for Professor Johnson technical progress was always bad for the country which experienced it, this was not necessarily true.

Professor Johnson said that what happened depended on elasticity of supply and the problem had been analysed by Tinbergen and Meade. The elasticity of supply might be low enough to worsen the position of the country experiencing technical progress. To him, this was not the most important problem, but Professor Mahr was entitled to his own view.

Professor Sohmen suggested that, so long as one assumed a Pareto-optimum result in static analysis, one could presumably extend it to dynamics in the following way. Economic agents would not undertake measures which meant that the country would move to a worse position than without growth. If it was seen that the result of growth would be to lower certain prices too rapidly, increased production of the commodities in question would not take place.

Professor Sohmen then turned to the treatment of capital in the Heckscher-Ohlin theory. On page 104 of this paper, Professor Johnson had said that the traditional Heckscher-Ohlin model was fundamentally incapable of dealing with the role of capital in international trade theory. The factor proportion equilibrium equated rents per unit of the various factors. Whether the rate of interest was equalized in all countries depended on whether capital goods were internationally mobile. If capital goods (machines, etc.) could be traded freely, the prices of these goods would be equalized also. The equalization of both the price per unit and the rental rate per unit necessarily implied the equalization of rates of interest. This would only be prevented if capital goods could not be moved between countries.

Professor Sohmen wanted to emphasize that the assumed mobility of capital *goods* did not imply that *capital* was mobile. The latter was equivalent to an imbalance in a country's current account with the rest of the world which the former did not require at all, for capital goods could be exported in exchange for consumer goods.

Professor Johnson said that Professor Sohmen was not right about immiserizing growth, because economic agents were in competition. Where elasticities were less than infinite, this made the producers worse off than they could be in monopoly. Applied to international trade, this meant that the results were worse where producers sold in a competitive international market than if they combined. There was no guarantee that all agents together would produce the output at which they could maximize income or refrain from actions which would reduce it. Professor Sohmen was assuming that producers acted as a class.

On the trading of capital goods, Professor Johnson said that with perfectly free trade in capital goods, one would get equal factor rents. One would then need to look at other conditions as well; for example, specifying the depreciation process. In the Heckscher-Ohlin theory, one needed to know how goods were produced. One usually needed to know this in terms of quantities of inputs to be employed, and one deduced equalization of the price of inputs. To say that the rate of interest was equalized involved bringing in other conditions. It was not that one could not do this, but to do so would go beyond what he had attempted in his paper. Capital was a produced means of production, and one way to handle the problem was to regard capital as an input in the production function. Alternatively, one could proceed in terms of the rate of return, which was a money relationship and not the same as the payment for capital goods used in the production function. Professor Johnson said that he had been working on recent books in capital theory, including that of Haavelmo. Professor Meade simplified the problem in his recent book by regarding the rate of interest as an own-rate of return on a self-producing machine. He could not assume this in his own paper, and therefore needed to make use of the market process. Treating capital as a quantity of a productive agent was not the equivalent of regarding capital as a factor producing a rate of return.

Professor Sohmen did not agree on the first point with Professor Johnson. There was a high degree of friction and, under perfect competition, even if elasticity of demand was zero, this prevented many factors moving out.

Mr. Bhagwati wanted to make it explicit that under 'laissez-faire', if all profits were equalized, then there would be a conflict between national welfare and what a particular industry did.

Professor Johnson said that this could be dealt with in terms of the old point that farmers wanted a short crop. The individual would produce as much as he could, but nevertheless hoped that, since elasticity of demand was less than one, the total supply would be a small one.

Professor Sohmen replied that his arguments still held, provided there was perfect foresight. *Professor Johnson* replied that in this situation perfect foresight amounted to collusion.

Dr. Savosnick wanted to point out that Professor Johnson was now dealing with a model where there was no factor price equalization. It was therefore a model which explained both trade and factor-movements. The Ohlin model of factor price equalization assumed that technical progress and production functions were the same in all countries. Professor Johnson assumed that technical progress occurred in one country, so that demand led both to commodity trade on an exchange basis and to an import of capital and labour. If the productivity of capital and labour increased in the U.S.A., but not elsewhere, there would tend to be an import of capital and immigration of labour. At the same time, there would be an export of American techniques and ordinary commodity exchange between the U.S.A. and the rest of the world. If there were some initial obstacles to factor movements, these might be overcome by the increased stimulus to factor movements given by the technical progress.

Dr. Savosnick said that in 1959 Professor Johnson had dealt with some other related problems in his *Manchester School* article. He had allowed for different scales of preference and tastes for capitalists and workers.

For Professor Johnson, technical progress meant a change in income-distribution and returns to factors. If one assumed different sets of indifference curves for different kinds of factor owners, and took into account the changes in income-distribution which would follow from a technological change and from a change in the production structure, one would overcome the objection put forward by Professor Byé to the use of indifference curves. Dr. Savosnick pointed out that Professor Johnson could also have dealt with a situation where one had technical progress in all factors or only in one of them, and that such slight changes in the assumptions would make important differences to the conclusions.

Professor Mikesell commended the statement on page 112 that 'instead of being firmly grounded in stable and enduring characteristics of national economies — inherent cost differences, as in the Ricardian model, or differences in factor endowments, as in the Heckscher-Ohlin model —

comparative advantage is the evolving consequence of the dynamics of technical progress, capital accumulation, and population increase, and their diffusion through the world economy'. This raised the problem not only of evolution, but also of interdependence. He was reminded of the statement by Hirschman in his *Strategy of Economic Development* where it was suggested that countries developed comparative advantages in what they imported. He thought there was some truth in this and that it was amplified in Professor Johnson's paper.

On future trends in trade in industrial production, Professor Mikesell thought there might be a tendency to substitute movements of capital, technology and entrepreneurship for movements of commodities. He wondered whether one day movements of ideas, techniques and skills would largely replace movements of goods. He felt that more and more exports of industrial products would take the form of new products, or of products of new processes developed in a particular country; but that after a time these commodities would be produced abroad as a consequence of the transfer of technique. Their place would be taken by other products representing new innovations.

Professor Neumark said he had been drawn by Professor Ohlin. He had recently been taking part in an EEC study of the effects of taxation on foreign trade. As Professor Ohlin said, discussions of international trade theory and policy now often argued as though there were no taxes at all. However, international trade theorists had always had something to say about customs and excise duties, but not about direct taxes, which they tended to leave aside.

In the EEC committee, the question being considered was whether there could be different repercussions on the movements of people, goods and capital from direct, as opposed to indirect, taxes. It had also considered whether the general level of taxation had a direct effect on international capital movements, etc. This was an important question for members of EEC, because the difference in the percentage of G.N.P. going on taxation and social insurance contributions varied from 23 per cent in Belgium to about 32 per cent in France and Germany in 1958. The committee had concluded that there was no serious distortion effect upon international trade from these different levels of taxation. On the other hand they did think that the way in which the tax revenue was used had important effects.

Probably the structure of taxation also affected international activity. For example, in Germany and the Netherlands taxes on income and capital represented more than 50 per cent of total taxation; they represented only 36 per cent in France and 27 per cent in Italy. All depended on whether the effects of taxation on movements of capital were important. Marshall had held more than a century ago that commodity taxes could be shifted, but that income taxes could not. Recently, there had been much discussion of this proposition, but now most economists agreed that there was a difference between income taxes and commodity or turnover taxes. However, even if one agreed that income taxes did not affect prices very much, one had to admit that the method of depreciation of capital assets, the fiscal treatment of losses, etc., were very important. So, in comparing *effective* rises in taxation, one had to allow for stock valuation, depreciation, etc.

We knew that nowadays all countries tried through their tax systems to favour saving and innovation, but the degree of differentiation and variation between countries was very great.

Professor Gudin felt that the main interest of Professor Johnson's paper for an economist from an under-developed country was in the benefits derived from technical progress. These might go to consumers, to entrepreneurs or to workers. Professor Gudin suggested, with all deference to the economists from the U.S.S.R., that the U.S.A. represented the only real example of a dictatorship of the proletariat. In the U.S.A. the benefits from technical progress were absorbed by the workers, so that under-developed countries did not benefit from lower prices in America resulting from better productivity.

Furthermore, the tendency in the U.S.A. seemed to be that of entrepreneurs adding a margin to their prices in order to provide capital for extensions instead of obtaining it from the capital market. This again raised prices. Professor Gudin thought difficulties in U.S. balance of payments might be related to these facts.

Sir Donald MacDougall drew attention to the point that Professor Johnson's model assumed that the balance of payments looked after itself, and therefore ruled out a crucial question in advance. For a balance of payments deficit was less tractable than he implied. Sir Donald said that, having spent the last year in the U.K. and India, he might be over-impressed with balance of payments difficulties. But these could have a serious effect on production and growth, by leading to government policies to restrain demand, as in the U.K., or by causing shortages of imported supplies which created bottlenecks, as in India. The adverse effects of balance of payments difficulties on the national income could be considerably more serious than those of worsening terms of trade.

Professor Johnson's analysis might suggest that one should encourage technical progress in import-competing rather than in exporting industries. But, if there were balance of payments difficulties, one would welcome technical progress in both types of industry — in internationally traded goods generally rather than in non-traded goods. This once again illustrated the need for a theory which allowed for the latter type of good.

Sir Donald recognized the necessity, in any analysis, to deal with one problem at a time, but he would like a more integrated theory which recognized that something which was bad for the terms of trade might be good for the balance of payments and for the economic welfare of the country.

Professor Robinson wanted to discuss changes of technique and comparative advantage. He wondered if Professor Johnson was not a little too agnostic in what he said about export- and import-biased invention and thought there was some asymmetry between backward and advanced countries. He agreed with all that Professor Johnson said about developed areas, where technical progress depended on advancing knowledge within the country in question. In the under-developed areas, however, there was a stock of techniques which could probably be transmitted more by entrepreneurs than by research. Perhaps one should think in terms of adapting that stock of technique to local use in import-saving industries. Since most under-developed areas were doing this, he presumed that there was an import-saving bias in this kind of technical progress.

On page 112 of his paper, Professor Johnson said that 'there is no reliable presumption as to whether continuing technical progress will tend over the long run to increase or decrease comparative cost differences'. Professor Robinson did not think this was true, because there was both this process of the invention of new techniques and the question of the speed of transfer of techniques between countries. He thought the speed of transfer was increasing as time went on, and it was important to discover the reason why countries had increasing ratios of foreign trade to national income over a given period, followed by a fall. The U.K., for example, had reached a peak in this ratio in the 1870s and 1880s since when it had fallen. Perhaps the explanation was the degree of industrial leadership which Britain had shown in the nineteenth century; this had been much more permanent than one could possibly hope for nowadays.

Professor Kindleberger commented that this was precisely what Professor Johnson said briefly in his next sentence.

Professor Johnson replied he had been thinking of a country sitting tight on technology, its monopoly position being undermined by the international transmission of technical change. He agreed that one could give no general rule on the ratio of trade to income, because this ratio did rise and fall from time to time and there was no general presumption one way or the other. An important question was how important the transmission of technology would be compared with invention and natural advantage within the country itself.

Dr. Savosnick said that at the end of Professor Johnson's paper came the statement that 'Various reasons have been suggested, however, for believing that in the long run no country is likely to enjoy increasing gains from trade at the expense of its trading partners, since such gains are likely to be undermined by the development or transmission of countervailing technical change'. Professor Johnson's model was concerned with only two countries and he had himself found that with three countries one got a situation where it was perfectly conceivable, and even likely, that one country might be lagging continually behind a competitive country with rapid technical progress. This would cause a lasting structural change and would be a very painful process. The lagging country would lose its markets in third countries and also suffer from worsened terms of trade.

A second point was whether technical progress made sense without rapid capital accumulation. It seemed that a rich country which was rapidly accumulating capital had a greater opportunity to implement technical change than a poor and laggard country. It was therefore quite possible that Myrdal was right in his theory that the rich countries would get progressively richer and the poor relatively poorer over a long period.

Professor Johnson replied to the discussion. He did not disagree very greatly with what Professor Ohlin had said. He might have introduced the variable factor too quickly, but had tried to show what would happen if, instead of taking a fixed supply of a factor, one allowed it to alter. He had therefore chosen two alternatives for advanced and under-developed areas and this gave the essence of his results.

On methodology, Sir Donald MacDougall had criticized his assumptions about the balance of payments. He had not assumed that the balance of payments would look after itself, but that it depended on a correct balance between aggregate demand and aggregate supply. This was not the central problem of technical change, and he had therefore not considered it an important point in the analysis. Professor Johnson said that it was conceivable that this was a wrong-headed attitude, but that nevertheless it was the one he had taken.

Professor Johnson said that Mr. Bhagwati had partially answered the suggestion that we needed a large number of models. There was obviously a delicate line between having a large number of models covering a great number of situations, and producing a model which showed which factors were most relevant. As for his emphasis on technical progress, this was consistent with some of the models which Professor Ohlin had suggested. For example, economies of scale and technical progress went together very well. Taxation was difficult to relate to technical change, but it had a big influence, especially on capital movements. Professor Johnson thought that the structure of tariffs was important and that a great deal of work remained to be done on it. We talked of tariffs a great deal without having a satisfactory analysis of the influence of economic policy on international trade.

Professor Johnson said there was a basic difference between Professor Byé and himself on the use of economic theory. Professor Byé was really saying that he had not dealt with all aspects of the problem of technical change. This was not the purpose of economic analysis ; a theory was not intended to cover every aspect of a problem but to abstract all the relevant elements. What comparative statics was concerned with was discovering which forces were at work, and no economist since Schumpeter had suggested that it could do any more than discover which forces were at work. Professor Johnson agreed that capital was probably needed when technical change took place, but he did not think that this could be accepted as a universal principle. He was not particularly interested in whether one had an initial burst of investment to bring in an innovation. If one were dealing with the transitional effects of innovation, the question of investment and of the balance of payments would be very important, but this would be a minor part of a full analysis. Finally, Professor Johnson asked Professor Gudin why he thought it was that technical progress led to higher wages in the U.S. and nowhere else. The question was not what technical progress did, but why it did it.

THE DISCUSSION OF THE PAPER BY
SIR ROY HARROD

Dr. Patel introduced the paper saying that the central question Sir Roy dealt with was obviously very important. There was general agreement that the less-developed countries should be helped to reach the point of what had come to be known as the take-off. The questions Sir Roy raised in his paper were how long and how costly the process of assisted take-off would be and under what conditions it would succeed. Though Sir Roy gave several models in his paper, he was perhaps particularly concerned with model *A*. Dr. Patel therefore concentrated on it.

This model showed that it was possible for an under-developed country to reach the point of self-sustaining growth over a period of twenty years. In the process, savings would have to increase from about 5 to 20 per cent of national income and foreign capital equal to about four times the initial income would have to be provided. On this basis, total national income could be trebled over the twenty-year period. While the task of reaching the point of take-off over a reasonable period of time was thus manageable, it would require strict control over increases in consumption and a sizeable inflow of foreign capital.

The total amount of foreign capital required under Sir Roy's model was obviously large and the model implied that something like £5000 million per annum would be required for all under-developed areas. In view of the largeness of this figure it was no merely academic question to inquire whether Sir Roy's model, and the conclusions based upon it, were realistic. Dr. Patel had therefore tried to compare Sir Roy's Scheme *A* with the assumptions in India's Third Five Year Plan which sought to give a model of economic development in India over the twenty-five years since the beginning of the First Five Year Plan in 1951. Although the assumptions in India's third plan were not always explicit, a rough comparison with Sir Roy's model was possible.

Broadly speaking, while there were surprising similarities between Sir Roy's model and India's plans, there were also some important differences. The main similarity was that India also hoped to achieve self-sustaining growth within roughly twenty years. Over the period, the rate of saving was expected to increase from 5 to almost 20 per cent of national income and total national income was expected to treble, as in Sir Roy's model. Another, rather surprising, similarity was that, like Sir Roy Harrod in Scheme *A*, India had allowed (at least for the third and the fourth plan periods) an increase of 4 per cent per annum in total consumption to take care of population growth and the minimum rise in consumption required to stimulate incentive. There was a minor difference in that Sir Roy had allowed for a deterioration in terms of trade, whereas India had not. However, Sir Roy had assumed a somewhat slower rate of growth in population. The over-all 'seepage' of 4 per cent per annum through increased consumption was the same in both the cases.

Despite these similarities, there was one major difference. While Sir Roy had concluded that the amount of foreign capital required for the take-off would be four times the initial level of income, it was hoped in India that the external capital needed for this purpose would not be significantly greater than the initial income. It was, therefore, of practical importance to try to discover why this important difference arose.

This difference between the two schemes seemed to result mainly from three factors : one methodological and two substantive. Though Sir Roy assumed a 5 per cent rate of domestic saving before the beginning of assisted take-off, this was not reflected in the starting-point of his model because he assumed a two-year time-lag between investment and the resultant income. In the first year of his model all the investment required was assumed to be financed by an inflow of foreign capital. In reality, one would expect that the savings and investment in the years before the initial year would provide some domestic resources in the first year of the period under consideration so that only part of the investment required in the first year would need to come from abroad. This was implicit in the Indian plans. It was difficult to say what difference would be made to Sir Roy's conclusions if the starting-point of his model were changed to take account of the effect of earlier investment in the economy, but it might be useful to rework his model with this modification.

The second difference was on the capital-output ratio. Dr. Patel thought that Sir Roy's assumption was a little awkward. Sir Roy assumed that since the capital-output ratio in developed areas was 3 : 1, this was the average ratio that the under-developed countries should reach by the time they reached the point of take-off. This required him to assume a marginal capital-output ratio higher than 3 : 1. In India, on the other hand, while the marginal capital-output ratio was assumed to increase from 1·8 : 1 initially to 3 : 1 in the latter part of the take-off period, there was no suggestion that the average capital-output ratio over the period, as a whole, should be 3 : 1. Clearly, Sir Roy's assumption required much more investment than had been assumed in India. While Dr. Patel was inclined to agree that the assumptions about capital-output ratios in the Indian plans were somewhat optimistic, Sir Roy's assumption seemed to err on the other side.

Another major difference was over the service charge on foreign capital. Sir Roy assumed a 7 per cent service charge per annum. Although at one point in Sir Roy's paper it was mentioned that the service charge included a certain amount of amortization, a closer look at his model showed that his calculations, at any rate, made no allowance for this. If, therefore, the 7 per cent figure was assumed to refer to service charges proper, this assumption was much more pessimistic than that made in India's plans. Although a precise figure for the service charge assumed in the Indian plans could not be given, it was clear that considering that a significant part of external assistance already received or expected to be received by India was in the nature of grants and loans repayable either in rupees or at low rates of interest, the average service charge on the total inflow of capital in India would certainly be substantially lower than 7 per cent.

Dr. Patel explained that his main purpose in contrasting Sir Roy's model with India's plans was not to suggest that the assumptions underlying the latter were more realistic. Perhaps the truth lay somewhere between Sir Roy's conclusions and India's aspirations. The important point, however, was that the requirements for foreign aid, as suggested by Sir Roy's paper, were much larger than those assumed at present either in India or in aid-giving countries generally. Even if Sir Roy's conclusions were modified somewhat, much would need to be done to augment the present flow of capital to the developing countries. Dr. Patel did not share Sir Roy's judgement that the actual requirements for aid might be less than his model implied in view of the fact that not all under-developed countries had the absorptive capacity needed to reach the point of take-off over the next twenty years. Since the giving of aid was motivated essentially by political rather than economic considerations, it would not be possible to apportion available funds for assistance among the developing countries strictly in accordance with their absorptive capacity. If the countries which were well on the way to take-off were to be given all the aid that they could usefully absorb, the total requirements for external assistance would necessarily have to exceed the amounts that would be required if assistance were to be distributed strictly on the basis of absorptive capacity. In view of this, it was especially important to give more attention to the terms on which foreign aid was supplied.

The question was not simply that of keeping the service charges low in order to reduce the total amount of assistance required during the period of assisted take-off. There was also the fact that service charges of the order shown by Sir Roy would require an altogether unmanageable increase in the exports of the developing countries. On a quick calculation, it would appear that under Sir Roy's model, India, for example, would need to increase her exports ninefold over a period of twenty years. This was clearly unmanageable. In this connection, Dr. Patel drew attention to Professor Lundberg's remark that an extraordinary degree of statesmanship in developed countries would be required if the exports of the developing countries were to increase satisfactorily. Professor Kitamura had suggested that some under-developed areas might be able to achieve a surplus with other under-developed areas which in turn could have a surplus with the industrialized countries. Since the service charges, however, had in the main to be paid to industrialized countries, Dr. Patel saw no escape from the necessity of a rapid increase in the exports of the developing countries as a group to the industrialized countries. There was little point in adding to the difficulty of this problem by allowing a heavy burden of service charges to grow.

If the argument was that private foreign capital could not move without the expectation of a satisfactory reward, we should have to accept a smaller role for private foreign capital. If the burden of service charges were not kept low, a period of at least ten years would probably be required after one reached the point of take-off. During this period the developing countries would still need to borrow abroad in order to meet service charges. Sir Roy had rightly emphasized that the great danger in prolonged reliance on foreign capital was that, beyond a certain point, the ownership of a country's capital assets by foreigners would be intolerable. The escape from this lay in keeping service charges low from the outset and in not emphasizing too much the role of private foreign capital.

Finally, Dr. Patel wished to draw attention to the many valuable incidental comments Sir Roy had made in his paper on the general problem of development. He referred in this connection to Sir Roy's emphasis on the importance of factors other than capital in stimulating development. Sir Roy's main thesis about the extremely narrow margin that separated the chances of success from those of failure in enabling the developing countries to reach the point of take-off was also undoubtedly sound. There was one point, however, on which he found it difficult to agree with Sir Roy. Sir Roy had suggested that developing countries should concentrate on their export industries. While Dr. Patel had no objection to emphasizing the importance of exports, he doubted whether Sir Roy's reasons for this emphasis were correct. If the emphasis on exports was contrasted with the emphasis on import-substitution, it should not be forgotten that comparative advantage might dictate reducing the reliance on imports as well as for increasing exports. The only general rule one could give was that countries should concentrate on producing those commodities in the production of which they would have a comparative advantage. Whether this implied emphasis on exports or on import-substitution was a question of fact rather than of theoretical presumption.

Professor Johnson had reworked the table for Sir Roy's Scheme *A*.[1]

[1] The following table gives Professor Johnson's recalculation of Sir Roy Harrod's Scheme *A*. The assumptions are the same as Sir Roy Harrod's except that : (*a*) Allowance is made for the fact that, before the crash programme, net saving is going on and the economy is growing, though slowly. It is assumed

Years	Income (i)	Income not available for capital formation (ii)	Amortization less replacement expenditures (iii)	Service charges on foreign borrowing (iv)	Domestically available for capital formation, viz. (i) − (ii) + (iii) − (iv) (v)	Capital stock (excluding land) (vi)	Saving required (vii)	Foreign borrowing required, viz. (vii) − (v). Borrowing : − repayment : + (viii)	Accumulated foreign borrowing (ix)
0	97·5	92·6	—	—	4·9	200·0	19·6	−14·7	−14·7
1	100·0	95·0	0·0	1·0	4·0	219·6	21·0	−17·0	−31·7
10	164·0	137·2	7·4	10·9	23·3	456·1	34·3	−11·0	−166·8
15	215·8	168·0	8·8	13·8	42·8	647·6	45·1	−2·3	−198·9
20	283·9	205·4	10·5	12·2	76·8	900·0	60·0	+16·8	−157·2

As the table stood, it ignored savings before period 1. He had therefore constructed his own table to show what happened if saving in period 1 was allowed to finance part of investment. One could then assume that 100·5, rather than 104·5, was required consumption.

Sir Roy Harrod said that he had begun by producing tables similar to Professor Johnson's but had scrapped these because they allowed no time for the construction of capital assets. This allowed one to have a rise in income in year 1. He had then decided that this was too simple a model and would be severely criticized by members of the Round Table. He had therefore scrapped the table which Professor Johnson now wanted.

Professor Johnson explained that all he wanted to do was to assume that growth was continuing at its own slow rate to begin with. The point was that when one made his two changes and allowed for previous saving, one reached a maximum amount of foreign borrowing of about 200 units in period 15, after which foreign borrowing fell. One therefore had not Sir Roy's 4 : 1 ratio between foreign borrowing and initial income, but a maximum 2 : 1 ratio which was closer to the figures of the Indian plan. The only significance of what he had done was that it showed that the timing affected the results. For there was a cumulation of initial borrowing because of service charges.

Sir Roy Harrod was still puzzled about what Professor Johnson had done. He had deducted 5 units for initial saving throughout his model. He admitted that there was an anomaly over what happened in year 0 and year 1, but did not see how Professor Johnson's change made such a difference.

Professor Gudin said that Sir Roy had rendered an important service by emphasizing the predominant importance of the human element — of the human 'cadres' for economic development. Capital would always flow to the countries where the capable human beings were available.

that the growth rate initially is $2\frac{1}{2}$ per cent, corresponding to a savings ratio of 5 per cent and a capital-output ratio of 2 : 1. (This is an approximation, since the time-lags in Harrod's model reduce the growth rate slightly below $2\frac{1}{2}$ per cent.) (b) The 4 per cent growth rate of income not available for capital formation is assumed to start simultaneously with the 5·6 growth rate of income entailed in the crash programme, instead of a year earlier as in Sir Roy Harrod's model.

Sir Roy Harrod has made the following written reply :

'As regards (a), I stated that I assumed some moderate growth rate (including a percentage of saving varying in the tables — 5 per cent in A) prior to the crash programme. The contribution by this 5 per cent saving out of initial income occurs yearly in my tables throughout the twenty years. But I ought to have made some allowance for domestic saving in year 0. This once-over omission can only make a slight difference to the final result.

'As regards (b), in my preparatory work for the Conference I got out a series of tables allowing the income resulting from the crash programme to grow *simultaneously* with the expedited charges on income as specified in column (ii), as in Professor Johnson's table. I feared, however, that this would expose one to the charge of having ignored the gestation period in capital formation. Wanting to recommend assisted take-off, I felt that I must be especially on my guard against making things look easier than they in fact are. I accordingly scrapped all these tables. I still feel that I was right to do so.

The surprisingly large difference made by this change of assumption was rightly explained by Professor Johnson as due to the high gearing incurred in the model, including the effect of foreign service charges.'

Where Professor Gudin did not find himself much in agreement with Sir Roy was when he said (on page 116) that 'foreign borrowing should be regarded as a burden on the balance of payments'. For the borrowed capital was used to increase exports, or to reduce imports, or to raise domestic production.

In the two first cases, the balance of payments would be taken care of and, in the third, *if there was no inflation* the part of monetary purchasing power absorbed by the new domestic production would reduce the demand for imports, as Alfred Kahn had clearly demonstrated.

Professor Gudin said further that he did not see any danger in the increase of the flow of foreign capital into the country. If the country's income grew at the same pace, the *proportion* of borrowing remained the same, and if it did not grow, and the country did not develop, foreign capital would simply not be forthcoming.

A country that borrowed money and did not default, would, of course, always pay back more than it received, because of interest. But if the money was productively invested, the rise of output resulting from investment would provide for that. Furthermore, if the borrowing country was a 'good risk', the increment in the inflow of foreign investment would largely compensate for the outflow in respect of interest. The fact that increased foreign investment and home prosperity run together dissipated any real danger of disequilibrium.

Professor James said that he wanted to congratulate Sir Roy Harrod on an interesting and realistic paper. He would like to ask one question : at the end of the paper, Sir Roy proposed a levy on profits and on foreign capital, to be used by a national investment bank. He thought that such a levy would be easier to operate if made on a multilateral basis. When a big foreign company had a monopoly and a large investment in a particular country, it was often keen to reduce reinvestment in the country where it operated. However, he thought that such companies were perfectly prepared to make loans either to the country in question or to others, to help them to advance and to increase prosperity in the particular country. He thought that one should try to organize this system internationally, thereby obtaining capital for growth.

Professor Gudin pointed out that in some countries there was a differential tax which was heavier on profits which were remitted than on profits which remained within the country.

Professor Delivanis said Sir Roy Harrod was perfectly right in stressing that a shortage of capital was not always the most important factor limiting growth in under-developed countries. Many people now took this view and it would be a common opinion in the near future. He would like to recall that before 1939 it was generally accepted that inflation was unavoidable unless a growth programme could be completely financed from abroad. This view had been abandoned since the IBRD had met all spending outside the borrowing country. Sir Roy was right to insist on the importance of amortization funds for economic development. In this particular situation they were very important, since in under-developed economies those concerned were uncertain about the future, afraid of nationalization and in the habit of making big speculative profits.

He would like to add how much he agreed with Sir Roy's provision for an increase in consumption as the economy grew. Professor Vakil's argument in the opposite direction was wrong, as had been shown by setbacks in Bulgaria and Yugoslavia, particularly in the agricultural sector where those concerned had not experienced an improvement in living conditions and were therefore uninterested in increasing output and improving efficiency.

He could not accept Sir Roy's contention that excessive saving was the cause of the rather low growth rates in some countries, unless by saving he meant hoarding. He also found Sir Roy rather unjust to the monetary authorities of mature countries, suggesting that plans for growth would reduce their ability to hold down growth by pursuing unduly restrictive policies in order to avoid inflation or balance of payments difficulties. Both these latter could be pernicious phenomena, especially if people had considerable experience of inflation. He thought this was shown by the example of Germany in the 1930s and of the U.K. since 1945 except, of course, where exchange control was very efficient.

He would finish with a further argument in favour of encouraging those industries in under-developed countries which competed with imports. This was the inability of exporters to conquer and hold new markets. Finally, he thought that long-term purchase contracts for increasing exports were only effective if production was in the hands of a few large firms and administration was neither inefficient nor corrupt.

Mr. Lamfalussy suggested that it would be useful to include some explicit assumptions about the time-pattern of exports and imports. We had the figure which Sir Roy gave for the net balance of payments deficit, but this was not sufficient, particularly if we had to make a choice about the distribution of investment between industries. Since Sir Roy might be thought to favour investment in import-replacing industries, Mr. Lamfalussy thought that it was necessary to trace the pattern of exports and imports more explicitly. Perhaps one should introduce an import function into the model. Mr. Lamfalussy also thought that the difference between Sir Roy and Professor Johnson lay in the fact that Professor Johnson was assuming that the economy was already growing without the foreign borrowing. After Sir Roy's crash programme, growth became much more rapid.

Professor Johnson agreed. His assumption of net saving implied that the economy was already growing.

Professor Robinson said that after the IEA's Take-off Conference, he was interested in the relation between Sir Roy's model and the kind of take-off model discussed in the work of Professor Rostow and other economic historians. His impression was that the historians were thinking in terms of a much longer time-scale. The general impression seemed to be that the period of preconditioning would take about fifteen years and required considerable investment in infra-structure. The subsequent take-off process could take at least twenty years, and he thought that Sir Roy's crash programme was much too short to allow the development of co-operating factors of production. If Sir Roy was right in his assumption that it was the co-operating factors which were important, then the period was much too short. A second puzzle was why one never approached the Arthur Lewis net savings ratio of 10 per cent of net income.

Sir Roy Harrod pointed out that in Scheme *A* marginal saving increased all the time ; it was unlike some models, which assumed constant marginal saving.

Professor Kindleberger pointed out that in year 21 Sir Roy's scheme assumed a savings ratio of 20 per cent. He did not think that this was a realistic figure for a country like India. Indeed, this kind of representation was one of the main failings of all models of this kind. It was always necessary to make some realistic assumptions about the relationship between a rise in income and the effect on the balance of payments. If there were extra productive resources available, it was important to know how these were used and whether they went into exports or domestic production. As for the question of repayment, Professor Rosenstein-Rodan, in the appendix to *A Proposal : Key to United States Economic Foreign Policy* by Professors Millikan and Rostow, had worked out a model where repayments began after thirteen years. Unfortunately, it was easy to show in this kind of model that after about thirty years one country could own the whole of the world !

Sir Roy Harrod said he would be much more sceptical of his model if it had assumed a 20 per cent savings ratio throughout. While this did not seem to be an unreasonable savings proportion at the end of the process, it might well be unrealistically high, and it was perfectly possible to reduce it a little.

Professor Johnson pointed out that Professor Kindleberger had put his finger on the sensitivity of the model. There were two explosive forces. One was the growth of income in excess of consumption ; the other was the rapid accumulation of debt. After fifteen to twenty years, a small change swung the balance very sharply.

Professor Neumark recalled the stress on human resources in Sir Roy Harrod's paper. The proposal for a levy on foreign companies suggested to him that, if this was to be used for investment in the under-developed area it would be most valuable if it were partly invested in improving the efficiency of human capital. No one seemed to have suggested the possibility of investment in civil servants. In many under-developed countries, the standards set by civil servants were very low, both intellectually and morally. He thought there was a strong correlation between the salary levels and the honesty of civil servants. This was particularly pertinent in times of inflation, which made otherwise low salaries quite insufficient. An aggravating factor was that income taxation was much more effective for civil servants, who had tax deducted at source, than for independent business men, who found it much easier to avoid taxes. He would therefore suggest using some foreign aid to under-developed areas to raise the salaries of civil servants.

Mr. Liesner wanted a small change which would make the amount suggested for total aid more realistic. One ought to define more closely what the goal of development aid was. He thought that the aim was to get the under-developed areas in thirty to fifty years to the kind of standard of living which developed areas had at present. A model which studied this problem was contained in an article by H. Theil which had appeared in *De Economist* in 1953.[1] This was a simpler model and perhaps of the kind that Professor Kindleberger would criticize, but it did pose some of these crucial questions about the direction we were going.

Professor Weiller was grateful that Sir Roy had left aside the geo-metrical progression used in former theories. Sir Roy had assumed the need for capital to grow relatively to output only up to a ceiling level where an optimum was reached. Professor Weiller was grateful to Sir Roy for his stress on factors other than capital and for clearing up the question whether balance of payments problems would arise if growth took par-ticular forms. He thought especially of African countries which had gone just beyond the first stage of development. They were obliged to sell on a market for raw materials which was not growing fast enough. He would not therefore put all stress on exports, but would emphasize the need to make new arrangements for taking surplus exports off the 'world' market. For example, one might consider African common markets which would make regional arrangements via preferential tariffs or customs unions.

As for import substitutes, we were now back to the idea that pro-tection was not always bad. However, once a protected local industry had been built up, there would be a tendency towards trade liberaliza-tion. He did not think that the creation of home industries should be neglected, but a mere tariff would probably not stimulate the economy sufficiently.

Professor Ohlin said that Sir Roy had suggested in his introduction that a capital deficiency did not impede growth in a developed country. In one sense this appeared to imply that the marginal productivity of capital was zero. Yet Sir Roy was assuming a capital-output ratio of 3 : 1. Perhaps Sir Roy was assuming some discontinuity in the marginal pro-ductivity of capital curve. It then seemed that the developed countries would advance just as rapidly (assuming no excess of savings) if they exported more of their capital. Or perhaps Sir Roy meant that the marginal productivity of capital was considerable if we reduced investment, but zero if we raised it. He wondered whether it really *was* true, as this implied, that the marginal productivity of capital curve in advanced countries had a kink in it, and if so what forces and systems had led us to produce at the point where this kink was. Professor Ohlin suggested that developed countries often did lack capital and that if, for example, more houses could be built in Sweden, labour would become more mobile.

[1] An English version appeared in *International Economic Papers*, No. 10.

Professor Robinson wondered whether Sir Roy's remarks about the greater importance of co-operative factors were intended to apply to both developed and under-developed countries.

Sir Roy Harrod replied that he was not implying that the marginal productivity of capital in developed areas was zero, but only that if these countries invested more but did not also increase the supply of other factors, there would be a rapid fall in marginal returns. It was not that marginal productivity was currently zero, but that without more co-operating factors, any further increase in the rate of investment would rapidly push returns down to zero.

As for the question whether developed areas would advance more rapidly if they exported more capital goods, he thought that the answer was, yes. There was a considerable margin of unused resources in the U.S.A. and, more moderately, in the U.K. Germany was probably more fully extended and was certainly growing rapidly. But some part of the German effort was being devoted to selling goods in exchange for gold or, more recently, dollars. She would certainly benefit the world as a whole by acquiring less foreign exchange and investing more overseas.

Professor Johnson pointed out that Sir Roy was working in terms of growth models in which the system approached an equilibrium path where the rate of growth depended on technical progress and population growth. In a sense, advanced countries had already reached a point of capital saturation not attained by under-developed areas. The theory assumed little substitutability between labour and capital. One had a rate of interest which represented an optimum rate of growth and that fixed the level of investment.

Professor Haberler inquired whether Sir Roy was contending that there were no investment opportunities in the U.S.A. and the U.K.; in other words, that capital was a free good.

Sir Roy Harrod replied that a change of heart by the authorities could raise the rate of growth in both countries to a point where there were no resources to spare. But at the moment there was excess capacity in both countries. The under-developed countries could be given more aid without reducing the rate of growth in either the U.S.A. or the U.K. below the level of the last five years.

Professor Ohlin agreed that where there was excess capacity, there were many ways of increasing activity and employment, of which this was one. He had suggested in Sweden that the OEEC should adopt a policy of making capital exports over and above any normal level to under-developed areas whenever excess capacity rose above a certain level. This would help to counter stagnation in OEEC countries and would be a useful item in a combination of methods.

Professor Ohlin agreed with Professor Neumark that we must invest to produce a stable *milieu* in under-developed areas and that efficient civil servants were necessary for this. In acquiring capital from abroad, stable administration was an important factor, since it had a big effect in reducing risk. When Sir Roy spoke of a 10 per cent worsening in the terms of trade of an industry being better than a 20 per cent tariff on its products he did not think that this was a correct measure of the loss. It was true that Sir Roy had a 50 per cent margin which was probably enough to save him, but if there was protection all round, this would raise the minimal prices of factors of production so that the loss of efficiency was only 10, 12 or 15 per cent. The remainder of the tariff was needed because protection increased factor prices.

Professor Haberler said that if there really was *general* excess capacity and *general* unemployment in the U.S.A., this was a short-run cyclical phenomenon. Such a condition, if it did not clear up by itself sufficiently fast, could be cured by various schemes of spending at home or abroad. However, the export of capital or foreign aid was still a burden because the resources transferred abroad could always be used at home. He was not saying that there should be no foreign lending or foreign aid, but he could not agree that there was no burden in sending resources abroad instead of using them at home.

Sir Roy Harrod did not altogether accept Professor Ohlin's suggestion about an OEEC policy for exporting capital during a recession. He did not think that it would be good for the receiving countries to be supplied with capital goods during a recession, but then to experience a sudden ending of this supply when the recession finished. However, he was not interested *only* in curing recessions. His real point was that the poor growth rates in the U.S.A. and the U.K. could be increased, if only demand were greater. Though there might be some difficulty in doing this in the U.K., he thought there was sufficient spare capacity in the U.S.A. It was possible to increase the rate of growth there by increasing the export of capital goods.

Dr. Olano said that he had found Sir Roy's paper both interesting and stimulating. If, as he hoped, Sir Roy's recommendations were accepted, both advanced and developing countries would benefit. He thought two points were particularly important. First, he agreed completely with Sir Roy that the main factor governing the optimum rate of investment was the growth potential of the economy. In developing countries, this depended especially on the rate at which cadres of entrepreneurs, engineers and foremen could be increased. He thought that this was absolutely fundamental. He also agreed with Sir Roy (on page 117) that the introduction of extra capital and other highly qualified factors of production could be looked upon as *fertilizing* the productivity of labour. He intended to use the expression fertilizing frequently in future.

Dr. Olano said that his experience in reviewing UN plans for technical assistance and his studies of economic growth in Latin America had convinced him that no effective results would be obtained unless technical and managerial cadres were improved and capital borrowed simultaneously. On the one hand, if technicians were trained, but there was no increase in investment, many of them would be frustrated from lack of suitable work and would migrate to developed countries. On the other hand, if capital was available, but technicians not trained, resources would be wasted.

Dr. Olano noted that Sir Roy estimated that the developing countries needed total loans of $14 billion a year. While he had not had any opportunity to make such a global calculation, an ECLA report which he had helped to prepare in 1954 put Latin-American needs at a minimum of $1 billion. A later and, he thought, rather foolish request asked for $3 billion a year. Finally, the important conference at Punta del Este in 1961 had pledged $2 billion. He thought this was the correct figure but would like to know more about how it had been calculated.

When he had worked with the United Nations, he had calculated that a fair share of technical assistance funds for Latin America would be 15 or 20 per cent of the total available. Applying this percentage to the figure of $2 billion, one got a total for foreign lending to the developing countries of $10-$13$\frac{1}{2}$ billion a year, which was practically the same as Sir Roy's.

Finally, he wanted to say that he particularly agreed with the statement that foreign borrowing should normally be regarded as imposing a long-run burden on the borrower's balance of payments and that one could not deal with the problem by progressively increasing the amount borrowed. He knew that his own country was trying very hard to expand exports and this was what Sir Roy recommended. However, there were many difficulties in exporting, particularly because of protection in the U.S.A. and in Europe. Did Sir Roy believe that if Argentina persisted in this policy of expanding exports, the U.S.A. and Europe would be prepared to increase their imports of food and raw materials?

Professor Kindleberger wanted to raise a question on the concept of absorptive capacity. Professors Millikan and Rostow suggested that this was limited, but for political reasons. His own question was where on a smooth investment demand curve, one would come to rest. He did not think that this question was settled and did not agree with those who suggested that there might be a kink in the curve. If Sir Roy suggested that other factors of production set the limit, he doubted whether one really could use an incremental capital-output ratio. It would be better to talk in terms of the marginal efficiency of capital.

Professor Tsuru wondered whether Sir Roy was assuming a 'mixed' economy. In a capitalist country a unit of capital in the hands of a private entrepreneur would have a dimension not only of a physical and monetary nature, but also of enterprise — of will power, with the by-product of bringing in foreign technicians and foremen. In other words, private capital had its own dynamism. He had been impressed by the emphasis on non-capital factors by Sir Roy, such as the need to provide incentive, but felt that he implied a mixed economy. He was sceptical of the ability of a mixed economy to provide such an incentive. What did Sir Roy assume?

He agreed with what Professor Neumark had said about the importance of an efficient civil service, but doubted whether the high salaries in the Indian civil service needed to be copied elsewhere. These salaries were, for example, almost ten times higher relatively to average incomes than was the case in the U.S.A., Japan or Latin America.

Sir Donald MacDougall did not think there was any *a priori* reason for supposing that the terms of trade would turn against the developing countries. Nevertheless, he agreed with Sir Roy that they would need a great deal of foreign capital over a long period. Sir Roy had presented several schemes for this, some of which he regarded as acceptable and others as unacceptable. On what basis did he make this choice? The answer appeared to be that he regarded a scheme as unacceptable if it required dependence on foreign borrowing on too large a scale and for too long a period, or where the foreign debt became too high a proportion of the national capital. These criteria gave certain results if one were thinking of a crash programme financed by lending at a rate of interest and if the capital had to be repaid. On the other hand, if one was thinking in terms of the international redistribution of income, the problem would be very different. Reworking Sir Roy's tables, one found that the need for aid would end much sooner if interest and capital repayments did not have to be allowed for. Sir Roy had questioned whether the developed countries could afford to lend as much as £5-10 billion per annum to under-developed countries. One had to allow for the fact that incomes in the developed countries would also be growing a great deal in the next twenty years. It followed that £5-10 billion would not represent nearly so large a proportion of their much higher incomes in the latter part of the period.

On page 134, Sir Roy asked whether the lessons learned from his macro-economic schemes could be applied on a micro-economic scale — to specific capital projects. He thought one reason why they could *not* be applied was that there were many projects where the capital equipment, once installed, lasted a long time and required little labour to operate it — for example, hydro-electric schemes. The capital-output ratio was thus very high. Yet such projects could not be rejected for this reason since they were essential to a country's development.

Dr. Savosnick said that Sir Roy Harrod emerged as a strong internationalist. He would like to suggest that Sir Roy's schemes for increasing capital might be linked with movements of labour. This was not a popular view, but he would suggest that if one took the growth of the whole world economy as one's aim, the obvious thing would be to move capital in one direction and labour in the opposite one. For example, the movement of West Indians to England had been good for both England and the West Indies. The movement of capital alone to the West Indies would probably not have been as effective.

Professor Morgan said that if one assumed a given level of employment, the granting of aid compelled a fall in the total of home consumption and investment. The assumption that development within a country could be just as fast with as without foreign aid was not necessarily true. In fact, the level of employment and the pace of price increases in the

U.S.A. since World War II had doubtless been somewhat greater with foreign aid being granted, than without it. Legislators were often more disposed to spend money on India than on Mississippi.

Professor Morgan thought Sir Roy's emphasis on co-operating factors valid and important and suggested that it was desirable to consider what kinds of factors these were. One could say that anything which raised the productivity of labour or land was investment. If one did not adopt such a catholic definition, but rather followed the standard national income-accounts concept of investment, he was forced to conclude that much of growth — probably well over half — could not be explained by increase in physical-capital-per-unit-of-labour-input. Among these other 'co-operating factors' were spending on food, medical attention and education.

Professor Kitamura returned to Professor Kindleberger's doubts on the absorptive capacity of under-developed countries. Sir Roy's model came close to assuming away absorptive capacity as a direct problem. The limitation on absorptive capacity appeared in Sir Roy's model as a low marginal productivity of capital and resulted simply from moving from a low capital supply at the beginning to a fixed capital-output ratio at the end. In many Asian countries the problem of absorbing capital was difficult and required a more direct attack than Sir Roy had suggested. Perhaps this could be introduced into the model by allowing more directly for the influence of non-capital factors. Professor Kitamura also pointed out that the 2 per cent annual increase in *per capita* consumption for which Sir Roy allowed was rather high compared with that which actually occurred in under-developed areas.

Professor Byé suggested that the use of G.N.P. in the analysis of development was often ambiguous. The export sector in an under-developed area was using foreign capital to some extent and this would add something at least to the G.N.P. of the lending country. Some of the earnings of its industry would go to foreign technicians and some would be repatriated. He therefore thought that the aim of development ought not always to be regarded as giving a maximum rate of growth of G.N.P. but should rather be looked at in terms of the standard of living of a particular part of the population.

So far as export industries were concerned, many of these were complementary and created external economies. One therefore had the paradox that while such industries might not be desirable in themselves, they had beneficial effects on other sectors of the economy. For example, it was accepted that the development of railways in the U.S.A. had helped to train engineers. Where there was disguised unemployment there was a great deal to be said for establishing textile industries for the internal market. One had to weigh the degree of protection required against the rise in employment.

Sir Roy Harrod replied to the discussion. He had been interested that the Indian plan came so close to his own model, since he had never studied the plan carefully. On the question raised by Professor Johnson, he was still puzzled over the contention that he was not allowing the 5 per cent net saving to raise capital at the beginning of the crash programme. As for the question of the time-lag, he still thought he was right. While it was true that the figures for the first year were sketchy, they could have been carried backward. In any case it seemed most sensible to allow some considerable period before new investment gave rise to new income.

Dr. Patel had pointed out that the assumed size of the capital-output ratio was important. He would like to remind Dr. Patel that in Table *D* he had assumed no change in the capital-output ratio of 3. This meant that borrowing was only twice initial income at the highest level of borrowing, which occurred after about fifteen years. While Sir Roy hoped that this brighter view was correct, he thought that in this kind of economic problem it was safer to be too pessimistic rather than too optimistic. As for service charges, while his figure of 7 per cent might be wrong, he did not think that, with some private borrowing inevitable and necessarily taking place at a high rate of interest, one ought to push the assumed service charge too low. It might be possible, though not easy, to eliminate private borrowing, and he thought that much the safest assumption was again that averaging out the cost of borrowing, with a high rate of interest charged by private lenders and a lower rate by others would lead to an average rate in the region of 7 per cent. However, he had once again made a calculation in Scheme *C* where service charges on foreign borrowing were only 4 per cent.

Sir Roy stressed that he attached great importance to the figures, not least because he had shown in his paper that a rise in the rate of increase in consumption from 2 per cent to $2\frac{1}{2}$ per cent would have a bigger effect than a rise in the foreign service charges from 4 per cent to 7 per cent. This was very important. Only Professor Johnson had taken up this particular point when he had stressed that the reason why a small change in consumption had such a big effect was that there were two explosive factors in his (Harrod's) scheme. One was the growth of income in excess of consumption and the other the rapid accumulation of debt. It might be that these assumptions were quite realistic and that this was why it was a question of touch-and-go whether countries took off successfully in the real world.

Dr. Patel had suggested that, while it would be very difficult indeed to finance the take-off of the whole under-developed world at once, and while it would therefore be better to concentrate on assisting only a small number of countries to develop, political factors meant that one had no choice but to lend to everyone. Sir Roy suggested that this made it all the more necessary for economists to show that it was impossible to aid all under-developed countries at once. They should stress the truth that capital ought to be channelled towards those countries where co-operating factors were increasing in amount most rapidly. While several participants had disagreed with his stress on the need to concentrate on developing exports, he felt that too much emphasis was usually put on the development of import substitutes. He would agree whole-heartedly with

Dr. Patel that what was needed was for each country to concentrate production where its comparative advantages lay.

Professor James had asked about his proposal for a levy. He would just stress the essence of his proposal which was that he wanted under-developed countries to become more self-dependent. He wanted increased incomes to go into domestic investment. A major problem was that incomes could increase in two ways. One was through increased distribution of income, where a major danger was the low marginal propensity to save of higher income earners. The alternative was to plough back profits, but this raised the point that such profits might often be remitted to the country which owned the investment and Professor Gudin had already given the objections to this. All he had tried to do in his paper was to suggest one way of solving the problem of increasing investment overseas while at the same time giving some part of the ownership of the capital goods created to the country where the capital was.

Professor Delivanis had criticized his suggestion for curbing the monetary authorities in mature countries. He knew that the monetary authorities in such countries were faced with difficult problems, but he did not want them to go on contending that the only way to cure the problems which growth caused was to check growth itself. Some kind of plan would be desirable because it could forbid the monetary authorities to check growth in order to cure the balance of payments or inflation. They should be made to deal with these problems in other ways.

Professor Robinson had suggested that the time scale in Scheme *A* was too short. This might well be true, but he had also given Scheme *H* where the crash programme lasted thirty years. Though annual lending was less, total lending was considerably greater than in Scheme *A*.

Replying to Professor Tsuru, Sir Roy said that he was assuming a 'mixed' economy because he was talking in terms of international agencies like the World Bank which gave development loans for specific purposes. Since this implied 'mixed' lending one would need a 'mixed' economy to receive such lending. Sir Roy agreed that the capital-output ratio would sometimes be very high, and he wanted to stress the need to look at productivity and not to argue that labour-intensive projects were always the right ones.

THE DISCUSSION OF THE PAPER BY PROFESSOR BYÉ

Professor Giersch introduced the paper, saying that Professor Byé's argument started with the contention that the classical theory of international trade was static, and that its explanatory and normative validity was limited to the special case, where there is no difference between short-term and long-term comparative advantage. Professor Byé thought that a more realistic theory should take into account changes in the composition of effective demand caused by growth, economies of scale, external economies and differences between sectors of the economy in such matters as self-financing and the length of the planning period.

The emphasis in the paper was on changes in the structure of demand and on the division of the economy into production sectors. Professor Giersch thought that this was a correct emphasis because many problems of international trade and growth arose from the fact that changes in production to meet changes in demand took time, owing to limited factor mobility within the countries. In so far as the classical trade theory ignored this, one could say that it assumed complete factor mobility within the countries concerned and not, as Professor Byé had said on page 144, absolute factor immobility.

Professor Giersch went on to say that Professor Byé adopted a sector approach in dealing with long-run comparative advantage. For Professor Byé, a sector not only produced goods, but also new kinds of labour, new capital and new techniques. Professor Giersch translated this into the language of traditional theory by saying that there were differences in external and internal economies which had to be accounted for if one was asking the question why, and how far, long-run and short-run comparative advantages were different from each other. On capital formation, Professor Byé obviously generalized from French experience by assuming a very low mobility of capital between sectors. Savings in one sector were not likely to flow elsewhere. This was in strong contrast to classical theory, where sector boundaries were considered to be much less important than international frontiers. The mobility of factors of production between sectors would be unimportant if the ratio between the rates of profits in the different industries always reflected comparative advantage. This was not the case, because of different degrees of monopoly, government intervention, etc.

On pages 156-7 of Professor Byé's paper, Professor Giersch could not understand the reference to imperfect competition between national economies. He found it difficult to make sense of the sentence, 'If a country like Belgium has a permanent deflationary climate and at the same time the formation of savings continues to be large, an abnormally low interest rate will cause certain activities to be financed which, in the same real conditions would not be financed elsewhere in the world'. He wondered why, in a country with abundant capital supply, investment in low-profit industries represented a distortion. He thought the question was rather why the low-interest country did not develop new industries favoured by growing world demand. He also wondered why there should not be more outflow of capital from a country like Belgium since, according to Professor Byé, the international mobility of capital was greater than that between sectors. Part of the answer might be that the market rate of interest was largely a monetary phenomenon and that, even in a perfect international capital market, there would be different rates of interest with higher rates in countries where the value of money was expected to fall and lower rates in countries with stable money. Belgium, like Switzerland, probably ought to be included in the latter category of countries.

Professor Giersch then drew attention to the problem of defensive investment and to Professor Byé's observation on page 154 that the percentage of self-financing was high in industries which were acutely threatened by decline. This might be an aspect of the immobility of capital between sectors in so far as entrepreneurs wanted to stay in their business rather than maximize the rate of profit. Apart from that, they might estimate the long-run prospects of their line of business more favourably than outsiders did. In an uncertain world, who could have better information on the chances for cost-reducing innovations and other possibilities of adjustment than those with experience in a particular industry? The fact that such industries could change over to new products surely suggested that the concept of a threatened industry was too clumsy. This concept ignored those possibilities of adjustment which were only brought to light if we talked about individual firms or production products. These remarks might be of some relevance for textile production in the more advanced countries. Finally, it might well be that the percentage of self-finance in a threatened industry was high mainly because the rate of investment there was so low due to a lack of outside funds.

Professor Giersch then enlarged on what Professor Byé had called the 'paradox of the active defence of threatened sectors in the older countries'. Several factors had to be considered here. There was protection afforded to a country by transport costs as well as government intervention and external economies. Professor Byé did not regard this as sufficient to show why agriculture or the textile industries were continuing to increase production in developed countries. He introduced the notion of what he called 'structural permanence', which included imperfections in the capital market and the unwillingness of producers to adjust to what they regarded as temporary changes in comparative advantages. Efforts were directed to restoring traditional comparative advantage and therefore served to distort the economy. To the means mentioned by Professor Byé — the creation of cartels, and the search for improved methods of production — Professor Giersch added the use of persuasive advertising. Although some of these methods were wasteful, one should not be too critical of such activities. Threatened industries were after all faced with severe foreign competition, and one might argue that this competition was as good for economic growth as the international specialization which had been so much stressed in the traditional theory of international trade.

The counterpart of active defence in industrialized countries was, of course, what Professor Byé called 'the premature appearance of advanced sectors in under-developed countries'. We could explain this by recognizing that — in contrast to classical theory — the international mobility of capital within one sector could be greater than the intersectoral mobility of capital within one country. By investing abroad, the growth of developed countries was carried beyond their national boundaries and new plants were established where natural resources were available and cheap labour could be trained. With this flow of capital would go managers and engineers using the same technique as in their home countries, although this technique might not imply the optimum combination of factors from the point of view of the developing country in present circumstances. This went far to explain why many poor countries exported their most capitalistic products, a fact which could be considered as the counterpart of the Leontief paradox.

For the Leontief paradox itself Professor Byé had given a dynamic explanation. It might happen that in a highly developed country additional demand called for the creation of very capital-intensive industries. They would be producing for the home market, while the more labour-intensive industries continued to form the main part of exports. If the new demand grew so fast that the domestic industry could not meet it, there would be room for imports of capital-intensive goods from less developed countries which — according to classical theory — were supposed to concentrate mainly on the export of labour-intensive goods. But in a dynamic setting, with innovations, new products and lags of adjustment almost anything might happen, and conclusions derived from a few simplifying assumptions could be irrelevant and misleading if applied to the numerous different cases in the real world.

Professor Byé's concluding section asked for a model to explain the development of international trade in the world economy. This should probably include not less than three countries, each of which had at least three sectors. There should also be a number of factors of production in each sector and country, a recognition of different economies of scale and external economies, of different propensities to save and to invest in the different sectors and so forth. Economists with comparative advantages in model building would probably not find much encouragement in reading Professor Byé's list of requirements, particularly since they were reminded that the list was far from exhaustive. Professor Byé's only hope of having his demand satisfied was probably to produce the model himself.

As for the principles and rules which Professor Byé deduced from his argument, Professor Giersch wanted to make only a small point. If anyone asked him what was most important in order to bring about the structural changes which a growing international economy required, he would simply advocate the removal of most artificial obstacles to the movement of factors of production between sectors and between countries and a positive programme for easing the adjustment process. Under such circumstances, the rough-and-ready principles following from a qualified version of the classical theory and the theory of external economies would after all not be the worst guide for the problems of trade policy at least of the more advanced countries.

Mr. Bhagwati said that Professor Byé's was an important paper with many good ideas. He would try to avoid discussing details and concentrate on the central question of statics versus dynamics. Statics was a method of analysing a problem rather than the problem itself. It was perfectly possible to deal with growth and technical progress in these terms. Economists like Professor Johnson and himself had dealt with the effect of growth on international trade by using comparative statics. One took some autonomous change in data and worked out the effect of this for the new equilibrium position. One was not concerned with the path by which the economy moved from one situation to another, but merely looked at the properties of the new equilibrium position.

Professor Byé was dealing with a similar problem but by implicitly adopting a dynamic approach. He focused on the question of how factor endowments in one period depended on the magnitudes of certain variables in the preceding period, thereby relating variables at one point of time to variables at another. However, sometimes Professor Byé's paper seemed to suggest that the mere fact of bringing in factors like shifts in pattern of demand made a theory 'dynamic'; this was not correct.

The interactions between variables at different points of time were of great importance and trade theory should focus more on them. One could get far more interesting results, for instance, if the question of the effect of technical changes abroad were considered in a dynamic context. 'Competitiveness' in a country's export markets might depend on her rate of innovation which, in turn, depended on her rate of investment. Then, to deal with an imbalance caused by foreign technical change by using a restrictive monetary policy which, while balancing the accounts currently affects the rate of investment adversely, would cause the payments difficulty to recur in some subsequent period. Perhaps this type of sequential process could illuminate British experience in recent years.

Professor Byé had also touched on the welfare aspects of growth, by distinguishing between short-run and long-run advantage. However, the question of welfare, once time was introduced into the picture, was much more tricky than was implied there. One complication, mentioned by Professor Byé, was the relation of the rate of saving to the pattern of production *via* the resulting income-distribution. This showed how there might be a conflict between maximizing current income and maximizing income at some specified future date. In principle, the theorists had tried to cope with this question by introducing inter-temporal utility functions, but any attempt at specifying these, along the lines of Arrow's a-temporal analysis, would probably be equally futile. Indeed, genuine difficulties concerning myopia and inconsistency in behaviour over time emerged which made the whole question extremely complex. These were questions of genuine importance. Professor Byé, in raising the problem of dynamic analysis in both its positive and welfare aspects, had written a stimulating paper.

Professor Mikesell considered the question of the early appearance of advanced sectors in under-developed areas and compared the results on pages 163-4 of Professor Byé's paper to Chenery's findings that the industries which progressed most rapidly were those competing with imported goods. Professor Mikesell thought there was a tendency for foreign firms with established export markets to wish to protect these markets at all costs. Studies of the motivation of foreign investment suggested that if one ignored firms investing in raw materials, which inevitably had to invest wherever those raw materials were, the main point was that, once a foreign investor developed a market, he would hold on to it by investment abroad even though he could obtain a higher rate of return in his home country by investing in something else.

As for whether progress was most rapid in the industries competing with imports, Professor Mikesell thought that this might be true in manufacturing but was not always true where one was dealing with raw materials produced for a rapidly rising world market. Once a market had been created for manufactured goods the advantages of location and of economic aid from the government became very important. Nevertheless, one found in many under-developed areas that if the expansion of an industry was based solely on sales to the domestic market, stagnation began to set in. As the rate of growth of the industry slowed, one needed a shift from import-competing products to exportable ones. If this conclusion was correct, a manufacturing industry in an under-developed country needed to become an exporter after a time if it was to continue to grow. Professor Mikesell said that the distinction between import-competing and export industries disturbed him because it implied, especially for an under-developed area, that the line between these two categories was fixed for ever and that some industries could never become export competing. He would therefore stress the view that there was a need to develop import-competing industries which could become exporters later on.

Professor Robinson commented that the history of Japan was rich in such examples, including the production of transistors and cameras.

Mr. Lamfalussy raised a question based on the concrete case of a country he would call Belgium, although any similarities with the real Belgium were purely coincidental. In this hypothetical country, the structure of exports seemed to correspond to the comparative advantage of the country in a *static* sense. This coincidence had been imposed by habit, the results of trade, etc. Accepting that this structure of exports suited the country in question, there might be a very difficult situation because the products where the country had a comparative advantage were not necessarily those for which international demand was growing rapidly. For example, the country might be well suited to producing textiles or non-ferrous metal where the long-run growth of demand was slower than in, say, electronics or engineering products. The problem was therefore whether economic policy could introduce new comparative advantages and turn the country's exports away from the old lines. In particular, could it do this by setting up a new infra-structure or by granting protection in the initial stages of the industry's growth?

Mr. Lamfalussy said that this was a very practical problem and he would therefore like to ask Professor Byé, first, how one could make reasonable forecasts of demand in the long run. Second, if it were possible to do this, could one also predict what would be the parallel developments of supply in other countries? For example, if Belgium were to establish a petro-chemicals industry, world consumption of petro-chemicals might be growing faster than demand for more traditional products, but what would be the growth of *supply* in other countries ? Apart from these two practical difficulties, Mr. Lamfalussy saw some conceptual problems. First, how could one calculate the sacrifice required to obtain the necessary change in infra-structure and, if one were able to calculate this sacrifice, how could one decide whether it would be justified in terms of the results it gave ? Second, there was the problem of horizons and the difficult, related question of welfare. The problem was that what might be true ten years ahead need not be true in twenty years. Mr. Lamfalussy therefore wondered how far one could go in making statements about welfare and trade on a long-run basis.

Mr. Lamfalussy said that several of the points made by Professor Giersch had been related in some ways to his own book on Belgium. Belgium was already making important capital exports and these represented a relatively high percentage of domestic capital formation. So far as defensive investment in Belgium was concerned, this happened not only because of the relative rate of interest but also because of uncertainty. Uncertainty was especially high in Belgium because of the high percentage of exports to income. Mr. Lamfalussy thought that there were two kinds of defensive investment. One kind happened where there was an error of judgement because an industry thought that its prospects were better than they really were. He thought that this kind of defensive investment was important in practice but not in theory. In theory, another possibility had to be considered, namely, defensive investment which could be regarded as the rational outcome of profit maximization. This could be shown by distinguishing between a firm which was starting from scratch and investment by existing firms. It was currently assumed, for example, that there was no need to replace fixed assets *continuously* and that in this way firms could move their capital resources from one industry to another, by accumulating depreciation allowances. Although this sounded easy, in fact it was not. One needed to replace tools continually because these wore out or because technical progress brought in new tools. With strong competition, a firm which did not renew its tools (out of current replacement allowances) as progress took place would find itself priced out of the market. It was therefore forced into defensive investment, instead of being able to 'release' capital. This kind of behaviour might be completely rational, but this did not mean that it did not lead to problems, especially to the 'freezing' of a country's industrial structure.

Dr. Myint discussed the question of mobility of resources between sectors. He suggested that there was a similarity between the concept of very low mobility between sectors and Taussig's concept of non-competing groups. Taussig had suggested that competition for labour between industries might well be greater than within an industry. We had to remember that when we spoke of mobility it was not merely capital that we were concerned with but also technical knowledge. He thought this was connected with the apparent paradox of the growth of advanced industries in under-developed areas. Dr. Myint pointed out that there were two kinds of industries set up in such countries. Some were established on government initiative, like the Indian steel mills. Others represented a kind of overflow from developed to under-developed areas. Dr. Myint wondered whether this second kind of industry was not the most important in helping under-developed countries to expand their exports. It might well be that, if under-developed countries would take more foreign capital of this kind, they would stand a much better chance of making exports within the under-developed world than if they concentrated at present on producing import substitutes.

Professor Nakayama said that Professor Byé's paper represented a bold new attempt to take up the fundamentals of growth. A major question was taken up in the second part of the paper where Professor Byé considered the sectoral structure of the economy and the way in which this led to international trade problems. Professor Nakayama was worried about the connection between growth and changes in patterns of international trade. He wondered whether one accepted the aim of growth first and then faced problems of exporting, or whether one increased exports first and then suffered problems of growth. The statistics for Japan showed that a slow rate of growth in exports might be the reason for the high rate of growth in the Japanese economy as a whole. What connection did Professor Byé see between growth in general and exports in particular ?

Professor Johnson thought the difference between Professor Byé's approach and that of the classical economists was not as great as Professor Byé appeared to think. The main question which needed discussing on Professor Byé's paper was that of the units which were used in international trade analysis. The International Economic Association Conference at Lisbon in 1957 had considered the economic consequences of the size of nations. The main conclusion seemed to be that the most important unit was not the nation but the individual sectors of particular economies. One had to look at industries or even firms because these were of increasing importance. In the past much trade had been carried out by large-scale enterprises and this had led to the development of international corporations. Professor Byé himself had been one of the first to call attention to their importance. However, Professor Johnson thought that the result of this new development might be to increase rather than decrease the extent to which classical analysis applied. The large enterprise took great care in calculating the costs and advantages of particular countries and particular factors of production. Professor Johnson thought this was a very important influence and that the solution of the dollar problem had been largely a result of the movement of U.S. investment to other countries.

Professor Johnson felt one could legitimately say that international trade theory was backward. It had long been encumbered with the labour theory of value at a time when general economic analysis had gone far beyond such a naïve concept. Now the theory of international trade ignored education and learning. He wondered why it should be assumed that industries continued to produce their existing products in competition with imports if they had acquired sufficient ability to move into new lines of activity as a result of the somewhat expensive process of learning. Similarly, allowance ought to be made for the differing degree of progress in different sectors of the economy. It was well enough known that knowledge and skill were not the same in all countries and all parts of the economy. These questions were important for international trade theory, especially where there was growth, and he suggested that the application of traditional theory was rather wider than Professor Byé appeared to think.

Dr. Marsan expressed some doubts on Professor Byé's claim that capital was immobile between sectors in mature economies. This was not always true. In Italy, for example, immobility was not due to the reluctance of capital to move so much as to other reasons. For example, there was resistance from organized labour because of unemployment. However, capital did move, for instance, from the textile and from the electric power industries into chemicals, electronics and other lines of activity.

Dr. Marsan did not see the distinction which Mr. Lamfalussy made between defensive investment and structural change. The replacement of old machinery with new could often lower costs without necessarily raising output. In Italian textiles, for example, output had remained roughly the same, while costs had fallen substantially. One interesting development in Italy had been that the largest manufacturer of type-writers was rapidly moving into the production of computers, while at the same time setting up typewriter plants in foreign countries. This was an interesting example of an industry diversifying its traditional production and seemed to show that capital was not the immobile factor of production. Dr. Marsan suggested that a most important factor was the size of the market. In a small country like Belgium, expansion would often mean an increase in the already high ratio of exports to output. A big country, however, could rely to a greater extent on sales at home, and this was an important argument in favour of international economic integration.

Professor Ohlin said that in some respects Professor Byé's conclusion about protectionism was good, accepted doctrine. It was possible to increase income by protection if one could thereby reduce unemployment, eliminate monopoly or bring about a better supply of factors of production. One way of obtaining that better factor supply was by acquiring foreign capital, technical knowledge and labour. One might also improve the factor supply by changing its distribution within the economy or by giving training, improving experience, etc. Professor Byé had stressed that one might improve the factor supply in the long run by protection, and Professor Ohlin wanted to point to the historical fact that export industries in small countries usually grew from industries originally supplying the home market. This supported Professor Byé's view. One would acquire efficient factors of production through training and experience. For example, one could not build up a selling organization in the U.S.A. until one had a strong industry with strong firms at home.

Professor Ohlin said he would like to make yet another plea for more attention to be paid to the theory of location. Professor Byé's analysis was excellent, but if one looked back at earlier development the great question was why particular industries were located as they were. This was the biggest problem in international trade theory and the answer was that it depended on the phenomena analysed in location theory. If one asked why iron and steel were produced in the Ruhr, the answer was not protection, but that raw materials like iron and coal were there. Labour moved to those places where producers could find the weight-losing raw materials that were necessary to produce particular products. He therefore thought that location theory was of great help in showing why the pattern of industry was as it was. Professor Ohlin hoped that participants would forgive his rather monotonous insistence on the importance of location theory. He thought one could easily build up a theory of fashion movements in economics. Location theory was not now fashionable, but it was important and he thought that economists should therefore diversify their theoretical clothing.

Professor Robinson inquired whether Professor Ohlin would deny what Professor Mikesell had said, namely, that the big exporters now had grown out of industries which were originally intended to save on imports. Typical examples were the way in which the cotton industry in the U.K. had grown up to replace Indian textiles, and the way in which the U.S. metal industry had replaced imports from Britain.

Professor Ohlin replied that, far from disagreeing, he thought this view supported his own position. He did not think it was necessary to be first in the field to build up an effective export industry, but in the second case Professor Robinson had quoted there had already been a strong American mechanical industry before the metal industry grew. All he was trying to say was that the kinds of factors of production needed to establish comparative advantage in a particular line of activity were the result of developments which could not take place unless considerable initial experience had been acquired.

Professor Mikesell pointed out that his initial remarks about the motivation of investors were intended to stress that in under-developed areas, and also in the EEC, the main aim was to protect markets. Once this aim was accepted, then one had to go on to consider factors like location.

Professor Ohlin commented that what Professor Mikesell was saying could be explained in terms of Weber's location theory. Since the U.S.A. had a large market in Europe, American producers were likely to set up factories there rather than try to sell from America over the European tariff.

Professor Robinson reported that much had been heard of these problems in the Addis Ababa Conference. A question which kept arising was the smallness of the African market and the question of which industries could operate on a small enough scale to thrive there.

Professor Weiller underlined the fact that under-developed areas were planning to set up new industries in the light of present and future needs, while continuing traditional exports of primary products. He went on to say that the theory of 'the permanence of structures' had been ascribed to him. When he used the concept of 'preference' for internal economic structures and international patterns of trade, he did not rule out short-run flexibility in national economic policies. He thought that economic policy would be flexible in the short run despite some long-run continuity of tendencies, expectations and preferences. In favourable periods, countries would engage in trade negotiations which moved them from protection towards liberalization.

Dr. Ferrero returned to the question of the low mobility of capital between sectors. He doubted whether this occurred in under-developed countries like Peru, where profits from agriculture and mining went to finance industry, trade and commerce. Indeed, in such a country one knew exactly who was making investments. Taking a historical view, in any country capital to start industry came mainly from the profits of previously existing enterprises in agriculture and mining.

Dr. Ferrero said that as for the correctness or otherwise of classical international trade theory the proof of classical theory which was given on pages 144-6 Professor Byé's paper struck him as being completely satisfactory. He did not think that Professor Byé's later criticisms were fair. If a country were to have a long-run comparative advantage, the rate of creation of factors of production must be maximized in the interim.

Then Professor Byé went on to say: 'Suppose . . . that specialization on agriculture generates no saving but that specialization on industry does. It is then not certain that specialization on agriculture in accordance with the comparative advantage in the given conditions of t_o and subsequent specialization according to the same principle will also maximize long-term comparative advantage by the time t_n.'

Dr. Ferrero thought it was unrealistic to assume that a country would specialize according to comparative advantage and yet generate no savings. A country would engage in what was most profitable so that the supply of savings would come from profits. He therefore thought that the theory of comparative advantage was perfectly correct.

Professor Bechin said that there were many interesting questions on the relationship between international economic development and inter-national trade. He wanted to remind participants that concepts like elasticity of demand, the allocation of resources, the structure of industry, imports and exports all had different meanings in the different stages of economic development. He wanted to stress that the relationship between such things changed in the long run and in the short run, for example, even within one business cycle. The history of long-run development in nearly all countries showed that in the first stages a country needed to import basic capital goods. Later, the structure of economies changed and a point arrived at where economic development proceeded on a new basis. Professor Bechin said he knew the writings of most present-day economists and understood that developed countries needed to import raw materials. However, Mr. Mikoyan had expressed the important idea that the U.S.S.R., with its highly developed production, could provide raw materials for countries like Japan. This could be achieved through long-term trade agreements, like that between Japan and the U.S.S.R. The U.S.S.R., with her huge mineral and agricultural reserves and the productive power to make them available, was in a position to provide raw materials not only for herself, but for other industrially developed countries as well.

The existing ways in which the industrially advanced countries were provided with raw materials were based on unequal relations between nations. Professor Bechin stressed that the main point was that if economists were to make theoretical or political studies of the growth of correct and world-wide economic relationships they would not only need to make formal statements of equal rights between countries but must allow for real equality. Then the ideas of the classical theory of comparative costs would be relevant and could serve as a reasonable basis for developing international trade.

Professor Delivanis thought Professor Byé was right in asserting that specialization by countries led to a disproportion in the growth of the various sectors and not to the absence of any of them. However, Professor Byé was a little too severe on traditional trade theory in contending that it was static. It presupposed equal increase in and extent of the various sectors and of cost and demand. Of course, Professor Byé regarded this as unrealistic. However, while it might not be correct for individual sectors, traditional theory might be correct for the whole economy.

So far as long- and short-run advantage was concerned, Professor Delivanis thought that in practice one could not accurately predict the long run, and had to base oneself on short-run factors. Predictions might prove to be wrong and non-economic phenomena might intervene. Similarly, there might be expropriation and monetary difficulties, either external or internal or both. These might either cover and conceal a real disequilibrium or neutralize one, for example, through increased imports leading to a deficit in the balance of payments. In view of all this and in view of time-lags and of the impossibility of comparing present and future advantage or sacrifice, planning for the future at the expense of the present became even less advisable, for discoveries took place continuously.

He wanted to finish by supporting Mr. Bhagwati's contention that the location and not the ownership of factors of production was what mattered. An example of this was the Greek building of ships in shipyards belonging to Greeks living abroad, and their export.

Sir Roy Harrod offered an essay in classification. There was a recognized division in economics between macro- and micro-economics. Most attempts, so far, at dynamics could be regarded as macro-economics. He suggested that Professor Byé's paper was a first essay in micro-dynamics.

Professor Byé thought it was clear that his paper had been as unsatisfactory to himself as it was to others in the discussion, which had shown the kinds of doubts which people had. He would therefore know in which directions to continue his researches. He wanted to make clear, in replying to several participants, what his position was on the link between traditional theory and his own views. He regarded traditional theory as indispensable and by traditional theory he meant not only comparative advantage but also factor proportions. However, it seemed to him that traditional theory was only valid in one given period of time, showing what happened spontaneously. On the other hand, that theory did not contain the hypothesis necessary to explain what happened over a series of periods. It was a method of analysing a given situation and not a process of evolution. We would need to go beyond what had been said about the kind of hypothesis made in macro-dynamics and allow for additional supply and demand, and for the creation of new factors of production. These were three aspects of the same global quantities and there was therefore a clear link between them. Specialization at point of time T_o would evolve with the appearance of new factors of production in various periods of time between T_o and T_n. However, one could not forecast which factors would appear and transform the situation at T_l.

In reply to Dr. Ferrero, Professor Byé said that the former point would be valid only if savings were the same in all the sectors of the economy and specialization in agriculture, for example, gave rise to the same savings as specialization in industry. Dr. Ferrero had said that savings would shift from one sector to another. For this to be true, one would have to shift agricultural savings into industry and, if this happened, the theory of specialization would soon not be valid. Savings could be more easily used in the same sector abroad. A study of the balances of payments of Latin-American countries showed considerable lending from Latin America to North America. Similarly, in Africa, the producers of primary products were more willing to lend outside Africa altogether, especially in Europe, rather than in new industries within the African continent.

So far as long-run advantages were concerned, he admitted that initial specialization was able to promote development. Nevertheless, this required reinvestment within the economy and we knew where, for example, the Emir of Kuwait lent his funds. They were lent to the London County Council and not within Kuwait. There was also the contention that different industries were unequal in creating and training skilled labour. Industry in particular required trained labour much more than agriculture did. Industry needed technicians and these were not trained at school. In Brazzaville, a high percentage of the population went to school, but there was no market for technical skills and therefore school children were given only general training. Such people made good civil servants, but not technicians, and there was no point in training people to be technicians if there were no industries in the country where they could work.

Mr. Lamfalussy had said that his model was too complicated. Professor Byé wanted to make it clear that he had not so far constructed a model on the basis of the elements he suggested. Nevertheless, excellent models had been constructed, for example by Lief Eriksen in the Tinbergen volume. These were many-sector models and underlay the analysis in his paper. They allowed for comparative advantage and for factor proportions and Professor Byé thought this was the way theory should develop.

Professor Byé agreed that it was hard to forecast the future and thought that two factors were important. First, the big firms which Professor Johnson had mentioned were not under the influence of normal market forces. The oil industry, for example, made plans over ten years. If industry could use such plans, why could not economists do the same? The economist after all was much better placed and often had a wider range of information available to him than an individual industry. French economists took the plans of individual industries and built up a comprehensive plan for the whole economy, showing what each branch of the economy would do. A second problem was that if one planned on the basis of the general interest or community welfare one was bound to go beyond purely economic questions. I. M. D. Little, for example, thought that one would end by discussing ethics.

Replying to Professor Bechin, Professor Byé said it was clear that the theory of comparative advantage would not apply in the same way to situations where countries traded on a basis of equality and situations where one country was dominant. The dominant economy would create demand for its output at home rather than induce the development of industries abroad in dependent countries. For example, without tariff protection in the British Empire there would have been no industry in Canada and New Zealand. In other words, a conscious effort had been necessary involving planning for industrialization in these countries. In Africa the position of the French was similar. In order to build up industry in Algeria it had been necessary to offer subsidies as high as 70 per cent. Similarly, the U.S.A. gave tax benefits to countries like Puerto Rico. Professor Byé also thought that the back-wash effect of new industries to which Dr. Myint had referred was a vital phenomenon.

Professor Byé agreed with Professor Ohlin that location theory ought not to be ignored. However, historically, he suggested that the growth of the Ruhr, which Professor Ohlin had mentioned, showed how large a role the decisions of big enterprises could play in the development of an industrial centre, although it was also true that the Prussian government had supported the creation of this centre. Similarly, the British industrial system had been built up since the seventeenth century with some public support through the Navigation Acts and by the activities of large enterprises, for example, in India. Such things were extremely important in developing the pattern of British industry. Professor Byé thought that Professor Delivanis was right in his remarks about the role of monetary disequilibrium. There was not only the problem of payments disequilibrium but of the distortions in the economy which this caused. Such distortions were considerable during wars, and he wondered how many industries had been created because of such wars. He was interested in the example of the Greek shipbuilders which showed how such distortions could occur.

Professor Byé concluded by saying that he did not regard what he called traditional theory as a punch-ball which one should keep hitting. He knew that this was not the whole of classical theory and that Mill, for example, had noted the export of capital from the U.K. to the Caribbean, and thereby provided us with a very early study of capital flows.

THE DISCUSSION OF THE PAPER BY DR. MYINT

Professor Mahr said he would not refer to the argument for the protection of a single, infant industry but rather to the protection of manufacturing as a whole. It was agreed that the basic condition for successful industrialization was a sufficient supply of good management, effective labour, efficient transport, ample credit, etc. To develop these, countries needed to produce behind protective tariffs in order to avoid competition from nations at a higher stage of economic development. Professor Mahr did not think this kind of reasoning would apply to individual industries in developed areas, even if they were new industries. However, it did apply to modern under-developed areas.

The other way to encourage development would be by direct methods such as the supply of technical assistance or foreign capital. This was precisely the method which was being followed at present and he wondered which of the two was the more effective. He believed there was some criterion on which one could base an answer. Everyone knew that it was possible to build up successful enterprises in under-developed areas so long as one had workers and foreign capital. Without such foreign aid, he thought that progress through protectionism would be very slow. The Zollverein had been set up in 1834 without any such technical assistance. It had been forty years before German industry could end protectionism and even now it had not entirely vanished. We must also remember the European countries at that stage had not lagged behind England quite so far as under-developed countries at present were lagging behind Europe and the U.S.A. He therefore thought that one could not wait for protectionism to bring about economic development but that direct measures would work much more quickly and effectively. Speed was necessary, since the under-developed countries were living at a subsistence standard and population was increasing rapidly.

Professor Mahr agreed with Dr. Myint that the only other case where protectionism could be successful was the case of serious balance of payments difficulties. Here, however, he felt a great deal of scepticism. Nor did he think that this particular argument was in any way related to the question of infant industries.

Professor Mikesell wanted to support the view that economic assistance was more desirable than protectionism. As for whether protection, if it had to come, should be applied across the board or only in strategic sectors, he would support the latter against the former. Professor Mikesell thought that protection could inhibit development, hurting some industries while benefiting others, and the fact that there was protection gave no guarantee of development. The problem of adjusting factor costs could frequently be dealt with without devaluation. Nevertheless, many countries had overvalued currencies, and devaluation could go a long way in helping them to adjust and to make their products more competitive. Professor Mikesell called attention to special cases such as Venezuela, where equilibrium had been achieved without severe import controls and despite high labour costs, which occurred because the oil industry paid high wages and so caused wages in general to be high. Devaluation appeared to be the solution to this problem. One might object that devaluation would raise the incomes of primary producers and so would lead either to no more investment — because the money was spent on luxury imports — or to investment in lines of activity like coffee-growing, which the government wanted to discourage. Perhaps the solution was to tax such windfall income. Professor Mikesell did not think that there was any guarantee that a tariff would lead to investment in the desired quantities. More than that, protectionism might direct investment into the wrong industries. He thought a much better solution was to offer selective inducements to investors.

Professor Robinson commented that, while Professor Mikesell appeared to dislike import duties in Africa and other countries, such duties were essential for revenue purposes. It was much easier in an under-developed country to tax commodities rather than income, for purely administrative reasons. This meant that customs duties, possibly with matching excise duties, were inevitable.

Professor Kindleberger did not think there was any problem here, provided one raised the bulk of the revenue from goods which could not be produced at home.

Professor Johnson reflected that opposition to tariffs often took very strange forms. Economists would advocate a subsidy to capital as an alternative, while making much of the argument that too little labour was being employed. He thought economists should not suggest policies which would push factor proportions even farther in the wrong direction.

Professor Neumark wondered whether participants were trying to explain what was going on in modern under-developed areas by analogy with the situation in the U.K. before the repeal of the Corn Laws. The situation today was quite different. Most under-developed countries imposed import duties as important revenue raisers, which often accounted for as much as 50 per cent of indirect tax revenue. However, there had been no general fiscal policy in the U.K. before the 1840s so that any analogy was bound to be misleading.

Professor Kindleberger said one could argue that all that Dr. Myint was looking at was various kinds of external economies. It was very desirable, analytically, to show the form of these and to this extent he would like to defend what Dr. Myint said.

So far as balance of payments as a ground for tariffs was concerned, he would comment that economists often used equations of the Harrod-Domar type to show the way in which capital could lead to growth. He wondered whether growth would be achieved more effectively through an increase in output which competed with imports or by increasing exports. The first would require protection, the second would not. Professor Kindleberger therefore suggested that there was a big difference between nineteenth-century growth where exports had led, and where balances of payments were therefore not a major problem, and the present situation where there was a need for building up infra-structure. Perhaps the real question was whether Dr. Myint had not ignored the model of growth which allowed for technical progress and the effect of protection or its removal on technical progress.

Most economic historians said that growth had been slow in France in 1860 because tariffs were sustaining the existing industrial structure and that the reduction of these tariffs completed the industrial revolution in France. He thought that the reduction of protectionism in present-day developed areas could be of some use, as the British government seemed to think in contemplating joining the Common Market, but that in an under-developed area any stimulus *could* help it to grow, whether this led to a rise or a fall in exports or imports. Any stimulus could spur on a country which was on the verge of new technical advances. In the U.K., however, mere exporting without technical progress might divert the country from its basic problem. As Professor Robinson had pointed out in his article in the *Economic Journal* in 1954, the U.K. was continuing to specialize *too* much on the fossilizing export products like cotton textiles or galvanized iron sheets.

Professor Gudin called attention to what Professor North had said in the IEA Conference on take-off at Konstanz, showing that in many instances take-off began with a leading sector in the export trade. Professor Gudin thought protection was beneficial for under-developed areas which needed time to build up external economies. His objection was that the infants were so slow in growing. List had spoken of a 25 per cent tariff for twenty-five years, while he himself had seen tariffs of 100 per cent. He thought that developing industries needed both the carrot and the stick, the latter consisting of a gradual reduction in the role of protection. One argument for protection included the existence of disguised unemployment. While there might be disguised unemployment in India or other over-populated countries, Professor Gudin did not believe that there was any in Latin America, where low productivity was taken for unemployment. Similarly, he did not think it right to say that industry was more productive than agriculture when one compared the result of a large amount of capital behind the industry with virtually no capital in agriculture. He believed that a mistake was being made in Latin America by extending protection to all sorts of industries at the same time. Not only consumption but capital industries were heavily protected. The result was that when a textile factory, for instance, wanted to renew its machinery, it was burdened by the high prices of that machinery made in the country behind a high tariff.

Professor Kitamura thought that the paper put protection in perspective, particularly by distinguishing between permanent protection and that required to build up infant industries and by showing that the purpose of protection was to lead to development. Professor Kitamura was intrigued by the fundamental question of the strategy of development planning. Having re-read the paper, he found some confusion between the idea of the big push and that of balanced growth. Dr. Myint treated these together, but he thought that the latest statement of Professor Rosenstein-Rodan's views was very nearly the reverse of the balanced-growth argument. Professor Rosenstein-Rodan stressed the indivisibility of investment, while Fleming's criticism of the balanced-growth doctrine was not in terms of demand but in terms of competition for scarce resources. In other words, this was a cost and not a demand argument. Dr. Myint, however, regarded balanced growth as a demand question which suggested that his reasoning on cost and demand conditions was not fully blended. Professor Kitamura thought that most of the arguments were cost rather than demand ones.

Professor Kitamura was rather worried that Dr. Myint saw a conflict between development planning and protection. If a development plan used only over-all import controls then he would accept it, but if protection was selective then he felt that Dr. Myint was taking a very narrow view of what protection was. In any case, if protection slowed down development he was sure that under-developed countries did not want to pursue this kind of policy.

Dr. Savosnick recalled the point made twenty-five years before by Professor Ohlin, who had pointed out that infant industries were not worth protecting unless they were able to repay at a later date what had been spent on them. If one established an infant industry with decreasing costs, would it be necessary to foster monopoly conditions in order to enable it to grow ? He thought it would be ridiculous to allow a struggling infant industry to fight a long and costly battle for survival.

Professor Morgan wanted to raise a background question, namely, what were the costs of supporting an infant industry ? If the costs were incurred once and for all, and the gains were large, then the venture was justified. But if the costs continued and the gains were modest, a mistake was being made. Professor Haberler's Cairo lectures offered impressive arguments as to the ways in which free trade caused growth (and did not simply give rise to maximum income in static economies). Free trade encouraged the international transfer of financial and physical capital, furthered the international transfer of skills and provided an effective anti-monopoly policy. Professor Morgan felt that in Dr. Myint's paper one missed the sense that the optimum use of resources in a static sense was important, and that distortions of the optimum were a burden to be weighed against possible gains.

On page 192 of his paper, Dr. Myint suggested that if one were pursuing the policy of the big push and concentrating on strategic sectors, quotas applied to selected areas of the economy represented the most flexible and effective control over development. Professor Morgan questioned this. Would not tariffs, subsidies or even exchange-rate variations provide a more supple and flexible control?

Professor Byé wondered what Dr. Myint thought of the argument that, if one had tariff protection, this would enable one to draw in foreign capital and establish new industries. He thought that the question was of the greatest practical importance for those dealing with the economic policy of recently independent African countries. The Treaty of Rome gave these countries certain tariffs which they could impose to attract European firms. It would be particularly interesting to compare this with the situation in Latin America, where he believed that most of the industry in São Paolo had been attracted by a tariff.

Professor Gudin replied that this was correct. Protection could attract foreign capital, and the results of attracting such capital could be either good or bad, depending on the kind of protective policy adopted.

Mr. Bhagwati questioned the validity of the contrast drawn by Dr. Myint, on page 192, between the trade policy implications derived from the big-push (balanced-growth) doctrine and the Hirschman strategic-sector approach. It was quite possible to have a selective tariff policy with the big-push approach. The quantitative restrictions, where used, were primarily due to inflationary pressures and overvalued exchange rates. These could very well arise under the Hirschman type of approach. Indeed, if the Hirschman strategy, whose rationale consisted solely in promoting the inducement to invest, were successful, the problem of inflationary pressure would arise inevitably and the government would be forced to resolve the ensuing balance of payments difficulties by quantitative restrictions or alternative measures.

Professor Tsuru thought one could avoid some of the confusion which appeared to exist in some participants' minds if one remembered that the theory of protection was not intended to apply to a centrally planned economy. Many under-developed countries had mixed economies with some planning and some free enterprise, and he therefore stressed that both the Hirschman policy and balanced growth were intended as devices for mixed economies. The whole problem should be set in a much broader context than that of classical trade theory, and to consider the Hirschman argument in a setting which assumed that there was no government control at all was forcing it into a very narrow context.

Professor Tsuru suggested that if countries operated on the basis of free enterprise, then Professor Haberler's classical recommendations would apply. He also thought it was interesting that Japan had had no tariff at all until 1899, by which time, according to Professor Rostow, take-off had been completed. It was clear that in this instance foreign trade had been able to provide a stimulus, but he did not think that such examples were in any way relevant to today's conditions. A stronger argument against protection was the big difference in the wage-productivity relationship between present-day developed and under-developed areas. The wage rate varied a great deal internationally. An Indian engineer was as competent as an American one, but there was an extremely big differential in income per head. Professor Tsuru therefore thought that it was possible for an infant industry to develop quite rapidly and yet be competitive in export markets.

Professor Robinson thought it important to ask the question, *when* one should act in supporting an infant industry. If it was merely a question of imposing protection and allowing firms to grow when they were ready to do so, the problem would be simple, but in many countries the demand for the protection of an infant industry was often confused with arguments for general protection. If one took some African examples where the market was very limited, the question of the correct moment to intervene was closely related both to the level of costs at the scale on which the plant began to operate and to the quality of the product produced. Quality was especially hard to predict and it was clear that some industries had been established prematurely.

Professor Robinson suggested that there were therefore two factors at which one had to look. First, there was the scale on which the infant industry was likely to operate, and, second, the period required for managers and workers to learn their jobs. If the aim of protecting an infant industry was to provide a sufficient learning period, then one would need to start protection somewhat before the point at which the industry was intended to produce effectively. With diffidence, he suggested that once one thought of infant industries in terms of Africa the main limit was the size of the market. It might be easier to create infant industries there if a number of countries, all at the same stage of development, each helped one or two infant industries in the other countries by giving these access to their markets. He thought there were important implications here for the relative stage of development which ought to have been reached by the countries which were assisting infant industries. Countries which were more industrialized would, he thought, be more likely to foster infant industries effectively.

Sir Donald MacDougall said he had been puzzled by the discussion on the balance of payments argument for protection. He would like to suggest that when under-developed countries were embarking on rapid development there might be a marked shift in demand towards imports, particularly of capital goods and industrial raw materials. If imports were free, one would then expect the ratio of imports to income to rise rapidly. Even allowing for all the aid that was likely to be granted, to pay for these imports would require a big rise in exports. He thought that the situation might be somewhat parallel to that in developed countries during a war. The shift from peacetime to wartime production required some degree of planning and this was a view which even the most *laissez-faire* economists would accept. Without planning and control, enormous relative price changes would be needed to move resources from peacetime to wartime production. The absolute price level would rise and inflation would be severe. In addition, the use of the price mechanism would be unfair because, even though prices had risen, the rich would still be able to buy as much as they wanted of many goods, for there were limits to the degree of redistributive taxation that was feasible. It was for these kinds of reason that the U.S.A. and Europe had imposed wartime controls.

Sir Donald suggested that the position might be rather similar in under-developed areas which had embarked on crash programmes for development. Relying entirely on devaluation would involve large changes in the prices of export and import goods relatively to those of non-traded goods, and would in practice lead to inflation as in developed countries during a war. More than this, it would be even more difficult for the under-developed countries to tax the rich sufficiently to satisfy the desire for reasonable equity. He therefore thought it was inevitable that many of these countries would have to use controls, including import controls and controls over the consumption of exportables.

It was true that, if one imposed controls over less-essential imports, then domestic production of substitutes would be stimulated. If the goods in question were luxuries this might be regarded as undesirable. It might be possible to prevent or limit such production through a licensing system, as in India, or by imposing excise taxes. Even if such measures were impracticable, or had limited success, it might nevertheless be desirable to control imports of less-essential goods. Whatever distortion this caused in the economy might be a price worth paying.

Sir Donald suggested that, if one looked at these problems in terms of a second-best theory, it would be a very different second-best theory from the kind considered thus far in the Round Table. He doubted whether Professor Haberler's assertions took sufficient account of the restraints under which such policies were pursued.

Dr. Patel questioned the contention that the low income-elasticity of demand for primary products was no bar to the under-developed countries' specializing in the production of such goods since historically there was little evidence to suggest that the terms of trade had moved against primary-producing countries. He suggested that even if historical evidence did disprove the thesis of a worsening of the terms of trade for primary-producing countries, it could still be argued that the impact of a low income-elasticity of demand for their exports was felt by these countries in the form of a slower rate of growth for these exports. That this was the case was amply borne out by facts. If growing import requirements required increased exports and if the income-elasticity of demand for traditional exports was low, there would be every justification for the developing countries to try to channel their growing resources into the production of commodities for which income-elasticities were high. While this did not mean that developing countries should stop producing primary products, it did mean that in allocating resources in future an attempt should be made to diversify production and exports.

Professor Weiller stressed that in the writings of List, the word protection had been understood in the widest sense and not merely to cover duties on imports. But List discarded the problems of the tropical areas of the world which nowadays represented a big challenge because it was not easy to see how the world demand for their products would grow. He thought it was not merely a question of contrasting agriculture with industry but that one had to consider a number of sectors. In his opinion, this was an advantage of Professor Byé's analysis which distinguished four sectors.

In discussing export crops, many participants had suggested that agriculture could not hope to grow because there was no rapidly increasing demand for agricultural produce on the world market. However, the first need was to convert a large part of food crops into cash crops on a national and inter-regional basis. Professor Weiller therefore thought that undeveloped countries, especially in Africa, should look carefully at ways and means of expanding their food industries as well as at the diversification of their production of basic commodities. He also referred to what Professor Byé had said about protection as a way of building up the supply of foreign capital for the industrialization of under-developed countries.

Professor Nakayama wanted to support Professors Mahr and Mikesell on the correct way of supporting an infant industry. As Professor Tsuru had said, Japan had been unable to impose a tariff for thirty years because of a one-sided treaty with the U.S.A. which meant that concessions had to be extended. Since it was unable to use a tariff, the Japanese government had used many methods to foster development, sometimes setting up more than 400 model factories in various industries at the same time. Professor Nakayama thought that, even if circumstances had changed, one could still apply such measures usefully in fostering infant industries. He wondered whether one possible help would be to lower the exchange rate. In Japan, this had happened fortuitously because the price of silver had fallen when the gold standard ended, and he wondered whether the stimulus which this had given to Japanese industry was the equivalent of present-day devaluation. On the one hand, he was not sure whether devaluation would be very effective in increasing exports. On the other hand, he thought that protection after take-off might still be needed, as it had been in Japan.

Professor Sohmen wanted to question Sir Donald MacDougall's view on the use of protection for balance of payments purposes as an alternative to devaluation. The reason why countries suffered inflation was that, with given aggregate demand, either their resources were too limited, or they were badly allocated, or both. Trade restrictions could neither make more resources available at home nor improve their allocation, and would therefore have to reduce imports by as much or more than would devaluation. The latter possibility could easily arise, for one might attract more foreign capital by devaluation than by trade restrictions. Restrictions on trade and payments implied, moreover, that trade would be less than if one had a lower exchange rate and freer trade, and the efficiency of resource allocation would necessarily be lower.

Dr. Myint replied to the discussion. So far as the distinction between static comparative cost theory and more dynamic analyses was concerned, he looked at the problem as follows. If one had free trade and an income of 100, protection might reduce this income to 95. However, with protection one might be able to train and improve the factors of production. There might then be a loss of 5 per cent in current income, but a greater rate of growth in the future. If, under free trade, the rate of growth was 2 per cent, but under protection it was $2\frac{1}{2}$ per cent, one had a situation similar to that analysed in Professor Byé's paper. It might be better to suffer a reduction of income at present from 100 to 95, but to achieve a $2\frac{1}{2}$ per cent growth rate on that base rather than to continue with the rate of expansion of 2 per cent on a base of 100.

So far as the prospects for primary producers were concerned he thought that the idea of an export bias had been overplayed. Nevertheless, Nurkse's idea that trade transmitted growth was a substantial one in which Nurkse tried to supplement cost factors by stressing the importance of demand.

Dr. Myint said he wanted to clarify some points. First, there was the question whether free trade was the ideal condition for transmitting ideas. This implied that protection prevented the transmission of some ideas, and he was not sure that this was true. This bore on the question whether one would get more stimulus into an economy through protection. It was impossible to be certain what the correct answer was, and more than this it was clear that sometimes protection would help to stimulate an economy and at other times it would not.

A second question was raised by Professor Robinson, who wanted to know *when* one should stimulate an infant industry. This was another very important question but, once again, Dr. Myint was not sure that one could have a clear answer. List had suggested that many under-developed areas grew in the first stage of development with free trade and that only later on, as had happened in Japan, did they need the benefit of protection. Dr. Myint thought that economists and politicians all tended to show that their own countries needed protection most. He thought that with many countries still in the pre-take-off period free trade or a small degree of government intervention was all that was needed to accelerate growth. However, there were arguments on both sides. Countries certainly could benefit from new ideas which free trade would bring, but other stimuli were required as well and, if a new industry was needed, it was conceivable that some protection might be desirable. Everything depended on how the actual situation was managed.

Dr. Myint said that many participants had questioned the contrast between protection, which was not likely to be balanced, and an over-all plan or balanced growth. His own view was that there *was* a conflict and that this occurred at a practical level. It was not just a question of logical analysis but of judgement about the real world. However, Dr. Myint thought that there was some logic in the notion that balanced growth and the big push were very similar. For example, Professor Rosenstein-Rodan in his early discussions of the big push had suggested that, in order to get the economy across the hump, it was necessary to increase the size of markets. It was clear, of course, that more investment would be needed than if one tried only to expand certain sectors, and the opponents of the big push contended that it meant that investment would exceed savings so that in the end there would be inflation and the process would be self-destroying. Dr. Myint was inclined to agree that there probably would be balance of payments difficulties and a need for over-all restriction. Except perhaps in India, he thought that over-all development plans were likely to lead to balance of payments troubles. However, he did not think it was true that there were no textbook rules which one could apply to developed areas, and he agreed with Professor Tsuru that discussions of protection were usually carried out on the assumption of general free enterprise rather than of planning.

Finally, Dr. Myint said that so far as the general issue of free trade or protection was concerned, much of the argument for protectionism was not as dynamic as one would wish. In the real world, one had to start with an existing situation where there was a great deal of waste and then attempt to rationalize trade restrictions and concentrate on certain areas. Given the rather complicated and confused situation from which countries began, he thought that the only solution was not to embark on free trade but to proceed to a logical but discriminatory treatment of certain sectors.

THE DISCUSSION OF THE PAPERS BY
MR. LIESNER AND PROFESSOR MIKESELL

Dr. Ferrero said that the papers dealt with a subject which was of great interest for Peru as a member of the Latin American Free Trade Area. He would concentrate on Professor Mikesell's paper, but would like to make a few brief comments on Mr. Liesner's. Mr. Liesner was concerned, first, with the welfare effects of regional free trade agreements, and, second, with how one could bring about the conditions one required to attain particular ends. Dr. Ferrero believed that Mr. Liesner was right in suggesting on page 196 that the original Viner criteria were still correct and that welfare was more likely to increase if the main effects of the agreement were trade-creating. He thought that this was more true where tariffs were high than where they were low. Similarly, he agreed with the contention that the wider was the range of industries covered the greater were the trade-creating, as opposed to trade-diverting, effects. In Latin America a wide range of commodities was covered, but the mechanism for lowering trade barriers was not operating satisfactorily.

As for the conditions required if one was to obtain welfare ends,

Mr. Liesner had said very little about this. Dr. Ferrero thought it was interesting to set out these conditions and see whether arrangements for regional preference fulfilled them.

Turning to Professor Mikesell's paper, Dr. Ferrero said that he agreed with almost all of it and had only two points of disagreement. As Professor Mikesell had said on page 206 of his paper, 'the theoretical analysis of customs unions or of regional preference arrangements generally should be directed more toward the problem of their impact on the direction of investment in the developing countries for future output rather than limited to an analysis of the welfare implications of shifting present trade patterns'. This was very important in Latin America where trade within the area accounted for only 10 per cent of the total international trade of the region. This low percentage was very different from that in the EEC. Other difficulties in Latin America were a low population density, high transport costs, monetary instability and so on. The Latin American Free Trade Area looked more to the future and was intended to develop new trade on new lines. On the other hand, in Europe the intention was to increase competition and efficiency and to reallocate resources.

Professor Mikesell had rightly stressed the importance of competition in regional trade agreements. Unfortunately, opinion in Latin America was frequently not inclined to accept this view, and free trade in Latin America was regarded as being more a way of planning regionally than a way of increasing competition. The system for reducing tariffs in the Latin American agreement did nothing to ensure increasing trade and increasing competition. Tariff cuts did not take place across the board as they did in the EEC but through very elaborate arrangements. Each country should cut duties every year on products traded with other member countries by 8 per cent on average, but cuts were not related to the whole of the members' trade.

Dr. Ferrero thought that it was necessary to increase trade in all possible goods and if there was no assurance that all duties would be reduced there was no guarantee that there would be a market for new goods which member countries began to produce or trade among themselves. Those who had set up the Latin American agreement claimed that the system assured flexibility, but he would prefer to say that it gave insecurity. No one would want to begin to produce a product unless there was some assurance that there was a market for it. Besides, the system made it difficult to lower trade barriers in existing industries and Professor Mikesell was right in stressing the need for competition. This competition was needed not only within the regional area but also between countries within that area and the rest of the world. If outside competition were excluded, this would mean that high-cost industries would grow up. A major good point was that the Latin American scheme was not a customs union but a free trade area, which gave some protection against this danger to low tariff countries, and he was worried that if in the end it became a customs union this would lead to a greater danger of inflation.

Dr. Ferrero thought it important to note that Peru was the only South

American country with a completely convertible currency, and therefore felt it necessary to defend her situation. He did not believe that a customs union or a free trade area whose purpose was to foster specialization could operate efficiently unless countries had currencies whose external and internal values were in line, and payments were free. However, general feeling in Latin America was very different because of a long history of widespread exchange restrictions, and the first draft of the Treaty had therefore established the obligation of maintaining equilibrium in the trade between each individual country and the rest of the area. He had never understood why this particular notion of equilibrium was necessary, and Peru had indeed claimed that this would mean, not a free trade area but a *forced* trade area. Perhaps Peru's views were somewhat different from those of other countries because she was a creditor country within the area. He thought that the problem of how trade and payments should be kept in balance had only been postponed.

Dr. Ferrero said that there were some minor points where Professor Mikesell and he took somewhat different views. He thought that perhaps Professor Mikesell had built up a false antithesis between self-sufficiency and regional agreements. In the middle of page 209 Professor Mikesell had said, 'In the absence of intra-regional trade in manufactures, each member will seek to produce as many commodities as possible for sale in the domestic market and import the rest from abroad. In order to save exchange, many commodities that cannot be produced domestically (because of limitations on investment capital and foreign exchange or otherwise) will be subjected to heavy duties or restrictive quotas or prohibitions.' And he said much the same on page 212 where he had written, 'This conclusion would be wrong, however, because the alternative to increased intra-regional trade is not reduced trade with the outside world but, rather, the production of a larger proportion of each country's requirements within its borders', and again on page 214, 'Again, so far as the future is concerned, it is not so much a matter of trade diversion as between the outside world and the regional group, but rather whether policies will be adopted which favour regional specialization as against those which favour the maximum degree of self-sufficiency at whatever cost on the basis of domestic markets alone'. Dr. Ferrero said that he did not agree with such a 'second best' attitude. If it was impossible to develop greater *world* trade he would agree, but why should one exclude this possibility, which was the best solution?

On another point, Professor Mikesell said that internal investment would lead to foreign exchange shortages, import restrictions or depreciation. Dr. Ferrero denied that investment could cause disequilibrium — unless it was excessive. He did not see why one type of investment should lead to balance of payments problems and others not.

On pages 208-9, when he discussed the balance between trade-diverting and trade-creating effects, Professor Mikesell came out in favour of regional arrangements because he made implicit assumptions which were incorrect in terms of actual agreements. For example, he quoted Viner to show that the net effect on welfare depended on the contrast between trade-diverting and trade-creating effects. On page 208, Professor Mikesell said that 'By and large the traditional primary exports of developing countries to the rest of the world will not be significantly affected by the creation of a regional trading arrangement'. Dr. Ferrero thought that they could be affected. The protection of a high-cost area affected its ability to export. If a regional agreement improved the competitive prospects of a country's manufactures this might help its exports to the rest of the world, but he did not believe that a regional trade agreement would make such industries efficient. Behind high protection it was more likely that the country would only produce for its home or regional market and not move into world markets. This was particularly true if the individual countries had high tariffs, which was the case in the Latin American Free Trade Area but not in EEC. For example, an ECLA study had shown that Latin American countries had no tariffs of less than 30 per cent on capital goods, and a much higher minimum for other manufactured goods.

Quoting Professor Mikesell's comment on page 209 that 'the long-run impact of a regional trading arrangement is not to decrease trade with the rest of the world but rather to change its pattern and possibly to enlarge it', Dr. Ferrero said that he was not sure of this because if strongly preferential treatment forced member countries to buy within the area, this might reduce trade with the rest of the world.

Professor Kitamura said that so far the theory of customs unions had been worked out only in terms of static welfare gains, assuming that other optimum conditions were satisfactory and ignoring effects on growth. This was true of analyses of industrially advanced areas. For the under-developed countries, the theory could only make a limited contribution to solving real problems. What Mr. Liesner had said about welfare effects was greatly affected by the state of trade theory. He concentrated first on gains from the reallocation of resources and second on the enforced efficiency effect. Professor Kitamura said he found the paper's discussion of the practical problems of creating conditions for attaining welfare gains very interesting. Mr. Liesner proceeded mainly in terms of a given income, not specifying the degree of integration, and talked as if the choice of a degree of integration made no difference to the policy of co-ordination. Actually, the author considered two different stages of integration ; a commodity common market, as in the ECSE, and a full economic union, as in Benelux. Professor Kitamura thought that the author could have made it more clear how great a degree of integration he was assuming and shown how welfare gains could be reached for each form of integration.

Professor Kitamura thought that Professor Mikesell made out a well-balanced case for regional trade agreements in an under-developed area. Dr. Ferrero's scepticism had to be considered, remembering that he was speaking of Peru which was a happy country. However, there were many more-unfortunate under-developed countries. These had no export surplus and no transferable currency. Professor Kitamura wanted to take Professor Mikesell's remarks out of the Latin American context and speak for less-fortunate under-developed areas in general. As Professor Mikesell had rightly said, the starting-point of any regional trade agreement was an existing system of trade restrictions, and it was this which had to be contrasted with the agreement which was to be created. One did not begin with either free trade or optimum welfare conditions. On the contrary, one had to analyse regional agreements against the possibility that in their absence the situation would grow progressively worse. The slow rise in the world demand for traditional export products made it hard for primary producers to rely on the existing trade pattern. Nor were there good prospects for expanding exports of other goods. It followed that primary producers had to aim at diversified expansion, and where import-substitution had to be organized on a limited national scale this was scarcely practicable.

The essence of the problem was that if countries were prepared to organize import-substitution at a regional level this might be beneficial. But the existing possibilities for such trade collaboration were not entirely encouraging. He thought that the final situation would be one where, for the region taken as a whole, imports had to be kept down to a level compatible with the available supply of foreign exchange. Such restraint would be compensated, on the other hand, by a greater volume of trade within the region. If one started from a disequilibrium position, there was also the question of the transition from a situation where there were restrictions to a situation where there were fewer restrictions. What we learned from Mr. Liesner's paper was that customs-union theory had so far been based on conditions for maximizing welfare, and he did not think that this was particularly relevant to regional free trade agreements between under-developed areas. Professor Kitamura thought that Professor Mikesell was right on page 210 when he said, 'While a customs union will not establish the optimum relations between internal prices of domestic and internationally traded goods for maximizing welfare, intra-regional trade and specialization will change relative prices and consumption patterns toward optimum conditions'.

Sir Roy Harrod had raised an important question. Since the capital goods required for development were bound to come mainly from outside the region, one could legitimately ask whether regional agreements between under-developed countries would help their balances of payments. On page 209, Professor Mikesell gave the answer: 'The additional foreign exchange required for the larger imports of capital goods, raw materials and fuel not produced by the regional partners will become available as a consequence of the reduced demand for consumers' goods and other commodities (including some capital goods) from outside the region'. The usual analysis of such questions referred to a change in the trade pattern and it was certainly important for under-developed areas to look beyond the existing trade pattern. He would like to refer to page 213 of Professor Mikesell's paper where the latter rejected the traditional idea that one could make useful generalizations about welfare gains from customs union by using the ideas of complementarity, competitiveness and existing trade patterns as the basic criteria. Professor Kitamura thought that the problems of under-developed areas were of a different dimension.

Professor Kitamura suggested that the alternative to regional trade arrangements for the under-developed areas would be that the situation would get steadily worse. Any regional preference scheme had a strong bias towards trade diversion. This was well recognized by Professor Mikesell, though it was not clear how far he agreed that this was inevitable. Professor Mikesell appeared to argue that ultimately one had trade creation. However, in connection with the payments problem and the choice between free trade area and customs union, Professor Mikesell tended to favour a solution where the degree of preferential discrimination against the outside world was considerably reduced. This problem was dealt with on pages 223-4 and in the second paragraph on page 225 in Professor Mikesell's paper. Professor Kitamura thought that Professor Mikesell's view was politically very sensible and he only wanted to offer a comment on the difference between customs unions and free trade areas. Professor Kitamura suggested that under preferential trade agreements there was always a tendency for these to evolve from a lower and looser form of agreement to a higher and tighter one.

With regard to the payments problem, Professor Kitamura pointed out that there was a high degree of bilateral trade in Latin America which, according to ECLA, appeared to have reached as high a level as 66 per cent of all trade. In these circumstances, there was some reason to assume that the EPU experience in Europe, particularly with the system of automatic credit expansion, might be relevant to Latin America.

In Europe, Professor Kitamura thought it was important to notice that this payments arrangement had come first, and then trade liberalization in OEEC. In other words, the EPU had been important as an engine or a lubricator for the expansion and liberalization of trade. Here, his own view conflicted with what Dr. Ferrero had said.

Regional trade *was* a second-best solution. Mr. Liesner held that regional agreements represented a defence mechanism and Professor Kitamura thought that this was more true of under-developed than of industrial countries. The important thing in helping under-developed areas was to enable them to escape from the stagnation into which circumstances forced them through limited export prospects. The economic rationale of a preferential free trade area in under-developed regions could only be seen in the dynamic context of growth. However, in many under-developed areas liberalization was not sufficient, but one needed a conscious attempt to create mutual complementarities and specialization, and to exploit economies of scale. Such arrangements were buttressed by regional co-ordination. For advanced areas like Europe, regionalism was rather more than a defence mechanism, because developed countries had greater freedom of action. Nevertheless Professor Kitamura thought there was a great deal to be said for the view that regional agreements

were no longer a matter of choice. They were imposed by the requirements of science, technology and economics in the contemporary world.

He thought that these had changed the whole character of the international division of labour and called attention to Professor Johnson's
paper, which held that technical progress and innovation were playing
an increasing role in determining the pattern of trade. We were now
witnessing greater trade between countries at the same or a similar stage
of development. This raised a fundamental question, namely, whether or
not the principle of economies of scale predominated over that of factor
proportions in determining the pattern of trade. He wondered whether,
in future, the division of labour would be less stable and more subject to
change than under the classical pattern of trade between developed and
under-developed areas. He thought this was possible but that there were
dangers in such a situation. Specialization must be created by mutual
agreement and negotiation, and was far from being a spontaneous result of
underlying economic conditions. It was necessary to present an economic
justification for the growth of regional trade agreements since the under-
developed countries needed more dynamic versions of the regional arrangements which developed areas were now creating.

Professor D' Alauro said that Mr. Liesner looked at the economics of
regional free trade areas, but an important question was what happened
if such arrangements took not only the simple form of a customs union,
but of a really general economic union.

So far as the customs union was concerned, Mr. Liesner could find
value in Viner's distinction between trade creation and trade diversion.
While this was a most important question for economic welfare, Professor
D'Alauro did not think that the parameters with which Viner dealt were
so important nowadays. He agreed with Professor Kitamura that wherever
one had a customs union one found that trade was created rather than
diverted. This could be seen if one looked at the Rome Treaty. Under
GATT, a common external tariff could not be higher than the previous
average tariffs of the countries forming the Common Market. However,
he thought this would have happened even without GATT. It was not
politically feasible to have a new common tariff which was higher than the
previous individual tariffs. Professor D' Alauro therefore agreed with
Professor Mikesell when he said that Viner's pronouncements were
pompous and perhaps dated.

Turning to some general considerations on Mr. Liesner's paper,
Professor D' Alauro said that one question was how one should calculate
the gains or losses of customs union. He thought it could be shown that
gains predominated, with prices and incomes falling when the tariff was
abolished. He also thought that if a country gave up indirect taxation
and replaced this with direct taxation, the result for the welfare of that
country would be favourable. Professor D' Alauro did not believe that
calculations of the gains and losses of a customs union were really possible
because there was too much room for error. Instead, calculations had
to be based on figures for the G.N.P. and we all knew how hard it was to

calculate this correctly. He thought it was Morgenstern who had said that one could easily get differences of 15-20 per cent in a calculation of the G.N.P. for the same country at some moment of time. This showed that any results which economists obtained for the net gain from a customs union based on national income calculations were unlikely to be very significant. Professor D' Alauro did not think it was necessary to make statistical calculations, since it was easier to see the obvious favourable effects of a customs union. With the EEC, notwithstanding that the arrangement had only been operating for three years, the results had been, although modest, decisively favourable. The external balance on current account of the EEC had improved; the volume of international trade of the 'Six' had increased: however, trade within the area had grown more than trade with the rest of the world.

Mr. Liesner had spoken of difficulties, especially within the ECSC, and he thought it was true that there had been such difficulties. Any specific scheme would encounter problems which would be difficult to solve, even within a partial union like the ECSC. It was known that the recommendations of the Tinbergen Committee were still up in the air. If this kind of difficulty could arise where only two products were concerned, it was clear that an over-all economic union would lead to much greater problems. Professor D' Alauro thought that if, in the EEC, integration happened without autarkic aims, helping on equilibrium growth in time and space and following the compensation principle for gains and losses, the result would necessarily be positive for the 'Six'. The EEC, as the Treaty established, would allow the ending of many monopolistic positions and would make easier the best and most adequate utilization of the natural and human resources, the most economic combination of factors of production and the most convenient extension of productive units. Professor D' Alauro was an optimist, and thought that the third countries — and the EFTA too — should be favourably impressed and approach more closely to the EEC. Generally, he hoped that what was happening in the EEC would show the way to the rest of the world.

Professor Johnson said that Mr. Liesner claimed that there was no specific analysis of the forced-efficiency effects. There were, however, studies of the effects of tariffs on the industrial structure, for example, that by Stykolt and Eastman. The problem was also dealt with in Scitovsky's book. Professor Johnson found it difficult to see why Mr. Liesner thought that the forced-efficiency effect was important and wondered whether Mr. Liesner had found such effects in his studies.

As for the problem of measuring welfare losses or gains, Professor Johnson thought it could be shown that any such measure would give an answer that was a low percentage of total national income. An easy way of showing why was to take the Stigler law that elasticity of demand was small and the Harberger rule that if one multiplied a lot of small fractions one could forget the answer. It followed that the answer one got would inevitably be a small one, but the cost of accelerating growth by protection might nevertheless be large in relation to the rise in the rate of growth that one achieved. He therefore thought that the cost-savings resulting from a customs union could be significant, even if they were small.

Professor Johnson defended the whole basis of making such estimates. Viner's contribution had not been merely to lay down a series of rules of thumb — for example, that countries which were similar were more likely to gain from a customs union. He did not want economists to translate findings of this kind into conclusions about the benefit of customs unions depending on the similarity or dissimilarity of countries. There was a strong case for saying that measurement was necessary, for if one did not measure one had to use one's judgement, and this led one from scarcity economics into policy decisions with the likelihood that one would be able to reach no conclusions which would stand up to criticism.

Professor Johnson thought that Dr. Ferrero had shown that this was true of Professor Mikesell's analysis. Professor Mikesell began with the assumption that the Latin American Free Trade Area was desirable, though without saying why. He then went on to say that the part of the theory which was applicable was not relevant, but that what was relevant were questions of growth, export bias, etc. Professor Mikesell then went on to assume that things were effects which were not effects — for example, that a common market would not lead to a fall in exports. Finally, he concluded that, even though the arrangement might be a failure, the effects on the location of industry between countries would make it very efficient. He also made pronouncements on the effects of common markets on the inducement to invest.

In other words, Professor Mikesell was producing a series of arguments based on factual assumptions which were never produced. He was operating in terms of pure faith, believing that the Latin American common market would at some time become efficient and that this would make up for its present failure. The difficulty was that it was equally possible to reverse the argument, and this meant that the argument led nowhere. If one proceeded in this way one had to rely on individual judgements as to how important and relevant certain facts were. This surely meant that one ought to measure wherever possible. Professor Johnson admitted that there were difficulties, but this meant not that we should evade the problem of measurement altogether, but that we should devote more effort to our measurements and make better estimates of margins of error. A similar kind of analysis would apply to growing economies which wanted to calculate growth on certain assumptions about how the setting up of a common market would alter future income. Although difficulties arose when one had to compare a current loss of income with a future increase in income, it was perfectly possible to do this and he had been surprised how little empirical analysis of the problem there had been. One could legitimately argue that economists were useless if none of them was prepared to measure any of these things.

Professor Giersch said he realized that Mr. Liesner had been hampered by the limit imposed on him by the title of his paper. Some further points should, therefore, be considered in the discussion. First of all, so far as trade diversion was concerned, Professor Giersch thought that it would not be so strong if the formation of a customs union meant that third countries lowered their prices in order to maintain their sales within the Common Market. This would happen in the short run and would change the terms of trade in favour of the member countries and against the outside world.

If one looked at the effects of a customs union on international capital movements, Professor Giersch suggested that in order to keep their markets, firms in third countries would do their best to jump over the common tariff wall and establish subsidiaries in the Common Market. The Common Market would become an artificial magnet for international capital and would thereby change the usual pattern of international capital movements. He thought that this would be disadvantageous for third countries, and particularly for those in an early stage of economic development. A natural reaction would be the formation of countervailing customs unions and other regional trading arrangements.

His third point referred to the effects of customs unions on internal trade and on the location of industries. He had shown in an article published in 1949/50 that tariff walls in continental areas tended to make for a geographical decentralization of production, hurting particularly locations near the borders. It followed that the removal of tariffs within the EEC, and the erection of a common tariff wall around it, would increase the attractiveness of the existing industrial centres around the Benelux frontiers and along the French-German frontier. This would be at the expense of industries on the periphery of the Common Market. Such a shift might be undesirable for political reasons, and cause a particular problem of regional economic policy within the EEC.

So far as the flow of capital within the Common Market was concerned, he would revert to what Professor Byé had said about the mobility of capital between sectors being rather low and fairly high between countries within a particular industrial field. This implied capital movements within the EEC along the lines of existing industries and sectors, and should be looked at together with Professor D' Alauro's point about competition within the EEC. Increased competition had resulted from the reduction of customs duties, but it could be argued that this effect would only last so long as customs duties were being reduced, that was, during the transition period. Even so, he thought that producers would find ways of avoiding increased competition through collusion, mergers and particularly through agreements on specialization. Professor Giersch said that international trade was supposed to bring about specialization under the pressure of competition, but it could also bring about agreements to specialize in order to avoid competition. Although the Rome Treaty contained provisions against cartel agreements and monopolies it was still uncertain how they would be implemented. Professor Giersch thought that the final outcome could be quite different from what the letter of the Treaty required. The ECSC had also rules for making competition more perfect. Firms had to submit price lists in order that the market might become more 'transparent'. In effect, this had contributed to changing imperfect oligopoly into an almost perfect oligopoly, or into a market structure which had similarities with an open-price association.

Sir Roy Harrod wanted to raise a point of practical importance, bringing out doubts and anxieties which there had been no time yet to air fully. He was not happy about the United Kingdom joining the EEC. This was not yet a *fait accompli*; all that had happened was that the U.K. had asked for terms. Sir Roy said he did not want terms very different from those suggested three years ago, namely, that the EEC should be a free trade area with agriculture excluded. He thought it was essential to safeguard the traditional pattern of imports of food and raw materials from overseas countries, and did not want any restraints on these except for revenue duties. Sir Roy thought that the Commonwealth, as distinct from other overseas countries, had been overstressed. Perhaps it was right to stress it, because this had a persuasive effect in the U.K.; but we were really concerned with the whole overseas world, including Latin America, from which Britain imported; and it was with the effects of the U.K. being a member of the EEC on all these countries that he was concerned. The question of Commonwealth preference was a very small one by comparison.

Sir Roy said that, unless there were big changes in the Rome Treaty, the U.K. would have to put a tariff on all these imports. While there might be many good effects from Britain joining the Common Market, these would not be the same as the effects of regional arrangements between under-developed areas which needed bigger markets. The biggest effect would be the switch of its import trade from the rest of the world to Europe. In static terms this might not seem too bad, but one ought to look at it dynamically. For example, the Continent was modernizing its agriculture and, although output per head there had not reached British levels, modernization in France and Germany was bound to lead to increasing agricultural surpluses and we should be forced to take these in preference to buying from the rest of the world. Indeed the surpluses in continental Europe would become greater because, with Britain as a market, Europe would be less worried about over-production. Sir Roy said that his views were contrary to some of those expressed earlier in the Round Table, but he was worried about the likelihood of relatively high-cost surpluses becoming an important problem. This was the main thing that disturbed him as he looked at Britain's desire to join the EEC.

Professor Byé agreed with the essential conclusions of Professor Mikesell's paper and thought that it was good to introduce unusual notions into this kind of discussion. He would suggest only that among the questions which one ought to ask about the role of the Latin American Free Trade Area was the role of 'poles de développement'. There were many countries in the Rio de la Plata, and if a development pole could be established there, this would be extremely valuable to many countries, including Argentina, Uruguay and Peru. Professor Mikesell had suggested that if a customs union led to a true economic union this would help planning. Professor Byé said that planning was difficult, but the more similar the countries one was dealing with, the easier it would be.

Professor Byé thought that Mr. Liesner should have defined more clearly the difference between free trade areas and customs unions. The main distinction that one should make was between federal and contractual types of agreement. For example, Germany after Bismark was probably federal in the sense that she had now become conscious of her unity, and that the whole state therefore had an importance greater than that of individual regions. This attitude was not yet present in Europe and, although he regretted this, he thought that one should not pretend that the situation was better than it really was. He also added that under the Rome Treaty each of the 'Six' countries could achieve its own optimum development and the same was not true for a federal system.

Professor Byé found it difficult to discuss what Mr. Liesner had said about the ECSC because Mr. Liesner had ignored the writings of a number of important authorities.

Professor Byé wanted to associate himself with Professor Johnson in insisting that economists should measure all that was measurable and then add what could not be put into figures. It was necessary to go to the limit in making measurements, even though the measures that we had included big margins of error. He also thought that one should make measures both *ex post* and *ex ante*.

Professor Byé thought it important not to overlook the fact that the countries in the EEC now had the biggest internal rate of growth *and* the biggest rate of growth of exports. None of the countries in the Common Market intended to leave it and he noted that the young lady of Europe now had a number of suitors.

Professor Haberler said that in making the contrast between trade diversion and trade creation it had to be remembered that trade diversion merely represented the protectionist effects of the regional agreement. It was therefore natural that free trade economists like Viner and Meade should say that trade diversion was bad. However, even if one accepted that a given arrangement was trade-diverting, it was not necessarily true that for this reason it was bad. One could put forward valid arguments for protection as such, and these would be true whether they related to a region or an individual country.

Professor Haberler said there had been several references to the fact that free trade could be defended on several partly dynamic grounds, not merely on the ground that it led to a better allocation of resources. Dr. Myint had written an important article in the *Economic Journal* in 1958, in which he had shown that free trade was defensible on other grounds, for example, on the ground that it stimulated competition. Thus he thought that probably Professors Johnson and Scitovsky were right when they stressed that a common market had more advantages than merely in bringing about a better division of labour. Professor Haberler wondered whether there really was a conflict between the objective of an optimum or a better allocation of resources and hence avoidance of trade diversion on the one hand, and the objective of maximizing or stimulating economic growth on the other hand. If one accepted that a particular customs union was likely to lead to large trade diversion, income would be less than in the absence of the scheme. *Prima facie* this must be bad for growth.

Turning to another question, Professor Haberler said that when a common market led to the importation of capital, this was not necessarily desirable, even for the importing countries. One should not forget that investment was not an end in itself; it was never better than the purpose for which it was made. True, if there was mass unemployment capital imports induced by protection would create employment. But as Keynes had once said, a tariff could do no better in such cases than an earthquake did. Under full employment the situation was different. One would have to introduce external economies or something similar to justify tariff-induced capital imports.

Moreover, if integration stimulated investment, disintegration would stimulate it even more. If the American market were split up, with New England nurturing an automobile industry by protection, the Middle West a textile industry and so on, investment could be stimulated enormously. But what would happen to the division of labour and to economic welfare?

Professor Kaigl said that, with the rapid growth of skill and technique, output was increasing and new markets were needed. This was why the West was creating common markets and customs unions. On page 197 of his paper Mr. Liesner said, 'The upshot is that an economic union may bring benefits not only because an actual reallocation of resources between different uses takes place, but also because resources are employed more efficiently in their existing uses'. Professor Kaigl thought this was a purely theoretical statement. He wondered whether a customs union would bring benefits and, if so, to whom? To all countries? to consumers? He thought consumers could only benefit if greater efficiency led to lower prices. However, in most cases prices did not fall and the customs union only benefited the profits of the biggest monopolists. A customs union allowed the growth of the big firms and the big countries at the expense of the small. Professor Kaigl said that Professor Mikesell also implied that in a free trade area the big firms and countries would be able to oppress the smaller ones.

If this was one of the effects of a free trade area under capitalism, how was the problem met in planned socialist economies? There a rise in output was allowed to reduce prices, and planning to allow specialization helped to increase trade and strengthen the inter-dependence of socialist countries. The aim was to raise output and achieve balanced growth in the whole socialist world. Planning was therefore good for clear-cut specialization which would give greater benefit to the whole group. The more-developed socialist countries transferred more and more branches of production to the less-developed parts of the bloc, thereby increasing output and productivity. Aid by socialist countries was advantageous not only to the givers but also to the receivers, who were able to obtain goods which they could not make, or could make only at higher costs, thereby freeing resources for other sectors of the economy. Future markets were also created and the division of labour between socialist countries improved.

Mr. Liesner summed up the discussion on his paper. Professor Kitamura had said that in order to discuss the practical problems of free trade areas one needed to say how much integration there was. He agreed in a way with this ; for instance, there were some problems in the ECSC which did not arise in other economic unions. This was not just an abstract question, but depended on actual cases. One difficulty was that it was often impossible to forecast what problems would arise. For example, indirect taxation was leading to difficulties in the ECSC which had not been foreseen. The Treaty had made no reference to them ; yet they were a problem within six weeks, and much confusion had followed. However, he could point to examples which went the other way. Some difficulties which had been expected to arise in the ECSC had not materialized. The adjustment of the French coal industry to conditions of free trade provided an example.

Mr. Liesner said the question had been asked how far economic regionalism was a defensive mechanism. He thought that regional agreements had progressed a long way since the creation of the Sterling Area, Benelux, OEEC and EPU. All of these were primarily defensive, intended to overcome adverse economic conditions. Professor D' Alauro had said that trade diversion was not the most important problem and suggested that, if a customs union were now being set up, it would not have a higher average tariff than previously. Mr. Liesner pointed out that in a strict sense anything less than complete free trade represented some diversion. He also disagreed with Professor D' Alauro's criticism of attempts to measure the gains from trade in a rough-and-ready kind of way. In this context he thought that one must beware of the reasoning of both Professor D' Alauro and Professor Byé. One should not draw any significant conclusions from the fact that trade within the EEC had risen most. In the first place, statistics were not conclusive. In the second place, if one looked at the development of trade within Europe and at European industrial production over the last ten years one found that there was no break in the trend in 1958. In a short paper on this subject, Mr. Lamfalussy had shown that trade within the area had not increased relatively to industrial production. Mr. Liesner agreed that this proved nothing, but there was no greater support for the other view expressed by Professor Byé.

Replying to Professor Johnson Mr. Liesner said that he had tried to give the reasons why he thought the forced efficiency effect was not very important. Scitovsky had thought that forced efficiency was significant, but had made no attempt to quantify the problem in his interesting analysis. On the question of economies of scale, Mr. Liesner said he was an agnostic ; there were no statistics, and in the absence of figures, he preferred not to make a guess. Mr. Liesner agreed with Professor Giersch, especially in his scepticism over the likelihood of increased competition in the EEC. The rules which had been written into the Rome Treaty were difficult to enforce and the anti-monopoly provisions of the ECSC did not appear to have worked well either.

Sir Roy Harrod feared trade diversion if the U.K. signed the present Rome Treaty. Mr. Liesner agreed that there would be some trade diversion, but was not prepared to guess how much. Professor Byé had attacked his treatment of the ECSC. All he had done was to try to choose examples of problems which were important not merely for the Coal and Steel Community but also for the Common Market. Transport was an example. Mr. Liesner said that he studied relatively few authorities ; no doubt, like most, he read less than he should. However, on this particular problem he felt he was on fairly firm ground.

Professor Kaigl had asked who benefited from forced efficiency. He agreed that increased efficiency did not often lead to absolutely lower prices, but there was a logical jump in Professor Kaigl's argument when Professor Kaigl suggested that increased profits went only to big firms and big countries. This question of polarization was a big issue, and he would therefore confine himself to two remarks. First, observers often forgot that chronic balance of payments difficulties were involved ; second, his own guess would be that the benefit of increased productivity mainly went to the smaller firms. In many countries small firms tended to be less efficient and the fact that competition forced them to increase their efficiency meant that this was the point where free trade might bring benefits. Also, although he would agree that prices did not often fall when efficiency increased, they might well fail to rise as rapidly as they otherwise would have done.

Professor Mikesell said that in contrasting the effects of customs unions on investment with the welfare effects of short-run trade shifts, he was not saying that welfare was of no importance. In Europe, the longer-run effects of the shifts in the pattern of investment and the allocation of resources would show up years later and might well be important. He certainly did not want to disparage welfare.

So far as the Latin American Free Trade Area was concerned, Dr. Ferrero had said that this was limited. He agreed that it had its defects and did not want to defend the Montevideo Treaty. He had been very critical of it in other writings. Professor Johnson had disparaged his faith, but unless one had faith there would be nothing for Professor Johnson to measure !

Dr. Ferrero had accused him of saying that the alternative to regional free trade was maximum self-sufficiency, while Dr. Ferrero thought that it was trade with the world on a multi-lateral basis. Professor Mikesell said that he would go one better and say that multi-lateral world trade was his first choice. However, he had tried to make it clear that, in Latin America, policies of maximum import-substitution had been adopted on the basis of production for domestic markets. He challenged this, but thought one had to accept it as a fact of life for most Latin American countries. It was not a universal phenomenon, but was nearly so in Latin America. Dr. Ferrero doubted whether exports of primary produce to the rest of the world would be affected. Professor Mikesell thought that a free trade area might reduce exports of primary produce by reducing investment in that sector and increasing it in manufacturing. This was not necessarily desirable and he pointed to the case of Argentina where it proved disastrous. Nevertheless, although it was undesirable, his answer would be that it was necessary under any system. It did not spring from regional arrangements as such. It was important to increase exports to the rest of the world and he had tried to stress that this would have to be encouraged in any ideal arrangement.

Sir Roy Harrod had asked in an earlier session how an increase in trade within the region could help to solve the problems of foreign exchange for under-developed countries and bring in capital from the rest of the world. He would give a twofold answer. In the higher stages of industrialization the problem was not an inability to produce given goods but to produce a greater variety of such things as capital goods which had limited markets. It was difficult for many of these goods to be produced on the basis of a country's own market, so that a broader regional market would help to foster specialization within the region and reduce import requirements from outside the region. Professor Mikesell also thought that production for a regional market tended to make commodities competitive with those sold by industrialized countries in world markets, and to encourage exports to countries outside the region. A regional market was therefore a first step towards diverting resources to exports to the rest of the world.

THE DISCUSSION OF PROFESSOR
BECHIN'S PAPER

Professor Tsuru said he would begin with the general comment that Professor Bechin's paper was based on Marxian concepts of political economy. Under capitalism, where the over-all social consequences of economic policy were achieved without planning, the ideal situation was one where the 'invisible hand' led to maximum social welfare, despite the fact that each individual unit in society behaved in a selfish way. Under capitalism, the instruments available to the government were limited. Its intervention was usually indirect and not very effective unless its social aims coincided with the laws of capitalist development. Professor Bechin thought that there was an objective law of historical development. If so, there was a real problem when Professor Bechin criticized direct investment by private capitalists. In so far as direct investment was successful in obtaining a high rate of return, there was an economic rationale within the framework of the capitalist system. It would be extremely hard for a capitalist state to discourage the successful investment of capital abroad. Yet Professor Bechin proposed that the capitalist state should either discourage or oppose direct investment, turning instead to making loans at a low rate of interest.

If one believed that the capitalist system had its own logic and that whatever was profitable should be encouraged, how could one reach the situation Professor Bechin proposed? Professor Bechin would argue that capitalism should take an enlightened long-run view but it was difficult to imagine that he would be able to produce arguments which were sufficiently convincing to persuade capitalist states to take measures against direct investment. He would like to hear what Professor Bechin's arguments were. The paper did not produce them and he thought that this was one of its deficiencies. The paper assumed coexistence (whether peaceful or not) between the capitalist and socialist systems, but this would require some modification of the capitalist economies, so as to enlarge the public sector and create 'mixed' economies. At the same time, the socialist economies would have to be modified so as to introduce greater decentralization in decision-making. There would have to be some use of the price mechanism, shadow prices, etc.

Professor Tsuru said he would like to refer to the letter written by Franklin D. Roosevelt to Lamont in 1944. This referred to a conversation which Roosevelt had had with Litvinov in 1933. Having discussed the possibility of sending a U.S. clergyman to Moscow, Roosevelt had remarked despairingly that there seemed little hope of understanding since the U.S.S.R and the U.S.A. were poles apart. Litvinov had replied that he did not feel that way. In 1917, the U.S.A. had been 100 per cent capitalist and the U.S.S.R. 0 per cent capitalist. By 1933, the U.S.A. was 80 per cent capitalist and the U.S.S.R. 20 per cent capitalist. By the middle 1950s the ratio would be 60 per cent to 40 per cent. Litvinov therefore felt that while the two countries might never come closer than that, there was nevertheless the hope of much greater understanding. Roosevelt had commented that this statement would remain in history. Professor Tsuru said he had quoted this to support his own view that peaceful coexistence required some modification of both systems. He would therefore like more persuasive arguments to support Professor Bechin's call for enlightened capitalism.

Professor Tsuru said that as in the next ten years the socialist, capitalist and semi-capitalist countries would all become more concerned with trading with each other, two major problems had to be considered. First, there was the question of price competition. Professor Johnson had pointed out that increased productivity could either be taken out in the form of increased money wages with profits constant or in the form of lower prices. Professor Johnson had referred to two sectors in the economy, agriculture and manufacture. He believed that by the nature of their system the socialist countries were the only ones which were likely to take out rising productivity in the form of lower profits. It was much easier for the capitalist countries to allow money wages to rise and profits to remain stable. If this were true, there should be an increase in the degree of price competition between capitalist and socialist countries. This kind of problem could already be seen in trade between Japan and China. If this was the long-run trend, serious problems were likely to arise, because there was likely to be a limit to the willingness of capitalist countries to lower their exchange rates. He would like Professor Bechin to say how far he was right in supposing that it would be easier for socialist countries to lower prices.

He thought that there was a similar difference in the flexibility of the industrial structure between socialist and capitalist countries. Capitalist countries often found it difficult to accept particular goods from under-developed countries, but there was greater flexibility in socialist countries, which often found it easy to accept cheap manufactured goods from under-developed countries. If this were true, we should probably see growing trade between under-developed and socialist countries and this might well pose a serious problem for capitalist countries, which were also interested in obtaining markets in under-developed areas. He wondered what Professor Bechin thought about this.

Professor Tsuru said that although it was a somewhat non-economic question, he wondered whether it was possible to separate trading questions from political ones, where socialist countries were concerned. Professor Bechin held that increased trade between all countries was desirable, whether these countries were socialist or capitalist. Professor Tsuru wondered whether this point really had been or could be demonstrated. It was just here that he found it difficult to separate trade, for example between Japan and the U.S.S.R., from political questions. If the two could be separated, then he was sure that trade would grow.

On a statistical point, Professor Tsuru said that Professor Bechin criticized the exploitation of under-developed areas by capitalist countries and wrote of such exploitation representing as much as 40 per cent of the gross value of the product in question. He thought this was quite possible, in the case of oil, but doubted whether it could happen with other products. He would like Professor Bechin to expand on this. There was also the question of the theoretical meaning of exploitation where there was direct investment. For example, on page 232 of his paper Professor Bechin implied that much of the value of goods like oil or ores could be withdrawn completely from the country without any equivalent return. He did not quite understand how more could be taken out than profits and would like Professor Bechin to be more specific. What could be taken out? Was it simply that wages were lowered?

Professor Bechin said that Professor Tsuru had not made any objections to the principal points of his paper, but wanted him to clarify some of the details. First, there was the question whether the state could persuade capitalists to refrain from direct investment. He had concentrated in his paper on different aspects of this question. He had not intended to call for enlightened capitalism; nor had he been concerned with persuasion, but only with the objective scientific analysis of existing economic relationships and their consequences. He had also given different examples of government interference in direct investment in developing countries. Many under-developed countries already limited direct investment, as indeed they were fully entitled to do.

Professor Bechin wanted to stress that he was not suggesting that the only alternative to direct private investment was socialism. The capitalist system had created many different forms of economic relationship and he was only analysing those which existed and not inventing them. Recently, new forms of economic relationship had been developed. For example, the U.S.S.R., the U.K. and Germany were all building steel mills in India, which, when finished, would be the property of India.

Professor Tsuru had asked whether it was possible to treat economic and political problems separately. Professor Bechin thought that one could put part of the answer by saying that bad policy could harm the economy. He regarded politics as a concentrated expression of economics. We should give scientific economic explanations for phenomena and base policy on these. This was our task as scientists.

As for the Roosevelt letter, he did not agree with the idea that reasonable economic relations between countries required their political systems to be quite similar. Our task was to take capitalism and socialism as they were and to explain how economic relationships could be extended in the existing circumstances.

Professor Tsuru had raised the problem of pricing. Trade between socialist and Western countries was carried out on the basis of world market prices. The question of how prices were fixed in particular countries was very difficult to answer, and was not the question we were at present discussing. Professor Bechin regarded the fixing of prices largely as a matter of the distribution of income. As for planning, the U.S.S.R. was aiming at a very high rate of growth in wages and consumption over the next twenty years, and he did not think that these factors bore much relation to prices on the world market. Soviet discussions of trade were based on existing world market prices.

Professor Tsuru had questioned his statistical measure of exploitation. He had put this into his paper, but agreed that exploitation could not be measured precisely. Various experts had attempted to provide such a measure, but he used different methods. He had analysed balances of payments and had found that 40 per cent of the value of export earnings of some under-developed areas was taken from them in various forms. This was only a rough approximation which he gave to illustrate the point he was making and not a precise measurement. In many cases, this was not necessary. The international distribution of gain could not be measured solely in terms of profit. Goods like oil were removed not as profits but as physical commodities.

Professor Bechin stressed that he was not trying to discuss what was desirable or undesirable, but to give an objective analysis of the consequences of different economic policies which had influenced economic relations between countries.

International Trade Theory in a Developing World

Mr. Lamfalussy said that he wanted to comment on the possibility of measuring exploitation through balance of payments figures. He had been puzzled by Professor Bechin's 40 per cent, and had made some calculations of his own from the latest GATT report. He thought that it was important to have a rough idea of the possible degree of exploitation, because if this turned out to be large we could then decide whether, by putting an end to it, we could raise the investment potential of under-developed countries. The figures for 1958 showed that export receipts of under-developed countries (including Australia and some similar countries) from developed, capitalist countries in North America and Western Europe totalled about $20 billion. The under-developed countries had to pay out to these same developed countries $2·5 billion in profits and interest payments and $1 billion for shipping, insurance, etc. The total of $3·5 billion represented 17·5 per cent of the export earnings. Mr. Lamfalussy did not think that one could regard the whole of the $3·5 billion as representing exploitation, since someone obviously had to pay for shipping, insurance, etc. The true figure for exploitation lay therefore between 0 per cent and 17·5 per cent. No doubt the correct figure would still be quite a sizeable percentage, but it must be considerably less than 40 per cent.

One could, no doubt, also contend that primary producers were exploited by being paid very low prices for their raw materials, but whether this really was exploitation was quite another story. One check was to go back to 1951 when there was no question of primary-product prices being unfairly low. In that year, export receipts were $18·8 billion and the various payments made by under-developed countries totalled $3 billion. This percentage was a little smaller than the one for 1958, and he would therefore conclude that while there was some exploitation, whose removal might raise the import capacity of under-developed areas, this was not the only, or even the greatest, burden on them.

Professor Kitamura said that this raised the question of what was the maximum permissible debt charge that one could impose on under-developed areas. Professor Bechin had mentioned a figure of debt service which equalled a third or a half of exports. Professor Kitamura said that he had met several Ministers of Finance in under-developed areas who suggested that 15-20 per cent of exports might be required to pay for the servicing of debt and regarded 25 per cent as the maximum.

Professor Kitamura said that the United Nations World Economic Survey showed that between 1950 and 1959 there was a tendency for the less-developed countries in the socialist bloc to grow faster than the more developed ones, thereby narrowing the gap in income between them. By contrast, the tendency in the non-socialist world was in the opposite direction, and the difference between the rates of growth of developed and under-developed capitalist countries was not helping to close the gap between these countries. This raised serious questions for under-developed countries, not least that of what institutional arrangements would give them a higher rate of growth. The attempt to co-ordinate national development plans under COMECON through trade policy had met with great difficulties in the initial period, but joint trade planning was now developing rapidly. He wondered how this co-ordination of planning for trade was effected. The answer to this question might throw some light on the problems confronting many other under-developed countries which were now beginning to grow together.

Professor Gudin suggested that one of the best ways of increasing under-standing and clarifying views was to exchange information on the matters discussed in Professor Bechin's paper. Professor Gudin then informed the meeting that, in Brazil, exports were equivalent to some 20 per cent of G.N.P. whereas profits of foreign investors were 1-2 per cent of G.N.P. This meant that foreign profits represented less than 10 per cent of exports. As for American profits in Brazil, he gave the information that 52 per cent of these profits had been reinvested in the last few years. Professor Gudin thought that the important effect of foreign investment in under-developed areas was not on the balance of payments but on the national income.

Professor Bechin had compared the amounts repaid to capitalist countries with the amounts received. He could not check Professor Bechin's figures but wondered whether he could quote any example of people who borrowed and did not pay back more than their initial borrow-ing (because of interest). So far as exploitation was concerned, he would like to inform Professor Bechin that the U.S.A. had helped Brazil, and other coffee-producing countries, to sustain the price charged to the American consumer.

Dr. Skorov said he would like to speak as a scholar, and not as a representative of UNESCO, on Professor Tsuru's remarks. Professor Tsuru had suggested that coexistence was impossible without considerable modification of both capitalism and socialism. He doubted whether this was correct. He rather believed that capitalism was evolving towards socialism. As for the evolution of the socialist system, he believed that this would logically develop into a fully communist system. In any case, the decentralization in a socialist system was on an entirely different basis from anything under capitalism. He thought that for coexistence the important thing was not so much the modification of the two systems as non-interference in each other's affairs. If one accepted the principle of non-interference and also that the world was developing constantly, then coexistence was possible. Besides all these theoretical considerations, co-existence was the only basis for any existence at all in the thermo-nuclear age.

Professor Tsuru had inquired about the possibility of falling prices in socialist countries. If the U.S.S.R. exported capital goods somewhat below world prices, this was entirely the result of the way in which prices were fixed in the socialist system. Capital goods were produced on a very large scale and bore no or very little turnover tax. Since most of the loans to under-developed areas were intended to give them capital goods, this represented a clear advantage to them. In this sense, price competition with the capitalist countries was already keen. At the same time, the

U.S.S.R. represented a large and growing market for goods from primary-producing countries. In the coming decade this market would be enlarged even more with the steadily increasing standard of living in socialist countries, coupled with a change in the structure of domestic production, especially that of agriculture. For example, now that Russia imported much Cuban sugar, she was able to lay less emphasis on growing beet for sugar. Similarly, the import of Egyptian long-staple cotton meant that it was possible to reduce her own production. New and potentially very big markets for cocoa, bananas and other tropical goods were being opened in the socialist world.

As to whether one could separate commercial and political relationships, the answer was that one ought to separate them, though it was by no means easy to do so. Since the war, it has been impossible to persuade the U.S.A. to ignore political considerations in developing trade with the U.S.S.R., though countries like the U.K. had not taken such a rigid view. The keen debate on Britain's wish to join the Common Market was just one more example of the close links between economic and political relationships.

Professor Ohlin contended that when Professor Bechin asserted that direct investment in primary production was bad, this was in contradiction of historical facts. Professor Gudin had already mentioned Brazil, but one could also quote what had happened in the U.S.A. a hundred years ago, in Canada, Sweden, Australia and New Zealand. He was surprised that Professor Bechin could assert the opposite so flatly without discussing such cases. The technical knowledge which foreign investment brought with it was also something which needed stressing. Professor Bechin suggested that if an under-developed country did not get the whole value of its exports, it was being robbed. Surely it was better to get 90 per cent of the total and use the remainder for interest payment than to be content with smaller exports and less-rapid development, and refuse to borrow foreign capital. One could always say that foreign control of one's raw material resources was risky and this was the real case for many nationalistic policies.

Professor Gudin had stressed that the important effect of foreign investment was not on the balance of payments, but on income. Many economists on the other hand tended to suggest that the necessity for making interest payments represented a permanent burden. One was reminded of Keynes' view that an indemnity payment was impossible. Surely it was all a question of size. With proper domestic policy there should be no real problem, and on this he agreed with Sir Roy. Professor Ohlin said he was puzzled that Professor Bechin was even more opposed to investment in export industries than in industries supplying the home market. If the balance of payments was causing difficulty, surely investment in exports was very desirable.

On the relation of economic and political questions, Professor Ohlin said he thought that Lenin's doctrine held that trade was not a matter of economics, but of politics, and part of the external policy of a socialist state. This must be even more the case with overseas investment. Professor Bechin claimed that we should regard the policy pursued as the outcome of the state of the economy, so that there was no contradiction between economic development and political actions. Did this mean that Professor Bechin thought there was no problem over whether Soviet external policy had economic aims only, or political ones as well? If so, this was surely a socialist form of Adam Smith's argument about the hidden hand, with complete harmony between the economic and political views of the leading political group in the U.S.S.R. Were we really being taught that what was in the economic and political interest of the U.S.S.R. was also in the interest of under-developed countries? We then seemed to have a very strange world in which only the activities of capitalist countries were motivated by political aims. He suggested that Russian trade policy in the last forty years had been relatively autarkic and not a policy for expanding economic relations with the outside world. Professor Ohlin stressed that he was not being critical, but merely asking a question on historical fact. As for the Common Market, an offer had been made to lower the tariff envisaged in the Rome Treaty by 20 per cent, and the U.S. government intended to negotiate a tariff reduction under GATT. He thought that predictions about world trade should not ignore such things.

Professor Robinson said that many economists thought that one virtue of direct investment in under-developed countries which normally traded with those making the direct investment was that the latter bore the risks and uncertainties of the investment. They only earned any reward when there was also a gain to the under-developed country. He stressed that there were many cases in Latin America in the nineteenth century where British investors did not receive back as much as 100 per cent of their initial investment. Britain had built many of the railways in the world at a return of less than 100 per cent of what they put into them. Similarly, a study by Professor Frankel of British investment in Africa showed that over a wide range this yielded an average return of less than the gilt-edged rate of interest. This was certainly true in gold mining. One should not look just at the spectacular successes of certain direct investments, but at the whole range, remembering that there was always a high degree of uncertainty.

Dr. Patel wanted to stress the points of agreement between Professor Bechin and economists from both developed and under-developed countries. First, everyone agreed that the economies of the primary producers needed strengthening and that this implied industrialization. The differences were only over the pace and direction of industrialization. Again, there was general agreement that the development of the less-developed countries would require some transfer of capital from the richer countries and that while foreign aid was necessary, it was equally important to enable the developing countries to expand their exports rapidly. Meanwhile, it was clear that most developing countries were willing to accept aid equally gladly from socialist as well as capitalist sources.

Differences began to arise only over the kind of capital transfer that was needed and the extent to which reliance could be placed upon private foreign capital. It was not easy to answer these questions in general terms. Professor Bechin was certainly right that in assessing the role of private foreign capital, allowance should be made for profits and interest earnings on the capital imported. However, the under-developed countries were sovereign states and should be able to decide for themselves the conditions under which they would allow the import of private foreign capital. While they were prepared to borrow private capital, they were also anxious to ensure that the direct and indirect returns on such investment over the long run would be larger than the loss implied in periodic payments to foreign capitalists. If the achievement of self-sustained growth was the objective, the inflow of private foreign capital could clearly be permitted only by using definite criteria to judge the net benefit to be derived by the developing countries. He was inclined to think that there had been too much emphasis on private foreign capital in the past and that in the future greater reliance would need to be placed on official capital. But, again, most of lending countries and institutions had accepted the principle that greater reliance should be put on the kind of aid which imposed less burden on the balances of payments of developing countries.

The argument that direct private investment was superior to official capital in so far as private foreign entrepreneurs brought with them technical knowledge as well as capital could easily be exaggerated. An inflow of technical know-how could come with official capital as well. The arrangements for setting up of steel plants in India were a case in point.

On page 234 of his paper, Professor Bechin had stressed that loans from the U.S.S.R. carried a low rate of interest and were repayable in local currency, that was to say, ultimately in goods. He did not know whether Professor Bechin was trying to draw a contrast with aid from other countries. But he did not think that, taking everything into account, the terms on which assistance was offered by the United States, for example, were more onerous than those attaching to assistance from the U.S.S.R.

Professor Byé had the same reservations as Professor Ohlin about what Professor Bechin had said about the Common Market. He also agreed with Dr. Patel that it was important not to define the respective positions in a brutal way. Most of the developing countries, excluding some in Latin America, would inevitably have to plan their economies and that some degree of socialism would be inevitable. He thought one should distinguish direct investment in under-developed and developed areas. Direct investment in developed countries was a competitive question, with the investor and the borrower on equal terms. This happened, for example, with U.S. investment in France or Germany which held no disadvantage for the borrowing country and was altogether excellent. Direct investment in under-developed areas was not in the same category. Most classical economists agreed that there was sometimes a case for a monopoly over the production of some raw material. Oil was a good example. Even the most liberal economist could not claim that the oil industry was perfectly competitive, or that it automatically reached the optimum situation for either producing or consuming countries.

There should therefore be a long-term plan for petroleum production and it was right to look for and guard against exploitation. This could happen not only through prices charged and paid, but also by the timing of production. It was necessary for such an industry to regulate the production rate in order to safeguard reserves. Planning of production over time might well be in the general interest. It followed that when direct investment was being made in under-developed countries it should be planned, and the country where the investment took place should control the plan. If planning was not possible, it was better to avoid direct investment altogether.

Professor Morgan said that since he had read Professor Bechin's paper, he had tried to find statistics which were relevant to the concept of 'exploitation' dealt with on page 232. Professor Bechin said that between 1946 and 1958 the U.S.A. had exported $11·4 billion of capital. It was not clear how his data could be reconciled with those of the Department of Commerce of the U.S.A., which give 'U.S. private long-term and short-term capital outflow, including private remittances' as $27·5 billion for this period. U.S. government's foreign economic assistance (grants plus loans) for the same period added up to $50·1 billion. The total of private and governmental capital outflow was therefore $75·6 billion.

As to 'profits' returned to the United States, Professor Morgan understood Professor Bechin to give the figure of $19·6 billion for the years 1946–58. Department of Commerce data gave 'income on investments' at $24·9 billion. But the two totals were not necessarily inconsistent : the Bechin figures might be for dividends only (excluding interest). In any case, it was clear that the outflow of private and government capital, including gifts, was about three times as great as income from investments.

It was suggested that loans, direct investments and gifts were a useful stimulus to the U.S. economy. But this was a period of generally excessive demand in the United States ; the need was to check demand rather than increase it. Hence, to the extent the capital outflows were spent in the U.S.A., they were generally a burden on the economy. In some of these years aggregate American demand was deficient. In such times, higher domestic spending — for example, government outlays in appropriate areas — could be more prompt, better adapted to the available resources, and so more effective in that they gave both higher employment and a higher growth rate than foreign grants and loans.

Sir Donald MacDougall returned to the question of exploitation. When one talked of exploitation in Professor Bechin's sense, one presumably implied that foreign private investment brought gains to the investing country and losses to the country receiving the investment. In capitalist countries it was broadly true, subject to a good many qualifications, that capital flowed to where it could earn the highest return, thereby tending to equalize private rates of return on home and foreign investment after allowance for risk had been made. Now if extra investment was carried out within a developed country, the profit earned was approximately equal (according to capitalist theory) to the additional benefit derived by the nation. Part of the profits earned would go to the government in taxation, and part to the private investor.

If, on the other hand, the capital were invested instead in an under-developed country, a substantial part of the profit would be taken by the government of that country. Given the existence of double taxation agreements, the investing country's government would often give tax credit for the tax already paid in the under-developed country. It followed that the benefit to the nation was less than if the investment had been carried out at home. If this was true, then developed countries were being altruistic in making private investments abroad. He agreed that there were many other considerations which might tell in the other direction, but this was nevertheless one important offsetting factor.

If the developed countries stopped direct investment, and put nothing in its place, this might well be advantageous economically, if not politically, to the developed countries. There were certainly many in the U.K. who took this view, on both balance of payments and other grounds. On the other hand, he suggested that the ending of direct investment would be disadvantageous to the under-developed countries not only because it would reduce their tax receipts, but also because they would be unable to use their labour and natural resources so fully and would therefore forgo the various external economies that resulted from direct investment. The aggregate gains from such investment were often much more important than any subsequent balance of payments difficulties that might arise. As Dr. Patel had said, India had decided, after careful consideration, that it was in her interest to accept direct private investment from abroad along with other types of aid, although she did not accept all investment indiscriminately.

If Professor Bechin said that private direct investment should be stopped and replaced by government loans, there might be more to be said for his argument. But there would still be the difficult question of how certain types of technical know-how could then be acquired. He would like to remind Professor Bechin that much government aid was already being given on generous terms, and often in greater quantities than direct private investment.

Professor Kaigl disagreed with Professor Tsuru's view that capitalism and socialism were becoming more similar. Of course there was de-centralization on an increasing scale in socialist countries, but this was always of a socialist character and linked with the central direction of the economy. More and more decisions were being left to the enterprises, after the proportions of investment, consumption and other major items had been settled centrally. All these decisions were taken under the influence of the views of the man in the street. Before the government took major economic decisions, nation-wide discussion was organized and the government took account of the views expressed in framing its future plans. The everyday policy of enterprises was controlled by workers and by the inhabitants of the region. The main feature of the evolution of the socialist countries was a more and more far-reaching democratization. In capitalist countries, however, the evolution of the system meant that more and more of the economic power was concentrated in a few hands. It followed that the evolution of the two systems was leading them in opposite directions. Nevertheless, he believed that mutual trade was to the advantage of both.

Professor Bechin said that the discussion had shown great interest in the problems touched upon in his paper. Differences of opinion were quite natural, and he hoped that economists would continue to study and discuss these problems, finding a solution in conformity with the aims of economic and social progress. He thought that Professor Kitamura had raised a very real problem in showing that the gap in wealth and incomes between different capitalist countries was not narrowing. If one looked at past developments, one could see that there were several reasons why these differences existed. First, there were internal conditions, including feudal forms of social organization. There was also external economic dependence and colonial exploitation. In recent years, with most of these countries independent, their rates of growth had risen and were continuing to increase. When all the internal and external obstacles were removed, it would be possible to raise growth rates even further. Professor Bechin thought that the main prerequisite of growth was genuine independence.

Professor Bechin agreed with Mr. Lamfalussy that the removal of profits from under-developed countries limited their power to import, but he could not accept the figure of 18 per cent, which was too low. One had to allow for sums appropriated by foreign owners of the capital assets of a developing country which did not appear in the balance of payments. His own figure related only to some selected countries, but he was pleased that Mr. Lamfalussy agreed that the withdrawal of profits by foreigners *had* held back the development of certain countries.

Professor Ohlin had spoken of the favourable effects of direct investment on the development of the U.S.A., Sweden and other countries in the last century, but Professor Bechin thought that similar direct investments in the colonies of Asia or Latin American countries had had an opposite effect. That was the point he had tried to stress in his paper. Again, while Professor Robinson had noted that Britain had not earned as much as even the value of her original lending to some countries, one had to remember that Britain had experienced a wide variety of results in her foreign lending.

Professor Bechin shared Dr. Patel's hope that there would be less private direct investment in future. Nor did he disagree with Professor Gudin that one had to pay something when one borrowed. This was not what he had meant. He was merely saying that high interest charges hampered the development of under-developed countries. He was also glad that Professor Byé agreed that direct investment had different effects in developed and in under-developed countries.

R
497

Professor Bechin knew the figures which Professor Morgan had given for the capital grants of the U.S.A., but his own figures had compared net exports of capital and the interest earned on it.

Finally, he wanted to stress that revolutionary changes were now occurring in the forms of economic relationship between nations. The favourable results of these changes were obvious, and a scientific study of the factors lying behind their improvement would make a great contribution to economics.

THE DISCUSSION OF THE PAPER BY
MR. LAMFALUSSY

Mr. Liesner said he would try to comment fairly on Mr. Lamfalussy's paper, although to do so one really needed a statistical library at hand. The basic aim of the paper was to explain why the effects of recessions in the U.S.A. and pauses in Western Europe on world trade and incomes were not cumulative. On page 249 of his paper, Mr. Lamfalussy said that such movements could be caused either by the working of the international trade multiplier or by balance of payments difficulties leading governments to apply import restrictions. In the second case, the result would not be a fall in income so much as one in world trade. Looking at these two possibilities Mr. Lamfalussy concluded that neither of them had operated to any significant extent. The main reason why there had been no cumulative movement in international trade was the generally inflationary character of the period. A slight fall in exports could be met either by increasing home consumption or by switching exports to other markets. Although there had been pauses in economic activity in Western Europe, levels of income had stood up well. This left the question whether balance of payments policies had led to any cumulative results. If one allowed for anything like normal propensities one would expect that a country suffering from a recession would experience an improvement in its balance of payments while other countries suffered a deterioration. If countries were not prepared to deflate, one naturally wondered why measures to offset resulting balance of payments difficulties did not lead to a fall in world trade.

Mr. Lamfalussy argued in terms of a model where one had implied trade between two countries which were trying to keep up their incomes, and the foreign trade position of both of these was affected by what went on in a third country. It seemed obvious that the first two countries would run into balance of payments difficulties unless they could substitute trade with each other for imports from the third country whenever this had a lower level of activity than they had. Mr. Lamfalussy's answer to the question why had this not happened in practice was that non-trading items in the balances of payments of most countries had been important in the 1950s and that they had been unaffected by changes in the general level of economic activity. Private capital movements, foreign aid and defence expenditure had all been highly significant. Mr. Liesner would have put more emphasis than Mr. Lamfalussy on the effects of the rather discriminatory import restrictions of the period.

Another important question was that of international liquidity. Mr. Lamfalussy wrote as though the effects of the EPU were restricted to Western Europe. In fact, they affected the whole of the sterling area and after 1954 transferable sterling also. In other words, virtually all non-dollar trade with Europe went through the EPU.

Mr. Liesner noted that on page 257 of his paper, Mr. Lamfalussy said, 'it is the growth of its gold and dollar reserves that enabled Western Europe to resume its expansion and to develop its imports from the Non-Industrial Areas'. He would like to say that imports from non-industrial countries were not paid for in either gold or hard currency.

When Mr. Lamfalussy considered the effects of shifts in income he looked at the results of visible trade only. However, one ought to look at all payments made out of income in the importing country and paid over to exporting countries. For example, in 1954 the trade balance of Western Europe with the U.S.A. worsened by $700 million, but the current surplus fell by only $100 million. The deflationary effect was therefore less than the pure trade figures suggested.

Mr. Liesner was not too happy with the theoretical analysis on pages 244-8, especially in so far as it considered the effect of the price level on the propensity to import. What it seemed to say was that with a high price level and low incomes a rise in income would lead to a big increase in imports. It seemed to follow that if incomes increased there would be a balance of payments deficit. On the other hand, Mr. Lamfalussy held that if income fell the analysis would not be reversible. A country which had a high price level would experience only a small fall in imports, the argument being that consumers would be more price conscious if incomes were declining. Some of the difficulties arose because Mr. Lamfalussy began with a disequilibrium situation where devaluation seemed imminent. But Mr. Liesner did not think American experience would bear out this analysis.

Turning to some statistical questions, Mr. Liesner wondered why in Appendix III on currency reserves Mr. Lamfalussy considered the gold reserves of the U.K. only. Why not include dollars as well? On a more substantial point, Mr. Liesner wondered whether one should not subtract outstanding sterling balances. Certainly, if one looked at Western Europe as a whole he thought one ought to deduct sterling balances held by countries outside Western Europe. In Appendix IV, Mr. Liesner was not happy about the division into Western Europe, North America and other countries. He would have thought that non-industrial countries should be put into a separate category. Again, Mr. Lamfalussy had chosen 1951 as a starting-point on some occasions and 1950 on others. One usually thought of the first year in any series or any study as being normal. However, 1950 was not a normal year, and 1951 even less so.

Finally, Mr. Liesner said that he would just like to comment briefly on the pause in Western Europe in 1952 which Mr. Lamfalussy labelled a textile recession. This might be largely true, but it still left open the question whether the recession was natural or was induced by government restrictions. Mr. Liesner's view was that the recession was rather wider than Mr. Lamfalussy had indicated, and that government restrictions affected many imports directly. He therefore thought it was wrong to conclude from examining the statistics that the marginal propensity to import was high because imports fell off rapidly.

Mr. Maizels said he would make some empirical observations on an empirical study which tried to tie in theoretical generalizations with the statistics. He thought that Mr. Lamfalussy's theory, especially on relative price levels, was very hard to link with the statistics at all and it was perhaps not surprising that as the paper went on Mr. Lamfalussy left these questions aside. One reason was probably that this kind of analysis was very hard to apply, for example, if one wanted to know whether a particular country's general price level was out of line and therefore whether its currency should be devalued or revalued. To put this question in the forefront of the argument led one straight into considerable difficulty. Another problem was that, while Mr. Lamfalussy's statistics related to groups of countries, his argument ran in terms of individual countries. This meant that his grouping was not sufficiently refined and one should, for example, look at the U.K., Western Europe and Japan separately. The marginal propensity to import was different in the U.K. and in Western Europe, and the U.K. had special links with non-industrial countries which meant that her position was directly connected with the effects of falling primary-product prices on the balance of payments of the rest of the sterling area. On the other hand, the growth of Western Europe and Japan had its main effect in increasing the export-earning capacity of non-industrial countries. Again, *within* non-industrial countries, what happened to those countries which produced oil had a big effect on the trade figures. Yet the basis of any changes in such figures was the ability of the oil companies to switch production as they wanted. It was by no means clear that changes in the trade of oil-producing countries were related in the same way, or indeed at all, to recessions in industrial countries as were changes in the main primary products.

Mr. Maizels pointed out that since the war no recession had been completed within a year, which meant that using annual figures obscured time-lags in the transmission of cycles. This was especially serious for econometric analysis, where there were two kinds of lag. First, there was a lag between the onset of a recession in industrial countries and a fall in their imports. On the other hand, there was a lag between a fall in the imports of primary produce by industrial countries and a fall in their exports to primary producers. If a recession in the industrial countries proceeded very rapidly this could more than outweigh the relatively slow reactions of non-industrial countries.

Mr. Maizels did not think one could usefully carry out this kind of analysis solely in terms of value. One must separate the influence of a recession on the volume of trade from its effects on the prices of the goods traded. We all knew that the effects of recession were different in industrial and non-industrial areas, and there had been several remarks about recessions hitting prices of primary products and employment in industrial countries. Mr. Maizels thought the facts were rather more complex than this. In the early post-war recessions, imports of primary products to the U.S.A. fell in both volume and price. Later, this was not so true, and he thought one should divide post-war recessions into two groups. It might be that the change in American reactions was a once-for-all event. In some industries, the U.S. companies were concerned with safeguarding their own resources and this was particularly true of non-ferrous ores and oil. Instead of being marginal sources of supply, U.S. imports were becoming permanent and stable sources, and it was the production of home industries which was now marginal. Perhaps this was why falls in U.S. activity had affected trade less than had been anticipated. If one looked at prices, one found that in 1953–54, contrary to expectations, prices of primary produce had not fallen and Mr. Maizels thought that this was partly due to the asymmetrical role of imports. He agreed with Mr. Liesner that the analysis was best carried out in terms both of commodity trade and of current balances. The figures in the appendix suggested that there was some cyclical movement in invisible trade items, which meant that more detailed statistics were needed for these.

Professor Delivanis thought that the reason why many economists mistakenly forecast a depression at the end of the 1940s was that they underestimated the importance of continued public spending when reconstruction was over but economic development and military spending continued. Mr. Lamfalussy was wrong in ignoring the invisible items in the balance of payments and in being astonished that U.S. capital exports to Western Europe continued when equilibrium had been almost achieved towards the end of 1960. These exports were not so much the expression of fears of a dollar devaluation but a result of expectations of high profit at a time when stock exchanges in Western Europe were booming and European interest rates were high. Mr. Lamfalussy was right in admitting the part that chance had played in monetary developments in the 1950s in the Western world, but he underestimated the importance of independent monetary policy, thanks to substantial gold reserves and the extent of international liquidity. Last, but not least, there was the stabilization by law of U.S. agricultural prices, the pledge of Western governments to maintain full employment and increased possibilities of obtaining loans from international organizations. Professor Delivanis said that on international liquidity in particular he strongly disagreed with Mr. Lamfalussy.

Professor Weiller thought that the cyclical role of change in trade policies was always understressed, especially by economists in the U.K. and U.S.A. where, for different and opposite reasons, this phenomenon could not be noticed. He recalled that in his book *Europe and the Money Muddle*, Professor Triffin agreed that long-term capital flows could generally have a stabilizing effect, but denied the possibility of a cyclical element in the change towards more or less protection before 1914. Professor Weiller considered trade policy an important factor for the 'long waves' and major turning-points. One question was the long-run level of protection, which ought to be as low as possible; another question was the need for some flexibility in economic policies. All this had indeed existed both before 1914 and in the 1950s, when liberalization had been carried out within the OEEC framework.

Professor Weiller also thought that foreign aid had played a large part in preventing more serious disturbances in international trade. However, countries which had received considerable aid very often channelled it elsewhere — to countries which did not need it so badly — and this had accelerated the redistribution of reserves between industrial countries. For non-European countries the problem was more difficult. In his opinion at the moment, the need was not for more and more foreign capital, but for greater co-operation in providing international aid. This was especially important for the under-developed countries and to strengthen co-operation in this field Professor Weiller thought that an institution like OECD could usefully regulate the flow of aid.

Sir Roy Harrod said that Mr. Lamfalussy's was fine, detailed work which it would be hard to controvert. Objections had been made to Mr. Lamfalussy's method, but he thought that so far no hole had been made in the argument. It was right to suggest that luck was mainly responsible for the fact that post-war recessions had not gained momentum, but, if this was true, it had to be remembered that luck always came to an end. Past experience was by no means conclusive; and one needed built-in stabilizers.

The initial piece of good luck was that there had been no big recession in the early 1950s. Instead, the Korean war had postponed the onset of any recession and its effects had been good in the sense that they got the U.S.A. out of step with Europe. This lack of synchronization had continued until 1958, with excellent results. The immediate reaction to the Korean war had been stock-piling and rising real spending, followed in 1952–53 by European recessions whose effects had been rather wider than Mr. Lamfalussy's reference to textiles suggested. However, the U.S. economy had continued to boom because of defence spending during this period; whereas the additional defence spending in Europe was not sufficient to offset the deflationary forces. Only after the big American defence spree had tailed off was there the 1953–54 recession in the U.S.A.; but by then Europe had recovered. The world had therefore been protected from the effects of the 1953–54 recession simply because things were out of step in this way. Most of Europe was by then experiencing a strong boom. This was caused by long-term post-war reconstruction, and the fixed investment boom to which it gave rise meant that the out-of-phase movement as between Europe and the U.S.A. continued.

In the U.K., strong anti-boom measures were taken in 1955 so that our boom ended; but the boom had not ended in Europe, and things remained out of phase. However, in 1957, a pause in Europe began in the sense of a fall in the rate of growth early in that year, with output flattening out in the second half of 1957. There was an associated fall in the prices of primary produce, and Sir Roy argued that recently Europe and Japan had been having a bigger effect on primary-product prices than had the U.S.A. The expectation of continued increases in exports of primary produce had been disappointed and this absence of a continued rise had led to big price movements. In 1957, there had also been a fall in U.S. investment and exports. Mr. Liesner had suggested that the Suez crisis had had little effect on trade. Sir Roy, however, thought the crisis must have meant that late in 1956 and early in 1957 U.S. exports had been sustained and that, but for Suez, the emergence of the U.S. balance of payments deficit would have come earlier.

Professor Sohmen thought that important lessons could be learned from the behaviour of the U.S. balance of payments in the 1950s, when it had worsened as income fell. A simple explanation was that the U.S.A. had been suffering from cost inflation. Only this could explain the unusual behaviour of the balance on current account. Indeed Professor Sohmen thought that the deterioration of the balance of payments simultaneously with a fall in domestic activity was the only criterion available for distinguishing cost push from demand pull. Objections to the use of other criteria, especially those raised by Haberler and Machlup, were well known. Professor Sohmen thought one could use this particular criterion without even having to look at price indices. A major difficulty when using over-all price indices for international comparisons was that, in any case, they included many goods which were not traded, and so could not give an adequate picture of a country's competitiveness in world markets.

This was, of course, not true of export price indices. They gave quite a different picture of developments in the U.S. economy. In addition, he suggested that they provided interesting evidence on the values of elasticities of demand in international trade. If a relative increase in U.S. export prices led, as it had, to a deterioration of the balance on current account in the U.S.A., this showed that demand elasticities in international trade were high and that devaluation would therefore be effective in solving balance of payments difficulties.

Then, unfortunately, in 1958 all areas were back in phase, and there was recession both in the U.S.A. and in Europe. However, he thought one could be more cheerful in the light of what had happened in that year. Strong measures were taken to cure what looked like developing into a big depression and these were successful. The U.K. and the U.S.A., faced with a formidable recession at a time when primary-product prices were low and Europe was pausing, did extremely well to deal with matters so effectively.

Sir Donald MacDougall commented especially on Professor Sohmen's remarks. In the recessions of 1953–54 and 1960–61, the U.S. balance of payments on current account had improved, not worsened. In the recession of 1957–58 it had worsened, but various factors were unusually favourable in 1957 and unusually unfavourable in 1958–59. The U.S. balance was helped in 1957 by the closing of the Suez Canal, by an inflationary boom in Europe, by bad harvests in Europe in 1956 and by shipments of cotton well in excess of current needs abroad. In 1958–59 all these conditions were reversed and the U.S. balance was further worsened by such special factors as a temporary decline in the domestic supply of meat, the switching over of the aircraft industry from propeller to jet planes, a steel strike and the delay in introducing the 'compact' car. It was easy to show that much of what had happened depended on special factors and he thought it was difficult to deduce anything about cost-push inflation from these events.

Sir Donald thought it would be difficult to carry out an econometric analysis of, for example, the marginal propensity to import, with the limited information we had, since it was hard to isolate special factors. However, if one were to attempt such an analysis, one should look not only at the relation between trade and income but also the relation between trade and the percentage of unemployment, since this gave some indication of the extent of shortages or surpluses. An important factor determining U.S. exports was the level of unemployment in Europe and not just the level of industrial production or income there. U.S. coal and steel exports to Europe were frequently marginal.

So far as built-in stabilizers were concerned, Sir Donald drew attention to the possibility of equilibrating capital movements in the trade cycle. For example with a recession in the U.S.A. and a boom in Europe, low interest rates in the U.S.A. would send capital to Europe. Money would also flow in order to buy ordinary shares, and he thought it was important to look carefully to see how far share prices were in phase.

Sir Donald was perplexed by Mr. Lamfalussy's assumption that the marginal propensity to import was a function of relative prices. He saw two possible explanations. First, if the price level were low in some sense, the balance of payments would tend to improve, with exports rising quickly and imports slowly. This would lead to the cyclical behaviour described by Mr. Lamfalussy, though not if one were measuring trade in terms of deviations from the trend. Secondly, if the relative price level was abnormally high, then the average propensity to import might be greater than usual and the marginal propensity might also be high.

Professor Giersch was also puzzled by what Professor Sohmen had said. He agreed that one could use the cost-inflation hypothesis to explain why the U.S. balance of payments had worsened in a recession, but how could one explain an improvement of the balance of payments in recovery unless one brought in such factors as time-lags or capital movements?

Dr. Savosnick referred to the statement on page 261 of Mr. Lamfalussy's paper that 'Western Europe, as a whole, has not suffered from this development until now. The deflationary effect of the fall of its exports to North America has been more than offset by the rise in its sales to the Non-Industrial Areas. At the same time, the spectacular increase in intra-European trade has no doubt resulted in a substantial net addition to total demand.' He did not see how one could say that there was *no doubt* that this development resulted in a net addition to total demand. The fact that Europeans could obtain things more cheaply by importing from other European countries, rather than from domestic sources, might have led many of them to demand other things at home which otherwise would not have been bought. But there was no guarantee that this would be the result, and one might reasonably suspect that reductions in many incomes would have occurred when high-cost producers were supplanted by low-cost producers. He would not wish to contradict Mr. Lamfalussy's conclusions if these were made slightly less categorically.

There might, however, be another explanation why the increase in internal trade within Europe had acted as a stabilizer. The individual European exporter was increasingly selling in both a foreign-European and an American export market. The growth of the individual European market might make him less nervous when the American barometer dropped. He might therefore be more inclined to carry on with investment plans. Investment demand in Europe had therefore been kept up and the marginal propensity not to spend might have been smaller than otherwise.

Professor Byé said that for several years U.S. industry had had considerable increased capacity and this might help to explain the asymmetric behaviour of the balance of payments and demand. For example, the U.S. steel industry knew that if there was an increase in domestic demand this would reduce the amount of unused capacity, while, if there was a depression, the main effects of this would be on the external surplus. So far as structural changes were concerned, all agreed that these were important in the period in question. They were not only connected with the liberalization of exchange but with other questions too. Professor Byé was sorry that the question of shifts in the German economy had not been studied. He thought one reason for the good export performance of the Germany economy since the war was that even before 1939 the economy had been oriented towards exporting to a greater extent than had happened in countries like France. This was partly a spontaneous movement, but had been helped on by the state. He thought that in the reconstruction period deliberate attention had been given to increasing exports. France had only actually begun to achieve these later, but since 1953 there had been a vigorous movement towards exporting, partly supported by government action. For example, it was seen that an export market would have to be built up by, for example, setting up organizations like the Renault Chain in the U.S.A. Success in exporting to the U.S.A. required a great deal of investment. There were thresholds to pass and 'development poles' to be set up abroad. Among elements supporting continued structural change, Professor Byé thought that the setting up of the Common Market was responsible for the strong growth of inter-European trade in 1960.

Turning to the question of transfers, Professor Byé said that one had to remember that in addition to the kind of capital flow which had already been discussed there were financial flows which had no counterpart within the period of time in question. Nor should one forget that transfers were still mainly bilateral. While there had been a fall in transfers from the U.S.A. to Europe, grants to under-developed countries had been maintained. Although there was not always an obligation for the under-developed country to buy in the lending country the fact was that most purchases would be made in that country. Professor Byé explained that in a report to the Economic Council in France he had insisted on the need to distinguish between the trade balance and transfers.

Professor Tsuru had been stimulated by the theoretical part of the paper. Although Japan was not specifically considered, he was worried about how one would apply an analysis in terms of relative price levels to such a country. For example, since 1957 wholesale prices in Japan had been steady or had been rising rather slowly at 1 or 2 per cent per annum. Yet export prices had fallen 22 per cent. If one took a ratio of f.o.b. export prices and wholesale prices, one obviously would get very big fluctuations. It would obviously not be easy to integrate the price level into any analysis when there were such divergent movements. Professor Tsuru added that since both Sir Roy Harrod and Mr. Maizels had mentioned her as an important market for primary producers he would like to say that, apart from oil and rubber, Japan was not an important buyer of primary produce.

Professor Bowen had read the paper with non-industrial countries in mind, including Australia. Australia was a country which was growing rapidly and setting up new industries both to replace imports and develop exports. Although the IMF had helped countries like Australia in recent years the major factor had been the relative stability of the U.S.A. and Europe. He did not believe that this was due to the operation of built-in stabilizers, since these usually worked well *except* when conditions were really bad and they were needed. He therefore thought that, even if there was a fair degree of stability in some parts of the world, economic de-stabilization was likely to occur elsewhere as the bad effects of industrial depression on non-industrial countries showed. The export of recession to under-developed areas meant a fall in the rate of growth, and one effect was the imposition of long-period import restrictions. As a result of the relatively stagnant demand for primary produce, the rate of growth of real income was rather slow in Australia at present.

Mr. Lamfalussy summed up the discussion. His paper represented a first step in a bigger study and that he would consider all the suggestions made in the discussion as he proceeded with his work. Mr. Lamfalussy said he would like to clear up what had been said about his theoretical digression, which it seemed to him now was perhaps a little cryptic. Ambiguity arose because he had made no specific assumptions about levels of employment or the balance of payments. One could therefore object to his conclusions on grounds of the asymmetry, on page 247 of his paper, where he argued that differences in costs would either lead to full employment in the low-cost country (and hence to a higher propensity to import when income was rising, just as if the country had higher costs), or to a steady balance of payments disequilibrium which obviously could not last for ever. Thus this asymmetry argument could not hold in the long run.

Mr. Lamfalussy admitted that this was true, but answered the criticisms by saying that the 1950–60 period was not a long-run one either. We could, in fact, observe that the presumably low-cost countries (continental Europe) had come steadily closer to full employment during the period and yet had simultaneously enjoyed a steady surplus on their current external accounts. It was this situation that he was trying to 'rationalize' in his theoretical section. Though this situation was unlikely to last for ever, and hence to represent an equilibrium position — either the growing labour shortages or the external surplus must go — it had lasted long enough to be taken into account, rather than to be dismissed as a theoretically uninteresting or meaningless case.

Mr. Lamfalussy said he would also take into account the comments of Mr. Liesner and Mr. Maizels on his statistics. In particular, he would use quarterly figures and improve his triangular model by a more detailed geographical breakdown.

Mr. Lamfalussy thought that all Mr. Liesner's points were valuable, especially what he had said about the links between the EPU and the sterling area. He also agreed with Professor Delivanis that there had been considerable mistakes in forecasts of activity over the last fifteen years and that public expenditure had been an important factor ensuring stability in individual countries. Nevertheless, he thought there was considerable instability in the international mechanism. So far as institutions were concerned, he was not sure that taking them into account made one feel any more optimistic, because of the way in which the gold exchange standard system worked.

Replying to Professor Weiller, Mr. Lamfalussy said that he thought it was very hard indeed to generalize about the influence of trade policies but he thought that trade policies, like export drives, reduced rather than increased stability. Mr. Lamfalussy agreed with Professor Byé that there was considerable unused capacity in the U.S.A., but thought that his theory could allow for this. He also thought Professor Byé had made an essential point in stressing the links between non-commercial transfers and political decisions. This was certainly important and he intended to pay great attention to it in his further study.

Replying to Professor Tsuru, Mr. Lamfalussy said he thought it was not possible to deal easily with either export or domestic prices when making statistical studies, and that it was better to try to deal with costs. This would not help one to solve all problems but might give a partial solution. He also suggested that, so far as the exports of primary producers were concerned, continental Europe was more important than either the U.K. or Japan.

Replying to Dr. Savosnick, Mr. Lamfalussy said he did not claim that an increase in trade within Europe had no effect on its balance of payments, but he was uncertain about the effect on income. He thought that the big rise in inter-European trade in 1958 had stimulated income.

Dr. Savosnick suggested that the opening of trade within a region might have a depressing effect.

Mr. Lamfalussy replied that in Europe the ending of restrictions and the lowering of tariffs took place in a period of full employment, and he therefore thought there was a presumption that its effects, working through the accelerator, would be beneficial.

Sir Roy Harrod suggested that if the rise in trade within Europe took place at the expense of countries outside Europe then the effects within Europe must be beneficial. However, if countries simply imported from each other what they had previously made for themselves, he did not see why there should be any net change within the European group.

Mr. Lamfalussy ended by saying that so far as Professor Bowen's comments were concerned he did not think that, if there was a reasonable degree of stability in Europe, this could have very bad effects on underdeveloped areas.

THE DISCUSSION OF DR. SERGEYEV'S PAPER

Professor Kindleberger said he was sure the Conference was very grateful for Dr. Sergeyev's valuable description of the growth of trade both between the socialist countries and between them and the rest of the world. The rapid growth of such trade made it important for economists to take its potentialities into account. We must allow for the fact that the structure of production in socialist countries would change and affect the trade pattern in the rest of the world. For example, Morris Adelman expected big increases in exports of petroleum and natural gas by the U.S.S.R. We should be better able to approach the pattern of development of such future trade if we had a clearer understanding of the principles on which socialist trade was conducted. Since Dr. Sergeyev's paper did not explain these principles concretely, Professor Kindleberger wanted to put some specific questions about how they were applied in practice.

First, there was the principle of equality, mutual advantage and noninterference. Non-socialist economies, while they realized that the price system had its weaknesses, believed that, when competitive, it provided for all these things. The market operated through an invisible hand, each participant trying to maximize his own advantage in consumption and production. Such advantage must be mutual, or there would be no trade. Equality was more illusive, since it was the equality of purchasing power in demand and units of output supplied rather than equality between countries or firms which was important. Monopolies and external economies or diseconomies would distort the price system, but economists could suggest ways of correcting these which did not imply abandoning price calculation.

Socialist countries used prices in trade, but it was not clear how they calculated these. Professor Bechin had said that there were world prices for many world products, but there was not a single world price, regardless of location. Dr. Sergeyev said that these prices were fixed for long periods with no 'free play'. Did such prices reflect marginal social costs? Dr. Olano and the other UN experts found it hard to define equitable prices in Dr. Sergeyev's sense, but finally concluded that the long-run equilibrium price was what they were concerned with. However, values were changed in the short run and the U.S.S.R. had recently been forced to sell products like sugar, cotton or aluminium below the long-run price in order to clear the market. It appeared that the U.S.S.R. charged different prices to different customers. If this was true, it might be due to pure price discrimination or, more likely, to having to balance separate bilateral trade accounts. How could one be sure that in these circumstances trade was mutually advantageous or equal? It would have been more helpful if Dr. Sergeyev had discussed such differential pricing rather than the 'most-favoured nation' clause.

Professor Kindleberger thought it unnecessary to speak particularly on non-interference. Mutual planning was surely mutual interference, voluntary though it was. More generally, traditional theory regarded prices as indeterminate in bilateral monopoly, but determinate in competition. How could there be a determinate solution with bilateral state trading? Should one divide the gains from trade equally between the seller's lowest monopoly supply price and the buyer's highest offer price? Or should one stay somewhere in between? Without competitive prices, trade became a matter of bargaining rather than economics, with no single solution which could give equality and mutual advantage.

Despite talk of planning, he suspected that socialist trade contained a strong element of empiricism. In its early days the U.S.S.R. had used the law of planned, proportional development to free itself from overseas markets and suppliers. To build up heavy industry and the production of machinery, it had exported traditional products as and when necessary. During the late 1920s, an attempt to expand trade failed because of depression, and the U.S.S.R. turned inward again. After 1945, the larger number of socialist countries all attempted to emulate this early development of the U.S.S.R., but this made little sense. Slowly and empirically specialization and exchange had developed. While one could not call the COMECON system planning, it did appear to try to measure and trim national plans to balance imports and exports. But there was no apparent principle of planning, for example, the linear programming of eight or ten countries' input and output of materials. Only Professor Frisch's article in 1949 gave a crude solution, and even it required each country to specify demands and supplies of fixed quantities of goods without saying what changes would be made if price-ratios altered.

Professor Kindleberger thought socialist literature recognized the need for planning multilateral trade, despite the success to date of empirical methods. To solve problems like whether Czechoslovakia should sell shoe machinery to Bulgaria and thereby reduce Polish and Hungarian sales of shoes, a price system approximating marginal social cost would be helpful. For example, because Marxian economics regarded capital as unproductive, there was a bias towards capital-intensive goods ; having zero value, such a factor could be used intensively. In fact it was limited, and this created problems. There was also a bias caused by uncertainty, at least until the last revaluation, over the purchasing power of the rouble. This must have inhibited clearing through the rouble. A third bias was the pressure to fulfil the plan, even though it might be better to alter it. Perhaps most important was the difficulty of moving from bilateral balance to a multilateral system, balancing trade both within the socialist bloc and between it and the West. While it seemed that some surpluses in socialist bloc trade were met in convertible currencies, a truly efficient system would provide for such clearing automatically. As it was, the system must remain half planned and half unplanned, because socialist countries traded with non-socialist ones. Would this imply that the socialist plan for the next twenty years would have to be altered if unspecified trade changes took place ? Or would trade with non-socialist countries have to be restricted to unimportant items to safeguard the plan ?

Many of these questions might seem academic and trivial, since socialist trade was large and growing. However, since socialist economies contrasted their system with the classical one, it would be valuable if they could explain in detail how the system actually worked in particular, specified situations.

Dr. Olano did not believe it was as hard to define equitable prices as Professor Kindleberger suggested. Professor Kindleberger had mentioned the UN report which he had helped to produce. The problem of definition had not turned out to be as difficult as Professor Kindleberger had implied, but the report had said that one should use the American economists' concept of 'reasonably stable' prices.

Professor Kitamura understood that in early trade with Eastern Europe the main idea was that the U.S.S.R. should supply machinery while the other countries produced food and raw materials. Apparently the Eastern European countries had found it hard to implement this idea. Food was in short supply in Eastern Europe, but ample in the U.S.S.R. The recent trend had been to reverse this pattern, with Eastern Europe exporting mainly capital goods or semi-manufactured goods to the U.S.S.R., which was now a major supplier of food. There was reason to assume that this reversal of the trend was based not on factor proportions but on economies of scale and technical progress, which might become more important for the international division of labour. However, the main reason was understood to be that the planned change in production had implied difficult adjustments and some waste of resources. He wondered how far Soviet trade planning was learning from such experience. The paper emphasized that there was increasing industrialization in all socialist countries and he was not sure what the final pattern would be if all of them increased industrial exports. It seemed clear, however, that the importance of factor proportions tended to decline. On the basis of a changed situation there now seemed to be a need to create a pattern of specialization on the basis of negotiation and agreement. Professor Kitamura thought that what had happened in Eastern Europe could teach some lessons to the rest of the world. Where it was merely a question of exploiting natural resources it was easy enough, for example, to use East German and Czech capital goods to mine Polish coal. With manufactured goods, however, very difficult policy decisions were involved, as for instance in Professor Kindleberger's example of the shoe industry. There might well be a waste of resources, because duplication in some countries led to excess capacity. This was the kind of situation that planning should have avoided. His main question was therefore what particular principle was applied when a decision was being taken as to which industries should be located in particular countries. Where these countries were independent, each would have views on the development which it regarded as desirable. How far could there be real regional planning without reducing the sovereign decision-making power of each individual country?

Professor Delivanis asked Dr. Sergeyev how the multi-price system was combined in the socialist countries with the practice of multiple exchange rates which appeared to have been greatly used before 1954. He also wondered whether Dr. Sergeyev would explain how his figures on page 278 would be altered if they were calculated at constant prices, and how prices were calculated in trade between socialist countries. Finally, what would buyers have done if they had been allowed to choose freely between goods made outside the socialist bloc and goods made within it? In Bulgaria, it had seemed to him that consumers preferred the former. He also wondered how long-term purchase agreements were altered in the light of unforeseen developments.

Professor Haberler was glad that Dr. Sergeyev favoured the most-favoured-nation principle. This principle, cherished by the liberal classical economists, had been under strong attack by nationalistic, protectionist and left-wing economists in the West. He wondered whether Dr. Sergeyev could explain what precisely the most-favoured-nation principle meant under the Soviet trading system. In capitalist countries it meant that imports from all countries paid the same customs duties. However, once one moved away from tariffs towards quotas and other quantitative controls, it was hard to give a meaningful definition of the most-favoured-nation clause. In the defunct ITO charter, which it had been hoped Russia would accept, an attempt had been made to apply the most-favoured-nation principle to state trading. This could be done, it was thought, by means of the so-called 'commercial considerations clause'. That was to say, state trading countries would promise to be guided in their trade solely by 'commercial considerations'. Some Western economists pointed out, however, that this would sanction the sharpest monopolistic practices on the part of the state trading agencies — for monopoly pricing surely might stem from highly 'commercial' considerations. The upshot was that nobody in the West really knew what the most-favoured-nation principle meant when applied to government trade. Professor Haberler therefore wondered what Dr. Sergeyev had in mind when he recommended application of the most-favoured-nation principle.

Dr. Savosnick wanted to know more about the planning principles in Soviet trade. Perhaps Dr. Sergeyev could say whether he believed that Soviet trade would turn out *very* differently if each Soviet enterprise were allowed to buy and sell as it chose, either at home or abroad. He was assuming that internal Soviet prices would remain much as at present. Did Dr. Sergeyev believe that the result would be a considerable increase or decrease in the volume of Soviet trade or that the U.S.S.R. would accumulate a balance of payments surplus or deficit in the absence of government intervention? Obviously, it would be very naïve to suppose that nothing would change or that such trade liberalization could occur without a period of adjustment. However, he thought that the Soviet economy was similar to the American and that liberalization would lead to increased similarity. In any case, since they believed in the superiority of Soviet planning, the planners must have some idea of what a more capitalistic alternative would look like. What did Dr. Sergeyev think it would look like?

Dr. Sergeyev said that Professor Kindleberger treated trade as an activity whose aim was advantage or profit. In his paper, he regarded trade as a part of the economic relations between nations. That was why all the problems touched on by Professor Kindleberger really needed a different explanation.

Professor Kindleberger treated trade in a very narrow sense. He treated it as the trade of an individual firm, but not as that of a branch of the economy or as a form of international economic relations. For Professor Kindleberger, trade was not an integral part of the economy, and its main purpose was profit, rather than a contribution to the development of the economy and the raising of living standards. One's view of the principles of the international economic relations was wrong. Professor Kindleberger considered equality as equality of purchasing power or of the number of units of output supplied, and not as the equality of the contracting countries. He applied this understanding and treatment to socialist foreign trade. Professor Kindleberger defended the spontaneous method of pricing, insisting that the market was guided by an 'invisible hand' and that benefit from trade and equality were secured only by spontaneous competition.

In fact, trade was part of the economy. No country could live on trade alone, however important foreign trade was for a particular country. The main thing was production, and countries could buy or sell whatever other countries were producing. We should therefore approach the problem of planning trade as part of the problem of planning in general.

Planning of foreign trade depended on planning the whole economy of a country, and this was one of the most important factors lying behind the continuous growth and expansion of foreign trade. In the general socialist market, demand and supply was characterized by the plan.

The main function of COMECON was to co-ordinate the economic planning of the member countries. This did not mean COMECON was a sort of general planning institute for these countries. Each of them independently planned economic development. In the socialist bloc, the co-ordination of plans took into account the specific character of each country and was aimed at increasing and extending the planned and rational division of labour among them.

The essence of co-ordination in planning was that the socialist countries concerted their decisions on developing the most important branches of their economies in order to maximize rates of the growth of output.

Dr. Sergeyev therefore had a completely different view of the role of COMECON, which was not a supreme planning establishment but only co-ordinated the development of different socialist countries by co-ordinating their trade. Each country had its own plan, which allowed it to make the most efficient use of its own productive resources. These plans were then co-ordinated on the basis of the principles of the division of labour, but this did not imply that COMECON was a supreme planning establishment.

In answer to Professor Kitamura it should be stated that the Soviet Union was delivering to the European socialist countries not only food, but above all the important industrial raw materials and various modern machines and equipment.

Professor Kitamura had asked how, if all countries were simultaneously increasing their exports of capital goods, the division of labour could be based on factor proportions. Dr. Sergeyev explained that the apparent contradiction was removed if one remembered that the industrial goods group included industrial raw materials, capital goods and consumption goods. For example, the development of the socialist international division of labour would result in increasing the share of machinery and equipment in exports from 29 per cent in 1958 to 36 per cent in 1965, and in reducing the shares of fuel and raw materials from 50 per cent to 39 per cent, respectively.

It should be stressed that the planned distribution of resources in the socialist bloc was carried out by expanding and strengthening various forms of economic co-operation—foreign trade, credits, the co-ordination of plans, technical assistance, etc.

As for the practical principle on which resources were allocated, in practice, this was achieved by co-ordinating the development plans of all socialist countries. Specialization was taken into account, as was co-operation between countries. Every socialist country was first of all developing those branches of its economy for which natural and economic conditions were favourable and in whose development other socialist countries were interested. International specialization in the socialist bloc had always been linked with the creation of the optimum national economic complex for each country. The international socialist division of labour presupposed the development of many industries within the economy of each country, including primary and manufacturing industries and supplying both consumption goods and capital goods.

Professor Delivanis had asked what price was used for price fixing in international trade. The trade of socialist countries was carried out on the basis of world prices in the main markets, but these prices were not automatically used. Commodity prices, fixed in roubles, were mutually agreed by the trading state organizations for a certain period. These prices were net of elements caused by speculation or short-run fluctuations. Agreed prices usually remained constant at least for a year and many commodity prices were fixed for several years. However, the stability of prices in the trade of socialist countries did not mean that prices should be absolutely invariable. With important changes in the world value of commodities, the prices of certain goods were periodically revised. The principle of uniform prices represented an important advantage of socialist foreign trade. While there was a multiplicity of prices in the world capitalist market, pricing in the general socialist market was characterized by equality. Each country sold its commodities to other socialist countries at an identical price. As a rule, variation was allowed only within any difference in transport and insurance charges, resulting from different terms of delivery.

To answer Professor Delivanis one could cite data for the expansion of the Soviet foreign trade with the other socialist countries. In 1960, as compared with 1946, the volume of Soviet trade with socialist countries had risen more than eight times at constant prices and more than eleven times at current prices.

To Professor Haberler, Dr. Sergeyev said that he thought socialist economists gave a slightly different meaning to the most-favoured-nation principle. This was applied fully between socialist states and covered not only trade in the narrow sense but other forms of economic relation. In economic relations between socialist and capitalist countries the principle was applied more narrowly. It was restricted to the problems of exports and imports, customs duties, marine transportation and some legal issues.

Professor Robinson wondered if Dr. Kaigl would elaborate on the way in which plans were co-ordinated in terms of a concrete example. Czechoslovakia made machinery. When the Soviet Union was planning, did it ask how much of particular kinds of machine Czechoslovakia could produce and how far it might be desirable for the Czechoslovak production capacity to be increased ? Did it also try to discover kinds of machinery which Czechoslovakia could not produce, or for which Czechoslovakia had no spare capacity, and arrange for these to be supplied by the U.S.S.R. ?

Professor Kaigl stressed first of all that the planning of foreign trade was not separate, but an integral part of the over-all plan for the economy. Foreign trade was balanced, in the sense that it reflected the international division of labour in production. Nevertheless, the foreign trade plan did not determine every foreign trade transaction, but only gave physical indices for the main targets; total value indices were also given with the aim of balancing imports, exports and foreign exchange requirements. Within this framework, individual firms carried out their transactions on the basis of profitability. As Dr. Savosnick had pointed out, trade could not be liberalized, since this would interfere with the over-all plan. Trade must be carried out within the framework of a general foreign trade plan which must therefore combine several principles. First, there must be a balanced development of the particular country and its socialist partners. Second, one must look at profitability from the point of view of the whole national economy. Various accounting methods were used, especially in determining what kind of goods should be exported. One method was to compare the export price with the cost of production. Another was to compare it with the cost of production minus the cost of imported raw materials or with costs in the last stage of production if one was dealing with a finishing industry. One also had to allow for the fact that a stable, though less profitable, price might be more desirable than a price which gave a high return to an individual transaction. Profitability from the point of view of the individual enterprise could therefore be looked upon only as the last of these principles.

Professor Kaigl said that two main fields had to be considered. The first was raw materials and energy ; the second was the finishing industries. With raw materials, the aim was to make the best use of the resources of each socialist country. With coal, socialist countries which needed it supplied capital goods to Polish coalmines and received coal as payment. Another example was Bulgaria, which had copper resources. The aim was not only to allow the best possible use of this ore by all socialist countries, but also to enable Bulgaria to produce both copper ore and electrical engines. Czechoslovakia was giving aid to Bulgaria, partly by renouncing the production of some electrical machinery and obtaining this from Bulgaria. In the finishing industries, the main principle was to achieve such specialization as would allow mass production and high productivity.

Replying to Professor Robinson, Professor Kaigl explained the division of labour between Czechoslovakia and the U.S.S.R. by instancing the common effort to build up a large chemical industry. When this was applied to particular trade agreements, it meant that Czechoslovakia would concentrate on producing particular chemical equipment where she had a special advantage or experience. This machinery would be sold not only in Czechoslovakia but also in the U.S.S.R., and even the rest of the world. The Soviet Union would specialize on other types of chemical machinery which would be sold to Czechoslovakia and the total trade between the two countries would be in bilateral balance.

Professor Weiller thought that some progress had been made in increasing East–West understanding of trade matters since 1934 when he had taken part in discussions at the Ministry of Foreign Affairs in Paris on a commercial treaty with the U.S.S.R. which never came into being. The main obstacle had been the problem of what most-favoured-nation treatment meant. There had been two approaches, with the U.S.S.R.

taking a legalistic point of view that this implied equal treatment at the particular moment when any given exchange was taking place. The French took the view that most-favoured-nation treatment implied the much more liberal principle of allowing free play to the price mechanism. Professor Weiller thought that, despite this difference, it should be possible to find ways and means of expanding trade. Western countries had sufficient protection and government interference to make them understand the difficulties in the way of socialist trade planners.

So far as scales of prices and quantities to be traded were concerned, we must be ready to plan over a long period at stable prices. This was particularly true of primary producers, and made it desirable for them to be able to plan their sales. Professor Weiller thought that in relations with the U.S.S.R. the principle to be accepted should be that of concluding long-run agreements based on stability of prices and quantities for specific products.

Mr. Bhagwati stressed that difficulties could arise if contractual agreements, fixing both prices and quantities of traded commodities, were entered into. One was eliminating trade uncertainty; but one might simply transfer uncertainty elsewhere. For instance, if India agreed to supply the U.S.S.R. with coal and had domestic difficulties in coal production, the trade agreement would require that India should export the coal and go without it herself.

Professor Weiller explained that his point had not been intended to apply generally and that long-run planning would be much more successful with some goods than with others.

Professor Robinson said that in long-term planning of trade by the U.K., difficulties had arisen because countries like Australia and New Zealand wanted to keep their freedom to purchase whatever manufactured goods they happened to want several years ahead. This made it extremely difficult to write into an agreement what the primary producers would take from Britain, though it was easier for Britain to say what her primary product imports would be fairly far ahead. Thus, bargains were made in money terms and had on several occasions subsequently proved inequitable in real terms, owing to a rise in the price of British manufactured exports.

Professor Mikesell said that since trade agreements in Eastern Europe aimed mainly at bilateral balance, it would be a miracle if such trade could be planned on an entirely rational basis. Multilateral trade, even in a planned system, would need a multilateral payments system. Failure to meet planned trade targets was inevitable, and it would help the development of the socialist bloc if particular countries could hold accumulated balances for use in third countries. In his studies of trade targets under bilateral agreements in Eastern Europe, he had found a wide disparity between the targets and actual trade. This raised the question of the role of the rouble as a means of multilateral settlement and also how far it was recognized in Eastern Europe that a bilateral balance of trade was very difficult to achieve. There would be great benefit from multilateral trade, whether planned or unplanned, but this implied the need for multilateral settlements.

Professor Ohlin thought it would be valuable if Dr. Sergeyev could say a little more on how the U.S.S.R. regarded the most-favoured-nation principle, since he was asking for its universal application. Could Sweden rely on being able to export to the U.S.S.R. if it could produce particular products more cheaply than, say, Czechoslovakia? He knew of examples where the U.S.S.R. had taken machinery at prices higher than those in Sweden. Were these the exceptions which proved the rule? It was also possible that the U.S.S.R. might pay for Western goods by, for example, supplying motor-cars, and these were harder to sell in Western markets than cars from other countries. If this was more than an exception, it contradicted the operation of the most-favoured-nation principle.

Professor Ohlin did not see how planning could be carried out in Eastern Europe in the way Dr. Kaigl wanted if the U.S.S.R. did not treat Czechoslovakia as better fitted than East Germany for setting up a chemical industry. Was it possible to alter the whole planning of Eastern Europe if it turned out that East Germany could produce more cheaply? And what did 'more cheaply' mean? Were prices used in the same way when considering the comparative advantages of every country? Professor Ohlin also wondered if socialist countries considered whether in some sense (and in *which* sense) goods could be bought more cheaply outside the Soviet bloc, and who made such investigations. If this was not done, then most-favoured-nation treatment was not being given.

Dr. Sergeyev contended that Russia had a different understanding of most-favoured-nation treatment which was applied fully in the socialist bloc. Surely, more-favoured treatment was given to the least wealthy countries in Eastern Europe. Such behaviour could be very easily forgiven, but it still meant that there was not complete most-favoured-nation treatment within the bloc. With capitalist countries, the principle must be less fully applied, because one then had to take account of customs duties, freight rates, etc. Did this not mean that capitalist countries were inevitably treated differently? There must be some similarity between preferential treatment within the socialist bloc and arrangements in the Common Market, which socialist economists criticized so severely.

Professor Ohlin wondered how the socialist countries decided where conditions for producing a particular commodity were best, and whether their accounting system regarded interest as a cost. If not, capitalist countries would be delighted, because it would mean that they could buy capital goods from socialist countries with no allowance for capital cost in the price. It seemed to him that there must be an accounting system which was used for deciding on trade within the bloc, but that a modified world market price was introduced for trading with other countries. If this were so, he did not see how there could possibly be equal treatment for both types of country.

Professor Kaigl explained that when socialist economists spoke of most-favoured-nation treatment they also took account of planning. He had been asked whether adjustments would be made if East Germany could produce goods more cheaply. The answer was that the price for each good was fixed among all socialist countries for a long period. Such a choice between countries could therefore be made only when long-run trade agreements were being discussed, and was therefore made every 3-5 years. He would also like to say that socialist countries *did* investigate prices outside the socialist system. If it was found that a particular product could be acquired more cheaply outside the bloc, a long-term trade agreement would be made. However, there were big difficulties in trading with capitalist countries. Some would make long-term agreements, but it was dangerous to abandon the production of any particular good because one might then find that the capitalist country was unable or unwilling to go on supplying it. Stability was a most important element in trade agreements, and great care was taken to ensure stable supplies in trading with capitalist countries. If one did not find a particular country willing to make a long-term agreement, one turned elsewhere.

Sir Roy Harrod wanted to know whether, when Dr. Kaigl said that some countries were less willing to make trade agreements, he was including in that statement the willingness of individual firms to commit themselves for the distant future.

Professor Kaigl said that long-term contracts with individual firms were concluded within the framework of a long-term agreement with a government. These agreements and contracts could cover both capital and consumer goods. Individual enterprises would make cost calculations about the profitability of trade. While the calculations of these enterprises relating to internal transactions would be based on the prices which were fixed for considerable periods, calculations for external trade would be based on the quite separate concept of modified world prices.

Professor Lipinski thought that a socialist organization of the economy was best for rapid growth but that one should not imagine that planning could not produce as well as solve problems. Planning was not simple, and all the problems of socialist planning had not yet been solved. International trade was a very important limiting factor for Poland. The main Polish problem was not the training of cadres or innovation, but the balance of payments and the possibility of increasing imports. There were also many problems in organizing trade with capitalist countries. He was not sure whether world prices were a good basis for trade, because he was not an expert on that subject. But he felt that this was just as important a question as that of fixing prices *within* the country. Poland was trying to solve the problem of how to price her exports and there was now an Institute for Foreign Trade. One of its tasks would be to devise methods for measuring the efficiency of exports and imports.

Professor Lipinski said that some of the contributors to the discussion had raised the implied question of how independent Poland was economically. The answer was that Poland was as independent on questions of economics and economic development as it was possible to be. Only two countries were truly independent in economic matters — the U.S.S.R.

and the U.S.A. However, Poland was not dependent on planners in other countries when she decided on her own plans. He thought that Poland and Czechoslovakia were the only countries in the Soviet bloc which had received no loans from the U.S.S.R.

So far as the international division of labour was concerned, Poland could set her own targets for development, but there were agreements between the socialist countries on co-ordinating plans. Nevertheless it was not true that one country was prevented from developing entirely as it wished ; targets were entirely free, as was the degree of development. Professor Lipinski said it was hard to accelerate economic development in the most efficient way, and particularly to decide on the correct size of new investment and how new industries should be introduced. He thought that even the socialist countries probably did not achieve an entirely rational solution. But the solution was not entirely rational in capitalist countries either, and he thought there was a greater possibility of being right where there was planning. The fact that it was not money profit which determined all investment in a planned economy made it easier to accelerate the rate of economic growth.

Mr. Hellberg said that socialist countries regarded trade as being very beneficial and their plans for the next seven years looked forward to a big increase. This expansion was to be concentrated on trade within the socialist bloc and it would therefore have been interesting to know more about the principles lying behind this expansion. Dr. Sergeyev had stressed the high proportion of capital goods in exports. This was understandable in view of their high rate of growth and the great difficulties in establishing some form of international specialization in consumer goods. As for long-term agreements, economists from socialist countries often gave the impression that their plans were extremely inflexible. However, he found this difficult to believe, since it was clearly impossible to plan accurately five years ahead when trade was so greatly dependent on rapid technical changes. For example, the long-term trade agreement between the U.S.S.R. and West Germany had originally made no allowance for trade in steel pipes ; a quota for steel pipes had already been introduced after only six months. This showed that flexibility was possible. However, Mr. Hellberg felt that multilateral trade between socialist countries would be extremely difficult to arrange. All these countries were heavily in debt to the U.S.S.R. and this would make it difficult to introduce a multilateral payment system.

Professor Bechin said that a major problem in the discussion had been that we often understood the same words to mean different things. For instance, two kinds of phenomena had often been confused. First, there were short-run factors, including, for example, particular trade agreements or cyclical fluctuations on the world market. Second, there were the interests of long-run economic development. It was not easy to reconcile these two and indeed the one often contradicted the other.

For example, the Korean war had led to a boom in the raw materials markets, but after 1957 the long-run effects had been that supplies had expanded and it had been difficult to sell raw materials on the world market. It followed that when one was concerned with fixing the prices of exports or imports, both long-run and short-run questions had to be considered. This was why the U.S.S.R. preferred to make long-term trade agreements, whether these were bilateral or multilateral. Only in a long-term agreement could price questions be correctly decided. According to the economic position of the countries concerned, a trade agreement should allow for the exchange of a certain quantity of goods and for an increase in output, with investment carried out to allow this rise in output to take place. He therefore felt that mutual advantage in trade could only be achieved on the basis of long-run agreements. He could not agree with Professor Kindleberger, who thought of mutual advantage in terms only of the short run.

Dr. Sergeyev thought that some understanding had been reached during the discussion. Replying to Dr. Savosnick, he said that he would put the question somewhat differently. He would ask whether it was good for the U.S.S.R. to have a state monopoly of trade. The answer was that under centralized planning, the only way to trade was through a state monopoly. Such trading was not only indispensable, but also good.

The foreign trade of the socialist countries, where the main export resources and import commodities were the people's own property, could be based only on the principle of a state monopoly, the essence of which was to concentrate all foreign trade operations in the hands of the state. The intervention of the state in foreign trade secured the exact fulfilment of all commitments at the proper time. Pre-war experience in the U.S.S.R. proved that the state monopoly had never damaged trade relations between the U.S.S.R. and the capitalist countries.

It was necessary to clarify once more the question of most-favoured-nation treatment. This principle meant that any international agreement made by a particular country should include a provision for granting to a contracting country all the economic rights and privileges, which it agreed to grant to a third country. The socialist countries based their treaties and agreements with each other and with the capitalist countries on the most-favoured-nation principle unconditionally and free of charge.

In the great majority of the agreements between socialist and capitalist countries the operation of the most-favoured-nation clause was limited to commodity exports and imports, and to questions of navigation and international law. However, in agreements between socialist countries, the arrangement covered not only trade in the narrow sense but the whole multiplicity of economic relations. For example, in the agreements between the U.S.S.R. and the Democratic Republic of Vietnam, the German People's Republic and Bulgaria, the U.S.S.R. and the Chinese People's Republic it was stated that the contracting parties granted each other most-favoured-nation treatment in all questions of trade and navigation, and in other forms of economic relation between both states.

In settling a number of important questions on their economic relations, the socialist countries based their agreements on the principles of the most-favoured nation. But this was not national treatment and it differed substantially from their agreements with capitalist countries. National treatment meant granting equal rights to foreign citizens, firms and goods and to one's own citizens, firms and goods. Granting national treatment to the industry and trade of an under-developed country practically meant depriving it of the protection of its own government.

In contrast to the trade agreements between the socialist countries, capitalist trade agreements were characterized by a large number of the important exceptions to the general rules of most-favoured-nation treatment, for example, on preferential treatment, and on advantages and privileges based on custom treaties and multilateral international agreements.

In trade agreements between socialist countries there were virtually no exceptions to the rules of most-favoured-nation treatment. This showed that these agreements were based on the impossibility of there being economic blocs within the socialist system.

In agreements between the socialist and capitalist states there were some exceptions to the most-favoured-nation treatment. These exceptions included rights and advantages granted by customs treaties, and such restrictions were included in the agreements by no means at the initiative of the socialist countries. The socialist countries were seeking the most-favoured-nation principle in their trading and economic relations with all countries. The member countries of COMECON had no treaties for customs and other trade privileges other than those which were in force for other countries.

It was necessary to stress again the importance of long-term agreements, which helped to expand the volume of commodity trade. Owing to the long-term agreements with the socialist countries, and with the non-socialist countries (including Sweden), they were guaranteed being able to buy and sell various goods, including modern machinery and equipment.

As for the settlement of accounts, money settlements between socialist countries could be carried out both by bilateral and by multilateral clearing. These were affected somewhat by the fact that the bigger part of the trade turnover of the socialist countries was based on bilateral agreements. However, in 1957 the member countries of the COMECON signed the multilateral clearing agreement.

A country having roubles on its clearing account might transfer them through the multilateral clearing account with the consent of the debtor country. The sum transferred in this way could be used for purchasing commodities in any member country. The rouble used for money settlements in socialist international economic relations was secured by gold and was not subject to devaluation or other spontaneous fluctuations. Export and import prices in roubles were stable over long periods, and that was why the rouble had a stable purchasing power in the socialist market.

A policy of autarky was not characteristic of the socialist countries.

They had been fighting against the discriminating policies and defending the expansion of mutually advantageous trade with all countries on the basis of both bilateral and multilateral agreements, defending international trade by long-term agreements. The expansion of socialist foreign trade turnover was equally based on the growth of trade in production and consumption goods and traditional and new export and import items. For example, the share of non-food consumption goods in Soviet imports increased from 14 per cent in 1958 to 18 per cent in 1959.

At present, the socialist countries were achieving their far-reaching programmes for economic development. The forms of socialist economic co-operation were steadily developing and improving and the rational international division of labour was expanding.

The steadily accelerating growth of social production in the socialist countries was an important factor. It was increasing the mutual trade turnover of the socialist countries, and contributing to the expansion of trade between them and non-socialist countries on a basis of mutual advantage and equality.

THE DISCUSSION OF THE PAPERS BY DR. PATEL AND DR. SAVOSNICK

Dr. Sohmen had found both the papers highly stimulating and useful. The approaches of the two authors to the problems posed in the topics assigned to them differed a great deal. Whereas Dr. Patel's paper dealt with virtually every aspect of the external economic relations of less-developed countries, Dr. Savosnick followed in the footsteps of Professors Hicks and Harry Johnson. He provided a purely theoretical survey of growth in one country and of a few selected variables in others, assuming that no autonomous expansion took place in these latter countries. Dr. Sohmen said that if his comments referred more often to Dr. Patel's paper this should not be interpreted as a value judgement but rather as a reflection of the fact that he was a rather critical spirit by temperament and had found less to disagree with in Dr. Savosnick's than in Dr. Patel's paper. However, disagreement on some fundamental issues did not prevent him from finding himself very much in agreement with other arguments set forth by Dr. Patel, among them some which were rarely heeded by policy-makers in less-developed countries.

There was first of all the fundamental question whether balance of payments problems were more natural for under-developed countries. Most economists seemed to say yes, and Dr. Patel, unlike Dr. Savosnick, certainly belonged to this group. He drew the inevitable corollary that such countries would necessarily have to impose controls on trade to a much greater extent than their more advanced trading partners.

Pure theory provided no justification for this view, plausible though it seemed at first sight, and economists of more classical persuasion might take some satisfaction from recent evidence that even the most affluent societies were not immune from balance of payments difficulties. Dr. Sohmen believed that many people unconsciously extended to the balance of payments as a whole what was certainly true of the balance on goods and services. It was a most natural state of affairs that a country in which capital was scarce should have a substantial deficit on the latter, just as it was most unnatural that a highly industrialized country should not have a substantial surplus. All that was needed to make this a state of equilibrium was a sustained flow of capital or of unilateral aid from the latter to the former. Dr. Patel did not like to see under-developed countries depend too much on donations, and Dr. Sohmen believed that his reasons for this were very sound.

In the absence of a sufficient volume of foreign aid, and with the limitations imposed by finite gold and foreign exchange reserves, every country would have to adjust its deficit on trade and services to the voluntary private capital inflow. A number of measures were available to do this and Dr. Patel had classified them under the headings of 'import policy', 'export policy' and 'exchange rate policy'.

Leaving aside the possibility of exchange rate adjustments for a while, measures to increase exports were always somewhat more difficult than measures to restrict imports. In order to be exported, goods had first to be produced and then had to be offered at a reasonably competitive price. Open or hidden subsidies for exports to aid their sales abroad, a measure towards which Dr. Patel did not seem to be wholly disinclined, did not strike Dr. Sohmen as a very useful solution for less-developed countries. Their fiscal systems were usually as under-developed as everything else, and it seemed wise to reserve their public expenditure for better uses. To the extent that goods subsidized by less-developed countries were also subjected to import duties in the more-developed ones, this method of promoting exports amounted to a direct transfer from poor to rich, which most of us probably found a somewhat awkward arrangement. The easiest, least imaginative and hence by far the most popular method of dealing with external payments troubles remained the restriction of imports. At least in a very superficial sense, balance of payments difficulties could always be mitigated in this way. At the same time, import restrictions satisfied a deeply rooted conviction of most people that they represented a particularly appropriate measure to be used by under-developed countries for other reasons as well. There was no need to list these reasons in detail before the Round Table, but he believed that all of them could be subsumed under the headings 'infant industry protection' and 'improvement of the terms of trade'.

To his mind, this rationalization of the use of trade restriction for balance of payments purposes was thoroughly mistaken. Whatever protection could be justified on general grounds involved selected commodities. The items usually most severely affected by controls imposed for balance of payments reasons belonged to an entirely different category. Governments tried to keep out those luxury goods which, in their opinion, were needed least of all. Dr. Patel correctly pointed out that few governments seemed to be aware of the fact that this practice obviously induced domestic production of luxury goods. In other words, there was the creation or preservation of those industries which the country needed least of all. The goods produced need not be the same, but he was certain that there were appropriate Indian or Indonesian equivalents of tail-fins or maraschino cherries. There was an anti-demonstration effect on consumption through the prohibition of luxuries, but he was sceptical whether this could ever outweigh the impact on the pattern of production. In any case, the obvious remedy was not import restriction but a stiff excise tax on all goods considered as luxuries, whether they were produced domestically or imported.

Another feature which made trade restrictions rather unattractive when imposed for balance of payments purposes was that typically they implied quantitative controls to a much greater degree than did restrictions to protect infant industries. Dr. Patel rightly stressed as one of the most unattractive aspects of quotas that the artificial scarcity rents they created went into private pockets in most cases, whereas tariffs would at least be a welcome source of additional and badly needed government revenue. It was, of course, true that part of this scarcity rent served to supplement through bribes the inadequate salaries of government officials in many countries, a problem to which Professor Neumark had called attention. But he was certain that more appropriate methods could be found to tackle this problem.

On the terms of trade argument for protection, Professor Sohmen found that many people rather uncritically considered that any fall in the terms of trade was disadvantageous to the country in question. There was no doubt that deterioration in the terms of trade would usually prove to be a loss if it was due to developments in the outside world. To the extent that the terms of trade deteriorated because of more extensive trade with other countries, however, this held only once the optimum degree of restriction had been exceeded. The optimum degree of restriction was itself a concept without operational significance in the real world. Otherwise complete autarky would always be the best policy for a country. For this would maximize its terms of trade.

For under-developed countries, trade restrictions with the aim of improving the terms of trade struck him as particularly inappropriate. In so far as trade controls hit other under-developed countries all the expected gains cancelled each other out, as Dr. Patel also reminded us. In so far as import controls affected industrial nations, the imposition of trade restriction by any single under-developed country was likely to have an infinitesimal effect on export prices. This might not be so for larger trading blocs of developed nations, however, and regional customs units might serve a useful purpose for that reason.

Having disposed of all these alternatives, only the imposition of tariffs on the grounds of infant industry protection seemed to him to be left as an even-debatable policy measure. He thoroughly agreed with Dr. Patel and with the overwhelming majority of economists that the development of backward economies required a determined and sustained effort by their authorities. This would have to be an effort on a broad front, beginning with public education and the creation of social overhead capital and judicious assistance to private as well as public enterprise. However, Dr. Patel had not converted him from being the incorrigible liberal that he was in matters of trade policy. He was not ashamed to say that he regarded even protective tariffs as one of the least defensible measures of development policy. What he supported were active measures of encouragement. He believed there was a strong presumption that the principal effect of policy measures which prevented activity taking place was the protection of the lame and dumb rather than the encouragement of the strong.

Several participants had called for more empirical research, and he joined them — adding a plea for really convincing empirical demonstrations of the way in which protective policies had contributed to the growth of different countries in the course of history. Against examples such as the U.S.A., which was sometimes quoted, one could set others, like Japan, whose development started with the opening of its economy to world trade and whose most rapid period of growth was one of free trade, as our Japanese friends had reminded us.

A simple theoretical consideration provided an alternative and perhaps superior method of encouraging infant industries. If an industry had any justification for existing at all it should be able, as participants had said in previous discussions, to pay for itself over its life, if all its true social costs were fully accounted for. Nothing more ought to be required in infancy than long-term loans from the rest of society or the rest of the world to be repaid when the industry was established. Strict accountability for all benefits received seemed to be an incomparable and almost indispensable advantage, particularly for a free-enterprise economy. Only this could ensure that government was not being degraded to become an instrument for filling private pockets.

The reason why severe trade restrictions were now widely regarded as entirely normal in under-developed countries might well be that the currencies of almost all of them were unmistakably overvalued and that imports were consequently artificially encouraged. So long as exchange rates were not adjusted, some measure of import restriction would help to redress the balance to some extent. Though all the circumstances he described as typical for under-developed countries were characteristic phenomena of currency overvaluation, Dr. Patel, unlike Dr. Savosnick, and perhaps out of sense of allegiance to the institution he represented, denied that exchange rate adjustment would be a feasible solution in these countries. One reason was that devaluation would be equivalent to a uniform rate of duty and subsidy respectively on all imports and exports. On the other hand, other factors would dictate different rates for individual commodities.

Apart from the objection that one could have devaluation as well a different rates of positive and negative duties, Professor Sohmen wanted to ask Dr. Patel what calculus ought to be used to determine the appropriate rate of duty for each commodity. He fully agreed, on the other hand, that small and frequent changes in the foreign exchange rate were not convenient instruments of economic policy. The question was whether less frequent and consequently larger adjustments were any more helpful. Such adjustments would be the only alternative if, as many people seemed to believe, some degree of inflation was unavoidable for under-developed countries, and if all of them, and all advanced countries as well, did not undergo inflation at approximately the same pace. Variation in exchange rates, if perhaps not a sufficient, was an absolutely necessary condition for confining the disequilibrium in external accounts to at least manageable dimensions.

Discontinuous exchange rate adjustments were so disruptive to both trade and capital movements that it was understandable that governments shied away from them as long as they could — and often much longer. The system of the 'adjustable peg' inaugurated at Bretton Woods had nowhere, he believed, made itself felt more painfully than in the under-developed countries. It did this through the restrictions of trade it forced both upon them and on the more advanced countries when they experienced balance of payments difficulties. It did it also through the under-use of resources caused by the monetary and fiscal restrictions which had to be imposed when a currency became overvalued and the authorities wanted to preserve convertibility at pegged exchange rates.

The two countries in the Western world whose post-war growth had been most spectacular, West Germany and Japan, had, if anything, had undervalued currencies during most of the 1950s. This saved them from the oppressive trade restrictions that other countries had to apply. One had to reckon with the fact that economic growth in many countries where such restrictions were applied was very disappointing, despite the valiant efforts of the governments in question.

What was often overlooked in discussions of the balance of payments, including Dr. Patel's, was that exchange rates also had a great deal to do with the direction and size of capital movements. There was no better mechanism for driving private capital away from a country than currency overvaluation. This held especially for the portfolio investment that used to play such an important and fruitful role in the economic development of overseas territories. It was hardly pure accident that Canada, whose currency was prevented from being overvalued by flexible exchange rates, received the largest capital inflow during the 1950s. Professor Sohmen was convinced that the maintenance of equilibrium exchange rates, either through determined monetary and fiscal policy or through abandoning pegged par values, was an indispensable condition for securing a sufficiently high volume of capital inflow. Without such capital inflow development programmes would, in most cases, be doomed to failure. He could give at least five dozen other reasons for believing that the pegging of exchange rates ought to be forbidden, but he thought he had already made out a convincing case.

Turning to Dr. Savosnick's paper, Professor Sohmen said that the principal objective was to extend the Hicks-Johnson analysis of economic growth and its effects on the balance of payments and the terms of trade from two or three countries, one of which was a competitor of the single, growing country while the other was complementary to it. The former would, of course, find that its terms of trade had worsened and that it was more certain to experience balance of payments difficulties than the latter. Dr. Savosnick had investigated the relative advantages of different policies designed to restore equilibrium and, not surprisingly, had found that devaluation was likely to be a less painful alternative than inflation.

However, Professor Sohmen disagreed with the conclusion Dr. Savosnick reached at the end of his paper, namely, that the imposition of import-tariffs, presumably recommended here only as a temporary measure, might be used to speed-up adjustment to the new equilibrium. In the context of pure theory, to which his paper was confined, producers would be led to the correct pattern of production for the long run by the change in the terms of trade alone. Incidentally, Dr. Savosnick's conclusion conflicted with the view expressed by Professor Byé a few days before, with which Professor Sohmen also wanted to register his disagreement, that the principle of comparative advantage guaranteed the optimum allocation of production in the short but not in the long run. The close association of this principle with the name of Ricardo in itself suggested that it must be interpreted to imply a state of long-run equilibrium. For the preoccupation with the long run was perhaps the principal hall-mark of Ricardo's work, and indeed he had been reproached with this ever since. This was not to deny that in the real world changes in technology and tastes would continuously prove that adjustments in the past had been wrong. This could not only be seen *ex post*, however, and did not of itself provide a case for interference with the market, that was to say unless it could be demonstrated that clairvoyants were more frequently found among government officials than among private entrepreneurs.

Professor Kindleberger wondered what the Savosnick model implied. If this was a Keynesian model then it was important whether increased exports had priority. If, however, it was a full employment model, then there was more to be told. Professor Kindleberger said that he admired brevity, but that this must be combined with clarity and precision, and he wondered whether Dr. Savosnick could expand on what was said in his paper.

Dr. Savosnick said that his was a full employment model, though later in the paper he allowed for unemployment.

Sir Roy Harrod said he would concentrate on questions which arose from Dr. Patel's statement, in page 312 of his paper, that, 'given the balance of payments constraint that generally operates in developing countries, a course of action designed to strengthen progressively the balance of payments may be preferable to any available alternative even if the immediate consequences of such preference imply a smaller increase in production'. Sir Roy wondered whether the distinction between investments which helped the balance of payments and those which improved production could be maintained. This was linked with Joan Robinson's distinction between the balance of payments barrier and the inflation barrier in under-developed countries. It seemed clear that the balance of payments was more important for under-developed countries, and he wondered whether the consequence was that one had to divert investment to improving the balance of payments instead of raising productivity. He was not clear about the difference between the two policies. There was obviously a contrast between investment in tradeable goods and in infrastructure, and a major difficulty was the problem of assessing the value of infra-structure. The value of a tradeable commodity could be assessed at world prices, but it was hard to see how one could measure the increase in productivity arising from investment in infra-structure.

Similarly, if one looked only at traded goods, how did one split off those which helped the balance of payments from the others? All traded goods had some relationship to imports and exports. Was Dr. Patel suggesting that there was no point in investing in some goods with high productivity because the elasticity of demand for them as exports was less than one? He found it hard to see how Dr. Patel could draw this kind of distinction.

Sir Roy recalled the contention in his own paper that in the process of development one must give an incentive by raising the standard of living. If productivity could be successively increased, this would allow such an incentive to be given and, indirectly, would allow a rise in the standard of living without a burden on the balance of payments. For this reason one would suppose that the stress should be put on investment in those goods in which productivity was greatest. One would then have a margin which could be used either to increase consumption or to raise investment. Sir Roy thought it was better to avoid both tariffs and export subsidies if the idea was to expedite development. Professor Nakayama had told the Round Table about 400 pilot factories set up in Japan and he thought that this was a good way to develop. Some would not be successful, but those that were would provide an example to private entrepreneurs and be places where 'cadres' could be trained. However, to be successful such pilot factories would need to operate with free-trade prices as a criterion of success or failure. He doubted whether such a scheme would promote the development of the country if it was not carried out under free trade.

Sir Roy said that inflation was bad for under-developed areas especially, because it destroyed amortization funds and caused these countries' meagre savings to be used for mere replacement instead of for net investment. He thought tied loans could be useful where, for example, a country like the U.K. was suffering from balance of payments difficulties but had surplus capacity. In such a situation there was some case for tied loans, but not otherwise.

Dr. Ferrero said that, like Dr. Sohmen, he was a liberal. He did not think there could be any special balance of payments difficulties, provided that global demand was kept within the available resources. Usually, balance of payments difficulties arose because of excessive consumption, investment or, more frequently, excessive government expenditure. This question had been well discussed by Professor Nurkse in the IEA meeting at Rio in 1957. Even if there were balance of payments difficulties, however, the best way of dealing with them was not Dr. Patel's. Indeed, he was surprised that Dr. Patel supported exchange controls and other restrictions since it was precisely these that the IMF was intended to abolish. He thought that if there was a balance of payments problem the solution suggested by Dr. Patel would be much more difficult than the natural one. Dr. Patel argued that devaluation was less flexible than subsidies and tariffs, but in effect subsidies and tariffs, when selective, acted in the same way as did multiple exchange rates, which had been discredited by experience. The economic effects would be the same. Nor did he see how government planning could work more efficiently than market forces. It would be necessary to plan import substitution, export promotion, subsidies, tariffs, etc.

Dr. Ferrero suggested that experience in Latin America told against Dr. Patel's arguments. If one compared countries with high import duties and exchange controls, like Argentina, Brazil and Chile, with others like Mexico and Peru, one found that the countries with controls had not been able to increase their exports in the past fifteen years. Similarly, their cost of living had risen more than in the other countries and changes in exchange rates had therefore been greater.

Professor Robinson was disappointed that the meeting had paid so little attention to the problem of introducing dynamic concepts into the theory of international trade. This was what the IEA had hoped for, but perhaps it had been over-optimistic. Professor Robinson said he would like to start with the proposition that international trade was not an end in itself but subsidiary to the maximization of income and the rate of growth of income. There were possible conflicts between a perfect international trade policy and growth. The Calvinists, like Dr. Sohmen, must prove that a country would not suffer in terms of a reduction of the rate of growth. Professor Robinson thought it was necessary to be clear how measures to reduce balance of payments deficits affected growth. If the exchange rate were fixed, then a balance of payments deficit was nearly always cured by reducing growth. In the U.K., this was done through higher interest rates and less investment in infra-structure and these were the result of marginal balance of payments difficulties. If one pursued a policy of becoming less dependent on international trade, the rate of investment could be increased and growth encouraged. A major question which one had to ask was what would be the consequences of cutting down, say, the marginal 5 per cent of foreign trade. If its value was equal to 5 per cent of income, he doubted whether doing without it, and forfeiting the gain from specialization and trade, would cause a loss of more than

$2\frac{1}{2}$ per cent in national income. It followed that if one could grow 1 per cent faster each year, even after making a sacrifice equal to $2\frac{1}{2}$ per cent of income, at the end of a decade one would be much better off, with smaller international trade and faster growth.

Professor Robinson said that the interesting question was what made the ratio between international trade and income the size that it was in a given country at a particular moment. There was also the question of how this ratio changed over time. He thought that the size of trade was partly a result of the size of the country itself. In countries with populations of about 200 million, for example the U.S.A., trade represented 5 to 7 per cent of national income. In countries of 50 million, like the U.K., it represented 15 to 20 per cent, occasionally reaching 25 per cent. In countries of 15 million it represented 25 to 30 per cent. However, the percentages showed interesting and significant changes over time, and this was not a question of size alone but of changing factor endowments. He thought that one should take a dynamic view of this question as well. For example, a country which exported minerals might find these exhausted, as the U.K. had with tin. There were also changes in the relative importance of products through technical progress. For example, there was the development of oil, and more recently of nuclear power, as a source of energy. This had helped, for example, to modify the position of coal in the U.K. Similarly, artificial rubber affected the factor endowments of rubber-growing countries. He therefore suggested that it was most important to apply the theory of international trade dynamically.

If one looked at countries which had taken off into sustained growth, most of them showed a particular period in which the rise in the rate of growth took place, and this phase of take-off was in a number of cases also a phase of growing exports relatively to income. In the U.K., exports had risen from 10 per cent of national income in 1740 to 16 per cent in 1800. In Japan, the ratio had risen from 3 per cent in 1868 to 11 per cent in 1900. The U.S. ratio had been stable at 7-8 per cent in the relevant period. However, if one turned to what one knew regarding the largely under-developed areas whose growth rates one was anxious to see improved, one found that nearly all of them were dependent on exports of primary products and, partly in consequence of this, had a falling ratio of exports to income. This was more significant because, as Dr. Patel had said, most of them would want to increase their imports, especially of capital goods, if their foreign trade position allowed. These countries were therefore faced, not as Professor Sohmen suggested with a short, temporary period of adjustment in the balance of payments, but with a long-run trend in which exports were falling relatively to income.

If one looked at the history of countries which had taken off, both exports and imports had risen. In the U.K., exports of manufactured goods had been used to bring in imports of food, reducing dependence on home-produced food and allowing increased specialization on industries with a comparative advantage. These industries achieved external economies and increased productivity. With the under-developed areas today, take-off was being attempted with a falling ratio of exports to income and this led to all sorts of planning difficulties. While the rich countries had been able to rely on their exports to bring in imports whenever shortages arose, modern under-developed countries constantly found that there were bottlenecks in particular parts of the economy, caused by the difficulty of meeting shortages through importing. This made it most important to get proportions right and to achieve the correct balance in planning for development. It was easy to have wasted effort in India because foreign exchange could not be used if particular shortages arose. Improvisation was necessary and Dr. Patel was right in showing that India had to make the maximum effort to increase exports. Any activity which was competitive with exports must be restricted. However, having done this in the longer run, India would be faced with the need to make progressive adjustments.

There was little hope of a sufficient increase of India's traditional exports in the longer run and he doubted whether her new exports would be able to rise fast enough to increase the export-income ratio. To find new and dynamic exports, India must try to develop production of manufactured goods which could first be sold on the home market in order to reduce costs. Then, at a later stage, these import-saving industries might be turned over to exporting. The problem should be handled on an infant industry basis and the fact faced that we were dealing with a progressive development and not merely a short-run disequilibrium. It was not just a question of increasing the freedom of trade but of sustaining the export-income ratio in developing countries. This was a more fundamental problem, related to factor scarcity and comparative advantage. It would occur whether or not trade was free. It was a problem which arose even with complete free trade and which was not easy to deal with by constant and continuous devaluation. Professor Robinson was less persuaded than the supporters of fluctuating exchange rates that speculation always exerted a favourable interest on foreign exchange rates. Countries like India and the U.K. faced a situation where the ratio of imports to income was high and devaluation was thus inflationary.

Professor Morgan wanted to comment on that part of Professor Sohmen's introduction where he took it for granted that tariffs had assisted American growth. It was by no means clear that historical evidence supported this judgement; internal growth had not depended on protection. The Mid-West grew without a tariff protecting it from Eastern competition; nor was the Far West protected from the rest of the country as it developed. And with falling transportation costs as efficiency in transport had increased, there had been steadily less 'natural' protection to newer areas as the years went by.

Professor Morgan also said that growth meant a rise in real income in the form of goods people *wanted*. If, instead of people choosing for themselves, bureaucrats chose for them — through tariffs, quotas, allocations, subsidies and the like — the significance of increased output became conjectural.

International Trade Theory in a Developing World

Sir Donald MacDougall wanted to stress that Dr. Savosnick's analysis bore little resemblance to the real problems of the U.K., Germany, etc. This was not intended as a criticism of the analysis as such, but Dr. Savosnick's concentration on the terms of trade was not very appropriate. The problem in the real U.K. was not the result of a worsening in the terms of trade; these had been improving for a good many years. The difficulty was that costs per unit of output were rising faster than in Germany, and perhaps the U.K. was less vigorous in innovating, selling and so on.

If there was a balance of payments deficit in the U.K., and full employment was to be maintained, the orthodox remedy was devaluation plus deflation. This would reduce total expenditure and also raise the prices of traded goods relatively to those of non-traded ones, thereby switching production from non-traded to traded goods (and consumption in the opposite direction). It was not a question of moving along the transformation curve between importables and exportables but of inducing a shift of production towards both types of traded goods.

Sir Donald wondered how this applied to what Dr. Savosnick and Dr. Sohmen had said. If one relied on a flexible exchange rate, this might lead to a considerable depreciation in order to get payments balanced in the short run. A much smaller depreciation, or perhaps none at all, might be required in the longer run if one now took special steps to encourage production of exportables and importables. It might not be sufficient to look merely at the immediate profitability of various investments, but might be necessary to take special steps to get the structure of the economy right.

In India, such an analysis might be even more useful. It was not certain whether or not it was necessary for India to devalue the rupee to achieve equilibrium in the long run. But to achieve a balance entirely by this means in the short run would involve large changes in relative prices which would be disruptive, inflationary and inequitable. Controls, as well as high excise taxes, were thus necessary. It would be politically very difficult to allow, for example, rich Indians to travel freely abroad when there was a serious shortage of foreign exchange for purchasing imported materials and capital goods.

Dr. Ferrero had spoken with some pride about Peru, but Sir Donald wondered how income distribution in Peru compared with that in less fortunate countries. It was sometimes possible to have a good balance of payments position because the gains from growth went to a narrow part of the population. Development in under-developed countries needed to be widespread.

If Professor Sohmen were to look at the orders of magnitude of the Indian problem, he might feel that an analysis in terms of marginal changes was not very appropriate. India had to more than double her exports to achieve equilibrium in her balance of payments. She had to raise the ratio of exports to income and, in the light of Professor Robinson's remarks, this was clearly a very formidable task.

Sir Donald did not deny that some currencies might be overvalued and should be devalued. He was attracted by Dr. Patel's idea of finding an exchange rate around which one could operate various types of control, taxes and subsidies. One possible criterion was that when such controls became ineffective and unworkable, one should devalue.

Sir Donald agreed with Dr. Patel that there was a balance of payments barrier to growth. If one sought only to provide the savings necessary to finance development, and ignored the balance of payments, difficulties were likely to occur. Sir Roy Harrod's paper had allowed for a fall in the terms of trade of $\frac{1}{2}$ per cent per annum. An alternative approach would be to allow for balance of payments difficulties which would lead to bottlenecks in the economy and thereby slow development.

Professor Johnson wanted to protest against the tendency of participants to identify the problems of India and the U.K. and especially the methods of dealing with these problems. So far as the U.K. was concerned, he thought Professor Sohmen's remarks were more relevant than what Professor Robinson and Sir Donald MacDougall had said. The two latter thought that the level of the sterling exchange rate and the role of the U.K. as a world financial centre were both entirely satisfactory. Professor Johnson thought the problem of the U.K. was particularly one of the exchange rate, but this did not lead him on to identify under-developed with developed areas.

Professor Robinson's main opposition, with which he agreed, was to looking at international trade as the only cause of economic welfare, and at interference with trade as the most serious kind of intervention in the economy. The main thing was to find the most satisfactory ways of accumulating capital, knowledge and so on. At the margin, he thought that the difference in welfare made by trade restrictions was small, so that if one removed intervention in international trade one would be affecting something purely marginal.

Nevertheless, one should not go on to imply that interference with trade would necessarily give growth. In order to obtain the extra 1 per cent of growth per annum about which Professor Robinson spoke, one would have to interfere with many other things, and it did not necessarily follow that such interference would flow easily from restrictions on trade. The main issue seemed to be whether one could plan an economy better than the market system could run it. On this, Dr. Patel balanced the various opinions very ably. A commitment to planning was irrational if what one really needed was to make good deficiencies in the market system. One also required sufficient faith in those who would administer the plan to be sure that they would do this without great inefficiency. What Dr. Ferrero was really asking was how far one could maintain that planning was better than the free price mechanism if prices reflected real costs.

What Professor Sohmen appeared to have said was that if one had flexible exchange rates everything else would follow. Professor Sohmen disliked using the exchange rate as an instrument of central planning. However, if one was committed to planning for growth, the question was whether or not the exchange rate could be used effectively from a purely technical point of view. Professor Johnson thought that when one looked at balances of payments one should distinguish the central reserve countries from the others, whether these others were developed countries or not. The real problems of growth were not balance of payments problems, and much of the discussion had been concerned with real problems of growth which appeared in the form of balance of payments difficulties. In some circumstances, therefore, it was better to start with these real problems and to work back to the balance of payments. Dr. Savosnick, for example, had not shown how real problems led to balance of payments deficits. Such deficits represented the running down of assets, and to build up a satisfactory model for studying balance of payments problems one needed to start in a situation where a country possessed such assets and show how adjustment to change reduced them. Professor Johnson thought modern theory had a great deal more to say on these questions than the discussion so far had made it appear.

In his honest attempt to strike a balance between planning and not planning, Dr. Patel had shown that there was much logic in the market system. One of the greatest dangers was that people would say that economic theory showed that planning should be avoided ; that nevertheless they themselves wanted to plan, and that this meant that economic theory was wrong. He was enraged by the views of many planners but, if one looked at the question more open-mindedly, perhaps it could be resolved. On balance, Dr. Patel took a refreshing view in not holding a dogmatic position but insisting that one should apply what logic there was in the operation of the market.

Professor Ohlin agreed that Professor Robinson was right in stressing the need for a dynamic approach to international trade questions, but thought that Professor Sohmen was also right in stressing the relevance of some existing international trade doctrines even in this context. For example, currently accepted doctrine included the infant-industry argument and therefore considered long-run effects on resources, monopoly problems and the impossibility of reallocating resources in under-developed areas. If one considered that conditions in under-developed countries were somehow special and that intervention of some kind was necessary, the question arose whether intervention should be through international trade or other methods. As economists, we thought that intervention in trade was the most interesting and rational form of intervention, but why should one concentrate on foreign trade ? If one said that the U.K. needed a higher rate of growth, he could see an easy path. One began with a deficit, introduced protection and obtained relief. One might then get greater progress over two or three years, but perhaps other reliefs would be as desirable, and perhaps these would give better long-run advantages by allowing greater trade. One could justify similar interference with trade in under-developed areas to increase mobility and so on. However, if one restricted foreign trade too much, one would lose both the direct advantages of trade and those which flowed from the import of foreign capital and know-how. Industrialists in Sweden, for example, said that they would be more ready to build factories in India if India relied on a more stable and less restrictive trade policy.

Professor Ohlin suggested that other forms of intervention would be less risky. As for Professor Johnson's question whether those who planned or who acted on plans would do so more effectively than the price system, he thought it conceivable that the answer was yes. Dr. Patel himself was a good argument in favour of planning and, if all planners were Patels, many liberals would be converted. He therefore agreed with Messrs. Sohmen and Ferrero that the kind of mechanism which bureaucrats in under-developed areas were being asked to handle was much more difficult than that dealt with by the price mechanism in other countries. When new and untried administrators were asked to handle this kind of situation with the results the planners expected, it was clearly asking too much of them. One could hardly expect super-intelligence and immense wisdom from them. He thought that this was one argument against intervention. There were many kinds of international equilibrium, with more or fewer import restrictions. Perhaps the main thing was to try to avoid having an overvalued currency.

Professor Robinson had said that devaluation was inflationary and he would agree for a country like England where virtually all consumer goods had an import content. But countries like Brazil and India were big enough, and wages were sticky enough, to make it possible to adjust the foreign exchange rate. If we were discussing really violent forms of intervention perhaps one should consider wage control to prevent internal cost inflation resulting from devaluation.

Professor Ohlin agreed with Dr. Savosnick that it would be very desirable if one could prevent inflation from leading to devaluation, but he thought that Professor Robinson's analysis of elasticity of demand was too static. A small country achieved a big rise in exports in the long run from a 10 per cent devaluation. He thought the overvaluing of a currency could be correct only in very special circumstances. Perhaps the price system would work more effectively if relative cost levels could be kept more in balance.

Professor Ohlin thought that consumption was important not merely to give incentives but because it affected the ability to work, improved skills, etc. He had always admired the under-developed countries, in the sense that their inhabitants did very well with such low consumption standards. There had been much evidence in Europe that increases in consumption raised the quality of labour in both the short and the long run. This was a formidable problem for under-developed areas. If savings were increased as fast as some people hoped, perhaps it could be done only at the cost of reducing the rate of increase in the skill of labour. There was also the question of population increases. He wondered whether, in view of their rising populations, some under-developed areas were trying to go too fast. Perhaps they should choose between a less rapid rate of growth of income or a less rapid rate of growth of population.

Professor Robinson stressed that he was not anxious to reduce the long-run volume of world trade. The real question for a country like Britain was how to balance the balance of payments while continuing full employment. He was more concerned with easing the problems of transition within the economy, and this required that adjustments should be made before the crises occurred. What one needed was for a country to be able to see what its long-run comparative advantage was and to adjust its economy with that particular destination as the final goal.

Professor Mikesell said that, because many economists were against protection, they tended to fall back on classical arguments for free trade. He thought that a more useful approach to the balance of payments problem was to consider positive inducements as an alternative to protection. Both represented interference with free market forces, and both meant planning and therefore had long-run implications. It was not necessary to recite all the difficulties which arose from protection. For example, the fact that it tended to foster the development of the wrong industries. However, it was very important to make sure that protection did not foster the use of domestic resources to make goods whose consumption the government wanted to reduce. There might well be a clash here between balance of payments and basic development objectives.

So far as devaluation was concerned, he did not feel that completely flexible exchange rates were the answer. He regarded these as an engine of inflation and thought that Canada had been a very special case. An occasional, 'once-for-all' change in the exchange rate from time to time might, however, be necessary because some inflation would almost inevitably occur in most under-developed countries.

Professor Johnson commented that Professor Mikesell was not presenting the exchange rate issue as others would. Many economists would say that complete flexibility in the exchange rate was better than occasional big changes.

Dr. Myint had been struck by the difference between India and other countries. He thought that India was nearly unique as an under-developed area and that one should not generalize from Indian experience. The basic problem was to be able to interchange domestic resources and foreign exchange. India was in a particularly bad position here, though he realized that she had special difficulties and rigidities. Other under-developed countries had much greater flexibility and, if one were looking at the long run, this flexibility was important. He therefore thought that one should separate the real problems of development from the balance of payments difficulties which often arose from short-run speculation. On the other hand, India had much better administrators and planners than most other under-developed countries and Mr. Patel's suggested mixture of remedies was therefore much too complex for these other countries.

Professor Giersch said he wanted to elaborate on the conflict between trade and growth, not for under-developed areas or the U.K., but for countries like Western Germany. Apart from the balance of payments crisis of 1949–50, Germany had experienced no conflict of this kind, and he wondered why this was. One reason was a happy accident : the structure of production inherited from the past was such that Germany could easily supply goods for which world demand was growing fast. Second, the structure of production was sufficiently flexible, and this was largely due to a high rate of growth of the economy. Most adjustments could therefore take place at the growth margin. On the other hand, in the U.K., one probably had the vicious circle of a low rate of growth leading to low mobility and in turn perpetuating the low rate of growth. Professor Giersch suggested that devaluation might change the attitude of entrepreneurs towards growth. This seemed to have happened, for example, in France after 1958, when devaluation had made entrepreneurs much more optimistic about their chances in the EEC. However, he wanted to stress that flexible exchange rates were no substitute for flexibility in the structure of production and for an economic policy designed to foster the working of the price mechanism.

Professor Bechin said that, as he saw it, the scientific approach to economic growth was the only one which would enable one to diagnose the phenomena of growth. The modern world situation was worse than in earlier times for two main reasons. First, there was the long-run tendency for primary-produce prices to fall. Second, there were cyclical movements in these prices. Together, these created the difficulties mentioned by Dr. Patel. Professor Bechin reported that the U.S.S.R. had experienced similar difficulties when realizing her plans for industrialization during the 1920s and 1930s. She had had to increase imports of capital goods at a time when primary-produce prices were low and she had nothing else to export. He therefore understood Dr. Patel's difficulties both as an economist and as a citizen of a country which had faced similar problems. In modern conditions, such measures as import restrictions on non-essentials might give good results. He agreed with many of Dr. Patel's solutions, but would particularly stress the necessity of long-term loans at low rates of interest on a purely commercial basis. It would also be good if under-developed countries could pay their debts not only in foreign exchange but by exporting the goods which they could produce most easily.

Dr. Patel replied to the discussion on his paper. On the contrast drawn by Dr. Ferrero between liberals and others, Dr. Patel's impression was that differences among participants often appeared exaggerated through the anxiety of many participants to correct what they regarded as the mistaken notions of others. If participants clarified their own position without trying to knock down dummies set up by themselves, actual differences would seem less sharp. He was therefore particularly grateful to Professor Johnson for pointing out that in this he was trying to reach a correct balance between opposing views often expressed in India.

The basic point was that balance of payments difficulties in developing countries did not simply reflect inadequate or misdirected fiscal or monetary policies for mobilizing resources. The narrow base of the economy and the comparatively low substitutability of resources made it impossible to overcome balance of payments difficulties in less-developed countries simply by attempting to increase domestic savings. Perhaps, in these circumstances, a country should live within the constraint imposed by the balance of payments, but the consequences for growth could not be disregarded. Professor Sohmen had pointed out that one could deal with this situation by foreign aid. Dr. Patel would add that so far as foreign aid was available its contribution was larger than one would normally suppose in terms of the usual savings — investment models where a given inflow of foreign capital was reckoned to add a corresponding amount to the total resources available for investment (or consumption). On a dynamic view the contribution of foreign aid should be reckoned higher, since an attempt to replace it by a similar rise in domestic savings would give a less satisfactory over-all result.

Again, if one suggested using devaluation or a fall in the terms of trade, one should still ask whether a proper ordering of investment priorities would not obviate the necessity for large or frequent devaluations which inevitably damped down growth. However, a fall in the terms of trade might improve the short-run situation or developing countries might not need to devalue their currency in certain circumstances. Again, even when balance of payments difficulties could be overcome by devaluation or worsened terms of trade, the short-run degree of devaluation required might be so severe as to reduce long-run growth. Devaluation in one developing country might produce a favourable response in its balance of payments, but the net advantage when countries in similar circumstances followed suit would be small and would have to be offset by a deterioration in the terms of trade for poorer countries. While resistance to devaluation was often seized upon by critics, perhaps the greater danger of competitive and suicidal devaluation was not generally recognized.

If there was any merit in his basic point, two conclusions seemed to follow. First, measures to correct balances of payments in developing countries must represent part of a long-term strategy for overcoming the basic structural weakness of their economies. This might imply preferring a short-run solution (for example, foreign aid) even though other, at least partial, cures were available (for example, devaluation). Second, a pattern of investment which strengthened the balance of payments might be preferable in the long run even if it implied a lower short-run production. He was interested here in what Sir Roy said, particularly about the difficulty of distinguishing between traded and non-traded goods. Certainly one should always be cautious in accepting arguments which purported to show that what was not so good in the short run would still be better in the long run. Nor did his basic point necessarily imply that the objective of strengthening the balance of payments would always require sacrificing productivity for some time. Whether this was true could not be asserted *a priori*, but only by looking at real situations. However, circumstances could exist where long-term growth would be slowed unless the short-run balance of payments was strengthened even at an immediate cost in terms of over-all productivity.

If the balance of payments barrier emerged before the savings barrier, in that some potential savings in the economy could not be realized because of balance of payments difficulties, restrictions on luxury imports would accelerate growth. Such restrictions would also moderate the demonstration effect and so promote a growth in savings. Sir Roy contended that even a half per cent difference in the rate of consumption growth would be decisive for the successful take-off in developing countries. These countries were walking a dangerous tight-rope and anything which helped to modify the pattern of demand so as to increase savings should be welcomed. All this, of course, was not an argument for protecting luxury industries but for curtailing luxury consumption.

On the argument that import restrictions might impair incentives, Dr. Patel agreed that restrictions on necessities could do this, but thought it too much to argue that the richer groups in developing countries need incentives through imported luxuries.

Dr. Patel thought one could prove little by considering Germany and Japan, as some participants suggested. Historically, most countries which had developed had relied on some restrictions, and, even now, countries which seemed to avoid restrictions adopted other devices with similar effects.

Sir Roy's comment on countries with balance of payments difficulties granting tied loans was justified. However, Dr. Patel felt that the case for tied loans should not be accepted *in toto*. For example, creditor countries with balance of payments difficulties should not object to their aid funds being used for purchases from other countries with balance of payments difficulties. This would be particularly true for other developing countries. There was clearly danger that a policy of tied loans, administered without any rational exceptions, would help some countries at the expense of the trade of others which were similarly in need of assistance. Equally, if the use of aid funds were tied to purchases from the aid-giving country, there was no point in adding to the disadvantages of tied assistance by stipulating that assistance would be tied to specific projects rather than be available for purchasing any relatively not-too-expensive commodities from the aid-giving country.

Dr. Ferrero had raised many points. First, Dr. Patel wanted to say that the IMF was a democratic and dynamic organization, and those associated with its work found it useful to exchange differing views. Dr. Ferrero had claimed that Dr. Patel's main recommendation on combining import duties with export subsidies came to the same thing as multiple exchange rates. If Dr. Ferrero's contention was that any arrangement according different treatment to different imports and exports had the same economic consequences as multiple exchange rates, Dr. Patel would agree. The substantive question, however, was whether one could dispense altogether with systems of differential incentives and disincentives. Despite all that was said about distortions caused by differential tax devices, hardly any country's fiscal system failed to discriminate between different lines of production or consumption. The basic objection to multiple exchange rates was that they were not a very effective or equitable instrument for such discrimination as might be needed.

The question raised by Professor Morgan was a good one, but was difficult to discuss. Dr. Patel did not intend to suggest that in matters of economic planning one could rely entirely either on market forces or on decisions of bureaucrats and politicians. Without some attempt to look ahead it would be impossible to meet future problems. This did not mean that one should try to plan the future in minute detail. The kind of decision one wanted to arrive at by planning or programming consisted essentially in broad questions such as the rate of growth to aim at, the pattern of investment, the degree of tax effort, the requirements for external assistance, etc. Within the framework of decisions relating to these broad questions a great deal, even in a planned economy, could and should be left essentially to the operation of market forces.

He agreed very much with what Professor Ohlin had said about population, but its growth was no reason for lowering one's sights. While everything must be done to control population growth — and India, at any rate, was trying to do what it could — the very fact that population would inevitably grow rapidly for some years required that the targets should be high.

Dr. Patel recalled a remark by Professor Lipinsky that there was no such thing as perfect planning. What was feasible in one country might not be feasible in others. But imperfections in planning, or differences in the ability to plan, did not themselves imply that it would be wise to dispense with planning altogether.

Dr. Savosnick said that Swedish business men used to tell him that when growth in Sweden was slow the Swedish economy would actually suffer because other countries were growing faster. He had argued that this was not necessarily so because it was not allowed for in the Johnson model. In that model the terms of trade and the standard of living would improve in the slower-growing country. However, the combined weight of a number of business men suggesting the same thing had begun to change his views and this paper tried to take a fresh look at this problem. Perhaps the choice of names for his countries was unfortunate and he agreed with Sir Donald MacDougall that the balance of payments of the U.K. was influenced by a domestic cost inflation accompanied by improving terms of trade. His was therefore a very hypothetical model, but did seem to have some relation to reality, though overlaid by the effects of inflation in the U.K.

When one analysed this problem in a three-country model, one found that the commodity terms of trade of the U.K. would worsen when the other countries were growing fast. There would therefore be a fall in the standard of living in the U.K., which found itself having to run faster in order to stay in the same place. It followed that the balance of payments problem resulting from a deterioration in the terms of trade was part of the process of industrial readjustment. There were many ways of dealing with the balance of payments, which was less important. In the end, it would correct itself and the aim of policy must be to ease such correction.

Dr. Savosnick disagreed with those who opposed devaluation as a policy measure because it led to inflation. It was quite true that devaluation was inflationary but one could use a number of deflationary policy measures in addition to devaluation, though this obvious truth was often forgotten. Dr. Savosnick agreed with Professor Sohmen that devaluation coupled with general disinflation should be sufficient. It was not necessary to have a tariff as well in order to step up adjustment. However, if the policy-makers had greater foresight than business men, the planners should stimulate business men to make changes towards the situation in which they would find themselves in the long run. For example, import-restrictions, tariffs, devaluation or export taxes could all be used and he would favour any such intervention if the planners did possess the necessary foresight.

In the hypothetical situation where a country was inside its production possibilities curve, the other question was what would happen to the balance of payments of the laggard country as it increased its rate of growth. There were two ways of reacting. First, the country could accept the fact that its technology was lagging and achieve a second-best solution ; second, it could speed up its rate of growth. In the short run, an increase in the rate of growth here would worsen the balance of payments. If restrictions were then imposed, a fall in consumption and/or investment might make entrepreneurs pessimistic and they would not use whatever resources had been released. A new form of thinking was required to discover how private investment could be stimulated while consumption was being deliberately reduced.

Dr. Savosnick thought that the discussion on Dr. Patel's paper had been somewhat confused. Growth and foreign investment from abroad were not necessarily the same thing. If India could grow from her own domestic resources there would be no balance of payments problem. He was therefore not satisfied that concentration on the balance of payments and on foreign aid was necessary. Dr. Savosnick thought that investment in developed countries was more profitable than investment in under-developed areas, which meant that humanitarian and political factors could be the only basis for aid. Once one admitted the non-economic nature of aid it was necessary to scrap the requirement of charging commercial interest rates. He therefore agreed with Professor Bechin that the whole question of the servicing and repayment of foreign-aid loans needed to be reconsidered.

THE DISCUSSION OF THE PAPERS BY PROFESSORS WEILLER AND DELIVANIS

Professor Mikesell said that the analysis of the existing international monetary organization needed to be approached historically. In fact, they made sense only in the light of their historical development. For example, the development of the EPU had changed the whole financial basis of the sterling area by allowing special sterling settlements. Similarly, convertibility in 1958 had changed the nature of the sterling area still further. He therefore thought that it would be helpful if economists could produce a more systematic analysis of the sterling, French franc and dollar areas, and perhaps of the rouble area too, if there was one. So far as the emergence of payments systems was concerned, recent developments in Latin America resulted from arrangements for the creation of a free trade area. He therefore thought that payments systems were related to trading relations and to financial and even political relationships. Payments arrangements did not provide a magic formula for assuring a desirable trade pattern, and the authors had looked at payments systems in terms of the best way of organizing them in order to promote growth. Capital flows were necessary but it was also important to devise ways of preventing these from leading to difficulties for reserve countries.

Professor Delivanis thought that the sterling and the French franc areas were better than the IMF or the dollar system. The latter represented multilateral payments systems to provide liquid funds rather than to allow deficit financing. However, Professor Mikesell doubted whether London really did provide limitless finance to the sterling area.

Professor Delivanis held the remarkable view that foreign exchange reserves were of more use than foreign capital. Professor Mikesell disagreed both on policy and theoretical grounds. It was true that some countries might need foreign exchange temporarily if they ran into balance of payments difficulties, but this did not necessarily require unlimited liquidity. He was not denying that there was a liquidity problem, but did believe that there was a distinct difference between foreign exchange and capital.

On page 344, Professor Weiller suggested that for any single country affiliated with a particular currency area, growth was more important than the rules of either the dollar or the Bretton Woods system. Professor Mikesell did not understand this, because since the war the U.S.A. had provided the bulk of foreign aid and had run up deficits of more than $12 billion. Professor Mikesell was confused, because at times both Professor Delivanis and Professor Weiller appeared to suggest that we should group countries into discriminating systems with each group going on inflating the supply of its trading currency without limit. He would certainly prefer a world arrangement for dealing with the liquidity problem to any national or regional one.

So far as inflation was concerned, Professor Weiller suggested on page 349 that a country with neither voluntary saving nor total planning would need a much higher rate of inflation than had previously been thought. Professor Mikesell said that several statistical studies suggested an inverse correlation between growth and inflation, and he wondered whether Professor Weiller would deny this.

Finally, on page 363, Professor Delivanis discussed the IMF arrangements, stressing that the IMF would grant credits to members whenever their balance of payments were strained by growth. Professor Mikesell thought there were many occasions on which the IMF had sought agreements to restrain the financial policies of borrowers and had gone far into interfering with their credit policies.

Professor Weiller said he would like to comment on the form, as distinct from the fact, of his paper. One difficulty was that whenever the dollar problem was discussed it was treated in quasi-mythical terms. In periods of accumulation of hot money the funds which remained in the U.S.A. were attributed both by the public and the press to a surplus of the balance of payments and so long as the gold exchange standard operated, the confusion persisted. After these quasi-mythical delusions of a psychological or sociological character, and the collapse of the 'financial myth', we returned to the tangible reality, only partly vitiated by these delusions.

Sir Donald MacDougall said that Professor Weiller's paper was rather philosophical and illustrated the somewhat different approaches of French and Anglo-Saxon economists. It was useful to have such different approaches and important for each group to discover what contribution the other had to make. The French were perhaps less bound by the classical framework, and more interested in problems of classification. Their approach was often historical. Professor Weiller was a rebellious type of historian and painted with a broad brush.

This paper reminded us of various important things. For example, a few years ago any Round Table meeting of this kind would have treated as central the problems of trade discrimination and of the inconvertibility of currencies imposed for balance of payments reasons. This time they had hardly been mentioned. The discussion of the discrimination involved in customs unions had been largely concerned with long-run effects, assuming that balance of payments problems could be overcome.

This suggested some interesting questions. Had the need for discrimination and inconvertibility after the war been a purely temporary phenomenon, or might it return ? Could such weapons safely be forsworn for all time ? Was the philosophy of the scarce-currency clause obsolete ? Similarly, quantitative restrictions on imports had been regarded as quite normal balance of payments weapons until fairly recently, but this was becoming less and less the case, at least among the more advanced nations. Then again, in the wartime discussions that led to Bretton Woods, it had often been assumed that international short-term capital movements could, and should, be controlled. The changes of view on these various matters affected the need for international liquidity, and whether they were wise would no doubt be discussed in connection with Professor Kindleberger's paper.

Turning to Professor Delivanis' paper, Sir Donald said it raised the question whether a rapidly increasing demand for exports was important for growth. He shared Professor Mikesell's doubts whether it was as important as foreign capital, but still thought that a rising export demand was highly beneficial. Secondly, Professor Delivanis seemed to imply that growth was necessarily bad for the balance of payments. Sir Donald was surprised at such a dogmatic conclusion. Professor Johnson (whose article on the subject was quoted by Professor Delivanis) had shown that, while more rapid growth might imply a more rapid increase in imports, it also normally meant a faster increase in productivity and so, quite probably, a slower rise in the price level. This would normally help the balance of payments. Perhaps Professor Delivanis would care to enlarge on this question.

Professor Delivanis also seemed to favour a policy, such as that usually followed by the IBRD, of granting loans only for the purchase of imported capital equipment. But in a country like India this could lead to awkward and wasteful results. India might not be typical, but the amount of foreign aid she needed to supplement domestic savings tended to be greater than the value of the capital goods which she wanted to import. Therefore, in order to absorb aid on the terms Professor Delivanis was suggesting, India would have to import more machines than she wanted and keep some of them idle for lack of foreign exchange to buy the raw materials required to feed into them. So far as capital from the U.K. to the sterling area was concerned, he could tell Professor Mikesell that such movements had been almost completely free in the past, but now seemed likely to be somewhat curtailed.

He wanted to ask Professor Bechin some questions about the operation of the rouble area. First, how much scope was there for multilateral trade within the area? Second, how far could a capitalist country use a surplus with one socialist country to finance a deficit with another? Finally, how far could a socialist country use funds earned in one capitalist country to finance a deficit with another?

Professor Kindleberger thought a fundamental question which needed answering was what the payments system meant. The fact that all accounts were settled in dollars did not in itself mean that one had a dollar payments system. We had all learned, as students, that money had three functions: as a medium of exchange, unit of account and store of value. Professor Weiller suggested, on page 340, that changes in the direction of trade flows would have a big effect on the pattern of international monetary systems. However, he thought some light could be thrown on this by considering one of the three functions of money, namely, money acting as something which could be held. Many people held Swiss francs, but this did not mean that there was a Swiss franc area.

Professor Kindleberger was not certain that it was necessary for an effective international currency system to create credit. Perhaps one could operate on the basis of 100 per cent reserves with transfers moving from the centre to the periphery and back again. Would the IMF be sufficient to solve international monetary problems, provided it was re-organized every five years to enlarge quotas? Or could the system be managed over time with fixed money reserves?

Professor Kindleberger thought there was a big difference between

British and French views on the nature of their currency areas. The French were perfectly happy with the idea of a franc area, but British economists were uncertain about the value of the sterling area. They had once claimed that it was important because of the interest and service charges which entered the balance of payments but, as time went on, the British became more and more doubtful. They felt that the U.K. would have to divert resources unduly in order to give savings to other sterling area countries. Moreover, trade flows were far from being financed entirely in sterling. If one asked the question, what did a regional arrangement provide, the answer was that it meant a great deal for those who got convertibility. If one asked what the cost of giving convertibility was, the answer might well be that one had to form a free trade area supported by an external tariff. Professor Kindleberger suggested that before long much more capital would have to be supplied by France to her African colonies and that with this drain French happiness might vanish.

Professor Kindleberger recalled that there was a two-year cycle in foreign trade crises in the U.K. This was blamed on the inventory cycle and on a two-year lag between the passing of decisions from the centre to the periphery of the sterling area. Would Professor Weiller say there was a prospect of this developing in the French area? Would the pre-occupation with prestige not become less important? This raised another interesting and important question, namely, whether there always had to be a centre and a periphery in international currency areas. Could one set up an area in which all members were equal, for example, an EPU for Latin America or Asia? One had to remember that in the EPU in Europe a great deal of the initial credit had come from outside. Such ideas were being propounded for Asia, with the suggestions that U.S. aid to India might be used to buy goods in Japan, but Americans were not happy about this.

Mr. Lamfalussy wondered whether, if one had to choose between different types of international monetary arrangement, the correct choice would be for a world-wide arrangement or a number of regional ones. Or should one combine the two? Assuming that growth was the main aim, Professor Delivanis had shown the advantages of a regional agreement. What did Professor Weiller think?

Mr. Lamfalussy also wondered how far the success of a regional grouping depended on either a preferential customs arrangement or some kind of free trade area. He wondered whether such a preferential system based on developed countries alone could be a success. So far as the European Common Market was concerned, he wondered whether it would be desirable to have monetary unification. He was concerned here with general rather than technical points.

Dr. Ferrero recalled that Professor Weiller suggested that the inflationary assistance to growth would have to be greater in countries at an earlier stage of development. He thought the opposite, because in poor countries the marginal propensity to consume would be high and elasticity of supply low.

Professor Delivanis had begun his paper by suggesting that disequilibrium in the balance of payments was unavoidable only when the trading countries were growing at substantially different rates and this difference was not neutralized by factors working in the opposite direction. He did not agree. In Europe, the rate of growth was highest in countries like Germany and Italy where there were no balance of payments problems. The same was true of under-developed areas; Peru and Mexico had grown more rapidly than Argentina and Chile, which had greater balance of payment problems.

Also, on page 354 of his paper, Professor Delivanis suggested that exchange control, if handled efficiently, was more effective than devaluation. Dr. Ferrero doubted whether, even if exchange control was efficient, it would lead to a more rational use of foreign exchange by the government of an under-developed country. If one merely used foreign exchange to bar non-essential imports, this would shift demand to the domestic market and would lead to the production of these same goods for the internal market. Then one type of control would inevitably lead to others. As for whether this would lead to a more rational use of foreign exchange, what mattered was the amount of savings the country could accumulate. Would they be increased by the controls? He also thought, unlike Professor Delivanis, that exchange control made people more willing to hoard and to transfer their capital abroad, especially if there was a great difference between the free and the black market exchange rate. There was thus a danger of a capital outflow at the same time as the inflow of capital would be reduced because foreign lenders became afraid that their money would be trapped. Exchange control assumed that the existing rate was more favourable than the equilibrium rate and only helped to worsen the situation.

Finally, on page 355, Professor Delivanis said that 'there is a likelihood that the internal monetary equilibrium will also be upset when growth is abnormally fast. In effect, in these circumstances monetary incomes increase and are generally spent, even though prices start rising, as a result of the reduced elasticity of demand caused by the increase of money incomes.' This raised again his question whether the most rapidly growing countries were not also the ones with the most stable price levels. It also raised the question of what was normal growth. In one sense, it was possible to argue that the growth rate was above normal only if countries were trying to grow faster than their available resources would allow, which meant excess spending and inflation.

Dr. Patel said he would like to begin by pointing out that IMF policy was not quite so restrictive as some participants made it appear. It did not refuse credits to members whenever their balance of payments was strained by growth. What the IMF took into account was not so much the cause of the balance of payments difficulty as the prospects of repayment within three to five years. As for the IMF's assistance being conditional, a member country could borrow almost automatically within the limits set by its gold contribution. In practice, it was allowed to borrow a further 25 per cent of its quota without much question. Only for accommodation beyond this did the Fund apply special scrutiny.

Dr. Patel wondered whether it was right to say that external assistance should finance merely the foreign exchange component of a project. Unfortunately, expressions like balance of payments loans raised images of support for wasteful policies. However, where the over-all plans and policies of a developing country were sound, it would be appropriate to make loans for buying raw materials and components as well as equipment. Even the World Bank was coming round to this view.

Speaking of the sterling area, Dr. Patel felt that with the advent of convertibility the importance of the sterling area as an arrangement for pooling scarce currencies had diminished. Its main importance now lay in providing a forum for exchanging views on matters of common interest.

As for the setting up of a Latin American or Asian version of EPU, Dr. Patel thought that since countries of these regions were in no position to provide credit to each other, funds for the revolving credit required to start such an arrangement would have to come from outside. He was not sure that any existing agency would be willing to provide it.

Professor Weiller said that the parts of his paper with which participants had disagreed were often connecting passages which brought in psycho-sociological concepts, so that to defend them would be a little outside the real purpose of the discussion. He wondered whether Professor Mikesell agreed on some basic points. In particular the thesis of the second part of his paper was that the important thing would be to economize in international liquidity. For example, the international monetary system had operated in the decades before 1914 with very small movements of gold. Many balance of payments items were cleared on the foreign exchange markets outside the mechanism of gold transfers. Only big centres like London could use the rate of interest to control monetary flows and it was important to recognize that before 1914 the operation of the gold standard had been supported by other adjustments. Professor Weiller suggested that more and more long-term capital flows were of an equilibrating — or at least self-equilibrating — kind. Those who lent had practically enabled those who needed loans to smooth adjustments. He wondered whether nowadays one could reduce the extent to which countries would resort to the ultimate means of payment, namely, gold or reserve currencies.

According to Professor Weiller, protectionism was not always bad for under-developed countries with inconvertible currencies. The movement towards free trade could be successful only in the most favourable circumstances. During unfavourable periods one had to realize that there would be little progress. He drew attention to a choice between flexible protectionism and flexible monetary or fiscal policies. Moreover, if one were to reintroduce something like the gold standard he would advocate definite indulgence towards the problems which under-developed areas had to face in any clearing system. In order to economize international liquidity, it was important to regulate the flows of aid, investment, and, eventually, repayment.

Professor Mikesell wanted to clarify one point. He had not said that he favoured making only loans tied either to investment in fixed capital or to the purchase of raw materials for specific projects. He agreed that lending needed to be more flexible, but he did not favour general balance of payments loans which did not support well-formulated projects.

Professor Bechin said that trade between socialist countries and capitalist countries was based on long-run balance. On the basis of this, each country supplied some goods to the other and no system of clearing was necessary. Deficits were met by long-run loans which could be paid off in later years when the country in question had a trading surplus. It was perfectly possible for a capitalist country having a surplus with a socialist country to use the accumulated funds to finance trade with other socialist countries.

Mr. Rip pointed out that the IBRD had made 40 per cent of a recent loan to Yugoslavia in the form of foreign exchange. He thought this was a valuable practice and that the operations of the bank were becoming more elastic. However, at the same time, the bank would not finance state-owned firms in under-developed areas on the grounds that these were not efficient. This was hard to understand, not least because the basic industries in under-developed areas must inevitably be financed by the state. Only the state's resources were big enough to meet the requirements of under-developed areas. If development was leading to a fall in subsistence production, then both internal and external trade would benefit.

Mr. Liesner said that Professor Delivanis claimed that if a scarce currency was pooled by a regional arrangement this would lead to stability. On *a priori* grounds, he could not agree. Indeed, it could be argued that pooling was a de-stabilizing factor. If there was a pool, the need for each country to tailor demand to the supply of the scarce currency was lost and a process of general overspending was therefore possible. This had happened to some extent in the sterling area since 1945.

Sir Donald MacDougall wondered if Dr. Kaigl could elaborate on a question of socialist trade. If, for example, the U.K. had a surplus with Czechoslovakia, could it use this to finance a deficit with Poland?

Professor Kaigl replied that this was perfectly possible because all trade would take place in the capitalist country's currency. Trade with the U.K. would therefore be in sterling and it would be possible to use this to buy goods from Poland.

Professor Delivanis replied to the comments on his paper. He had not examined the systems of payments in historical retrospect but as they were operating in the spring of 1961. He had avoided dealing with all those questions which had been considered specifically and extensively elsewhere, for example, the sterling area. He had never intended to say that the London market could grant unlimited credits to the sterling area, but he believed strongly in the difference between foreign exchange and foreign capital. The latter, but not the former, could be replaced by compulsory saving within the country concerned. He was in favour of free trade and believed that the U.K.'s relatively elaborate trade policy had aided the smooth functioning of the sterling area. His contention about the IMF's lending policy had been confirmed by Dr. Patel.

Mr. Lamfalussy had asked about preferential treatment within a regional payments area. This was necessary, he thought, in times of foreign exchange scarcity. He would like to point out that Dr. Ferrero had not considered the substantial balance of payments difficulties experienced by Germany in the early 1950s nor the contribution of expenditure by American soldiers in eliminating these. Dr. Ferrero was right in his views about the reactions of people who had experienced inflation when foreign exchange control was applied as it was in Latin America or Greece. The situation was very different in India where monetary history had been less unstable. International monetary disequilibrium was reached when a country became over-employed. His reference to Professor Johnson's article was concerned with the difference between stocks and flows.

Replying to the discussion on his paper, *Professor Weiller* said he would remind Sir Donald that, in many papers, economists played the fascinating game of going back to orthodox theory and then picking holes in it. It would be of no use to put together all the proposed models in order to explain the real phenomena of international trade. He hoped he would be forgiven for having taken an historical view, in that way eliminating a number of problems while trying to throw some light on the actual working of the payments and exchange system. When he had spoken of the lack of restrictiveness in the dollar zone he had meant that it was a system without fixed rules. On the other hand, during the same period, the IMF had laid down rules, but there had been many exceptions in practice to the rules it was supposed to follow, and its goal had been reached only by a series of detours. However, this had been very successful, and we had to remember that around 1958 balance had been achieved in an unorthodox way.

Dr. Ferrero had asked the important question about which underdeveloped countries found inflation most valuable for growth. What he had said had been based on the facts as he saw them and also on an analysis for certain countries made by the younger French economists, Ducros, Chabat and Lambert. In an article published in the *Revue d'Économie Politique* (January 1961) Ducros had shown that if one took a group of under-developed areas in the very early stages of development, inflation could have been beneficial to growth. The reason was that in these particular countries there was a class of absentee land-owners with large hoardings. Inflation helped to reduce the real value of these accumulated hoards.

Professor Weiller thought that all the questions raised on the operation of the franc zone were important and he had given more study to this problem since he had written his paper. However, his conclusions had not changed. The zone was losing its former significance as new countries obtained their independence, and most of their economic claims corresponded to what one could call normal desire. For example, African countries often wanted separate dollar accounts. This would have been a problem during the period of dollar shortage but now it was less important. It could also happen that such countries wanted to devalue or to make other monetary changes separately. However, he looked forward to a period of monetary co-operation on a very different basis from that of the 1950s. Professor Kindleberger had suggested that any currency zone needed a currency strong enough to be safely hoarded as a currency reserve. It was not possible to claim that the French franc had ever been a completely stable reserve currency. However, as various African countries wanted to be able to transfer into French francs he thought that this should not be neglected and could help to solve the problem of international liquidity. Once a currency became strong enough to be used as a reserve currency, it represented not so much a zone but an international payments system with a centre of gravitation. What economists meant today when they spoke of a 'currency area' might correspond to what he had tried to explain in his paper.

THE DISCUSSION OF PROFESSOR KINDLEBERGER'S PAPER

Mr. Lamfalussy said there were many points in the paper with which he agreed, especially on technical problems. However, he also agreed with Professor Kindleberger on at least one major point of principle. Both of them disliked measuring the adequacy of international liquidity in terms of the internationalized version of the quantity theory of money. However, even at this stage there was a basic difference. Professor Kindleberger objected to such a crude over-all quantitative measure, not because he thought it inadequate as a measure, but because he apparently did not believe that it was really possible to ask meaningful questions about international liquidity. Professor Kindleberger took this view even though he admitted that there might be a liquidity problem for individual countries. However, this would resolve itself into a balance of payments problem, which should be solved in a more or less empirical way according to the particular situation. One could not add together such individual liquidity problems into a *world* liquidity problem.

Mr. Lamfalussy believed that one could ask meaningful questions about international liquidity provided one avoided the mere aggregation of reserves and did not simply make crude comparisons with actual or desirable developments in international trade. Mr. Lamfalussy pointed out that international reserves (which he defined as liquid external assets, gold or any convertible currency) were there, not to finance the total volume of international trade, but balance of payments *deficits*.

This led to the question, what kind of deficits should be financed through the transfer of international reserves. Mr. Lamfalussy did not want to give a complete list, but made some suggestions based on two criteria. First, that deficits should be self-liquidating in a broad sense ; second, that they should not add to international excess demand. Examples were a cyclical stock deficit of the kind dealt with by Harry Johnson in one of his earlier articles, which tended to be rather important for trading-manufacturing countries like the U.K. or Belgium. Another example was that of speculative capital movements (a stock deficit on capital account) like that of Belgium in August 1960. These were becoming increasingly important as capital movements were liberalized, especially if such liberalization applied to residents.

Another example was a 'structural' deficit like that of the U.K. Labour costs per unit of output rose relatively to those of other countries because productivity was increasing slowly. Devaluation did not necessarily solve the problem because it did not always provide a stimulus to shift resources towards industries where productivity was high and growth rapid. It was at least arguable that one might tolerate the deficit and maintain full employment, giving a breathing space during which resources could be re-allocated.

Counter arguments could be advanced against recognizing the necessity for financing such deficits through the transfer or creation of liquid reserves. A deficit on current account could be eliminated by adequate public or private capital movements. The difficulty, however, arose if the capital movements did not occur or did not occur fast enough to prevent unwarranted deflationary policies. However, Mr. Lamfalussy said we had to remember his second condition, namely, that the deficit was not to add to international excess demand. Financing was desirable only if world resources were not fully employed. Otherwise, deficits ought to be cured either by disinflation or by transfers and capital movements which released an equivalent volume of real resources.

Mr. Lamfalussy said there was disagreement between Professor Kindleberger and himself on how a situation could be handled where some areas were fully employed, others not. Professor Kindleberger argued that, at present, international 'monetary' financing of under-developed countries might lead to an excess demand for European goods, without bringing any relief to the relatively under-employed U.S. industry. Mr. Lamfalussy suggested that there were two possible answers to this dilemma. The U.S. could make tied loans ; or else we could encourage financing by international monetary authorities, even if this led to additional inflationary pressure in Europe. For the coexistence of inflation in Europe with excess capacity in the U.S.A. meant a basic imbalance between Europe and the U.S. which ought to be dealt with by a differential rise in wages or in productivity, or by currency readjustments.

Mr. Lamfalussy thought that if balance of payments deficits of his 'authorized' version were frequent, or of long duration, and if they could not be financed through the depletion of external reserves, one would be entitled to call such a situation a 'world' liquidity problem.

Mr. Lamfalussy thought there was a problem here for empirical investigation. For example, in the autumn of 1961 the U.K. was obviously short of reserves, but the desirability of devaluation was questionable to say the least, because of what he had said about this being a structural deficit. One had also to remember that a year before there had been no problem of the U.K. balance, but a deficit in the U.S.A. There could then have been no question of disinflating the U.S. economy, and devaluation of the dollar would not have been practicable. It was not advisable to cut capital spending in third countries, and it was quite impossible to cut capital exports to Europe. An increase in capital exports from Europe was desirable, but this raised the problem of how to persuade them to move, the dating of such movements and their size. He thought there was a strong presumption that an increase in liquidity would do no harm. While the U.S.-U.K. see-saw was the result of the instability of the gold exchange standard, he agreed with Professor Kindleberger that a gold exchange standard with two or several polar centres was unstable. It was the shortage of liquid reserves in both countries which made this otherwise harmless and 'normal' see-saw so dangerous.

Turning to solutions and policy measures Mr. Lamfalussy said that Professor Kindleberger cherished the idea of swapping reserves. Mr. Lamfalussy could not understand the swap system. What about leakages towards third countries? Surely these increased the instability of the gold exchange standard. Reserves could only be created when they were not needed, unless there was a closed circuit — i.e. if the U.S.'s and the U.K.'s consolidated balance showed no deficit. If this were so, why should not one cancel out debt rather than incur it? The present Basle Agreement was not a swap, but a unilateral holding of sterling balances on the part of creditor countries. It would become a swap only if the Continental countries started incurring deficits, and the U.K. surpluses, and if the U.K. were prepared to accept Continental currencies as a means of settlement. Otherwise, Continental countries would have to give up their sterling holdings, or dollar holdings, or gold reserves, and over a complete 'cycle' of revolving balance of payments deficits, there would be no creation of liquidity. Now, even if this happened (which was at the least doubtful), there would be a real increase in international liquidity *only* if the holding of the currencies of other countries became a steady habit by *all* countries involved in swapping. Mr. Lamfalussy suggested that short of this steady habit, which could not be created overnight, we would need some formal institutional arrangements. Otherwise, each individual country would continue to look at its *net* reserves, and the whole process of swapping would have little meaning for the makers of economic policy.

As for the general question of balance of payments discipline, this leads inevitably to value judgements. According to Mr. Lamfalussy, one ought to be consistent with one's own value judgements, and apply them to all monetary systems. If Professor Kindleberger had a preference for balance of payments discipline, he ought to take into account the historical experience which clearly showed that the present unregulated gold exchange standard very often led to inflationary developments.

Sir Roy Harrod said that this was a paper which covered a number of problems and that he agreed with much of it. However, on the question of liquidity he disagreed virtually *in toto*. One had to recognize that the need for liquidity was the result of the chops and changes of economic circumstance; it was impossible to try to reduce such unpredictable things to rule, or to classify them. When one had a turnover of more than $150 billion a year and much possibility for changes in the direction of trade, no exact balancing was possible. The amount of new gold coming forward each year was worth $500 million, which meant that whenever all the surplus countries in the world had a total surplus of more than that size (i.e. 0·3 per cent of world turnover), there must be some deficit countries somewhere.

Sir Roy agreed that the solution to a country's deficit was often to encourage development within that country, or to devalue the currency. However, this did not cover all cases and in particular it did not cover what he had referred to as the 'chops and changes of circumstance'. For example, in the U.K. in 1961, the fundamental problem was that the economy had not yet adjusted itself to the recent abolition of restrictions on imports. He was sure that this adjustment would happen in due course, but one could not expect it to do so immediately. Similarly, in the U.S.A. in the years 1956–58, there had been a big rise in U.S. foreign investment, coupled with certain complex changes in merchandise trade. Given time, natural forces or government action would enable the country to assimilate such changes and there was no need for drastic remedies. Again, each recession, even if it were only moderate, produced dislocations in balances of payments, but did not require that these should be met by deflation or devaluation.

Sir Roy disagreed with Professor Triffin, who thought that the difficulties over international liquidity would arise only in the future. He thought that the problem of a shortage of international liquidity was already with us. There were several reasons why these liquidity problems had not come to the fore. On the one hand, countries with good reserves did not see that there was a problem. On the other hand those who had weak reserves, if they were to complain, invited the taunt that the real solution was for them to improve their own competitive position. Central bankers rather liked a shortage of liquidity since it gave them an extra stick to brandish in their favourite role as deflationists. Over the last ten years every country in Europe had, at some time, found it necessary to pursue a cautious growth policy because of a shortage of liquidity. There had also been a tendency for the international rate of interest to rise in recent years. Sir Roy thought that all this was very bad for developing countries which needed an increasing demand from mature countries if they were to grow. If two or three developed countries were having to deflate, this was bad for under-developed areas. He had already shown the importance of service charges on international lending and it was clear that the over-all amount of investment from abroad which under-developed countries could afford to receive was less if the rate of interest rose. He knew that the World Bank had been impeded in its raising of money by high rates of interest and thought this represented *prima facie* evidence for saying that international liquidity was too small.

Sir Roy pointed out that no one had claimed that liquidity was excessive in the 1930s and he remembered Keynes advocating the issue of international gold notes. Again, in discussions of a Clearing Union after the war, the big theme had been that if this were to lead to free trade, greater liquidity would be necessary. Yet, since the pre-war years the value of international liquidity had fallen by 30 or 40 per cent because of the reduced commodity value of gold. This situation must surely become worse in the future. For various reasons there had been adventitious aids to liquidity in the non-dollar world in the form of accumulations of sterling and dollar balances over the last twenty years, but Sir Roy thought that in the future it would be necessary to depend much more on gold.

He therefore wanted to raise the price of gold, which was at present less than half of its pre-war commodity value. Sir Roy said that the biggest argument against this was that when one raised the value of gold, the biggest gain went to the countries who happened, for various reasons, to hold most gold at that particular moment. However, the real gain was not the initial rise in value of gold, but the greater production and trade to which greater liquidity would lead. He pointed out also, that the existing distribution of loans and grants in the world was by no means perfect.

Sir Roy agreed that there were other ways to increase international liquidity and people said that it was irrational to continue to use gold. He agreed that there were alternatives to using gold, but thought it was quite impossible for us to persuade those who had to make decisions to accept any of these. The three ways of solving the problem through the IMF, without raising the price of gold, were first, to use open-market operations; second, to finance the creation of buffer stocks; and third, long-term lending. It was necessary to contrast long- and short-term lending, since short-term lending meant that repayments of debt became oppressive at once. He did not think, for example, that Professor Triffin's idea of achieving $15 billion worth of continuously outstanding short-term lending after ten years was practicable. Sir Roy also pointed out that if one used open-market operations, then one raised, in an even more acute form than when one raised the price of gold, the question of whose open-market securities one was going to buy. Once again, it was likely that the rich countries would gain most. Sir Roy thought that it would be better to finance buffer stocks because this would also represent a way out of the oscillations of primary protected prices. The issue of notes against goods would represent a genuine way of increasing liquidity. Sir Roy thought that the Stamp Plan was a good one, but it had the failing that it stressed long-term loans. There seemed to be appalling difficulties here, not least the perennial question of who would get the loans. Despite the attitudes of the U.S.A. and indeed of the world central bankers, he thought that on balance the easiest procedure would be to raise the price of gold.

Professor Robinson was glad that Sir Roy had stressed that it was not necessary to make all under-developed countries live within their primary-produce earnings. If one looked at 1938, the reason why there had been no major crisis, whereas today there would have been one, was probably that world liquidity was so much greater.

Professor Tsuru also disagreed with Professor Kindleberger. In Japan, imports were $6 billion per annum and reserves were 30 per cent of imports. Japan hoped to increase imports to $10 billion which would require reserves of $3 billion. In other words, Japan needed to raise her reserves by $1 billion. If twenty countries were trying to attract similar amounts of gold simultaneously they would obviously fail. It followed that the U.S.A. would have to supply the necessary dollars. So if at any point in the next five years the U.S.A. felt it necessary to correct its balance of payments problems by raising exports and reducing imports, this would cause deflation in many countries. Professor Tsuru was therefore convinced that there was an acute problem of world liquidity.

Professor Tsuru said he was reminded of the well-known remark by Schumpeter that a claim on a horse could not be ridden. On the other hand a claim to money *was* money. He saw a difference between institutional arrangements for economizing liquidity within a country and similar arrangements on a world scale. Professor Kindleberger said that perhaps it was necessary to increase IMF quotas, swap funds between central banks and so on. However, when Professor Kindleberger said that the quantity theory of money had no greater relevance internationally than internally, Professor Tsuru did not agree. There was a very big difference — many ways of economizing on liquidity internally did not apply internationally. He wondered if Professor Kindleberger would oppose methods of economizing on international means of payment. If he did, then he was being consistent with his paper. *Professor Kindleberger* replied that this was the case.

Professor Morgan pointed out that Professor Kindleberger had, on page 381 of his paper, reasoned that instability of exchange rates depressed both trade and capital movements. But one should add the proviso that fluctuating exchange rates should be compared with possible alternatives. When this was done, it might not be so clear that fluctuating exchange rates were the worst of the alternatives.

Professor Morgan was also worried over Professor Kindleberger's ideas on monetary discipline. A drop in world liquidity was neither necessary nor sufficient to lead to internal monetary restraint. In fact, the general trend was to give monetary authorities greater discretion. Perhaps Kindleberger was unnecessarily provocative in comparing extremes. A reasonable compromise on middle ground might be discoverable.

Professor Sohmen thought that the false impression had arisen in this conference that liberals regarded an increase in world trade as an end in itself. He wanted to stress that, as far as he was aware, they all regarded it simply as a means of achieving increased growth, both for the world and for particular countries. It was true that foreign trade could lead to balance of payments difficulties and he agreed that it would be disastrous for both individual countries and for the world as a whole if such balance of payments difficulties were corrected by restrictive monetary and fiscal policies. Restrictive trade policies were not the answer, however, because they affected the allocation of resources adversely.

He thought it unfortunate that exchange rates were seen only as a means of curing balance of payments difficulties. They ought also to be recognized as a powerful tool of employment policy. If exchange rates were constant, a country whose currency was overvalued had no alternative but to adopt deflationary policies or to impose trade restrictions.

Professor Sohmen regretted the exclusive emphasis on macro-economic policies for full employment : we tended to forget the role of exchange rates. Devaluation had a certain effect on employment, while its effect on the balance of payments was uncertain, at least in pure theory. He did not agree with the frequent objection that devaluation by one major country would lead only to competitive devaluation by everybody. If some currencies were overvalued, then others must, by definition, be undervalued.

The usual charge that devaluation was a beggar-my-neighbour policy was not true, even on the evidence of the great depression. Exchange depreciation allowed more expansionary policies and in the 1930s its principal aim had usually been to increase the flexibility of monetary and fiscal policies. For example, if one looked at the evidence presented in *Exchange Depreciation*, Seymour Harris' book of 1936, one saw that countries with depreciated currencies had, on the whole, increased imports as much as exports. Most of the increase in employment in these countries could not, therefore, have taken place at the expense of other countries.

Professor Sohmen thought that two false issues had been raised during the Round Table meeting. The first was that devaluation necessarily led to a fall in the terms of trade. Mrs. Joan Robinson had considered this problem in 1937, and given an exact statement showing that either a fall or a rise was possible. Second, there was a contention that devaluation inevitably meant accelerated inflation. He would refer to his own article in the *Quarterly Journal of Economics* of 1958, where he had shown that there was no presumption that devaluation would lead to inflation if a country had imposed trade restrictions before the devaluation. By removing these restrictions, it might be possible to reduce prices.

Most of the legitimate objections to devaluation rested on the necessary unpredictability of its timing and extent. Governments were forced to keep it secret until the last moment under the system of the 'adjustable peg', and considerable risks were thus imposed on trade and capital movements. One ought instead to look at the alternative policy of flexible exchange rates. Professor Sohmen emphasized that if one wanted to avoid all changes in exchange rates, the system was the same as the gold standard. The only basis for preferring the 'adjustable peg' to flexible exchange rates was that, if there was speculation, inflation might be less than with flexible rates, *provided that* speculators looked neither backwards nor forwards. He did not think this was a very realistic assumption. He did not want to go into detail, but would also point out that flexible exchange rates, coupled with an appropriate monetary policy, could direct private speculative capital in such a way that the much debated problem of 'international liquidity' would disappear.

Professor Johnson thought Professor Sohmen had raised an important issue since the whole problem of liquidity stemmed from the use of fixed exchange rates. When economists produced purely theoretical analysis they came out in favour of flexibility; yet when they looked at the world they found that most exchange rates were fixed. This suggested that there must be some good reason for having fixed exchange rates. It was notable that within countries also exchange rates were fixed and did not differ between different areas and towns. He thought it had already been agreed by the Round Table that the nation was not always the most useful unit for economic analysis, but there might be virtues in fixed exchange rates which did carry over from the national to the international level.

Professor Johnson did not want to go all the way in advocating floating exchange rates, but he did agree with Sir Roy Harrod that the slowing down of growth since the war had been closely connected with the shortage of liquidity. Economists saw this situation as implying a need to increase reserves and he agreed that the question of what exactly liquidity comprised was a very difficult one to answer. There were many alternative ways of increasing liquidity and several widely discussed plans. Indeed, one could argue that there were too many plans with the Triffin plan, the Bernstein plan and the Harrod no-plan.

Faced with so many alternatives, no one was willing to do anything and we stumbled along, always solving problems after they had arisen — the Haberler plan. The ultimate answer must be the use of open-market operations by a world central bank to provide a steady increase in world reserves; this was the Friedman or Chicago plan applied on a world scale. The World Central Bank would increase its stock of assets at a fixed annual rate. One could not reach this kind of solution merely by taking one step at a time and this was the objection to what Professor Kindleberger said. It was necessary to look at the whole world situation and he could not see the IMF evolving in this way.

Replying to Sir Roy Harrod, Professor Johnson opposed the use of notes to finance buffer stocks. What was needed was an increase in liquidity of about $1 billion. The goods that went into buffer stocks were products, like gold itself, and the only virtue of the Harrod notion was that it gave subsidies to under-developed areas. It might therefore be better to give these outright.

Sir Roy Harrod argued that it was reasonable for aggregate buffer stocks to increase in proportion with aggregate production and consumption, so that one would get the right kind of figure.

Professor Johnson agreed that the volume of buffer stocks was likely to rise at the same rate as production and consumption did, but argued that production and consumption of primary products would not rise as rapidly as production in general, and as world trade. Therefore, the rate of growth of buffer stocks would lag behind the need for liquidity.

Professor Mikesell was more puzzled by Professor Kindleberger than in disagreement with him. However, he disagreed with Professor Johnson's suggestion of a machine to pour out liquidity at a constant rate of growth. This was not the answer. He had great doubts on the case for a regular, or a once-for-all, increase in world liquidity in the form either of a rise in the price of gold or of a steady 3-5 per cent per annum increase. Within an economy the monetary system did adapt to changing circumstance, for example, by the development of financial intermediaries. These did not yet operate internationally, but they had developed internally and might well do so internationally in the future. The IMF would clearly evolve further, and might well develop means of economizing on liquidity.

Professor Mikesell was a little worried about the U.S. balance of payments deficit. Although this deficit had been greatly reduced, there were heavy foreign aid and military expenditures. However, the major problem arose from the fact that the surplus of dollar payments over receipts was being absorbed by developed countries like Germany or Switzerland, which already had ample reserves. One solution might be for the U.S.A. to grant tied loans, but this was not the preferred approach. No one wanted foreign aid to decline, but it was hard for the U.S.A. to achieve a large enough current account surplus to finance it.

Professor Mikesell said that economists should not advocate the U.S.A. taking deflationary measures in the face of unemployment to achieve a large enough foreign surplus. Countries like Germany might want to increase their reserves and the Triffin plan, which in a sense would allow the U.S.A. to lend long and borrow short, had some appeal. Alternatively, West Germany might lend its surpluses to the IMF, which in turn would make loans to, or invest in, the deficient countries.

Professor Mikesell asked whether it was better to deal with the problem by continually increasing the volume of liquidity, or whether we should seek some kind of co-operative planning to balance the world's balances of payments. Perhaps we needed co-operation among debtors and creditors such as was achieved under the OEEC, *and measures for expanding liquidity*. However, he had very great doubts also about the idea of regularly increasing the volume of world liquidity and also about the desirability of raising the price of gold.

Dr. Patel had no doubt that greater international liquidity was needed. Those who objected to the application of the quantity theory in the field of international liquidity generally approved of it in the internal sphere. There were, of course, many ways for increasing international liquidity. For one thing, IMF quotas could be increased periodically. If no part of the increased quotas had to be paid in gold, he could see no objection to increasing international liquidity periodically through a revision of IMF quotas. As matters stood, however, the stipulation that a part of the increase in quotas should be paid in gold amounted to the application of a means test and the main benefit from quota increases went to the richer countries who could put up the gold. If the nexus with gold were broken and if the lending policy of the IMF were to become more automatic, the IMF would become a credit-creating institution through a periodic expansion of its resources. Professor Kindleberger had suggested that the IMF would have no use for the large amount of local currencies contributed by the less-developed countries. This was not a helpful way of looking at the problem as the local currencies contributed by the weaker members represented their drawing rights on the Fund.

He could see no particular merit in increasing the price of gold as a way of increasing international liquidity and indeed thought that a strong objection to this procedure was that another increase in the price of gold would strengthen the fetish of gold.

While he himself was in favour of the IMF becoming a credit-creating institution, there was little likelihood that the present discussions on the reform of the IMF would take that turn. The practical question, therefore, was simply of ensuring that any arrangements for enabling the IMF to borrow the currencies of its stronger members would keep the door open for future reform along the lines he preferred.

Short-term capital movements posed a problem not merely for the pound or the dollar or for the industrialized countries as a whole but for the under-developed countries as well. Since the under-developed countries depended greatly on the flow of capital from the richer nations, any strain imposed on the payments position of the advanced countries by short-term capital movements would have repercussions on the developing countries, unless steps were taken to enable the richer countries to continue their assistance programmes in the face of temporary difficulties.

There were suggestions that the problem of short-term capital movements could be taken care of by informal understanding among central banks. However, even with the U.K., the agreement with the European central banks proved to be only of temporary value and the whole transaction had to be settled finally by the U.K. drawing on the Fund. It might be better if the IMF were enabled to act effectively in such situations from the very beginning. The current discussions in the Fund assumed that while the Fund would make arrangements to borrow the currencies of its stronger members, actual borrowing from the Fund by members would continue to take place only through the normal quota system. There would be no increase in total international liquidity beyond what was implicit in the existing quotas. If, instead, the IMF had adopted the Bernstein plan, loans made from currencies newly borrowed by the Fund to counteract short-term capital movements would have been separated from the normal transactions of the Fund made through its quota system. There would at least have been the advantage that the constituting of a separate fund for special operations would have made for greater flexibility and would have left room for further modifications.

On Professor Kindleberger's point about the importance of reserves, Dr. Patel agreed that under-developed countries did not always appreciate their importance. However, while it was natural for developing countries to draw down reserves unduly to support their development plans, the responsibility for helping them to maintain adequate levels of reserves would have to be accepted by the aid-giving countries as well. With foreign aid now so important in the balances of payments of the developing countries, creditor countries must avoid the temptation to reduce their own aid commitments by encouraging under-developed areas to draw down their reserves. Indeed, it would often be appropriate for aid-giving countries to ensure that some of their aid was used to build up reserves. As things stood, however, there was considerable resistance among aid-giving countries to giving assistance for this purpose. Dr. Patel thought that this very complex problem could only be solved by greater understanding on the part of creditor as well as debtor nations.

Professor Bowen wondered why, when Professor Kindleberger suggested that we were far from solving the balance of payments problems of under-developed countries, he also implied that the problems of developing countries were unrelated to the shortage of liquidity. Professor Bowen thought there was a serious liquidity problem and that it was first necessary to look at this as a world-wide problem. What impressed him in looking at the developing countries was the need, in the next five or six years, to get a big increase in their exports. There was no great technical difficulty in doing this since the countries had resources, but some aid was needed to activate them.

The great problem was where the increased exports could go to. Perhaps one reason why liquidity was needed was to absorb these exports and therefore the timing in the increase in liquidity was important. The existing institutions would no doubt solve the problem in ten or twenty years, but this would be too late. He therefore supported Professor Johnson in the view that there was a need for an international central bank as a new venture.

Mr. Maizels said that, unlike the self-liquidating deficit considered by Mr. Lamfalussy, a long-run deficit was much more difficult to deal with, because the time-perspective differed. There was a need not just to find liquidity, but to convince others that the deficit would liquidate itself. So far as the U.K. and Belgium were concerned, the Belgian solution of deflation would not work in the U.K. It was true that the results of liberalizing imports were part of the U.K.'s problem as Sir Roy Harrod suggested, and the U.K. was obviously finding difficulty in absorbing them.

However, the root of the problem was why this difficulty in absorbing the imports had occurred at all. The basic trouble was that the over-all rate of growth was too low. The ratio between imports and income was lower than in the 1930s and the U.K. was therefore only returning to what had been the pre-war normal. The problem was not an excess of imports but a deficit of exports. Should an economy like this be provided with liquidity to support its deficit over the period? There was a great danger that there would be too little change in the economy, and a rapid rate of growth was needed to stimulate innovation and productivity. There was no reason why other policies, for example devaluation, should not be used, but these were no substitute for growth.

In the short run the main problem in under-developed areas was that the free market had been broken in the sense of allowing sharp falls in primary-product prices. Mr. Maizels thought that it was not simply a problem of reserves and liquidity, but also one of fluctuations in the prices of primary products. He wondered whether it was possible to create an institutional scheme for all primary products which would allow short-term compensation for fluctuating prices. On the whole he did not believe that it could be done.

Professor Weiller suggested that what we were looking for was some kind of synthesis and of course this meant considerable simplification. He agreed very much with Professor Kindleberger and, strange though it might seem, with Sir Roy as well. In practice one might adopt two approaches. One could either separate the problems of the developed and the under-developed areas ; or one could take both together. Looking at the under-developed areas one had the important question of foreign aid and its distribution and, in this respect, he agreed with Sir Roy.

The second method was Professor Kindleberger's, namely, that of looking at the problem country by country and region by region. This meant a much more global approach and led to the question of world liquidity. Professor Weiller suggested that even if we solved the problem for individual countries, we would still need a world solution.

Sir Donald MacDougall said he agreed with a good deal of what Sir Roy had said. On the question of whether liquidity was inadequate there was a tendency to argue that, because the change in the ratio of reserves to trade since before the war did not prove it conclusively, there was therefore no shortage. This was a *non sequitur*. Much more empirical work was needed on the probable size of the swings in balances of payments against which reserves had to be held. Even this could not prove the need for more liquidity, but it did not follow that nothing need therefore be done. A crude quantity theory of money was admittedly as unsatisfactory in the international as it was in the national field. But one had a feeling that the ratio between reserves and international transactions could not decline steeply and continuously without causing trouble ; and it would fall steadily if nothing were done, because new gold production was limited and there could be only a slow increase, if any, in foreign holdings of sterling and dollars.

If one could not accept statistical arguments on the inadequacy of liquidity, what other arguments could be used? The contention that growth had been held up by shortage of liquidity was not completely convincing. It might be true of the U.K., but not of most other advanced nations in Europe and North America. Some under-developed countries might have been held up, but most of them did not wish to hold large

T

561

reserves; it would be more true to say that they had been held back by a shortage of aid rather than by a shortage of liquidity. Another possible argument was that few countries thought they had too big reserves, that many would like more, and that a good many would probably react quickly, and in an unfavourable way, if they ran into deficit.

The problem of short-term international capital movements was a serious one. If one thought of the possible size of these movements in the future, including movements associated with stock exchange speculation, it was clear that tremendous shifts were possible and we needed to consider how these could be damped down. He would go further than Professor Kindleberger in suggesting that more formal exchange guarantees would help (although he appreciated the practical difficulties), but there was still the problem of divergent rates of interest. Perhaps we should go back to Bretton Woods and agree that countries were responsible for controlling international capital movements.

Some participants had suggested that because there were no inter-regional balance of payments problems within a country, there could therefore be no real international problem. But intra-national conditions were quite different. For example, within a country interest rates were much more uniform, there were large equilibrating capital movements, and there was what one might call 'Marshall Aid' between regions through the system of taxation and unemployment benefits.

Sir Donald believed that there *was* a need to increase international liquidity. How to do this was a technical and political problem. Like Professor Johnson, he felt there was a danger that, if one spent too much time comparing rival plans, nothing would be done at all. Since for reasons given by Sir Roy Harrod it was very difficult to increase international credit facilities sufficiently, the only hope might be to raise the price of gold. One fundamental problem was that countries were still reluctant to give very large blank cheques or to hold large amounts of each others' currencies or of 'bancor'. The problem within a country was quite different; notes issued by the Central Bank were legal tender so that only a very small gold backing, if any, was necessary. The same would be wholly true of international money issued by a world central bank only if there were also a world government. Otherwise, national governments were bound to prefer reserves of gold to reserves of 'bancor', or of another country's currency; for in a political crisis the use of gold could not be so easily blocked by a hostile nation or international organization. Perhaps some people liked the Triffin plan because they were idealists about the possibility of world government; but we were far from this.

Mr. Bhagwati had reservations about the value of flexible exchange rates. For instance, if there were no floor to the fall in the exchange rate, de-stabilizing speculation, undertaken in the expectation of a big wage rise, could lead to a fall in the exchange rate which, in turn, could lead to the feared wage increase. De-stabilizing speculation could then be self-justifying. It might be argued that, in such an event, an appropriate monetary policy could be adopted to check the price increase ; however, this could easily create unemployment, in which case it could not be maintained that the freely fluctuating exchange rate could combine full employment with external balance and efficiency.

Mr. Bhagwati further said that one essential ingredient of the Triffin plan appeared to be the provision of an annual increase in the supply of liquidity. One should ask whether this was really necessary. Countries often seemed to work in terms of given *levels* of reserves ; these levels were revised upwards only periodically, when the *proportions* got out of line, beyond some minimum, through expanding trade. Unless this sort of argument could be answered, it seemed that the current method of expanding liquidity, by *periodic* increases in IMF quotas and the like, might be adequate, as Professor Kindleberger seemed to argue. Of course, one did need some plan to handle the problem of instability caused by the gold exchange standard ; but that was a separate issue, as Professor Kindleberger had rightly emphasized.

Professor Kindleberger thought it was necessary to divide the question into two parts dealing, on the one hand, with hot money and on the other with structural change. His real quarrel with Professor Tsuru was that the Triffin plan mixed the two. This was unfortunate, because it led those with quantity-of-asset problems to say that they had liquidity problems. The basis question was why we needed certain kinds of assets with certain liquidity attaching to them. Professor Kindleberger thought that Professor Tsuru had made a big contribution on the problem of hot money. However, he would himself favour a more pragmatic approach than that of Dr. Patel, though he preferred the Bernstein to the IMF plan. Perhaps if one were dealing with an individual cycle the IMF scheme was a good one. What was needed was not to increase international assets each year, but to develop arrangements on the lines of the Bernstein plan or the Basle agreement. Professor Kindleberger thought that the greatest need was for discount facilities. These worked domestically and therefore should work internationally too. If there were a run on the currency, lending freely at high rates of interest would break speculation. Professor Kindleberger explained that Professor Sohmen and he had explored the merits and deficiencies of flexible exchange rates for a number of years and he was not anxious to take this particular debate any further during the Round Table. He feared speculators much more than Professor Sohmen did, but this was why he preferred fixed exchange rates *plus* discount facilities.

On the structural problem, Sir Roy Harrod thought that foreign capital was hard to absorb in under-developed areas. Under-developed countries did not need cash and there was no justification for using this as an excuse for increasing the balances of the IMF year by year. One then had merely a kind of poker game and increasing the balances was merely the same thing as adding extra chips. He rejected the notion that under-developed areas had a liquidity problem and not merely a quantity-of-total-money-assets problem.

So far as developed countries were concerned there were two kinds of problem, namely, the British-Belgian and the Japanese. He thought that the solution to the British problem was almost entirely a question of growth. He disagreed with both Sir Roy Harrod and Professor Robinson in that he thought that this and not liquidity was the greatest need of the U.K. The heart of the British problem was growth and the technical change which growth brought about. It was clear that British growth was restricted by the balance of payments, and not by liquidity, and the reason why Britain had a growth problem was that she had not used Marshall Aid to modernize her economy.

As for how one could solve a problem like Britain's, he suggested that perhaps the use of swaps might be helpful. The transactions demand for foreign exchange could alter and this was the essence of the remarks by Professor Weiller and Mr. Lamfalussy. If our problem was a liquidity shortage like that between 1873 and 1896, which might cause a world depression, the problem could be met by swapping arrangements enabling two swapping countries to acquire claims on each other. The changes in the IMF quotas had already added to long-run reserves. Professor Kindleberger thought that speculators could be dealt with and that the real question was the transactions demand for foreign currency. He was not sure that a shortage of gold had held back growth and stressed that there was a major difference between most British economists and himself, because he thought that there was great confusion in British minds between the problems of international liquidity and of structural imbalance. Growth needed long-run and not short-run assets.

Sir Roy Harrod said he would like to take a specific case in answer to Professor Kindleberger. It was wrong to say that growth had not been held back by a liquidity shortage. Britain had removed restrictions from her imports as a contribution to the cause of world prosperity. It was evident that it would take Britain four or five years to become adjusted to this by increasing her exports as much as imports had already increased. With sufficient liquidity, the U.K. could have afforded to wait. He could not see what other assets Britain could have sold in order to finance the readjustment. This was definitely a liquidity problem and not an asset problem.

INDEX

Entries in the Index in Black Type under the Names of Participants in the Conference indicate their Papers or Discussions of their Papers. Entries in Italics indicate Contributions by Participants to the Discussions

Index

Index

Index

PRINTED BY R. & R. CLARK, LTD., EDINBURGH